THE CHILD CLINICIAN'S HANDBOOK

THE CHILD CLINICIAN'S HANDBOOK

SECOND EDITION

WILLIAM G. KRONENBERGER

Indiana University School of Medicine

ROBERT G. MEYER

University of Louisville

ALLYN AND BACON

Boston   London   Toronto   Sydney   Tokyo   Singapore

Executive Editor: Rebecca Pascal
Series Editorial Assistant: Whitney Brown
Marketing Manager: Caroline Croley

Copyright © 2001, 1996 by Allyn & Bacon
A Pearson Education Company
Needham Heights, MA 02494

Internet: www.abacon.com

Library of Congress Cataloging-in-Publication Data

Kronenberger, William G.
    The child clinician's handbook / William G. Kronenberger, Robert G. Meyer.—2nd ed.
        p.   cm.
    Includes bibliographical references and index.
    ISBN 0-205-29621-1
    1. Child psychiatry—Handbooks, manuals, etc.   I. Meyer, Robert G.   II. Title.
    [DNLM: 1. Mental Disorders—diagnosis—Child—Handbooks.   2. Mental
    Disorders—therapy—Child—Handbooks. WS 39 K93c 2001]
    RJ499.3 .K76 2001
    618.92'89—dc21

                                                                      00-038066

Printed in the United States of America
10 9 8 7 6   07 06 05

DEDICATION

To my grandparents Harold and Mary,
George and Rosella.
—WGK

To Christopher, Sean, and Eric
—RGM

CONTENTS

PREFACE

Our goal in writing the first edition of this book was to provide a practical, clinical reference for child mental health clinicians and students based on current research. The first edition of *The Child Clinician's Handbook* covered diagnosis, evaluation, testing, and treatment of childhood mental disorders so that busy students and clinicians could use it easily and efficiently as a reference in their clinical courses and day-to-day work. Therefore, we aimed to keep the practical, clinical issues of assessment and treatment paramount while integrating major advances in theory and research.

The second edition of this book follows in the footsteps of the first while adding some components that should make it both more comprehensive and easier to use for learning and reference. The second edition of *The Child Clinician's Handbook* is intended to facilitate clinical work by anticipating the questions of practitioners and students: What are the characteristics of the disorder? Are there any tests that I can use to assess it thoroughly? How do I treat the disorder? For each major childhood mental disorder, these questions are answered in a structured presentation that is uniform throughout the text. Hence, the book is designed for quick and easy use with tables and clearly identified sections to use as summaries and content guides. Extensive references for each disorder direct clinicians to other sources if additional readings are desired.

In writing this second edition, we have also integrated the major contributions of research over the past several years. The explosion of empirically validated treatments, outcome research, practice guidelines, and treatment reviews has provided much more information about which treatments work for various disorders. Major journals such as the *Journal of Clinical Child Psychology*, the *Journal of Pediatric Psychology*, and the *Journal of the American Academy of Child and Adolescent Psychiatry* have published special issues and articles about empirically supported treatments and practice parameters. It is, therefore, important for clinicians and students to be aware of new findings and reviews of treatment outcomes.

Paralleling the improvements in treatment outcome research, new and significant developments have taken place in assessment tools and assessment research. The past few years have seen the introduction of numerous psychological tests by the major test publishers, and several new assessment-focused or assessment-related journals have been launched. A major aim of this revision was to review this new information, applying it to the major childhood mental health diagnoses. To do so, we have updated information about existing checklists (e.g., the Child Behavior Checklist), replaced former versions of tests with new revisions (e.g., Conners' scales, WAIS-III), and added newer instruments that are becoming widely used (e.g., Behavior Assessment System for Children). We have also provided more extensive information about intelligence and neurocognitive testing for disorders that have a strong cognitive component, such as Attention-Deficit/Hyperactivity Disorder and Learning Disorders, reflecting the improvements in research in cognitive testing.

Our readers have also provided us with valuable input for this second edition. More information about epidemiology and prognosis has been added for several disorders. New appendices in this edition, developed with the feedback of graduate students and practitioners, show samples of an intake background and clinical information form, as well as parent handouts for several major behavioral techniques. We hope that this specific clinical information will further increase the utility of the book.

The material contained in this book is drawn from several sources, ranging from well-constructed research studies to our own clinical observations. Obviously, child mental health is a constantly evolving field, and we expect the research and clinical database to advance. Hence, we welcome comments, feedback, and suggestions about new research and clinical directions in this field. Please send these to William Kronenberger, Ph.D., Riley Child and Adolescent Psychiatry Clinic, Indianapolis, IN 46202-5200.

We appreciate the permission of the American Psychiatric Association to use the DSM-IV categories and diagnostic criteria to structure our presentation of child psychopathology. Readers who are interested in an extensive discussion of the formal diagnosis of childhood psychiatric disorders should consult the DSM-IV.

We are grateful to several students and colleagues who provided us with invaluable comments, assistance, and written contributions to this book. Laura Bolte deserves special mention for her coauthorship of the Anxiety Disorders chapter from the first edition of this book. David Sabine and Stacy Cambron also provided assistance with the writing of the Disruptive Behavior Disorders chapter for the first edition of this book. Sherrie Bloemendaal's help with library work was much appreciated. We reserve special thanks for Sue Hutchinson, Mylan Jaixen, Carla Daves, Sean Wakely, Jill Jeffrey, and Becky Pascal for their help with the editorial process. We also acknowledge the professors and colleagues who have been instrumental in our clinical learning experiences: Bob Thompson, Dick Lawlor, George McAdoo, Gina Laite, Suzanne Blix, A. J. Spoerner, Jim Rizzo, Diane Lanman, Rosemary Collins, Ted Petti, Bob Ten Eyck, Chris McDougle, Ann Giauque, Karen Meighen, Lori Hines, Naomi Swiezy, David Dunn, Pat Brearton, Kelda Walsh, Mark Bangs, George Karwisch, Greg Zimet, Ron Stachler, Paul Deardorff,

David Hellkamp, Vytautas Bieliauskas, A. I. Rabin, Bertram Karon, and many others—their influence is no doubt incorporated in this work as it is in our therapeutic styles. Finally, the support, input, and specialty knowledge of our colleagues Earl Kronenberger, Bryan Carter, and Linn LaClave were essential in our work.

LIST OF TABLES

CHAPTER 1

Diagnosis, Assessment, and Treatment in Clinical Practice

■ ## Introduction

This book is intended to be a practical reference and teaching text for child mental health clinicians and trainees. Every day, these clinicians face a common scenario: A child walks in the door, accompanied by (usually at the insistence of) a parent. The child and parent are at the clinician's office because the parent or another adult finds the child's behaviors to be problematic or because the child is showing some distress. The mental health clinician (*clinician* will be used in this book to refer to a psychologist, psychiatrist, physician, social worker, family therapist, psychiatric nurse, counselor, or advanced student in one of these areas) is expected to perform an evaluation and to provide recommendations in a timely, professional, and informed manner.

The task of the clinician is enormous: The clinician must, in a limited period of time, provide a diagnosis, background information, formulation of the case, and therapeutic recommendations. In many cases, the clinician is then called on to explain the diagnosis to parents and to intervene, which requires additional expertise. Added to this increasingly complex picture are the facts that diagnostic systems change every few years, psychotherapy is evolving, and a mountain of assessment and clinical outcome research is published every year. In order to stay current and competent, clinicians must be skilled in therapy, adroit at observation, and knowledgeable about research and clinical literature.

Even if all children presented with similar problems, the clinician's job would be complicated and intellectually demanding. However, diagnostic categories for childhood disorders are growing in number and refinement. The clinician must be prepared to recognize and address problems as varied as Mental Retardation, Separation Anxiety Disorder, and Conduct Disorder. Perhaps the only similarity across children is the clinician's starting point. This starting point usually involves three basic questions:

1. What are the characteristics of the child's problem?
2. How should the child's problem be evaluated in depth?
3. Based on the evaluation results, what can be done to address the child's problem?

Guidelines and suggestions for answering these questions can be found in numerous sources. Question 1 involves establishing a diagnosis and/or description of the child's behaviors, as well as a history of the symptoms and related problems. Traditionally, the clinician has referred to the current Diagnostic and Statistical Manual of Mental Disorders (since 1980, DSM-III, DSM-III-R, and DSM-IV; American Psychiatric Association, 1980, 1987, 1994) and to psychopathology books for assistance with this initial question. However, although DSM-IV provides important information about symptoms, features, and epidemiology, it falls short on in-depth evaluation (particularly psychological testing) and therapy recommendations. Hence, the clinician has to look elsewhere to answer Questions 2 and 3.

Question 2 reflects the focus on more in-depth, individual evaluation of the child's problems. For this evaluation, clinicians rely on observation, clinical interviews, psychological assessment, and behavioral assessment. Clinical interviews tap general background information, but they also focus on specific factors common to a diagnostic group. For example, the interview of a child with Attention-Deficit/Hyperactivity Disorder (ADHD) might include observation and questions related to the child's ability to concentrate, sit still, listen, and follow directions. These components would be much less emphasized in the interview of a child with Separation Anxiety Disorder. Clinical interviews with parents would be similarly tailored to the child's problems. Psychological testing, on the other hand, might focus on test patterns typical of the child's diagnostic group and on the selection of specific test instruments to assess the child's problem in detail. Behavioral assessment investigates the child's behaviors, the events that preceded the behaviors (antecedents), and the events that followed the behaviors (consequences).

In order to address Question 2, then, the clinician needs current knowledge about general interviewing questions, diagnosis-specific features to investigate in the interview, general psychological tests (such as IQ tests and broad personality tests), and diagnosis-specific tests (those designed to evaluate a particular cluster of problems, such as ADHD). To use the ADHD example again, the clinician would need background information about the child's development and current circumstances; specific interview information about ADHD features; (ideally) IQ and achievement testing; and tests of attention, concentration, and other ADHD-related behaviors. Hence, in addition to DSM-IV, the clinician draws on knowledge contained in a basic interviewing book, books about the major tests (such as IQ tests and personality tests), and books (or articles) about diagnosis-specific tests to answer Question 2.

Finally, after completing the evaluation process that answers the first two questions, the clinician must provide recommendations for intervention. In many cases, interventions are conducted by the evaluating clinician. Hence, the clinician often must know in detail how to address the problem in therapy. As with the first two questions, many excellent books have been written to address Question 3. Books exist, for example, about cognitive-behavioral, psychodynamic, play, and family therapy to address child behavior problems. In many cases, however, these books deal with general therapy techniques but lack specific application or modification for different problems.

Looking at the clinician's ideal bookshelf, then, one can see diagnostic books, interviewing books, testing books, and therapy books. Clinicians have probably used these books in the course of their initial learning and continuing education. Unfortunately, however, they rarely take their basic books down to assist with day-to-day clinical issues, except, perhaps, to doublecheck on a diagnostic criterion. Why does this situation exist?

Clinicians need the information in their basic books, but they often do not use basic books in their daily practice. Books that have been so important in learning are relegated to the status of decorations in the clinical office.

There appear to be at least three reasons for this state of affairs: First, time is a factor. Busy clinicians do not have time to read a new book (or to review an old one) for each patient; they do not have daily time to do a literature search or to enter a scholarly debate. This is not to belittle the importance of these endeavors. Indeed, it is very important for clinicians to keep up with their field and with scholarly advances. But the everyday office environment is typically not the place for such efforts; continuing education classes, case conferences, seminars, and professional holidays provide opportunities for more basic learning. In the office, interacting with patients, the clinician needs access to practical summaries, descriptions, and brief recommendations.

Second, many child mental health books do not integrate the topics of diagnosis, interviewing, assessment, and treatment. More commonly, these topics are the subjects of separate, lengthy, detailed books. Although such books provide essential in-depth information, they leave a gap between diagnosis, assessment, and therapy. Assessment-therapy gaps, however, are not present in the clinical setting. Rather, the clinician uses assessment to plan, evaluate, and modify therapy; assessment and therapy are part of the same process. Hence, clinicians need a book that addresses diagnostic, assessment, and therapy issues in a brief, practical, integrated manner.

Third, in day-to-day practice, clinicians need to find information quickly. Often, the clinician has 5–10 minutes between appointments in which to review the patient's chart and plan for the session. If questions arise in this brief time, the clinician must find answers immediately or wait until later to search for them. To provide quick answers, a book for the busy clinician must have a well-defined organization and structure. The structure should be the same from chapter to chapter, with clear, consistent headings from one chapter to the next. In short, the clinician should be able to easily predict where information can be found in a reference book. If a book does not adhere to this strict organization, chances are that it will not be used as a quick reference.

■ Rationale

The problems just outlined are the impetus for the writing of this book. Meyer and Deitsch (1996) have dealt with many similar issues for adult mental health clinicians in their *Clinician's Handbook*. This work is intended to apply their approach (with some modifications) to the situation of the child mental health clinician. Addressing these issues and providing a resource that will be useful to busy clinicians has required the definition of a clear set of goals and organizing principles for this book:

1. Integrated consideration of diagnostic, assessment, and therapy issues in each chapter
2. Broad organization of chapters by diagnosis according to DSM-IV
3. Use of consistent structure and headings within each chapter
4. Critique, when possible, of assessment instruments and intervention modalities based on research findings

Adherence to these goals means that this book is intended to be problem-focused, practical, easy-to-use, concise, and current with the literature. Familiarity with the organizational principles outlined here and with the philosophy of the book will help clinicians use the book as a reference in everyday practice. Because of the organization of the book, clinicians should have a sense of *what* is covered in each chapter and *where* such information can be found. Issues of diagnosis, evaluation/assessment, and therapy are covered in every chapter. Chapters are organized based on the DSM-IV diagnostic system, with which almost every clinician is familiar. All major DSM-IV childhood diagnoses, including some that affect children and adults (such as Mood Disorders) are covered. The age range is approximately birth to 16 years of age; clinicians who are interested in disorders of late adolescence and adulthood are referred to Meyer and Deitsch's (1996) *Clinician's Handbook*.

Although DSM-IV provides extensive and useful diagnostic information, the use of the DSM-IV diagnostic system as one of the organizing components of *The Child Clinician's Handbook* is not intended as a blanket endorsement of all of the contents of the DSM-IV. Certainly, some DSM diagnoses and assumptions have been both criticized and acclaimed. However, an extensive discussion of the advantages and disadvantages of the DSM system is beyond the scope of this book. DSM-IV was chosen to organize the chapters of this book because it is the most widely used and widely accepted system of mental disorders for both clinical and research purposes. Hence, it offers not only a comprehensive diagnostic system, but it also serves as a common language for mental health practitioners and researchers.

■ Some Assumptions

Because this book is intended to be a resource for practicing and training clinicians, it assumes a basic level of clinical knowledge. Essentially, this basic level of knowledge means that the user of this book will probably have had (or will be currently taking) introductory courses in counseling or psychotherapy, diagnosis, and assessment. Hence, major interventions and assessment instruments are reviewed in the following section, but comprehensive discussions of specific assessment and intervention techniques are avoided in this introductory chapter. Later chapters discuss assessment instruments and treatment techniques in greater depth, as they pertain to specific clinical problems. Clinicians looking for additional information concerning specific assessment instruments should refer to the test manuals and to Sattler (1993). Books containing overviews of treatment techniques are referenced in the following Treatment Options section.

■ Basic Organization

□ INTRODUCTION

All of the chapters in this book follow a similar outline (Table 1.1), which is designed to facilitate the process of rapidly locating and understanding information pertaining to childhood mental health disorders and treatment. The subject of each chapter is a major category of DSM-IV disorders, such as Mood Disorders or ADHD. Depending on the breadth of the major category, there will be descriptions of one or more disorders con-

TABLE 1.1   Outline of Chapters in *The Child Clinician's Handbook*

I. Clinical Description
   A. Diagnostic Considerations
   B. Appearance and Features
   C. Etiology

II. Assessment Patterns
   A. Broad Assessment Strategies
      1. Cognitive Assessment
      2. Psychological Assessment
      3. Behavioral Assessment
      4. Family Assessment
   B. Syndrome-Specific Tests

III. Treatment Options
   A. Behavioral Interventions
   B. Psychotherapy
   C. Family Interventions
   D. Medication
   E. Inpatient Hospitalization
   F. Special Education
   G. Referral

tained within the chapter. In the Mood Disorders chapter, for example, are the diagnoses Bipolar I Disorder, Bipolar II Disorder, Cyclothymic Disorder, Major Depressive Disorder, and Dysthymic Disorder. The ADHD chapter, on the other hand, contains only a single disorder. Characteristics that are shared by all of the disorders within the major category are covered in an introductory section. Then characteristics of the diagnosis, assessment, and treatment of each specific disorder are described.

CLINICAL DESCRIPTION

Coverage of each specific disorder begins with a Clinical Description section. This section gives clinicians an overall picture of the disorder that may be used to guide the clinical interview and initial formulations. Within this section, three major topics are considered, each of which is labeled with a subheading: Diagnostic Considerations, Appearance and Features, and Etiology.

Diagnostic Considerations

The Diagnostic Considerations section begins with a basic description of diagnostic criteria specified in DSM-IV. However, the Diagnostic Considerations section does not cover the criteria verbatim (you can use the DSM-IV for that), and it is *not* a substitute for DSM-IV. Rather, diagnostic criteria are summarized in descriptive form to supplement the formal DSM-IV listings. For example, DSM-IV includes numerous subtypes and specifiers for some disorders. Much of this detail is omitted or only briefly summarized in the Diagnostic Considerations section. In short, the clinician should have and use the DSM-IV.

Instead of simply repeating DSM-IV criteria, the Diagnostic Considerations section addresses issues related to making a diagnosis. These issues include a broad description of the disorder, difficult differential diagnoses, prevalence of the disorder, course, and subtypes of the diagnosis. In some cases, competing diagnostic systems are so commonly used (as with diagnoses of Autistic Disorder and Learning Disorders) that the clinician needs to be aware of how these fit with the DSM-IV criteria. Over all, then, the Diagnostic Considerations section provides additional information that the clinician can use in making a diagnosis of the child's problem and in understanding this diagnosis. A table describing epidemiology, subtypes, and course is included in each Diagnostic Considerations section to assist with rapid retrieval of these facts.

Appearance and Features

Following the description of diagnostic issues, the discussion turns to the psychological, behavioral, and social appearance of a child with the disorder. Diagnostic criteria, of course, begin to give a picture of the child's appearance, but they are of necessity restricted to broad and/or key features of the disorder. In addition to key features, the Appearance and Features section describes behaviors, psychosocial characteristics, and risks associated with the child's condition but not necessarily required for diagnosis. For example, children with ADHD are at increased risk for learning disabilities, although this is not a diagnostic criterion for the disorder.

The Appearance and Features section also attempts to bring the diagnosis "to life" by describing features typically seen in a child with the disorder. This section should be clinically useful in two ways: First, it should familiarize clinicians with what they are likely to see from a child with the diagnosis. Second, the Appearance and Features section suggests targets for specific questions in the clinical interview. These questions may probe the details and associated features of the disorder, helping the clinician to gain a more comprehensive picture of the child's problems. The Appearance and Features section, then, is intended to assist the clinician with the interview and observation facets of the initial evaluation. In order to improve the usefulness of the Appearance and Features section, a table summarizing the primary and associated features of each disorder is included in each Appearance and Features section.

In addition to investigating the Appearance and Features pertaining to specific disorders, there is certain background and interview information that clinicians typically will want to obtain regardless of the child's presenting problem. Appendix A provides an example of the typical components of background information that are helpful in understanding and formulating clinical data (as well as important for ruling out medical diagnoses and screening for danger); the appendix is organized in the format of a blank form to facilitate the organization of background information as it is obtained. Appendix B contains a form to assist with conducting and documenting a focused interview known as a Mental Status Examination (MSE). The MSE is routinely used in medical settings to gather clinical data relevant to psychological and behavioral symptoms and well-being.

Etiology

The Diagnostic Considerations section concludes with a discussion of the etiology of the disorder. Rather than adopting a set pattern of describing biological, then psychological, then social theories of etiology, the emphasis of the Etiology section differs from chapter to chapter, based on the weight of empirical research and theory. For example, if biological theories of etiology have received more empirical and theoretical attention for a particular disorder, these will be emphasized in the Etiology section of that disorder.

An overview of disorder etiology can be extremely helpful to clinicians, who are frequently asked by parents "why" their child has a behavior problem. Even if clinicians do not want to answer that question directly (or confidently!), chances are that they will want to have tentative etiological hypotheses for their own clinical use. In fact, some etiological formulations are standard in intake report summary sections. In addition, knowledge about possible etiology can help clinicians select targets for the clinical interview. Awareness about potential causal issues can guide clinicians' observations and questions. Finally, etiological hypotheses are often important in choosing an intervention. Family etiology, for example, may result in a recommendation for family therapy.

☐ ASSESSMENT PATTERNS

Following the basic description of the disorder, an Assessment Patterns section provides recommendations about how the child might be assessed using standardized psychological instruments. The major problem for the clinician at this stage is not finding a test to use, but selecting among the multitude of tests that are available to assess children. Many tests (such as IQ tests, broad personality tests, self-esteem tests, and broad-band behavior problem checklists) are used in the assessment of multiple disorders, whereas other tests may be designed for a specific disorder or behavior problem. Likewise, tests may assess cognitive, psychological, behavioral, or familial-social characteristics of the child. Finally, tests differ based on who responds to the questions. In the case of a child, the parent is often called on to respond to questions about the child's behaviors. Other respondents are the clinician, the teacher, other adults, or the child.

Clearly, the selection of tests poses a complex situation for the clinician. To simplify and organize the presentation of assessment instruments for each disorder, tests are classified based on the breadth of their application (broad application vs. application to a specific disorder), the major type of information that they provide (cognitive, psychological, behavioral, or familial-social), and the major source of information and formulation (clinician, child, parent, or other person) (Table 1.2). To assist the clinician with the selection of tests, a sample assessment battery is included in the Assessment Patterns section for each disorder. This sample battery is illustrative of useful tests for *most* children presenting with the disorder. However, tests may need to be added or deleted based on the particular characteristics of each child.

Broad Assessment Strategies

The Broad Assessment Strategies section reviews tests that are useful in the assessment of more than one disorder. Such tests tap broad psychological, behavioral, and social characteristics of the child, which may pertain to multiple disorders. Specifically, clinicians frequently want information about the child's cognitive functioning, internal psychological functioning, external behavioral functioning, and family environment, regardless of the child's specific problems. Information about these areas can be critical in formulation, diagnosis, and intervention.

TABLE 1.2   Organization of Psychological Assessment Instruments

TARGET OF ASSESSMENT	PRIMARY INFORMATION SOURCE			
BROAD ASSESSMENT STRATEGIES	**Clinician**	**Child**	**Parent**	**Other**
Cognitive				
Psychological				
Behavioral				
Family				
SYNDROME-SPECIFIC TESTS				

The selection of which tests to include in the Broad Assessment Strategies section was guided by several criteria: popularity with clinicians, quantity of empirical research, usefulness in the clinical situation, and importance of the data for diagnosis and therapy. If empirical data exist to support the use of the test or presence of a test pattern in a diagnostic group, research references are provided. In some cases, hypothesized test patterns can be inferred for a diagnostic population based on clinical experience and observations (but no current empirical support); these hypotheses are stated as being "expected" or "likely," and they are not referenced. Hence, expected assessment patterns that are described without reference to a book, article, chapter, or study are based on clinical experience and expectation as opposed to research data.

Of course, the relevance and importance of each test will vary somewhat based on the features of a specific disorder. Thus, no broad assessment strategy or test cuts across *all* diagnoses. Some chapters, for example, will not consider internal psychological assessment, whereas others will not cover family assessment. Only relevant assessment strategies are described for each diagnosis.

Although no test is useful for all childhood diagnoses, many broad tests show up repeatedly throughout the book. Summaries and descriptions of these tests are provided later in this chapter. In subsequent chapters, when broad tests are recommended for a specific diagnosis, only a description of their application to the diagnosis will be given. No basic information (e.g., reference, number of items, scoring, etc.) will be provided for broad tests in the later chapters, because the reader may refer to the basic test description in this introductory chapter (see Table 1.3 for a list of broad assessment instruments and corresponding references).

In order to simplify the organization of the Broad Assessment Strategies section, broad tests are divided into four groups based on the type of information that they give: Cognitive Assessment, Psychological Assessment, Behavioral Assessment, and Family Assessment. These four test groups have specific definitions in this book, which are described later. Within each group, attention is given to the primary respondent and/or administrator of the test. Tests

TABLE 1.3   Broad Assessment Instruments

NAME (ABBREVIATION)	REFERENCE	INFORMATION SOURCE
Cognitive Assessment		
Bayley Scales of Infant Development: Second Edition (Bayley-II)	Bayley, 1993	Clinician
Stanford-Binet Intelligence Scale: Fourth Edition (SB:FE)	Thorndike et al., 1986	Clinician
Wechsler Preschool and Primary Scale of Intelligence—Revised (WPPSI-R)	Wechsler, 1989	Clinician
Wechsler Intelligence Scale for Children— Third Edition (WISC-III)	Wechsler, 1991	Clinician
Wechsler Adult Intelligence Scale—Third Edition (WAIS-III)	Wechsler, 1997	Clinician
Kaufman Brief Intelligence Test (K-BIT)	Kaufman & Kaufman, 1990	Clinician
Wechsler Abbreviated Scale of Intelligence (WASI)	Psychological Corporation, 1999	Clinician
Woodcock-Johnson Tests of Educational Achievement—Revised (WJ-R)	Woodcock & Johnson, 1989	Clinician
Wechsler Individual Achievement Test (WIAT)	Psychological Corporation, 1992	Clinician
Vineland Adaptive Behavior Scales (VABS)	Sparrow et al.,1984	Clinician
Adaptive Behavior Evaluation Scale (ABES)	McCarney, 1995	Parent, Teacher
Psychological Assessment		
Minnesota Multiphasic Personality Inventory (MMPI, MMPI-2)	Hathaway & McKinley, 1967; Butcher et al., 1989	Clinician
Minnesota Multiphasic Personality Inventory—Adolescent Form (MMPI-A)	Butcher et al., 1992	Clinician
Rorschach Inkblot Test (Rorschach)	Exner & Weiner, 1995	Clinician
Thematic Apperception Test (TAT)	Murray, 1943	Clinician
Diagnostic Interview for Children and Adolescents (DICA)	Reich et al., 1997	Clinician
Diagnostic Interview Schedule for Children (DISC)	Shaffer et al., 1993	Clinician
Child Assessment Schedule (CAS)	Hodges, 1985	Clinician

(continued)

NAME (ABBREVIATION)	REFERENCE	INFORMATION SOURCE
Schedule for Affective Disorders and Schizophrenia for School-Age Children (K-SADS)	Puig-Antich et al., 1983	Clinician
Piers-Harris Self Concept Scale (PHSCS or Piers-Harris)	Piers, 1984	Child
Symptom Checklist-90—Revised (SCL-90-R)	Derogatis, 1994	Child

Behavioral Assessment

Child Behavior Checklist (CBCL)	Achenbach, 1991a, 1992	Parent
Teacher's Report Form (TRF)	Achenbach, 1991b	Teacher
Youth Self-Report (YSR)	Achenbach, 1991c	Child
Conners' Parent Rating Scale—Revised (CPRS-R)	Conners, 1997	Parent
Conners' Teacher Rating Scale—Revised (CTRS-R)	Conners, 1997	Teacher
Conners-Wells' Adolescent Self-Report Scale (CASS)	Conners, 1997	Child
Behavior Assessment System for Children—Parent Rating Scales (BASC-PRS)	Reynolds & Kamphaus, 1992	Parent
Behavior Assessment System for Children—Teacher Rating Scales (BASC-TRS)	Reynolds & Kamphaus, 1992	Teacher
Behavior Assessment System for Children—Self-Report of Personality (BASC-SRP)	Reynolds & Kamphaus, 1992	Child
Symptom Inventories—4 (ECI-4, CSI-4, ASI-4)	Gadow & Sprafkin, 1997a, 1998a	Parent, Teacher
Personality Inventory for Youth (PIY)	Lachar & Gruber, 1995	Child

Family Assessment

Family Environment Scale (FES)	Moos & Moos, 1994	Parent, Child

that require administration or extensive formulation by the clinician are considered to be *clinician-administered*. Examples of such tests are IQ tests, achievement tests, neuropsychological tests, projective tests, and interviews. Although all clinician-administered tests use data provided by the child and/or parent, considerable effort, expertise, and/or observation are required by the clinician. Hence, these are grouped under the clinician-administered rubric to alert clinicians that these tests require additional time and expertise.

Tests that are essentially self-administered are grouped into three additional categories: *Child-report* tests involve the self-report of the child; essentially, the child reads (or is read) questions and provides answers. In many cases, these tests are susceptible to bias, social desirability, difficulty understanding questions, limited vocabulary, lack of insight, and other factors that may distort the meaning of the data obtained. The clinician must consider these factors in evaluating the meaning of child-report tests. On the other hand, self-report measures are essential in the direct assessment of internal states (which can only be inferred from observation), and they provide valuable information about the child's view of the problem. *Parent-report* tests involve the parent's response to questions involving the child, parent, or family. Again, the clinician must consider effects of social desirability, bias, lack of insight, lack of observational skill, and other personality factors in interpreting the data obtained. *Other-report* tests are face-valid tests completed by other persons familiar with the child. Inpatient unit staff, teachers, and siblings are examples of such persons. These tests carry the same caveats as child and parent-report tests.

The organization of tests into clinician-administered, child-report, parent-report, and other-report categories has several advantages. First, interpretation of the tests should involve a consideration of who is the respondent to the test. A growing body of research indicates that different informants differ considerably on ratings of behavior problems for the same child. Correlations between almost any combination of parent, child, teacher, and mental health worker ratings of the same behavior tend to be quite low (usually in the 0.20's; Achenbach, McConaughy, & Howell, 1987), although mother-father correlations may be somewhat higher (Kaslow & Racusin, 1990). Child self-ratings of symptoms often do not correspond with parent, teacher, or professional ratings. Research suggests that observers may not be as accurate at reporting internal symptom states of a child (such as depression, which observers tend to underestimate; Kaslow & Racusin, 1990), whereas observers may be more accurate than children at reporting external behavioral symptoms. Furthermore, reports of symptoms tend to be consistent within but not between respondents. In other words, parent ratings of depression on one test tend to correlate highly with parent ratings of depression on a different test, but not with child ratings of depression on the same test. Hence, a comprehensive assessment must integrate information from multiple sources.

Second, interpretation should involve a consideration of the degree to which the items are face valid, projective, and/or interpreted by the clinician. Projective tests and tests requiring additional inferences take clinical formulation into account, whereas face-valid instruments are more direct measures of what the child or parent wants to say to the clinician. Third, tests involve varying degrees of preparation, time, and effort. Clinician-administered tests almost always require the use of the clinician's (or a technician's) time in order to gather data. Hence, these tests must be worked around clinical interviews and the rest of the clinician's schedule. Child-, parent-, and other-report tests may be completed without requiring significant additional clinical time. Fourth, the tests give different types of information, all of which can be valuable. Children and parents, for example, can have different viewpoints on the same behavior. Therefore, it is usually important to give a variety of tests based on the respondent and the type of information obtained. Such a multimethod approach can give a more complete clinical picture.

Cognitive Assessment

The broad assessment strategies for each disorder can be divided into four major categories (cognitive, psychological, behavioral, and family) based on the type of information obtained. Cognitive assessment is defined in this book as tests that provide information about a child's intellectual abilities, specific cognitive abilities, understanding of the environment, ability to engage in adaptive behavior, and level of basic knowledge. With few exceptions, cognitive assessment tests are clinician-administered and require considerable expertise to administer and interpret.

Intelligence Tests.   Perhaps the most widely used cognitive assessment tests in the clinical setting are intelligence tests. Intelligence tests are used to gain an overall impression of the child's cognitive ability as well as to measure specific intellectual abilities, such as verbal comprehension and nonverbal reasoning. Although numerous intelligence tests exist, the most extensively used are the *Bayley Scales of Infant Development: Second Edition* (Bayley-II; Bayley, 1993) for children age 0–42 months, the *Wechsler Preschool and Primary Scale of Intelligence—Revised* (WPPSI-R; Wechsler, 1989) for children age 3–7 years, the *Wechsler Intelligence Scale for Children—Third Edition* (WISC-III; Wechsler, 1991) for children age 6–17 years, the *Wechsler Adult Intelligence Scale—Third Edition* (WAIS-III; Wechsler, 1997; The Psychological Corporation, 1997) for adolescents and adults over age 16, and the *Stanford-Binet Intelligence Scale: Fourth Edition* for age 2–adult (SB:FE; Thorndike, Hagen, & Sattler, 1986). Some of the research that applies to the most recent versions of the Wechsler scales is based on earlier revisions of these scales: the *Wechsler Preschool and Primary Scale of Intelligence* (WPPSI; Wechsler, 1967), the *Wechsler Intelligence Scale for Children—Revised* (WISC-R; Wechsler, 1974), and the *Wechsler Adult Intelligence Scale—Revised* (WAIS-R; Wechsler, 1981). Although research using these earlier versions can be applied to more recent revisions (with appropriate caution), the earlier versions of intelligence tests generally should not be used in place of their revisions in the clinical setting.

The Bayley-II is a measure of mental-behavioral development in infants age 1 month to 42 months. Its items require the presentation of a stimulus or request to the child, followed by observation and scoring of the response. Items test age-appropriate mental and motor development. The Bayley II yields a Mental Developmental Index (MDI), a Psychomotor Developmental Index (PDI), and a Behavior Rating Index (BRI). The MDI may be used as an approximation of IQ, although IQ at very young ages is only moderately predictive of IQ at later ages. Based on a large normative sample, Bayley-II MDI, PDI, and BRI raw scores may be converted to standard scores with a mean of 100 and standard deviation of 15 (Bayley, 1993).

At older ages (roughly 3 or 4 years and up), the Wechsler scales (WPPSI-R, WISC-III, and WAIS-III) become the measures of choice for child intelligence and cognitive status. Each Wechsler scale consists of a variety of subscales; most subscales appear on all three age-based versions of the Wechsler IQ tests (Tables 1.4 and 1.5). As measures of specific cognitive abilities, the Wechsler subscales may be helpful in the diagnosis and understanding of certain disorders. More importantly, however, subscales may be combined into higher-order ability composites.

The most well known and widely used composites are based on Wechsler's a priori conceptualization of intelligence as having Verbal and Performance components. Hence, in

TABLE 1.4   Wechsler Intelligence Scale Verbal Subtests

SUBTEST	WPPSI-R	WISC-III	WAIS-III
Sentences (short-term auditory memory for sentences)	O	N	N
Digit Span (short-term auditory memory for numbers)	N	O	S
Information (fund of basic information)	S	S	S
Comprehension (practical knowledge and judgment)	S	S	S
Arithmetic (mental computation)	S	S	S
Vocabulary (word knowledge)	S	S	S
Similarities (relationships between concepts)	S	S	S
Letter-Number Sequencing (short-term auditory memory during mental operations)	N	N	O

S—Standard Subtest
O—Optional Subtest
N—Not on Test

addition to an overall measure of intelligence (Full Scale IQ or FIQ), the WPPSI-R, WISC-III, and WAIS-III yield measures of Verbal IQ (VIQ—comprehension and knowledge of verbal concepts) and Performance IQ (PIQ—visual-spatial, visual-motor, and visual sequencing ability). However, the Verbal-Performance differentiation of subtests appears to hold empirically only for the WPPSI-R (Sattler, 1990).

Factor analyses of the WISC-III and WAIS-III support the existence of Verbal (usually called Verbal Comprehension or VC) and Performance (usually called Perceptual Organization or PO) clusters of subtests, but additional clusters have also been identified (Psychological Corporation, 1997; Sattler, 1993; Wechsler, 1991). The most widely accepted "other" factor-analytically derived clusters of subtests are Freedom from Distractibility (FFD, a measure of attention, concentration, and short-term memory; Arithmetic and Digit Span subtests) and Processing Speed (PS, a measure of rapid response to simple visual-motor tasks; Coding and Symbol Search subtests) (Sattler, 1993; Wechsler, 1991). Recent research on the FFD factor indicates that it may be a stronger measure of short-term memory during mental operations than of freedom from distraction (Psychological Corporation, 1997). Hence, the FFD factor was renamed "Working Memory" (WM) in the WAIS-III, and an additional subtest (Letter-Number Sequencing) was found to load on the WM factor in the WAIS-III.

In summary, the WISC-III and WAIS-III give FIQ, VIQ, PIQ, VC, PO, FFD (or WM), and PS scores in addition to subtest scores. Subtest raw scores are converted to scaled scores (mean = 10; standard deviation = 3) based on excellent normative samples. FIQ, VIQ, PIQ, VC, PO, FFD, and PS scores are reported as standard scores (mean = 100; standard deviation = 15). The VC, PO, FFD, and PS "Index" scores are factorially more "pure" (stronger internal consistency with less overlap) than the VIQ and PIQ "IQ" scores. Therefore, the index scores can sometimes provide more information about ability strengths and weaknesses than the VIQ and PIQ scores. Overall, the WPPSI-R, WISC-III, and WAIS-R

TABLE 1.5 Wechsler Intelligence Scale Performance Subtests

SUBTEST	WPPSI-R	WISC-III	WAIS-III
Geometric Design (visual-motor organization)	S	N	N
Animal Pegs (concentration, finger dexterity, and persistence)	O	N	N
Mazes (planning and perceptual organization)	S	O	N
Object Assembly (synthesis of parts into meaningful wholes)	S	S	O
Block Design (analysis and synthesis of abstract part-whole relationships)	S	S	S
Picture Completion (identification of essential detail)	S	S	S
Picture Arrangement (social-temporal sequencing)	N	S	S
Coding/Digit-Symbol (psychomotor speed of symbol association and reproduction)	N	S	S
Symbol Search (psychomotor speed of matching of details)	N	O	O
Matrix Reasoning (nonverbal logical reasoning)	N	N	S

S—Standard Subtest
O—Optional Subtest
N—Not on Test

provide excellent data concerning the cognitive-intelligence status of children age 3 and older. Additional interpretive strategies and tables for these tests may be found in Wechsler (1989, 1991, 1997) and Sattler (1993).

Other than the Wechsler scales, the SB:FE is a widely used intelligence test in the clinical setting. The SB:FE consists of fifteen subtests that cluster into four broad intelligence areas: Verbal Reasoning (VR), Abstract/Visual Reasoning (AVR), Quantitative Reasoning (QR), and Short-Term Memory (STM). Depending on age, children are administered from eight to fifteen of the subtests. Based on a large normative sample, subtest scores are converted to Standard Age Scores (SASs), which are standard scores with a mean of 50 and a standard deviation of 8. Area (VR, AVR, QR, and STM) standard scores and an overall IQ score are reported based on a population mean of 100 and standard deviation of 16.

The SB:FE has received criticism for its normative sample, factor structure, difficulty of administration, and length of administration (which can exceed 2 hours). Sattler (1993) found no evidence to support the existence of the four area composites. He proposed an alternate grouping of subtests into Verbal Comprehension, Nonverbal Reasoning/Visualization, and Memory areas. Despite these problems, the SB:FE is still widely used. Its widespread use is probably a result of its historical significance, broad age range, extensive sampling of abilities, and utility with mentally retarded individuals. However, psychometrically and practically, the SB:FE is a less desirable test than the Wechsler scales except in special cases (which are noted in later chapters).

In addition to the more extensive, comprehensive tests of intelligence, several excellent, brief measures of intelligence may be used in situations that require screening assessment of cognitive ability. In addition to shorter administration time, brief IQ tests may be used when the child's performance is adversely affected by the length and elaborate nature of the more extensive scales. The *Kaufman Brief Intelligence Test* (K-BIT; Kaufman & Kaufman, 1990) takes about 20–30 minutes to administer and consists of two subtests. The Vocabulary subtest contains questions about single-word expressive vocabulary (picture naming) and identification of words from verbal and letter-placement cues. The Matrices subtest consists of pictorial analogies and matching problems. Hence, K-BIT results provide an estimate of verbal (Vocabulary subtest) and nonverbal (Matrices subtest) ability, as well as an overall IQ Composite score.

Another brief intelligence test, the *Wechsler Abbreviated Scale of Intelligence* (WASI; Psychological Corporation, 1999), provides Verbal and Performance IQ as well as Full Scale IQ estimates for individuals of ages 6–89 years. The WASI consists of four subtests that are identical in format (although specific content is different) to WISC-III/WAIS-III subscales: Vocabulary, Block Design, Similarities, and Matrix Reasoning. Administration of the full WASI (4 subtests) takes approximately 30 minutes, but a two-subtest (Vocabulary-Matrix Reasoning) form can be administered in about 15 minutes. An additional advantage of the WASI is its inclusion of Matrix Reasoning, which has no counterpart in the WISC-III and is an excellent measure of nonverbal logical reasoning. Because the WISC-III has no subtest that specifically measures nonverbal logical reasoning, WASI Matrix Reasoning can be added to the WISC-III to provide this information.

Confidence intervals (95%) for K-BIT IQ composite scores range from ±4 to ±9 points from the obtained IQ score, while those for the WASI range from approximately ±4 to ±7 for the 2 and 4 subtest Full Scale IQ. Comparable values for the WISC-III are approximately ±5 to ±6 points (Kaufman & Kaufman, 1990; Psychological Corporation, 1999; Wechsler, 1992). K-BIT Composite and Vocabulary IQ scores correlate strongly with WISC-R IQ scores (Kaufman & Kaufman, 1990). WASI subtest scores correlate at about a 0.65–0.85 level with corresponding WAIS-III and WISC-III subtests, whereas WASI composite scores correlate at an approximately 0.80–0.90 level with corresponding WISC-III and WAIS-III composite scores (Psychological Corporation, 1999). Hence, both the WASI and the K-BIT provide reliable and valid information about cognitive ability for children and adolescents.

Several other, less widely used measures of intelligence have good psychometric properties and provide clinically relevant data. These scales will not be covered extensively in later chapters, but they deserve mention because they may provide valuable information for specific disorders. The *McCarthy Scales of Children's Abilities* (McCarthy, 1972; ages 2½ to 8½), the *Kaufman Assessment Battery for Children* (K-ABC; Kaufman & Kaufman, 1983; ages 2½ to 12½), the *Differential Abilities Scales* (DAS; Elliott, 1990; ages 2½ to 17), and the *Woodcock-Johnson Tests of Cognitive Abilities—Revised* (Woodcock & Johnson, 1989a; McGrew, 1994; ages 2 to 90 years) are excellent measures of global and specific cognitive abilities. The DAS and K-ABC are widely used in place of the WPPSI-R, which has received criticism for its length and uninteresting content for preschool children. In addition, selected subtests from the SB:FE and the *Woodcock-Johnson Tests of Cognitive Abilities—Revised* can be used by clinicians to assess specific areas of cognitive functioning as well as global intelligence.

Achievement Tests. Whereas intelligence tests seek to evaluate intellectual ability (reflected in basic knowledge and skills obtained in the everyday environment), achievement tests focus more on academic knowledge gained in the school and home settings. These tests measure the extent to which children have learned what they have been formally taught. At later ages, achievement tests reflect the effects of formal schooling. Like intelligence tests, there are many achievement tests, several of which are psychometrically quite good. Two such tests are the *Woodcock-Johnson Tests of Educational Achievement—Revised* (WJ-R; Woodcock & Johnson, 1989b) and the *Wechsler Individual Achievement Test* (WIAT; Psychological Corporation, 1992). Several other excellent tests exist, such as the *Kaufman Test of Educational Achievement* (K-TEA; Kaufman & Kaufman, 1985; a 1997 normative update is also available) and the *Peabody Individual Achievement Test—Revised* (PIAT-R; Markwardt, 1989; a 1997 normative update is also available). The WJ-R and WIAT will be considered in more detail here because they are widely used with many subtests and excellent psychometric properties.

The WJ-R is an individually administered achievement test with nine standard subtests that fall into four achievement clusters: Reading (pronunciation and comprehension), Mathematics (basic arithmetic and applied problems), Written Language (spelling and writing skills), and Knowledge (science, social studies, and humanities). Subtest and cluster scores are converted to standard scores (mean = 100; standard deviation = 15) based on a large, representative normative sample. In addition to the nine standard subtests, the WJ-R includes a variety of "supplementary" subtests that are not required in order to obtain cluster scores. However, they can be useful in detailed analysis of a problem in a specific achievement area (such as reading or math). Like standard subtests, supplementary subtests yield standard scores relative to a normative sample.

The WJ-R covers an extremely wide age range, from age 2½ to adulthood, and it yields an extensive body of scores. In addition to standard scores, the WJ-R gives age-equivalent, grade-equivalent, percentile, confidence interval, and Relative Mastery Index (RMI) scores. The RMI is a measure of the percentage of mastery of a topic obtained by the tested child when the average child would score a 90%. For example, an RMI of 95 on Calculation indicates that, when the average child has achieved a 90% mastery level of Calculation, the tested child is likely to show 95% mastery of Calculation.

Like the WJ-R, the WIAT has excellent psychometric properties, although its age range is substantially smaller than that of the WJ-R (age 5 to 19-11). The WIAT consists of eight subtests and four composite areas: Reading, Mathematics, Language, and Writing. The Reading, Mathematics, and Writing areas are similar to those on the WJ-R. However, the Language area includes tests of listening comprehension and oral expression that are unlike any test in the WJ-R achievement battery (although there are tests of Oral Vocabulary and Listening Comprehension in the *Woodcock-Johnson Tests of Cognitive Abilities*). In addition, the WIAT does not include Knowledge tests like those on the WJ-R.

WIAT subtest and composite raw scores yield age- or grade-based standard scores (mean = 100; standard deviation = 15) based on a representative normative sample. Unlike the WJ-R, the WIAT includes no supplementary subtests, but the WIAT may be used as a brief, screening test by eliminating some of the more lengthy and complex subtests. Because the WIAT was co-normed with the WISC-III (i.e., some of the children in the WIAT and WISC-III standardization samples took both the WIAT and WISC-III), WIAT scores can be directly linked to WISC-III scores. In other words, a "predicted" score for each WIAT area can be calculated from the WISC-III IQ score, and the statistical significance of the IQ-achievement difference can be calculated.

Adaptive Functioning Tests. It is sometimes important to consider the results of an adaptive functioning test in addition to the results of intellectual testing, particularly for children with low IQ. Adaptive functioning reflects the extent to which a child functions effectively within the environment. Specifically, adaptive functioning tests investigate the child's performance of daily living skills, communication with others, functioning in social situations, and use of motor skills to interact with the environment. Hence, tests of adaptive functioning can give the clinician an idea of the child's ability to engage in self-care and interaction with the environment. Children with adequate adaptive functioning skills can interact appropriately with their environment and can care adequately for themselves. A child with low IQ but high adaptive functioning would be treated quite differently than a child with low IQ and low adaptive functioning.

Most adaptive functioning tests have significant psychometric or practical drawbacks. In the clinical setting, a widely used and psychometrically sound adaptive functioning test is the *Vineland Adaptive Behavior Scales* (VABS; Sparrow, Balla, & Cicchetti, 1984). The VABS assesses social competence and adaptive behavior in children from birth to 19 years old. It is administered in interview format to a respondent who is familiar with the child's behavior. Adaptive behavior is tapped by four VABS subscales: Communication (receptive and expressive language, written language), Daily Living Skills (hygiene, personal care, independence in personal living), Socialization (social behavior), and Motor Skills (gross and fine motor coordination). Subscales can be combined to give an Adaptive Behavior Composite. In addition to adaptive behavior scores, the VABS also gives a score for Maladaptive Behavior (behavior problems).

All VABS scales can be converted to standard scores (mean = 100; standard deviation = 15) based on a normative sample. In addition to the Expanded Form, there is a briefer Survey Form of the VABS and a Classroom Edition for teachers. The Expanded or Survey forms are typically given to the primary caretaker (usually a parent) and take from 30–90 minutes to administer. The VABS has good psychometric properties and is the most widely used adaptive behavior scale. However, its norms have been criticized (Sattler, 1990).

The *Adaptive Behavior Evaluation Scale* (ABES; McCarney, 1995) is a questionnaire-format adaptive behavior scale with forms for parents and teachers. Because of its questionnaire format, it is much easier to administer than the VABS, and it is useful for broad assessment purposes (not exclusively focused on mental retardation). The ABES yields adaptive behavior scores in 10 areas: Communication Skills, Self-Care, Home Living, Social, Community Use, Self-Direction, Health and Safety, Functional Academics, Leisure, and Work. Scaled scores (mean of 10, standard deviation of 3) are provided for each of the 10 subscales, and an overall composite score (mean of 100, standard deviation of 15) is also given, based on a large, nonclinical, nonrepresentative sample. Although not as widely used as the VABS, the ABES provides a questionnaire-format alternative for assessing adaptive functioning.

Other than the VABS and the ABES, most adaptive behavior scales are strongly focused on mentally retarded populations. Thus, their usefulness as broad assessment instruments is very limited.

Psychological Assessment

Psychological Assessment instruments are defined in this book as tests that measure the internal psychological thoughts, affects, beliefs, issues, or states of the child. They differ from Behavioral Assessment instruments in that they are internally focused on the child's thoughts and feelings. Psychological Assessment instruments are valuable in the clinical setting because they provide a window on the internal states that are presumed to underlie the child's behavior. Thoughts, feelings, and beliefs are important in clinical formulations and in many treatment modalities, particularly psychodynamic and cognitive. Included in the category of Psychological Assessment are clinician-administered tests of personality and structured interviews, as well as child-report tests of self-esteem, stress appraisal, and coping. These tests share in common a focus on self-report information.

Clinician-Administered Tests of Personality. Clinician-administered tests of personality are often divided into objective and projective tests. Objective tests present the child with a structured set of questions and a finite set of answers. The child chooses a preworded answer for each question. Projective tests present an ambiguous or incomplete stimulus and ask the child to make something (e.g., a percept, story, or drawing) out of the stimulus.

An extremely useful objective personality test for adolescents is the *Minnesota Multiphasic Personality Inventory* (MMPI; Hathaway & McKinley, 1951, 1967). When the original MMPI was revised, a version was created specifically for use with adolescents, the *Minnesota Multiphasic Personality Inventory-Adolescent* (MMPI-A; Butcher et al., 1992). The MMPI is the most widely used and researched personality test, although most of its use has been with adults. The MMPI consists of 566 true-false items (478 items on the MMPI-A) that cluster into three validity and ten clinical scales (Table 1.6). A fourth validity scale, the "Cannot Say" scale (abbreviated as "?"), is a count of the number of items left unanswered by the respondent. In addition to the basic validity and clinical scales, hundreds of other MMPI validity, clinical, and content scales have been developed as well as subscales to enhance the interpretation of the basic clinical scales (see Greene, 1991, and Graham, 1990, for a description of additional MMPI scales). With the exception of the Lie (L) scale, the other basic validity and clinical scales were developed using an empirical approach for item selection. This approach selects items based on the extent to which they differentiate between a normal group and a target clinical group. For example, items for the Hypochondriasis (Hs) scale were selected because they differentiated between normals and psychiatric patients with functional somatic problems (the empirical item selection process was, in fact, not quite this simple or clean; see Dahlstrom, Welsh, & Dahlstrom, 1972, for a detailed analysis of item selection).

MMPI scale scores may be converted to T-scores based on a nonrepresentative Minnesota sample tested in the 1930s and 1940s. However, T-scores obtained using these norms are remarkably similar to those using more representative samples (Greene, 1991). Interpretation of the MMPI is complex because of the number of potential MMPI scales to interpret, the meaning of profile patterns, the variety of items contained in each scale, and the volume of MMPI research. At the very least, knowledge of psychometrics, a graduate-level course, and clinical supervision are required to use the MMPI competently. Readers interested in additional information concerning the MMPI are encouraged to consult Graham (1990), Greene (1991), and Dahlstrom et al. (1972).

TABLE 1.6   MMPI/MMPI-2/MMPI-A Validity and Clinical Scales

SCALE	ABBREVIATION (NUMBER)	DESCRIPTION
VALIDITY SCALES		
Lie	L	presents overly favorable picture of self; denies faults
Infrequency	F	exhibits unusual, atypical responding
Defensiveness	K	minimizes problems; denies distress
CLINICAL SCALES		
Hypochondriasis	Hs (1)	has somatic complaints
Depression	D (2)	exhibits dysphoria, tiredness, inhibition, low self-esteem, attention/concentration problems
Hysteria	Hy (3)	is self-centered, superficial, demands attention
Psychopathic Deviate	Pd (4)	is nonconforming, resists rules, authority conflict, socially maladjusted, impulsive
Masculinity-Femininity*	Mf (5)	is dependent, passive, sensitive, has traditional female interests, is nurturant
Paranoia	Pa (6)	is suspicious, self-righteous, guarded
Psychasthenia	Pt (7)	is anxious, self-critical, ruminates
Schizophrenia	Sc (8)	exhibits thought problems, alienation
Hypomania	Ma (9)	is impulsive, energetic, egocentric
Social Introversion	Si (0)	exhibits social discomfort, inhibition

*Scale is scored in the opposite direction for females. Note: This table is for review purposes and is not intended to serve as the basic resource for interpretation of the MMPI.

The lower age range of the MMPI has been a subject of disagreement between clinicians. Relative to adult norms, adolescents tend to elevate most MMPI scales. Marks, Seeman, and Haller (1974) addressed the problem of elevated adolescent scores by providing actuarial data and norms for children as young as 14. Using age 14 as the cutoff is probably wise, considering that the reading ability required for most MMPI items is approximately sixth to eighth grade. Marks et al.'s (1974) adolescent norms are probably the most widely used for the original MMPI. However, because those norms use non-K-corrected scores (adult MMPI norms use K-corrected scores), they should be interpreted with caution for adolescents with high K-scales.

The original MMPI was revised in 1989 to form a new (but very similar) instrument, the MMPI-2 (Butcher, Dahlstrom, Graham, Tellegen, & Kaemmer, 1989). The MMPI-2 retained most of the original items from the basic clinical and validity scales (although some of these were slightly reworded to reflect more modern views). However, many of the other items were changed, deleted, or added, requiring most other MMPI subscales to be changed as well. A new, modern, more representative normative sample was used, and the calculation of T-scores was changed for most scales (not scales 5 and 0) to achieve a somewhat more normal distribution of scores. These T-scores are called uniform T-scores and are not normalized T-scores *per se* (see Butcher et al., 1989, for a discussion of T-score derivation). T-scores of 65 (not 70 as on the original MMPI) and higher were considered clinically significant. The issue most relevant to child/adolescent assessment, however, was the authors' recommendation that the MMPI-2 not be used with adolescents under the age of 18 (Butcher et al., 1989).

The MMPI-A (Butcher et al., 1992) was developed as the adolescent companion to the MMPI-2. An effort was made to retain (with occasional wording changes) most MMPI items in order to maintain congruence between the MMPI-A and MMPI/MMPI-2, although some items were deleted because of offensive or inappropriate content for adolescents. Validity and clinical scales that are most changed on the MMPI-A are F (27 items deleted from the original MMPI), 5 (16 items deleted), and 0 (8 items deleted); other validity and clinical scales have only minor changes. Norms for the MMPI-A were derived from a national sample of 1620 adolescents between the ages of 14 and 18. Efforts were undertaken to make the normative sample representative of geographic region and ethnicity; however, the sample may be of somewhat higher SES than the national population of adolescents. Like the MMPI-2, the MMPI-A uses uniform T-scores for the most validity and clinical scales (not scales 5 and 0).

The MMPI-A is a 478-item, true-false instrument that can be administered to adolescents age 14 to 18. It includes the same basic validity and clinical scales as the MMPI and MMPI-2, and most scales retain their original interpretive meaning. Numerous new validity and clinical scales were also developed for the MMPI-A (Butcher et al., 1992). Unlike the MMPI-2 (but similar to earlier MMPI adolescent norms), non-K-corrected norms are used for all scales. T-scores of 65 and higher are considered clinically significant.

The decision of which form of the MMPI to use for adolescents is a complex one. Perhaps the easiest decision is that the MMPI-2 should never be used with an adolescent under age 18. For children age 14–18, the original MMPI has the advantage of decades of research and clinical use, but some items are inappropriate for adolescents, and norms are less than ideal. The MMPI-A, on the other hand, is briefer, has more appropriate items for adolescents, has better norms, and is a generally more modern test. However, it does not have the volume of research and clinical support of the MMPI. Overall, interpretation of MMPI scales L, K, 1, 2, 3, 4, 6, 7, 8, 9, and 0 should be similar for the MMPI and MMPI-A because only very minor changes were made in these scales. Scales F and 5, however, have undergone major changes on the MMPI-A. The MMPI-A also includes several content scales that are more relevant to adolescents than were scales from the original MMPI (Williams, Butcher, Ben-Porath, & Graham, 1992).

Of the projective personality tests, the most well known are the *Rorschach Inkblot Test* (Exner, 1993; Exner & Weiner, 1995) and the *Thematic Apperception Test* (TAT; Murray, 1943). The Rorschach consists of 10 cards, each of which is a picture of a symmetric inkblot. Although numerous systems exist for administering the Rorschach, all administrations ask initially for what is seen on the blot (the percept). Later, the subject is asked to show in detail the characteristics that led him or her to see the percept in the way that it was seen. Scoring is done on the basis of response characteristics (determinants) such as color, form, achromatic color, shading, dimensionality, and texture. The content and form quality of responses are also used in scoring. The widely accepted Exner (1993) Rorschach scoring and interpretation system is used in this book.

The TAT (Murray, 1943) is one of a multitude of storytelling tests. Numerous other such tests exist, several of which were designed specifically for children. However, the TAT is the oldest, best known, and most widely used of these tests. Hence, it serves as the prototypical storytelling test in later chapters of this book. Many hypotheses about TAT patterns may be readily applied to other storytelling tests.

The TAT presents the child with a picture of a person or people in a certain setting or activity. The child is asked to tell a story about the characters in the picture, what they are doing, what they are thinking, and what they are feeling. No widely accepted scoring system exists for the TAT. Stories are typically analyzed for repetitive, unique, intense, or problematic themes, beliefs, or affects. The TAT can provide a picture of how the child expects sequences of events to occur, as well as predominant affects and thoughts of the child related to these stories. Alexander (1990) presents a general approach to analyzing and interpreting storytelling information such as that obtained in the TAT or in biographical interview.

Projective tests have received criticism for questionable psychometrics, especially interrater reliability and validity. Transient state factors (such as hunger, mood, and frustration) can affect projective test results and should not be interpreted as enduring personality traits. On the other hand, children often have difficulty with questionnaire-type self-report tests, so projectives are often an essential source of information, as long as they are appropriately interpreted. Furthermore, projective tests have received clinical and research support for certain uses (Masling, 1997).

Clinician-Administered Structured and Semistructured Interviews. Structured and semistructured diagnostic interviews use an organized set of questions and probes to evaluate a child's behaviors and feelings. They are typically based on a diagnostic system (e.g., DSM-III-R or DSM-IV) and have as their major goal the delineation of a specific diagnosis. Examples of structured or semistructured interviews are the *Diagnostic Interview for Children and Adolescents* (DICA; Reich et al., 1997; Welner, Reich, Herjanic, Jung, & Amado, 1987), the *Diagnostic Interview Schedule for Children* (DISC; Costello, Edelbrock, Dulcan, Kales, & Klavic, 1984; Shaffer et al., 1993), the *Child Assessment Schedule* (CAS; Hodges, 1985, 1987; Hodges & Zeman, 1993), and the *Schedule for Affective Disorders and Schizophrenia for School Age Children* (Kiddie-SADS or K-SADS; Orvaschel & Puig-Antich, 1987; Puig-Antich, Chambers, & Tabrizi, 1983; Puig-Antich & Ryan, 1986). These interviews consist of a set of diagnostic questions that is asked directly to the child and/or parent and is used to arrive at a diagnosis for the child. They have both parent and child forms, although the integration of these forms varies between interviews. The interviews differ somewhat on the skill required of the interviewer, the diagnostic criteria covered, and psychometric properties.

The DISC and DICA undergo regular revisions based on updates of the DSM and updates of their psychometrics. Both of these questionnaires are available in computer-administered format, with revisions (of both paper and computer-administered versions) noted by a version number appended to the end of the name (such as DICA-IV and DISC-2.3). Currently, these semistructured interviews are the most widely used of their type in research and clinical settings. The development of the DISC traces back to studies funded by the National Institute of Mental Health (NIMH), and much DISC research continues to emerge from groups funded by NIMH grants. The DICA is published and promoted by a publishing company (Multi-Health Systems), with concurrent research and publications by scale authors and others.

The DICA and DISC consist of specific questions about symptom presence and severity, which are rated on a yes/no or frequency scale. The DICA may be administered to children age 6–17, whereas the DISC may be administered to children age 6–18. The K-SADS and the CAS, on the other hand, are less structured and, therefore, require a skilled interviewer and more clinical judgment than the DICA and the DISC (Mokros & Poznanski, 1992). The CAS contains open-ended as well as yes/no questions, and the K-SADS uses severity ratings as well as symptom presence questions. In addition, both the CAS and the K-SADS call on the interviewer to make a judgment as to the presence or absence of symptoms as opposed to simply recording answers.

In addition to these widely used interviews, other semistructured diagnostic interviews exist, such as the Child and Adolescent Psychiatric Assessment (CAPA-C; Angold & Costello, 1995) and the Interview Schedule for Children (ISC; Kovacs, 1985). In many cases, these interviews are used largely in the research programs of their authors and do not see widespread clinical use. Major test publishers have developed other semistructured diagnostic interviews, which are promoted for sale to clinicians.

Despite their potential utility as diagnostic tools, long, semistructured diagnostic interviews such as the DICA, DISC, CAS, and K-SADS are rarely used in actual clinical practice. A major problem is their length, which ranges in time from 1–4 hours. This significantly limits their clinical utility, and makes them unpleasant for clinicians and families. Computer administration of the DICA and DISC reduces demands on the clinician, but the interview nature of the scales is obviously reduced. A second problem with semistructured interviews is the questionable value of interview-based self-report of symptoms by children younger than 12 years. Several studies suggest that children under age 12 may not be reliable reporters of symptoms on structured interviews such as the DICA (Breton et al., 1995; Schwab-Stone, Fallon, Briggs, & Crowther, 1994). On the other hand, semistructured diagnostic interviews are vitally important for research, which demands standardization and replication. Hence, they have seen most widespread use in research. Because of their limited clinical applicability, these interviews are considered only in the context of diagnoses for which they have seen widespread clinical or research use. Because of their breadth, they could be used to assist with making almost any diagnosis covered in this book.

Child-Report Psychological Assessment Instruments. Child self-report instruments are sometimes used to gather information about internal psychological thoughts and feelings, but these instruments should be used with appropriate caution. Preadolescent children frequently answer questions in socially desirable ways out of concern for providing the "correct" answers. Because many young children lack understanding or motivation for therapy, their motivation to complete self-report scales accurately is questionable. Other problems with self-report include poor insight, reading difficulty, and word knowledge problems.

The Behavior Assessment System for Children (BASC; Reynolds & Kamphaus, 1992) includes self-report scales (BASC-SRP) for children age 8–11 and for adolescents age 12–18. The Personality Inventory for Youth (PIY; Lachar & Gruber, 1995; for age 8–18) and the Youth Self-Report (YSR; Achenbach, 1991c; for age 11–18) are other self-report questionnaires that include questions about internal thoughts and feelings. These questionnaires contain items about external behaviors as well as internal states, and they are described in greater detail in the next section.

For older children and adolescents, two additional useful self-report psychological tests are the *Piers-Harris Self Concept Scale* (PHSCS; Piers, 1984) and the *Symptom Checklist-90—Revised* (SCL-90-R; Derogatis, 1994). The PHSCS is an 80-item, self-report scale of self-concept/self-esteem in children (Piers, 1984). In addition to a Total Self-Concept Score, it yields subscale scores of self-concept in 6 areas: Behavior, Intellectual and School Status, Physical Appearance and Attributes, Anxiety, Popularity, and Happiness and Satisfaction. PHSCS subscale and Total Self-Concept raw scores convert to T-scores (mean of 50, standard deviation of 10) based on a large normative sample. For all scales, higher T-scores indicate better self-concept. However, the norms of the Piers-Harris may overestimate self-esteem; clinical experience suggests that T-scores of 55–60 are average, as opposed to T-scores of 50.

The SCL-90-R is a 90-item, self-report scale that asks the respondent to rate the subjective severity of psychological symptoms in nine areas: Somatization, Obsessive-Compulsive, Interpersonal Sensitivity, Depression, Anxiety, Hostility, Phobic Anxiety, Paranoid Ideation, and Psychoticism. It also yields a Global Severity Index of overall symptom severity. Items are face-valid and are rated on a 0–4 scale of severity. Subscale raw scores are converted to T-scores based on a normative sample of adolescents. The SCL-90-R may be administered to adolescents as young as age 13 and has been shown to be reliable and valid (Derogatis, 1994). It can be a useful instrument for quantifying the severity of an adolescent's symptoms along several symptom parameters. Although it is more face-valid (and, thus, more subject to manipulation) than the MMPI, the SCL-90-R is briefer and more symptom focused. Clinical experience with this scale suggests that the norms for adolescents may provide T-scores that are too low, minimizing the actual severity of symptoms.

Behavioral Assessment

Unlike psychological assessment instruments, behavioral assessment instruments focus on the external behaviors of the child. Behavioral assessment scales provide a structured, systematic way for the clinician to gather information about the child's behavior as it is perceived by an observer in a certain setting. Because they are usually administered in checklist form, some behavioral assessment scales are called behavior checklists.

In addition to using observer-report methods, behavioral assessment can also be obtained based on the self-report of the child. Most self-report behavior checklists contain a mixture of questions about external behaviors and internal thoughts and feelings. Thus, they may be considered as both psychological assessment instruments (because of self-report questions that focus on internal thoughts and feelings) and as behavioral assessment instruments (because of questions that focus on external behaviors). Furthermore, most of the major observer-report behavior checklists have a self-report version as well. To simplify the presentation of these behavior checklists, both observer-report and self-report versions are discussed in this section.

Achenbach Child Behavior Checklists.   One of the most widely used groups of behavior checklists is that developed by Achenbach: the *Child Behavior Checklist* for parents of children age 2–18 years (CBCL; Achenbach, 1991a, 1992), the *Teacher's Report Form* for children age 5–18 years (TRF; Achenbach, 1991b), and the *Youth Self-Report* for children age 11–18 years (YSR; Achenbach, 1991c). Recent efforts have standardized the format and meaning of the Achenbach scales across ages and respondents. Hence, the CBCL, TRF, and YSR share many similar items and yield essentially the same subscales. This congruence is extremely valuable when comparing data obtained from different respondents.

The CBCL has separate forms for children age 2–3 (CBCL/2–3; Achenbach, 1992) and children age 4–18 (CBCL; Achenbach, 1991a). CBCL items fall into two categories: competence items and problem items. The seven competence items (each item has several subparts) ask for information about the child's participation in sports, activities, groups, chores, peer relationships, and academics. Three competence scales are obtained based on sums of item scores: Activities, Social, and School competence. Higher scores on the competence scales indicate better adjustment in these areas.

In addition to the competence items, the CBCL contains 113 behavior problem items, one of which has eight subparts and one of which asks the parent to list up to three problems that are not covered on other checklist items. Each CBCL item describes a specific behavior or belief of the child. For the behavior problem items, the parent rates on a 0 (not true) to 2 (very or often true) scale the extent to which the item is true of the child's behavior during the past 6 months. Behavior problem items cluster into eight factor analytically derived subscales (with certain modifications to create congruence between the CBCL, TRF, and YSR), although items may appear on none, one, or more than one subscale. The CBCL subscales are Withdrawn, Somatic Complaints, Anxious/Depressed, Social Problems, Thought Problems, Attention Problems, Delinquent Behavior, and Aggressive Behavior. Certain subscale scores (adjusting so that items are not counted twice in a single scale or for both scales; see Achenbach, 1991a) are combined to yield two "higher-order" subscales: Internalizing (Withdrawn, Somatic Complaints, and Anxious/Depressed) and Externalizing (Delinquent Behavior and Aggressive Behavior). An overall Total Problem score is obtained by summing all CBCL items except items 2 (allergy item) and 4 (asthma item).

CBCL Competence and Problem Subscale raw scores are converted to T-scores based on a large national sample of children age 4–18. T-scores are normalized such that a large proportion of normal children receive high competence and low problem scores. Problem subscale T-scores of 67–70 and higher may be considered clinically elevated, whereas Total Problem T-scores of 60–63 and higher may be considered clinically elevated. In interpreting CBCL subscale scores, the clinician must look at what items are driving the subscale score. A high Anxious/Depressed score, for example, could reflect perfectionistic worry or feelings of isolation and worthlessness depending on item endorsement patterns.

The CBCL/2–3 resembles the CBCL, but it has no Competence items and fewer (100) problem items. Like the CBCL, it gives Anxious/Depressed, Withdrawn, Somatic Problems, Aggressive Behavior, and Destructive Behavior subscales, but it lacks the Social Problems, Thought Problems, and Attention Problems subscales. The CBCL/2–3 also has a Sleep Problems subscale. Internalizing (Anxious/Depressed and Withdrawn subscales), Externalizing (Aggressive and Destructive Behavior subscales), and Total Problem scores are obtained, and conversion to T-scores occurs as on the CBCL. Interpretation is also similar to the CBCL.

The TRF is the teacher-completed analogue to the CBCL. Although it lacks the Competence section of the CBCL, it includes an Academic/Adaptive Functioning section (Academic Performance, Working Hard, Behaving Appropriately, Learning, and Happy subscales, and a Total Adaptive score) and a Problem Items section (same subscales as CBCL, with very minor item differences on subscales). The TRF and CBCL have the same number of items, most of which are identical. Scoring and interpretation are essentially the same as for the CBCL.

The YSR has the same number and type of Competence and Problem items as the CBCL, with few exceptions. In fact, almost all YSR items are CBCL items worded in the first person. YSR subscales are virtually identical to CBCL subscales, with the exception of the School Competence subscale (missing on the YSR). Total scores, T-scores, and scale interpretation are similar to the CBCL.

Clinicians can use the different Achenbach scales to obtain a picture of the child's behavior from the viewpoint of multiple respondents in multiple situations. For example, a problem-ridden TRF profile coupled with a relatively normal CBCL profile suggests that the child may behave adequately in the less structured, more individualized home environment while becoming disorganized and misbehaving at school. Alternatively, the child may behave poorly only around a particular teacher, or the parent may be minimizing the child's behavior problems. In cases in which the YSR, TRF, and/or CBCL show markedly different profiles, the clinician should expect the child, teachers, and parents to disagree about the child's behavior problems.

Conners' Rating Scales—Revised. Like the Achenbach scales, the *Conners' Rating Scales—Revised* (CRS-R) are paper-and-pencil questionnaires for parents (*Conners' Parent Rating Scales—Revised;* CPRS-R), teachers (*Conners' Teacher Rating Scales—Revised;* CTRS-R), and the child (*Conners-Wells' Adolescent Self-Report Scale;* CASS) (Conners, 1997). As with their predecessors (Conners, 1990), several versions exist of the CRS-R; alternative (shorter) versions are derived by taking a subset of the subscales from the longer version of each parent-, teacher-, or self-report CRS-R scale. The CPRS-R and CTRS-R may be used with children age 3–17 years; the CASS is for adolescents age 12–17.

The CPRS-R long form (CPRS-R:L) consists of 80 behavior problem items rated by the parent on a 0 to 3 scale based on the degree to which each has been a problem in the past month. Items are summed to give several sets of subscales. Seven subscales are factor-analytically derived: Cognitive Problems (12 items measuring difficulty with school, difficulty completing cognitive tasks, and cognitive weaknesses such as problems with memory/attention), Oppositional (10 items measuring anger, irritability, defiance, aggressive behavior, and disobedience), Hyperactivity (9 items measuring overactivity and impulsivity), Anxious-Shy (8 items measuring fearfulness and social insecurity), Perfectionism (7 items measuring obsessive/compulsive behavior and difficulty tolerating change), Social Problems (5 items measuring isolation and social skills problems), and Psychosomatic (6 items measuring illness complaints and fatigue). Two subscales are rewordings of the 9 DSM-IV ADHD Inattentive symptoms (DSM-IV:Inattentive subscale) and the 9 DSM-IV Hyperactive-Impulsive symptoms (DSM-IV:Hyperactive-Impulsive subscale); these two subscales add to give a third DSM subscale, DSM-IV:Total, which consists of all 18 ADHD symptoms. Conners (1997) also provides a procedure for using the DSM-IV items to yield a count of the number of ADHD symptoms for which the child screens as positive.

Three additional subscales on the CPRS-R:L are the Conners' Global Index (CGI):Total subscale, the CGI:Restless-Impulsive subscale, and the CGI:Emotional Lability subscale. The CGI:Total (10 items) subscale is identical to the "Hyperactivity Index" (also called the "Abbreviated Symptom Questionnaire" or ASQ) from the previous version of the CPRS (Conners, 1990). The Hyperactivity Index (typically in the form of the ASQ) had sometimes been used as a brief screen for the diagnosis of ADHD. This use, however, has been criticized by authors who recommend that it only be interpreted in the context of other CRS subscales (Atkins & Pelham, 1991; Barkley, 1987). The CGI:Restless-Impulsive subscale (7 items measuring distractibility, restlessness, overactivity, poor frustration tolerance, and impulsivity) and CGI:Emotional Lability (3 items measuring moodiness, crying, and tantruming) subscale are nonoverlapping subsets of CGI:Total items suggested by factor analysis (Conners, 1997).

A final subscale on the CPRS-R:L is the ADHD Index, which was derived by selecting 12 items that were most sensitive in differentiating a sample of children diagnosed with ADHD from matched, nonreferred peers. The ADHD Index consists largely of items measuring inattention, distractibility, restlessness, impulsivity, hyperactivity, and disorganization. Because of the way in which it was derived, the ADHD Index is particularly well suited for screening for ADHD in large nonclinical populations. Hence, the CPRS-R:L yields 14 subscales, 7 of which are factor-analytically derived, 3 of which are based on DSM-IV symptoms, 3 of which are based on the former Hyperactivity Index (or ASQ), and 1 of which was developed to differentiate children with ADHD from nonreferred peers.

Although Conners (1997) recommends use of the long forms of the CPRS-R, CTRS-R, and CASS whenever possible, several shorter forms of these scales may be useful in specific situations. Alternative forms of the CPRS-R include the short form (CPRS-R:S), the Conners Global Index-Parent (CGI-P), and the Conners' ADHD/DSM-IV Scales-Parent (CADS-P). The 27-item CPRS-R:S contains the full ADHD Index and the highest-loading items from three CPRS-R:L subscales: Oppositional, Cognitive Problems, and Hyperactivity. The CGI-P consists of the 10 CGI items from the CPRS-R:L. The CADS-P contains the ADHD Index and the three DSM-IV subscales from the CPRS-R:L. These alternative subscales focus almost exclusively on inattentive, hyperactive, and impulsive behaviors typically seen in children with ADHD.

The CTRS-R long form (CTRS-R:L) contains the same subscales as the CPRS-R:L, with the exception of Psychosomatic, which is dropped on the CTRS-R:L. As with the CPRS-R:L, items are rated on a 0–3 scale based on behavior in the past month. Although the subscales have the same names and broadly similar interpretation, item content is identical only for the DSM-IV subscales, and clinicians should be aware of item content differences between the CPRS-R:L and CTRS-R:L. Furthermore, most subscales have different numbers of items than corresponding CPRS-R subscales (8 items for Cognitive Problems, 6 for Oppositional, 7 for Hyperactivity, 6 for Anxious-Shy, 6 for Perfectionism, 5 for Social Problems, 12 for ADHD Index, 10 for CGI:Total, 6 for CGI:Restless-Impulsive, and 4 for

CGI:Emotional Lability). The CTRS-R:L includes the same types of alternative forms as the CPRS-R: a short form (CTRS-R:S, 28 items), CGI form (CGI-T, 10 items), and ADHD/DSM-IV Scales (CADS-T). Subscales on the alternative CTRS-R forms are similar to those on the alternative CPRS-R forms.

The CASS scales are based on self-report. CASS items fall into 6 subscales: Family Problems (12 items), Emotional Problems (12 items), Conduct Problems (12 items), Cognitive Problems (12 items), Anger Control Problems (8 items), and Hyperactivity (8 items). An ADHD Index and three DSM-IV symptom subscales (Inattentive, Hyperactive-Impulsive, and Total) were derived based on procedures similar to those used for the CPRS-R. Short-form (27 items with Conduct Problems, Cognitive Problems, Hyperactive-Impulsive, and ADHD Index subscales) and ADHD/DSM-IV (ADHD Index and 3 DSM-IV ADHD symptom subscales) versions of the CASS also exist (Conners, 1997).

Raw scores on the Conners' scales are converted to T-scores based on a large normative sample. Extensive supporting psychometric data are provided in the manual (Conners, 1997). Conners (1997) refers to T-scores in the 61–65 range as mildly atypical; scores in the 66–70 range are called moderately atypical, whereas scores of greater than 70 are markedly atypical.

It is important to remember that Conners' T-scores are linear transformations of a skewed distribution of scores. In other words, most children have few reported problems, whereas a very small minority have many reported problems. The effect of this distribution is that a T-score of 50 usually corresponds to a percentile of greater than 50 (often in the 60–70 percentile range). On the other hand, a T-score of 70 typically corresponds to a percentile lower than 98 (which is the percentile associated with a +2 standard deviation elevation on a theoretical normal curve). Typically, the child's T-score matches the theoretical percentile on the normal curve at a T-score of around 55–65, with lower T-scores underestimating the child's *actual* percentile in the norm sample and higher T-scores overestimating the child's *actual* percentile in the norm sample. This problem is found on virtually any behavior questionnaire with linear T-scores based on norm sample data.

In addition to the revised versions of the CRS, earlier versions of the *Conners' Parent Rating Scales* (CPRS; Conners, 1990) and *Conners' Teacher Rating Scales* (CTRS; Conners, 1990) are still used in some research and clinical settings. Several forms of the original CPRS exist, differing primarily in breadth and in number of items. The CPRS has a 93-item form (CPRS-93; age 6–14) and a 48-item form (CPRS-48; age 3–17), which is a revised version of the 93-item form. The 10-item "Hyperactivity Index" (HI or ASQ; now called the CGI, as described earlier in this chapter), which is embedded in the longer CPRS forms (Conners, 1990), is also widely used.

As with most CRS-R subscales, items on the original Conners' scales fall into factor-analytically derived subscales, and parents rate each item on a 0–3 (CPRS-48) or 1–4 (CPRS-93) scale based on the past month. Norms (for conversion to T-scores) are available based on age-sex groups for all Conners' scales except the CPRS-93 (Conners, 1990). Norms are also not available for the HI on the CPRS-93.

Similar to the CPRS, two major forms of the CTRS exist, a 39-item form (CTRS-39) and a 28-item form (CTRS-28). Both forms of the CTRS use a 0–3 rating scale and one-month time frame for items. A short form of the CTRS-39, the IOWA-Conners Rating Scale, was developed to delineate problems of inattention/overactivity from problems of aggression/defiance. The IOWA-Conners consists of 10 items, five of which measure inattention/overactivity and five of which measure aggression.

Behavior Assessment System for Children. The Behavior Assessment System for Children (BASC; Reynolds & Kamphaus, 1992), like the CBCL and CRS-R, consists of parent-report, teacher-report, and self-report behavior questionnaires. The BASC Parent Rating Scales (BASC-PRS) and Teacher Rating Scales (BASC-TRS) each have three forms for different child ages: Preschool (age 4–5 years; 131 items on the PRS; 109 items on the TRS), Child (age 6–11 years; 138 PRS items; 148 TRS items), and Adolescent (age 12–18 years; 126 PRS items; 138 TRS items). Items are answered on a Never-Sometimes-Often-Always (0–3) scale based on the frequency with which the child has shown the behavior in the past six months. The BASC Self-Report of Personality (BASC-SRP) has two age-based forms: Child (age 8–11 years; 152 items) and Adolescent (age 12–18 years; 186 items). Items on the BASC-SRP are answered on a true-false scale based on whether the child feels the item is a true or false description of the child. The BASC also includes scales for coding behavioral observations (Structured Observation System) and for collecting developmental history (Structured Developmental History) (Reynolds & Kamphaus, 1992).

The BASC-PRS yields 12 clinical subscales: Aggression (oppositional behavior, harassing peers, hostility, aggressiveness), Hyperactivity (restlessness, impatience, impulsivity, overactivity), Conduct Problems (disregard for the feelings/rights of others and major rule-breaking such as running away, swearing, lying, school suspension; age 6–18 only), Anxiety (worries, perfectionism, many fears, concerns about school performance), Depression (lonely, isolated, labile, easily upset), Somatization (many pain complaints, trouble breathing, neurological and gastrointestinal complaints), Attention Problems (inattentive, distractible, forgetful, does not complete tasks), Atypicality (out of touch with reality, odd thoughts or behaviors, self-stimulating behaviors, pica, hallucinations), Withdrawal (avoidance of peers or social situations, shy, fearful in social situations), Adaptability (adjusts well to changes, easily calmed; age 4–11 only), Leadership (participates in activities, outgoing, creative, confident; age 6–18 only), and Social Skills (good manners, complementary toward others, helpful, good conversationalist). In addition to these clinical subscales, the BASC-PRS provides a validity (F) scale, which measures the tendency to adopt an overly negative response set to the items. Subscales may be combined to form higher-order composites such as Externalizing Problems, Internalizing Problems, School Problems, Adaptive Skills, and an overall Behavior Symptoms Index.

The BASC-TRS yields the same 12 clinical subscales as the PRS (although item content is not identical), as well as a Learning Problems subscale (difficulty learning academic material, poor performance in reading, math, and spelling; age 6–18 only) and a Study Skills subscale (reading, homework, effort on schoolwork, organized; age 6–18). Like the PRS, the TRS also includes the F validity scale and the higher-order composites.

The BASC-SRP yields 14 clinical subscales: Anxiety (worries, fears, feeling overwhelmed), Atypicality (odd thoughts and behaviors, obsessive-compulsive symptoms), Locus of Control (feeling that others control the child's environment and future), Social Stress (worry about social relationships, isolation, alienation), Somatization (multiple physical complaints; age 12–18 only), Attitude to School (anger, suspiciousness, unhappiness, and alienation directed toward school environment), Attitude to Teachers (suspiciousness, mistrust, hostility, and resentment directed toward teachers), Sensation Seeking (enjoyment and seeking of risks and excitement; age 12–18 only), Depression (unhappiness, dissatisfaction, pessimism, and other depressive symptoms), Sense of Inadequacy (feelings of inferiority and failure related to school, peers, and achievement areas), Relations with Parents (feeling of acceptance/liking toward and from parents), Interpersonal Relations (good relationships with peers), Self-Esteem (feelings of positive self-worth, competence, and self-respect), and Self-Reliance (confident, independent, decisive). The BASC-SRP also includes the F validity scale, as well as a validity scale measuring the tendency to portray oneself in an overly positive way (L scale; age 12–18 only) and a validity scale measuring lack of attention to item content, poor reading ability, or random responding (V scale). Subscales may be combined to form higher-order composite scales such as Clinical Maladjustment, School Maladjustment, Personal Adjustment, and an overall Emotional Symptoms Index.

The BASC has seen widespread use in school settings because of its developmentally appropriate items and focus on school-related problems and competencies. Furthermore, the validity scales provide important information concerning the integrity of results, and the clinical scales overlap somewhat with DSM-IV criteria for certain disorders (e.g., ADHD and Conduct Disorder). Advantages to the BASC-SRP include the extension of the lower age range to 8 years (vs. 11 years for the YSR and 12 years for the CASS) and the inclusion of validity scales to assess potential problems with self-report. BASC raw scores are converted to T-scores using age- and sex-based norms. T-scores in the 60–69 range are considered moderately elevated ("At-Risk Range"), whereas T-scores of 70 or greater are considered significantly elevated ("Clinically Significant Range").

Symptom Inventories—4. The Symptom Inventories—4 (Gadow & Sprafkin, 1997a, 1997b, 1998a, 1998b; Sprafkin & Gadow, 1996) are parent-report and teacher-report behavior checklists for children age 3–6 years (Early Childhood Inventory; ECI-4), 5–12 years (Child Symptom Inventory; CSI-4), and 13–18 years (Adolescent Symptom Inventory; ASI). SI-4 items are rewordings of all major behavioral DSM-IV symptoms for the disorders of childhood: ADHD, Oppositional-Defiant Disorder, Conduct Disorder, Generalized Anxiety Disorder, Obsessive-Compulsive Disorder, Specific Phobia, Tic Disorders, Enuresis, Encopresis, Schizophrenia (CSI-4 and ASI-4 only), Major Depressive Disorder, Dysthymic Disorder, Bipolar Disorder (ASI-4 only), Anorexia Nervosa (ASI-4 only), Bulimia Nervosa (ASI-4 only), Antisocial Personality Disorder (ASI-4 only), Schizoid Personality Disorder (ASI-4 only), Autistic Disorder (ECI-4 and CSI-4 only), Asperger's Disorder (ECI-4 and CSI-4 only), Social Phobia, Selective Mutism (ECI-4 only), Separation Anxiety Disorder (parent-report only), Post-traumatic Stress Disorder (ECI-4 only; single items screen for this disorder on the CSI-4 and ASI-4), and Reactive Attachment Disorder (ECI-4 only). Other items do not mirror DSM-IV symptoms exactly but screen for problems with panic symptoms (ASI-4 only), developmental delay (ECI-4 only), drug use (ASI-4 only), peer conflict (ECI-4 only), adjustment disorder (ECI-4 only), sleep problems, feeding problems (ECI-4 only), and somatization (CSI-4 and ASI-4 only).

Almost all SI-4 items are answered on a Never-Sometimes-Often-Very Often (0–3) scale, with no time period specified for the onset or duration of symptoms. In general, a symptom is considered to be present if the respondent endorses an item (symptom) as occurring "Often" or "Very Often." Hence, Symptom Count scores are obtained by counting the number of items (symptoms) answered "Often" or "Very Often" within each diagnostic category (with the exception of some of the more severe symptoms, such as Conduct Disorder items, which qualify as present if answered "Sometimes"). Total Symptom Count scores may then be matched to DSM-IV criteria for number of symptoms needed for a diagnosis. Symptom Severity scores are obtained by adding scores (0–3) for each item within a diagnostic subscale. The Symptom Severity scores, therefore, resemble subscale scores as typically calculated from behavioral questionnaires.

Recently published norms (Gadow & Sprafkin, 1997b, 1998b), using a nonrepresentative normative sample, allow the conversion of Symptom Severity scores to T-scores for the ASI and CSI. New psychometric data provide substantial information to assist in interpreting the Symptom Count and Symptom Severity scores obtained from the CSI-4 (Gadow & Sprafkin, 1997a, 1997b, 1998a, 1998b). Although CSI-4 norms are based on a sample for age 5–12, the items for the CSI-4 appear to be developmentally appropriate through the midteen years; thus, the major benefit of the ASI-4 and ECI-4 is their coverage of additional diagnoses more commonly seen in their age ranges.

The utility of the SI-4 to screen for DSM-IV diagnoses is clear: No other scales offer such direct correspondence to a wide range of diagnostic criteria. However, because no time is specified for onset or duration of symptoms, SI-4 items should not be considered as identical to all DSM-IV diagnostic criteria. Furthermore, exclusionary criteria must be taken into account, and the SI-4 should not substitute for a clinical interview. However, these inventories are widely used to assist in the interview and to quantify parent and teacher report of DSM-IV diagnostic criteria.

Personality Inventory for Youth. The Personality Inventory for Youth (PIY; Lachar & Gruber, 1995) is a 270-item, true-false self-report personality inventory for children age 9 to 18 years. PIY responses yield four validity scales and nine clinical scales; each clinical scale, in turn, is divided into several subscales. The four PIY validity scales measure nonsense/random responding (VAL scale), inconsistent responding (INC scale), exaggeration of psychological symptoms (FB scale), and denial, defensiveness, or socially desirable response set (DEF scale). The nine PIY clinical scales are Cognitive Impairment (COG), Impulsivity and Distractibility (ADH), Delinquency (DLQ), Family Dysfunction (FAM), Reality Distortion (RLT), Somatic Concern (SOM), Psychological Discomfort (DIS), Social Withdrawal (WDL), and Social Skills Deficits (SSK). Raw scores are converted to T-scores using sex- (but not age-) based norms. T-scores required for clinically significant elevations vary from 60 to 80, depending on the scale (Lachar & Gruber, 1995).

Ultimately, the clinician's choice of what behavioral and psychological assessment instruments to use depends on the needs and characteristics of a particular clinical case. In general, it is wise to gain input from parents, teachers, and, when possible, the child. The Achenbach (CBCL, TRF, YSR) and BASC scales provide broad symptom coverage, good norms, good psychometric properties, and measurement based on the perspectives of parent, teacher, and child. The Conners' scales give more detailed and circumscribed information about externalizing problems (particularly attention, hyperactivity, and conduct problems), with subscales based directly on DSM-IV criteria for ADHD. The CSI-4 provides information directly pertinent to DSM-IV diagnostic criteria. The PIY and BASC include validity scales, if there is concern about the accuracy of the respondent. Hence, these behavioral questionnaires are complementary, not redundant, with each providing unique advantages for a particular assessment goal.

Family Assessment

A final set of broad-band instruments that are commonly used in clinical practice with children are family assessment scales. Family assessment scales quantify family characteristics that are believed to be important in the adjustment of family members. They augment the clinician's observations of in-session family interactions and allow the clinician to assess different points of view of family members. Parents, for example, might see the family level of control much differently than children do. Because the respondent to a family assessment instrument must have an intimate knowledge of the family situation, parents and children are the primary information sources.

One of the most widely used tests of family environment is the *Family Environment Scale* (FES; Moos & Moos, 1994). The FES is a 90-item, true-false scale designed to assess basic characteristics of the family environment. It is composed of 10 subscales: Cohesion (commitment and support in the family), Expressiveness (open expression of feelings and behaviors), Conflict (open expression of hostility, conflict, and aggression), Independence (self-reliance, assertiveness, and acceptance of intrafamily differences), Achievement Orientation (values of competition and drive to succeed), Intellectual-Cultural Orientation (interest in intellectual and cultural activities), Active-Recreational Orientation (participation in recreational-social activities), Moral-Religious Emphasis (religiosity and use of religious rules to guide the behavior of family members), Organization (structure and planning in the family), and Control (firm rules and hierarchy in the family).

Kronenberger and Thompson (1990) factor analyzed FES subscales and found three higher-order factors: Supportive (Cohesion, Expressiveness, Independence, Active-Recreational Orientation, and Intellectual-Cultural Orientation scales), Conflicted (Conflict, Cohesion [reverse scored], and Organization [reverse scored]), and Controlling (Control, Moral-Religious Emphasis, Achievement Orientation, and Independence [reverse scored]). The Supportive factor measures a sense of openness, team spirit, and shared interests and activities. The Conflicted factor assesses family conflict and a lack of the support and organization that could control conflict when it arises. The Controlling factor measures the use of overt rules and implicit religious and achievement expectations to maintain family stability.

The FES may be completed by parents or adolescents. Raw scores are converted to T-scores based on a large normative sample of families. The sample is not nationally representative, however. Factor scores are sums of subscale T-scores (T-scores of scales with negative factor loadings are subtracted; Kronenberger & Thompson, 1990). It is often instructive to compare the results of parent- and child-reporting to see discrepancies in how the family is viewed. These discrepancies can be helpful in formulations and interventions.

In addition to the FES, many other family scales exist, and assessment of parents may provide information about key family characteristics. For example, if a parent's MMPI may be particularly useful for a diagnosis, parental MMPI patterns are described in the Family Assessment section. Parent assessment can be helpful in planning family interventions and in formulations of a case.

Syndrome-Specific Tests

Syndrome-specific tests are instruments designed to assess features characteristic of a single diagnosis or a very closely related group of diagnoses. In each chapter, following a discussion of broad assessment test patterns, syndrome-specific tests are described for each disorder. Like the broad assessment instruments, syndrome-specific tests differ based on respondent, with some tests administered and interpreted by the clinician, whereas others are completed by other adults, parents, or the child. Hence, the division of clinician-administered, child-report, parent-report, and other-report is retained under each chapter heading of Syndrome-Specific Tests. Syndrome-specific tests can be invaluable in the detailed evaluation of a particular problem or diagnosis. It is notable that the quantity and quality of syndrome-specific tests vary greatly from one diagnosis to another. Depression and ADHD, for example, have a number of extremely good syndrome-specific tests, whereas there are fewer tests for enuresis, encopresis, and somatoform disorders. Syndrome-specific tests are presented and critiqued under their respective diagnoses.

TREATMENT OPTIONS

Coverage of each disorder concludes with a consideration of treatment options. For each specific disorder, this section covers only treatment options that have been the topic of widespread or promising theoretical, clinical, or research work. Furthermore, each treatment option is discussed as it pertains directly to the disorder. Thus, later chapters do not contain basic descriptions of therapies such as family therapy and behavioral interventions.

Behavioral Interventions

Behavioral interventions focus on the child's problem behaviors, the antecedents of behaviors, and the consequences of behaviors. Internal psychological processes, developmental history, and past stressors are usually not significant for behavioral evaluation or treatment. External behaviors and environmental characteristics, manifest in the A-B-C approach (Antecedents-Behaviors-Consequences), are the main focus.

Behavioral interventions are often used with children because adults have a great deal of control over their environment. Furthermore, behavioral interventions require little understanding or thought on the part of the child. Hence, even very young or intellectually impaired children can benefit from behavioral interventions. Although the exact content and form of behavioral interventions vary widely depending on the specific target behaviors, at a basic level, they take a similar approach.

First, the problem behavior is operationalized. It is analyzed in detail with specific descriptors. Vague, overly inclusive language is discouraged. Disobedience, for example, may be reconceptualized as "sticks out tongue following a request to perform a behavior." Second, the behavior is monitored, with attention also given to the situation that leads up to the behavior (antecedents) and to the situation that follows the behavior (consequences). Third, reinforcing and punishing consequences are identified. Fourth, antecedents and consequences are modified. This may involve removing some antecedents that encourage the behavior and removing some consequences that reinforce it. In addition, negative consequences may be added. Alternatively, the child may be encouraged to perform different behaviors that are incompatible with the problem behavior. Reinforcing consequences are attached to these incompatible behaviors.

In addition to this basic intervention outline, other behavioral interventions such as desensitization and positive practice exist (see O'Donohue, 1998, for additional comments about behavioral interventions). Many authors have published behaviorally based plans for treatment of certain types of problem behaviors. These plans often appear as self-help books for parents (Phelan, 1995) or as treatment manuals for therapists working with teachers or parents (Barkley, 1997). Although parents are most often responsible for implementing a behavioral plan in the child's environment, teachers and other authorities are used for behavioral plans that are implemented out of the home. Behavioral treatments are some of the most widely used and studied methods of intervening to change child behavior, and some work with parents is routine in many clinical child interventions. Often, behavioral interventions are used in conjunction with one or more of the other treatment modalities discussed later in this chapter. Sample behavior modification (parent) handouts are contained in Appendix C.

Psychotherapy

Psychotherapy may be defined in various ways. For the purposes of this book, the term *psychotherapy* will be used to group techniques that directly or theoretically address the thought processes, affects, or beliefs of the child. One could argue that behavioral interventions fit into this definition. However, there are several valid reasons for separating behavioral interventions from psychotherapy. The first is pragmatic. Behavioral interventions for childhood disorders are so important and prevalent that they merit their own heading. The second reason is the strict behavioral approach's repudiation (or at least avoidance) of a focus on internal psychological processes. If behavioral interventions affect thought, it is not because they directly intended to. A final reason for separating behavioral interventions from psychotherapy is that the child can be much less of an active participant in most behavioral interventions (other than receiving the directives and contingencies of authorities) than in other psychotherapeutic interventions.

Five types of psychotherapy are mentioned with some regularity throughout the following chapters. *Psychodynamic psychotherapy* involves a focus on internal, sometimes unconscious or automatic, conflicts, drives, and thought processes that underlie behavior. The goal of psychodynamic psychotherapy is to process the child's conflicts, drives, and memories such that the child gains insight into their effects on beliefs and behavior. In some cases, psychodynamic psychotherapy also involves having a corrective experience with the therapist, in which the therapist is a stimulus for the child to re-experience a stage of development or an important relationship. For example, the therapist could give the child the experience of an accepting parental figure.

Play therapy involves the use of play to allow the child to demonstrate and experience conflicts, affects, fears, hopes, and other thought/affect processes. The experience occurs in the context of an accepting therapist who validates the child and, ideally, teaches the child self-acceptance. Some therapists interpret the child's play behavior in the hopes of facilitating insight (a psychodynamic technique), whereas others are staunchly nondirective and accept any nondangerous, nonaggressive, nondestructive behaviors from the child. The child presumably benefits from increased self-acceptance and insight, which is learned from and encouraged by the play therapist (see Axline, 1969).

Cognitive or cognitive-behavioral interventions encompass a variety of techniques that seek to increase the child's awareness of how thought processes drive behavior and affect. The child is taught to monitor, challenge, and alter thought processes (see Kendall, 1991). Unlike psychodynamic interventions, cognitive-behavioral interventions place less emphasis on the past history of the development of behavior. Rather, they focus on how current thought drives present feelings and behaviors.

There is some inevitable overlap between behavioral and cognitive-behavioral interventions, because both focus on the behaviors of the child. Self-monitoring, for example, may serve the behavioral purpose of evaluating performance and dispensing reinforcement, or it may serve the cognitive purpose of enhancing insight into one's behavior and the situations in which it occurs. Such overlapping interventions may be described in either of the categories for which they are relevant.

Hypnotic techniques involve the use of hypnosis to allow the child to gain greater control over physiological or thought states. Following induction of hypnosis, suggestions are made to experience physiological change, to view a situation differently, or to have a hypnotic experience that will assist with memory and/or insight into problems. Hypnotic techniques are frequently used for child disorders that have a physiological or anxiety component (see Olness & Gardner, 1988).

Group therapy is a generic term used to refer to delivery of a psychotherapeutic intervention in a group format. In many cases, the presence of the group is used to facilitate the intervention. For example, group members may model disclosure, affect, and change for other group members. On the other hand, interaction between group members may facilitate insight into a personal or social problem. Group members can also act as motivators for other group members. In some cases, the group is used to deliver another type of intervention; behavioral and cognitive-behavioral techniques, for example, are often taught in a group format. Hence, group therapy and the other psychotherapy techniques sometimes overlap (see Yalom, 1985). Certain problems, especially involving social skills, empathy, and interaction problems, are best dealt with in a group setting. Groups are also used to facilitate discussion, to provide support, to normalize disorders, and to motivate otherwise disinterested children.

Family Interventions

Family interventions refer to the group of psychological interventions that focus on the family as the unit of change for the child. This focus may result in the entire family being present for therapy, or it may result in one other family member (usually a parent) entering therapy in order to benefit the child by changing his or her own behavior.

Family therapy follows the theory that the child's problems emerge in and are shaped by a family system. Eventually, the problem comes to serve a role in the family system, and the family system is reluctant to give up the symptom. The family may be especially reluctant to give up the child's problem if it is deflecting the family's energy and attention from an even greater family problem, such as conflict between the parents. To address the child's problems, then, the therapist must address the problems inherent in the family system. It is these problems and the family's reluctance to change that is maintaining the child's problem.

Family therapists seek to change the family system by pointing out the role of the child's symptom, by restructuring the family, and by encouraging more positive styles of family interaction. Structural family therapists (Minuchin, 1974) seek to create appropriate boundaries between family subsystems (such as the parental and child subsystems) and to weaken boundaries that isolate certain family members. Power, boundaries, and coalitions between family members are the main focus of structural therapists. Family therapists with a more interactional focus show how the communication in the family creates problems for members. Strategic family therapists (Haley, 1976) emphasize the importance of the child's symptom in maintaining the family system's integrity. Regardless of specific orientation, however, the family therapist's focus is on the family as the source of the problem and not on the child. Change in the child's symptoms can and will occur only when the family changes.

Parent psychotherapy involves a referral for the parent to work on individual issues that may or may not directly relate to the child. This therapy may be focused on a diagnosis carried by the parent or on parent behaviors that are provoked by interactions in the parent-child relationship (see Meyer & Deitsch, 1996, for a summary of adult assessment and intervention).

Like parent psychotherapy, *marital therapy* centers on the parents as opposed to the child. Marital therapy is warranted for families in which parental conflict contributes to the child's problems or to the parents' inability to manage the child's problems. Open parental conflict, for example, is stressful to children and provides models of hostile interaction. In addition, conflict between parents is often played out in the family in the form of inconsistent discipline and lax rules (see Weeks & Treat, 1992).

Medication

Medication is used to treat a number of childhood disorders, with clearly documented effectiveness for some disorders (such as ADHD). Medications that are commonly used to treat childhood disorders are briefly summarized in the Treatment Options section for each disorder. The rationale, effectiveness, and pros/cons of medication are considered along with the types of medication used for particular disorders. However, dosages and detailed administration instructions are not described in this book. Furthermore, only medications that have received significant research or clinical attention in published sources are considered.

Inpatient Hospitalization

Inpatient hospitalization is sometimes used as a "last resort" for children with severe behavioral and psychological problems. Children are typically hospitalized only when they are unmanageable in the home environment, dangerous to themselves or others, severely incapacitated by their disorder, and/or unresponsive to outpatient management. Overall, it is generally wise to use inpatient hospitalization sparingly because it labels the child as "very sick," it places the child in an environment that sometimes contains negative behavioral models, it separates the child from potential social support in the family, it creates a discontinuity of care, and it is costly. Nevertheless, inpatient treatment is warranted for some children, and many children benefit from it.

Of course, inpatient hospitalization is not actually a treatment modality but rather an environment in which various treatments can be administered. Medication is a very common treatment on inpatient units, as is group psychotherapy. Also common (but not universal) are individual psychotherapy, behavior modification plans, and milieu therapy. Less common are family therapy and marital therapy.

Special Education

For some childhood disorders (such as Mental Retardation and Learning Disorders), special provisions must be made in the academic content and process of the child's schooling. When the targets of intervention are behavior problems at school, interventions are covered under the Behavioral Interventions section. However, when the targets of intervention are the child's abilities and achievement, these educational interventions are considered in the Special Education section.

Referral to Other Professionals or to Authorities

Certain disorders are associated with medical, legal, or other risks that require close work with other disciplines. When these risks exist, they are noted in the introductory paragraphs of the Assessment Patterns or Treatment Options sections. More detailed information about referral needs may also be covered in a special Referral to Other Professionals or to Authorities subsection in the Treatment Options section. Examples of medical and legal risks are mental health conditions that are associated with neurological complications and conditions that are associated with abuse/neglect.

Medical and legal issues, however, may arise in any child therapy case, and the clinician must be observant for warning signs. A few of the warning signs for organic impairment include recent severe injury/illness, sudden behavioral change, lack of psychosocial explanations for behavior, very severe symptoms, loss of consciousness, and significant change in mental status. Warning signs of abuse include fearfulness toward adults, physical signs (bruises, etc.), use of clothing or absence from school to hide injury, social withdrawal, avoidance of certain people or situations, extreme parental defensiveness over discipline, family stress, aggression, fixation on sexual themes and behaviors, and repeated complaints of injury or illness. The clinician must be cautious, however, about jumping to conclusions based on the presence of only a few warning signs. The warning signs noted here could indicate other problems as well.

In general, children being seen for mental health assessment and interventions should— like all children—be regularly seen by a pediatrician. Any psychological or behavioral complaint that may have a physical basis (such as an eating problem) should be referred to a pediatrician for specific medical evaluation concurrent with psychological evaluation.

■ Conclusion

The aim of this book is to provide clinicians with an up-to-date handbook for daily use in the diagnosis, assessment, and treatment of children's mental health problems. To this end, the remaining chapters are focused on the assessment and treatment of specific DSM-IV diagnoses. Of course, no book can anticipate the variety of individuals presenting with a specific diagnosis. Furthermore, some individuals will respond to certain treatments, whereas others will not. Ultimately, the clinician must marshal all available resources for assessment and treatment of the child, using a mix of clinical skill and knowledge. This book is intended to be on the front line of those resources.

■ References

Achenbach, T. M. (1991a). *Manual for the Child Behavior Checklist/4–18 and 1991 Profile*. Burlington, VT: University of Vermont Department of Psychiatry.

Achenbach, T. M. (1991b). *Manual for the Teacher's Report Form and 1991 Profile*. Burlington, VT: University of Vermont Department of Psychiatry.

Achenbach, T. M. (1991c). *Manual for the Youth Self-Report and 1991 Profile*. Burlington, VT: University of Vermont Department of Psychiatry.

Achenbach, T. M. (1992). *Manual for the Child Behavior Checklist/2–3 and 1992 Profile*. Burlington VT: University of Vermont Department of Psychiatry.

Achenbach, T. M., McConaughy, S. H., & Howell, C. T. (1987). Child/adolescent behavioral and emotional problems: Implications of cross-informant correlations for situational specificity. *Psychological Bulletin, 101,* 213–232.

Alexander, I. E. (1990). *Personology.* Durham, NC: Duke University Press.

American Psychiatric Association. (1980). *Diagnostic and statistical manual of mental disorders, third edition.* Washington, DC: Author.

American Psychiatric Association. (1987). *Diagnostic and statistical manual of mental disorders, third edition (revised).* Washington, DC: Author.

American Psychiatric Association. (1994). *Diagnostic and statistical manual of mental disorders, fourth edition.* Washington, DC: Author.

Angold, A., & Costello, E. J. (1995). A test-retest reliability study of child-reported psychiatric symptoms and diagnoses using the Child and Adolescent Psychiatric Assessment (CAPA-C). *Psychological Medicine, 25,* 755–762.

Atkins, M. S., & Pelham, W. E. (1991). School-based assessment of attention-deficit hyperactivity disorder. *Journal of Learning Disabilities, 24,* 197–203.

Axline, V. M. (1969). *Play therapy.* New York: Ballantine.

Barkley, R. A. (1997). *Defiant children: A clinician's manual for assessment and parent training* (2nd Ed.). New York: Guilford.

Bayley, N. (1993). *Bayley Scales of Infant Development: Second Edition.* San Antonio: Psychological Corporation.

Breton, J., Bergeron, L., Valla, J., Lepine, S., Houde, L., & Gaudet, N. (1995). Do children aged 9 through 11 years understand the DISC version 2.25 questions? *Journal of the American Academy of Child and Adolescent Psychiatry, 34,* 946–954.

Butcher, J. N., Dahlstrom, W. G., Graham, J. R., Tellegen, A. M., & Kaemmer, B. (1989). *MMPI-2: Manual for administration and scoring.* Minneapolis, MN: University of Minnesota.

Butcher, J. N., Williams, C. L., Graham, J. R., Archer, R. P., Tellegen, A., Ben-Porath, J. S., & Kaemmer, B. (1992). *MMPI-A: Manual for administration, scoring, and interpretation.* Minneapolis, MN: University of Minnesota.

Conners, C. K. (1990). *Conners' Rating Scales manual.* North Tonawanda, NY: MHS.

Conners, C. K. (1997). *Conners' Rating Scales-Revised technical manual.* North Tonawanda, NY: MHS.

Costello, A. J., Edelbrock, C. S., Dulcan, M. S., Kales, R., & Klavic, S. H. (1984). *Report on the NIMH Diagnostic Interview Schedule for Children (DISC).* Bethesda, MD: National Institute of Mental Health.

Dahlstrom, W. G., Welsh, G. S., & Dahlstrom, L. E. (1972). *An MMPI handbook: Volume 1. Clinical interpretation.* Minneapolis, MN: University of Minnesota Press.

Derogatis, L. R. (1994). *SCL-90-R administration, scoring, and procedures manual—Third edition.* Minneapolis, MN: NCS.

Elliott, C. D. (1990). *Differential Ability Scales.* San Antonio: Psychological Corporation.

Exner, J. E., Jr. (1993). *The Rorschach: A comprehensive system* Volume 1: Basic Foundations (Third Edition). New York: Wiley.

Exner, J. E., Jr., & Weiner, I. B. (1995). *The Rorschach: A comprehensive system* Volume 3: Assessment of children and adolescents (Second Edition). New York: Wiley.

Gadow, K. D., & Sprafkin, J. (1997a). *Adolescent Symptom Inventory-4 screening manual.* Stony Brook, NY: Checkmate Plus, Ltd.

Gadow, K. D., & Sprafkin, J. (1997b). *Child Symptom Inventory-4 norms manual.* Stony Brook, NY: Checkmate Plus, Ltd.

Gadow, K. D., & Sprafkin, J. (1998a). *Child Symptom Inventory-4 screening manual.* Stony Brook, NY: Checkmate Plus, Ltd.

Gadow, K. D., & Sprafkin, J. (1998b). *Adolescent Symptom Inventory-4 norms manual.* Stony Brook, NY: Checkmate Plus, Ltd.

Graham, J. R. (1990). *MMPI-2: Assessing personality and psychopathology.* New York: Oxford University Press.

Greene, R. L. (1991). *MMPI-2/MMPI: An interpretive manual.* Boston: Allyn & Bacon.

Haley, J. (1976). *Problem-solving therapy.* San Francisco: Jossey-Bass.

Hathaway, S. R., & McKinley, J. C. (1951). *The Minnesota Multiphasic Personality Inventory Manual.* New York: Psychological Corporation.

Hathaway, S. R., & McKinley, J. C. (1967). *The Minnesota Multiphasic Personality Inventory Manual.* New York: Psychological Corporation.

Hodges, K. K. (1985). *Manual for the Child Assessment Schedule.* Unpublished manuscript, University of Missouri-Columbia.

Hodges, K. K. (1987). Assessing children with a clinical interview: The Child Assessment Schedule. In R. J. Prinz

(Ed.). *Advances in behavioral assessment of children and families* (pp. 133–166). Greenwich, CT: JAI Press.

Hodges, K., & Zeman, J. (1993). Interviewing. In T. H. Ollendick & M. Hersen (Eds.), *Handbook of child and adolescent assessment.* Boston: Allyn & Bacon.

Kaslow, N.J., & Racusin, G. R. (1990). Childhood depression: Current status and future directions. In A. S. Bellack, M. Hersen, & A. E. Kazdin (Eds.), *International Handbook of Behavior Modification and Therapy* (2nd ed., pp. 223–243). New York: Plenum.

Kaufman, A. S., & Kaufman, N. L. (1983). *Kaufman Assessment Battery for Children (K-ABC).* Circle Pines, MN: American Guidance Service.

Kaufman, A. S., & Kaufman, N. L. (1985). *Manual for the Kaufman Test of Educational Achievement (K-TEA) Comprehensive Form.* Circle Pines, MN: American Guidance Service.

Kaufman, A. S., & Kaufman, N. L. (1990). *Kaufman Brief Intelligence Test.* Circle Pines, MN: American Guidance Service.

Kendall, P. C. (1991). *Child & adolescent therapy: Cognitive-behavioral procedures.* New York: Guilford.

Kovacs, M. (1985). The Interview Schedule for Children. *Psychopharmacology Bulletin, 21,* 991–994.

Kronenberger, W. G., & Thompson, R. J., Jr. (1990). Dimensions of family functioning in families with chronically ill children: A higher order factor analysis of the Family Environment Scale. *Journal of Clinical Child Psychology, 19,* 380–388.

Lachar, D., & Gruber, C. P. (1995). *Personality Inventory for Youth (PIY) manual.* Los Angeles: Western Psychological Services.

Marks, P. A., Seeman, W., & Haller, D. L. (1974). *The actuarial use of the MMPI with Adolescents and Adults.* Baltimore, MD: Williams & Wilkins.

Markwardt, F. C. (1989). *Manual for the Peabody Individual Achievement Test—Revised (PIAT-R).* Circle Pines, MN: American Guidance Service.

Masling, J. M. (1997). On the nature and utility of projective tests and objective tests. *Journal of Personality Assessment, 69,* 257–270.

McCarney, S. B. (1995). *The Adaptive Behavior Evaluation Scale Home Version Technical Manual—Revised.* Columbia, MO: Hawthorne Educational Services.

McCarthy, D. A. (1972). *Manual for the McCarthy Scales of Children's Abilities.* San Antonio: Psychological Corporation.

McGrew, K. S. (1994). *Clinical interpretation of the Woodcock-Johnson Tests of Cognitive Ability—Revised.* Boston: Allyn & Bacon.

Meyer, R. G., & Deitsch, S. E. (1996). *The clinician's handbook* (4th ed.). Boston: Allyn & Bacon.

Minuchin, S. (1974). *Families and family therapy.* Cambridge, MA: Harvard University Press.

Mokros, H. B., & Poznanski, E. O. (1992). Standardized approaches to clinical assessment of depression. In M. Shafii & S. L. Shafii (Eds.), *Clinical guide to depression in children and adolescents* (pp. 129–155). Washington, DC: American Psychiatric Press.

Moos, R. H., & Moos, B. S. (1994). *Manual for the Family Environment Scale* (3rd ed.). Palo Alto, CA: Consulting Psychologists Press.

Murray, H. A. (1943). *Thematic Apperception Test manual.* Cambridge, MA: Harvard University Press.

O'Donohue, W. (1998). *Learning and behavior therapy.* Boston: Allyn & Bacon.

Olness, K., & Gardner, G. G. (1988). *Hypnosis and hypnotherapy with children* (2nd ed.). Philadelphia: Grune & Stratton.

Orvaschel, H., & Puig-Antich, J. (1987). *Schedule for Affective Disorders and Schizophrenia for School-Age Children—Epidemiologic Version (Kiddie-SADS-E (K-SADS-E)).* Unpublished manuscript, University of Pittsburgh.

Piers, E. V. (1984). *Piers-Harris Children's Self-Concept Scale Revised manual 1984.* Los Angeles, CA: Western Psychological Services.

Phelan, T. W. (1995). *1-2-3 Magic: Effective Discipline for Children 2–12.* Glen Ellyn, IL: Child Management Inc.

Psychological Corporation. (1999). *Wechsler Abbreviated Scale of Intelligence manual.* San Antonio, TX: Author.

Psychological Corporation. (1997). *WAIS-III/WMS-III technical manual.* San Antonio, TX: Author.

Psychological Corporation. (1992). *Wechsler Individual Achievement Test manual.* San Antonio, TX: Author.

Puig-Antich, J., Chambers, W., & Tabrizi, M. A. (1983). The clinical assessment of current depressive episodes in children and adolescents: Interviews with parents and children. In D. Cantwell & G. Carlson (Eds.), *Childhood depression* (pp. 157–179). New York: Spectrum.

Puig-Antich, J., & Ryan, N. (1986). *Schedule for Affective Disorders and Schizophrenia for School-Age Children (6–18 years)—Kiddie-SADS-Present Episode (K-SADS-P).* Unpublished manuscript, University of Pittsburgh.

Reich, W., Welner, Z., Herjanic, B., & MHS Staff (1997). *Diagnostic Interview for Children and Adolescents Computer Program (DICA-IV).* North Tonawanda, NY: MHS.

Reynolds, C. R., & Kamphaus, R. W. (1992). *Behavior Assessment System for Children manual.* Circle Pines, MN: American Guidance Service.

Sattler, J. M. (1990). *Assessment of children* (3rd ed.). San Diego, CA: Jerome M. Sattler, Publisher.

Sattler, J. M. (1993). *Assessment of children* (revised and updated 3rd edition). San Diego, CA: Jerome M. Sattler, Publisher.

Schwab-Stone, M., Fallon, T., Briggs, M., & Crowther, B. (1994). Reliability of diagnostic reporting for children aged 6–11 years: A test-retest study of the Diagnostic Interview Schedule for Children—Revised. *American Journal of Psychiatry, 151,* 1048–1054.

Shaffer, D., Schwab-Stone, M., Fisher, P., Cohen, P., Piacentini, J., Davies, M., Conners, C. K., & Regier, D. (1993). The Diagnostic Interview Schedule for Children Revised Versions (DISC-R): Preparation, field testing, inter-rater reliability, and acceptability. *Journal of the American Academy of Child and Adolescent Psychiatry, 32,* 643–650.

Sparrow, S. S., Balla, D. A., & Cicchetti, D. V. (1984). *Vineland Adaptive Behavior Scales.* Circle Pines, MN: American Guidance Service.

Sprafkin, J., & Gadow, K. D. (1996). *Early childhood inventories manual.* Stony Brook, NY: Checkmate Plus.

Thorndike, R. L., Hagen, E. P., & Sattler, J. M. (1986). *Guide for administering and scoring the Stanford-Binet Intelligence Scale: Fourth Edition.* Chicago: Riverside.

Wechsler, D. (1967). *Manual for the Wechsler Preschool and Primary Scale of Intelligence.* San Antonio: Psychological Corporation.

Wechsler, D. (1974). *Manual for the Wechsler Intelligence Scale for Children—Revised.* San Antonio: Psychological Corporation.

Wechsler, D. (1981). *Manual for the Wechsler Adult Intelligence Scale—Revised.* San Antonio: Psychological Corporation.

Wechsler, D. (1989). *Manual for the Wechsler Preschool and Primary Scale of Intelligence—Revised.* San Antonio: Psychological Corporation.

Wechsler, D. (1991). *Manual for the Wechsler Intelligence Scale for Children—Third Edition.* San Antonio: Psychological Corporation.

Wechsler, D. (1997). *Wechsler Adult Intelligence Scale—Third Edition: Administration and Scoring Manual.* San Antonio: Psychological Corporation.

Weeks, G. R., & Treat, S. (1992). *Couples in treatment: Techniques and approaches for effective practice.* New York: Brunner/Mazel.

Welner, Z., Reich, W., Herjanic, B., Jung, K., & Amado, H. (1987). Reliability, validity, and parent-child agreement studies of the Diagnostic Interview for Children and Adolescents (DICA). *Journal of the American Academy of Child and Adolescent Psychiatry, 26,* 649–653.

Williams, C. L., Butcher, J. N., Ben-Porath, Y., & Graham, J. R. (1992). *MMPI-A content scales: Assessing psychopathology in adolescents.* Minneapolis, MN: NCS.

Woodcock, R. W., & Johnson, M. B. (1989a). *Woodcock-Johnson Psycho-Educational Battery—Revised, Tests of Cognitive Abilities.* Allen, TX: DLM Teaching Resources.

Woodcock, R. W., & Johnson, M. B. (1989b). *Woodcock-Johnson Psycho-Educational Battery—Revised, Tests of Achievement.* Allen, TX: DLM Teaching Resources.

Yalom, I. D. (1985). *The theory and practice of group psychotherapy* (3rd ed.). New York: Basic Books.

CHAPTER 2

Attention-Deficit/ Hyperactivity Disorder

■ **Attention-Deficit/Hyperactivity Disorder**

□ CLINICAL DESCRIPTION

Diagnostic Considerations

Attention-Deficit/Hyperactivity Disorder (ADHD) is one of the most common Axis I childhood disorders (see Table 2.1), occurring in as many as 1–5% of children (American Psychiatric Association, 1994; Conners, 1998). It is characterized by inattention, disorganization, restlessness, impulsivity, and hyperactivity. These symptoms are disruptive or create social-environmental problems for the child (American Psychiatric Association, 1994; Barkley, 1998; Munoz-Millan & Casteel, 1989). The disorder is much more common in boys than girls, with ratios of 2:1 to 10:1 reported in the literature (American Psychiatric Association, 1994; Barkley, 1991a).

DSM-IV divides ADHD criteria into two groups. The *Inattention* group consists of symptoms reflecting lack of attention to details, difficulty sustaining attention, failure to listen, organizational problems, distractibility, failure to complete activities, and forgetfulness. The *Hyperactivity-Impulsivity* group consists of excessive behavior, squirming, difficulty remaining seated, inappropriate noise/vocalization, and difficulty waiting. Children must meet *either* six of the Inattention symptoms *or* six of the Hyperactivity-Impulsivity symptoms to qualify for ADHD diagnosis. Furthermore, the symptoms must be present in two or more situations. Children who meet only Inattention criteria in a 6-month period are coded as being Predominantly Inattentive Type, while those who meet only Hyperactivity-Impulsivity criteria in a 6-month period are coded as being Predominantly Hyperactive-Impulsive Type. Children who meet both the Inattention and the Hyperactivity-Impulsivity criteria are coded as being Combined Type. Hence, ADHD is coded in DSM-IV as having three subtypes, depending on whether the predominant features are Inattention, Hyperactivity-Impulsivity, or both. An additional ADHD Not Otherwise Specified (ADD NOS) category

TABLE 2.1   Epidemiology and Course of ADHD

Prevalence: 1–5%

Sex Ratio (Male:Female):   2:1 to 10:1

Typical Onset Age: 3–7 years

Course: Symptoms persist in moderate form into adulthood in estimated 30–66% of cases. Increased risk of antisocial and related behavior in ADHD-CD subtype.

Common Comorbid Conditions:	1. Conduct Disorder
	2. Oppositional-Defiant Disorder
	3. Learning Disabilities
	4. Mood Disorders
	5. Anxiety Disorders
	6. Sleep Disorders
Relevant Subtypes:	1. Inattentive vs. Hyperactive-Impulsive
	2. With Comorbid Conduct/Oppositional Problems
	3. With Comorbid Learning Problems
	4. With Comorbid Social Disability

may be used for children who have problems with attention, hyperactivity, or impulsivity but who do not meet ADHD criteria.

The DSM-IV criteria differ from DSM-III-R, which listed a single group of 14 criteria for ADHD and required the presence of 8 for a diagnosis (American Psychiatric Association, 1987). The use of a single list of ADHD symptoms in DSM-III-R had been criticized based on factor analytic studies that suggested that ADHD symptoms fall into two categories: inattention-restless and impulsive-hyperactive (Barkley, 1998). DSM-IV more closely approximates factor analytic findings by splitting ADHD symptoms into two groups and allowing for an Inattentive subtype. In fact, DuPaul et al. (1997) have shown that teacher ratings of the 18 DSM-IV ADHD criteria factor into the two categories identified in DSM-IV.

The age of the child is critical in making the ADHD diagnosis. Moderate levels of diffuse activity and a short attention span are not uncommon in very young children. Attention, concentration, and purposeful, controlled activity increase with age. Nevertheless, half of ADHD cases have onset before age 4, and onset of some symptoms must occur prior to age 7 for a diagnosis to be made (American Psychiatric Association, 1994). For some children, the disorder is not apparent until the child begins school. The school environment can magnify or illuminate ADHD symptoms because school activity is more structured and a large amount of comparison children are present. ADHD usually is diagnosed before the age of 7 (Biederman, 1991). When the diagnosis is made after age 7, retrospective accounts show the onset of the behaviors to be prior to age 7.

As noted earlier, DSM-IV recognizes subtypes of ADHD based on whether the child's symptoms are predominantly inattentive or hyperactive-impulsive. In addition to the core symptoms of the disorder, children with the Hyperactive-Impulsive or Combined subtypes of ADHD are more likely to have a concurrent diagnosis of oppositional-defiant disorder or conduct disorder, compared to children with the Inattentive subtype. Children with the Hyperactive-Impulsive or Combined subtypes are also more likely to be placed in special classes for children with behavior problems, and they are more likely to have a family history of aggressive, hyperactive, or substance abusing behaviors. Children with the Inattentive subtype, on the other hand, tend to have more problems in cognitive ability areas, including an increased incidence of memory problems, learning disorders, and sequential processing problems. They also are more likely to have a family history of learning disabilities and anxiety disorders (Barkley, DuPaul, & McMurray, 1990).

ADHD is associated with a plethora of medical, behavioral, cognitive, and academic disorders. Children with ADHD frequently do poorly in school; they are more likely to have physical problems than other children; they have increased difficulties with peer acceptance; and they are more likely to be anxious and depressed (Barkley, 1998; Biederman, 1991). ADHD sometimes co-occurs with low IQ, in which case ADHD criteria should be applied based on the child's mental age. Perhaps the most common features associated with ADHD, however, are those of Oppositional-Defiant Disorder (ODD) or Conduct Disorder (CD). Stated simply, many children with ADHD have difficulties with compliance and rule-breaking behavior.

The large but incomplete overlap between ADHD and CD/ODD suggests that subtypes of ADHD may exist in addition to those recognized by DSM-IV. Several authors have noted the heterogeneity of the ADHD population (Whalen & Henker, 1991), which argues for the importance of delineating ADHD subtypes. A first division of subtypes is based on the degree to which the child with ADHD shows conduct problems. As many as 50% of children with ADHD have an associated CD or ODD (Barkley, 1991b; Biederman & Steingard, 1989). These children (hereafter referred to as ADHD-CD) channel their overactivity into oppositional, aggressive, antisocial, or dangerous behavior; children with ADHD alone present with more attention/impulsivity problems (Carlson & Rapport, 1989). Some of the overlap in ADHD-CD symptoms in this group may be secondary to the relationship between impulsivity (a symptom of ADHD), frustration tolerance, and fighting (a symptom of CD/ODD). Research indicates, for example, that more impulsive children (regardless of whether they are diagnosed with ADHD) tend to get into more fights (Halperin et al., 1995) and to have difficulty delaying gratification (Barkley, 1998). Furthermore, children with ADHD-CD are at risk for later antisocial-aggression problems, whereas those with simple ADHD are not (Biederman, 1991).

Learning disabilities are another set of diagnoses that frequently co-occur with ADHD or are mistaken for ADHD. Children with ADHD may be vulnerable to learning problems because of their difficulty sustaining attention to school tasks and difficulty organizing information. Conversely, because children with learning disabilities are frequently frustrated and upset in school, they may be more behaviorally active and show more off-task behavior in the school environment. Deficits in acquiring and processing incoming information, a hallmark of learning disabilities, can interfere with attentional processes, contributing to the presentation of symptoms consistent with ADHD. Between 10% and 20% of children with ADHD appear to have comorbid learning disorders (Hinshaw, 1992).

Studies show that about 9–11% of children with ADHD have dyslexia (reading learning disability), whereas up to 33% of children with dyslexia have ADHD (Pennington, 1991). It has been suggested that in cases when ADHD and dyslexia co-occur, the ADHD is most likely secondary to the dyslexia (Pennington, 1991). In addition to dyslexia, some authors (Rourke, 1988) have noted some overlap or possible diagnostic confusion between ADHD and Nonverbal Learning Disabilities (NVLD) in preschool children. The NVLD syndrome is characterized by weaknesses in visual perception, complex motor tasks, novel problem solving, mathematics, reading comprehension, and nonverbal reasoning, in the context of strengths in rote verbal skills, rote verbal memory, overlearned verbal facts, word knowledge, and overlearned verbal academic material (such as reading recognition). Especially at young (preschool) ages, children with NVLD tend to be hyperactive, with poor visual attention processes. This presentation often leads to suspicion that the child has ADHD. When ADHD co-occurs with a learning disability, it is essential that treatment focus on the learning disability as well as the ADHD. In many cases, the learning disability will be a significant cause or contributor to the ADHD symptoms.

Biederman (1991) suggests two other subtypes of ADHD based on co-occurring diagnoses: ADHD with major depression symptoms (as many as 30% of ADHD cases; Barkley, 1991b) and ADHD with anxiety disorder (as many as 30% of ADHD cases; Barkley, 1991b). These subtypes represent children who have emotional difficulties superimposed on their inattention-hyperactivity problem. Such children may experience an exacerbation of their anxiety-depression if they are discouraged, intimidated, or frustrated by the structure of a behavioral modification plan. Thus, treatment may need to be modified to accommodate the child's comorbid depression-anxiety. The delineation of ADHD subtypes suggests that children with ADHD should routinely be evaluated for related conduct, mood, or anxiety problems. The presence of an associated problem may require more intensive intervention and may signal increased risk for negative long-term outcome.

Consistent with the DSM-IV division of ADHD into Inattentive and Hyperactive subtypes, several authors suggest distinguishing ADHD subtypes based on whether symptoms are primarily cognitive or behavioral (August & Garfinkel, 1989; Halperin et al., 1990). Children with behavioral ADHD show features of inattention, impulsivity, and hyperactivity, with no associated learning or other disability. These children are at high risk for associated Conduct or Oppositional-Defiant Disorder. Children with cognitive ADHD, on the other hand, have significant learning and/or other cognitive disabilities in addition to milder problems with inattention, impulsivity, and hyperactivity. However, they typically have fewer problems with CD than the behavioral group (August & Garfinkel, 1989). Evaluation, educational programming, and psychological interventions should differ between these groups.

A final subtyping of ADHD is based on the extent of comorbid social problems. Greene, Biederman, Faraone, Sienna, and Garcia-Jetton (1997) characterize children with ADHD as "socially disabled" (ADHD + SD) if measures of their adaptive social functioning are substantially discrepant with their intelligence testing scores. Children with ADHD + SD have been shown to have elevated rates of mood disorders, conduct problems, anxiety disorders, smoking, family problems, adaptive functioning deficits, and substance abuse, compared to children with ADHD who do not have the SD component. These differences persisted at 4-year follow-up (Greene et al., 1997).

Appearance and Features

Despite considerable variability in symptoms across the population of children with ADHD, certain features are frequently seen (see Table 2.2). One very common feature is difficulty sustaining attention during relatively long, monotonous, group-oriented, or repetitive tasks (Barkley, 1998; Frick & Lahey, 1991). Research suggests that deficits in task

TABLE 2.2   Appearance and Features of ADHD

COMMON FEATURES

1. Attention problems
2. Overactivity: restlessness, inability to sit still, fidgeting, constant movement
3. Impulsivity: interrupting others, difficulty waiting for turn, blurting out answers, making simple mistakes because of impulsive answers, acting without considering consequences
4. Deficits in executive functioning, goal formulation, problem solving, and arousal
5. Organizational deficits: problems staying on schedule, messiness, slow completing tasks, often off-task
6. Poor school performance and/or learning disability
7. Peer relationship problems
8. Oppositionality/defiance or conduct problems
9. Able to attend to interesting, changing, reinforcing activities that are chosen by the child
10. Responsive to immediate and salient reinforcement
11. Negative interactions and relationships with authorities
12. Negative reputation among authorities
13. Sleep disturbance (rule out apnea)
14. Adoption of an acting as opposed to reflective style
15. Risk of negative adolescent/adult outcome
16. Onset prior to age 7

OCCASIONAL FEATURES

1. Onset prior to age 4, although often not identified until school age
2. Problem becomes more apparent at child's entry to school
3. Physical problems, including higher injury risk and motor coordination problems
4. Aggressive and/or antisocial behavior
5. Problems adjusting to changes

Note: The features listed in the table are often seen but are not universal. Some features may be diagnostically relevant or required, whereas others may not be required for diagnosis. "Common" features are typical of the disorder; "occasional" features appear frequently but are not necessarily seen in a majority of cases.

persistence and sustained attention, as opposed to distractibility, are primarily responsible for the observation that children with ADHD fail to complete tasks before moving on to more interesting stimuli (Pennington, 1991). On tasks that are interesting, tasks that involve shifts of focus, tasks that allow freedom to choose activity, or tasks that provide immediate reinforcement, behavioral differences between children with ADHD and other children may be unnoticeable. Thus, a child with ADHD may appear focused at home or in front of a video game but be quite inattentive and disruptive at school. These situational differences suggest that behavioral data must be gathered from multiple observers in multiple settings in order to diagnose ADHD. Diagnostically, the ADHD behavior need occur in only two settings, although children with ADHD often manifest the behavior in more than two situations (American Psychiatric Association, 1994).

In addition to showing poor sustained attention, children with ADHD frequently manifest difficulty with impulse control (Barkley, 1998; Carlson & Rapport, 1989). Barkley

(1997a) cites neurologically based self-control deficits and disinhibition as the core features of ADHD; children with ADHD have difficulty monitoring, planning, and regulating themselves and their behavior. Impulse control and self-control deficits underlie behaviors such as interrupting others, difficulty waiting for turn, poor performance on tasks requiring waiting or thoughtful decisions, and failure to complete tasks in a timely and planned manner (Barkley, 1997a; Brown & Quay, 1977; Carlson & Rapport, 1989). Impulsivity also affects the child's compliance with rules or requests, especially when the child acts before considering consequences. Such impulsive behaviors can be dangerous to the child or others, possibly explaining the higher frequency of injury in children with ADHD (American Psychiatric Association, 1994). Impulsivity may decrease in situations involving immediate and valued consequences (Barkley, 1998).

A third common feature of ADHD is overactivity, which may be more prevalent in younger children with ADHD. Overactivity is particularly noticeable in situations requiring the child to sit still or to remain in the same place for an extended period of time. At these times, children with ADHD tend to squirm, stretch, change position, make noises, play with anything within reach, and stand. The extent of this hyperactivity, however, varies considerably with time, stress, and situation (Barkley, 1998).

Some authors suggest that the ADHD features of inattention, impulsivity, and overactivity reflect general deficits in executive functioning and arousal (Barkley, 1997a; Conners, 1995; Pennington, 1991). Children with ADHD frequently have difficulty with tests of executive functioning (Pennington, 1991), which is defined as the ability to purposefully engage in planned, meaningful, goal-directed behavior. Lezak (1983) identifies four parts of executive functioning: formulating goals, planning, acting on goal-directed plans, and performance of the desired behavior. Barkley (1997a) notes that deficits in executive functioning may underlie some of the problems in self-control, impulsivity, and temporal planning frequently seen in children with ADHD.

Although not inherent in the ADHD diagnosis, noncompliance, aggression, and other antisocial behaviors are also common features of children with the hyperactive-impulsive and combined subtypes of ADHD (Battle & Lacey, 1972; Frick & Lahey, 1991). These behaviors may result from difficulties with sustained attention, impulsivity, or an associated CD. Not surprisingly, the disruptions, interruptions, noncompliance, and antisocial behaviors of children with ADHD create social problems for them. Interactions with adults are frequently aversive and involve cycles of commands, noncompliance, and punishment. Empirical study indicates that children with ADHD often receive harsh and controlling responses from parents and teachers, who may ignore periods of good behavior (Danforth, Barkley, & Stokes, 1991; Frick & Lahey, 1991). Children with ADHD who exhibit antisocial behaviors such as aggression and interruption also have problems with peer relationships (Carlson & Rapport, 1989). Excessive talking, interruption of ongoing activity, failure to wait for turn, and provocative behavior are all annoying to peers, leading to social problems for over 50% of children with ADHD (Barkley, 1991b). Despite talking more, children with ADHD listen and respond less to peers, robbing their social interactions of a sense of balance (Barkley, 1991b). In some cases, peer rejection leads to anger, alienation, and further antisocial behavior from the child with ADHD, causing a vicious circle of rejection (Frick & Lahey, 1991).

In the academic realm, the effects of ADHD are significant and pervasive. In fact, many children with ADHD present initially because of academic difficulties. Academic difficulty among children with ADHD is common, with 20–30% of children with ADHD having a learning disability (Barkley, 1991b; Barkley, DuPaul, & McMurray, 1990; Lambert & Sandoval, 1980). Overall, children with ADHD have achievement testing scores 10–15 points below scale norms, and 35% of children with ADHD will be retained a grade at least once before high school (Barkley, 1991b). Expressive language and organization of ideas may be particular problems (Barkley, 1998), although studies show deficits across virtually all academic areas (e.g., Barkley, Anastopoulos, Guevremont, & Fletcher, 1991). The academic difficulties of children with ADHD have been attributed to motivational problems, attention problems, lower IQ, and poor test-taking skills (Barkley, 1998).

In addition to academic problems, ADHD is associated with a host of other risks. Children with ADHD show a higher rate of motor coordination problems (as high as 52% have coordination difficulty) and sleep difficulties such as problems falling asleep, frequent waking, and tiredness after waking (Barkley, 1991b). In some cases, problems with sleeping or with the sleep-wake schedule contribute substantially to the ADHD symptoms. For example, sleep apnea (temporary cessation of breathing during sleep) can, in some cases, cause disorganized, inattentive behavior during waking hours, and children with suspected ADHD should always be screened for sleep problems (Hansen & Vandenberg, 1997). Health problems and injuries are also common for children with ADHD. Between 10 and 25% of children with ADHD experience multiple serious accidents or poisonings (Barkley, 1991b).

Recently, more attention has been given to the persistence of ADHD throughout adolescence and adulthood. As many as 30–50% of children with ADHD show symptoms persisting through adolescence and into adulthood (Biederman, 1991; Weiss, Hechtman, Milroy, & Perlman, 1985); 50–80% of children with ADHD continue to meet ADHD criteria in adolescence (Barkley et al., 1991; Barkley, Fischer, Edelbrock, & Smallish, 1990). Behavioral symptoms such as impulsivity, inattention, immaturity, oppositionality/defiance, social skills deficits, and distractibility often endure into adolescence. However, symptoms of hyperactivity decline (Barkley et al., 1991; Hechtman, 1991). Elevated rates of academic failure, antisocial personality, substance abuse, criminal behavior, and depression have been reported in adolescents and adults who were diagnosed with ADHD as children, although the risk of these negative long-term outcomes is largely limited to the ADHD-CD subtype (Barkley et al., 1991; Biederman, 1991; Hechtman, 1991; Klein & Mannuzza, 1991). These negative outcomes are less prevalent in adults than in adolescents (Klein & Manuzza, 1991).

Hechtman (1991) reviews literature supporting three types of ADHD adult outcome: normal functioning (probably fewer than half of children; Weiss et al., 1985), moderate disability (serious concentration, social, and emotional problems, low self-esteem, anxiety, and irritability; perhaps as high as 66% [Weiss et al., 1985]), and significant disability (major depression, substance abuse, antisocial behavior). Those with co-occurring CD or Mood Disorder diagnoses are particularly at long-term risk. Factors related to positive adult outcome are higher IQ, internal locus of control, better social skills, higher family SES, supportive family, and good health (Hechtman, 1991).

Etiology

Biological Theories

A growing body of research suggests that children with ADHD have a neuroanatomical or neurophysiological abnormality in the brain regions that regulate attention and motor behavior, particularly the frontal lobes and parts of the limbic system (Barkley, 1997a, 1998; Pennington, 1991). Initially, researchers noticed that brain damaging conditions such as closed head injury, perinatal oxygen deprivation, poor prenatal care, and hydrocephalus often resulted in overactivity and attention deficits (Hynd, Hern, Voeller, & Marshall, 1991). These observations led to the hypothesis that ADHD may be caused by damage affecting brain regions responsible for attention and behavioral control. However, fewer than 5% of children with ADHD have a history of documented brain injury. Hence, more recent research focuses on developmental or genetic deficits in brain structure or physiology, regardless of injury history (Barkley, 1998).

The dysfunctional brain areas implicated most consistently are the frontal lobes and the limbic system. Research has shown smaller frontal lobe areas in children with ADHD, decreased frontal lobe blood flow and metabolism, functional abnormalities suggesting frontal lobe dysfunction, and possible EEG abnormalities in certain frontal lobe areas (Barkley, 1991b; Hynd et al., 1991; Pennington, 1991). Zametkin et al. (1990) used positron emission tomography (PET) scanning techniques to show that adults with ADHD had significantly less activity in the frontal lobe areas, compared to adults without ADHD. Although some results of ADHD-neuroanatomy studies are not always consistent (Hynd et al., 1991), the bulk of the research supports the hypothesis that neuroanatomical or neurophysiological abnormalities contribute to the development of most ADHD cases (Barkley, 1998).

Genetic factors have been implicated as one cause of neurological abnormalities underlying ADHD. Research shows increased incidence of ADHD in biological relatives of children with ADHD. First-degree relatives of children with ADHD show an increased incidence of ADHD, depression, alcoholism, conduct problems, and antisocial disorders (Barkley, 1991b; Barkley, 1998; Biederman, 1991; Biederman, Faraone, Keenan, Knee, & Tsuang, 1990). Furthermore, 20–32% of immediate family members of children with ADHD show symptoms of ADHD (Barkley, 1991a; Barkley, 1991b; Zametkin, 1989). Hyperactivity in particular appears to have a significant genetic basis, with heritability studies showing greater concordance for hyperactivity among monozygotic (genetically identical) than among dizygotic (not genetically identical) twin pairs (Goodman & Stevenson, 1989). These results suggest a genetic link, but some of the increased family incidence of ADHD could also be a result of environmental factors that remain stable from generation to generation (e.g., poor parenting, low SES).

In addition to genetics, damage to the developing fetus has been implicated as a risk factor for some cases of ADHD. For example, mothers who smoke during pregnancy appear to be at higher risk for having children with ADHD (Milberger, Biederman, Faraone, & Jones, 1998). Attention problems and hyperactivity are also found in some other fetal syndromes.

Differences in neurotransmission may explain some of the neurological findings in studies of the etiology of ADHD. Because the neurotransmitters most responsible for attention and motor behavior are the catecholamines (dopamine, norepinephrine, epinephrine), they (especially dopamine) have received the most attention. Most of the evidence supporting the catecholamine hypothesis of ADHD comes from studies showing that medications that reduce the symptoms of ADHD (dextroamphetamine [Dexedrine], methylphenidate [Ritalin], and pemoline [Cylert]) increase the amount of catecholamines in the brain (Barkley, 1998; Hynd et al., 1991). Furthermore, the prefrontal cortex and parts of the limbic system, which have been implicated in PET and MRI studies as having deficient activity in individuals with ADHD, have many dopamine pathways (Barkley, 1998).

Nutrition and toxins have created occasional excitement in the mass media, but little evidence exists to support their causal role in more than a handful of cases. Lead poisoning can create overactivity, but very few cases of ADHD have been attributed to lead. Other ingested substances, such as food additives and sugar, have been suggested as reasons for the development of ADHD. Although it is conceivable that food allergies or sugar cause overactivity in an occasional child, empirical research has not supported the role of food as a factor causing ADHD in most children (Barkley, 1991b; Hynd et al., 1991).

Behavioral Theories

Although biological factors are thought to have a significant role in the development of most cases of ADHD, psychological and environmental factors are likely to contribute to the severity and specific characteristics of the disorder. Chaos in the environment may mean that the child is rarely exposed to structure and organization, reducing social learning experiences in these areas. Parents may inadvertently reinforce symptoms of ADHD by giving a child added attention (often negative) following hyperactive behaviors.

Psychological Theories

Hyperactive or inattentive behavior may also result from environmental stress, such as family dysfunction or traumatic stress. It is unlikely, however, that the full ADHD syndrome would result from such problems in the absence of a biological predisposition to ADHD. Instead, these factors are likely to exacerbate existing ADHD symptoms or to create transient overactivity in an otherwise normal child (Frick & Lahey, 1991).

☐   ASSESSMENT PATTERNS

Broad Assessment Strategies

Cognitive Assessment

Clinician-Administered IQ Testing.   Cognitive measures used with children who have ADHD seek to identify deficits of attention, cognitive control, memory, and global intelligence that may be associated with the disorder. They also provide a baseline estimate of intellectual functioning, from which the extent of an attention deficit may be evaluated. Cognitive tests may also help to identify ability strengths and weaknesses that explain the child's attention problems in the school setting. Clinicians must remember that, although children with ADHD as a group score lower on a variety of cognitive tests, they are a heterogeneous group with regard to test score performance.

As a group, children with ADHD score about 1/3 to 3/4 of a standard deviation lower than matched controls on measures of intelligence, although most children with ADHD score in the broad average range (Loge, Staton, & Beatty, 1990; Lufi, Cohen, & Parish-Plass, 1990). Loge et al. (1990) found children with ADHD to score lower than nonreferred controls on WISC-R Full Scale IQ, Information, Arithmetic, Digit Span, Block Design, and Coding. However, virtually all IQ scores and subtest scores from the ADHD sample were in the average range. This result reflects the so-called *ACID* (Arithmetic; Coding, Information, Digit Span) profile frequently seen in children and adults with learning disabilities and ADHD (Kaufman, 1990; Sattler, 1990). Lufi et al. (1990) found children with ADHD to score lower than controls on virtually all WISC-R subtests, with the largest differences occurring on the Arithmetic, Block Design, Digit Span, and Coding subtests. On the Arithmetic and Coding scales, children with ADHD also scored lower than a mental health clinic sample.

The WISC-III Arithmetic and Digit Span subscales have been found in factor analytic studies to constitute a "Freedom from Distractibility" (FFD) or "Working Memory" factor that measures memory during periods of mental effort and concentration (earlier studies with the WISC-R included the Coding subscale on this factor) (Psychological Corporation, 1997; Wechsler, 1997). Although several studies have found that children with ADHD score lower on the scales composing the FFD factor (Loge et al., 1990; Lufi et al., 1990; Rispens et al., 1997), substantial research also indicates that FFD is not a specific marker for ADHD (Cohen, Becker, & Campbell, 1990; Pennington, 1991).

With the addition of the Symbol Search subtest to the WISC-III and WAIS-III, the Coding subtest has moved from the FFD factor to a new factor, named Processing Speed (Coding and Symbol Search). Processing Speed (PS) subtests demand focused, rapid, visual association/discrimination and motor response. An element of task persistence and sustained attention is also present on the PS tests. It appears that children with ADHD score lower on these (and similar) tests compared to nonreferred controls (Loge et al., 1990).

In addition to (or in place of) the WISC-III, the K-BIT or WASI may be particularly helpful for children who cannot sustain attention to a longer IQ test or who have difficulty with the greater expressive and understanding demands of the comprehensive IQ tests. Some children with ADHD provide underestimates of ability on the Wechsler scales because they do not maintain attention and motivation long enough to provide accurate results.

The results of cognitive or neuropsychological testing should not be used in isolation to make the diagnosis of ADHD. Many children with ADHD do well in the one-on-one situation of individual psychological testing, and their results may not reflect their behavior in groups or in less stimulating situations. Recent reviews indicate that no cognitive or neuropsychological test has sufficient power to be used in isolation to diagnose ADHD (Shelton & Barkley, 1995). On the other hand, cognitive testing provides an important component to be integrated with the results of behavioral checklists, observations, and interview data. Cognitive testing can also provide valuable information about the child's abilities and neuropsychological functioning, as long as the clinician is mindful of the influence of the controlled conditions of the testing situation. (A sample assessment battery is shown in Table 2.3.)

Clinician-Administered Achievement Testing. Achievement tests are routinely administered to children with suspected ADHD because of the risk of learning difficulty associated with the disorder. The WJ-R, WIAT, and Kaufman Test of Educational Achievement (K-TEA; Kaufman & Kaufman, 1985) are commonly used broad achievement tests for assessing learning problems in children with suspected ADHD (Sattler, 1990). More specific tests capture areas such as reading and mathematics in a briefer format or in greater detail (Sattler, 1990). The *Wide Range Achievement Test—Third Edition* (WRAT-III; Wilkinson, 1993) is also sometimes used for assessment of learning problems in children

TABLE 2.3   Sample Assessment Battery for ADHD

COGNITIVE

1. Wechsler Intelligence Scale for Children—Third Edition (or other Wechsler test based on age)
2. Kaufman Brief Intelligence Test
3. Woodcock-Johnson Tests of Achievement—Revised
4. California Verbal Learning Test for Children—Revised

BEHAVIORAL

1. Symptom Inventory—4 (Parent-Report and Teacher-Report)
2. Behavior Assessment System for Children (Parent-Report and Teacher-Report)
3. Conners' Rating Scale—Revised (Parent-Report and Teacher-Report)
4. Personality Inventory for Youth

SYNDROME SPECIFIC

1. Conners' Continuous Performance Test or T.O.V.A.
2. Home Situations Questionnaire
3. School Situations Questionnaire

Note: Assessment instruments are intended to supplement (not substitute for) a good clinical interview and, when possible, a structured diagnostic interview.

with ADHD, but its predecessor, the WRAT-R (Jastak & Wilkinson, 1984), has received some criticism for poor psychometrics (Kaufman, 1990; Sattler, 1990). Chapter 11 includes more detailed information about the strengths, weaknesses, and uses of achievement tests for assessing learning disorders.

As a group, children with ADHD tend to score lower on achievement tests than do nonreferred control groups. Barkley et al. (1991), for example, found a sample of adolescents with ADHD to show WRAT scores in the 88–99 standard score range, with the lowest scores in mathematics; these scores were lower than those of a nonreferred control group. However, August and Garfinkel (1989) note that there are subgroups of children with ADHD who score in average ranges on achievement tests. Using the WRAT-R, August and Garfinkel (1989) found that behavioral ADHD subtypes scored in the 96–104 standard score range in reading, spelling, and arithmetic. The cognitive subtype, by contrast, scored in the 80–91 range.

Behavioral Assessment

Parent-Report/Other-Report.   Although child behavior checklists are essential for the comprehensive assessment of a child with ADHD, they should be used with several caveats. Most importantly, the clinician must remember that checklists are affected by the motives and personality of the adult completing them. Factors such as social desirability, exasperation with the child, parental psychopathology, and halo effects can affect scores. This may be particularly true in the case of the child with ADHD, who places stress on the parent. A related problem is the lack of agreement between respondents about the child's behavior.

The Achenbach scales (CBCL and TRF) include some items that reflect essential or associated features of ADHD (predominantly contained on the Attention Problems subscale), as well as other items that may be associated with ADHD, such as symptoms of Disruptive Behavior Disorders (Aggressive Behavior, Delinquent Behavior, and Social Problems subscales) and Internalizing disorders (Anxious/Depressed subscale). CBCL and TRF subscale items do not, however, correspond directly to DSM-IV criteria. In fact, content analyses indicate that only 1–2 items on the Attention Problems scale overlap with the 9 DSM-IV ADHD-Inattentive criteria, and only 2–3 items on the Attention Problems scale overlap with the 9 DSM-IV ADHD-Hyperactive criteria (Kronenberger, 1997). Thus, the majority of DSM-IV ADHD symptoms do not overlap with the content of the CBCL and TRF. Other Attention Problems subscale items reflect immaturity, anxiety, and disengagement from the environment (Kronenberger, 1997).

Despite this discrepency in content from DSM-IV, the Achenbach scales discriminate children with ADHD from nonreferred and other clinically referred children (Barkley, 1987). A typical child with ADHD would be expected to elevate the Attention Problems scale, with other elevations likely on the Aggressive Behavior scale and the Social Problems scale. Social competence scores are often low relative to norms. Adolescents with ADHD tend to elevate CBCL/TRF Internalizing subscales (in addition to Attention Problems and Aggressive Behavior), whereas children with ADHD have a greater tendency to elevate the Externalizing subscales alone. For example, adolescents show lower social competence scores and higher Anxiety-Depression, Somatic Complaints, Withdrawal, and Aggressive Behavior scores (Barkley et al., 1991).

The Conners' scales (parent- and teacher-report) include items measuring both diagnostic criteria and associated features of ADHD. The 18 DSM-IV ADHD symptoms are directly reflected in 18 items on the Conners' scales, which form DSM-IV Inattentive, DSM-IV Hyperactive-Impulsive, and DSM-IV Total subscales. These subscales allow for direct measurement of parent-report of ADHD symptoms and comparison of parent ratings to national norms. Hence, the degree to which the child's behavior, as reflected by DSM-IV ADHD symptoms, is abnormal (as rated by parent) can be obtained from the Conners' scales.

The Conners' scales also contain items measuring associated cognitive (Cognitive Problems subscale) and behavioral (Hyperactivity subscale) features of ADHD, many of which do not overlap with DSM-IV diagnostic criteria. Other subscales can assist in identifying comorbid Oppositional-Defiant/Conduct Disorder (Oppositional subscale), Anxiety-Depressive Disorders (Anxious-Shy, Perfectionism, and Psychosomatic subscales), and/or social problems (Social Problems subscale). A Conners' ADHD Index scale was derived empirically by selecting items that discriminated most significantly between groups of children with and without ADHD; this subscale is a good measure of a child's risk of having an ADHD diagnosis, particularly if nonreferred groups of children are being screened. The 10-item Hyperactivity Index (HI), from the earlier versions of the Conners' scales (Conners, 1990) is retained in the revised versions, under the new name Conners' Global Index (CGI). Although the CGI has been used separately to assess for ADHD, it does not have appropriate coverage of symptoms to be used alone in ADHD assessment (Barkley, 1987; Conners, 1990).

Children with ADHD would be expected to elevate the Conners' DSM-IV symptom subscales in accordance with the degree to which their symptoms are in the inattentive category, the hyperactive-impulsive category, or both. A similar pattern of elevations would be expected on the Cognitive Problems and Hyperactivity subscales. It is important to remember that elevation of the Cognitive Problems subscale may also indicate a learning disability or low IQ. Elevation of the Oppositional subscale along with the ADHD-related subscales suggests a likely ADHD-CD subtype, and concurrent Oppositional-Defiant Disorder or Conduct Disorder should be investigated. The CGI and Conners' ADHD Index are screening subscales that are typically elevated by children who have the classic spectrum of inattentive, hyperactive, and impulsive behaviors. Preliminary results have shown the ADHD Index to be quite sensitive (above 90% sensitivity and specificity) in identifying children with ADHD from their nonreferred peers (Conners, 1997).

The "short" versions of the Conners' scales were developed to provide a briefer assessment of the narrow band of symptoms directly associated with ADHD. They contain only the ADHD Index and abbreviated versions of the Oppositional, Cognitive Problems, and Hyperactivity subscales. The CADS-P includes only the ADHD Index and 18 DSM-IV symptom-items. The CGI-P contains the 10 items from the CGI. These short scales may be useful in focused situations when time is crucial, such as repeat monitoring of symptoms following diagnosis. Whenever possible, however, use of the full CPRS-R is recommended.

Like the Conners' scales, the BASC parent- and teacher-report scales contain separate subscales measuring Attention Problems and Hyperactivity. Although the items on these scales do not overlap exactly with DSM-IV criteria, they are very similar to the criteria, with the inclusion of a few additional associated features of ADHD (Kronenberger, 1997). The BASC also includes subscales that can assist in identifying comorbid or alternative internalizing (Anxiety, Depression, Somatization) or externalizing (Aggression, Conduct Problems) problems. The adaptive subscales on the BASC (Adaptibility, Social Skills, Leadership) provide additional information about the child's resilience and social behavior.

Children with ADHD tend to produce peak elevations on the BASC Hyperactivity and Attention Problems subscales. Group mean scores for the Aggression, Conduct Problems, and Depression subscales are elevated in ADHD samples, but individual children vary significantly in their relative elevations of these subscales. Interestingly, elevations of the Hyperactivity and Attention Problems subscales, relative to a mean T-score of 50, are characteristic of most clinically referred children, with or without ADHD. It is the relative elevations of these scales over the scores of other subscales (especially Aggression and Conduct Problems) that is most characteristic of ADHD (Reynolds & Kamphaus, 1992). There is also a short (45-item) version of the BASC, which includes only items pertinent to Attention Problems, Hyperactivity, Internalizing Problems and Adaptive Skills; this version (called the BASC Monitor for ADHD) may be used when a more focal assessment is desired.

The ECI-4, CSI-4, and ASI-4 cover all 18 DSM-IV ADHD symptoms, in addition to the symptoms of Conduct Disorder, Oppositional-Defiant Disorder, and several anxiety and mood disorders. Thus, they assess possible comorbid or alternative diagnoses as well as ADHD. Within clinical samples, the parent-report CSI-4 is a relatively sensitive (0.80 sensitivity in one study) and specific (0.74 specificity value in one study) instrument (Gadow & Sprafkin, 1997).

Comparison of results from parent-report and teacher-report checklists can provide insights into the child's relative behavior at school and at home. A problem-ridden teacher-report profile coupled with a relatively normal parent-report profile suggests that the child may behave adequately in the less structured, more individualized home environment while becoming disorganized and hyperactive at school. In cases in which parent- and teacher-reports show markedly different profiles, the clinician should expect parents and teachers to disagree about the accuracy of the ADHD diagnosis. Additionally, research has shown that teachers tend to exaggerate the presence of ADHD symptoms in a child who is showing oppositional behavior (Abikoff, Courtney, Pelham, & Koplewicz, 1993). Hence, teacher-report of ADHD symptoms should be interpreted very cautiously for children who have known problems with oppositional, defiant, rule-breaking, or other (nonhyperactive) disruptive behavior.

Child-Report.   In addition to parent- and teacher-report checklists, child self-report behavior checklists are used as a standardized means of assessing the child's view of his or her ADHD symptoms and concurrent problems. The YSR form of the CBCL, for example, allows older children and adolescents (age 11–18) to self-report on symptoms corresponding closely to the items and subscales of the CBCL and TRF. On the YSR, adolescents with ADHD typically elevate the Attention Problems, Social Problems, Aggressive Behavior, and Delinquent Behavior subscales; elevations of other scales vary based on individual variability in comorbid symptoms (Barkley et al., 1989).

The CRS-R also includes a self-report version, the Conners-Wells' Adolescent Self-Report Scale (CASS), for adolescents age 12–17. The CASS measures ADHD symptoms and related problems in more depth and breadth than the TRF, including questions that correspond directly to DSM-IV. Elevations of the DSM-IV:Hyperactive-Impulsive, Conduct Problems, and Anger Control subscales of the CASS are typical of the hyperactive-impulsive or ADHD-CD subtype of the disorder. Elevations of the DSM-IV:Inattentive, Cognitive Problems, and Hyperactivity subscales are indicative of the inattentive subtype of ADHD. Other subscales can alert the clinician to the presence of comorbid or alternative Family Problems and/or Emotional Problems (distress and dissatisfaction).

The BASC-SRP has the advantage of a broader age range than most other self-report questionnaires (age 8–18 years), although it includes no subscales corresponding to the primary symptoms of ADHD. Several BASC-SRP subscales can provide information about symptoms that are typically associated with ADHD, including alienation from school (Attitude to School and Attitude to Teachers subscales), internalizing problems (Anxiety and Depression subscales), social problems (Social Stress, Relations with Parents, and Interpersonal Relations subscales), and self-esteem (Sense of Inadequacy, Self-Esteem, and Self-Reliance subscales). Hence, the advantages of using the BASC-SRP in assessing children with ADHD are its coverage of social, self-esteem, and anxiety-depression problems that may be associated with the disorder. As a group, children with ADHD produce moderate elevations of all BASC-SRP subscales, with no clear pattern of elevations (Reynolds & Kamphaus, 1992). There is little item or subscale correspondence between the BASC-SRP and the parent- or teacher-report BASC scales.

The PIY includes an Impulsivity and Distractibility (ADH) scale, which is divided into Brashness (ADH1, bragging, showing off, bothering others), Distractibility/Overactivity (ADH2, inattention, difficulty waiting, failure to learn from punishment or mistakes, difficulty delaying gratification), and Impulsivity (ADH3, restlessness, impulsivity, failure to complete things) subscales. Another PIY scale with direct relevance to ADHD symptomatology is the Cognitive Impairment scale, which encompasses the Poor Achievement/Memory (COG1, memory and concentration problems that cause difficulty in learning), Inadequate Abilities (COG2, sense of intellectual and academic inferiority relative to others), and Learning Problems (COG3, poor school achievement) subscales. Other PIY subscales tap symptoms of oppositional-aggressive behavior (Delinquency scale, DLQ), family problems (Family Dysfunction scale, FAM), anxiety-depression (Psychological Discomfort scale, DIS), and social problems (Withdrawal [WTH] and Social Skills [SSK] scales). Children with ADHD tend to elevate the ADH subscale, with elevations of the COG, DLQ, FAM, DIS, and SSK subscales varying based on each individual child's presentation (Kronenberger, 1997; Lachar & Gruber, 1995). Like the BASC-SRP, the PIY applies to a broad age range (8–18 years) and includes validity scales measuring overreporting (F scale) and underreporting (L scale) of symptoms, as well as defensive responding (K scale).

Family Assessment

Parent-Report. Because ADHD is a stressor for families and because the family is often involved in the treatment of ADHD, family assessment can be helpful for formulations and intervention. The Family Dysfunction scale of the PIY gives information about family problems from the perspective of the child. Elevations of this scale should be investigated with further interviewing and/or tests.

Although there is no characteristic profile for families of children with ADHD, high levels of stress would typically be reflected by elevations on the PIY Family Dysfunction scale, and the Conflict subscale of the FES. FES results may also indicate whether the family is overly authoritarian (high Control subscale, low Independence subscale) or chaotic (low Control and Organization subscales, high Independence subscale). Diminished family support and high family stress would result in low FES Cohesion subscale scores and high Conflict subscale scores. This information would guide both behavioral and family interventions.

As noted earlier in the chapter, parent-child relationships can be significantly strained by the presence of ADHD. Standardized, detailed testing information about the parent-child relationship can be obtained by using the Parenting Stress Index (PSI; Abidin, 1995), which measures stressful child behaviors, parent adjustment problems, and strains in the parent-child relationship. Parents of children with ADHD have been found to significantly elevate the Distractibility/Hyperactivity, Adaptability, Reinforces Parent, Demandingness, Mood, and Acceptability subscales of the child domain of the PSI, with peak scores on the Demandingness subscale (Abidin, 1995).

Syndrome-Specific Tests

Clinician-Administered

Continuous Performance Tests (CPT). A CPT is a test that assesses attention, impulsivity, and distractibility using target stimuli. Stimuli are typically visual (letters, numbers, shapes, or other stimuli) or auditory (words or tones, usually on an audiotape). The object of the task is to execute a response (such as pushing a button) when a certain stimulus or sequence of stimuli is presented. Attention factors are measured by seeing how consistently and correctly the child is able to track and respond to the stimuli.

Typical scores derived from CPT tasks are based on the accuracy and speed of the child's response to the target and nontarget stimuli. Accuracy is measured with hits (correct responses to target stimuli), misses (omissions that occur when the child fails to respond to a target), and commissions (responses to nontarget stimuli, as if they were targets). Hits measure accurate, sustained attention and response to the stimulus; misses measure distractibility, disengagement from the task, or wavering attention; commissions measure impulsivity or poor attention to the stimuli. Hence, a child with many hits, few misses, but many commissions is showing good sustained attention but significant impulsivity. On the other hand, a child with few hits, many misses, and few commissions is showing distractibility and poor sustained attention but less impulsivity. Some CPTs (Leark, Depuy, Greenberg, Corman, & Kindschi, 1996) also measure anticipatory responses (responses made so close after the presentation of a stimulus that they must be "lucky guesses") and multiple responses (more than one response to a stimulus). These types of responses typically indicate a failure to follow task directions and can alert the examiner to validity problems with results.

In addition to accuracy of response, speed of response is a parameter frequently measured by CPTs. Response speed may be more sensitive to attention problems than accuracy because reaction time tends to deteriorate significantly with impaired attention (Conners, 1995). Response speed measures typically assessed by CPTs (Conners, 1995; Leark et al., 1996) include response time (RT; time from the presentation of a target to the child's response), variability of response time (RTV; the standard deviation or variance of all of the child's response times throughout the test), interstimulus interval response time change (RTISI; change in response time based on the speed with which stimuli are presented), and test duration response time change (RTTD; speeding or slowing of response time from the beginning to the end of the test). Slower, more variable response times indicate likely attention problems. High RTISI scores indicate that the speed of the child's response was significantly negatively affected when stimulus presentation was slowed; hence, they indicate children who have difficulty maintaining arousal during slower, more boring stimulus presentation (Conners, 1995). High RTTD scores indicate that the child's response speed slowed significantly during the course of the test; these scores, therefore, indicate problems with sustained attention. Some tests also measure the speed of the child's response following a commission response (Leark et al., 1996); hypothetically, children should slow their response after a commission because their error has taught them to be more cautious.

Some CPTs speed up the presentation of the stimuli when the child is doing well or slow down the presentation of stimuli if the child is doing poorly. These CPTs yield a fourth score, the interstimulus interval, which is a measure of the average speed at which numbers were presented to the child. Shorter interstimulus intervals indicate that the child was able to attend to briefer, more rapid stimuli. Other CPTs vary the interstimulus interval according to a predefined pattern, to give a standardized assessment of variability in the child's speed and accuracy of response depending on the interstimulus interval.

Another parameter along which CPTs vary is the proportion of target to nontarget stimuli. In target-frequent conditions, the target occurs far more frequently than the nontarget (typically in a 3:1 to 10:1 ratio), requiring many responses from the child and vigilance to withhold responses on the rare nontargets. In target-infrequent conditions, the nontarget occurs far more frequently than the target, requiring few responses from the child and vigilance to respond to the rare targets.

Commonly used visual CPTs are the Conners' Continuous Performance Test (CCPT; Conners, 1995), the Test of Variables of Attention (TOVA; Leark et al., 1996), and the Vigilance Task of the Gordon Diagnostic System (GDS; Gordon, 1983; Gordon & Mettelman,

1987). The CCPT presents letters in a target-frequent, single-target condition, with measurements on both accuracy and response time indices (yielding most, but not all, of the scores described earlier). The child must press the space bar for every letter except the letter *X*. Interstimulus interval is varied in a patterned, counterbalanced way throughout the test, independent of the speed or accuracy of the child's responses. Normative scores are based on a large but not well-described sample age 4 years through adult. Administration time is under 15 minutes on computer. Research (Conners, 1995) has shown a 74% sensitivity and 87% specificity rate for a regression model of CCPT scores discriminating children with ADHD from nonreferred children, although these values are probably much lower for discriminating ADHD from clinic-referred children with other diagnoses (DuPaul, Anastopoulos, Shelton, Guevremont, & Metevia, 1992). The CCPT was also found to be sensitive to Ritalin effects (Conners, 1995).

The TOVA (Leark et al., 1996) uses a square for its stimulus. The target occurs when the square is at the top of a larger square on the computer screen; the nontarget occurs when the square is at the bottom of a larger square on the computer screen. The TOVA uses a fixed interstimulus interval (2 seconds) but varies the target-infrequent (first half of test) and target-frequent (second half of test) conditions. Most CPT scores described earlier (with the exception of interstimulus interval scores) are provided by the TOVA. Administration time is about 23 minutes on computer. Norms are based on a large sample age 4 through adult; adult norms for the TOVA appear to be better than those for the CCPT, although this has not been extensively researched (Leark et al., 1996). Sensitivity (0.72) and specificity (0.85) values for the TOVA (discriminating ADHD and nonreferred groups) were very similar to those for the CCPT. TOVA scores were also sensitive to Ritalin and caffeine effects (Leark et al., 1996).

The GDS is a small, computerized device that assesses sustained attention and impulsivity in children with ADHD, using several tests. The 9-minute CPT measure in the GDS (Vigilance Task) requires the child to press a button when the sequence 1, then 9, appears on the screen; an auditory version of this task requires responses to numbers presented in the auditory modality but is otherwise identical (Gordon, 1997). Scores are obtained for hits, misses, and commissions, as well as for variability of performance across three, 3-minute time intervals (Gordon, 1983). The Distractibility Task of the GDS is a variant of a CPT (Gordon & Mettelman, 1987), which also discriminates children with ADHD from nonreferred children (Loge et al., 1990). This task is identical to the Vigilance Task of the GDS except that number stimuli flash in three separate columns at the same time (giving the appearance of a three-digit number). The child is to respond when a 1 appears followed by a 9, but only when *both* numbers are in the center column. Numbers in the other columns are intended as distractions. Number correct and errors of commission are scored. Finally, an Auditory Interference Task requires the child to complete the visual Vigilance or Distractibility Tasks, while random numbers are presented aloud as interference stimuli (Gordon, 1997).

Auditory CPTs were developed much more recently than visual CPTs and, therefore, there is less research on their validity. Auditory target and nontarget stimuli range from tones to words to mathematics problems. In addition to the auditory version of the TOVA (Leark et al., 1996), other auditory CPTs include the Intermediate Visual and Auditory Continuous Performance Test, the Auditory Continuous Performance Test, and the Paced Auditory Serial Attention Test. Auditory CPTs yield the typical CPT scores based on accuracy and speed of response.

CPTs are good measures of inattention and distractibility. CPT scores generally correlate moderately with observer measures of ADHD symptoms as well as with other cognitive measures of attention, distractibility, and impulsivity (Barkley, 1987; Conners, 1995; Guevremont, DuPaul, & Barkley, 1990; Klee & Garfinkel, 1983; Leark et al., 1996; Newcorn et al., 1989), although the overlap of CPT scores and observer measures of ADHD is far from perfect (DuPaul, Anastopoulos, et al., 1992). DuPaul, Anastopoulos, et al. (1992) found that CPT (GDS) scores are relatively poor predictors of ADHD symptoms as rated by parents and teachers. On the other hand, Grant, Ilai, Nussbaum, and Bigler (1990) found scores from the GDS Vigilance Task to correlate with Verbal IQ, Performance IQ, Freedom from Distractibility, finger oscillation, auditory perception, visual-motor integration, and nonverbal reasoning scores in a sample of children with ADHD. Furthermore, children and adolescents with ADHD do more poorly on the CPT than nonreferred children (Conners, 1995; Leark et al., 1996; Loge et al., 1990), and CPT scores improve with stimulant medication (Conners, 1995; Fischer & Newby, 1991; Leark et al., 1996). There have been some data suggesting that the Ritalin dose that produces optimum effects on TOVA scores is similar to the Ritalin dose that produces optimum effects in the environment (Leark et al., 1996). This finding has led some clinicians to use the TOVA to decide Ritalin dosing, although information from other sources should be used as well. Interestingly, CPT measures of impulsivity have also been found to predict the tendency to get into fights with other children (Halperin et al., 1995).

Matching Familiar Figures Test.   The MFFT (Kagan, 1966) is a 12-item (short-form) or 20-item (long-form) measure of impulse control, visual discrimination ability, and attention to detail (Cairns & Cammock, 1978). The child is shown a picture of an object and then must choose from a group of six nearly identical pictures the one that exactly matches the target picture. The child is scored for latency time (mean time taken to respond to each picture) and number of errors. Raw scores may be compared to norms (Salkind & Nelson, 1980). The MFFT discriminates children with ADHD from nonreferred children, and it relates to behavioral measures of activity (Barkley, 1987). However, at least one study questions the MFFT-20's ability to discriminate between adolescents with and without ADHD (Barkley et al., 1991). The MFFT has been criticized because of its high correlations with intelligence and achievement as well as for reliability problems (Barkley, 1987; DuPaul, Anastopoulos, et al., 1992; Milich & Kramer, 1984). Furthermore, MFFT scores show limited overlap with teacher-reported ADHD symptoms (DuPaul, Anastopoulos, et al., 1992). Nevertheless, the MFFT appears to be sensitive to impulsive responding in many children with ADHD, despite its limited value for making a diagnosis.

Waiting Tasks.   Waiting tasks require the child to wait a specified amount of time before executing a simple response. For example, in the Delay Task from the GDS (Gordon, 1983) the child must wait, then press a button after a certain amount of time. The child is not told that the amount of waiting time is 6 seconds. When the child presses the button after the requisite amount of time, he or she receives a point, the time is reset, and the waiting period starts again. If the child presses the button before 6 seconds have elapsed, a point is not awarded, and the timer returns to a 6-second delay. Scores are given for the number of correct responses, the number of times that the button was pressed, and a ratio of correct responses to button presses. Waiting tasks such as the Delay Task measure impulsivity, although their ability to discriminate children with ADHD from nonreferred children is uncertain (Barkley, 1987; Loge et al., 1990).

Verbal Learning and Memory Tests. Memory and verbal learning tests, such as the California Verbal Learning Test for Children (CVLT-C; Delis, Kramer, Kaplan, & Ober, 1994), are very useful in the assessment of children with ADHD because they test for patterns of auditory attention, memory, and learning. The CVLT-C consists of a 15-word shopping list, which is read to the child five times. After each reading of the list, the child is asked to repeat as many of the words as possible. Following these five trials, a new (interference) list is read once, with the child again asked to recall as many words as possible from the new list. Then the child is asked to recall as many words as possible from the original list (the one that was read five times), without having the list read by the examiner. Next, the child is given semantic cues to remember the words. Following a 20-minute delay, the child is again asked to recall words from the original list. This recall is followed by a cued trial and, finally, by a recognition task in which the child must pick out the original words from a long list of target and decoy words.

Children with ADHD tend to show less consistency in words recalled across the five trials of the CVLT-C and to do most poorly (relative to peers) on the first and last of the five trials of the original list. They are also less adversely affected by interference effects on memory (caused by the interference list), compared to children with verbal learning disabilities or mental retardation (Delis et al., 1994). Because the CVLT-C measures auditory attention and learning, it can provide information important in understanding the academic functioning of a child with ADHD.

Executive Functioning Tests. Cognitive tests that measure executive functioning, goal direction, planning, cognitive flexibility, and verbal and nonverbal fluency are sometimes referred to as "frontal lobe" tests because these cognitive abilities seem to be most affected in known cases of frontal lobe dysfunction. These tests typically require some degree of planned, flexible problem solving, while restraining inappropriate responses. For example, maze tests measure planning ability and inhibition of inaccurate responses (entering dead ends of mazes). Maze tests, such as the WISC-III Mazes subtest, discriminate children with ADHD from controls and are responsive to medication effects (Barkley, 1991a).

Other tests of frontal lobe functioning include the Stroop Color and Word Test (Golden, 1978), which requires the child to attempt three tasks: reading a page of color words printed in black ink, labeling colors on a page of X's printed in different colors of ink, and reading a page of color words that are printed in ink of different colors than the colors named by the words. The main score of the Stroop is based on the degree to which the child's performance on the third page (with the different color names and inks) deteriorates, compared to performance on the first two pages. This interference measure reflects the degree to which the child can maintain cognitive focus and flexibility in the face of distracting information (the fact that the words are printed in colors different from the name of the word). Tests of verbal fluency (such as the Controlled Oral Word Association Test; Borkowski, Benton, & Spreen, 1967) and response shift, concept formation, and abstract problem solving (such as the Wisconsin Card Sorting Test [Heaton, 1981] and the Children's Category Test [Boll, 1993]) are also frequently used to assess the ability areas grouped under frontal lobe functioning.

Deficits in executive (frontal lobe) functioning may be at the center of the attention-organization problems characteristic of ADHD. Pennington (1991) notes that children with ADHD have been found to score lower than controls on fluid problem-solving tasks such as the WCST and the Tower of Hanoi task. Both of these tasks require planning, problem solving, and nonverbal reasoning.

Parent-Report/Other-Report

ADHD Rating Scales. ADHD rating scales consist of a list of the DSM ADHD symptoms, which are rated by an observer or by the child as to the frequency of their occurrence (DuPaul & Stoner, 1994). DuPaul et al. (1997) and DuPaul, Power, Anastopoulos, & Reid, (1998) have developed the ADHD Rating Scale-IV (ADHDRS-IV), a stand-alone, parent- or teacher-report ADHD rating scale based on DSM-IV criteria. Normative data are provided for the parent- and teacher-report ADHD rating scales based on a representative sample, divided by sex and age.

Research using the ADHDRS-IV has shown that both parent-report and teacher-report of ADHD symptoms are useful in assisting with a diagnosis of ADHD. Using various combinations of percentile cutoffs (usually in the 80th to 90th percentile ranges) for parent and teacher ratings on the ADHDRS-IV subscales of Inattention and Hyperactivity-Impulsivity, Power et al. (1998) found that approximately 70–80% of cases of ADHD could be reliably identified with minimal numbers of false positives. Of course, alternative diagnoses and clinical information need to be integrated with ADHDRS-IV results to arrive at an accurate diagnosis.

Home Situations Questionnaire/School Situations Questionnaire. The Home Situations Questionnaire (HSQ; Barkley, 1981) consists of 16 items that describe situations around the home in which children with ADHD may have behavioral difficulties. A revised version of the HSQ has 14 items (DuPaul, 1990). Parents state whether their child has a problem in that setting and the severity of the problem. Scores are obtained for the number of problem situations and the mean severity of these problems when they occur. Scores may be compared to norms derived by Barkley and Edelbrock (1987) or DuPaul (1990). The HSQ provides information about the pervasiveness, severity, and location of the ADHD symptoms at home. Such situation-specific information can be helpful in behavioral interventions. Children with ADHD score higher on the scale than nonreferred children, and the scale is sensitive to treatment effects (Barkley, 1987; Fischer & Newby, 1991).

The School Situations Questionnaire (SSQ; Barkley, 1981) is a 12-item scale consisting of school situations that could be problematic for the child with ADHD. A revised version of the SSQ has 8 items (DuPaul, 1990). As with the HSQ, teachers state whether the child has a problem in each situation and rate the severity of the problem. Number of problem situations and mean severity are scored and compared to norms (Barkley & Edelbrock, 1987; DuPaul, 1990). Children with ADHD score higher than nonreferred children on number of situations and situation severity (Barkley, 1987), and the SSQ is sensitive to treatment effects (Fischer & Newby, 1991).

Unlike other rating scales, the HSQ and SSQ provide information about the situations in which inattention, impulsivity, or hyperactivity are likely to occur. This delineation of situational differences tends to fit the observations of most parents or teachers, who have difficulty completing global items about behavior. Frequently, for example, observers state that a child is "sometimes" impulsive, meaning that the child shows impulsivity, but not in all situations. The HSQ and SSQ allow the clinician to investigate whether "sometimes" means that the child is somewhat impulsive (or inattentive, or hyperactive) in all situations, or whether "sometimes" means that the child is very impulsive in some situations but not in others.

Attention Deficit Disorders Evaluation Scale (ADDES; McCarney, 1989a; 1989b; 1995a; 1995b). The ADDES is a 46 (Home Version) or 60- (School Version) item questionnaire of typical ADHD behaviors. Raters use a 0–4 scale to rate the frequency with which a child age 4 ½–18 years shows various behaviors. No time frame (e.g., past week or past month) is suggested for reporting on the child's behaviors, although the rating anchors suggest that the rater should be familiar with the child's behavior over a period of over one month. Item scores are summed to yield two subscales (Inattentive and Hyperactive-Impulsive) as well as a Total Score, which are compared to scores from large normative samples to give standard scores and percentiles. Subscale scores 1 standard deviation below the mean are considered to have be atypical, whereas scores more than 2 standard deviations below the mean indicate a serious problem in that subscale area. The ADDES subscales are based on DSM-IV criteria for the Inattentive and Hyperactive-Impulsive subtypes of ADHD. Unlike other scales (e.g., the CSI-4 and CRS) that contain one item for each DSM-IV ADHD criterion behavior, the ADDES contains multiple items for each ADHD criterion behavior. However, individual ADDES items do not directly correspond to individual ADHD criteria. Hence, the ADDES reflects specific ADHD criteria loosely, although its subscales correspond fairly well to the DSM-IV ADHD subtypes. Because there are several ADDES items for each DSM-IV criterion behavior, it is also possible to obtain a summed item score for each of the 18 DSM-IV ADHD criteria. The psychometrics of the ADDES appear to be good (McCarney, 1995a, 1995b).

The ADDES has several companion scales for ADHD assessment. The Early Childhood Attention Deficit Disorders Evaluation Scale (ECADDES; McCarney, 1995c, 1995d) is a downward extension of the ADDES for children age 2–6 years. Like the ADDES, it includes a School Version (56 items) and a Home Version (50 items) and provides scores for Inattention and Hyperactivity-Impulsivity based loosely on DSM-IV diagnostic criteria. An adult version of the ADDES, the Adult Attention Deficit Disorders Evaluation Scale (A-ADDES), can assist with the standardized assessment of attention problems and related difficulties in adults (McCarney & Anderson, 1996a, 1996b, 1996c). An advantage to the ADDES family of scales is a set of corresponding intervention manuals (Jackson, 1997; McCarney, 1994; McCarney & Johnson, 1995) for use based on ADDES results. These manuals provide specific suggestions (divided by ADHD symptom) for home and school-based treatment of the child with ADHD. The intervention manuals may also be used for any patient who has been assessed for DSM-IV symptoms of ADHD.

ADD-H Comprehensive Teacher Rating Scale. (ACTeRS; Ullmann et al., 1997). The ACTeRS scales are teacher- (24 item) and parent- (25 item) report measures of attention problems, hyperactivity, and related behaviors. Items are rated on a 5-point scale (almost never to almost always) and add to give subscale scores for Attention, Hyperactivity, Social Skills, Oppositional, and Early Childhood (the latter scale measures difficult temperament and is on the parent-report version only). No time frame is provided for evaluating the child's behavior. Subscale scores are converted to percentiles based on a large norm group, with lower scores reflecting greater problems. The ACTeRS is very easy and convenient to administer, score, and interpret.

Because of its brevity, content, and the lack of a specified time frame reference, the scale may be given several times per day, in order to monitor changes in the child's behavior throughout the day. Relative elevations of the subscales may suggest symptom groups that are the most significant problem for the child at different times of day. The ACTeRS differentiates children with ADHD from nonreferred children and is sensitive to treatment effects (Ullmann et al., 1997).

Attention-Deficit/Hyperactivity Disorder Test. The ADHDT (Gilliam, 1995) is a 36-item observer-report (typically parent or teacher) measure of ADHD in children and adolescents age 3–23 years. Items fall into three subscales: Hyperactivity, Impulsivity, and Inattention. Raw scores are converted to standard scores based on a large national normative sample.

Brown Attention-Deficit Disorder Scales. The BADDS (Brown, 1996) are 40-item self-report and observer-report scales for adolescents and adults age 12 and older. Separate forms (with slightly different content and wording) are used for adolescents and adults. Problems (items) characteristic of attention-deficit disorder are read to the patient, who rates each on a 0–3 scale of frequency of occurrence in the past 6 months. Items may also be read to an observer (typically a parent of an adolescent or a spouse of an adult) to record observer ratings. The BADDS yield five subscales: Organizing and Activating to Work, Sustaining Attention and Concentration, Sustaining Energy and Effort, Managing Affective Interference, and Utilizing Working Memory. Raw scores are converted to T-scores based on norm samples, and the total scale score is compared to values indicating risk of having ADHD. The BADDS are especially useful for gathering self-perceptions of adolescents and adults about their ADHD symptoms.

TREATMENT OPTIONS

Treatment options for ADHD are shown in Table 2.4.

Medication

Medication is the most well-known, most widely used, and one of the most effective interventions for ADHD (Greenhill, 1992). Specifically, psychostimulant medications are frequently prescribed to assist in the management of ADHD, with improvement rates of 70–80% (Anastopoulos, DuPaul, & Barkley, 1991; Barkley, 1977; Greenhill, 1989, 1992; Munoz-Millan & Casteel, 1989), compared to placebo response rates of 10–18% (Greenhill, 1989, 1992). The stimulant medications most prescribed for children with ADHD are methylphenidate (Ritalin), dextroamphetamine (Dexedrine), and Adderall (a mixture of dextroamphetamine and levoamphetamine salts) (Greenhill, 1992; Swanson et al., 1998).

Adderall appears to have clinical and side effect profiles similar to those of Ritalin or Dexedrine, but preliminary research has shown that Adderall (in doses higher than 5 mg) has longer-lasting effects than Ritalin. Specifically, Ritalin was found to have peak effects in 1.5–2.0 hours, whereas Adderall at 10 to 20 mg doses had peak effects in 2.5–3.0 hours. In

TABLE 2.4   Treatment Options for ADHD

1. Medication
   a. Psychostimulants
   b. Tricyclic antidepressants
   c. Selective serotonin reuptake inhibitors (Prozac)
   d. Other medications (Clonidine, Thioridazine)
2. Behavioral Interventions
   a. Eight Component Home-Based Plan
      (1) Assessment
      (2) Psychoeducation
      (3) Goal Setting and Monitoring
      (4) Parent Skill and Relationship Building
      (5) Contingency Management
      (6) Generalization to Other Settings
      (7) Maintenance and Relapse Prevention
      (8) Follow-Up
   b. School-Based Plan
      (1) Antecedent Management
      (2) Contingency Management
      (3) Token Economies
      (4) Daily Report Cards
      (5) Academic Interventions
3. Family Interventions
   a. Structural Family Therapy
   b. Problem-Solving Communication Training
4. Psychotherapy
   a. Cognitive-Behavioral Interventions
      (1) Self-Talk
      (2) Self-Monitoring
      (3) Cognitive Problem Solving

Note: This outline of options summarizes major treatments covered in the text. Specific treatments are often combined into an intervention package. Refer to the text for additional descriptions of each treatment. This table is not necessarily an exhaustive list of all treatments available.

addition, the duration of action of Ritalin was found to average 4 hours, whereas that for Adderall ranged from 4.8–6.4 hours in a linear dose-dependent relationship for doses of 10, 15, and 20 mg (Swanson et al., 1998). Because the effects of methylphenidate and dextroamphetamine wear off in several hours, sustained-effect forms of these medications have been developed, under the names "sustained release" (for Ritalin) and "spansule" (for Dexedrine). Clinically, variable effects have been reported for Ritalin-SR (sustained release), whereas more consistent positive effects tend to be reported for the Dexedrine spansule.

Cylert (pemoline) is a longer-lasting stimulant that is less addictive at high doses than the faster-acting stimulants. However, findings of liver toxicity in some patients have greatly curtailed its use. Furthermore, it may not be as effective as the other stimulants (Greenhill, 1989). Because of these problems, Cylert is rarely prescribed today.

Stimulants have been shown to produce increased attention, reduced impulsivity, decreased overactivity, decreased restlessness, increased compliance, reduced aggressiveness, improved memory, improved social interaction, and improved classroom behavior (Anastopoulos et al., 1991; Barkley, Fischer, Newby, & Breen, 1988; Danforth et al., 1991; Greenhill, 1992; Rapport et al., 1988). Teachers report that 75% of children with ADHD improve in global behavior following medication with stimulants (Greenhill, 1992). Evidence also exists that Ritalin has positive effects for adolescents and adults as well (Biederman, 1991; Greenhill, 1992; Klorman, Coons, & Borgstedt, 1987), and Ritalin has been shown to decrease ADHD symptoms and aggressive behaviors (including symptoms of Oppositional-Defiant Disorder) in lower SES, urban children (Bukstein & Kolko, 1998). Stimulants improve basic cognitive attentional functioning and motivation during academic tasks in half or more of the children who take them (Swanson, Cantwell, Lerner, McBurnett, & Hanna, 1991; Swanson et al., 1998). CPT scores generally improve following medication (Fischer & Newby, 1991; Greenhill, 1992), and children taking stimulants are able to attempt and accurately complete more mathematics problems in a classroom situation (Swanson et al., 1998).

The most common side effects of stimulants are decreased appetite, weight loss, headache, increased crying, heart rate elevation, slowing of growth, irritability, increased tension, and difficulty sleeping in some children (Anastopoulos et al., 1991; Greenhill, 1992). Furthermore, a "behavioral rebound" (Greenhill, 1992) may occur when children experience stimulant withdrawal, usually at the end of the school day. This behavioral rebound consists of irritability, hyperactivity, and excitability. It is usually managed by administering the child an additional dose of the stimulant or by using a longer-lasting stimulant (Greenhill, 1992). More severe but less common side effects are an increase in hyperactive behavior and the development of tics (Greenhill, 1989). The latter effect is rare but argues against the use of stimulants with children who have a positive family history for tic disorder (Biederman, 1991; Greenhill, 1989). There have also been warnings of stimulants provoking manic episodes in children with comorbid ADHD and depression or in children at risk for mood disorders. Lombardo (1997) recommends that children be carefully screened for risk factors for bipolar illness (especially family history of bipolar disorder and depression) prior to initiation of stimulant treatment. The severity of some stimulant side effects can be managed by altering the doses or providing "drug holidays," during which stimulant use is discontinued (Anastopoulos et al., 1991). Parents should be informed about possible side effects and should be instructed to monitor them, with severe effects brought immediately to the attention of the prescribing physician.

Despite their effectiveness with many children with ADHD, psychostimulants may not be the drug of choice for certain children with ADHD. Some children, for example, fail to respond to stimulant medication (20–30% of cases), whereas other children are at risk for tics. Sometimes, children or family members may abuse the stimulant medication. Finally, some children need longer-acting medications or have co-occurring depression (Biederman, 1991; Greenhill, 1989, 1992).

Other than stimulants, antidepressants such as tricyclics (TCAs) and selective serotonin reuptake inhibitors (SSRIs such as Prozac and Zoloft) are occasionally used to treat ADHD. The efficacy of SSRIs awaits more research, but case studies have shown improvement when ADHD is comorbid with depression. TCAs tend to be prescribed when depression and/or sleep problems are concurrent with ADHD. TCAs are longer lasting, may have an effect on depression, generally do not affect tics, and do not result in addiction. One common TCA for ADHD is desipramine (Norpramin), which has been found to have a 68% improvement rate for children with ADHD (Greenhill, 1992). Imipramine (Tofranil) has also shown response rates greater than those of placebo (Pliszka, 1991). Like stimulants, however, problems exist with TCA treatment. Side effects of TCA treatment are cardiotoxicity, dry mouth, decreased appetite, headaches, tiredness, dizziness, insomnia, and abdominal discomfort (Biederman, 1991). Furthermore, almost one-third of children will show no response to TCAs (Greenhill, 1992; Pliszka, 1991). Because of side effects and lack of placebo-controlled studies, Greenhill (1992) recommends that TCAs be used with caution for preadolescent children, and parents should closely monitor the child for side effects.

Numerous other medications, including clonidine (Catapres), monoamine oxidase inhibitors (MAOIs), thioridazine (Mellaril), lithium, and bupropion (Wellbutrin), have been suggested as potential treatments for ADHD, although little data exist on the use of these medications (Greenhill, 1992). Clonidine may be promising for children with ADHD who have high levels of motor activity and aggression, as well as for children with co-occurring ADHD and Tourette's syndrome (Biederman, 1991; Greenhill, 1989). MAOIs are effective but rarely used because they require strict dietary adherence that children are prone to violate (Biederman, 1991; Greenhill, 1989). Studies of lithium for ADHD treatment have produced disappointing results (Greenhill, 1989).

Behavioral Interventions

Home-Based Behavioral Interventions

Eight-Component Behavioral Plan. A variety of therapist-directed behavior management plans have been proposed for children with ADHD and related problems. Behavioral intervention manuals developed for families of children with externalizing problems are also easily modified to address common problems seen in children with ADHD (Anastopoulos et al., 1991; Anastopoulos, DuPaul, & Shelton, 1996). Barkley (1997b) and Bloomquist (1996), for example, provide two systematic, well-documented treatment manuals for children with oppositional-defiant, undercontrolled, disorganized, or social-problem behaviors. Barkley's (1997) manual is written for therapists and focuses mainly on parent behavior training to manage externalizing child behaviors. Bloomquist's (1996) manual is tailored for both therapists and parents; it emphasizes family and social interventions in addition to behavior modification for problem behaviors. McCarney (1994; McCarney & Johnson, 1995) provides manuals containing specific interventions based on the symptoms of ADHD being shown by the child.

Most behavioral treatments for children with ADHD follow a patterned approach to intervention (Anastopoulos et al. 1996; Barkley, 1997; Bloomquist, 1996; Kronenberger, 1999). The major components of behavioral treatment for ADHD are summarized next.

Component 1: Assessment. Before any intervention is initiated, it is important to thoroughly assess the child and family for ADHD, for related problems, and for unrelated comorbid conditions. Initial assessment is also important for the establishment of baseline functioning and for the process of operationally defining treatment goals. Operational definitions of symptoms and goals typically take the form of symptom counts or ratings that have some reliability across time and informant. For example, the amount of time that a child spends focusing on homework per evening could be an operationalized goal. Assessment continues throughout the behavioral treatment, with regular monitoring of treatment goals using the operational definitions developed at the initial assessment.

Component 2: Psychoeducation. Prior to initiating behavioral plans, it is important that parents are taught the basics of behavior management in general and of the ADHD treatment plan in particular. ADHD is explained in detail, with attention to specific symptoms, etiology, appearance, features, prevalence, course, and treatment. Handouts and books may be used to facilitate understanding and retention of information. Recommended books for explaining ADHD include Barkley's (1995) *Taking Charge of ADHD* or Phelan's (1996) *All About Attention Deficit Disorder.* Videotapes, such as Barkley's (1993a) *ADHD: What Do We Know?* and *ADHD: What Can We Do?* (1993b), are excellent psychoeducational tools. Following explanations of ADHD, behavior management is explained as a general technique. Principles of reinforcement, reinforcement schedules, attention as reinforcement, punishment, and operant conditioning are then explained. Then these principles are specifically applied to ADHD, with particular attention to the effects of ADHD on the parent-child relationship. During this discussion, the automatic nature of parent-child interaction and conflict is explored. Examples of sequences in which children and parents act (usually in a mutually hostile or aggravating way) are given. Parents are taught that the goal is for them to reduce automatic, negative behavior and to increase purposeful, positive contingencies in the environment. Emotion is taken out of the delivery of consequences, with parents encouraged to deliver negative consequences in a matter-of-fact way. At this stage, parents often benefit from reading books such as *1-2-3 Magic* (Phelan, 1995) or *SOS: Help for Parents* (Clark, 1996). Finally, three special issues about the use of behavior techniques with children with ADHD are covered: need for immediate reinforcers, need for consistency, and need for the identification of specific behaviors. Contingencies must also be able to change to fit changes in the child's behavior.

Component 3: Goal Setting and Monitoring. With this treatment component, parents explicitly set goals for their child's behavior. These goals are used to monitor progress throughout the child's treatment. Ideally, these goals are a logical extension from the problem behaviors identified in the initial assessment.

Component 4: Parent Skill and Relationship Building. Prior to implementing contingency management, it is generally wise to put some relationship-building techniques in place. Anastopoulos et al. (1991), for example, suggest a period of attention training, in which parents are taught the power of parental attention and techniques for harnessing this power. Techniques such as Special Time (see Appendix C) seek to build the parent-child relationship by encouraging a fixed period of accepting, positive interaction between parent and child. In addition to Special Time, Positive Attention (see Appendix C) is also used to improve the parent-child relationship by increasing pleasant parent-child interactions.

Parents are eventually encouraged to provide attention when their child is behaving appropriately on task and to ignore inappropriate, off-task behavior. Punishment is not used at this time. Parents are also encouraged to use attention as a reinforcer in other situations, providing attention to the child during periods of positive behavior and withdrawing attention during hyperactive, off-task behavior. Finally, parents are taught to increase the child's frequency of independent behavior by giving occasional attention reinforcement when the child is not depending on the parent for entertainment. The largest obstacle to this task is the parental inclination to leave the child alone during periods of good behavior. These times typically allow the parent to take a break, and parents sometimes fear provoking their child with parental attention. Parents are taught that providing attention during times of positive behavior increases the probability of future positive behavior, bringing additional benefits.

Component 5: Contingency Management. Initially in this phase, parents select a single behavioral goal or target, and this behavior is tied to a clear reinforcement system (see Appendix C). A system of token reinforcement may be used, or praise or other primary reinforcers may be provided at the time of the behavior. Some therapists (Barkley, 1997b) recommend that praise be used initially as a reinforcer, with more concrete reinforcers used later to supplement praise. The behavior target selected should be easily observable, clearly defined, and relatively frequent. Anastopoulos et al. (1991), for example, select "compliance with initial parental requests" (p. 216) as the target behavior, using a token system for reinforcement. In addition to having a specific, observable target behavior, a reinforcer must be selected and administered. Reinforcers that have shown the greatest effect on the behavior of children with ADHD are delivered immediately following the behavior (Hersher, 1985), are easily noticed by the child (concrete or obvious), and are highly meaningful to the child. The plan is fully explained to the child before its implementation. Behaviors are charted by the parent and discussed each week, with appropriate modification of the plan. One or two weeks after the instigation of contingency management, negative reinforcement and punishment techniques are phased into the plan (following explanation to the child). Specifically, time-out (see Appendix C) and response cost (in which a reinforcer, such as a token, is removed) are used to reduce the frequency of negative behaviors. As with reinforcement, punishment must be immediate and tied to specific behavior. Time-out, for example, typically involves sitting on a chair in a relatively unstimulating part of the room immediately following the target negative behavior. The time-out period should be relatively brief (one minute for each year of the child's age is a rough guideline, although this often must be modified for individual children), with extensions of the period for noncompliance with the time-out directive. Pelham and Hoza (1996) recommend that the time-out period be shortened slightly if the child's behavior in time-out is good. This "early release" encourages the child to maintain behavioral control during a period of correction. Continued careful charting and flexibility in the implementation of the plan are essential. Finally, parents are encouraged to extend the principles of the plan to other child behaviors.

Component 6: Generalization to Other Settings. A common complaint about behavioral interventions for ADHD-related behaviors is the lack of generalization to other behaviors or environments. In other words, the child follows "the letter of the law" of the behavioral plan but fails to improve any other behaviors. Home-based plans sometimes do not produce specific change in the school, and vice versa. Techniques to improve generalization include the following:

1. Change the target from a specific behavior to a general principle. Once a child has achieved the goal for a specific target behavior, the therapist may want to abstract from that specific behavior to all instances of the general principle that underlies the behavior. For example, if being on time in the morning is the initial target, the therapist might abstract to being on time for everything.

2. Teach the child to recognize opportunities to show target behaviors in novel situations. Children need an initial period of learning how to apply the general principle to specific situations. Practicing the identification of target situations (examples) with the therapist can help with this. Additionally, parents and teachers can help the child to recognize the general principle *in vivo*. For example, a parent might remind the child that the family has an outing in one hour and that the child should be on time for the outing in order to receive a reward. Eventually, children should be rewarded for times that they remember the target behaviors without being told or warned.

3. Open lines of communication and coordinate efforts across environments. Adults in different environments should communicate about the child's target behaviors to provide consistency in the behavior plan across situations. Barkley (1997b), for example, uses a Daily Report Card to facilitate communication between teachers and parents, with both teachers and parents implementing a behavioral plan. This encourages generalization of behavior to home and school environments.

4. Use cognitive-behavioral techniques (explained later in this chapter) to give the child the ability to monitor and direct behavior in multiple settings. Cognitive-behavioral techniques increase the child's awareness and control over behavior. Because the child is a constant across settings (even if the authorities change), any consistency within the child will assist with generalization of behavior across settings.

5. Teach safe practice. Kronenberger (1997, 1999) recommends the use of a technique called "safe practice" to promote generalization of positive behavior to socially sensitive situations. These situations typically occur when the child's disruptive behavior would be either dangerous or a major nuisance to a significant amount of innocent bystanders. For example, a child who misbehaves loudly for 30 minutes in the middle of a church service cannot be ignored until the child quiets down. Safe practice involves practicing the target behavior in the target situation at a time when negative behaviors would not be disruptive or dangerous to others. In the previous example, the family may go and sit in the church at a time when a service is not underway and when no other people are in the church. The child would then be rewarded or punished based on behavior, without having the power to control the parents' behavior by disrupting a church service.

Component 7: Maintenance and Relapse Prevention. This behavioral component involves the anticipation of problems, practice at problem solving, and the development of skills to deal with problems without help from the therapist. Parents review and plan with the therapist the future of behavioral management in the home, anticipating problems and events. Parents are encouraged to develop and implement their own behavioral plans, with the therapist acting as a monitor and advisor but less active than before. Signs of and risk factors for relapse are reviewed with parents: the tendency to become lax in contingencies, parental stress and frustration, testing of limits by the child, introduction of new authorities into the child's environment (and the need to discuss behavioral plans with new authorities), and the tendency for behavior and behavioral plans to deteriorate under stress. Kronenberger (1997, 1999) recommends that parents be taught to systematically vary components of a behavior modification plan (reinforcers, appearance of tokens or charts, schedule of reinforcement) in order to prevent the child's habituating (becoming bored with) to the behavioral plan. Follow-up sessions are scheduled, and the parents are encouraged to continue monitoring behaviors for discussion at follow-up. The therapist and parents set criteria for unscheduled "booster" sessions (usually, these criteria are signs that the child's behavior is relapsing and that the family cannot prevent the relapse without the therapist's help). It is important at this stage to reassure the parents about their competence and ability to manage the child without frequent visits to the therapist; their fears and concerns need to be addressed. Therapy sessions gradually become less frequent, until meetings are held only once per month or 6 weeks.

Component 8: Follow-Up. Finally, once the therapist and family have cut meeting times to once every month to 6 weeks, therapy consists of a few final sessions of monitoring and reassurance. These sessions focus on ensuring that the goals of maintenance and relapse prevention have been achieved. Follow-up observational data are collected and problems are discussed. Therapy may be restarted if the concerns about relapse begin to emerge. Typically, follow-up sessions occur at 2–3 month intervals for 4–6 months.

School-Based Behavioral Interventions

ADHD symptoms are often initially identified at the school, and schools are frequently a major locus of pressure on the child to improve behavior. Hence, school-based interventions are a common part of treatment for the child with ADHD. DuPaul and Stoner (1994) and Morriss (1996) provide excellent, comprehensive summaries of diagnostic, assessment, and treatment issues pertaining to ADHD in the school setting. McCarney (1994) and Morriss (1996) also give very specific and useful suggestions for managing individual ADHD symptoms in the school setting. Behavioral techniques applied at school are often used for children with ADHD (DuPaul, Guevremont, & Barkley, 1992), and communication between parents and teacher is essential for managing the child's behavior across environments (and for evaluating the generalization of treatment effects). Some common school-based behavioral interventions are as follows:

Antecedent Management Techniques. One group of school-based techniques targets stimuli that may elicit inattention, impulsivity, or hyperactivity (antecedents to ADHD behavior). Stimulus reduction, for example, involves buffering the child from extraneous stimuli, presumably reducing distractibility and impulsivity. In stimulus reduction, the child is put in a quiet room or in a well-defined (often screened) area within the classroom (Morriss, 1996). Stimulus reduction techniques have received little empirical support, and they are rarely used to treat ADHD (Abramowitz & O'Leary, 1991). A second school-based technique is seating modification, in which the child's seat is moved to a place that will provide more task-appropriate stimulation and less extraneous stimulation. Typically, seating modification involves moving the child to the front of the room or away from other overly active groups of children. In other cases, the seating arrangement of the entire classroom may be changed to reduce distractions from other children (Abramowitz & O'Leary, 1991). Seating modification apparently does produce less off-task behavior. Other specific techniques suggested by Abramowitz and O'Leary (1991) include reducing background classroom noise, reducing difficulty of tasks, allowing the child to self-pace on tasks, increasing task structure, and increasing the stimulation of tasks by using audio or visual components.

Contingency Management. In addition to techniques directed at stimuli, school-based behavioral techniques also emphasize modification of contingencies to change ADHD behavior (DuPaul, Guevremont, et al., 1992). Teacher attention and access to enjoyable classroom activities are preferred reinforcers for shaping the child's behavior (DuPaul & Stoner, 1994). Teachers are encouraged to praise appropriate behavior and to ignore or punish inappropriate behavior. Praise may be verbal-direct (a statement that the child is engaging in good behavior), verbal-indirect (a pleasant verbal interaction with the child that does not specifically refer to good behavior but is contingent on it), nonverbal-direct (a smile or friendly nod), or nonverbal-indirect (standing near the child or otherwise engaging in pleasant nonverbal interaction). Ideally praise follows good behavior as soon as possible and never follows inappropriate behavior.

Behaviors that are inappropriate but not dangerous, destructive, or disruptive may be ignored by the teacher, although research indicates that some punishment adds to the effectiveness of a praise-ignore plan (Abramowitz & O'Leary, 1991; DuPaul, Guevremont, et al., 1992). It is essential that the teacher's method of ignoring be carefully studied for subtle reinforcing components.

Certain behaviors exhibited by the child with ADHD cannot be ignored or do not respond to ignoring. Generally, these behaviors are disruptive, dangerous, destructive, or impinge on the freedom of other children. In some cases, merely alerting the child that the behavior is unacceptable is sufficient to produce change. Morriss (1996), for example, suggests the use of a "secret signal" between teacher and child to alert the child that the child is to stop the negative (or off-task) behavior and to return to task.

In cases of more severe or persistent problems, punishment techniques can be effective, if properly administered. Reprimands, for example, are particularly effective if they are administered in a brief, matter-of-fact, consistent, firm, direct (standing close to the child and requiring eye contact), private, and immediate manner (Abramowitz & O'Leary, 1991; DuPaul & Stoner, 1994), and if the reprimand is backed with the potential of losing privileges (Morriss, 1996). Because teachers must deal with large classes, anger, delay, and inconsistency are common problems for teachers in administering social punishment to children with ADHD. Furthermore, overly long explanations are aversive and irritating to the child, reducing the likelihood that they will be heard and understood. Teachers should think in terms of presenting one to two major points to the child in the course of an explanation about good or bad behavior; additional statements are likely to be ignored by the child.

In addition to reprimands, time-out techniques can be used to punish negative behavior at school. Because time-out involves restricting the child from access to reinforcement, time-out is perceived by the child as negative, and it produces the same effects as other punishment techniques. School-based time-out may take the form of ineligibility for reinforcers that are being distributed to the class for a specified period of time (Abramowitz & O'Leary, 1991). For example, if each child is given a piece of candy for solving a math problem correctly, the punished child would not be eligible for the candy. Alternatively, time-out may be delivered by restricting access to a favored activity, such as the computer (DuPaul & Stoner, 1994). Social time-out involves removing the child from the class, either by moving the chair to a remote area of the room or out into the hall. Time-out is most effective when it is announced in a firm, brief, clear, matter-of-fact way, when the child does not desire isolation, when the amount of time for the punishment is clear, when the duration is reasonable for age, and when the child receives additional punishment (an extension of the time-out period) for anything short of immediate compliance with the time-out order (Abramowitz & O'Leary, 1991; DuPaul & Stoner, 1994). Because of its severity and duration, time-out should be used sparingly and only for severe, negative behavior. If implemented properly, time-out can have a significant effect on the target child's behavior.

Token Economies.   In some cases of ADHD, a token economy may be established in the classroom. This technique awards the child points for desirable behaviors (usually on-task behavior) and, sometimes, removes points for undesirable behaviors (response cost). Although response cost is not included in all token interventions, it appears to be a critical component of token interventions for children with ADHD (DuPaul, Guevremont, et al., 1992). Points may then be exchanged for rewards.

Token economies are powerful shapers of behavior, particularly when the response-cost component is included. However, they are not without risk: First, other children in the classroom may be jealous of the child with ADHD and misbehave in the hopes of getting their own token economy. Second, if the parameters of good and bad behavior are too stringent, the child with ADHD may be unable to earn any tokens. Such failure may lead to frustration and an increase in negative behavior. This scenario can be avoided by making the target behaviors initially very simple and increasing their difficulty with time. Third, the token economy motivates the child with external rewards, which will not always be present throughout the child's life. Ultimately, the child must acquire an intrinsic motivation for good behavior. Fourth, the token economy must be simple enough for the child to understand. Fifth, the token economy may not generalize to the home or to other classrooms. Sixth, token economies require attention and consistency from the teacher, which may be difficult in large classes. Despite these risks, a well-designed token economy can be a potent modifier of children's behavior, justifying its use with children who do not respond to less intense interventions (DuPaul, Guevremont, et al., 1992).

One well-designed token-type intervention is the Attention Training System (ATS; Gordon, Thomason, Cooper, & Ivers, 1991; Rapport & Gordon, 1987). The ATS uses an apparatus to deliver and deduct the reinforcement points in a token-type behavioral modification plan. The apparatus displays on a screen (placed on the child's desk) points earned by the child for on-task behavior. Each minute a point is automatically added to the total on the screen. If the teacher observes the child in off-task behavior, the teacher pushes a button on a remote-control device, triggering a red light on the child's screen. The red light remains lit for 15 seconds, and a point is subtracted from the child's point total. Thus, as long as the teacher observes on-task behavior, points accumulate automatically at a rate of one per minute. A response-cost procedure deducts one point when the teacher observes off-task behavior. At the end of the class (or day), the child may trade points for rewards.

The ATS has several advantages over traditional token systems (Gordon et al., 1991). First, rewards are frequent and require no modification of the teacher's behavior. Second, rewards are prominent and immediate. Third, the target behavior is not difficult for most children with ADHD. Fourth, response cost is built into the program and requires little teacher effort. However, the ATS suffers from many of the same problems of other token interventions, and the apparatus costs several hundred dollars (DuPaul, Guevremont, et al., 1992). Children can also become frustrated and angry when points are deducted, leading to outbursts or refusal to work. Nevertheless, the ATS has been found to result in large improvements in on-task behavior for children with ADHD (DuPaul, Guevremont, et al., 1992; Gordon et al., 1991). Several authors (DuPaul, Guevremont, et al., 1992; Gordon et al., 1991) note the importance of response cost in the ATS and in other token-type procedures. Response cost, as used in the ATS, is an essential component for significant change and has no demonstrable negative long-term effects.

Daily Report Cards.   Daily report cards are rating sheets for target classroom behaviors, which are completed by teachers and sent to parents on a daily basis. Typically, 3–4 academic and behavioral goals are identified as targets. Each target is rated on a scale (e.g., 1–5 rating) based on the child's behavior, with separate ratings given for different periods throughout the day. Parents then deliver positive or negative consequences to the child based on the report card (Barkley, 1997b; DuPaul & Stoner, 1994).

Academic Interventions.   A variety of interventions are used to structure the teaching task to match the strengths and weaknesses of the child with ADHD, with the goal of improving grades and learning. Shortened assignments, frequent breaks, more frequent feedback on accuracy of answers, frequent changes of learning tasks, and interspersing "fun" activities with learning activities have all been used to promote the learning of children with ADHD. Morriss (1996) and McCarney (1994) provide other examples of these interventions.

Multisite Behavioral Packages

Pelham and Hoza (1996) describe an intensive (9 hours per day, 5 days per week) 8-week summer treatment program for children with ADHD. As a part of this program, children receive classroom instruction, group treatment, social skills training, sports participation, and other structured activity in the general context of an overall behavioral plan. The behavioral components of the plan include a point system, use of clear commands by adults, time-out, and parent behavior training. Follow-up consists of Saturday meetings with the children (every other week throughout the school year), follow-up behavioral meetings with parents, and collaboration with teachers to develop school-based behavioral modification plans. Pelham and Hoza (1996) report very positive outcomes for this intervention.

Overall, behavior modification plans are effective in managing the behavior of many children with ADHD, provided that they are consistently implemented (Anastopoulos et al., 1996; Barkley, 1991a; Pelham & Hoza, 1996; Whalen & Henker, 1991). Abramowitz, Eckstrand, O'Leary, and Dulcan (1992), for example, used a simple method of social punishment (immediate reprimand) and achieved effects comparable to those of medication in one child. Abramowitz et al. (1992) conclude that individual differences in children determine the relative effectiveness of behavior modification versus medication and that a multimodal (e.g., behavior modification *and* medication) approach may be wisest. Greenhill (1989) also suggests that a combination of medication and behavior management may have the greatest effect on ADHD.

The additive effects of medication and behavior management may occur because both interventions reduce the frequency of aversive interactions between the child and parent. This reduction breaks the cycle of misbehavior, power struggles, and negative attention. Medication reduces the frequency of aversive behavior on the part of the child, which is complemented by the behavior plan's effects on the behavior of the parent. Each member of the parent-child system sees the other as improved, leading to positive interaction (Danforth et al., 1991). Thus, behavioral techniques may be particularly important in cases of ADHD that are seen as annoying or aversive by the parents (such as cases with oppositional-defiant features [Biederman, 1991]). In addition to beneficial effects on the child, parents may feel more efficacy and parenting self-esteem as they see the beneficial effects of the behavior plan that they implement.

Ultimately, the success of a behavior plan depends on how well it is carried out in the environment. Factors such as parental psychopathology, family dynamics, sibling rivalry, and peer relationships can affect a behavioral plan. Furthermore, behavioral plans are demanding on parents and teachers, particularly because children with ADHD require frequent monitoring and immediate response (Munoz-Millan & Casteel, 1989). Hence, the clinician should conduct a careful environmental evaluation prior to implementing a behavior plan for ADHD.

Family Interventions

In addition to the parent-training components of behavioral treatments for ADHD, more family-oriented interventions may be helpful in some cases, especially when family dynamics interfere with behavioral treatments. Family resistance should be considered as a possible reason for the failure of a behavioral intervention program. If resistance is present, the clinician should evaluate the family for systemic influences that support or encourage the child's symptoms. For example, the child's negative behaviors may deflect attention from a conflictual marital relationship, or the parents' disagreement about the behavior plan may reflect an underlying animosity toward each other. In such cases, couples psychotherapy or structural or strategic family therapy may be warranted. Family interventions may also be helpful for families struggling with the integration of behavioral techniques into the developmental transition of adolescence. Adolescents may resist the structure of a behavioral plan, and they may respond to a different set of reinforcers.

Barkley et al. (1992) used a structural family therapy model to work with families of adolescents with ADHD. Interventions consisted of typical structural techniques: joining and evaluating the family; identifying alignments, boundaries and power; altering family structure to strengthen appropriate boundaries and to weaken inappropriate boundaries; and reducing enmeshment and disengagement in the family (Minuchin, 1974). The structural intervention resulted in significant improvement, although not to the degree found with a typical behavioral treatment (Barkley et al., 1992).

Problem-solving communication training (PSCT; Barkley et al., 1992; Robin, 1998) involves the use of a structured, five-step approach to problem solving within the family: identify the problem, suggest possible solutions, evaluate each possible solution, select the best solution, and implement the solution. Additionally, family members are taught to communicate with direct, accurate statements that minimize provocation and negative emotion. Irrational beliefs and misinterpretations of statements of other family members are identified and discussed, with particular attention to multiple levels of communication (e.g., content, implication, and emotion) within the family. Structural techniques are used to address recurrent problems or resistance to change. A modification of PSCT was found to be equally effective to behavioral interventions in treating adolescents with ADHD (Barkley et al., 1992).

Psychotherapy

Cognitive-Behavioral Interventions

Cognitive-behavioral interventions for ADHD attempt to directly address attention and concentration deficits with cognitive self-awareness, self-perception, and self-control strategies (Hinshaw, 1996; Kendall & Braswell, 1993). These interventions teach children to use a combination of self-talk, self-monitoring, and cognitive problem-solving strategies that enhance attention, motivation, and behavioral self-control. Self-talk generally takes the form of reminding oneself of the cognitions and behaviors to be executed in order to achieve a goal. Additional self-talk uses are for self-reinforcement and for encouraging planful, systematic problem solving over reflexive, maladaptive behavior. Self-monitoring, on the other hand, involves increasing the child's awareness of situations, behaviors, and cognitions that precede or accompany ADHD symptoms. This increased awareness is used to anticipate problems and circumvent them. Finally, cognitive problem-solving consists of systematic efforts to generate and select behaviors that will result in positive consequences for the child and a reduction of ADHD symptomatology (Hinshaw & Melnick, 1992).

Self-talk is present in most cognitive-behavioral treatments. It is used to enhance self-monitoring and problem solving as well as to assist the child in controlling thoughts. Self-talk is typically used to teach children to remind themselves about cognitive control strategies and to stay on task (Baer & Nietzel, 1991). For example, the child may mentally go through a list of problem-solving steps. Another use of self-talk is for positive self-statements (e.g., I *can* control my behavior) and self-reinforcement (e.g., I did really well in class paying attention to the teacher).

An example of *self-monitoring* or self-evaluation is provided by Hinshaw and Melnick's (1992) description of the Match Game. In this game, a target behavior (sitting still, for example) is chosen, and positive and negative examples of the behavior are demonstrated by the therapist, along with ratings for each behavior on a 1 (bad) to 5 (good) scale. The child is then engaged in an activity with other children. Following the activity, the therapist and the child independently rate the child's performance on the target behavior. The ratings are then compared, along with the rationale for each. Discussion promotes the child's self-awareness and self-monitoring of the target behavior. Reinforcement for correct matches may be used to increase the motivation of the child. A variant of the Match Game may be used when child and parent independently rate goals that were set as a part of a behavioral intervention.

Cognitive problem-solving strategies are exemplified by a group intervention developed by Fehlings, Roberts, Humphries, and Dawe (1991). Fehlings et al. (1991) taught children with ADHD to use a five-step process for problem solving: define the problem, set a goal, generate solutions, choose a solution, and evaluate the outcome. Various techniques, including modeling, role playing, homework, and reinforcement, were used to teach the problem-solving process. This process was applied to specific problems, which were eventually generalized to include several areas of particular difficulty for children with ADHD. Parents were also taught the problem-solving process and encouraged their children to use it at home. Bloomquist, August, and Ostrander (1991) also used a five-step problem-solving process, although their steps differed from Fehlings et al. (1991): recognize the problem, generate solutions, think of consequences for the solutions, anticipate obstacles to the solutions, and implement the solution. Teachers and parents encouraged children to use the strategies. Horn, Ialongo, Greenberg, Packard, and Smith-Winberry (1990) added relaxation training and self-monitoring to their problem-solving intervention to increase the ability of the children to recognize and manage threats to adaptive problem solving.

Several *integrated/manualized cognitive-behavioral treatment packages* for ADHD have been developed. These packages use a structured approach to cognitive-behavioral intervention, integrating several cognitive-behavioral techniques in a treatment plan. Kendall (1992), for example, has developed a 20-session, workbook-based program to help children learn to control and decrease impulsive behaviors. His Stop and Think program relies heavily on self-talk and cognitive problem-solving techniques. Children are taught five problem-solving steps, which are applied to increasingly complex and social problems. Stop and Think also includes a self-monitoring component and requires practice between sessions. The child is rewarded for accurate self-monitoring and for using the problem-solving techniques. A workbook is used to structure the intervention and to provide the child with practice in using the cognitive-behavioral techniques. Kendall and Braswell (1993) provide a comprehensive overview of cognitive-behavioral techniques used in the Stop and Think Program and related self-instructional and problem-solving interventions.

Hinshaw (1996) has developed a cognitive-behavioral treatment package that emphasizes self-monitoring and social competence. Using the Match Game (described earlier) to rate target behaviors during group interaction, along with feedback from peers and therapists, children are taught to monitor and evaluate their behaviors. Reinforcement is provided for accurate matching of the child's rating of behavior with the therapist's rating of the child's behavior (provided that the child's behavior exceeds some minimum criterion level). Hinshaw's program also includes an anger management component. In this component, children learn to control anger by recognizing anger cues, by learning coping strategies for managing anger once cues are present, and by practicing these monitoring and coping techniques during actual provocation by other group members. Extensive reinforcement is used to encourage mastery and effective performance by the children. Hinshaw's program has received some empirical support (Hinshaw, 1996).

The excitement generated by the theoretical underpinnings of cognitive treatments for ADHD is often not matched by outcome studies. Studies of the efficacy of several types of self-instructional (a combination of self-talk and cognitive problem solving) therapy for ADHD have been discouraging (Hinshaw, 1996). Cognitive-behavioral interventions are often found to be less effective than medication or behavioral treatment (Abikoff, 1987, 1991; Hinshaw & Melnick, 1992). In many cases, cognitive-behavioral treatments generally have not resulted in improvements in the cognitive functioning, academic performance, or impulsive behavior of children with ADHD (Abikoff, 1991). Furthermore, cognitive-behavioral treatments require an adequate level of cognitive development in the child, which excludes many preschool and early-school age children (Whalen & Henker, 1991). Finally, cognitive treatment alone is almost always ineffective for ADHD symptoms; a behavioral (reinforcement) component is almost certainly necessary to motivate the child to make cognitive gains.

On the other hand, self-monitoring and self-evaluation techniques have produced encouraging results (Hinshaw, 1996), and some other integrated treatment plans (Fehlings et al., 1991) have resulted in improvement in ADHD symptoms (Baer & Nietzel, 1991; Fehlings et al., 1991; Kendall & Braswell, 1993). Furthermore, the combination of cognitive-behavioral techniques with more traditional behavioral techniques may result in an additive therapeutic effect, although preliminary findings suggest that the additive effects of cognitive and behavioral therapy for ADHD are likely to be small (Horn et al., 1990). Finally, the existence of some studies demonstrating positive effects of cognitive-behavioral therapy for ADHD suggests that these treatments deserve further study (Abikoff, 1991; Baer & Nietzel, 1991; Barkley, 1991a) and that development of more refined and appropriate cognitive-behavioral techniques may result in more consistent positive outcomes (Hinshaw, 1996).

In addition to effects on primary ADHD symptoms, cognitive-behavioral interventions have been shown to be effective for anger management, social skills, and oppositional behavior (Hinshaw, 1996; Hinshaw & Melnick, 1992), which are common and significant associated features of ADHD. Systematic cognitive-behavioral treatment plans for social skills deficits are described by LeCroy (1994) and Forman (1993). Anger and aggression management programs include those of Feindler (1991; Feindler & Guttman, 1994) and Lochman, White, & Wayland, (1991). These programs have received empirical support and could be very useful for children with ADHD who have certain associated problems.

Play Therapy/Psychodynamic Psychotherapy

The current literature suggests that the use of play or psychodynamic therapy alone for ADHD is usually not appropriate, unless the hyperactivity is resulting from some traumatic event that needs to be processed by the child. However, play therapy may be warranted to address anxious, depressed, or angry symptomatology resulting from the experiences of a child with ADHD.

Other Treatments

In addition to the major treatments covered here, numerous other treatments have been suggested for ADHD. Many of these amount to fads that generate considerable pop-psychology interest but little scientific support. Others have shown promise and need further investigation.

In the fad category are most dietary interventions. Although it is true that certain toxins (e.g., lead, mercury) can lead to disorganized or overactive behavior, toxins are very rarely responsible for the development of ADHD behavior. Nevertheless, families in particularly hazardous or toxic living situations should be screened for the possibility of toxic effects. Food additives, vitamins, and sugar have also received attention, but the scientific data in these areas generally do not support their role in ADHD (Barkley, 1991; Conners, 1980).

More promising are relaxation and biofeedback techniques that encourage children with ADHD to gain some measure of control over their impulsivity and overactivity. The development and evaluation of treatment packages using these techniques is in its infancy, so their efficacy is largely unknown. Nevertheless, case studies and clinical experience have been encouraging (Barkley, 1991; Lubar, 1991).

■   ## References

Abidin, R. R. (1995). *Parenting Stress Index* (3rd Ed.). Odessa, FL: Psychological Assessment Resources.

Abikoff, H. (1987). An evaluation of cognitive-behavior therapy for hyperactive children. In B. B. Lahey & A. E.

Kazdin (Eds.), *Advances in clinical child psychology* (Vol. 10, pp. 171–216). New York: Plenum.

Abikoff, H. (1991). Cognitive training in ADHD children: Less to it than meets the eye. *Journal of Learning Disabilities, 24,* 205–209.

Abikoff, H., Courtney, M., Pelham, W. E., & Koplewicz, H. S. (1993). Teachers' ratings of disruptive behaviors: The influence of halo effects. *Journal of Abnormal Child Psychology, 21,* 519–533.

Abramowitz, A. J., Eckstrand, D., O'Leary, S. G., & Dulcan, M. K. (1992). ADHD children's responses to stimulant medication and two intensities of a behavioral intervention. *Behavior Modification, 16,* 193–203.

Abramowitz, A. J., & O'Leary, S. G. (1991). Behavioral interventions for the classroom: Implications for students with ADHD. *School Psychology Review, 20,* 220–234.

Achenbach, T. M. (1991). *Manual for the Child Behavior Checklist/4–18 and 1991 profile.* Burlington, VT: University of Vermont Department of Psychiatry.

American Psychiatric Association. (1987). *Diagnostic and statistical manual of mental disorders, third edition (revised).* Washington, DC: Author.

American Psychiatric Association. (1994). *Diagnostic and statistical manual of mental disorders, fourth edition.* Washington, DC: Author.

Anastopoulos, A. D., Barkley, R. A., & Shelton, T. L. (1996). Family-based treatment: Psychosocial intervention for children and adolescents with Attention Deficit Hyperactivity Disorder. In E. D. Hibbs & P. S. Jensen (Eds.), *Psychosocial treatments for child and adolescent disorders: Empirically based strategies for clinical practice.* Washington, DC: American Psychological Association.

Anastopoulos, A. D., DuPaul, G. J., & Barkley, R. A. (1991). Stimulant medication and parent training therapies for Attention Deficit-Hyperactivity Disorder. *Journal of Learning Disabilities, 24,* 210–217.

August, G. J., & Garfinkel, B. D. (1989). Behavioral and cognitive subtypes of ADHD. *Journal of the American Academy of Child and Adolescent Psychiatry, 28,* 739–748.

Baer, R., & Nietzel, M. T. (1991). Cognitive and behavioral treatment of impulsivity in children: A meta-analytic review of the outcome literature. *Journal of Clinical Child Psychology, 20,* 400–412.

Barkley, R. A. (1977). A review of stimulant drug research with hyperactive children. *Journal of Child Psychology and Psychiatry, 18,* 137–165.

Barkley, R. A. (1981). *Hyperactive children: A handbook for diagnosis and treatment.* New York: Guilford.

Barkley, R. A. (1987). The assessment of Attention Deficit-Hyperactivity Disorder. *Behavioral Assessment, 9,* 207–233.

Barkley, R. A. (1991a). Diagnosis and assessment of attention-deficit hyperactivity disorder. *Comprehensive Mental Health Care, 1,* 27–43.

Barkley, R. A. (1991b). Attention-deficit hyperactivity disorder. *Psychiatric Annals, 21,* 725–733.

Barkley, R. A. (1993a). *ADHD—What do we know?* New York: Guilford.

Barkley, R. A. (1993b). *ADHD—What can we do?* New York: Guilford.

Barkley, R. A. (1995). *Taking charge of ADHD: The complete, authoritative guide for parents.* New York: Guilford.

Barkley, R. A. (1997a). *ADHD and the nature of self-control.* New York: Guilford.

Barkley, R. A. (1997b). *Defiant children: A clinician's manual for assessment and parent training* (2nd Ed.). New York: Guilford.

Barkley, R. A. (1998). *Attention-Deficit/Hyperactivity Disorder: A handbook for diagnosis and treatment* (2nd Ed.). New York: Guilford.

Barkley, R. A., Anastopoulos, A. D., Guevremont, D.C., & Fletcher, K. E. (1991). Adolescents with ADHD: Patterns of behavioral adjustment, academic functioning, and treatment utilization. *Journal of the American Academy of Child and Adolescent Psychiatry, 30,* 752–761.

Barkley, R. A., DuPaul, G., & McMurray, M. B. (1990). Comprehensive evaluation of attention deficit disorder with and without hyperactivity as defined by research criteria. *Journal of Consulting and Clinical Psychology, 58,* 775–789.

Barkley, R. A., & Edelbrock, C. S. (1987). Assessing situational variation in children's behavior problems: The Home and School Situations Questionnaires. In R. Prinz (ed.), *Advances in behavioral assessment of children and families* (Vol. 3, pp. 157–176). Greenwich, CT: JAI Press.

Barkley, R. A., Fischer, M., Edelbrock, C. S., & Smallish, L. (1990). The adolescent outcome of hyperactive children diagnosed by research criteria, I: An 8-year prospective follow-up study. *Journal of the American Academy of Child and Adolescent Psychiatry, 29,* 546–557.

Barkley, R. A., Fischer, M., Newby, R., & Breen, M. (1988). Development of multi-method clinical protocol for assessing stimulant drug responses in ADHD children. *Journal of Clinical Child Psychology, 17,* 14–24.

Barkley, R. A., Guevremone, D.C., Anastopoulos, A. D., & Fletcher, K. E. (1992). A comparison of three family therapy programs for treating family conflicts in adolescents with ADHD. *Journal of Consulting and Clinical Psychology, 60,* 450–462.

Battle, E. S., & Lacey, B. (1972). A context for hyperactivity in children, over time. *Child Development, 43,* 757–773.

Biederman, J. (1991). Attention Deficit Hyperactivity Disorder (ADHD). *Annals of Clinical Psychiatry, 3,* 9–22.

Biederman, J., Faraone, S. V., Keenan, K., Knee, D., & Tsuang, M. T. (1990). Family-genetic and psychosocial risk factors in DSM-III attention deficit disorder. *Journal of the American Academy of Child and Adolescent Psychiatry, 29,* 526–533.

Biederman, J., & Steingard, R. (1989). Attention-Deficit Hyperactivity Disorder in adolescents. *Psychiatric Annals, 19,* 587–596.

Bloomquist, M. L. (1996). *Skills training for children with behavior disorders: A parent and therapist guidebook.* New York: Guilford.

Bloomquist, M. L., August, G. J., & Ostrander, R. (1991). Effects of a school-based cognitive-behavioral intervention for ADHD children. *Journal of Abnormal Child Psychology, 19,* 591–605.

Boll, T. (1993). *Children's Category Test.* San Antonio, TX: Psychological Corporation.

Borkowski, J. G., Benton, A. L., & Spreen, O. (1967). Word fluency and brain damage. *Neuropsychologia, 5,* 135–140.

Brown, R. T., & Quay, L. C. (1977). Reflection-impulsivity of normal and behavior-disordered children. *Journal of Abnormal Child Psychology, 5,* 457–462.

Brown, T. E. (1996). *Brown Attention-Deficit Disorder Scales manual.* San Antonio, TX: The Psychological Corporation.

Bukstein, O. G., & Kolko, D. J. (1998). Effects of methylphenidate on aggressive urban children with Attention Deficit Hyperactivity Disorder. *Journal of Clinical Child Psychology, 27,* 340–351.

Cairns, E., & Cammock, T. (1978). Development of a more reliable version of the Matching Familiar Figures Test. *Developmental Psychology, 11,* 244–248.

Carlson, G. A., & Rapport, M. D. (1989). Diagnostic classification issues in Attention-Deficit Hyperactivity Disorder. *Psychiatric Annals, 19,* 576–583.

Clark, L. (1996). *SOS: Help for Parents* (2nd Ed.). Bowling Green, KY: Parents Press.

Cohen, M., Becker, M. G., & Campbell, R. (1990). Relationships among four methods of assessment of children with Attention Deficit-Hyperactivity Disorder. *Journal of School Psychology, 28,* 189–202.

Conners, C. K. (1980). *Food additives and hyperactive children.* New York: Plenum.

Conners, C. K. (1990). *Conners' Rating Scales manual.* North Tonawanda, NY: MHS.

Conners, C. K. (1995). *Conners' Continuous Performance Test Computer Program 3.0 user's manual.* North Tonawanda, NY: MHS.

Conners, C. K. (1997). *Conners Rating Scales—Revised technical manual.* North Tonawanda, NY: MHS.

Conners, C. K. (1998). Overview of Attention Deficit Hyperactivity Disorder. *Abstracts of the NIH Consensus Development Conference on Diagnosis and Treatment of Attention Deficit Hyperactivity Disorder,* 21–24.

Danforth, J. S., Barkley, R. A., & Stokes, T. F. (1991). Observations of parent-child interactions with hyperactive children: Research and clinical implications. *Clinical Psychology Review, 11,* 703–727.

Delis, D.C., Kramer, J., Kaplan, E., & Ober, B. A. (1994). *California Verbal Learning Test, Children's Version (CVLT-C) manual.* San Antonio: Psychological Corporation.

DuPaul, G. J. (1991). Parent and teacher ratings of ADHD symptoms: Psychometric properties in a community based sample. *Journal of Clinical Child Psychology, 20,* 245–253.

DuPaul, G. J. (1990). *The Home and School Situations Questionnaire—Revised.* Unpublished manuscript. University of Massachusetts Medical Center, Worcester, MA.

DuPaul, G. J., Anastopoulos, A. D., Shelton, T. L., Guevremont, D.C., & Metevia, L. (1992). Multimethod assessment of Attention-Deficit Hyperactivity Disorder: The diagnostic utility of clinic-based tests. *Journal of Clinical Child Psychology, 21,* 394–402.

DuPaul, G. J., Guevremont, D.C., & Barkley, R. A. (1991). Attention Deficit-Hyperactivity Disorder in adolescence: Critical assessment parameters. *Clinical Psychology Review, 11,* 231–245.

DuPaul, G. J., Guevremont, D.C., & Barkley, R. A. (1992). Behavioral treatment of Attention-Deficit Hyperactivity Disorder in the classroom. *Behavior Modification, 16,* 204–225.

DuPaul, G. J., Power, T. J., Anastopoulos, A. D., & Reid, R. (1998). *ADHD Rating Scale-IV: Checklists, norms, and clinical interpretation.* New York: Guilford.

DuPaul, G. J., Power, T. J., Anastopoulos, A. D., Reid, R., McGoey, K. E., & Ikeda, M. J. (1997). Teacher ratings of

Attention Deficit Hyperactivity Disorder symptoms: Factor structure and normative data. *Psychological Assessment, 9,* 436–444.

DuPaul, G. J., & Stoner, G. (1994). *ADHD in the schools: Assessment and intervention strategies.* New York: Guilford.

Fehlings, D. L., Roberts, W., Humphries, T., & Dawe, G. (1991). Attention Deficit Hyperactivity Disorder: Does cognitive behavioral therapy improve home behavior? *Journal of Developmental and Behavioral Pediatrics, 12,* 223–228.

Feindler, E. L. (1991). Cognitive strategies in anger control interventions for children and adolescents. In P. C. Kendall (Ed.), *Child and adolescent therapy: Cognitive-behavioral procedures.* New York: Guilford.

Feindler, E. L., & Guttman, J. (1994). Cognitive-behavioral anger control training. In C. W. LeCroy (Ed.), *Handbook of Child and Adolescent Treatment Manuals.* New York: Lexington.

Fischer, M., & Newby, R. F. (1991). Assessment of stimulant response in ADHD children using a refined multimethod clinical protocol. *Journal of Clinical Child Psychology, 20,* 232–244.

Forman, S. (1993). *Coping skills interventions for children and adolescents.* San Francisco: Jossey-Bass.

Frick, P. J., & Lahey, B. B. (1991). The nature and characteristics of Attention-Deficit Hyperactivity Disorder. *School Psychology Review, 20,* 163–173.

Gadow, K. D., & Sprafkin, J. (1997). *Child Symptom Inventory—4 norms Manual.* Stony Brook, NY: Checkmate Plus, Ltd.

Gilliam, J. E. (1995). *Attention-Deficit/Hyperactivity Disorder Test.* Austin, TX: Pro-Ed.

Golden, C. J. (1978). *The Stroop Color and Word Test.* Chicago: Stoelting.

Goodman, R., & Stevenson, J. (1989). A twin study of hyperactivity, II: The aetiological role of genes, family relationships, and perinatal adversity. *Journal of Child Psychology and Psychiatry, 30,* 691–709.

Gordon, M. (1983). *The Gordon Diagnostic System.* Boulder, CO: Gordon Systems.

Gordon, M. (1997). *The ADHD/Hyperactivity newsletter* (Winter/Spring 1997 Issue, Volume 24). DeWitt, NY: Gordon Systems.

Gordon, M., & Mettelman, B. B. (1987). *Technical guide to the Gordon Diagnostic System.* DeWitt, NY: Gordon Systems.

Gordon, M., Thomason, D., Cooper, S., & Ivers, C. (1991). Nonmedical treatment of ADHD/Hyperactivity: The attention training system. *Journal of School Psychology, 29,* 151–159.

Grant, M. L., Ilai, D., Nussbaum, N. L., & Bigler, E. D. (1990). The relationship between Continuous Performance Tasks and neuropsychological tests in children with Attention-Deficit Hyperactivity Disorder. *Perceptual and Motor Skills, 70,* 435–445.

Greene, R. W., Biederman, J., Faraone, S. V., Sienna, M., & Garcia-Jetton, J. (1997). Adolescent outcome of boys with Attention-Deficit/Hyperactivity Disorder and Social Disability: Results from a 4-year longitudinal follow-up study. *Journal of Consulting and Clinical Psychology, 65,* 758–767.

Greenhill, L. L. (1989). Pharmacologic treatment of Attention Deficit Hyperactivity Disorder. *Pediatric Psychopharmacology, 15,* 1–27.

Greenhill, L. L. (1992). Treatment issues in children with Attention-Deficit Hyperactivity Disorder. *Psychiatric Annals, 19,* 604–613.

Guevremont, D. C., DuPaul, G. J., & Barkley, R. A. (1990). Diagnosis and assessment of Attention Deficit-Hyperactivity Disorder in children. *Journal of School Psychology, 28,* 51–78.

Halperin, J. M., Newcorn, J. H., Matier, K., Bedi, G., Hall, S., & Sharma, V. (1995). Impulsivity and the initiation of fights in children with Disruptive Behavior Disorders. *Journal of Child Psychology and Psychiatry, 36,* 1199–1211.

Halperin, J. M., Newcorn, J. H., Sharma, V., Healey, J. M., Wolf, L. E., Pascualvaca, D. M., & Schwartz, S. (1990). Inattentive and noninattentive ADHD children: Do they constitute a unitary group? *Journal of Abnormal Child Psychology, 18,* 437–449.

Hansen, D. E., & Vandenberg, B. (1997). Neuropsychological features and differential diagnosis of sleep apnea syndrome in children. *Journal of Clinical Child Psychology, 26,* 304–310.

Heaton, R. K. (1981). *Wisconsin Card Sorting Test manual.* Odessa, FL: Psychological Assessment Resources.

Hechtman, L. (1991). Resilience and vulnerability in long term outcome of Attention Deficit Hyperactive Disorder. *Canadian Journal of Psychiatry, 36,* 415–421.

Hersher, L. (1985). The effectiveness of behavior modification on hyperkinesis. *Child Psychiatry and Human Development, 16,* 87–97.

Hinshaw, S. P. (1992). Externalizing behavior problems and academic underachievement in childhood and adolescence: Causal relationships and underlying mechanisms. *Psychological Bulletin, 111,* 127–155.

Hinshaw, S. P. (1996). Enhancing social competence: Integrating self-management strategies with behavioral procedures for children with ADHD. In E. D. Hibbs & P. S. Jensen (Eds.), *Psychosocial treatments for child and adolescent disorders: Empirically based strategies for clinical practice.* Washington, DC: American Psychological Association.

Hinshaw, S. P., & Melnick, S. (1992). Self-management therapies and Attention-Deficit Hyperactivity Disorder. *Behavior Modification, 16,* 253–273.

Horn, W. F., Ialongo, N., Greenberg, G., Packard, T., & Smith-Winberry, C. (1990). Additive effects of behavioral parent training and self-control therapy with Attention Deficit Hyperactivity Disordered Children. *Journal of Clinical Child Psychology, 19,* 98–110.

Hynd, G. W., Hern, K. L., Voeller, K. K., & Marshall, R. M. (1991). Neurobiological basis of Attention-Deficit Hyperactivity Disorder (ADHD). *School Psychology Review, 20,* 174–186.

Jackson, M. T. (1997). *The Adult Attention Deficit Disorders Intervention Manual.* Columbia, MO: Hawthorne Educational Services.

Jastak, S., & Wilkinson, G. S. (1984). *Wide-Range Achievement Test—Revised.* Wilmington, DE: Jastak Associates.

Kagan, J. (1966). Reflection-impulsivity: The generality and dynamics of conceptual tempo. *Journal of Abnormal Psychology, 71,* 17–24.

Kaufman, A. S. (1990). *Assessing adolescent and adult intelligence.* Boston: Allyn & Bacon.

Kaufman, A. S., & Kaufman, N. L. (1985). *Kaufman Test of Educational Achievement.* Circle Pines, MN: American Guidance Service.

Kendall, P. C. (1992). *Stop and think workbook* (2nd Ed.). Available from the author.

Kendall, P. C., & Braswell, L. (1993). *Cognitive-behavioral therapy for impulsive children* (2nd Ed.). New York: Guilford.

Klee, S. H., & Garfinkel, B. D. (1983). The computerized continuous performance task: A new measure of inattention. *Journal of Abnormal Child Psychology, 11,* 487–496.

Klein, R. G., & Mannuzza, S. (1991). Long-term outcome of hyperactive children: A review. *Journal of the American Academy of Child and Adolescent Psychiatry, 30,* 383–387.

Klorman, R., Coons, H. W., & Borgstedt, A. D. (1987). Effects of methylphenidate on adolescents with a childhood history of attention deficit disorder: I. Clinical findings. *Journal of the American Academy of Child and Adolescent Psychiatry, 26,* 363–367.

Kronenberger, W. G. (1997, August). *Assessment advances in ADD: Current trends and tools.* Paper presented at the 1997 Building Bridges Symposium on ADD and LD, Louisville, KY.

Kronenberger, W. G. (1999). *Parent-Delivered Behavioral Treatment for ADHD (PDBT-A).* Unpublished manuscript.

Lachar, D., & Gruber, C. P. (1995). *Personality Inventory for Youth (PIY) manual.* Los Angeles: Western Psychological Services.

Lambert, N. M., & Sandoval, J. (1980). The prevalence of learning disabilities in a sample of children considered hyperactive. *Journal of Abnormal Child Psychology, 8,* 33–50.

Leark, R. A., Depuy, T. R., Greenberg, L. M., Corman, C. L., & Kindschi, C. L. (1996). T.O.V.A. Test of Variables of Attention Professional Manual, Version 7.0. Los Alamitos, CA: Universal Attention Disorders.

LeCroy, C. W. (1994). Social skills training. In C. W. LeCroy (Ed.), *Handbook of Child and Adolescent Treatment Manuals.* New York: Lexington.

Lezak, M. D. (1983). *Neuropsychological assessment* (2nd Ed.). New York: Oxford.

Lochman, J. E., White, K. J., & Wayland, K. K. (1991). Cognitive-behavioral assessment and treatment with aggressive children. In P. C. Kendall (Ed.), *Child and adolescent therapy: Cognitive-behavioral procedures.* New York: Guilford.

Loge, D. V., Staton, D., & Beatty, W. W. (1990). Performance of children with ADHD on tests sensitive to frontal lobe dysfunction. *Journal of the American Academy of Child and Adolescent Psychiatry, 29,* 540–545.

Lombardo, G. T. (1997). BPD and ADHD. *Journal of the American Academy of Child and Adolescent Psychiatry, 36,* 719.

Lubar, J. F. (1991). Discourse on the development of EEG diagnostics and biofeedback for Attention-Deficit/Hyperactivity Disorders. *Biofeedback and Self-Regulation, 16,* 201–225.

Lufi, D., Cohen, A., & Parish-Plass, J. (1990). Identifying Attention Deficit Hyperactive Disorder with the

WISC-R and the Stroop Color and Word Test. *Psychology in the Schools, 27,* 28–34.

McCarney, S. B. (1989a). *The Attention Deficit Disorders Evaluation Scale, Home Version, Technical Manual.* Columbia, MO: Hawthorne Educational Services.

McCarney, S. B. (1989b). *The Attention Deficit Disorders Evaluation Scale, School Version, Technical Manual.* Columbia, MO: Hawthorne Educational Services.

McCarney, S. B. (1994). *The Attention Deficit Disorders Intervention Manual.* Columbia, MO: Hawthorne Educational Services.

McCarney, S. B. (1995a). *The Attention Deficit Disorders Evaluation Scale Home Version Technical Manual Second Edition.* Columbia, MO: Hawthorne Educational Services.

McCarney, S. B. (1995b). *The Attention Deficit Disorders Evaluation Scale School Version Technical Manual Second Edition.* Columbia, MO: Hawthorne Educational Services.

McCarney, S. B. (1995c). *The Early Childhood Attention Deficit Disorders Evaluation Scale Home Version Technical Manual.* Columbia, MO: Hawthorne Educational Services.

McCarney, S. B. (1995d). *The Early Childhood Attention Deficit Disorders Evaluation Scale School Version Technical Manual.* Columbia, MO: Hawthorne Educational Services.

McCarney, S. B., & Anderson, P. D. (1996a). *The Adult Attention Deficit Disorders Evaluation Scale Self-Report Technical Manual.* Columbia, MO: Hawthorne Educational Services.

McCarney, S. B., & Anderson, P. D. (1996b). *The Adult Attention Deficit Disorders Evaluation Scale Home Version Technical Manual.* Columbia, MO: Hawthorne Educational Services.

McCarney, S. B., & Anderson, P. D. (1996c). *The Adult Attention Deficit Disorders Evaluation Scale Work Version Technical Manual.* Columbia, MO: Hawthorne Educational Services.

McCarney, S. B., & Johnson, N. (1995). *The Early Childhood Attention Deficit Disorders Intervention Manual.* Columbia, MO: Hawthorne Educational Services.

Milberger, S., Biederman, J., Faraone, S. V., & Jones, J. (1998). Further evidence of an association between maternal smoking during pregnancy and Attention Deficit Hyperactivity Disorder: Findings from a high-risk sample of siblings. *Journal of Clinical Child Psychology, 27,* 352–358.

Milich, R., & Kramer, J. (1984). Reflections on impulsivity: An empirical investigation of impulsivity as a construct. In K. Gadow & I. Bialer (eds.), *Advances in learning and behavioral disabilities* (Vol. 3, pp. 117–150). Greenwich, CT: JAI Press.

Minuchin, S. (1974). *Families and family therapy.* Cambridge, MA: Harvard University Press.

Morriss, R. (1996). *Attention disorders in children: School-based assessment, diagnosis, and treatment.* Los Angeles: Western Psychological Services.

Munoz-Millan, R. J., & Casteel, C. R. (1989). Attention-Deficit Hyperactivity Disorder: Recent literature. *Hospital and Community Psychiatry, 40,* 699–707.

Newcorn, J. H., Halperin, J. M., Healey, J. M., O'Brien, J. D., Pascualvaca, D. M., Wolf, L. E., Morganstein, A., Sharma, V., & Young, J. G. (1989). Are ADDH and ADHD the same or different? *Journal of the American Academy of Child and Adolescent Psychiatry, 28,* 734–738.

Pelham, W. E., & Hoza, B. (1996). Intensive treatment: A summer treatment program for children with ADHD. In E. D. Hibbs & P. S. Jensen (Eds.), *Psychosocial treatments for child and adolescent disorders: Empirically based strategies for clinical practice.* Washington, DC: American Psychological Association.

Pennington, B. F. (1991). *Diagnosing learning disorders: A neuropsychological framework.* New York: Guilford.

Phelan, T. W. (1995). *1-2-3 Magic: Effective Discipline for Children 2–12.* Glen Ellyn, IL: Child Management Inc.

Phelan, T. W. (1996). *All about Attention Deficit Disorder.* Glen Ellyn, IL: Child Management, Inc.

Pliszka, S. R. (1991). Antidepressants in the treatment of child and adolescent psychopathology. *Journal of Clinical Child Psychology, 20,* 313–320.

Power, T. J., Andrews, T. J., Eiraldi, R. B., Doherty, B. J., Ikeda, M. J., DuPaul, G. J., & Landau, S. (1998). Evaluating Attention Deficit Hyperactivity Disorder using multiple informants: The incremental utility of combining teacher with parent reports. *Psychological Assessment, 10,* 250–260.

Psychological Corporation. (1997). *WAIS-III/WMS-III technical manual.* San Antonio, TX: Author.

Rapport, M., & Gordon, M. (1987). *The Attention Training System (ATS).* DeWitt, NY: Gordon Systems.

Rapport, M. D., Stoner, G., DuPaul, G. J., Kelly, K. L., Tucker, S. B., & Schoeler, T. (1988). Attention deficit disorder and methylphenidate: A multi-level analysis of dose-response effects on children's impulsivity across settings. *Journal of the American Academy of Child and Adolescent Psychiatry, 27,* 60–69.

Reynolds, C. R., & Kamphaus, R. W. (1992). *Behavior Assessment System for Children manual.* Circle Pines, MN: American Guidance Systems.

Rispens, J., Swaab, H., Van Den Oord, E. J. C. G., Cohen-Kettenis, P., Van Engeland, H., & Van Yperen, T. (1997). WISC profiles in child psychiatric diagnosis: Sense or nonsense? *Journal of the American Academy of Child and Adolescent Psychiatry, 36,* 1587–1594.

Robin, A. L. (1998). *ADHD in adolescents.* New York: Guilford.

Rourke, B. P. (1988). The syndrome of nonverbal learning disabilities: Developmental manifestations in neurological disease, disorder, and dysfunction. *The Clinical Neuropsychologist, 2,* 293–330.

Salkind, N.J., & Nelson, C. F. (1980). A note on the developmental nature of reflection-impulsivity. *Developmental Psychology, 16,* 237–238.

Sattler, J. M. (1990). *Assessment of children* (3rd ed.). San Diego: Jerome M. Sattler, Publisher.

Shelton, T. L., & Barkley, R. A. (1995). The assessment and treatment of Attention-Deficit/Hyperactivity Disorder in children. In M. Roberts (Ed.), *Handbook of pediatric psychology* (2nd ed., pp. 633–654). New York: Guilford.

Swanson, J. M., Cantwell, D., Lerner, M., McBurnett, K., & Hanna, G. (1991). Effects of stimulant medication on learning in children with ADHD. *Journal of Learning Disabilities, 24,* 219–231.

Swanson, J. M., Wigal, S., Greenhill, L. L., Browne, R., Waslik, B., Lerner, M., Williams, L., Flinn, D., Agler, D., Crowley, K., Fineberg, E., Baren, M., & Cantwell, D. P. (1998). Analog classroom assessment of Adderall in children with ADHD. *Journal of the American Academy of Child and Adolescent Psychiatry, 37,* 519–525.

Ullmann, R. K., Sleator, E. K., & Sprague, R. L. (1984). A new rating scale for diagnosis and monitoring of ADD children. *Psychopharmacology Bulletin, 20,* 160–164.

Ullmann, R. K., Sleator, E. K., & Sprague, R. L. (1997). *ACTeRS manual.* Champaign, IL: Metritech

Wechsler, D. (1997). *Wechsler Adult Intelligence Scale—Third Edition.* San Antonio, TX: Psychological Corporation.

Weiss, G., Hechtman, L., Milroy, T., & Perlman, T. (1985). Psychiatric status of hyperactives as adults: A controlled prospective 15-year follow-up of 63 hyperactive children. *Journal of the American Academy of Child Psychiatry, 24,* 211–220.

Whalen, C. K., & Henker, B. (1991). Therapies for hyperactive children: Comparisons, combinations, and compromises. *Journal of Consulting and Clinical Psychology, 59,* 126–137.

Wilkinson, G. S. (1993). *Wide Range Achievement Test* (3rd ed.). Wilmington, DE: Wide Range, Inc.

Zametkin, A. J. (1989). The neurobiology of Attention-Deficit Hyperactivity Disorder: A synopsis. *Psychiatric Annals, 19,* 584–586.

Zametkin, A. J., Nordahl, T. E., Gross, M., King, A. C., Semple, W. E., Rumsey, J., Hamburger, M. S., & Cohen, R. M. (1990). Cerebral glucose metabolism in adults with hyperactivity of childhood onset. *New England Journal of Medicine, 323,* 1361–1366.

CHAPTER 3

Disruptive Behavior Disorders

Conduct Disorder (CD) and Oppositional-Defiant Disorder (ODD), referred to as Disruptive Behavior Disorders, are among the most common psychiatric disorders seen in children and adolescents (Shamsie & Hluchy, 1991). The CD and ODD diagnoses share the characteristics of disruptive, disobedient behavior and the breaking of societal norms. Although early research challenged the distinction between CD and ODD (Anderson, Williams, McGee, & Silva, 1987; Reeves, Werry, Elkind, & Zametkin, 1987; Rey et al., 1988), more recent work supports the CD-ODD distinction. Factor analytic studies, for example, consistently find separate groups of symptoms corresponding to CD (components of law-breaking and violation of norms) and ODD (components of aggression, anger, and disobedience) (Achenbach, 1991; Loeber & Schmaling, 1985; Quay, 1986). Reviews by Lahey, Loeber, Quay, Frick, & Grimm, (1992) and Loeber, Lahey, and Thomas (1991) summarize the relationship of ODD and CD as follows:

1. ODD and CD demonstrate distinct patterns of co-variation. Children who exhibit one of the symptoms of either of these disorders are more likely to have another of the symptoms of the same diagnosis than a symptom of the other diagnosis.

2. Age of onset for ODD symptoms is earlier than for CD symptoms.

3. ODD and CD are developmentally related. Many children with ODD do not ever develop CD, but almost all children with CD have had an earlier ODD diagnosis. CD, in turn, predicts Antisocial Personality Disorder in adulthood.

4. Familial correlates of ODD and CD are similar, but children with CD have a greater number or intensity of the correlates.

5. Treatments for ODD are more likely to be effective than treatments for CD, probably because of lower symptom severity and younger age of children with ODD.

■ Oppositional-Defiant Disorder

☐ CLINICAL DESCRIPTION

Diagnostic Considerations

DSM-IV defines ODD as "a recurrent pattern of negativistic, defiant, disobedient, and hostile behavior toward authority figures" (American Psychiatric Association, 1994, p. 91). Diagnostically, ODD is characterized by symptoms such as arguing with authorities, refusal to comply with requests, losing temper, irritability, externalizing blame for misbehavior, vengeful behavior, annoying and provocative behavior, and appearing angry or resentful. Because the disturbance must cause "significant" impairment, typical child oppositionality does not qualify for ODD. ODD is not diagnosed if the child qualifies for the CD diagnosis; without this exclusionary criterion, virtually all children with CD would also receive the ODD diagnosis (see Table 3.1 for epidemiology and course of Disruptive Behavior Disorders).

Appearance and Features

Unlike CD, which is more severe in its manifestation and consequences, ODD is more likely to be tolerated by some parents. Furthermore, because many ODD symptoms

TABLE 3.1 Epidemiology and Course of Disruptive Behavior Disorders

Prevalence: 6–16% of boys; 2–9% of girls

Sex Ratio (Male:Female):   2:1 to 4:1

Typical Onset Age: ODD has onset in the 4–8 year range. Onset of CD is typically later, with earliest onset in middle childhood and latest onset in adolescence.

Course: A significant proportion (at least 25–40%) of children with ODD develop CD. CD is associated with instability in school, job, relationships, and finances; chronic substance abuse is a risk; a large minority of cases of CD (estimated at nearly half) develop Antisocial Personality Disorder in adulthood; CD is associated with lifelong risk of rule-breaking behavior including lawbreaking.

Common Comorbid Conditions: 1. Attention-Deficit/Hyperactivity Disorder
2. Learning Disability/Academic Deficiency
3. Substance Abuse
4. Mood Disorders
5. Personality Disorders

Relevant Subtypes (ODD):   1. With vs. Without Early Symptoms of CD

Relevant Subtypes (CD):   1. Childhood-Onset vs. Adolescent-Onset
2. Overt vs. Covert
3. Group/Socialized vs. Solitary/Undersocialized
4. Aggressive vs. Nonaggressive
5. Impulsive vs. Psychopathic

Note: ODD = Oppositional-Defiant Disorder. CD = Conduct Disorder.

resemble typical childhood behavior, parents may be unaware that their child's "misbehavior" warrants a psychiatric diagnosis.

As previously noted, ODD behaviors differ from typical childhood disobedience in severity and frequency. (Appearance and features of ODD are listed in Table 3.2.) At preschool ages, this is manifest in frequent, severe temper tantrums and intolerance of frustration. The preschooler with ODD has difficulty delaying gratification; typically, he or she responds to frustration with an extremely hostile and vocal display. Kicking, thrashing, power struggles, and destruction of property are common. If the parent gives in to the child's demands, the child learns that escalation of the power struggle results in gratification.

At older ages, tantrum behavior may persist, but oppositionality and defiance usually become more sophisticated. "Talking back" and passive-aggressive refusal to comply are typical at latency and adolescent ages. Destructive and aggressive behaviors persist and are often incorporated into power struggles. Parents may feel held hostage by their child's threats to destroy property or to become physically aggressive. In many cases, parents fear making any request to the child because they know that it will lead to a bitter and exhausting power struggle. At times, the child may appear to be provoking or testing adults for the limits of acceptable behavior. The child may be described by parents as touchy, stubborn, argumentative, and provocative.

Oppositional behavior may be affected by environmental or social factors. Children with ODD tend to be most oppositional toward certain adults or in certain situations. Many parents, for example, can identify one parent who receives most of the oppositional and defiant behavior. Alternatively, the child may be oppositional at home but not at school. Many children with

---

TABLE 3.2   Appearance and Features of Oppositional-Defiant Disorder

COMMON FEATURES

1. Is short tempered and easily angered
2. Argues frequently
3. Provokes peers or authorities
4. Seeks revenge; is vindictive
5. Externalizes blame
6. Is defiant and noncompliant
7. Has poor frustration tolerance
8. Is stubborn
9. Is unwilling to compromise
10. Is angry/hostile
11. Is irritable

OCCASIONAL FEATURES

1. Has inconsistent caretakers
2. Has harsh or neglectful caretakers
3. Is hyperactive

Note: The features listed in the table are often seen but are not universal. Some features may be diagnostically relevant or required, whereas others may not be required for diagnosis. "Common" features are typical of the disorder; "occasional" features appear frequently but are not necessarily seen in a majority of cases.

ODD are adversely affected by hyperactive or disobedient peers who put them in situations of conflict with authority. If such conflicts occur repeatedly, the child may get a reputation for oppositional behavior. This reputation may lead to increased intolerance of oppositional behavior by authorities, worsening the child's relationship with adults in the environment. When alienation from authorities and adults occurs, children with ODD begin to make hostile attributions that lead to further resentment and thwarting of rules and authorities.

Children with ODD almost always come to clinical attention at the request of parents or teachers who are frustrated with their behavior. Parents usually describe a plethora of oppositional and defiant symptoms. They often report trying various interventions, although more extensive investigation usually reveals that the interventions were half-hearted, inconsistent, poorly timed, or doomed to fail for some reason. Children with ODD frequently present without symptoms in the clinical interview, unless they are upset by something said or done by the parent or clinician. Many children with ODD refuse to recognize that they have a problem, externalizing blame for their behaviors. For example, hitting a parent may be warranted, in the child's view, because the parent put an unreasonable constraint on the child. Despite a denial of problems, children with ODD may be at risk for comorbid depression or a developmental disorder. Hence, co-occurring or underlying problems should be carefully examined.

Children with ODD are at risk for the development of CD. One study found that 44% of boys with ODD developed CD within a three-year period (Loeber, Keenan, Lahey, Green, & Thomas, 1993). Other research has shown that younger children with significant CD or ODD behaviors are 16 times more likely than other children to develop CD-like syndromes in adolescence (Fergusson, Lynskey, & Horwood, 1996). Children with ODD who develop CD at later ages usually show a prodromal set of CD symptoms or may even qualify for the CD diagnosis at a young age, whereas children with ODD who have no symptoms within the CD spectrum are at much lower risk for developing CD (Biederman et al., 1996). Parental substance abuse, low SES, physical fighting, low IQ, poor academic performance, and inconsistent discipline further raise the chances of development of CD (Fergusson et al., 1996; Loeber, Green, Keenan, & Lahey, 1995). The peer group may be especially important in determining the continuation of CD-ODD behaviors or the late onset of these behaviors. Children with early CD-ODD symptoms that remit in adolescence tend to affiliate with less delinquent peer groups, compared to children who develop or continue to qualify for CD-ODD diagnosis in adolescence (Fergusson et al., 1996).

Etiology

Family problems and behavioral factors are frequently a factor in the development and/or maintenance of the oppositional, noncompliant, negative, and defiant behaviors typical of ODD. Families of children with ODD show a higher rate of parental depression, substance abuse, and Antisocial Personality Disorder than families of other clinic-referred children (Billings & Moos, 1983; Griest, Wells, & McMahon, 1980). Behavioral factors, such as parental discipline and parental involvement, are also associated with the development of ODD symptoms (Frick et al., 1992; Griest et al., 1980). Harsh physical punishment of children, for example, can create anger, reduce attachment, and provide a model of aggression. Inconsistent discipline can reward children for escalating until parents give them what they want; the children then learn to escalate the pattern of defiant, aggressive, and destructive behavior in order to be rewarded by getting their way (Patterson, 1982). Oppositional behavior is reinforced when the child gains attention and control as a result of it. To the extent that attention, control, and gratification result from oppositional behavior, the child will be prone to show ODD symptoms.

Despite the popularity of familial-behavioral explanations of ODD, some data suggest that genetic factors may also play a role. Epidemiologic studies indicate that adopted children of antisocial biological fathers are more likely to exhibit antisocial behavior than are other adopted children (Mednick & Hutchings, 1978). Twin studies also support a genetic component to ODD (American Psychiatric Association, 1994). Early temperament characterized by irritability, poor frustration tolerance, and attachment problems may also render a child vulnerable to the development of ODD in response to environmental behavioral factors. Nevertheless, biological factors appear to explain only a portion of the variance in emergence of ODD symptoms.

Certain disorders, such as ADHD, seem to put children at risk for ODD because their symptoms clash directly with the rules of society. Those children are more prone to be corrected and to have difficulty conforming, as compared to children with no psychiatric diagnosis. ODD develops out of the repeated negative interactions between the child and those who set limits on the child's behavior. Hence, ODD can develop as a result of comorbid psychiatric symptoms.

☐ ASSESSMENT PATTERNS AND TREATMENT OPTIONS

Although research supports the existence of ODD and CD as separate syndromes, they share the major characteristics of oppositionality, defiance, authority problems, and rule-breaking. Hence, ODD and CD are assessed and treated similarly. Furthermore, because ODD may develop into CD, any ODD assessment must take into account the possible presence of CD symptomatology. CD often warrants closer monitoring, involvement of authorities, and more intensive treatment than does ODD, but the basics of the interventions for the disorders are often quite similar. Hence, assessment and treatment of ODD and CD will be considered jointly, following a discussion of CD.

■ **Conduct Disorder**

☐ CLINICAL DESCRIPTION

Diagnostic Considerations

DSM-IV defines CD as "a repetitive and persistent pattern of behavior in which the basic rights of others or age-appropriate societal norms or rules are violated" (American Psychiatric Association, 1994, p. 85). This behavior occurs across multiple social arenas, including home, school, and community. Symptoms of CD include bullying, intimidating others, fighting, use of weapons, stealing (with and without confrontation of a victim), cruel behavior toward people or animals, sexual coercion, lying, fire setting, running away, breaking into a house or car, and truancy. CD occurs in 6–16% of boys and 2–9% of girls (American Psychiatric Association, 1994).

DSM-IV recognizes two CD subtypes: Childhood-Onset type requires at least one conduct problem prior to age 10. Adolescent-Onset type requires no conduct problem prior to age 10. Childhood-Onset type is typically more persistent and severe as the individual develops; it is more likely to evolve into Antisocial Personality Disorder. Children with Adolescent-Onset CD are more likely to be female, less likely to be aggressive, have less family adversity, are of higher socioeconomic status, and exhibit higher verbal and reading ability (McGee, Feehan, Williams, & Anderson, 1992; Moffitt, 1990). Adolescent-Onset CD is also less likely to be developmentally related to ODD (Lahey et al., 1992). Numerous other CD subtypings have been identified, including the following (Christian, Frick, Hill, Tyler, & Frazer, 1997; Lahey et al., 1992; Loeber, 1982; Loeber & Schmaling, 1985):

1. *Overt versus Covert Behaviors.* Overt CD behaviors include confrontational behavior such as fighting, stealing with confrontation of the victim, and being physically cruel. Covert behaviors include manipulating others, stealing without confrontation, destroying property, and running away.

2. *Group (Socialized) versus Solitary (Undersocialized) CD.* This division distinguishes between those who are likely to act out in the context of peer relationships (Socialized) and those who commit their antisocial acts in a solitary manner (Undersocialized). Undersocialized boys with CD tend to be more aggressive and to have a poorer prognosis (Jenkins & Glickman, 1947; Jenkins & Hewitt, 1944). There may also be physiological differences between the subgroups (Bowden, Deutsch, & Swanson, 1988; Rogeness, Hernandez, Macedo, & Mitchell, 1983), including lower resting heart rate for Undersocialized CD.

3. *Aggressive versus Nonaggressive CD.* Children with Aggressive CD tend to engage in more fighting, confrontation, and harmful behaviors directed at people. Children with Nonaggressive CD, on the other hand, are less confrontive and engage in more property-related misbehavior. There may be some interaction between the aggressive-nonaggressive and socialized-undersocialized subtypes of CD: Children with Aggressive CD who are also rejected by peers may be at greater risk for a variety of negative outcomes (such as risk for long-term behavioral problems, social rejection, and school failure), as compared to children with aggressive CD who are not rejected by peers (Bierman & Wargo, 1995).

4. *Impulsive CD versus Psychopathic CD.* Children with Psychopathic CD lack empathy, do not feel remorse for misbehavior, and appear unemotional, in addition to showing the typical symptoms of CD. Children with Impulsive CD have fewer problems with lack of empathy, remorse, or emotion, but they have the typical oppositional, aggressive, egocentric, rule-breaking, and impulsive traits of CD. When groups of children with CD and ODD are combined, more children with CD fall into the Psychopathic CD group, whereas more children with ODD fall into the Impulsive CD group (Christian et al., 1997). Children with Psychopathic CD engage in more severe misbehavior (destruction and aggression), are suspended more often from school, and engage in more criminal behavior. They also are more likely to have a parent with Antisocial Personality Disorder (APD) and may be at greater risk for APD themselves (Christian et al., 1997).

CD is associated with a number of other Axis I and II disorders. Myers, Burket, and Otto (1993) reported that a majority of their sample of hospitalized adolescents with CD also met criteria for substance abuse, ADHD, Major Depressive Disorder, and/or a personality disorder. In another clinical sample, one in three children with an Affective Disorder also qualified for a Conduct Disorder (Kovacs, Paulaskas, Gatsonis, & Richards, 1988; Puig-Antich, 1982). Comorbidity studies have shown that as many as 54% of adolescents with bipolar disorder also qualify for a diagnosis of CD (Kovacs & Pollock, 1995). Schneider, Atkinson, and El-Mallakh (1996), summarizing across several studies, report a "remarkably consistent rate of 37% to 42% of comorbid CD in children and adolescents with bipolar illness" (p. 1423). Because CD is more prevalent than bipolar disorder, the percentage of children with CD who have bipolar disorder is far less than the percentage of children with bipolar disorder who have CD.

The percentage of children and adolescents with comorbid CD and substance abuse problems has been estimated at 50% or more (Reebye, Moretti, & Lessard, 1995; Myers et al., 1993). Furthermore, adolescents treated in substance abuse programs are more likely to relapse if they carry a CD diagnosis (Myers, Brown, & Mott, 1995). Therefore, children with CD should be screened for alcohol or drug use.

CD or ODD is found in 20–60% of ADHD cases (Biederman, Munir, & Knee, 1987; Kazdin, 1996). When ADHD and CD co-occur, the onset of ADHD typically precedes the onset of CD. Furthermore, a co-occurring ADHD and CD condition is worse than either condition alone, with greater symptom severity, increased risk for later Antisocial Personality Disorder, more environmental problems, more social problems, and deficient processing of social information (Kazdin, 1996; Milich & Dodge, 1984).

Appearance and Features

Appearance and features of CD are listed in Table 3.3. Children with CD show a consistent pattern of rebellion and violation of societal norms. These norms may be formal (legal), informal (social mores), or specific to the household (parental rules). In most cases, CD develops as a gradual process of oppositionality that expands from oppositionality toward parents to oppositionality toward adults, all authorities, and eventually to society as a whole (Dishion, Patterson, Stoolmiller, & Skinner, 1991).

In the typical scenario of CD development, the young child displays ODD-type symptoms in the context of strained parent-child interactions. These patterns worsen as the child escalates defiance, disobedience, and aggression to "win" power struggles with the parent. As these interaction patterns become ingrained and severe, the child generalizes them to situations outside the home. The child fails to develop good tolerance for frustration, and any delay of gratification becomes cause for rule-breaking. The child expects that rule-breaking or oppositional-defiant behavior outside the home will bring reinforcement as it has in the home environment. This expectation can take on an air of entitlement, in which the child focuses on gratifying his or her own needs while ignoring the rules of society and the feelings of others.

Often, the school and/or peer group are the first non–home settings in which the child engages in oppositional and rule-breaking behaviors. Most CD-type school/social problems emerge in middle or junior high school. These antisocial behavior problems are annoying to teachers and most peers, leading to school and social failures. Such failures further alienate the child from peers, rules, and norms. The social skills, social involvement, and social competence of children with CD, therefore, drops with time (Renouf, Kovacs, & Mukerji, 1997). There is also evidence that children with comorbid depression and CD are at particular risk for declines in social functioning (Renouf et al., 1997) and for poor social relationships in general.

TABLE 3.3   Appearance and Features of Conduct Disorder

COMMON FEATURES

1. Physical aggression; fighting; intimidation
2. Cruelty to people or animals
3. Theft
4. Destruction of property; fire setting
5. Use of weapons or other means to cause serious injury
6. Lawbreaking
7. Truancy
8. Running away
9. Substance abuse
10. Friends with conduct problems
11. Manipulation; deceit; lying
12. Hostile attribution bias
13. Impaired social problem-solving ability

OCCASIONAL FEATURES

1. Harsh, neglectful, or inconsistent discipline
2. Criminal record
3. Thrill seeking, dangerous behavior
4. Academic problems; school drop-out

Note: The features listed in the table are often seen but are not universal. Some features may be diagnostically relevant or required, whereas others may not be required for diagnosis. "Common" features are typical of the disorder; "occasional" features appear frequently but are not necessarily seen in a majority of cases.

Separated from mainstream peers and norms, the child may then identify with a deviant peer group. The deviant peer group provides negative social modeling and reinforcement for antisocial behavior. Eventually, the child internalizes a self-concept of "troublemaker," seeks reinforcement in rule violation (e.g., lying, stealing, manipulation), and associates with other children who have CD. Activities that lead to immediate or effortless gratification are chosen (e.g., drug use, stealing) as alternatives to the "unattainable," socially acceptable means of gratification. Angry feelings resulting from alienation and isolation may also contribute to the emergence of CD in late childhood and adolescence.

In addition to behavioral problems with oppositionality and rule-breaking, there is ample evidence that children with CD score lower on intelligence tests, and they often perform poorly in school. In one study, low academic achievement and failing a grade occurred three times more frequently in conduct disordered junior high school students than in a matched control group (Safer, 1984). Deficits in various academic skills, especially reading, have also been correlated with adolescent delinquency (Dishion, Loeber, Stouthamer-Loeber, & Patterson, 1984; Sturge, 1982). Children with CD are often perceived by their teachers as uninterested in school, unenthusiastic, and careless. However, it is unclear whether CD arises as a reaction to educational failure or whether CD causes failure (Rutter, Tizard, & Whitmore, 1970; Sturge, 1982).

A number of studies indicate that the intellectual deficiencies of aggressive children extend to social problem-solving and processing skills (Dodge, 1985; Lochman, White, & Wayland, 1991). Compared to peers, aggressive children more often perceive neutral social cues as having aggressive meaning (Dodge, 1985; Milich & Dodge, 1984). Children with CD are less able to generate relevant means to a social end, to anticipate obstacles blocking a social goal, and to generate directly assertive social responses to a difficult social situation (Joffe, Dobson, Fine, Marriage, & Haley, 1990). Furthermore, aggressive boys are more likely to act aggressively when they respond impulsively, and they do not perceive obstacles to their problem solutions (Dodge & Newman, 1981). In short, children with CD tend to interpret neutral situations as hostile, to fail to generate appropriate solutions to problem situations, and to act inappropriately in problem situations.

Because they interpret neutral situations as hostile, aggressive children feel threatened by peers and adults. Their aggressive behavior, which they see as justified given their interpretation of the situation, may appear misplaced and excessive to others. These attributional distortions, coupled with an impulsive response style, contribute to a greater likelihood of antisocial and aggressive behaviors.

Many children with CD are in environments with a variety of stresses, negative temptations, and negative models. Parent antisocial behavior and alcoholism predict CD in children. Family life is often characterized by harsh or inconsistent discipline, by lack of warmth and support, by spousal conflict, by poor monitoring of the child, by instability (in finances and relationships), and by lack of resources (financial, educational, and external social support). In many cases, the children live in impoverished, disadvantaged, and/or dangerous neighborhoods, where negative role models and negative peer pressure abound. Parents may feel that efforts at home will come to naught when the child faces social temptations in the neighborhood and at school.

CD is often a precursor of Antisocial Personality Disorder (APD) in adulthood; almost half of children with CD develop significant APD symptomatology (Myers et al., 1993; Robins, 1966). One variable that predicts the development of APD is the number of CD symptoms the child exhibits; early age of onset of CD (especially before age 12) also predicts APD. CD may also predict later chronic substance abuse and overall poor quality of life in adulthood (American Psychiatric Association, 1994). For example, CD is associated with a high death rate, unemployment, marital conflict, financial instability, and poor interpersonal relationships (Robins, 1966).

Etiology

Biological Theories

Several biological theories have been proposed for CD, with mixed empirical results. Children with conduct problems show less reactivity to and faster recovery from laboratory stimuli (Mednick & Christiansen, 1977). Slow heart rate has also been linked to conduct problems (Wadsworth, 1976). Taken together, these findings suggest that children with CD may be less responsive to external stimuli and may need a higher level of external stimulation.

Additional support for biological etiology is found in neuroanatomical and neuropsychological studies. Researchers have found correlations between tests of frontal lobe functioning and delinquency (Moffitt & Henry, 1989). A well-known function of the frontal lobes is the inhibition and planning of behavior. Presumably, then, these findings suggest that children with CD have less frontal lobe–mediated inhibition of behavior, increasing the probability that they will behave impulsively.

Family and genetic studies also support a biological component to CD. Parental APD, for example, has been found to be associated with CD independent of maternal parenting behavior (Frick et al., 1992). Adoption and twin studies also show a concordance of CD in biologically related children (Cadoret, 1978; Cadoret & Cain, 1980; Jarey & Stewart, 1985; Mednick & Hutchings, 1978). Over all, results of biological studies are suggestive but preliminary in explaining the emergence of CD.

Family-Behavioral Theories

Virtually all major psychological theories of the etiology of CD cite a role for parent and family functioning in the emergence of symptoms. There is evidence that preschool children with ODD show more problems with security of attachment (based on behavior when reunited with the parent following separation) and with separation distress, compared to nonreferred controls (Speltz, DeKlyen, Greenberg, & Dryden, 1995). Many insecurely attached children with CD also have histories of negative parent-child interactions characterized by lack of warmth and negotiation, high defensiveness, harsh discipline, and inconsistent discipline (Henggeler et al., 1986; Kazdin, 1987). Because attachments formed during infancy and toddlerhood are the basis for later social behavior, disruption in the attachment process may produce later problems with social interaction and adherence to social norms. Examples of attachment disruptions and social deprivation, such as extended separation from the parent, multiple caretakers, marital conflicts, and poor child care, predict later antisocial behavior (Loeber & Dishion, 1983). The child develops little loyalty to rules and social relationships because attachment figures have done little to earn such loyalty. Instead of nurturance, the child expects rejection and punishment from authorities and society. Thus, the child attempts to meet his or her own needs, with little regard for the advice or rules of society.

In addition to the dyadic parent-child interaction, broader family factors may predispose the child to CD. Children of criminal or alcoholic parents are more likely to have CD (Quinton, Rutter, & Gulliver, 1990; Robins, 1966; Robins, West, & Herjanic, 1975; Rutter, 1985). Family factors such as large size, parental discord, excessive conflict, substance-abusing parents, parental psychopathology, and parental depression predict CD in the child (Frick et al., 1992; Kazdin, 1996; West & Farrington, 1977). Families who reward negative behavior by giving in to the child's demands are more likely to have children who engage in antisocial behaviors (Snyder, Schrepferman, & St. Peter, 1997). These factors may contribute to CD by disrupting attachment, by reducing parental attention to the child, by rewarding negative behavior, by encouraging inconsistent parenting, and/or by providing a negative model for the child.

The association between parental depression and CD could also be a result of distortions in the observational report of a depressed parent: Depressed parents tend to overestimate externalizing problems in their children, relative to teacher-reports and to observational coding (Fergusson, Lynskey, & Horwood, 1993; Griest, Wells, & Forehand, 1979). Hence, some children with apparent CD may come to the attention of clinicians because of catastrophizing on the part of a depressed parent.

Despite the intriguing associations of CD with attachment and family variables, poor parental disciplinary practices remain the single most emphasized factor in the development of CD. Patterson's (1982) coercion theory is one of the best-known and well-researched explanations of how inconsistent discipline may lead to ODD and CD. Coercion theory suggests that oppositional, aggressive, and antisocial behaviors emerge through a process of reciprocal, negative, coercive interchanges between the child and parent. The scenario begins with a child who exhibits distress behavior as a result of temperament, stress, or other factors. Such behaviors may be developmentally normal (such as crying in an infant) or responses to a negative environment. In healthy parent-child relationships, child distress behavior quickly shapes the behavior of caretakers, who respond to the needs of the child. As the child matures, more appropriate social and verbal skills replace the rudimentary negative distress behaviors, and the child learns to respond appropriately and positively to caretakers.

For some children, however, this rudimentary negative distress behavior is irritating to caretakers, who avoid and/or harshly discipline the child. The child responds to the avoidance or harsh discipline with increasingly hostile and unrewarding behavior, leading to further avoidance and mistreatment from parents. As the parents' avoidance and mistreatment increase, the child must increasingly escalate the behavior to gain parents' attention and force parents to attend to the child's needs. Eventually, the parent unintentionally reinforces the child's coercive behavior by giving in or modifying demands placed on the child whenever the child displays escalating, oppositional behavior.

This pattern of interaction evolves into a simple power struggle: The child makes a request, refuses to behave, or performs an undesirable behavior. In response, the parent imposes a consequence (punishment) or refuses a privilege. The child reacts by escalating forbidden, antisocial, or upset behavior, and the child persists at this behavior until the parent removes the consequence or restores the privilege. The escalation of conflict between child and parent may involve screaming, threats, and even physical fighting, but the child persists in the conflict until the parent gives in. Eventually, the child has difficulty with any tolerance of frustration and takes a similar approach to avoiding or disregarding the rules of society.

An example of coercion theory begins with a mother instructing her child to pick up his toys. The child whines and refuses. The mother yells and threatens to spank the child. The child throws a tantrum with loud screaming and thrashing. Finally, the mother withdraws and cleans up the toys herself. In this process, the child learns that if he tantrums enough, he can get his way with his mother. The mother learns not to upset the child, lest he throw a tantrum.

Such coercive interchanges are not always "won" by the child, but the intermittent reinforcement of periodic "wins" is sufficient to cause the negative behaviors to persist. Because intermittently reinforced behavior is difficult to extinguish, children with CD give up their symptoms slowly and reluctantly. Parental inconsistency and harshness can contribute to a relapse of such behaviors.

Psychodynamic Theories

Psychodynamic theories of CD are based on the assumption that children adopt rule-following behaviors as a result of internalizing and identifying with the beliefs and behaviors of significant others. Normally, children form strong attachments to their caretakers, who gratify their needs adequately. The experience of need gratification and caretaking creates a bond between the child and caretaker, which results in the child identifying with the identity and behaviors of the caretaker. This caretaking bond also encourages the child to please the caretaker and to retain the love and protection of the caretaker. The child thus learns to relinquish the desire for immediate and/or complete gratification in favor of more cooperative, trusting behavior and a strong bond with the caretaker. Over time, and after many instances of steady, nonpunitive caretaking, the child forms an internalized representation of the benevolent, available parent. This internal representation sustains the child's behaviors during separations from the parent and during times of frustrated needs (Matthys, Walterbos, Nijo, & van Engeland, 1989).

In some cases, the development of the internalized caretaker is disrupted, and the child is left without the representation of the benevolent authority. Traumatic events, inconsistent or harsh parenting, separation from parents, emotionally distant parenting, and family conflict, for example, may disrupt the internalization process, leaving the child with little regulation of his or her needs and impulses. Hence, the child is unable to tolerate limits, frustration, delayed gratification, and other rules. The child lacks respect for others because the child did not internalize the respect and understanding of caretakers. In the end, the child acts impulsively and immediately to gratify needs, constrained only by the limits of reality but not by the limits of internalized standards of behavior.

☐ ASSESSMENT PATTERNS

Overview

Because oppositional, rule-breaking behavior varies by context and social relationships, informants tend to differ on ratings of CD/ODD behaviors. Therefore, the symptom picture may vary somewhat based on the source and context of information. Discrepancies in observer reports may reflect influences as diverse as rater bias, secondary gain, social desirability, contextual differences, and rater psychopathology.

Interestingly, research has shown that teachers are accurate raters of CD/ODD behaviors whether or not ADHD is present (Abikoff, Courtney, Pelham, & Koplewicz, 1993). This result indicates that teachers do not inflate their report of CD/ODD behaviors for children with ADHD. Furthermore, teacher-report of CD/ODD symptoms correlates more strongly with objective impairment criteria (school suspensions, police contacts, peer rejection, aggressive behavior) than does parent-report or child self-report of CD/ODD symptoms. On the other hand, parent-report and child-self-report of CD/ODD symptoms adds to the validity of teacher-report of those symptoms (Hart, Lahey, Loeber, & Hanson, 1994). These findings argue strongly for the validity of teacher-report of CD/ODD symptoms and for the additive value of parent- and child-report of CD/ODD symptoms. Hence, assessment of a child with CD/ODD should use multiple methods completed by multiple informants in reference to multiple settings. This multirater-multimethod approach provides a good starting point for capturing the complexity of behavior of the typical child with CD/ODD. (A sample assessment battery for ODD and CD is shown in Table 3.4.)

| TABLE 3.4 | Sample Assessment Battery for Oppositional-Defiant Disorder and Conduct Disorder |

COGNITIVE

1. Kaufman Brief Intelligence Test

PSYCHOLOGICAL

1. MMPI-A

BEHAVIORAL

1. Child Behavior Checklist
2. Teacher's Report Form

FAMILY

1. Family Environment Scale

SYNDROME-SPECIFIC

1. Overt Aggression Scale
2. Means-End Problem-Solving Procedure

Note: Assessment instruments are intended to supplement (not substitute for) a good clinical interview and, when possible, a structured diagnostic interview.

Broad Assessment Strategies

Cognitive Assessment

Clinician-Administered. As a group, children with CD/ODD are more likely to suffer from academic deficiencies than their normal peers, and boys in residential settings are at greater risk for language deficiencies (Warr-Leeper, Wright, & Mack, 1994). Because poor school performance is characteristic of children with CD/ODD, it is important to assess intellectual deficits or learning disabilities that may be overshadowed by oppositional behavior. Additionally, in some cases the poor judgment shown by most children with CD/ODD is secondary to overall poor cognitive functioning.

Socialized children with CD/ODD tend to provide less variability between subtests of the WISC-III. On the other hand, less socialized, more aggressive children with CD/ODD may have higher Performance than Verbal IQ, reflecting weaknesses in vocabulary, in knowledge of learned facts, and in knowledge of social convention (Warr-Leeper et al., 1994). Truancy or school misbehavior may also result in lower WISC-III Verbal subtest scores (especially Information, Vocabulary, or Arithmetic) as well as in lower achievement test scores.

The ability to abstract can be important in curbing aggression because abstraction is important for social problem solving. Problems with abstract verbal thinking may be apparent on the Similarities and Comprehension subtests of the WISC-III. Undersocialized children may score lower on Picture Arrangement and Comprehension than those who are aware of social norms and expectations. On the other hand, children with CD/ODD who are more involved with passive or status offenses are likely to have higher intellectual abilities overall than those who commit more aggressive acts.

In cases in which only an intellectual screen is necessary, the K-BIT or WASI can provide estimates of verbal, nonverbal, and overall ability. IQ screening scores can indicate if the child's judgment is a part of a greater intellectual ability problem or if ability is in the average range or above. Relatively lower scores on the nonverbal reasoning subtests suggest difficulties in abstraction, whereas relatively lower scores on the verbal subtests may indicate a language disorder.

Psychological Assessment

Clinician-Administered. Psychological test responses in children with CD/ODD often are characterized by aggressiveness, alienation, disregard for rules, anger, and/or socialization problems. Such test patterns may alert the clinician to potential problems, situational interpretations, or personality predispositions that may put the child at risk to misbehave or to behave impulsively.

MMPI/MMPI-A profiles of adolescents with CD/ODD usually show family problems, problems with authorities, rebellion against expectations, anger, distrust, and a lack of identification with societal rules. Hence, the typical MMPI profile for an adolescent with CD/ODD includes an elevation on scale 4. The Persecutory Ideas subscale of MMPI scale 6 is also generally elevated, although the overall scale 6 score may be within normal ranges (because of the presence of many naively optimistic items on this scale—the Naivete subscale). An elevated scale 8 may indicate social alienation, impulsivity, and a feeling of being out of control, which may drive some of the antisocial behavior. Elevated scale 2, combined with depressed scale 9, typically reflects some unhappiness with the current situation, perhaps as a result of having needs repeatedly unmet or as a result of being punished (e.g., by the legal system). Herkov and Myers (1996), however, found that adolescents with comorbid depression and CD tended to have lower scores on scales 2 and 0, compared to depressed adolescents without CD. Hence, CD may hide some of the elevations on MMPI scales typically associated with depression. Elevation of scale 9, on the other hand, often suggests that the child acts on antisocial impulses, enjoys the thrill of antisocial behavior, and is extremely resistant to efforts to control behavior.

The Adolescent Conduct Problems Scale (A-con) of the MMPI-A taps specific conduct behaviors. A-con items include impulsivity, risk-taking behaviors, and antisocial behaviors. Elevated A-con scores may predict school suspension, legal difficulty, and conflict with societal norms (Butcher et al., 1992). Because A-con is a relatively face-valid scale, an adolescent with CD may deliberately answer questions to receive a low score. When this is the case, L and K scale scores should be inspected for a defensive response set.

In addition to A-con, several other MMPI-A content scales can be relevant in the understanding of the adolescent with CD/ODD. Elevation of the A-aln (Adolescent-Alienation) subscale typically indicates a feeling of being misunderstood and unliked. Adolescents with high scores on A-aln report that they do not receive their due in life and complain that they are not close to anyone. The A-ang (Adolescent-Anger) subscale detects anger control problems and impulsivity in anger-arousing situations. Adolescents with high A-ang scores report problems such as fighting, impatience, temper tantrums, and destructive behavior. Other relevant MMPI-A content subscales indicate suspiciousness (A-cyn), family conflict and disengagement (A-fam), and school problems (A-sch).

Behavioral Assessment

Parent-Report/Other-Report.   Almost all broad-band child behavior checklists include items measuring aggressive, oppositional, rule-breaking, and antisocial behaviors. Factor analyses and internal consistency studies indicate that these items cluster into one or two groups. The first group characterizes aggressive, disobedient, and mildly oppositional behaviors (ODD-type behaviors); subscales tapping this dimension generally carry labels such as *Aggression, Aggressive Behavior,* and *Oppositional Behavior.* The second group of behaviors represents more serious antisocial behaviors such as truancy, firesetting, destruction of property, and drug use; subscales tapping this dimension are labeled *Delinquent Behavior* or *Conduct Problems* (Achenbach, 1991).

On the Achenbach scales, children with CD/ODD tend to elevate the Delinquent Behavior and Aggressive Behavior subscales as well as the Externalizing score. Delinquent Behavior elevations are more typical of children with CD, whereas Aggressive Behavior elevations suggest ODD. On average, children with CD/ODD do not differ from other clinically referred children on other CBCL/TRF subscales (McMahon & Forehand, 1988). For any individual child, however, other subscale scores may suggest contributing or co-occurring behavior problems. It is important to note that many children who elevate the Delinquent Behavior and Aggressive Behavior scales do *not* qualify for a CD diagnosis. Hence, the Achenbach scales should not be used exclusively to make a CD or ODD diagnosis (McMahon & Forehand, 1988).

Because symptoms on the CBCL/TRF Delinquent Behavior subscale are rare in nonreferred samples, endorsement of only two or three of the Delinquent Behavior items can produce a borderline or clinical elevation on that subscale. Therefore, it is especially important to review specific answers and to follow up with parents on those items. The Aggressive Behavior subscale, on the other hand, requires endorsement of many items before scores reach elevated levels. This characteristic is expected because behaviors described by the Aggressive Behavior subscale items are more commonly seen in nonreferred samples than Delinquent Behavior subscale items.

On the Conners' scales, children with CD/ODD typically elevate the Oppositional and Social Problems subscales. Elevations of the Cognitive Problems, Hyperactivity, CGI, ADHD Index, and DSM-IV ADHD symptom subscales strongly suggest that ADHD should be considered as a diagnosis. Additionally, an elevation of the Cognitive Problems subscale is associated with risk of comorbid learning disorder.

On the BASC, children with CD/ODD tend to score highest (T-scores > 70) on the Conduct Problems subscale. Interestingly, the limited research to date has found only moderate (T-scores 60–70) elevations on the Aggression subscale, although the Aggression subscale tends to be the second-highest elevation for children with CD/ODD (Reynolds & Kamphaus, 1992). Mild elevations (T-scores of about 60) are generally found on the Hyperactivity, Depression, and Attention Problems subscales.

BASC profiles of children with CD/ODD differ from those with Depression by the CD/ODD group's lower scores on the Depression and Atypicality subscales. Children with ADHD tend to score higher (in the 65–70 range) on BASC Hyperactivity and Attention Problems subscales and lower on BASC Conduct Problems subscale than children with CD/ODD. Children with CD/ODD and comorbid ADHD and/or depression tend to show a blend of these BASC profiles (Reynolds & Kamphaus, 1992).

The ECI-4, CSI-4, and ASI-4 include all developmentally appropriate DSM-IV symptoms of ODD and CD. Responses to the individual CD items should be examined carefully because these items include some severe problems. Specificity values for the parent-report CSI-4 for ODD and CD have been found to be 0.75 and 0.83, respectively. Sensitivity of the parent-report CSI-4 for ODD was 0.69; sensitivity to CD has not been studied (Gadow & Sprafkin, 1997). For children who elevate the ODD or CD subscales on the ASI-4, the drug use items should be carefully inspected to warn of associated drug use. In addition the ASI-4 Antisocial Personality Disorder subscale is frequently elevated for adolescents with severe CD. On the ECI-4, children who elevate the ODD and CD subscales often elevate the Peer Conflict Scale, reflecting aggressive behavior and poor peer relationships. Feeding problems may also be indicated on the ECI-4.

Child-Report.   The self-reports of children with CD/ODD often suffer from low insight, denial of problems, or attempts to manipulate the test results. Hence, they should be interpreted cautiously. The PIY and BASC have the advantages of validity scales to detect defensive, random, and exaggerated responding. These validity scales should be closely examined when interpreting the profile of a child with CD/ODD. The YSR and CASS do not contain validity scales and are interpreted in the same way as their parent-report counterparts.

As a group, children with CD/ODD do not produce very different BASC-SRP profiles as compared to children with ADHD or depression. This could be due to the problems with self-report noted earlier. Individual BASC profiles, however, can be useful in understanding a child's view of his or her problems (Reynolds & Kamphaus, 1992). In the case of CD/ODD, the Attitude to School and Attitude to Teachers scales can provide valuable information about the child's degree of alienation from and hostility toward school and teachers, respectively. The Sensation Seeking scale can assist in understanding the degree to which stimulation drives the child's behavior. Other BASC-SRP scales can indicate the presence of comorbid internalizing, social, or other problems.

On the PIY, children with CD/ODD would be expected to elevate the Delinquency scale. Inspection of the subscales of the Delinquency (DLQ) scale can provide additional information about the type of antisocial behavior being reported by the child. The Antisocial Behavior subscale (DLQ1) measures severe conduct problems that are clear violations of laws or major social rules; children with CD typically elevate this scale. The Dyscontrol subscale (DLQ2) measures impulsivity, anger, temper outbursts, egocentricity, and unpredictable behavior, whereas the Noncompliance subscale (DLQ3) measures oppositional behavior and resistance to change. Children with CD or ODD tend to elevate these latter two scales. Many children with CD/ODD will not elevate the DLQ scale because of low insight or because they refuse to admit their problems. Therefore, elevated DLQ scores indicate some frankness about admitting behavioral problems and a realization that the problems are present. Other PIY scale and subscale scores can indicate comorbid social (Social Withdrawal, Social Skill Deficits scale), family (Family Dysfunction scale), and impulsivity (Impulsivity and Distractibility scale) problems.

For children who are unable to complete verbal self-report scales, Ernst, Godfrey, Silva, Pouget, and Welkowitz, (1994) and Valla, Bergeron, Berube, Gaudet, and St-Georges, (1994) have created separate pictorial measures of anxiety disorders, depression, psychosis, ADHD, CD, ODD, and substance abuse, based on the DSM-III-R criteria for these disorders. Children state the degree to which each picture is an accurate portrayal of their behavior or emotional state. Both measures discriminate children with CD/ODD from children with other diagnoses and are sensitive to comorbid diagnoses.

Family Assessment

Parent-Report.   Based on research indicating that inconsistent supervision and lack of household rules may contribute to CD/ODD (Wilson, 1980), the FES Organization subscale is likely to show deficits in families of children with CD/ODD. The Controlling factor and Control subscale may be elevated, especially in families with a strong hierarchy and harsh discipline. If this is the case, the child may be rebelling against the weight of expectations and lack of independence. Because parent-child interactions tend to show higher rates of conflict in families with a child with ODD (Fletcher, Fischer, Barkley, & Smallish, 1996), elevations of the Conflict scale are expected. Harsh discipline and family conflict also cause elevations of the Conflicted factor and Conflict subscale in some CD/ODD families. The Supportive factor and its components, on the other hand, may show deficits in the CD/ODD family, reflecting a dearth of mutual interest, expression of beliefs, and shared activities. The configuration of FES subscale and factor scores may suggest intervention targets and potential problems that may arise during the course of therapy.

In some cases (especially when the legal system is involved), the family may be motivated to present an overly positive picture of family environment. Because the FES is largely face-valid, deliberate attempts to present a positive characterization of the family will result in an inaccurate profile. A quick screen for defensive or socially desirable responding in these cases is to add the raw scores of the Cohesion and Expressiveness subscales to the reverse raw score of the Conflict subscale (e.g., reverse score every Conflict subscale item, or subtract the Conflict raw score from 9 because 9 is the maximum raw score on the Conflict subscale). The Cohesion and Expressiveness subscales are considered socially desirable by almost all families, and the Conflict subscale is considered undesirable. Hence, this sum is the number of "family relationship" items that the respondent answered in a socially desirable way, with the maximum score being 27. Scores of 25 or higher are extremely rare, even in model families, and they probably indicate some defensiveness or positive bias.

The PIY and BASC-SRP include validity scales (measuring defensive, exaggerated, and random responding) as well as scales measuring family functioning. Hence, some assessment of family functioning can be accomplished in the context of behavioral questionnaire measures. The BASC-SRP Relations with Parents scale assesses self-reported feeling of acceptance within the family. The PIY Family Dysfunction scale, on the other hand, measures parent-reported and self-reported (respectively) conflict and problems within the family.

Syndrome-Specific Tests

Clinician-Administered

Behavioral Coding Systems in a Clinic Setting. Direct behavioral observation is a valuable but expensive procedure for obtaining a reliable and valid description of parent-child interactions. Typically, clinic-based, structured observation systems code parent-child interaction in a playroom setting, in 5–10 minute intervals based on predefined parent-child tasks. The Dyadic Parent-Child Interaction Coding System (DPICS; Eyberg & Robinson, 1983), for example, uses "cleanup time" in which the parent attempts to direct the child to pick up toys in the playroom. The observer records the frequency of behaviors using twenty-three coding categories. Parent behaviors include direct and indirect commands, descriptive/reflective questions, acknowledgment, irrelevant verbalization, unlabeled and labeled praise, physical positive and negative, and critical statement. Child behaviors include cry, yell, whine, smart talk, destructive, physical negative, and change activity. Two behavioral sequences are scored: parental response to deviant child behavior (respond/ignore) and child response to commands (compliance/noncompliance/no opportunity). The DPICS successfully discriminates families of children with CD from those of children with no diagnosis. It also differentiates between children with CD and their siblings (Robinson & Eyberg, 1981) and is sensitive to treatment changes (Eyberg & Robinson, 1982; Webster-Stratton, 1984).

In addition to the DPICS, several other structured observation systems exist, such as the Forehand Observation System (FOS; Forehand & McMahon, 1981), the Clinic Task Analog (Roberts & Powers, 1988), and the Compliance Test (Bean & Roberts, 1981). These systems differ in the tasks that they require of parent and child, the behaviors and interactions that are coded, and the way in which the room is arranged for the task. Although their scoring systems differ, each provides a score that reflects the degree to which the child was compliant with parent requests. Brumfield and Roberts (1998) suggest that the Compliance Test may be the most accurate of these behavior coding tasks.

Behavioral Coding Systems in a Home Setting. Several behavioral coding systems have been developed to measure the behavior of children with CD/ODD and their families in the home setting. Two of the systems that have been most frequently used are the Family Interaction Coding System (FICS; Patterson, Ray, Shaw, & Cobb, 1969) and the Standardized Observation Codes system (SOC; Wahler, House, & Stambaugh, 1976). These coding systems are similar in that certain rules are imposed on the family during the observation period (e.g., all members present; no TV, radio, or telephone). During the observation period, the child's behavior and the responses by family members are coded in order to provide a sequential account of the child's interactions with family members.

Parent-Report/Other-Report

Eyberg Child Behavior Inventory (ECBI). The ECBI (Eyberg & Ross, 1978) is a parent rating scale of CD/ODD behaviors in children age 2–17. It contains descriptions of 36 behaviors commonly reported by parents of children who show oppositional, defiant, conduct-disorder behaviors. Parents rate each behavior on a 7-point scale indicating frequency of occurrence (Intensity score) and on a yes-no problem identification scale (Problem score). Based on factor analyses, the ECBI appears to be a unidimensional scale measuring conduct problems in children and adolescents. A cutoff criterion of 11 or more behaviors has been suggested for the identification of clinically significant conduct problems (Eyberg & Ross, 1978; McMahon & Forehand, 1988).

Parent Daily Report (PDR). The PDR (Chamberlain & Reid, 1987; Patterson, Reid, Jones, & Conger, 1975) is completed during a 10-minute telephone interview. It consists of thirty-three child behaviors and one item asking if the child has been spanked in the last day. The PDR yields two scores: Targeted Behaviors (the sum of occurrences of behaviors identified as problematic by parents at the initial interview) and Total Behaviors (the sum of all occurrences on the total list of behaviors).

A revised version of the PDR has been developed for the longitudinal investigation of children with CD and their families (Patterson & Bank, 1986). This version asks parents whether they have disciplined their child in the past 24 hours for twenty-three behaviors characteristic of ODD or CD. If a parent answers an item affirmatively, he or she is asked to describe the discipline procedure. The revised PDR also includes sections on parental monitoring of the child, positive reinforcement directed to the child, and the occurrence of crises and social support. A parallel, child-report version of this form asks the child about occurrence of the CD behaviors, the state of his or her mood, and whether the parents have engaged in any of several monitoring behaviors (Patterson & Bank, 1986).

Original Ontario Health Study (OCHS). The OCHS (Boyle et al., 1993) was developed to provide a simple, rapid means of identifying childhood psychopathology in the general population. The OCHS consists of thirty-four behavior problems that cluster into three subscales: CD (physical violence and severe violation of social norms), Hyperactivity (inattention, impulsiveness, and hyperactivity), and Emotional Disorder (tension, obsessions, and compulsive behavior). Each item is scored on a 0–2 scale from "never or not true" to "often or very true," and sums of items give subscale raw scores. Separate versions of the OCHS exist for parents, teachers, and adolescents age 12–16. The OCHS may be useful as a quick screen for conduct problems.

Overt Aggression Scale (OAS). The OAS (Yudofsky, Silver, Jackson, Endicott, & Williams, 1986) was developed for observer rating of child physical or verbal aggression. Aggressive behavior on the OAS is rated in four categories: Verbal Aggression, Physical Aggression against Objects, Physical Aggression against Self, and Physical Aggression against Others. For each category the OAS rater indicates the severity of the behavior on a four-level scale. For example, on the Verbal Aggression scale, "makes loud noises" is a first-level behavior, whereas "makes clear threats of violence" is a fourth-level behavior. The OAS may be used as a brief measure of the severity and frequency of aggressive behavior.

The OAS has been used on psychiatric units to monitor changes in behavior and efficacy of interventions. It is sensitive to behavior changes as a result of treatment with lithium and other medications. OAS scores also correlate with staff global ratings of improvement in behavior (Malone, Luebbert, Pena-Ariet, Biesecker, & Delaney, 1994).

Adolescent Antisocial Behavior Checklist (AABCL). The AABCL (Ostrov, Marohn, Offer, Curtiss, & Feczko, 1980) is a 350-item scale of antisocial behaviors typically displayed by adolescents in an institutional setting. Staff rate the occurrence and severity of behaviors on a 0–6 point scale. AABCL scores cluster into four subscales: (Activities Directed) Against Staff, Against Property, Against Rules, and Against Visitors. AABCL scores predict differences in antisocial behavior in the institutional setting (Ostrov et al., 1980).

Generalized Parental Expectancies Questionnaire (GPEQ). The GPEQ (Howe, Baden, Lewis, Ostroff, & Levine, 1989) measures parents' beliefs concerning the general effectiveness of four parenting actions: verbal or physical punishment, withdrawal of positive reinforcement, contingent reinforcement of alternative behavior, and ignoring child misbehavior. For each of nine hypothetical misbehaviors, the parent rates the effectiveness of the four parenting responses on a seven-point scale. The GPEQ yields four expectancy scores, one for each of the four types of parental actions. It can be used to gauge parental beliefs and preferences for responses to child misbehaviors. These beliefs and preferences may need to be addressed if a change in parenting behavior is required as a part of therapy.

New York Teacher Rating Scale (NYTRS). The NYTRS (Miller et al., 1995) is a 36-item teacher-report scale measuring oppositionality, peer rejection, aggression, and rule-breaking in children in the first through tenth grades. All items differentiate between children with CD and no psychiatric diagnosis. The NYTRS yields four factor-analytically derived subscales: Defiance, Physical Aggression, Delinquent Aggression, and Peer Relations. One higher-order subscale, Antisocial Behavior, includes the Physical Aggression and Delinquent Aggression items as well as some conduct disorder items that did not load on any factor; this subscale is a good indicator of CD. An overall score from the NYTRS, the Disruptive Behavior score, reflects all items except for Peer Relations and is a good index of CD/ODD behaviors. The Defiance subscale corresponds most closely to ODD.

The NYTRS has good content coverage of ODD and CD symptoms, and NYTRS scores differentiate between children with and without CD. Analyses also indicate that the NYTRS provides information that is not completely redundant with other major behavioral checklists and that it may be a better predictor of CD than other behavioral checklists (Miller et al., 1995).

Child Report

Social Attribution and Social Problem-Solving Measures. These tests assess the child's problem-solving abilities and attributional style toward ambiguous or challenging social situations. Measurement of social problem-solving ability may be particularly important for children with CD because social problem-solving deficits have been implicated in CD/ODD behavior (Dodge, 1985; Lochman et al., 1991). The *Means-End Problem-Solving Procedure* (MEPS; Platt & Spivak, 1975) requires children to provide a middle portion to stories that have a beginning and end, but no middle. Children must suggest behavioral means by which subjects can achieve the ending goals of the story. The means are then scored for relevance to achieving the goal, for awareness of obstacles to the goals, and for the child's awareness of sequencing and the passage of time. Children with CD/ODD give lower overall number of relevant means to the story ends and perceive fewer obstacles to the attainment of social goals.

Other tasks that present ambiguous situations that test the child's perception and reasoning related to hypothetical social situations include the *Social Situations Analysis* (SSA; Conolly, Burstein, Stevens, & White, 1987), the *Adolescent Social Problem Solving Scale* (ASPS; Kennedy, Felner, Cause, & Primavera, 1988), the *Assessment for Social Failure* (ASF; Guerra, Huesmann, & Zelli, 1990), and the *Problem-Solving Measure for Conflict* (PSM-C; Lochman & Dodge, 1994). The ASPS measures the number of problem-solving solutions generated by the child, as well as the quality of the solutions. The SSA and PSM-C code the child's solutions to hypothetical social problems into categories reflecting aggression, assertiveness, compromise, help seeking, passive response, vague response, and similar categories. Children also report outcomes from the situations. The ASF focuses more on the child's identified reasons for failure in hypothetical social situations. Children with CD/ODD tend to show problems in problem solving and attributions on all of these measures.

Anger-Aggression Inventories. Anger-aggression inventories are used to measure hostile attitudes, components of anger, and expression of anger, from the point of view of the child. They can be extremely helpful in assessing a child whose CD/ODD symptoms are largely secondary to anger problems, and they are widely used to track progress in anger management groups. The 75-item, true-false *Buss-Durkee Hostility Inventory* (BDHI; Buss & Durkee, 1957; for adolescents and adults) measures eight dimensions of anger (Assault, Indirect Aggression, Irritability, Negativism, Resentment, Suspicion, Verbal Hostility, and Guilt) that fall into two factors: Attitudinal Hostility/Suspicion (e.g., "I know that people tend to talk behind my back") and Motoric Hostility/Assault (e.g., "If somebody hits me first, I let him have it"). The 80-item *Novaco Anger Inventory* (NAI; Novaco, 1975; for adolescents and adults) asks respondents to rate the degree to which different situations would arouse anger on a 5-point scale. Similar to the NAI, the *Children's Anger Response Checklist* (CARC; Feindler, Adler, Brooks, & Bhumitra, 1993) asks about responses to 10 different anger-arousing situations, focusing on the child or adolescent's thoughts, feelings, and actions. The 71-item *Children's Inventory of Anger* (CIA; Finch, Saylor, & Nelson, 1987) also measures children's self-reported level of anger in response to different anger-provoking situations. Finally, the 44-item *State-Trait Anger Expression Inventory* (STAXI; Spielberger, 1988) measures adolescent-reported anger in six areas: State Anger, Trait Anger, Anger-In, Anger-Out, Anger-Control, and Anger-Expression. Typically on anger-aggression inventories, children with CD/ODD report more anger, less control over anger, and more aggressive reactions to anger-arousing situations.

☐   TREATMENT OPTIONS

Overview

Many approaches to the treatment of CD/ODD have been tried with varying success (Kazdin, 1997; Shamsie & Hluchy, 1991). In fact, the broad range of therapies attempted testifies to how difficult these disorders are to treat effectively. Effectiveness in the long term is a particularly difficult goal, especially when the child is returned to the environment that produced or maintained the disorder in the first place.

Another major difficulty in treating children with CD/ODD is comorbidity with other disorders (Holland, Moretti, Verlaan, & Peterson, 1993). Research on the relationship between CD/ODD and other disorders indicates that comorbidity is the rule rather than the exception (Biederman, Newcorn, & Sprich, 1991; Myers et al., 1993). Clinicians should be particularly alert for signs of ADHD and Depressive Disorders in the child with CD/ODD because these disorders are often masked by the more dramatic CD/ODD symptoms. When a comorbid condition is suspected, treatment should include components for both disorders.

Often children with CD/ODD symptoms are already extensively involved with the school, legal, or mental health system by the time that they present for psychological intervention. Because of this involvement with "the system," a rich database of the child's history often exists in the form of school, legal, and past mental health records. Review of these records may assist with preliminary formulations and selection of intervention techniques. Prior treatment failures should be examined closely so that earlier mistakes are not repeated in treatment. Consultation with school and legal agencies may be warranted in some cases as well, and appropriate permission to release information should be obtained from the parent or guardian.

Behavioral Interventions

Home-Based Behavioral Interventions

Because many CD/ODD behaviors violate rules set by authorities, behavioral interventions involving authorities are among the most common and most effective for CD/ODD. Behavioral interventions can take place both at home and at school. Home-based interventions are almost always delivered by parents. Such parent-delivered behavioral interventions, typically referred to as parent management training (PMT), have produced some of the most impressive research results on treatment efficacy, with one-third to two-thirds of children typically showing clinically significant improvement (Barkley, 1997; Kazdin, 1996; McMahon & Forehand, 1984; Patterson, Chamberlain, & Reid, 1982; Webster-Stratton, 1984, 1996). The rationale for PMT is founded in the theory that coercive parent-child interchanges and environmental contingencies are instrumental in the development and maintenance of oppositional, defiant, and antisocial behaviors. Improvements in parent ratings of child behaviors and in parent attitudes toward the child have consistently been obtained with PMT interventions, with effects often present at 1-year follow-up (Kazdin, 1996; Webster-Stratton, 1984). PMT approaches have been pioneered and refined by various professionals, including Patterson (1982), Clark (1985), and Kazdin (1996). Most PMT interventions are implemented in a 12–20 session (1–2 hour meetings between therapist and parents) treatment plan that includes some combination of the following components:

1. *Psychoeducation.* PMT programs begin with teaching of basic behavioral and CD/ODD concepts, such as coercion, reinforcement, punishment, rule violation, and operationally defined behaviors. Parents learn how their parenting behavior can increase or decrease oppositional-defiant behaviors in their child. Parents may also receive some background information about the disorder, such as symptoms, etiology, prevalence, and common treatments. Finally, an overview of the treatment plan is given, with clear expectations of the parents and child.

2. *Observation and monitoring.* Target problem behaviors are identified, and parents are asked to monitor the occurrence of these behaviors at home. This process clarifies the parents' views of the child's behaviors and establishes a baseline by which to measure the effectiveness of future intervention. Ideally, target behaviors are easily identifiable, discrete, and clearly operationally defined.

3. *Reinforcement of prosocial behavior.* In this third step, parents learn reinforcement techniques to focus the child's (and parents') attention from antisocial behavior onto prosocial goals. The provision of reinforcement for prosocial behaviors also encourages such behaviors. Examples of reinforcers include social, material, and activity rewards (Clark, 1985).

Social rewards consist of components of parent-child interaction, such as smiles, hugs, and praise. These rewards are implemented as specific parental behaviors that maximize their social impact on the child. For example, praise is more effective if specific feedback is given regarding the behavior rather than more general praise (e.g., "I'm so proud of you for picking up your room" as opposed to "What a good boy you are"). Material rewards include points, tokens, and other reinforcers that may be used by the child to "purchase" tangible objects. Alternatively, the child may be given such objects directly. Activity rewards include access to favored games, areas, or other things to do (e.g., staying up late). Social, material, and activity rewards are combined in this step to encourage specific prosocial behaviors identified by the parent and therapist. The connections of rewards and specific behaviors are planned and purposeful. (Appendix C provides parent handouts for implementing a similar form of contingency management.)

4. *Simple, effective commands.* Parents are taught to state commands simply, and one at a time. This is accomplished by the parent being in proximity to the child and having a stern facial expression (e.g., laughing or shouting from another room are discouraged). The parent then says the child's name and maintains eye contact to ensure that the child's attention is focused on the parent. Finally, the parent gives the command in simple, clear language. Angry, demanding, or irritated tone of voice is discouraged. Based on the child's compliance or noncompliance with the command, the child receives attention or time-out. Command control (Appendix C) is often used to implement these parenting goals, and Phelan's (1995) *1-2-3 Magic* program also focuses on these areas.

5. *Discipline of unacceptable behavior.* At this stage of parent training, parents are taught the correct use of time-out. Time-out consists of removal of the child from a reinforcing or stimulating situation and placement in a situation that is free of reinforcement or stimulation. Time-out should occur for a discrete period of time, and attempts on the part of the child to escalate behavior and escape time-out should be met with further punishment or ignoring. For example, if the child is screaming and taunting from the time-out room, the door may be shut and an extra two minutes added to time-out time. Physical punishment is strongly discouraged, and alternatives to physical punishment (especially time-out, withdrawal of privileges, and ignoring) are taught. Parents also learn to ignore mild attention-getting behaviors to avoid reinforcing the child's negative behaviors with attention. Phelan's (1995) *1-2-3 Magic* program, an integrated program that focuses on time-out and ignoring, can be used to help parents with this step of treatment. Appendix C of this book also provides a parent handout with descriptions of the use of time-out and ignoring.

6. *Supervision-monitoring.* Parents are encouraged to provide close supervision for their child, even when the child is away from home. This involves such behaviors as knowing where the child is at all times, what the child is doing, and when the child will be home. Supervision by other adults should occur only if the parent knows, trusts, and is comfortable with the adult.

7. *Generalization to other environments.* Following the implementation of home-based interventions, other environments of the child may be brought into the treatment. Typically, the school is the major focus of this effort. The child's performance in target areas (usually achievement and behavior) at school are monitored, with feedback provided regularly (ideally daily) to parents. Based on the child's reported performance, positive or negative consequences are then delivered at home.

8. *Communication strategies.* Finally, parents learn problem solving, negotiation strategies, and effective communication. Children often respond favorably to being made a part of the problem-solving process, and joint solutions are more likely to be adhered to than decisions imposed by parents without discussion. However, the parent must be careful not to allow the child to start a power struggle. Ultimately, the parent must retain responsibility and control for the decision, but the child should feel that his or her input is valued and important. In order to accomplish these goals, parents practice basic skills of reflective listening, negotiation, and avoidance of power struggles (Clark, 1985). Phelan (1998) and Robin (1998) provide good descriptions of these communication strategies.

Parents are taught these eight steps with a combination of techniques. Initially, a didactic role is adopted by the therapist, who teaches the parent a principle and answers questions about it. The therapist may then model the parenting behavior, anticipating problem situations and solutions. The parent may then practice and role play the new parenting behavior in therapy. When the parent and therapist are comfortable with the technique, the parent then uses it at home and reports on its effectiveness. The therapist then gives feedback, and, if necessary, parent and therapist may modify the technique.

Based on child age and developmental level, specific PMT interventions may have to be modified. In the case of adolescents, targeted behaviors should include those that put the adolescent at immediate risk for danger or delinquency. Parental monitoring and supervision may be more difficult because the adolescent expects greater freedom than the child. Chores and restriction of free time may be added to punishment procedures, and the adolescent may have a greater involvement in the therapy sessions. For example, the adolescent may be present as contingencies and reinforcers are developed, and the adolescent may be involved in the development of a behavioral contract with target behaviors and reinforcers (Clark, 1985). In addition to providing a therapeutic experience for the adolescent, involvement of the adolescent in decision making allows the therapist to model communication strategies. Communication and independence issues should be integrated into the therapy, using techniques such as reflective listening and family problem solving (Phelan, 1998; Robin, 1998).

In the case of the preschool child, PMT programs frequently include (in addition to the eight steps described earlier) a component of relationship building and nondirective play (Forehand & McMahon, 1981; Webster-Stratton, 1996). In nondirective play, the parent is taught to watch the child play as opposed to encouraging a certain type of play by the child. When the parent is engaged by the child, the parent behaves (within reason) in the manner suggested by the child. Parents are coached to reduce the frequency of competing verbal behavior (e.g., commands, questions, and criticisms) and to allow the child to lead the interaction. Parents are also encouraged to ignore minor inappropriate behaviors. Special time (Appendix C) is an example of a highly structured form of nondirective play.

Structured, manualized versions of PMT plans for CD/ODD have been developed by Barkley (1997), Bloomquist (1996), and Webster-Stratton (1981a, 1981b, 1982a, 1982b, 1996). Webster-Stratton's program uses videotape modeling methods for parents of preschool and early school-age children. The videotapes show parents and children of differing sexes, ages, cultures, socioeconomic backgrounds, and temperaments in an effort to promote positive modeling effects. Parent models in the tape provide examples of effective and ineffective parenting behaviors. Webster-Stratton's BASIC program includes a series of ten videotape programs of modeled parenting skills (250 vignettes of 1–2 minutes each, which are shown in 13–14 two-hour sessions), which focus on the skills of nondirective play, social rewards, setting limits, and discipline (command control, time-out, and ignoring; see also Appendix C for more information on these techniques). Based on the vignettes, the clinician leads a discussion of the interactions and encourages parents' ideas and problem solving, as well as role playing and rehearsal.

In addition to the BASIC program, Webster-Stratton has developed videotape programs to assist with parents' interpersonal skills (problem solving, anger management, communication, stress management, and social support), to train parents to improve the child's academic skills (homework, academic goals, setting limits about achievement, interaction with school and teachers), to train teachers to improve their management of students and parents, and to teach social skills to children. Each of these additional videotape treatment modules takes about 6–14 sessions to complete. As with the BASIC program, the additional modules consist of viewing the videotapes and engaging in group discussion of the content, modeling, and problem-solving process.

The effectiveness of the clinician-led group discussion of the BASIC modeling videotapes has been demonstrated in a series of studies (Webster-Stratton, 1984, 1991, 1996). More importantly, Webster-Stratton has shown that the BASIC program is as effective as individualized, intensive, one-to-one training with a therapist while requiring 80% less therapist time (Webster-Stratton, 1984). Although the combination of discussion sessions and videotapes has been the most effective treatment, the videotapes alone have also produced significant improvement.

Despite the impressive results of PMT outcome studies, a substantial proportion of families experience less favorable outcomes following PMT (Griest & Wells, 1983; Sanders & James, 1983). Limited initial and long-term improvement in families of children with severe CD is not uncommon, especially in severely disadvantaged or stressed families (Dumas & Wahler, 1983; Ferber, Keeley, & Shemberg, 1974; McMahon & Forehand, 1984). If the family is marked by socioeconomic disadvantage, if the mother is depressed, if the parents are socially isolated, or if there is marital conflict, PMT may have diminished effectiveness (Dumas & Wahler, 1983; Wahler, 1980; Webster-Stratton, 1985). The therapeutic success of parent training depends on the parent's ability and willingness to learn and implement the behavioral plan at home. Homes with stress, poverty, chaos, conflict, unmotivated parents, and social isolation are often poor sites for these plans. In these situations, additional intervention and/or a modification of PMT is warranted, typically with the introduction of family intervention components or, in severe cases, hospitalization or residential care. These treatments are reviewed later in this chapter.

Psychotherapy

Psychotherapeutic approaches to CD/ODD treatment have been dominated by the cognitive-behavioral model. This model targets the child's thoughts and behaviors relative to three primary, overlapping deficits found in children with CD/ODD: social relationships, problem solving, and anger management.

Social Relationships/Social Skills

Children with CD/ODD demonstrate social behavior deficits that can lead to negative interactions with others and alienation from societal rules (Webster-Stratton, 1991). Children with CD/ODD are not only aggressive within the family, but (compared to nonaggressive children) they are also less competent socially and more likely to be rejected by peers (Coie, 1990; Loeber & Dishion, 1983). There is some evidence of positive results from social skills training programs, but more efficacy research is needed (Kolko, Loar, & Sturnick, 1990).

Most socially oriented cognitive-behavioral approaches attempt to teach the child social behaviors based on a hypothesized social skills deficit. These programs coach children in play skills, friendship and conversational skills, academic skills, and behavior control strategies. A typical progression and content of a social skills training group may be as follows: reading social cues; starting and ending a conversation; giving and receiving compliments; expressing oneself nonverbally; asking questions to others; answering questions when asked; expressing emotions; entering a group or conversation; disagreeing with others; setting limits on others and resisting peer pressure; anticipating what others are thinking and feeling; developing empathy; and persuading others. Children learn in a group setting through modeling, giving support and suggestions, cooperating with other group members, and evaluating themselves and others. Therapeutic activities include cooperative projects, games, constructive activities with blocks and clay, and playing with toys. Successful skill performance is rewarded with praise or token reinforcers. In some cases, such interventions include a response-cost component, in which a child loses a previously gained reinforcer following performance of an undesired behavior. The addition of a response-cost component improves the effectiveness of a reinforcement program, but response cost alone tends to be ineffective (Bierman, Miller, & Staub, 1987). Social skills group interventions have been extensively described by LeCroy (1994) and Forman (1993).

In some cases, more specific, simple social skills are targeted for improvement. This approach may be necessary with children who have fundamental skills deficits or who are having difficulty learning more complicated social interaction skills. Specific social skills include eye contact, smiling, physical space, voice volume and inflection, content of conversation, compliments, acknowledgments, conversational openers, assertive requests, and ignoring. These simple skills are taught using an introductory explanation followed by videotaped modeling, role playing, repeated rehearsal of the skill, feedback, modification based on feedback, and/or anticipation of real-life situations in which the skill may be used. It is usually wise to include a reinforcement component in the skill-learning process in order to increase the child's motivation.

In addition to the more behaviorally oriented interventions described previously, some social skills interventions emphasize cognitive components. These interventions train children in the cognitive processes of problem solving, self-control, self-statements, empathy training, and perspective taking. Psychoeducational (including viewing of educational videotapes on social skills) and group discussion methods are commonly used to initially teach these techniques. Children then practice the skills with the therapist and other group members; games and stories can also be used to teach the cognitive skills. Finally, the children are given homework assignments to try the cognitive techniques in their everyday peer interactions. They report on their homework the next session, with feedback and reinforcement from the therapist and group (Webster-Stratton, 1991, 1996). Using a structured, videotape-based social skills training program, Webster-Stratton (1996) has shown that addition of these more advanced social skills training methods to conventional PMT results in more improvement in symptoms and, especially, in social interaction.

Problem Solving

Problem-solving interventions combine cognitive and behavioral techniques to teach problem-solving skills, such as generating alternative solutions, means-ends and consequential thinking, and taking the perspective of others (Kazdin, Esveldt-Dawson, French, & Unis, 1987a, 1987b; Kendall & Braswell, 1993). Typically, such interventions teach children to approach a problem using some variant of a six-step process (Kazdin et al., 1987a, 1987b; Kendall, 1992):

1. Define the problem.
2. Identify the goal.
3. Generate options.
4. Evaluate options.
5. Choose the best option.
6. Evaluate the outcome.

This process is applied primarily to social problems and is taught using a variety of techniques: didactic teaching, practice, modeling, role playing, feedback, social reinforcement, and therapeutic games. Response cost and token reinforcement are also frequent components of problem-solving interventions. Children are awarded tokens and praise for mastery of the goals of the treatment. Following successful learning of the problem-solving skill, children are given homework assignments to apply the skill in their daily lives. Reinforcement and response cost may again be used to encourage compliance with homework (Kazdin et al., 1987a, 1987b).

Kendall (1992) has developed a 20-session manualized treatment that teaches the problem-solving steps with a focus on slowing impulsive behavior. The child completes activities in a workbook during the therapy sessions, with homework included to promote practice and generalization to other settings. Kendall's (1992) "Stop and Think" program is easily modified to apply to CD/ODD behaviors. Kazdin (1996) also uses a 20-session program to teach problem-solving skills to children with CD/ODD. Both Kendall and Kazdin use games and problems to facilitate practice of the problem-solving techniques.

Problem-solving training produces more significant reductions in conduct symptoms and more significant improvements in prosocial behavior than either nondirective supportive therapy or no-treatment control (Kazdin, 1996). A combination of problem-solving training and PMT resulted in improvement at study completion and at 1-year follow-up. Behavioral improvement and reduced aggression following problem-solving training were obtained in hospitalized aggressive antisocial children, the majority of whom had a CD diagnosis. Improvements persisted at 1-month and 1-year follow-up (Kazdin et al., 1987a, 1987b). The combination of PMT and problem-solving training has been found to be more effective than either technique used in isolation (Kazdin, 1996), with about two-thirds of patients in the combined treatment group showing clinically significant improvement, compared to about one-third of patients in the PMT or problem-solving training groups only.

Anger Management

Anger management programs seek to reduce CD/ODD and anger-related behavior problems by directly addressing the emotional states that are associated with hostile attributions and aggressive behavior. These programs include cognitive and behavioral components that are taught to children in an 8–16 session group format Several anger management programs have shown promise in the treatment of children with CD/ODD. The typical components of an anger management program are as follows (Feindler, 1995; Feindler & Guttman, 1994; Forman, 1993; Goldstein, Glick, Reiner, Zimmerman, & Coultry, 1987; Lochman et al., 1991):

   1. *Psychoeducation and background.* Initial sessions focus on descriptions of the physiological, cognitive, and behavioral components of anger. Problems that anger has created for the children are raised for group discussion. The benefits of anger control are emphasized, and tangible reinforcers may be introduced. Games, rewards, and role playing are used to make the educational process fun and interesting to the children. Role models (e.g., sports stars, actors) are also sometimes introduced as examples of people who effectively control anger and are successful.
   2. *Goal setting.* Children set goals for control over their anger, for reduction of symptoms, or for attainment of rewards that are tied to anger management.
   3. *Arousal awareness.* Children are taught to recognize the physiological cues of arousal in themselves and others: sweating, clenched fists, muscle tension, heavy breathing, rapid heartbeat, and so on. Arousal is introduced as an early precursor to anger and other emotions, and children are told that if they can "catch" their anger early, it will be easier to stop an anger response.
   4. *Situational awareness.* Children next learn to identify situations and cues that lead to anger, behavioral responses, and the consequences of the behavior. Goldstein et al. (1987) and Feindler and Guttman (1994), for example, use an A-B-C model to illustrate this principle:

      a. Trigger (antecedent): What led up to it? What caused the problem? In what situation did the problem occur? Triggers may be either internal (self-statements, physiological states) or external (provocative situations or behaviors by others). Children practice identifying triggers throughout the anger management intervention.
      b. Response (behavior): How did the child react to the problem?
      c. Consequence: What were the results of the conflict situation and the child's behavior?

   5. *Cognitive awareness.* Cognitive awareness involves learning how the child's interpretation of events affects thought processes, which in turn affect emotions and behaviors. Anger is conceptualized as a result of these processes and not as an uncontrollable response to an unambiguous situation. Examples of hostile, neutral, and positive attributions are provided and discussed, with children predicting thoughts and outcomes that might follow from different attributions of the same situation. Children also learn to generate their own alternative beliefs and thoughts about ambiguous situations.

6. *Monitoring.* Children use monitoring in session and at home to track the cognitions, situations, and arousal states that are linked to anger. Rewards may be linked to completion of homework assignments to keep a log of these cognitions, situations, and arousal states. Later in treatment, monitoring is broadened to include the child's effortful responses to manage anger.

7. *Anger control strategies.* Once children learn the cognitive, physiological, and situational precursors of anger, they are taught a variety of techniques to diffuse these precursors. Different anger management programs introduce these anger control strategies at different times, but the most typical anger control strategies are the following:

a. Relaxation techniques: Deep breathing and visualization are taught as methods to promote physiological relaxation, which is incompatible with the arousal that accompanies anger.

b. Distraction techniques: Counting, visualization, focusing attention on other things, looking away, and seeking distracting stimuli (e.g., a friend, a book) are used to distract the child from a provoking situation and gain time to consider choices.

c. Self-talk. Children are taught positive self-statements to increase control in pressure situations (e.g., "slow down," "chill out," "stay calm"). Reminders are introduced to replace internal triggers.

d. Challenging beliefs. Children learn to identify beliefs that will lead to anger and to generate alternative beliefs that will not provoke an anger response. They then learn to challenge their angry beliefs with the alternative beliefs, slowing or stopping the cognitive process that leads to anger.

e. Reduction of provocative behavior. Children learn to identify behaviors that are likely to anger others. Alternative behaviors are identified.

f. Anticipation of consequences. Using the A-B-C method, children are encouraged to think of the consequences that may result from different choices of behavior. Identification of short- and long-term consequences is taught, with children focusing on external (loss of privileges), internal (loss of self-respect, disappointment), and social (alienation, rejection) consequences of aggression.

g. Assertion training. Assertion behaviors are taught as alternatives to aggressive behaviors. Assertion behaviors involve actions that express the child's opinion or that gain the child a desired outcome without provoking the other person. Feindler and Guttman (1994) cite techniques such as repeating requests, being empathic during assertions, and confusing the other person as examples of ways to be assertive or to diffuse anger situations.

8. *Self-evaluation.* Self-evaluation involves looking back on the anger-provoking situation and making an evaluation of one's behavior and the outcome. Alternative behaviors and alternative outcomes (both positive and negative) are considered, and a plan is formulated for the next time a similar situation is encountered. Children are also taught to make internal self-statements that are either congratulatory (e.g., "I really kept my cool"; for successful or desired behavior) or corrective (e.g., "I need to tune in to my cues"; for failure or undesired behavior).

9. *Problem-solving training.* Problem-solving training (described earlier) is often added to anger management, with a focus on solving problems in anger-arousing situations.

10. *Social skills training.* Some anger management programs include a component of social skills training such as that described earlier in this chapter. Some components of social skills training may be combined with assertion training as anger control strategies. Social skills training is particularly important when children are showing anger behaviors as a result of unsatisfying social interactions with peers.

11. *Review and integration of skills.* A final one to two sessions are typically spent reviewing anger management skills and anticipating future challenges. Methods to keep practicing and using skills are discussed with children (and sometimes parents). Follow-up or booster sessions may be scheduled.

Anger management skills are taught using a variety of techniques tailored to the developmental level of the child. Modeling, role playing, watching videotapes of oneself, watching videotapes of role models demonstrating anger control strategies, group discussion, competition games focused on practicing or learning skills, storytelling, drawing, rewards, keeping a diary at home, and completing homework assignments of practicing skills in the home environment are examples of techniques used to encourage children to learn, practice, and use their anger management skills. In some cases, parents may be involved to facilitate completion of homework assignments or to reward children for successful implementation of the skills at home and in the office.

Family Interventions

Family interventions are often needed to supplement PMT methods, especially for families who lack the cohesion, structure, resources, and/or adaptive interactions necessary to translate PMT techniques from the therapist's office to the home environment. Family interventions for CD/ODD range from traditional family therapy to innovative programs that involve intensive work with the family and home environment. Most family interventions include some component of PMT. There is some evidence that traditional family therapy alone is less effective than either PMT alone or PMT combined with family interventions (Estrada & Pinsof, 1995). Of the family intervention methods intended to supplement PMT, the most well known and researched are the ADVANCE parent intervention, parent-child interaction therapy (PCIT), functional family therapy (FFT), synthesis teaching (ST), and self-sufficiency training (SS).

PMT Adjunctive Family Treatments

The ADVANCE parent intervention consists of a videotape-discussion intervention developed by Webster-Stratton (1996) to supplement her BASIC program. ADVANCE focuses on the relationship and stress management skills necessary to maintain treatment progress and gains in high-risk families that have difficulty with traditional PMT alone. The ADVANCE videotapes and discussions emphasize methods of self-talk, anger management, communication skills, problem solving, and social support to improve the psychological wellness and social interactions of parents in a 14-session treatment plan. Preliminary outcome data have shown that use of the ADVANCE program results in improved communication and problem-solving skills in children and parents, as compared to parents who received only the BASIC component of PMT (Webster-Stratton, 1996).

Parent-child interaction therapy (PCIT; Eyberg, Boggs, & Algina, 1995; Schuhmann, Foote, Eyberg, Boggs, & Algina, 1998) combines the methods of PMT with in-session training in adaptive parent-child interaction. Parents learn to play in a warm and nondirective way with their child (similar to the technique described as "Special Time" in Appendix C), as well as how to manage child behavior effectively using the major tenets of PMT. In sessions, the parent and child play while the therapist observes and codes the interaction. The therapist then provides feedback to the parent, either through an ear speaker during the session or in a wrap-up time after the session. Supportive and behavioral characteristics of the interaction are targeted for improvement. Because of the focus on play interactions, PCIT is typically used with preschool children. Efficacy studies indicate positive results at treatment termination and four-month follow-up (Eyberg et al., 1995; Schuhmann et al., 1998).

Functional family therapy (FFT) combines the methods of PMT and structural family therapy to facilitate structure, rules, discipline, and communication in the family (Alexander & Parsons, 1982). Child behavior problems are addressed as symptoms of maladaptive interaction patterns in the family, with attention to the function that these symptoms serve in maintaining the family structure. To achieve change in the family, members are encouraged to understand the beliefs that underlie their behaviors toward other family members. Family members then learn to communicate clearly about their needs and about family problems. As family members respond appropriately to the needs/problems identified by other family members, they are rewarded with praise or tangible reinforcers. Adaptive change in beliefs, communication, and behavior are modeled, practiced, and encouraged in sessions. FFT treatment is superior to supportive treatment or to no treatment, although careful comparison of FFT and PMT has not occurred (Alexander & Parsons, 1982).

In ST (Wahler, Cartor, Fleischman, & Lambert, 1993), parents learn to discriminate between stressful stimuli emanating from the child care arena and other arenas. The procedure uses a conversational format in which clinician and parent discuss the parent's child care experiences and other experiences that affect child care. The purpose of this discussion is to accentuate the differences between child care and external (usually stressful) experiences, which influence the parent's emotional state. This discussion of differences in experiences enables the parent to approach the task of child care with greater objectivity, reducing the chances that parental stress will be displaced onto the child in the form of harsh or inconsistent discipline.

SS (Blechman, 1981, 1984) teaches parents to analyze their reactions to stressful events and to find practical solutions. A patterned problem-solving sequence is used to accomplish this goal. First, a particular life problem is targeted. Next, antecedents to the problem and consequences of the problem are identified through intensive discussion in therapy. As parents gain greater insight into the effects of stress on their behavior toward the child, they position themselves to anticipate and control their behavior in stressful situations. This enhanced control prevents the emergence of negative parent-child interaction patterns.

Studies of ADVANCE, PCIT, FFT, ST, and SS generally support their use as adjuncts to PMT. Marital therapy for parents appears to confer similar benefits but has not been as systematically studied. The effects of individual psychotherapy for parents of children with CD/ODD have not been studied extensively, but such treatment may also prove a useful adjunct to PMT (Estrada & Pinsof, 1995).

Integrative, Multisystemic Treatments

Henggeler and his colleagues have developed a family systems and ecological approach to intervention, called multisystemic therapy (MST; Henggeler & Borduin, 1990; Henggeler, Melton, & Smith, 1992; Henggeler et al., 1986; Henggeler, Schoenwald, & Pickrel, 1995). MST is an eclectic but systematic approach to intervening at the level of the individual, family, and broader systems. Family communication, structural components of the family system, the marital relationship of the child's caretakers, discipline within the family, family support, and parent-child interaction are common targets of family-level interventions in MST. Although the focus is on family-based interventions, MST also includes components of PMT and cognitive-behavioral interventions to assist the parents and child in improving child behavior. Interventions may also address other contexts of the child and family (school and neighborhood), often requiring home-based or school-based therapy and interventions. Hence, the family and child are viewed as being embedded in other contexts, which can have positive or negative influences on family environment and child behavior.

MST is one of the most well-documented and researched family interventions for severe CD/ODD. Although it draws on a number of possible interventions, it is a systematic approach that requires training in the principles and techniques of MST. Short-term and long-term outcome studies of children with serious criminal histories and CD/ODD have shown MST to be superior to incarceration, individual counseling, probation, and similar interventions for delinquent youth (Henggeler et al., 1986, 1992, 1995). Furthermore, although the intensity of MST intervention can be costly, studies of MST and similar family preservation programs have shown them to cost far less (as much as 2–8 times less) than residential treatment, incarceration, and hospitalization (Chamberlain & Rosicky, 1995), while producing better outcomes.

Medication

Abikoff and Klein (1992) conclude that there is uncertain benefit associated with stimulant treatment of CD/ODD. Some studies show significant improvement following stimulant treatment in institutionalized and outpatient antisocial adolescents (Eisenberg et al., 1963; Maletsky, 1974), whereas other research indicates no improvement (Conners, Kramer, Rothschild, Schwartz, & Stone, 1971). Stimulants may have the greatest effect on children with CD/ODD who have co-occurring attention problems, impulsivity, or hyperactivity, especially if these co-occurring symptoms are contributing to the oppositional, antisocial behavior. When stimulants are used, Ritalin (methylphenidate), Adderall (dextroamphetamine and amphetamine combination), and Dexedrine (dextroamphetamine) appear to be the most common choices; some authors have reported that Cylert (pemoline) may be effective for some children with comorbid ADHD-CD who do not respond to other psychostimulants (Shah, Seese, Abikoff, & Klein, 1994). Overall, however, stimulants are not a first-line medication treatment for CD/ODD. The benefit of stimulant medication for CD/ODD seems to be on an individual basis for children with comorbid ADHD.

Neuroleptics (such as risperidone [Risperdal], clozapine [Clozaril], haloperidol [Haldol], and thioridazine [Mellaril]) are sometimes used when agitation or excessively violent behavior is a primary feature of CD/ODD, but they also vary in effectiveness from individual to individual (Klein, Gittelman, Quitkin, & Rifkin, 1980). Furthermore, the side effects of neuroleptics, especially with long-term use, limit their utility with children. Hence, neuroleptics tend to be used only in cases of severe or dangerous behavior and/or associated neurological disorder.

Lithium has been used with some effectiveness in explosively aggressive children with CD/ODD and bipolar or depressive features (Campbell & Cueva, 1995). However, group research support for lithium treatment for CD/ODD in general is equivocal (Klein, Abikoff, Klass, & Shah, 1989). Antidepressants are occasionally used for CD/ODD with a strong affective component. Trazodone (Desyrel), for example, is sometimes used to control aggressive or destructive outbursts. Buspirone (Buspar) has been reported to be effective in a sample of children with comorbid ADHD and ODD (Gross, 1995). Anticonvulsant medications (particularly Tegretol [carbamazepine]) have also been used to control impulsive and aggressive outbursts in children with CD/ODD, but their effectiveness seems to be on a case-by-case basis (Campbell & Cueva, 1995).

Overall, there is no single, widely accepted pharmacological treatment for CD/ODD. Instead, multiple medications are used to treat severe or dangerous symptoms based on the individual presentation of the child. Medication is also often used when ADHD or Mood Disorders are comorbid with CD/ODD. Medication is rarely the sole treatment modality for the child with CD/ODD, unless the CD/ODD symptoms are felt to be exclusively the result of another disorder (e.g., Dysthymia or ADHD). In general, medication is used in conjunction with psychotherapy and behavior modification to treat the CD/ODD behaviors.

Inpatient Hospitalization

In some cases, the child's oppositional or antisocial behaviors are of sufficient severity or threat to warrant more intensive interventions. The most common of these interventions are hospitalization, partial hospitalization (day treatment), and residential placement. In the case of severe CD/ODD, the first decision for the clinician concerns the level of dangerousness presented by the child and/or situation. Children with co-occurring CD/ODD and depression, for example, should be evaluated for self-injurious or suicidal tendencies. Alternatively, some children with CD/ODD repeatedly place themselves in dangerous situations or engage in dangerous pursuits. In other cases, children with CD/ODD are a danger to others. Threats, revenge themes, or predatory behaviors may suggest behavior that will be dangerous to others. Finally, many children with CD/ODD are at risk because of their environment. Signs of physical, verbal, or sexual abuse in the home environment should receive immediate attention. The home environment may have a less overt but still negative effect by allowing CD/ODD behavior because of poor discipline. Peers and the neighborhood environment, especially in disadvantaged living situations, may present many opportunities and temptations to engage in antisocial behavior. If a child's behavior, safety, and psychological status are substantially deteriorating in the home environment, short-term inpatient or longer-term residential treatments should be considered. Three types of placements are commonly used for children with CD/ODD: inpatient hospitalization, day treatment, and residential placement.

Inpatient hospital settings provide an opportunity to remove children from the stresses and contingencies of their environment. Free of these factors, a new behavioral plan may be implemented in the relatively safe and controlled milieu of the hospital. Such a plan generally targets compliance, following rules, and prosocial behaviors. Rewards in the form of privileges, praise, and access to favored activity are used to reinforce positive change. Ideally, cognitive-behavioral techniques are taught in group or individual therapy, and family issues are addressed in family therapy. The inpatient hospital milieu tends to be a short-term (several days to several weeks) placement intended to break the negative cycle of behaviors at home, to protect the child from stress or danger, to give an initial exposure to cognitive-behavioral strategies, and to stabilize the child's behavior. The structured milieu of the inpatient unit alone may result in significant reductions in aggressive behavior in almost half of hospitalized children (Malone et al., 1997), although follow-up outpatient therapy and changes in the home environment are generally necessary for continued improvement and maintenance of gains.

Day-treatment programs provide an intensive (usually 5–8 hours per day, 3–5 days a week) outpatient experience and allow the child to spend nights and weekends at home. Like inpatient units, day treatment programs have special education, activities, individual therapy, group therapy, family therapy, and behavioral programs to encourage behavioral and psychological change. However, they cost far less than an inpatient stay and allow the child to maintain a daily connection with the family. Day treatment programs are effective in reducing CD behavior and improving social skills, self-perceptions, and family functioning, at both posttreatment and at 5-year follow-up (Grizenko, 1997; Grizenko, Papineau, & Sayegh, 1993). In some cases, children may participate in programs with many of the qualities of a day treatment program but with fewer, briefer meetings (2–4 days per week, 2–3 hours per day). These programs, often referred to as intensive outpatient programs, offer many of the advantages of day treatment with a less rigorous schedule for children who do not demand the intensity of a day treatment program. Children are most likely to benefit from a day treatment or intensive outpatient intervention if their initial problems are not excessively severe and if their parents are cooperative with the interventions (Grizenko, 1997). Day treatment may also be used immediately after discharge from an inpatient unit to help maintain the gains made during the acute hospitalization.

Residential placements are sometimes necessary for the most severe CD cases or for children with CD who are removed from abusive family environments. The Response Program (RP; Holland et al., 1993; Moretti, Holland, & Peterson, 1994), for example, is a time-limited residential program based on the belief that a bonding injury or attachment failure of some sort has occurred in children with CD. RP focuses on three goals: understanding the role of attachment and bonding insults in the development and maintenance of behavior problems, working to develop conditions within the child's environment that will lead to the development of attachment, and working to ensure the continuation of care for children regardless of the nature or persistence of their behavior problems. Two processes are central to the development of attachment based on the RP model: affiliation, the feeling of belonging and being connected with others; and mutuality, the understanding that the actions and feelings of one person affect others. Children are in residence at RP for four weeks at a time. Living arrangements, therapeutic experiences, and group activities are structured to achieve affiliation and mutuality in residents. Following treatment in RP, parents and children reported fewer symptoms of CD at 6-, 12-, and 18-month follow-up than at intake; parents reported fewer symptoms of oppositional and attention-deficit behaviors for that same time period (Moretti et al., 1994).

A second residential program is based on Aggressive Replacement Training (ART; Goldstein et al., 1987), which uses Goldstein et al.'s (1987) 10-step anger management technique. The ART program is based on the assumption that anger and aggression are last-resort methods of coping. ART groups consist of six to twelve boys (13–21 years of age) with CD/ODD. ART includes anger control training, "structured learning" (social skills intervention), and "moral education" (moral reasoning skills). Participants complete the program during an approximately 10-week residential stay. Outcome studies of ART suggest that it improves social skills and prosocial behavior while decreasing impulsivity and acting-out behaviors (Goldstein et al., 1987).

In addition to the two prototypical residential programs described previously, there are myriad residential programs and settings for delinquent children. These vary in quality from residential "warehouses," which do little more than provide lodging, to residential therapeutic settings, which include components of cognitive-behavioral interventions and behavior management programs. Although there is evidence that residential therapeutic programs such as ART and RP result in improvement in CD/ODD symptoms, residential settings without a clear intervention sequence may not have the same success.

An alternative out-of-home placement to residential programs is therapeutic foster care. The most well structured and well researched of the therapeutic foster care programs is the Treatment Foster Care (TFC) program (Chamberlain, 1996). This program places children with CD/ODD in trained foster families for about 6 months, with regular visits with the children's family of origin throughout the therapeutic foster treatment. Children are closely monitored by probation officers and case managers, who coordinate and support the foster placement and other therapy components of the treatment. Children also receive psychotherapy and psychiatric services, and family therapy is conducted with the family of origin. School consultations and interventions are also a part of the plan. Thus, a multisystemic plan is implemented, with temporary removal of the child from the home to facilitate change. Chamberlain (1996) provides additional detail about the specific components and treatment plan involved in the intervention. Compared to children receiving typical residential or hospital treatment intervention, children receiving TFC were less likely to be incarcerated (at 1-year follow-up), were more easily placed in the community, and showed a significant reduction in the number of behavior problems at home.

There has been considerable debate regarding the removal of children with CD/ODD from the home environment and treatment in inpatient or residential settings. Removal of children from their home environment may harm already fragile affiliations with others, including caregivers (Holland et al., 1993). In some cases (e.g., prison or some inpatient units), removal from the community is followed by placement in an environment in which the only attachments to be made are predominantly with an antisocial subculture. These attachments provide negative models and an "education" in antisocial behavior. An additional argument against intensive placements is based on economics: The cost of residential care and the large number of children with severe conduct problems make it impossible to provide residential treatment to all children in need. On the other hand, day treatment programs may be an alternative to higher-cost residential care. Grizenko et al. (1993) report that day treatment and residential treatment often have similar outcomes, although day treatment accomplishes its goals in a shorter time and with far less cost (approximately $9200 vs. $61,000 for residential).

Over all, then, inpatient/residential settings should be considered for children with CD/ODD in situations of danger or extreme deterioration in functioning. Because children with CD/ODD often are in situations of risk, the clinician should be aware of the potential need for an inpatient placement. However, such referrals should be made with prudence. Less restrictive day treatment programs may accomplish the same goals with less personal and financial cost, and intensive home-based programs may produce sufficient change with monitoring to ensure safety. Alternatives to hospitalization or residential treatment, of course, assume that the home environment is sufficiently safe for the child to remain in for at least part of the day.

Summary/Integration of Treatments

Treatment options for ODD and CD are listed in Table 3.5. Behavioral, cognitive-behavioral, and multisystemic treatments for CD/ODD have met with the greatest successes with

TABLE 3.5   Treatment Options for Oppositional-Defiant Disorder and Conduct Disorder

1. Behavioral Interventions
    a. Parent Management Training
        (1) Psychoeducation
        (2) Observation and goal monitoring
        (3) Reinforcement of prosocial behavior
        (4) Discipline and time-out for unacceptable behavior
        (5) Supervision-monitoring
        (6) Generalization to other environments
        (7) Communication strategies
    b. Modification for young school age and preschool children
        (1) Nondirective play
        (2) Simple, effective commands (command control)
    c. Videotape modeling (BASIC)
2. Psychotherapy
    a. Cognitive-behavioral interventions
        (1) Social skills training
        (2) Problem solving
        (3) Anger management
3. Family Interventions
    a. Videotape modeling (ADVANCE)
    b. Parent-child interaction therapy
    c. Functional family therapy
    d. Synthesis teaching—separation of child care stresses from other demands
    e. Self-sufficiency training—patterned problem solving applied to stressful situations
    f. Multisystemic therapy
4. Medication
    a. Psychostimulants (comorbid ADHD)
    b. Neuroleptics
    c. Antidepressants
5. Inpatient Hospitalization
    a. Traditional inpatient settings
    b. Day treatment/intensive outpatient
    c. Residential settings

Note: This outline of options summarizes major treatments covered in the text. Specific treatments are often combined into an intervention package. Refer to the text for additional descriptions of each treatment. This table is not necessarily an exhaustive list of all treatments available.

medication as a useful adjunct. Common factors across treatment modalities include close monitoring of the child by caretakers, modifying coercive family interactions, implementation of a family behavioral plan, changing the child's cognition system, teaching the child social problem-solving skills, providing positive models and removing negative peer models, reinforcement for attainment of therapy goals, and strengthening social relationships in general (Awad, 1985). The common problems in treatment appear to be resistance of the child to change, temptations and pressures in the neighborhood and peer groups, and difficulty for the family in following through on the therapy plan. Early intervention appears to produce greater results and prevents a downward spiral of deteriorating behavior; at older ages, CD/ODD is extremely difficult to change and requires extensive, persistent intervention. Selection of a treatment plan should be guided by the individual assessment, but it will probably include cognitive, behavioral, and, in the case of severe behavioral problems or co-occurring disorders, medication components.

■ References

Abikoff, H., Courtney, M., Pelham, W. E., & Koplewicz, H. S. (1993). Teachers' ratings of disruptive behaviors: The influence of halo effects. *Journal of Abnormal Child Psychology, 21,* 519–533.

Abikoff, H., & Klein, R. G. (1992). Attention-deficit hyperactivity and conduct disorder: Comorbidity and implications for treatment. *Journal of Consulting and Clinical Psychology, 60,* 881–892.

Achenbach, T. M. (1991). *Manual for the Child Behavior Checklist/4–18 and 1991 Profile.* Burlington, VT: University of Vermont Department of Psychiatry.

Alexander, J. F., & Parsons, B. V. (1982). *Functional family therapy.* Monterey, CA: Brooks/Cole.

American Psychiatric Association. (1994). *Diagnostic and statistical manual of mental disorders, fourth edition.* Washington, DC: Author.

Anderson, J. C., Williams, S., McGee, R., & Silva, P. A. (1987). DSM-III disorders in preadolescent children: Prevalence in a large sample from the general population. *Archives of General Psychiatry, 44,* 69–76.

Awad, G. (1985). Responsiveness in psychotherapy with antisocial adolescents. *American Journal of Psychotherapy, 39,* 490–497.

Barkley, R. A. (1997). *Defiant children: A clinician's manual for assessment and parent training* (2nd ed.). New York: Guilford.

Bean, A. W., & Roberts, M. W. (1981). The effect of time-out release contingencies on changes in child noncompliance. *Journal of Abnormal Child Psychology, 9,* 95–105.

Biederman, J., Faraone, S. V., Milberger, S., Jetton, J. G., Chen, L., Mick, E., Greene, R. W., & Russell, R. L. (1996). Is childhood Oppositional-Defiant Disorder a precursor to adolescent Conduct Disorder? Findings from a Four-Year Follow-Up Study of children with ADHD. *Journal of the American Academy of Child and Adolescent Psychiatry, 35,* 1193–1204.

Biederman, J., Munir, K., & Knee, D. (1987). Conduct and oppositional disorder in clinically referred children with attention deficit disorder: A controlled family study. *Journal of the American Academy of Child and Adolescent Psychiatry, 26,* 724–727.

Biederman, J., Newcorn, J., & Sprich, S. (1991). Comorbidity of attention deficit hyperactivity disorder with conduct, depressive, anxiety, and other disorders. *American Journal of Psychiatry, 148,* 564–577.

Bierman, K. L., Miller, C. L., & Staub, S. D. (1987). Improving the social behavior and peer acceptance of rejected boys: Effects of social skill training with instructions and prohibitions. *Journal of Consulting and Clinical Psychology, 55,* 194–200.

Bierman, K. L., & Wargo, J. B. (1995). Predicting the longitudinal course associated with aggressive-rejected, aggressive (nonrejected) and rejected (nonaggressive) status. *Development and Psychopathology, 7,* 669–682.

Billings, A. G., & Moos, R. H. (1983). Comparisons of children of depressed and nondepressed parents: A social-environment perspective. *Journal of Abnormal Child Psychology, 11,* 463–486.

Blechman, E. A. (1981). Toward comprehensive behavioral family interventions: An algorithm for matching families and interventions. *Behavior Modification, 5,* 221–235.

Blechman, E. A. (1984). Competent parents, competent children: Behavioral objectives of parent training. In R. F. Bangel & R. A. Polster (Eds.), *Parent training* (pp. 34–66). New York: Guilford.

Bloomquist, M. L. (1996). *Skills training for children with behavior disorders: A parent and therapist guidebook.* New York: Guilford.

Bowden, C. L., Deutsch, C. K., & Swanson, J. M. (1988). Plasma dopamine-beta-hydroxylase and platelet monoamine oxidase in attention deficit disorder and conduct disorder. *Journal of the American Academy of Child and Adolescent Psychiatry, 27,* 171–174.

Boyle, M. H., Offord, D. R., Racine, Y., Sanfors, M., Szatmari, P., & Fleming, J. E. (1993). Evaluation of the Original Ontario Child Health Study Scales. *Canadian Journal of Psychiatry, 38,* 397–405.

Brumfield, B. D., & Roberts, M. W. (1998). A comparison of two measurements of child compliance with normal preschool children. *Journal of Clinical Child Psychology, 27,* 109–116.

Buss, A. H., & Durkee, A. (1957). An inventory for assessing different kinds of hostility. *Journal of Consulting Psychology, 21,* 343–348.

Butcher, J. N., Williams, C. L., Graham, J. R., Archer, R. P., Tellegen, A., Ben-Porath, J. S., & Kaemmer, B. (1992). *MMPI-A: Manual for administration, scoring, and interpretation.* Minneapolis, MN: University of Minnesota.

Cadoret, R. J. (1978). Psychopathology in adopted-away offspring of biological parents with antisocial behavior. *Archives of General Psychiatry, 35,* 176–184.

Cadoret, R. J., & Cain, C. (1980). Sex differences in predictors of antisocial behavior in adoptees. *Archives of General Psychiatry, 37,* 1171–1175.

Campbell, M., & Cueva, J. E. (1995). Psychopharmacology in child and adolescent psychiatry: A review of the past seven years. Part II. *Journal of the American Academy of Child and Adolescent Psychiatry, 34,* 1262–1272.

Chamberlain, P. (1996). Intensified foster care: Multilevel treatment for adolescents with Conduct Disorders in out-of-home care. In E. D. Hibbs & P. S. Jensen (Eds.), *Psychosocial treatments for child and adolescent disorders: Empirically based strategies for clinical practice.* Washington, DC: American Psychological Association.

Chamberlain, P., & Reid, J. B. (1987). Parent observation and report of child symptoms. *Behavioral Assessment, 9,* 97–109.

Chamberlain, P., & Rosicky, J. G. (1995). The effectiveness of family therapy in the treatment of adolescents with conduct disorders and delinquency. *Journal of Marital and Family Therapy, 21,* 441–459.

Christian, R. E., Frick, P. J., Hill, N. L., Tyler, L., & Frazer, D. R. (1997). Psychopathy and conduct problems in children: II. Implications for subtyping children with conduct problems. *Journal of the American Academy of Child and Adolescent Psychiatry, 36,* 233–241.

Clark, L. (1985). *SOS: Help for parents.* Bowling Green, KY: Parents Press.

Coie, J. D. (1990). Adapting intervention to the problems of aggressive and disruptive rejected children. In S. R. Asher & J. D. Coie (Eds.), *Peer rejection in childhood* (pp. 309–337). Cambridge: Cambridge University Press.

Conners, C. K., Kramer, R., Rothschild, G. H., Schwartz, L., & Stone, A. (1971). Treatment of young delinquent boys with diphenylhydantoin sodium and methylphenidate. *Archives of General Psychiatry, 24,* 156–160.

Conolly, J., Burstein, S., Stevens, R., & White, D. (1987). *Interpersonal skill deficits of emotionally disturbed adolescents: Social problem solving, self-reports of social behavior, and self-esteem.* Unpublished manuscript.

Crittenden, P. M., & Ainsworth, M. D. S. (1989). Child maltreatment and attachment theory. In D. Cichetti & V. Carlson (Eds.), *Child maltreatment: Theory and research on the causes and consequences of child abuse and neglect* (pp. 494–528). Cambridge: Cambridge University Press.

Dishion, T. J., Loeber, R., Stouthamer-Loeber, M., & Patterson, G. R. (1984). Skill deficits and male adolescent delinquency. *Journal of Abnormal Child Psychology, 12,* 37–54.

Dishion, T. J., Patterson, G. R., Stoolmiller, M., & Skinner, M. L. (1991). Family, school, and behavioral antecedents to early adolescent involvement with antisocial peers. *Developmental Psychology, 27,* 172–180.

Dodge, K. A. (1985). Attributional bias in aggressive children. In P. C. Kendall (Ed.), *Advances in cognitive-behavioral research and therapy* (Vol. 4, pp. 73–110). Orlando, FL: Academic Press.

Dodge, K. A., & Newman, J. P. (1981). Biased decision making processes in aggressive boys. *Journal of Abnormal Psychology, 90,* 375–379.

Dumas, J. E., & Wahler, R. G. (1983). Predictors of treatment outcome in parent training: Mother insularity and socioeconomic disadvantage. *Behavioral Assessment, 5,* 301–313.

Eisenberg, L., Lachman, R., Molling, P. A., Lockner, A., Mizelle, J. D., & Conners, C. K. (1963). A psychopharmacological experiment in a training school for delinquent boys. *American Journal of Orthopsychiatry, 33,* 431–447.

Ernst, M., Godfrey, K. A., Silva, R. R., Pouget, E. R., & Welkowitz, J. (1994). A new pictorial instrument for child and adolescent psychiatry: A pilot study. *Psychiatry Research, 51,* 87–104.

Estrada, A. U., & Pinsof, W. M. (1995). The effectiveness of family therapies for selected behavioral disorders of childhood. *Journal of Marital and Family Therapy, 21,* 403–440.

Eyberg, S. M., Boggs, S. R., & Algina, J. (1995). Parent-child interaction therapy: A psychosocial model for the treatment of young children with conduct problem behavior and their families. *Psychopharmacology Bulletin, 31,* 83–91.

Eyberg, S. M., & Robinson, E. A. (1982). Parent-child interaction training: Effects on family functioning. *Journal of Clinical Child Psychology, 11,* 130–137.

Eyberg, S. M., & Robinson, E. A. (1983). Dyadic Parent-Child Interaction Coding System: A manual. *Journal of Clinical Child Psychology, 12,* 347–357.

Eyberg, S. M., & Ross, A. W. (1978). Assessment of child behavior problems: The validation of a new inventory. *Journal of Clinical Child Psychology, 7,* 113–116.

Feindler, E. L. (1995). Ideal treatment package for children and adolescents with anger disorders. *Issues in Comprehensive Pediatric Nursing, 18,* 233–260.

Feindler, E. L., Adler, N., Brooks, D., & Bhumitra, E. (1993). The development and validation of the Children's Anger Response Checklist: CARC. In L. VandeCreek (Ed.), *Innovations in clinical practice* (Vol. 12, pp. 337–362). Sarasota, FL: Professional Resources Press.

Feindler, E. L., & Guttman, J. (1994). Cognitive-behavioral anger control training. In C. W. LeCroy (Ed.), *Handbook of child and adolescent treatment manuals.* New York: Lexington.

Ferber, H., Keeley, S. M., & Shemberg, K. M. (1974). Training parents in behavior modification: Outcome and problems encountered in a program after Patterson's work. *Behavior Therapy, 5,* 415–419.

Fergusson, D. M., Lynskey, M. T., & Horwood, L. J. (1993). The effect of maternal depression on maternal ratings of child behavior. *Journal of Abnormal Child Psychology, 21,* 245–269.

Fergusson, D. M., Lynskey, M. T., & Horwood, L. J. (1996). Factors associated with continuity and changes in disruptive behavior patterns between childhood and adolescence. *Journal of Abnormal Child Psychology, 24,* 533–553.

Finch, A. J., Saylor, C., & Nelson, W. M. (1987). Assessment of anger in children. In R. J. Prinz (Ed.), *Advances in behavioral assessment of children and families* (Vol. 3, pp. 235–265). New York: JAI Press.

Fletcher, K. E., Fischer, M., Barkley, R. A., & Smallish, L. (1996). A sequential analysis of the mother-adolescent interactions of ADHD, ADHD/ODD, and normal teenagers during neutral and conflict discussions. *Journal of Abnormal Child Psychology, 24,* 271–297.

Forehand, R., & McMahon, R. J. (1981). *Helping the noncompliant child: A clinician's guide to parent training.* New York: Spectrum.

Forman, S. G. (1993). *Coping skills interventions for children and adolescents.* San Francisco: Jossey-Bass.

Frick, P. J., Lahey, B. B., Loeber, R., Stouthamer, M., Christ, M. A. G., & Hanson, K. (1992). Familial risk factors to oppositional defiant disorder and conduct disorder: Parental psychopathology and maternal parenting. *Journal of Consulting and Clinical Psychology, 60,* 49–55.

Gadow, K. D., & Sprafkin, J. (1997). *Child Symptom Inventory-4 norms manual.* Stony Brook, NY: Checkmate Plus, Ltd.

Goldstein, A. P., Glick, B., Reiner, S., Zimmerman, D., & Coultry, T. M. (1987). *Aggression Replacement Training: A comprehensive intervention for aggressive youth.* Champaign, IL: Research Press.

Griest, D., & Wells, K. C. (1983). Behavioral family therapy and conduct disorders in children. *Behavior Therapy, 14,* 37–53.

Griest, D., Wells, K. C., & Forehand, R. (1979). An examination of predictors of maternal perceptions of maladjustment in clinic-referred children. *Journal of Abnormal Psychology, 88,* 277–281.

Griest, D., Wells, K. C., & McMahon, R. J. (1980). An examination of differences between nonclinic and behavior problem clinic referred children and their mothers. *Journal of Abnormal Psychology, 89,* 497–500.

Grizenko, N. (1997). Outcome of multimodal day treatment for children with severe behavior problems: A five-year follow-up. *Journal of the American Academy of Child and Adolescent Psychiatry, 36,* 989–997.

Grizenko, N., Papineau, D., & Sayegh, L. (1993). A comparison of day treatment and outpatient treatment for children with disruptive behavior problems. *Canadian Journal of Psychiatry, 38,* 432–435.

Gross, M. D. (1995). Buspirone in ADHD with ODD. *Journal of the American Academy of Child and Adolescent Psychiatry, 34,* 1260.

Guerra, N., Huesmann, L. R., & Zelli, A. (1990). Attributions for social failure and aggression in incarcerated delinquent youth. *Journal of Abnormal Child Psychology, 18,* 347–355.

Hart, E. L., Lahey, B. B., Loeber, R., & Hanson, K. S. (1994). Criterion validity of informants in the diagnosis of Disruptive Behavior Disorders in children: A preliminary study. *Journal of Consulting and Clinical Psychology, 62,* 410–414.

Henggeler, S. W., & Borduin, C. M. (1990). *Family therapy and beyond: A multisystemic approach to treating the behavior problems of children and adolescents.* Pacific Grove, CA: Brooks/Cole.

Henggeler, S. W., Melton, G. B., & Smith, L. A. (1992). Family preservation using multisystemic therapy: An effective alternative to incarcerating serious juvenile offenders. *Journal of Consulting and Clinical Psychology, 60,* 953–961.

Henggeler, S. W., Rodick, J. D., Bordin, C. M., Hanson, C. L., Watson, S. M., & Urey, J. R. (1986). Multisystemic treatment of juvenile offenders: Effects on adolescent behavior and family interaction. *Developmental Psychology, 22,* 132–141.

Henggeler, S. W., Schoenwald, S. K., & Pickrel, S. A. G. (1995). Multisystemic therapy: Bridging the gap between university and community-based treatment. *Journal of Consulting and Clinical Psychology, 63,* 709–717.

Herkov, M. J., & Myers, W. C. (1996). MMPI profiles of depressed adolescents with and without conduct disorder. *Journal of Clinical Psychology, 52,* 705–710.

Holland, R., Moretti, M. M., Verlaan, V., & Peterson, S. (1993). Attachment and conduct disorder: The response program. *Canadian Journal of Psychiatry, 38,* 420–431.

Howe, G. W., Baden, A. D., Lewis, W. W., Ostroff, J., & Levine, B. (1989). *Parents' expectations of the efficacy of behavioral parenting techniques.* Unpublished manuscript available from George Howe, Center for Family Research, 613 Ross Hall, 2300 Eye St. N.W., Washington, DC 20037.

Jarey, M. L., & Stewart, M. A. (1985). Psychiatric disorder in the parents of adopted children with aggressive conduct disorder. *Neuropsychobiology, 13,* 7–11.

Jenkins, R. L., & Glickman, S. (1947). Patterns of personality organization among delinquents. *Nervous Children, 6,* 329–339.

Jenkins, R. L., & Hewitt, L. E. (1944). Types of personality structure encountered in child guidance clinics. *American Journal of Orthopsychiatry, 14,* 84–89.

Joffe, R. D., Dobson, K. S., Fine, S., Marriage, K., & Haley, G. (1990). Social problem-solving in depressed, conduct-disordered, and normal adolescents. *Journal of Abnormal Child Psychology, 18,* 565–575.

Kazdin, A. E. (1987). *Conduct disorders in childhood and adolescence.* Newbury Park, CA: Sage.

Kazdin, A. E. (1996). Problem solving and parent management in treating aggressive and antisocial behavior. In E. D. Hibbs & P. S. Jensen (Eds.), *Psychosocial treatments for child and adolescent disorders: Empirically based strategies for clinical practice.* Washington, DC: American Psychological Association.

Kazdin, A. E. (1997). Practitioner review: Psychosocial treatments for conduct disorder in children. *Journal of Child Psychology and Psychiatry and Allied Disciplines, 38,* 161–178.

Kazdin, A. E., Esveldt-Dawson, K., French, N. H., & Unis, A. S. (1987a). Effects of parent management training and problem-solving skills training combined in the treatment of antisocial child behavior. *Journal of the American Academy of Child and Adolescent Psychiatry, 26,* 416–424.

Kazdin, A. E., Esveldt-Dawson, K., French, N. H., & Unis, A. S. (1987b). Problem-solving skills training and relationship therapy in the treatment of antisocial child behavior. *Journal of Consulting and Clinical Psychology, 55,* 76–85.

Kendall, P. C. (1992). *Stop and think workbook* (2nd ed.). Available from the author.

Kendall, P. C., & Braswell, L. (1993). *Cognitive-behavioral therapy for impulsive children* (2nd ed.). New York: Guilford.

Kennedy, M., Felner, R., Cause, A., & Primavera, J. (1988). Social problem solving and adjustment in adolescence: The influence of moral reasoning level, scoring alternatives, and family climate. *Journal of Clinical Child Psychology, 17,* 73–83.

Klein, D. F., Gittelman, R., Quitkin, F., & Rifkin, A. (1980). *Diagnosis and drug treatment of psychiatric disorders: Adults and children.* Baltimore, MD: Williams & Wilkins.

Klein, R. G., Abikoff, H., Klass, E., & Shah, M. (1989). Preliminary findings from a controlled trial of lithium, placebo, and methylphenidate in children and adolescents with conduct disorders. Paper presented at the annual meeting of the New Clinical Drug Evaluation Unit, Key Biscayne, FL.

Kolko, D. J., Loar, L. L., & Sturnick, D. (1990). Inpatient social-cognitive skills training groups with conduct disordered and attention deficit disordered children. *Journal of Child Psychology and Psychiatry, 31,* 737–748.

Kovacs, M., & Pollock, M. (1995). Bipolar disorder and comorbid conduct disorder in childhood and adolescence. *Journal of the American Academy of Child and Adolescent Psychiatry, 34,* 715–723.

Kovacs, M., Paulaskas, S., Gatsonis, C., & Richards, C. (1988). A longitudinal study of comorbidity with and risk for conduct disorders. *Journal of Affective Disorders, 15,* 205–217.

Lahey, B. B., Loeber, R., Quay, H. C., Frick, P. J., & Grimm, J. (1992). Oppositional-defiant and conduct disorders: Issues to be resolved for DSM-IV. *Journal of the American Academy of Child and Adolescent Psychiatry, 31,* 539–545.

LeCroy, C. W. (1994). Social skills training. In C. W. LeCroy (Ed.), *Handbook of child and adolescent treatment manuals.* New York: Lexington.

Lochman, J. E., & Dodge, K. A. (1994). Social-cognitive processes of severely violent, moderately aggressive, and non-aggressive boys. *Journal of Consulting and Clinical Psychology, 62,* 366–374.

Lochman, J. E., White, K. J., & Wayland, K. W. (1991). Cognitive-behavioral assessment and treatment with aggressive children. In P. C. Kendall (Ed.), *Child and adolescent therapy: Cognitive-behavioral procedures* (pp. 25–65). New York: Guilford.

Loeber, R. (1982). The stability of antisocial and delinquent child behavior: A review. *Child Behavior, 53,* 1431–1446.

Loeber, R., & Dishion, T. J. (1983). Early predictors of male adolescent delinquency: A review. *Psychological Bulletin, 94,* 68–99.

Loeber, R., Green, S. M., Keenan, K., & Lahey, B. B. (1995). Which boys will fare worse? Early predictors of the onset of Conduct Disorder in a six-year longitudinal study. *Journal of the American Academy of Child and Adolescent Psychiatry, 34,* 499–509.

Loeber, R., Keenan, K., Lahey, B. B., Green, S. M., & Thomas, C. (1993). Evidence for developmentally based diagnoses of Oppositional Defiant Disorder and Conduct Disorder. *Journal of Abnormal Child Psychiatry, 21,* 377–410.

Loeber, R., Lahey, B. B., & Thomas, C. (1991). Diagnostic conundrum of oppositional-defiant disorder and conduct disorder. *Journal of Abnormal Psychology, 100,* 379–390.

Loeber, R., & Schmaling, K. B. (1985). Empirical evidence for overt and covert patterns of antisocial conduct problems: A meta-analysis. *Journal of Abnormal Child Psychology, 13,* 337–352.

Maletsky, B. M. (1974). D-amphetamine and delinquency: Hyperkinesis persisting? *Diseases of the Nervous System, 35,* 543–547.

Malone, R. P., Luebbert, J., Delaney, M. A., Biesecker, K. A., Blaney, B. L., Rowan, A. B., & Campbell, M. (1997). Nonpharmacological response in hospitalized children with conduct disorder. *Journal of the American Academy of Child and Adolescent Psychiatry, 36,* 242–247.

Malone, R. P., Luebbert, J., Pena-Ariet, M., Biesecker, K., & Delaney, M. A. (1994). The Overt Aggression Scale in a study of lithium in aggressive Conduct Disorder. *Psychopharmacology Bulletin, 30,* 215–218.

Matthys, W., Walterbos, W., Nijo, L., & van Engeland, H. (1989). Person perception in children with conduct disorders. *Journal of Child Psychology and Psychiatry, 30,* 439–448.

McMahon, R. J., & Forehand, R. (1984). Parent training for the noncompliant child: Treatment outcome, generalization, and adjunctive therapy procedures. In R. F. Dangel & R. A. Polster (Eds.), *Parent training: Foundations of research and practice* (pp. 298–328). New York: Guilford.

McMahon, R. J., & Forehand, R. (1988). Conduct disorders. In E. J. Mash & L. G. Terdal (Eds.), *Behavioral assessment of childhood disorders (second edition): Selected core problems* (pp. 105–153). New York: Guilford.

Mednick, S. A., & Christiansen, K. O. (1977). *Biosocial bases of criminal behavior.* New York: Gardner.

Mednick, S. A., & Hutchings, B. (1978). Genetic and psychophysiological factors in asocial behavior. In R. D. Hare and D. Schalling (Eds.), *Psychopathic behavior: Approaches to research.* Chichester, UK: Wiley.

McGee, R., Feehan, M., Williams, S., & Anderson, J. (1992). DSM-III disorders from age 11 to age 15 years. *Journal of the American Academy of Child and Adolescent Psychiatry, 31,* 50–59.

Milich, R., & Dodge, K. A. (1984). Social information processing in child psychiatric populations. *Journal of Abnormal Child Psychology, 12,* 471–490.

Miller, L. S., Klein, R. G., Piacentini, J., Abikoff, H., Shah, M. R., Samilov, A., & Guardino, M. (1995). The New York Teacher Rating Scale for disruptive and anti-social behavior. *Journal of the American Academy of Child and Adolescent Psychiatry, 34,* 359–370.

Moffitt, T. E. (1990). Juvenile delinquency and attention deficit disorder: Boys' developmental trajectories from age 3 to age 15. *Child Development, 61,* 893–910.

Moffitt, T. E., & Henry, B. (1989). Neurological assessment of executive functions in self-reported delinquents. *Development and Psychopathology, 1,* 105–118.

Moretti, M. M., Holland, R., & Peterson, S. (1994). Long term outcome of an attachment-based program for Conduct Disorder. *Canadian Journal of Psychiatry, 39,* 360–370.

Myers, M. G., Brown, S. A., & Mott, M. A. (1995). Pre-adolescent conduct disorder behaviors predict relapse and progression of addiction for adolescent alcohol and drug abusers. *Alcoholism Clinical and Experimental Research, 19,* 1528–1536.

Myers, W. C., Burket, R. C., & Otto, T. A. (1993). Conduct disorder and personality disorders in hospitalized adolescents. *Journal of Clinical Psychiatry, 54,* 21–26.

Novaco, R. (1975). *Anger control: The development and evaluation of an experimental treatment.* Lexington, MA: Lexington Books.

Ostrov, E., Marohn, R. C., Offer, D., Curtiss, G., & Feczko, M. (1980). The adolescent antisocial behavior checklist. *Journal of Clinical Psychology, 36,* 594–601.

Patterson, G. R. (1982). *Coercive family process.* Eugene, OR: Castalia.

Patterson, G. R., & Bank, L. (1986). Bootstrapping your way in the nomological thicket. *Behavioral Assessment, 8,* 49–73.

Patterson, G. R., Chamberlain, P., & Reid, J. B. (1982). A comparative evaluation of a parent-training program. *Behavior Therapy, 13,* 638–650.

Patterson, G. R., Ray, R. S., Shaw, D. A., & Cobb, J. A. (1969). *Manual for coding of family interactions.* New York: Microfiche Publications.

Patterson, G., Reid, J., Jones, R., & Conger, R. (1975). *A social learning approach to family intervention. Vol. 1: Families with aggressive children.* Eugene, OR: Castalia.

Phelan, T. W. (1995). *1-2-3 magic.* Glen Ellyn, IL: Child Management, Inc.

Phelan, T. W. (1998). *Surviving your adolescents.* Glen Ellyn, IL: Child Management, Inc.

Platt, N.J., & Spivak, G. (1975). *Manual for the Means End Problem Solving Procedure (MEPS): A measure of interpersonal cognitive problem solving skill.* Unpublished manuscript.

Puig-Antich, J. (1982). Major depression and conduct disorder in prepuberty. *Journal of the American Academy of Child Psychiatry, 21,* 118–128.

Quay, H. C. (1986). Classification. In H. C. Quay (Ed.), *Handbook of juvenile delinquency* (pp. 188–238). New York: Wiley.

Quinton, D., Rutter, M., & Gulliver, L. (1990). Continuities in psychiatric disorders from childhood to adulthood in the children of psychiatric patients. In L. N. Robins & M. Rutter (Eds.), *Straight and devious pathways from childhood to adulthood.* Cambridge: Cambridge University Press.

Reebye, P., Moretti, M. M., & Lessard, J. C. (1995). Conduct disorder and substance use disorder: Comorbidity in a clinical sample of preadolescents and adolescents. *Canadian Journal of Psychiatry, 40,* 313–319.

Reeves, J. C., Werry, J. S., Elkind, G. S., & Zametkin, A. (1987). Attention deficit, conduct, oppositional, and anxiety disorders in children: II. Clinical characteristics. *Journal of the American Academy of Child and Adolescent Psychiatry, 26,* 144–155.

Renouf, A. G., Kovacs, M., & Mukerji, P. (1997). Relationship of depressive, conduct, and comorbid disorders and social functioning in childhood. *Journal of the American Academy of Child and Adolescent Psychiatry, 36,* 998–1004.

Rey, J. M., Bashir, M. R., Schwartz, M., Richards, I. N., Plapp, J. M., & Stewart, G. W. (1988). Oppositional disorder: Fact or fiction? *Journal of the American Academy of Child and Adolescent Psychiatry, 27,* 157–162.

Reynolds, C. R., & Kamphaus, R. W. (1992). *Behavior Assessment System for Children manual.* Circle Pines, MN: American Guidance Service.

Roberts, M. W., & Powers, S. W. (1988). The compliance test. *Behavioral Assessment, 10,* 375–398.

Robin, A. L. (1998). *ADHD in adolescents.* New York: Guilford.

Robins, L. N. (1966). *Deviant children grow up: A sociological and psychiatric study of sociopathic personality.* Baltimore: Williams & Wilkins.

Robins, L. N., West, P. A., & Herjanic, B. (1975). Arrests and delinquency in two generations: A study of two black urban families and their children. *Journal of Child Psychology and Psychiatry, 16,* 125–140.

Robinson, E. A., & Eyberg, S. M. (1981). The Dyadic Parent-Child Interaction Coding System: Standardization and validation. *Journal of Consulting and Clinical Psychology, 49,* 245–250.

Rogeness, G. A., Hernandez, J. M., Macedo, C. A., & Mitchell, E. L. (1983). Biochemical differences in children with conduct disorder socialized and undersocialized. *American Journal of Psychiatry, 139,* 307–311.

Rutter, M. (1985). Family and school influence on behavioral development. *Journal of Child Psychiatry, 26,* 349–368.

Rutter, M., Tizard, J., & Whitmore, K. (1970). *Education, health, and behavior.* London: Longman.

Safer, D. J. (1984). Subgrouping conduct disordered adolescents by early risk factors. *American Journal of Orthopsychiatry, 54,* 603–612.

Sanders, M. R., & James, J. E. (1983). The modification of parent behavior: A review of generalization and maintenance. *Journal of Applied Behavior Analysis, 14,* 223–237.

Schneider, S. M., Atkinson, D. R., & El-Mallakh, R. S. (1996). CD and ADHD in bipolar disorder. *Journal of the American Academy of Child and Adolescent Psychiatry, 35,* 1422–1423.

Schuhmann, E. M., Foote, R. C., Eyberg, S. M., Boggs, S. R., & Algina, J. (1998). Efficacy of parent-child interaction therapy: Interim report of a randomized trial with short-term maintenance. *Journal of Clinical Child Psychology, 27,* 34–45.

Shah, M. R., Seese, L. M., Abikoff, H., & Klein, R. G. (1994). Pemoline for children and adolescents with conduct disorder: A pilot investigation. *Journal of Child and Adolescent Psychopharmacology, 4,* 255–261.

Shamsie, J., & Hluchy, C. (1991). Youth with conduct disorder: A challenge to be met. *Canadian Journal of Psychiatry, 36,* 405–414.

Snyder, J., Schrepferman, L., & St. Peter, C. (1997). Origins of antisocial behavior: Negative reinforcement and affect dysregulation of behavior as socialization mechanisms in family interaction. *Behavior Modification, 21,* 187–215.

Speltz, M. L., DeKlyen, M., Greenberg, M. T., & Dryden, M. (1995). Clinic referral for Oppositional Defiant Disorder: Relative significance of attachment and behavioral variables. *Journal of Abnormal Child Psychology, 23,* 487–507.

Spielberger, C. D. (1988). *Manual for the State-Trait Anger Expression Inventory (STAXI).* Odessa, FL: Psychological Assessment Resources.

Sturge, C. (1982). Reading retardation and antisocial behavior. *Journal of Child Psychology and Psychiatry, 23,* 21–31.

Valla, J. P., Bergeron, L., Berube, H., Gaudet, N., & St-Georges, M. (1994). A structured pictorial questionnaire to assess DSM-III-R-based diagnoses in children (6–11 years): Development, validity, and reliability. *Journal of Abnormal Child Psychology, 22,* 403–423.

Wadsworth, M. E. J. (1976). Delinquency, pulse rates, and early emotional deprivation. *British Journal of Criminology, 16,* 245–256.

Wahler, R. G. (1980). The insular mother: Her problems in parent-child treatment. *Journal of Applied Behavioral Analysis, 13,* 207–219.

Wahler, R. G., Cartor, P. G., Fleischman, J., & Lambert, W. (1993). The impact of synthesis teaching and parent training with mothers of conduct-disordered children. *Journal of Abnormal Child Psychology, 21,* 425–440.

Wahler, R. G., House, A. E., & Stambaugh, E. E. (1976). *Ecological assessment of child problem behavior: A clinical package for home, school, and institutional settings.* New York: Pergamon.

Warr-Leeper, G., Wright, N. A., & Mack, A. (1994). Language disabilities of antisocial boys in residential treatment. *Behavior Disorders, 19,* 159–169.

Webster-Stratton, C. (1981a). Modification of mothers' behaviors and attitudes through videotape modeling group discussion. *Behavior Therapy, 12,* 634–642.

Webster-Stratton, C. (1981b). Videotape modeling: A method of parent education. *Journal of Clinical Child Psychology, 10,* 93–98.

Webster-Stratton, C. (1982a). The long-term effect of a videotape modeling parent education program: Comparison of immediate and one year follow-up results. *Behavior Therapy, 13,* 702–714.

Webster-Stratton, C. (1982b). Teaching mothers through videotape modeling to change their children's behavior. *Journal of Pediatric Psychology, 7,* 279–294.

Webster-Stratton, C. (1984). Randomized trial of two parent-training programs for families with conduct-disordered children. *Journal of Consulting and Clinical Psychology, 52,* 666–678.

Webster-Stratton, C. (1985). Predictors of treatment outcome in parent training for conduct disordered children. *Behavior Therapy, 16,* 223–243.

Webster-Stratton, C. (1991). Strategies for helping families with conduct disordered children. *Journal of Child Psychology and Psychiatry, 31,* 737–748.

Webster-Stratton, C. (1996). Early intervention with videotape modeling: Programs for families of children with Oppositional-Defiant Disorder or Conduct Disorder. In E. D. Hibbs & P. S. Jensen (Eds.), *Psychosocial treatments for child and adolescent disorders: Empiri-*

cally based strategies for clinical practice. Washington, DC: American Psychological Association.

West, O. J., & Farrington, D. P. (1977). *The delinquent way of life.* London: Heinemann.

Wilson, H. (1980). Parental supervision: A neglected aspect of delinquency. *British Journal of Criminology, 20,* 203–235.

Yudofsky, S. C., Silver, J. M., Jackson, W., Endicott, J., & Williams, D. (1986). The Overt Aggression Scale for the objective rating of verbal and physical aggression. *American Journal of Psychiatry, 143,* 35–39.

CHAPTER 4

Elimination Disorders

Two elimination disorders are identified in DSM-IV: *Enuresis* is the inappropriate, usually involuntary discharge of urine after an age at which bladder control is expected. *Encopresis* is the discharge of feces into inappropriate places. Although these two disorders occasionally co-occur, they are different in presentation, etiology, and treatment, sharing few underlying characteristics. They do, however, share the common feature of being behavior patterns that are appropriate and expected at one age (infancy) and unusual, shameful, and deviant at another age. Hence, much of the informal, "parental" definition of these disorders hinges on the age at which a particular family believes that their child should be toilet trained. Parents who hold the unspoken opinion that toilet training must be achieved at a very young age may believe that their child has an elimination disorder when this is not the case; parents who err in the other direction may ignore or even foster an elimination disorder in their child.

■ Enuresis

☐ CLINICAL DESCRIPTION

Diagnostic Considerations

Functional enuresis (hereafter simply referred to as *enuresis*) is defined in DSM-IV as the inappropriate discharge of urine after an age at which bladder control is expected. In order to meet diagnostic criteria, a child must have at least two enuretic events a week for 3 consecutive months, or the enuresis must have a significant effect on the child's functioning. Enuresis cannot be diagnosed in children below age 5. If a child is developmentally delayed, the clinician should use the child's mental or developmental age instead of chronological age. Because physical disorders must be ruled out before a diagnosis of enuresis is made, examination by a physician is advised for any child presenting for enuresis.

Two overlapping groupings for enuresis exist: Primary-Secondary and Nocturnal-Diurnal. The term *primary enuresis* is used to denote a child with enuresis who has never had bladder control. "Having bladder control" is defined in various time frames ranging from 2 weeks to 6 months (Fritz & Armbrust, 1982; Scharf, Pravada, Jennings, Kauffman, & Ringel, 1987). *Secondary enuresis*, on the other hand, describes a child who had bladder control at one time before regressing to enuretic behavior. It is extremely rare for a child to have no accidents immediately following (or during) successful toilet training; secondary enuresis is diagnosed only when these accidents reach sufficient frequency to be diagnosed as enuresis.

As many as 80–90% of enuretic children are of the primary type (Houts, Berman, & Abramson, 1994; Scharf et al., 1987). A significant risk exists that primary enuresis may be the result of genetic, physiological, or developmental factors (Scharf et al., 1987). Hence, consultation with a pediatrician is extremely important in the case of a child with primary enuresis. Because the child with secondary enuresis had bladder control at one time, genetic-maturational causes are less likely. For these children, acute illness (or similar change in physiological status) and psychological-behavioral factors are considered as the strongest potential causes (Scharf & Jennings, 1988).

The nocturnal-diurnal distinction is based on whether wetting occurs during the day (diurnal enuresis) or at night (nocturnal enuresis); this distinction is coded in the DSM-IV diagnosis as Nocturnal Only, Diurnal Only, or Nocturnal *and* Diurnal. Nocturnal enuresis is much more common than diurnal enuresis (hence, the colloquial description of enuresis as "bedwetting"), and most enuresis treatment and research are directed at nocturnal enuresis. Diurnal enuresis is often regarded by parents as more intentional than nocturnal enuresis, and it is true that many cases of diurnal enuresis involve power struggles between the parents and child. However, diurnal enuresis can also be caused by factors such as failure of the child to recognize the need to urinate or poor sphincter control.

Studies of the prevalence of enuresis (reviewed by Fritz & Armbrust, 1982) indicate that 12–25% of 4-year-olds, 10–13% of 6-year-olds, 7–10% of 8-year-olds, 3–5% of 10-year-olds, and 1–3% of 12-year-olds and older are enuretic. Comparable but slightly lower prevalence rates are reported in other sources, with estimates of 7% for 5-year-old males and 3% for 5-year-old females; prevalence decreases to 2–3% at age 10 (American Psychiatric Association, 1994). The disorder is more common in boys, with estimates of the sex ratio ranging from 1.5:1 to 3:1 (Fritz & Armbrust, 1982; Scharf et al., 1987) (Table 4.1).

Appearance and Features

The appearance and features of a child with enuresis depend (see Table 4.2) on whether the enuresis is primary or secondary and whether it is diurnal or nocturnal. The most common enuresis presentation in the office of a mental health professional is a boy age 4–8 years with primary nocturnal enuresis. Ideally, the child will have had a full medical workup and physiological causes will be ruled out. Often, enuresis has created exasperation in the parents, who have tried interventions ranging from reward to punishment. The child usually sleeps through the bedwetting incident, only to find himself in a wet bed in the morning or some time after the enuretic incident is over. Because the wet bed must be changed, bedwetting is often an unpleasant occurrence in family life. The child's room (and the child) may smell, constantly reminding the parent and child of the problem. Parental upset and resentment of the child may be noticed by the child, and siblings may tease the child. In

TABLE 4.1   Epidemiology and Course of Enuresis

Prevalence: 3–13% of 5–6-year-olds

2–5% of 10-year-olds

Sex Ratio (Male:Female):   1.5:1 to 3:1

Typical Onset Age: 5–6 years

Course: Symptoms remit spontaneously or with casual treatment in some children but are persistent in other children. No typical long-term outcome pattern, but self-esteem problems are a risk if other children are aware of symptoms.

Common Comorbid Conditions: 1. Developmental Delays

Relevant Subtypes: 1. Primary vs. Secondary
                                                      2. Nocturnal vs. Diurnal

TABLE 4.2   Appearance and Features of Enuresis

COMMON FEATURES

1. Urinating into bed or clothes
2. Age 5 to 8 years
3. Child sleeps through bedwetting incident

OCCASIONAL FEATURES

1. Parental upset and/or resentment
2. Peer or sibling rejection

Note: The features listed in the table are often seen but are not universal. Some features may be diagnostically relevant or required, whereas others may not be required for diagnosis. "Common" features are typical of the disorder; "occasional" features appear frequently but are not necessarily seen in a majority of cases.

other cases, the parents give the child attention and nurturance after a bedwetting incident because they feel sorry for the child and do not want to shame him or her.

Diurnal enuresis typically has a different presentation. The child may inappropriately urinate only at certain times or in certain places while behaving appropriately at other times (e.g., at school). The reasons for the urination may be multiple. Common reasons are anger at parent, secondary gain for enuresis, and/or refusal to leave a fun activity to go to the bathroom until it is too late. Parents are often less forgiving about diurnal enuretic events than they are about nocturnal events, because they tend to perceive diurnal events as intentional. If the enuretic events occur in the presence of peers (or if the child does not change clothes before seeing peers), the child's odor may be a source of ridicule and isolation. Hence, the enuresis has significant social implications.

Etiology

Several potential etiological factors have been suggested for enuresis: medical problems, sleep disorder, bladder capacity, genetics, and psychological factors (Scharf et al., 1987).

Fritz and Armbrust (1982), for example, cite research indicating that 2–4% of enuresis cases result from urologic problems; urinary tract infections frequently account for secondary enuresis in girls. Other potential organic contributors to enuresis are diabetes, sickle cell disease, and spina bifida (Fritz & Armbrust, 1982).

At one time, nocturnal enuresis was thought to be the result of sleep disorders such as deep sleep, narcolepsy, and sleep apnea, but little evidence exists to support this view for the majority of children. In fact, enuresis occurs during any sleep stage and is unrelated to factors such as depth of sleep and dreams (Fritz & Armbrust, 1982; Scharf et al., 1987). Another etiological hypothesis for enuresis is that children with enuresis have a smaller bladder capacity than normal children. This hypothesis suggests that children with enuresis can hold less urine volume in the bladder before feeling the need to urinate (Scharf et al., 1987). Evidence for this etiological hypothesis is indirect and sketchy, although treatment programs have been designed to help children with enuresis by increasing functional bladder capacity (Geffken, Johnson, & Walker, 1986).

Genetic causes for enuresis are advocated by some authors (Fritz & Armbrust, 1982) and downplayed by others (Kanner, 1972). Enuresis does run in families, with as many as 70–85% of children with enuresis having a family member who is enuretic (Fritz & Armbrust, 1982; Scharf & Jennings, 1988; Shaffer, Gardner, & Hedge, 1984). The risk appears to increase with increasing genetic similarity. However, the extent to which this familial concordance is due to genetic factors or environmental factors is unclear. Enuretic families sometimes appear to regard the enuresis as normal, a type of "family tradition," which may encourage enuretic behavior in children (Kanner, 1972). The most reasonable conclusion at this point appears to be that genetic factors may contribute to some cases of enuresis, but they are neither necessary nor sufficient and must be activated by other etiological factors such as psychosocial factors. Unfortunately, the communication to parents that enuresis is genetic sometimes results in the mistaken belief that nothing can be done to treat the enuresis or that the only effective treatments will be medical. No evidence exists to support this belief.

Psychological factors are frequently cited as etiologically responsible for enuresis. Hypothesized factors range from permissive or restrictive toilet-training experience to emotional problems to faulty learning. Some cases of secondary enuresis may develop as a regressive response to stress; as many as four in five cases of secondary enuresis have encountered a significant stressor in the month prior to the development of the problem (Fritz & Anders, 1979). Evidence also exists supporting the notion that enuresis may arise because of faulty learning, particularly as a result of the failure to associate a full bladder with waking up at night. Many treatment modalities are based on this assumption (Mowrer & Mowrer, 1938). Psychodynamic factors such as toilet training history and emotional disturbance may be important in individual cases, but no research exists supporting these hypothesized factors for a majority of cases. Finally, family factors such as enmeshment or adoption of an infantile role by the child may account for the development of enuresis in some cases.

☐ ASSESSMENT PATTERNS

Prior to psychological assessment of a child with enuresis, physical causes of and/or contributions to the enuresis should be carefully evaluated. Among the relevant physical components to assess are functional bladder capacity (problems are usually indicated by frequent voiding of small amounts of urine), sleep disturbance, weakness of sphincter muscles, urinary tract infection, renal disorders, metabolic disorders, and neurological disorders. If these components have not been evaluated by a physician, referral for physical exam and urinalysis is important. Interview questions about schedule and type of urination, family history of enuresis, sleep problems, toilet training history, and family attitude about the enuresis can also provide information about possible physical influences (Rushton, 1993).

Broad Assessment Strategies

Cognitive Assessment

Clinician-Administered. WISC-III IQ scores of children with enuresis appear to be in normal ranges, with no consistent pattern of strengths and weaknesses (Shaffer et al., 1984; Steinhausen & Gobel, 1989). The finding of average intelligence levels in children with enuresis is at odds with the view that they may be developmentally delayed and suggests that their intellectual ability varies much like that of other children. Some children with primary enuresis, however, may have lower IQ scores and more developmental delays than children with secondary enuresis (Shaffer et al., 1984).

Achievement test scores of children with enuresis also appear to be average to slightly below average (Shaffer et al., 1984). Children with enuresis qualify for learning disability diagnoses at a lower rate than children with other psychiatric problems (Steinhausen & Gobel, 1989). Again, however, children with primary enuresis may be more at risk for a developmental disability diagnosis than children with secondary enuresis. Overall, current research suggests that children with enuresis show much the same performance and variability on intelligence and achievement tests as other children.

Psychological Assessment

Child-Report. Because of the young age of many children with enuresis, few self-report psychological tests apply to this group. Results of two studies using the Piers-Harris Children's Self Concept Scale (PHSCS) suggest that the broad self-reported self-concept of children with enuresis is in the normal range (total raw score 59–60; Wagner & Geffken, 1986; Wagner & Johnson, 1988). However, this result may reflect social desirability and denial as much as positive self-concept.

Behavioral Assessment

Parent-Report. Parent-report behavioral checklists are important components of the assessment of children with enuresis in order to rule out co-occurring or contributing psychological problems (Table 4.3). Studies report that as few as 15% or as many as 50% of children with enuresis may have accompanying emotional or behavior problems, although the emerging consensus is that children with enuresis, as a group, show no more significant behavioral problems than do children without enuresis (Shaffer et al., 1984; Steinhausen & Gobel, 1989; Warzak, 1993). The CBCL and BASC may be used to investigate the presence of other or associated behavior problems.

The ECI-4, CSI-4, and ASI-4 each include 2–3 items that measure diurnal and nocturnal encopresis. These are screening items, with no specifics about frequency or associated

TABLE 4.3   Sample Assessment Battery for Enuresis and Encopresis

BEHAVIORAL

1. Behavior Assessment System for Children (Parent and Teacher)

SYNDROME-SPECIFIC

1. Child Attitude Scale for Nocturnal Enuresis

Note: Assessment instruments are intended to supplement (not substitute for) a good clinical interview and, when possible, a structured diagnostic interview.

medical problems. Nevertheless, they can be helpful for warning clinicians about the possible presence of enuresis.

Syndrome-Specific Tests

Child-Report

The *Child Attitude Scale for Nocturnal Enuresis* (CASNE; Wagner & Geffken, 1986), consists of twenty-five yes-no items tapping four areas: knowledge of enuresis, feelings regarding enuresis, current child behaviors, and reactions of significant others. On the CASNE, most children with enuresis (65%) report unhappiness about their wetting behavior. In one study, all children reported the desire to overcome enuresis (Wagner & Geffken, 1986). Hence, although general self-concept (assessed by the PHSCS) appears to be positive, children with enuresis express some focal distress about their problem. The CASNE is also a useful measure of the child's perceptions of the environmental-parental response to their problem.

Parent-Report

A specific parent-report scale that can be useful in the assessment of enuresis is the twenty-item, yes-no *Tolerance Scale* (Butler, Brewin, & Forsythe, 1990; Morgan & Young, 1975), which measures parental attitudes toward and tolerance of enuresis. More intolerance has been found to be related to premature withdrawal from enuresis treatment (Morgan & Young, 1975). Because the scoring and psychometrics of the Tolerance Scale are not clearly explained in Morgan and Young's (1975) article, those interested in using this scale should also consult Butler et al. (1990) for more information.

☐   ## TREATMENT OPTIONS

Behavioral Interventions

Unidimensional Behavioral Interventions

Although numerous treatments for enuresis have been suggested, the treatment programs of choice for nocturnal enuresis rely on behavioral principles (Table 4.4). Ten unidimensional

TABLE 4.4   Treatment Options for Nocturnal Enuresis

1. Behavioral Interventions

   a. Unidimensional Behavioral Interventions
   - (1) Urine alarm (UA)
   - (2) Cleanliness training (CT)
   - (3) Positive practice (PP)
   - (4) Reinforcement for dryness (RD)
   - (5) Retention control training (RCT)
   - (6) Avoidance contingency (AC)
   - (7) Overlearning (OL)
   - (8) Waking schedule (WS)
   - (9) Intake schedule (IS)
   - (10) Stop/start training (SST)

   b. Multidimensional Behavioral Interventions
   - (1) Dry bed training—UA, PP, WS, CT, RD, OL
   - (2) Full spectrum home training—UA, CT, RCT, OL

2. Family Interventions

   a. Family therapy (systemic, dealing with enmeshment-disengagement issues)

3. Medication

   a. Imipramine
   b. DDAVP

4. Psychotherapy

   a. Hypnotic techniques
   b. Play therapy

Note: This outline of options summarizes major treatments covered in the text. Specific treatments are often combined into an intervention package. Refer to the text for additional descriptions of each treatment. This table is not necessarily an exhaustive list of all treatments available.

behavioral treatments have been consistently used for children with enuresis and have been systematically investigated in research: urine alarm; positive practice; intake schedule; reinforcement for dryness; retention control training; avoidance contingency; overlearning; cleanliness training; waking schedule; and stop/start training.

Urine Alarm (UA) and Cleanliness Training (CT).   The oldest and most widely used treatment for enuresis is the UA or "bell and pad" intervention (Mowrer & Mowrer, 1938). The bell and pad, sold commercially through several catalogs (see Mountjoy, Ruben, & Bradford, 1984, for a list of such devices and manufacturers), consists of two metal sheets separated by a cloth. The device is placed on (in the form of underwear) or under (in the form of a pad) the child. When the cloth is wet, an auditory alarm sounds. In most cases, the alarm wakes the child before the child has fully urinated; in other cases, the parents must wake the child.

UA is almost always accompanied by a concurrent CT intervention, which requires the child to go to the toilet, clean up, change clothing, strip and clean the bed, remake the bed, and reset the UA apparatus (e.g., Kaplan, Breit, Gauthier, & Busner, 1988). It is extremely important that the child carry out the CT in order to assume some responsibility for the bed-wetting behavior. In some cases, children's bedwetting behavior is subtly reinforced when the parent strips, cleans, and remakes the child's bed while having a pleasant interaction with the child. Parents should be neutral rather than punitive or pleasant during CT. Although numerous UA devices are commercially available, there is no evidence that one device is more effective than any other (Doleys, 1977).

Literature review studies indicate that the UA cures enuresis in 62–75% of cases but that the relapse rate is 25–41% (Doleys, 1977; Houts et al., 1994). Hence, the UA is an effective tool in initial arrest of enuresis with significant risk of relapse. The risk of relapse may be decreased if the alarm is programmed to sound on a variable ratio schedule of 70%; that is, the alarm sounds after 70% of wetting episodes and fails to sound after 30% of episodes. Use of a variable ratio schedule may reduce the percentage of relapse by 10–20% (Doleys, 1977). Supervision of the parents during treatment and follow-up also increases the effectiveness of the UA, possibly because it encourages the parents to follow the behavior plan closely (Doleys, 1977). The UA is less effective with children who have multiple wetting episodes at night, diurnal as well as nocturnal enuresis, unsatisfactory sleeping arrangements, family problems, fear of the UA apparatus, or parents with emotional problems (Butler et al., 1988; Dische, Yule, Corbett, & Hand, 1983; Fritz & Armbrust, 1982).

Two major theories exist concerning the mechanism by which the UA alleviates enuretic symptoms. Classical conditioning theory suggests that repeated presentation of the bell (unconditioned stimulus) while the child has a full bladder (conditioned stimulus) leads to association of a full bladder (conditioned stimulus) with waking up (conditioned response). Initially, a full bladder while asleep is a neutral stimulus for the child and is not associated with any behavior. On the other hand, the bell or tone sounded by the enuresis alarm, if sufficiently loud, is a stimulus that interrupts sleep in the absence of any prior learning. When the child wets the bed, the bell sounds immediately, waking the child while the bladder is still full. After numerous events such as this, the child begins to associate the full bladder with the sounding of the bell and waking up.

Classical conditioning theory suggests that the bell must sound immediately in order for the child to have a full bladder that is associated with waking; delayed sounding of the bell would allow the child to empty the bladder before waking. Evidence exists that immediate sounding of the bell is associated with faster and more complete training, supporting classical conditioning theory (Doleys, 1977). Classical conditioning theory also predicts that when the unconditioned stimulus (bell) is removed, extinction of the learned response (waking up) will occur. Extinction is less likely to occur when a criterion behavior has been learned under a variable schedule. This phenomenon may account for the increased effectiveness of variable schedules in preventing relapse in children with enuresis.

Operant conditioning theory posits that the UA causes behavior change by acting as an aversive event that follows a behavior. Hence, the child learns not to wet the bed in order to escape the aversive event of being awakened by a loud noise (Azrin, Sneed, & Foxx, 1974). In addition, many children regard components of cleanliness training, which follows the bell-waking sequence, as aversive. Evidence supporting this point of view is largely anecdotal and based on observations that children seem to dislike being awakened by the bell. In addition, some children express dislike and fear of the UA apparatus. In some cases, the child fears being shocked or harmed by the apparatus. Practice and desensitization should reduce these concerns.

Positive Practice (PP).   PP is a technique that involves the child repeatedly acting out the process of waking up, walking to the bathroom, and going to the toilet. One specific positive practice technique involves having the child lie in the bed for 3 minutes, then get up and go to the bathroom; this process is repeated nine times following each bedwetting incident (Azrin, Sneed, & Foxx, 1973). Modifications on this scheme are common. For example, another PP routine involves the child counting to 50, then getting out of bed, going to the bathroom, and trying to urinate; this sequence is repeated 20 times (Scharf et al., 1987). PP is rarely, if ever, used alone to treat enuresis, and its effectiveness when used alone has not been investigated. It is common as a part of multidimensional treatment packages for enuresis.

Reinforcement for Dryness (RD).   RD involves the use of praise or other rewards for dry nights. In its simplest form, RD involves having the child feel the dry sheets and then receive praise for having a dry night (Azrin et al., 1973). If the child needs more frequent reinforcement, RD may be combined with a waking schedule in which the child is awakened every hour or two and asked to check the sheets; dry sheets are rewarded with praise. More extensive RD interventions involve the parents, child, and therapist agreeing on some reward that the child will receive for each dry night. These rewards may reflect primary (i.e., going out for an ice cream cone) or secondary (i.e., star chart) reinforcers (Kaplan et al., 1988). Like PP, RD is rarely used alone to treat enuresis.

Retention Control Training (RCT).   RCT (Paschalis, Kimmel, & Kimmel, 1972) is based on the theory that children with enuresis have a smaller functional bladder capacity than normal children. This small functional bladder capacity may make it difficult for children with enuresis to sleep through the night without having the need to urinate. The goal of RCT is to eliminate enuresis by increasing the functional bladder capacity (Geffken et al., 1986). Functional bladder capacity is increased by having the child drink fluids and delay urination for increasing time periods. In one specific example (Houts, Peterson, & Whelan, 1986), children drank 8 ounces of water and practiced postponing urination for a 45-minute period. For each 3-minute period that they were able to postpone urination, the children received 5 cents. The criterion of adequate functional bladder capacity was considered to have been reached when the child could postpone urination for the entire 45-minute period.

Studies of the effectiveness of RCT have yielded mixed results, leading Doleys (1977) to conclude that "(the) data do not provide strong support for retention control training as a treatment procedure for enuresis.... Nevertheless, there appears to be enough evidence to warrant further investigation" (pp. 46–47). RCT has been more effectively used as one component of a treatment package (Houts et al., 1986). Some evidence exists that, as part of a treatment package, RCT can be an effective contributor to outcome, at least for children with small functional bladder capacity (Geffken et al., 1986; Houts et al., 1986). Hence, it does not appear to be advisable to use RCT as the exclusive treatment for childhood nocturnal enuresis.

Avoidance Contingency (AC).   AC treatments for enuresis involve the administration of a noxious stimulus or removal of a pleasant stimulus following a wetting episode. Although punishment-based treatments were common early treatments for enuresis (Glicklich, 1951), they are relatively unusual today, primarily because of the effectiveness of less aversive methods. Some clinicians conceptualize UA treatments as AC-type treatments because (according to operant conditioning theory) the child stops wetting to avoid being awakened by the bell. Time-out contingencies, which involve the removal of access to reinforcing places or activities following a wetting episode, may be an effective component in eliminating diurnal enuresis (Foxx, 1985). Although time-out does not involve the presentation of a noxious stimulus, it is a condition that the child avoids (hence, an AC treatment) because pleasant activities are removed. AC methods appear to have insufficient effectiveness to warrant their use in cases of nocturnal enuresis.

Overlearning (OL).　OL techniques are implemented after a child with enuresis has attained some criterion of dryness. They aim to reduce the relapse rate of children with enuresis by giving them large amounts of liquid prior to bedtime so that they learn to retain the liquid until waking. In a typical OL regimen, the child is trained (usually using a UA) until he or she achieves 14 consecutive nights of dryness. The child is then asked to drink up to 2 pints of liquid in the hour prior to bedtime and is monitored for enuretic accidents as before. Again, the child is trained to a criterion of 14 consecutive dry nights. Some evidence exists that this additional component reduces the relapse rate in children with enuresis (Taylor & Turner, 1975; Young & Morgan, 1972a, 1972b). OL may be modified in terms of the dryness criterion required before OL is implemented (7–14 days is typical) and in the amount of water the child drinks prior to bedtime (1–2 pints is typical) (Taylor & Turner, 1975). Given the relatively high relapse rate found in UA treatments, OL should be considered as an adjunct to UA treatment of any child at risk of having a relapse. By definition, OL is never used alone to treat enuresis.

Waking Schedule (WS).　Waking schedules are common components of multidimensional treatments of enuresis (Azrin et al., 1973; Fournier, Garfinkel, Bond, Beauchesne, & Shapiro, 1987; Whelan & Houts, 1990), although their design and implementation tend to vary widely. WS interventions share in common the characteristic of waking the child one or more times during the night and having the child attempt to urinate in the bathroom. In some cases, the WS involves waking the child every hour throughout the night, although this rigorous waking schedule is usually implemented for only the first night or two of treatment (Azrin et al., 1974; Whelan & Houts, 1990). Less rigorous, ongoing WS interventions require the parents to awaken the child one to three times at prescribed intervals throughout the night. Whelan and Houts (1990), for example, used an intensive, every-hour waking schedule for the first night of their intervention, but then had parents awaken the child once, approximately 3 hours after falling asleep. Following each dry night, the waking time was moved 30 minutes earlier to the child's time of falling asleep until the WS was not required. Controversy exists as to the value of including a WS in a treatment package (Whelan & Houts, 1990), but there is agreement that a WS alone is not an effective intervention (Fournier et al., 1987). The WS schedule should not be removed from effective treatment packages until more research data are available.

Intake Schedule (IS).　The intake schedule is a commonly used technique for toilet training or primary enuresis in young children. It is occasionally integrated with other treatments for older children as well. A typical IS intervention involves not allowing the child access to fluids for about an hour prior to bedtime. Immediately prior to bed, the child is then encouraged to urinate, emptying the bladder. This intervention reduces the chances of a full bladder during the night, which, in turn, reduces the chance that the child will urinate in bed.

IS interventions tend to work better if the child is encouraged to drink plenty of fluids about 2–3 hours before bed and if the child is restricted from salty or spicy foods in the evening. Drinking plenty of fluids several hours before bed will make urination immediately before bed an easier task and will reduce the chances that the child will be very thirsty in the hour before bed. Restriction from salty or spicy foods will help the child to feel less thirsty immediately before bedtime or during the night. IS interventions have not been as systematically studied as the other nocturnal enuresis interventions, probably because they are seen more as a toilet-training aid than as a treatment for significant enuresis. However, they are relatively easy to implement and are supported by clinical experience. Therefore, they are often present in many enuresis treatment plans.

Stop/Start Training (SST). Stop/start training is a less common, minimally effective treatment for enuresis, which is based on the belief that bedwetting results from a weakness of the bladder sphincter muscle (Bennett et al., 1985). In SST, children are told to stop and start the flow of urine at regular intervals during daytime urination. During urination, the child should pass a small amount of urine, then stop and count to three before continuing urination. Again, after the passing of a small amount of urine, the child should stop and count to three. The start-stop-count sequence should be repeated six times during each urination event. This exercise is assumed to strengthen the sphincter muscle, allowing the child to retain urine more easily while asleep. The child's compliance with this regimen is expected to be monitored and reinforced by parents (Bennett et al., 1985). SST is, at best, minimally effective, with a 17% effectiveness rate (14 consecutive dry nights) reported in one study (Bennett et al., 1985).

Multidimensional Behavioral Interventions

In actual clinical practice, it is rare to see one of the unidimensional behavioral treatments for enuresis applied alone. Even the venerable UA treatment is virtually always combined with CT, and RD is a common component of most clinical plans for enuresis. Most clinicians combine the unidimensional behavioral treatments based on considerations for the individual case or past experiences with the behavioral treatments. UA and CT are most likely to show up in these idiosyncratic treatment plans, largely because of their demonstrated effectiveness. Use of the UA with other behavioral treatments may increase its effectiveness by as much as 10% at posttreatment and follow-up (Houts et al., 1994).

Dry Bed Training. Several clinician-researchers have attempted to standardize multidimensional behavioral treatments so that they can be evaluated in outcome research. Probably the most extensively researched and well known of these is the Dry-Bed Training Procedure (DBT) developed by Azrin and colleagues (Azrin et al., 1973, 1974). DBT is a combination of UA, PP, WS, CT, RD, and OL techniques. It is implemented as follows:

The first night of training consists of intensive interventions in a variety of areas. One hour before bedtime, the child is given an explanation of the DBT procedure. Then the child is given a glass of liquid to drink and the UA is placed. Next, the child engages in PP, which consists of laying in bed and counting to 50, then rising and walking to the bathroom, followed by an attempt to urinate. PP is repeated twenty times. When PP is over, the child is asked to drink as much as possible and is sent to bed. At hourly intervals throughout the night, the child is awakened by parents and required to walk to the bathroom and attempt to urinate. Also at these hourly intervals, the parent feels the child's sheets and praises the child for dry sheets. The child is then given something to drink and sent back to bed (Azrin et al., 1973, 1974).

On subsequent nights, the UA is placed on the bed, and PP is given if an accident occurred on the previous night. Then the child is reminded of the goal of remaining dry and of the procedures that will occur if bedwetting occurs. Finally, the child is then sent to bed. The child is awakened at the parents' bedtime and sent to the bathroom to attempt to urinate; the awakening time is reduced by 30 minutes following each dry night. If the child sleeps through the night without a bedwetting incident, praise is given at least 5 times during the day for not wetting the bed. Praise is withheld if the child wets the bed (Azrin et al., 1973, 1974).

When a bedwetting incident occurs, the parent disconnects the alarm, awakens the child (if the child is not already awake), gives a brief verbal reprimand, and sends the child to the bathroom to finish urinating. The child then engages in CT, and the parent resets the UA. Finally, the child engages in twenty PP trials before going to sleep. The child must also then engage in twenty PP trials the next evening before bedtime (Azrin et al., 1973, 1974).

After 7 consecutive dry nights, the UA is no longer placed on the bed, and the parents inspect the child's bed each morning. If the bed is wet, CT occurs immediately and PP is implemented the following evening. If the bed is dry, the child is praised. If two accidents occur within a week, the child returns to the previous phase of treatment (Azrin et al., 1973, 1974).

Initial studies showed DBT to be extremely successful in eliminating enuresis in virtually all subjects within one month, with no major relapses at 3–6 month follow-up. Dry bed training has been shown to reduce enuretic accidents by as much as 85% within a week and 95% within a month (Azrin et al., 1973, 1974). No replication studies have duplicated Azrin et al.'s (1973, 1974) finding of 100% success rate and low (30%) relapse rate. Most replications find success rates of DBT of between 40% (Bennett et al., 1985; Fincham & Spettell, 1984) and 80% (Breit, Kaplan, Gauthier, & Weinhold, 1984; Butler et al., 1988; Kaplan et al, 1988), with relapse rates in the 40–50% range (Breit et al., 1984). Overall, effectiveness rates for DBT appear to be in the 70–80% effectiveness range, with relapse rates in the 30–50% range.

Studies investigating important components of DBT have shown that the mode of delivery (meeting with parents in therapist's office, therapist going to the child's home, meeting with parents and child in therapist's office) is unrelated to DBT effectiveness (Keating, Butz, Burke, & Heimburg, 1983). It appears that the UA is an important component of DBT (Azrin & Thienes, 1978; Besalel, Azrin, Thienes-Hontos, & McMorrow, 1980; Bollard, Nettelbeck, & Roxbee, 1982), although some variations of DBT call for omitting the UA (Azrin & Thienes, 1978). RCT does not appear to add to the effectiveness of DBT (Bollard & Nettelbeck, 1982), whereas a WS does appear to enhance DBT outcome (Kolko, 1987). Insufficient evidence exists to evaluate the other DBT components. Overall, the evidence appears to indicate that the UA should be included in DBT, whereas the other components should probably not be eliminated because of lack of knowledge in the literature to date.

Studies comparing DBT to other techniques have generally not shown DBT to be superior to UA-CT alone on initial treatment or relapse (Bennett et al., 1985; Butler et al., 1988;

Butler, Brewin, & Forsythe, 1990; Fincham & Spettell, 1984; Kaplan et al., 1988). The major disadvantage with DBT relative to UA is the commitment that DBT requires on the part of parents. The first night of intensive training, for example, allows virtually no sleep for parent or child. In addition, children sometimes rebel against the PP component of DBT, and parents sometimes find this component overly tedious. UA, on the other hand, requires minimal prebedtime preparation, and nighttime wakings occur only following bedwetting. Parents tend to rate UA more favorably than DBT, although there is no evidence that the effectiveness of UA or DBT is related to ratings of favorability (Fincham & Spettell, 1984). Regarding other treatments, DBT has been shown to be superior to SST and no treatment (Bennett et al., 1985). The relative effectiveness of DBT and other unidimensional behavioral treatments has not been extensively researched, but it is likely that DBT and UA-CT are the most effective treatments for enuresis. Unfortunately, it is not possible to predict for any single child whether DBT or UA-CT will be more effective, although across groups of children they seem to have similar effectiveness. UA is clearly the treatment of choice if parents seem less motivated or are unwilling to devote much time to treatment.

Full Spectrum Home Training. A second standardized multidimensional behavioral treatment package is Full Spectrum Home Training (FSHT; Houts et al., 1986; Whelan & Houts, 1990). FSHT consists of UA, CT, RCT, and OL components. The UA-CT components of FSHT are identical to the unidimensional UA-CT treatments previously described. The RCT component involves the child drinking 8 ounces of water during an "RCT Training Period" during the day. Then the child practices postponing urination for 3-minute increments of time, eventually building to a 45-minute period without urination (money at the end of each 3-minute period is used as a reward to encourage learning). The OL component is implemented following 14 consecutive dry nights. At this point, the child drinks 16 ounces of water in the hour before bedtime. FSHT is considered successful when the child has achieved 14 consecutive dry nights in the OL phase.

FSHT has initial success rates of 60–75% (Houts et al., 1986; Whelan & Houts, 1990), with very low relapse rates (Houts et al., 1986). In a study comparing FSHT to UA-CT and UA-CT-RCT, Houts et al. (1986) found similar initial success rates for all three treatments. However, FSHT resulted in significantly lower relapse rates than the other two treatments; relapse rate for FSHT was only 11% at 3- and 6-month follow-up, compared to 44% (3 month) and 33% (6 month) for UA-CT. The lower relapse rate for FSHT has been attributed to the OL component, although replication of this result is needed. Addition of a WS component to FSHT has not been shown to increase its efficacy (Whelan & Houts, 1990). Overall, FSHT should be considered as a relatively simple multidimensional treatment for enuresis that is initially as effective as UA and may result in lower relapse rates.

Family Interventions

The need for family therapy as a component of enuresis treatment is demonstrated by studies indicating that family difficulties are significantly related to the effectiveness of UA treatment for enuresis (Dische et al., 1983). Hence, it is advisable to assess the family prior to treatment for enuresis in order to identify families who may be in need of additional intervention. Self-report scales such as the FES may be particularly helpful in this regard. High scores on the FES Conflicted or Controlling factors and low scores on the FES Supportive factor may indicate the need for additional family intervention. In addition, the clinician's observations of a family structure that is covertly maintaining the enuretic behavior (Haley, 1976) would suggest the need for family intervention.

Protinsky and Dillard (1983), for example, suggest that in some cases enuresis is maintained by a coalition between one parent and the child with enuresis, with the other parent disengaged from the system. Although this coalition is not acknowledged overtly by the family, it results in characteristic repetitive sequences of behavior, such as enuresis, that bring the enmeshed parent and child together. In many cases, this family structure serves the purpose of deflecting attention away from the marital dyad, so marital issues must be carefully observed in therapy. Protinsky and Dillard (1983) suggest a multipart family intervention based on strategic family therapy (Haley, 1976). First, the therapist accepts the family's interpretation that the child is the presenting problem. In doing this, the therapist is able to join with and influence the family system. Second, the therapist assigns the family direct tasks that require the disengaged parent to join with the child with enuresis and that create some distance between the enmeshed parent and the child with enuresis. For example, the disengaged parent may be put in charge of handling the child's enuresis. Protinsky and Dillard (1983) note that other strategic techniques, such as paradox and prescribing the symptom, may be warranted in some cases of enuresis, but these techniques should be used with caution and by experienced therapists. Third, marital issues must be addressed, either through marital therapy or homework assignments that require more pleasant interactions. Protinsky and Dillard (1983) report success using this technique in individual cases.

Medication

The medications of choice for enuresis are imipramine (Tofranil) and desmopressin (DDAVP), although each medication has side effects that should be carefully considered prior to use. Imipramine is approved for use with children as young as 6 years of age and is more effective than placebo (Wiener, 1984), in addition to producing a therapeutic response sometimes faster than a UA (Fournier et al., 1987). The mechanism by which imipramine prevents enuresis is unclear, although it has been suggested that its antidepressant effects, effect on sleep patterns, and/or peripheral anticholinergic effects may be factors in its effectiveness (Fritz & Armbrust, 1982).

Most research reviews find imipramine (20–40% improvement rates) to be not as effective as UA (62–75% improvement rate) (Doleys, 1977; Fritz & Armbrust, 1982; Houts et al., 1994). Relapse rates following imipramine treatment are extremely high (40–60%; Fritz & Armbrust, 1987; Houts et al., 1994), probably reflecting the fact that no new behavior has been learned by the child. Combining imipramine and UA treatments appears to result in faster improvement but does not improve the overall success rate of UA.

Desmopressin (an analog of vasopressin [antidiuretic hormone]) has an antidiuretic effect that significantly reduces enuresis in children, adolescents, and adults. About 25–46% of children with enuresis become completely dry at night when taking desmopressin, with an average one-third reduction in bedwetting nights across the enuretic group as a whole (Bath et al., 1996; Houts et al., 1994; Thompson & Rey, 1995). Most children relapse when desmopressin is discontinued (Bath, Morton, Uing, & Williams, 1996; Houts et al., 1994; Thompson & Rey, 1995). Based on outcome studies for each treatment, desmopressin appears to be less effective than UA, although different patients may respond to one or the other treatment.

Treatment with imipramine or desmopressin is most appropriate for cases in which behavioral treatments are unsuccessful and for cases in which the child is extremely distressed or depressed (Weiner, 1984). Other indications for medication use include cases in which rapid response is necessary and cases in which the parents are unable to effectively carry out a behavioral intervention. Because of side effects, medication interventions for enuresis should be used with caution. Given the efficacy of behavioral approaches, initial use of medication for simple cases of enuresis is generally not warranted. Even following an initial failure of a behavioral plan, retrying behavioral interventions with increased effort may be as effective as using medication (Bath et al., 1996).

Other medications in the tricyclic antidepressant (desipramine [Norpramin], amitriptyline [Elavil], and nortriptyline [Pamelor]) and selective serotonin reuptake inhibitor (fluoxetine [Prozac] and sertraline [Zoloft]) classes are sometimes prescribed for enuresis, with positive results on a case-by-case basis (Mesaros, 1993; Sprenger, 1997; Wagner, 1987). Much less is known about the effectiveness of these medications (Fritz & Armbrust, 1982).

Psychotherapy

Hypnotic Techniques

Although not a first-line treatment for enuresis, hypnosis is occasionally cited as a treatment option for cases that have failed with standard behavioral treatment or that seem to have a strong psychodynamic component. Hypnosis treatments for enuresis usually combine relaxation with suggestions of waking up at night when experiencing a full bladder. The relatively few studies that address the use of hypnosis for children with enuresis report good success rates (often in the range of 70%; Banerjee, Srivastav, & Palan, 1993; Edwards & Van Der Spuy, 1985; Olness, 1975).

Other Psychotherapy Techniques

In addition to hypnotherapy, psychotherapeutic modalities such as play therapy (e.g., Axline, 1969), psychodynamically oriented therapy, or supportive psychotherapy are occasionally used for enuresis. Little has been written about any of these techniques, but what little evidence exists indicates that they have minimal effects on enuretic symptoms (Fritz & Armbrust, 1982; Werry & Cohrssen, 1965).

Psychotherapy is indicated in cases that involve other psychopathology in addition to enuresis. In these cases, psychotherapy should be used in conjunction with one of the behavioral interventions for enuresis. When enuresis is combined with other forms of psychopathology, the enuresis sometimes results from the psychopathology; as the psychopathology abates, the enuresis wanes as well. In addition, enuresis can create its own stresses, which can then be managed in play therapy.

Treatment of Diurnal Enuresis

In spite of the explosion of research and clinical techniques to address nocturnal enuresis, much less has been written on treatment of diurnal enuresis. Parents tend to regard diurnal enuresis as more deliberate, perhaps because sleep does not serve as an excuse for the enuretic episodes. The causes of diurnal enuresis, however, are multiple, ranging from poor monitoring of need to urinate to power struggles between the child and parents. In most cases, a reinforcement schedule for appropriate urination in the toilet and dryness during the day (RD), combined with cleanliness training (CT) and conspicuous monitoring of enuretic behavior, results in a remission of the diurnal enuretic behavior (Foxx, 1985). Regular bathroom trips during the day (somewhat akin to WS interventions at night, although referred to as toileting schedules [TS] during the day) also assist in the elimination of this behavior. RCT may be a treatment in cases of suspected small functional bladder capacity, although its effectiveness for diurnal enuresis has not been extensively studied. For cases in which the enuresis seems to be a result of other child or family psychopathology, psychotherapy or family therapy may be warranted (Table 4.5).

A common problem in the case of diurnal enuresis is the hiding of wet underwear by the child. This can undermine CT and RD interventions by giving the appearance of dryness when the child is actually continuing to have enuretic events. Hiding underwear can be discouraged by the use of two methods: First, each pair of the child's underwear may be labeled with a day of the week, with the child given access to seven labeled pairs of underwear for each week. Each morning when waking up and evening before sleeping, the child must show that he or she is still wearing the proper underwear. Alternatively, each pair of underwear may be numbered, and the number of the underwear for the day is then recorded and checked by the parent. When underwear is wet or soiled, the child is given a different pair of underwear, and the new number is recorded. A second method of discouraging underwear hiding (often combined with the first method) involves punishing the child (usually with time-out or restriction of privileges) if hidden underwear is found.

■ Encopresis

□ CLINICAL DESCRIPTION

Diagnostic Considerations

Functional encopresis is defined by DSM-IV as the discharge of feces into inappropriate places; the encopretic behavior may or may not be voluntary. As with enuresis, encopresis involves the diagnosis of a behavior that is normal at one stage of life (e.g., infancy) and

---

TABLE 4.5 Treatment Options for Diurnal Enuresis

1. Behavioral Interventions
   a. Cleanliness training (CT)
   b. Reinforcement for dryness (RD)
   c. Toileting schedule
   d. Retention control training (RCT)
   e. Underwear marking
2. Family Interventions
   a. Family therapy (systemic, dealing with enmeshment-disengagement issues)
3. Psychotherapy
   a. Play therapy

Note: This outline of options summarizes major treatments covered in the text. Specific treatments are often combined into an intervention package. Refer to the text for additional descriptions of each treatment. This table is not necessarily an exhaustive list of all treatments available.

abnormal at a later time in life. The stage at which such behavior becomes worthy of psychiatric diagnosis is set at age 4. In order to be diagnosed with encopresis, children must have one or more encopretic events per month for at least 3 months. Because functional encopresis cannot be diagnosed if the soiling is completely a result of a physical disorder (unless constipation is involved), a medical examination is recommended.

Encopresis can be subdivided based on several parameters: involuntary versus intentional; retentive versus not retentive; primary versus secondary; and diurnal versus nocturnal (Table 4.6). Involuntary encopresis is often the result of the retention of feces, which results in constipation and fecal impaction. When feces overflows the impaction (usually in liquid form), encopresis occurs. The retention of feces in the first place may be caused by a multiplicity of factors, including fear of defecating, oppositional tendencies, unwillingness to defecate, or a previous physical illness. Intentional encopresis usually occurs as the result of anger, oppositional behavior, or a power struggle between parent and child; it is rarely associated with constipation or impaction. Involuntary/retentive encopresis appears to be more common than intentional/nonretentive encopresis (Wald & Handen, 1987). Involuntary/retentive encopresis is subtyped and coded in DSM-IV as Encopresis "with constipation and overflow incontinence"; intentional/nonretentive encopresis is diagnosed as being "without constipation or overflow incontinence." There is some evidence that the latter subtype is associated with poorer long-term response to treatment (Rockney, McQuade, Days, Linn, & Alario, 1996).

As with enuresis, the primary-secondary distinction in encopresis is based on the prior acquisition of toileting skills. In order to qualify for a diagnosis of primary encopresis, a child must have had less than one year of total fecal continence. Secondary encopresis must follow a year of total fecal continence (Doleys, 1989). There is some evidence that children with primary encopresis are at greater risk for developmental delay, whereas those with secondary encopresis are at greater risk for high stress in the environment and for conduct problems (Foreman & Thambirajah, 1996). Also mirroring the enuresis classifications, diurnal encopresis occurs during the day, whereas nocturnal encopresis occurs at night.

TABLE 4.6   Epidemiology and Course of Encopresis

Prevalence: 1% for ages 5 and older

Sex Ratio (Male:Female):   As high as 6:1

Typical Onset Age: 4–5 years

Course: Symptoms remit spontaneously or with casual treatment in some children but are persistent in other children. No typical long-term outcome pattern, but self-esteem problems are a risk if other children are aware of symptoms.

Common Comorbid Conditions: 1. Developmental Delays

Relevant Subtypes:
1. Primary vs. Secondary
2. Nocturnal vs. Diurnal
3. Involuntary vs. Intentional
4. Retentive vs. Not Retentive

Estimates of the incidence of functional encopresis vary widely, from 1% to nearly 8% of children, becoming more rare at older ages (American Psychiatric Association, 1994; Doleys, 1989; Fritz & Armbrust, 1982). The 1% prevalence estimate for children age 5 and older is most widely accepted (American Psychiatric Association, 1994). The incidence of encopresis appears to decrease sharply at about age 7 to less than 1% (Knopf, 1979). Males outnumber females by as much as six to one (Doleys, 1989; Protinsky & Kersey, 1983). Most encopresis is of the diurnal type (Fritz & Armbrust, 1982; Protinsky & Kersey, 1983).

Appearance and Features

Appearance and features of encopresis are listed in Table 4.7. Children with encopresis may give advance notice that an encopretic event is occurring or about to occur by adopting characteristic postures or facial expressions. After the encopresis, they may resume their activity until it is convenient to change pants, or, more rarely, they may seek to change their clothing immediately. Typically, children with encopresis attempt to hide their problem, often by hiding the soiled clothing or by pretending that an event has not occurred. Upon confrontation by the parent, they may continue to deny the problem, even in the face of physical evidence. The degree of discomfort that the child has about the encopresis varies from child to child. Some children (probably more involuntary encopretics) are upset and ashamed about the episodes, but the majority (probably more intentional encopretics) act unconcerned about the symptom. Deliberate smearing of feces is unusual, although children with encopresis sometimes accidentally spread the feces in their attempt to clean it up or to hide it (Fritz & Armbrust, 1982).

Upon interview, it is sometimes found that the child with encopresis has unusual beliefs about toileting. Some children have a fear of the toilet, whereas others simply do not see the importance of using the toilet. In some cases, the child does not want to leave a

TABLE 4.7   Appearance and Features of Encopresis

COMMON FEATURES

1. Defecation into inappropriate place
2. Retention of feces with overflow of impaction (retentive type)
3. Use of defecation to manipulate environment (intentional type)
4. Age 4–7 years
5. Primarily males
6. Adoption of characteristic location, posture, or expression prior to encopretic event
7. Hiding soiled clothing

OCCASIONAL FEATURES

1. Unusual beliefs about toileting, and related anxiety
2. Not wanting to interrupt activity to defecate
3. Family contingencies rewarding encopresis (e.g., attention)
4. Peer rejection/isolation

Note: The features listed in the table are often seen but are not universal. Some features may be diagnostically relevant or required, whereas others may not be required for diagnosis. "Common" features are typical of the disorder; "occasional" features appear frequently but are not necessarily seen in a majority of cases.

favored activity to go to the bathroom, waiting until it is too late to make it to the toilet in time. Family responses to encopresis also may reveal insufficient motivation or discipline for the child to become toilet trained.

For older children, encopresis can have familial and social effects. Similar to enuresis, encopresis can become a significant family stressor, although many families with a child with encopresis simply incorporate the encopresis into usual family life. For example, the child may be sent to school with an extra pair of pants and underpants; in more extreme cases, the child may be forced by parents to wear a diaper or training pants. On family outings, a "clean-up kit" may be brought along, acting as a silent recognition that the encopresis will occur and nothing can be done about it. Parents may adopt an attitude of sympathy and indulgence toward the child with encopresis, particularly if one of the parents was encopretic. This adoption of encopresis as a family trait often indicates that the child and family will not give up the encopretic symptoms easily.

The social effects of encopresis depend on where the child has an encopretic event. Many children with encopresis have problems only in one situation. As long as they are cleaned up before leaving the situation, their problem does not affect their relationships in other situations. Other children with encopresis have unpredictable encopretic events that occur in many situations. When an event or its aftermath is noticed by peers, ridicule and isolation may result. The child with encopresis may be seen as "dirty" or as a "baby." Reputation effects may persist after the encopresis is cured.

Etiology

Multiple etiological factors are likely to be responsible for different cases of encopresis (Fritz & Armbrust, 1982; Protinsky & Kersey, 1983; Wald & Handen, 1987). The tendency for encopresis to run in families has been noted by several authors (Bellman, 1966; Wald & Handen, 1987), suggesting a possible genetic component. However, the family incidence of encopresis, while higher than chance levels, is relatively low (1% of mothers, 15% of fathers, and 9% of siblings of children with encopresis were found to be encopretic by Bellman [1966]). In addition, methods of and attitudes toward toilet training tend to run in families and could be as responsible as genetics for any family history of encopresis. Overall, existing evidence suggests that any genetic influence on functional encopresis is likely to be weak (Doleys, 1989).

Toilet-training behavior has also been suggested as a possible etiological factor (Bemporad, Kresch, Asnes, & Wilson, 1978). Wald and Handen (1987), for example, review studies suggesting that inconsistent toilet training approaches, such as alternating between rigidity and permissiveness, cause encopresis in children. Harsh or premature toilet training may also be responsible for some cases of encopresis (Fritz & Armbrust, 1982; Levine, 1975). Fritz and Armbrust (1982) suggest that the toddler may use encopretic behavior as one of the few outlets for demonstrating independence and retaliating against parents during toilet training. The potential etiological role of toilet training suggests that toilet training history should be carefully evaluated prior to treatment.

Other potentially significant etiological factors in the development of encopresis are family pathology (Protinsky & Kersey, 1983), co-occurring psychopathology in the child (Fritz & Armbrust, 1982), secondary gain for encopretic behavior (Wald & Handen, 1987), fear of using the toilet (Fritz & Armbrust, 1982), desire to remain in a dependent role, and stress. Some children are encopretic simply because their parents have not sufficiently emphasized the importance of going to the toilet. Although these factors may explain individual cases of encopresis, insufficient evidence exists to establish any of them as significant for a large percentage of children with encopresis. Stress has been the most consistently cited contributing factor in clinical and research work (Bellman, 1966; Fritz & Armbrust, 1982; Wald & Handen, 1987). Stressful events such as starting school, parental separation, birth of a sibling, and family conflict have been found to be present in a large percentage of children with encopresis (70% in Bellman's [1966] study). Stressful events may be more important in cases of secondary encopresis.

☐ ASSESSMENT PATTERNS

Broad Assessment Strategies

Cognitive Assessment

Clinician-Administered.   A first consideration in the assessment of the child with encopresis is developmental maturity. Encopresis cannot be diagnosed in a child with a mental age of less than 4 years. Informally, developmental maturity can be observed and discussed with the parent. More formal assessment would involve giving a brief intelligence test such as the K-BIT or WASI to screen for intellectual deficit. A subgroup of children with encopresis are developmentally delayed or have neurological problems that will emerge in lower performance on intelligence tests. However, the vast majority of children with encopresis are intellectually and neurologically normal and score in the average ranges (IQ of 90–109) on intelligence tests (Doleys, 1989; Fritz & Armbrust, 1982; Kolko, 1989). The risk that the encopresis is due to a medical or developmental problem is greater in the mentally retarded/neurologically impaired subgroup of children with encopresis.

Psychological Assessment

Child-Report.   A major concern in the assessment and treatment of encopresis is the effect of the disorder on the self-esteem of the child. Using the PHSCS, Owens-Stively (1987) found that children with encopresis had lower total, behavior, happiness, and popularity self-esteem than did children with no diagnosis. These results indicate that children with encopresis are at risk to feel that they are a problem, that they are disliked by other children, that they are unhappy, and that they are dissatisfied with themselves. On the other hand, Stark, Spirito, Lewis, and Hart (1990) found that the self-esteem of children with encopresis was higher than that of children with other psychiatric disorders. Hence, the self-esteem of children with encopresis appears to fall between that of nonreferred children and psychiatric outpatients. Children who are successfully treated report significant increases in self-esteem (Stark et al., 1990).

Behavioral Assessment

Parent-Report.   CBCL research has found elevated scores on most subscales for children with encopresis, with almost half of children scoring above the 90th percentile on the total score. Items reflecting immaturity, inattention-hyperactivity, and oppositionality tend to be the most often endorsed (Gabel, Hegedus, Wald, Chandra, & Chiponis, 1986; Johnston & Wright, 1993; Young, Brennan, Baker, & Baker, 1995). On the other hand, CBCL scores of children with encopresis are generally lower than those of other children brought for outpatient mental health services. No evidence exists that children with encopresis show a particular pattern of behavior problems such as stubbornness or social withdrawal (Gabel et al., 1986). CBCL behavior problem scores of children with encopresis have been shown to decline (improved functioning) following successful treatment, and children with higher CBCL scores at pretreatment are at greater risk for treatment failure (Young et al., 1995).

The different age-versions of the BASC include one to two items pertaining to enuretic/encopretic accidents, bedwetting, and abnormal behavior in the bathroom (playing in the toilet), although the specific items change across the different age-versions of the BASC. As with the CBCL, there is no characteristic encopretic profile on the BASC, and the BASC does not include a subscale that is specifically sensitive to encopresis. Rather, the usefulness of the BASC for evaluation of encopresis lies in its ability to identify concurrent or contributing behavioral problems. Low scores on the Leadership or Social Skills subscales, for example, could indicate concurrent social problems, whereas an elevated score on the Atypicality subscale could indicate immaturity or general oddity in behavior.

The ECI-4, CSI-4, and ASI-4 include a single item that screens for encopretic events but do not ask about the specifics of DSM-IV diagnostic criteria for encopresis. As with the BASC and CBCL, the SI-4 can assist in screening for comorbid behavior problems in a child with encopresis, but there is no classic encopresis profile on the CSI-4.

Studies have found that children with higher global behavior problem scores are at risk for poorer treatment outcome (Gabel, Chandra, & Shindledecker; 1988; Stark et al., 1990). In one study (Stark et al., 1990), 25% of treatment successes had other behavioral problems, whereas 80% of treatment failures experienced other behavioral problems.

Family Assessment

Parent-Report. Although there has been little empirical study of family assessment patterns of children with encopresis, administration of the FES may provide some insight into family dynamics. Families who are overly permissive may be expected to show low scores on the Control and Organization subscales, coupled with high scores on the Independence subscale. An overly restrictive/punitive family would be expected to show high Conflict, Control, Moral-Religious Emphasis, and Achievement Orientation scale scores, with low Independence scores. Particularly important to note are discrepancies between father- and mother-report of the family environment because these may indicate inconsistent parenting or subtle family conflict.

Syndrome-Specific Tests

Clinician-Administered. No widely recognized scale of encopretic behaviors and related issues exists. Therefore, the clinician must rely on interview to assess encopresis-specific issues. Important issues to assess in interview are frequency of encopretic episodes, time of occurrence, toilet training history, parental beliefs/attitudes about toilet training, family history of encopresis, whether the child had ever been toilet trained, current stresses, and antecedents and consequences of encopresis. Although no evidence exists that these variables are related to treatment outcome when a standard treatment regimen is used (Stark et al., 1990), knowledge of these variables may assist in the design of a treatment plan.

☐ TREATMENT OPTIONS

Overview

With the exception of medical treatments, it is rare to see only a single treatment modality used for encopresis (Table 4.8). Treatment for encopresis should always be accompanied by careful recording of encopretic and related behavior. Records typically include the time of encopretic event, type of stool, what the child was doing, antecedents and consequences of encopresis, and events of independent toileting. These records are used to monitor encopresis and to track the child's progress.

Medication and Related Medical Interventions

Because the majority of secondary encopresis cases involve or result from constipation, medical management of the encopretic behavior is routine. Often this is combined with a behavioral intervention, but medical treatment sometimes occurs alone as well. Medical

TABLE 4.8 Treatment Options for Encopresis

1. Medical Management
   a. Cathartic medications (enemas and suppositories)—for cases involving constipation
   b. Dietary changes (fiber)
2. Behavioral Interventions
   a. Self-monitoring
   b. Reinforcement for toileting (RT)
   c. Reinforcement for cleanliness (RC)
   d. Underwear marking (UM)
   e. Cleanliness training (CT)
   f. Toileting schedule (TS)
   g. Shaping/desensitization (SD)
   h. Punishment techniques
   i. Biofeedback
   j. Multidimensional treatments
3. Family Interventions
   a. Family therapy (systemic, dealing with enmeshment-disengagement issues)
4. Psychotherapy
   a. Play therapy
   b. Cognitive-behavioral challenges of irrational toileting beliefs

Note: This outline of options summarizes major treatments covered in the text. Specific treatments are often combined into an intervention package. Refer to the text for additional descriptions of each treatment. This table is not necessarily an exhaustive list of all treatments available.

treatment begins with the use of cathartic medications (enemas and suppositories) to eliminate constipation. This initial phase may last from several days to two weeks, depending on treatment protocol and response of the child to the medications. A typical regimen would involve the use of four enemas over a two-day period (Cox, Sutphen, Ling, Quillian, & Borowitz, 1996; Stark et al., 1990).

During (or sometimes following) the cathartic medication period, the child is administered mineral oil or another laxative two or three times per day in order to maintain adequate bowel functioning of about one soft stool per day (Cox et al., 1996; Stark et al., 1990). The laxative therapy varies in duration from 1–6 months. Finally, diet is changed to include more high-fiber foods that promote regular bowel functioning (Houts, Mellon, & Whelan, 1988; Wald & Handen, 1987). Behavioral components such as a toileting schedule (explained later in this chapter) are common additional components to these medical regimes.

Medical management of encopresis appears to be effective for 10–33% of children (Cox et al., 1996; Stark et al., 1990). Success rates for combined medical and behavioral treatment packages appear to be higher, in the 60–70% range (Cox et al., 1996; Wald & Handen, 1987). Because of the relative ease with which behavioral components can be added to medical treatments, a combined medical-behavioral approach appears to be the most prudent.

Behavioral Interventions

Behavioral treatments for encopresis generally focus on the use of monitoring, schedules, and reinforcement to shape or encourage appropriate toileting behavior. They are generally combined with medical treatments because retentive encopresis is common. Retentive encopresis generally necessitates the use of some type of enema and dietary plan, but the actual use of the toilet also needs to be shaped using behavioral principles. Common behavioral techniques include the following:

Reinforcement for Toileting (RT).   RT is the most commonly used and simplest initial intervention. The child is rewarded with praise or tangible reinforcers for defecating in the toilet. If an RT intervention is used, it is helpful to distinguish between independent trips to the toilet and trips that are requested or required by the parent. Independent trips should receive larger rewards (Cox et al., 1996; Kolko, 1989).

Reinforcement for Cleanliness (RC).   RC for encopresis corresponds to RD for enuresis. RC involves checking the child for soiled underwear at planned or variable intervals about 1–4 hours apart. Rewards and punishments are delivered based on the whether the underwear is clean or dirty. Praise and star charts are commonly used reinforcers, whereas time-out and restriction from favored activities are common punishers.

Bornstein et al. (1983) describe a combined RT/RC intervention that they call the "bathroom game." A variable reinforcement/punishment schedule is used because such schedules tend to produce more rapid and longer-lasting changes in behavior. In the bathroom game, the child is given a blank card with seven rows (one for each day of the week) and two columns (labeled "Soiling" and "Bowel Movement"), for a total of fourteen day-behavior cells. If the child soils on a particular day, a "Y" is marked in the "Soiling" column for that day; if the child has an appropriate bowel movement, a "Y" is marked in the

"Bowel Movement" column for that day. At the end of the week, the child's card is compared to a card held by the therapist. The therapist's card is identical to the child's, except that half (i.e., seven) of the therapist's day-behavior cells have stars in them. For each "Bowel Movement" cell in which the child has a "Y" and the corresponding cell on the therapist's card has a star, the child is awarded 50 cents; for each starred "Soiling" cell in which the child has a "Y," 25 cents are taken away (other reinforcers could be used as well). The proportion of stars on the therapist's card can gradually be reduced to allow fading of the treatment. Bornstein et al. (1983) report positive results of their technique in a case study, but common sense suggests that their complex technique could be used only with older or fairly intelligent children.

Underwear Marking (UM).   To assist with RC, UM is sometimes used to prevent hiding of dirty underwear. Solutions for preventing hidden underwear are also similar to those for diurnal enuresis: First, each pair of the child's underwear may be labeled with a day of the week, with the child given access to seven labeled pairs of underwear for each week. Each morning when waking up and evening before sleeping, the child must show that he or she is still wearing the proper underwear. Alternatively, each pair of underwear may be numbered, and the number of the underwear for the day is then recorded and checked by the parent. When underwear is soiled, the child is given a different pair of underwear, and the new number is recorded (if days of the week are used, the parent must have an additional supply of day-labeled underwear hidden for use if the primary underwear is soiled). Underwear marking is combined with punishment if hidden underwear are found.

Cleanliness Training (CT).   CT for encopresis, like CT for enuresis, involves cleaning self and clothes, with the primary responsibility for the cleaning left to the child. Typical encopresis CT consists of the child cleaning himself or herself, cleaning out and rinsing underwear, cleaning other clothes if needed, placing the dirty clothes in the appropriate place, cleaning the room or bed if needed, and redressing neatly (Knell & Moore, 1990; O'Brien, Ross, & Christophersen, 1986).

Toileting Schedule (TS).   The toileting schedule is a modification of the WS for enuresis. A typical TS begins with an evaluation of the time of day that the child tends to have bowel movements. If there is some regularity to the bowel movements, the child is placed on the toilet about 10 minutes prior to the regular bowel movement time and is required to remain on the toilet for 15 minutes or until a bowel movement occurs (whichever is shorter). The child is also placed on the toilet for 10–15 minutes every morning and about 15–45 minutes after each meal.

TS interventions assume some regularity to the child's bowel movements and are therefore less effective for overflow encopresis and other irregular encopresis symptoms. TS interventions are sometimes initiated or intensified following accidents. O'Brien et al. (1986), for example, require six hourly 5-minute toilet trips following an accident. TS interventions are most effective when combined with RT.

Shaping/Desensitization (SD).   SD techniques are most useful for children who are anxious about using the toilet. These interventions use successive approximations to the ultimate goal of independent toileting. They vary widely based on the specifics of the child's anxieties and misconceptions of using the toilet, but a sample intervention might include the following. First, the child is shown as the contents of a dirty diaper are dumped into the toilet and flushed. Next, the child could be rewarded for defecating into a diaper when in the bathroom, and then the diaper would be removed and its contents dumped in the toilet as before. The child would then be rewarded for sitting on the toilet lid while defecating in the diaper (again, with flushing of diaper contents). The child would then be encouraged to do the same thing with the lid open, and the diaper would be removed as the child sits over the toilet. Finally, the child would be encouraged to have the diaper removed prior to defecating in the toilet. Praise and other reinforcers are used to promote progress from one step to the next, and interventions to address the child's anxiety may be necessary at each step. Exceedingly anxious children may need an even more gradual introduction to such a desensitization plan, with milder and slower exposure. In cases of extreme anxiety about toileting, a thorough evaluation of the underlying causes of the anxiety and the possible effects of a desensitization plan should be conducted prior to implementing the plan.

Punishment Techniques.   Punishment techniques are incorporated into some treatments for encopresis, typically as a consequence for defecating in an inappropriate place or for attempting to hide the evidence of encopresis. When punishment is incorporated into a behavioral plan for encopresis, several points must be covered. First, the parents should speak with the child before the implementation of the plan. The child should be told that the encopretic behavior is no longer acceptable, and a description of the punishment contingency should be given. If an encopretic event occurs, the punishment should be administered matter-of-factly, and every effort should be made *not* to shame or scold the child. Examples of typical punishments are time-out (Appendix C), response cost (taking away a previously delivered reward), withholding TV time, or removal of a favored toy for a specified period of time. PP and TS are also seen by children as a form of punishment.

In many cases, events that are interpreted by the child as punishments are merely treatment-related logical consequences of the encopresis. Enemas or suppositories, for example, can often be skipped if the child has a bowel movement (negative reinforcement) but must be given if the child fails to have a bowel movement (punishment) (Knell & Moore, 1989; O'Brien, et al., 1986). PP (often seen by children as a punishment) in many cases is necessary only after an accident (O'Brien et al., 1986). Other restrictive dietary, medical, and scheduling interventions are necessarily more intense when the child is having problems with the encopresis. These logical consequences can be explained to the child as necessary for treatment. Although not intended as punishers per se, their presence in the behavioral plan can motivate a child in a similar fashion as a punishment intervention.

Punishment should be used extensively only if more basic medical or reward-based behavioral interventions have failed. Punishment is most likely to be appropriate in cases of voluntary encopresis when the child does not have sufficient negative contingencies to engage in normal toileting behavior. Such children are typically encopretic only at home and do not regard the smell or sensation of feces as aversive (hence, reducing the effectiveness of CT). Furthermore, they are not motivated by their parents' admonitions or by the responses of their siblings.

Biofeedback.   Biofeedback is becoming integrated into some behavioral packages for encopresis, particularly for use with children who appear to have difficulty monitoring rectal sensations or who have poor sphincter control (Kaplan, 1985). Another common problem occurs when children are anxious and reluctant to defecate because of pain associated with defecation following fecal impaction. Pain and anxiety can cause the child to reflexively tighten the sphincter and prevent defecation.

A typical biofeedback intervention involves the monitoring of tension and relaxation in the external anal sphincter. The child learns to control the degree of tension in the sphincter, based on feedback (usually in the form of a game) from the monitoring machine. Biofeedback aims to increase awareness of rectal sensations and to improve sphincter control (Wald & Handen, 1987). Based on review and empirical study by Cox et al. (1996), biofeedback success rates for most studies range from 63% to 73%. These rates have been shown to be clearly superior to medical management alone but not to a medical-behavioral-psychoeducational intervention (Cox et al., 1994, 1996). Cox et al. (1996) recommend that their multidimensional medical-behavioral intervention be tried first, with biofeedback added if improvement is not seen within two weeks.

Multidimensional Treatments. The individual behavioral interventions just described are typically combined into an integrated plan. Numerous multidimensional treatment plans exist, but all have in common the collection of behavioral data, control of access to underwear, RC, RT, CT, and eventual fading of the intervention (Doleys, 1989). Most include a simultaneous medical regimen of enemas, suppositories, and dietary change, whereas some have punishment as a component.

O'Brien et al. (1986), for example, describe a medical-behavioral intervention designed for treatment-resistant children. Their plan consists of initial evaluation for medical causes, followed by administration of two enemas to eliminate constipation. Each morning, the child is required to sit on the toilet for 5 minutes; if the child fails to defecate, a suppository is administered. Each afternoon, the child's pants are monitored for soiling at 90-minute intervals, and the child is required to sit on the toilet for 5 minutes once. CT is used after soiling. After appropriate toilet use, the child is reinforced by engaging with the parent in a preferred activity for 15 minutes. Finally, diet is modified to include more bulk and fiber foods. O'Brien et al. (1986) found their intervention to be highly effective with two of the four children in their study and mildly effective with the other two children. To address intermittent accidents in the other two children, they added a punishment component in which soiling incidents were followed by correction, ten positive practice (PP) trials, a 5-minute time-out, and six hourly 5-minute toilet sits. This mild punishment procedure further reduced soiling incidents.

Cox et al. (1996) describe an intervention called Enhanced Toilet Training (ETT). ETT uses components of medical interventions (enemas plus laxatives), RT, RC, TS, modeling and practicing of defecation behavior on the toilet, and psychoeducation about the physiology of defecation and the anatomical structures needed for defecation (especially relaxation of the anal sphincter). ETT resulted in significant improvement for 71% of patients and was superior to medical intervention alone.

The content and magnitude of a behavioral intervention is largely dependent on the symptoms, underlying causes, attitude, and motivation of the child. Some children are highly motivated to overcome encopresis and respond to simple self-monitoring, dietary change, and TS. Other children merely need encouragement from parents in the form of talking about the encopresis, explaining the need for the child to change behavior, and praising appropriate behavior. In reality, however, the previously mentioned types of children rarely come to the clinician's notice because they are "cured" by their parents. More extensive behavioral plans are designed for resistant and/or unmotivated children.

Wald and Handen (1987) review studies suggesting success rates of 61–78% for behavioral-medical treatments, although many of these studies rely on small samples. Some authors suggest that behavioral treatments are effective for nocturnal as well as diurnal encopresis (O'Brien et al., 1986), although the rarity of nocturnal encopresis makes systematic study of this point difficult. Perhaps because of these high success rates, behavioral treatments are commonly used for encopresis.

Family Interventions

Family therapy is occasionally used to treat encopresis, sometimes as an adjunct to behavioral therapy (e.g., Berrigan & Stedman, 1989). Family therapy is warranted when the family is significantly adversely affected by the encopresis, when family dynamics or structure interfere with the implementation of a behavior plan, or when family pathology (e.g., enmeshment) is maintaining the symptom. Protinsky and Kersey (1983) propose a family theory and strategic family therapy for encopresis that closely resembles the intervention proposed by Protinsky and Dillard (1983) for enuresis (see first section of this chapter). Protinsky and Kersey (1983) report success (86% success rate) in the implementation of their family therapy method in the clinical setting; however, no controlled research is available.

Psychotherapy

Play Therapy

Play therapy is a commonly used component of therapy for encopresis, although virtually no studies exist documenting its effectiveness for this particular disorder. Nondirective play therapy such as that described by Axline (1969) can be helpful in assisting young children with expression of feelings or fears related to toilet training. This goal may be particularly important in the case of the child who has endured overly restrictive toilet training and is rebelling against the structure imposed by parents.

Knell and Moore (1990) suggest a more directive form of play therapy that incorporates cognitive-behavioral principles to combat encopresis. Their technique begins with nondirective play. When specific encopresis-related themes emerge, the therapist addresses these with cognitive-behavioral techniques. For example, Knell and Moore (1990) describe a shaping technique in which the child is playing with a toy bear near the toilet. The child, however, avoids any toileting play with the bear. In response to this avoidance, the therapist has the bear gradually approach the toilet and use the toilet appropriately. If phobic or anxious behavior is played out (e.g., child flushes a doll down the toilet), the therapist can allow the child to experience the anxious situation by sitting the doll on the toilet (the cognitive-behavioral technique of exposure) but without the negative consequence of being flushed. Irrational beliefs are addressed by having the dolls express them and then having other dolls comment on their irrationality or model positive beliefs. Over all, the technique involves encouraging the child to express and address toileting problems through play. Although the initial free expression of feelings and concern is Axlinian, the directive play response of the therapist is designed to deliberately move the child to more adaptive toileting attitudes and behavior.

■ References

American Psychiatric Association. (1994). *Diagnostic and statistical manual of mental disorders, fourth edition.* Washington, DC: Author.

Axline, V. M. (1969). *Play therapy.* New York: Ballantine.

Azrin, N. H., Sneed, T. J., & Foxx, R. M. (1973). Dry Bed: A rapid method of eliminating bedwetting (enuresis) of the retarded. *Behavior Research and Therapy, 11,* 427–434.

Azrin, N. H., Sneed, T. J., & Foxx, R. M. (1974). Dry-Bed Training: Rapid elimination of childhood enuresis. *Behavior Research and Therapy, 12,* 147–156.

Azrin, N. H., & Thienes, P. M. (1978). Rapid elimination of enuresis by intensive learning without a conditioning apparatus. *Behavior Therapy, 9,* 342–354.

Banerjee, S., Srivastav, A., Palan, B. M. (1993). Hypnosis and self-hypnosis in the management of nocturnal enuresis: A comparative study with imipramine therapy. *American Journal of Clinical Hypnosis, 36,* 113–119.

Bath, R., Morton, R., Uing, A., & Williams, C. (1996). Nocturnal enuresis and the use of desmopressin: Is it helpful? *Child Care, Health, and Development, 22,* 73–84.

Bellman, M. M. (1966). Studies on encopresis. *Acta Paediatrica Scandinavia, 56* (Suppl. 170), 1–151.

Bemporad, J. R., Kresch, R. A., Asnes, R., & Wilson, A. (1978). Chronic neurotic encopresis as a paradigm of a multifactorial psychiatric disorder. *Journal of Nervous and Mental Disease, 166,* 472–479.

Bennett, G. A., Walkden, V. J., Curtis, R. H., Burns, L. E., Rees, J., Gosling, J. A., & McQuire, N. L. (1985). Pad-and-Buzzer Training, Dry-Bed Training, and Stop-Start Training in the treatment of primary nocturnal enuresis. *Behavioral Psychotherapy, 13,* 309–319.

Berrigan, L. P., & Stedman, J. M. (1989). Combined application of behavioral techniques and family therapy for the treatment of childhood encopresis: A strategic approach. *Family Therapy, 16,* 51–57.

Besalel, V. A., Azrin, N. H., Thienes-Hontos, P., & McMorrow, M. (1980). Evaluation of a parent's manual for training enuretic children. *Behavior Research and Therapy, 18,* 358–360.

Bollard, J., & Nettelbeck, T. (1982). A component analysis of dry bed training for treatment of bedwetting. *Behavior Research and Therapy, 20,* 383–390.

Bollard, J., Nettelbeck, T., & Roxbee, L. (1982). Dry bed training for childhood bedwetting: A comparison of group with individually administered parent instruction. *Behavior Research and Therapy, 20,* 209–217.

Bornstein, P. H., Balleweg, B. J., McLellarn, R. W., Wilson, G. L., Sturm, C. A., Andre, J. C., & Van Den Pol, R. A. (1983). The "Bathroom Game": A systematic program for the elimination of encopretic behavior. *Journal of Behavior Therapy and Experimental Psychiatry, 14,* 67–71.

Breit, M., Kaplan, S. L., Gauthier, B., & Weinhold, C. (1984). The Dry-Bed Method for the treatment of enuresis: A failure to duplicate previous reports. *Child and Family Behavior Therapy, 6,* 17–23.

Butler, R. J., Brewin, C. R., & Forsythe, W. I. (1988). A comparison of two approaches to the treatment of nocturnal enuresis and the prediction of effectiveness using pre-treatment variables. *Journal of Child Psychology and Psychiatry, 29,* 501–509.

Butler, R., Brewin, C., & Forsythe, I. (1990). Relapse in children treated for nocturnal enuresis: Prediction of response using pre-treatment variables. *Behavioral Psychotherapy, 18,* 65–72.

Cox, D. J., Sutphen, J., Borowitz, S., Dickens, M. N., Singles, J., & Whitehead, W. E. (1994). Simple electromyographic biofeedback treatment for chronic pediatric constipation/encopresis: Preliminary report. *Biofeedback and Self-Regulation, 19,* 41–50.

Cox, D. J., Sutphen, J., Ling, W., Quillian, W., & Borowitz, S. (1996). Additive benefits of laxative, toilet training, and biofeedback therapies in the treatment of pediatric encopresis. *Journal of Pediatric Psychology, 21,* 659–670.

Dische, S., Yule, W., Corbett, J., & Hand, D. (1983). Childhood nocturnal enuresis: Factors associated with outcome of treatment with an enuresis alarm. *Developmental Medicine and Child Neurology, 25,* 67–80.

Doleys, D. M. (1977). Behavioral treatments for nocturnal enuresis in children: A review of the recent literature. *Psychological Bulletin, 84,* 30–54.

Doleys, D. M. (1989). Functional enuresis and encopresis. In C. G. Last & M. Hersen (Eds.), *Handbook of child psychiatry diagnosis* (pp. 427–442). New York: Wiley.

Edwards, S. D., & Van Der Spuy, H. I. J. (1985). Hypnotherapy as a treatment for enuresis. *Journal of Child Psychology and Psychiatry, 26,* 161–170.

Fincham, F. D., & Spettell, C. (1984). The acceptability of Dry Bed Training and Urine Alarm Training as treatments of nocturnal enuresis. *Behavior Therapy, 15,* 388–394.

Foreman, D. M., & Thambirajah, M. S. (1996). Conduct disorder, enuresis, and specific developmental delays in two types of encopresis: A case-note study of 63 boys. *European Child and Adolescent Psychiatry, 5,* 33–37.

Fournier, J. P., Garfinkel, B. D., Bond, A., Beauchesne, H., & Shapiro, S. K. (1987). Pharmacological and behavioral management of enuresis. *Journal of the American Academy of Child and Adolescent Psychiatry, 26,* 849–853.

Foxx, R. M. (1985). The successful treatment of diurnal and nocturnal enuresis and encopresis. *Child and Family Behavior Therapy, 7,* 39–47.

Fritz, G. K., & Anders, T. F. (1979). Enuresis: the clinical application of an etiologically based classification system. *Child Psychiatry and Human Development, 10,* 103–113

Fritz, G. K., & Armbrust, J. (1982). Enuresis and encopresis. *Psychiatric Clinics of North America, 5,* 283–296.

Gabel, S., Chandra, R., & Shindledecker, R. (1988). Behavioral ratings and outcome of medical treatment for encopresis. *Journal of Developmental and Behavioral Pediatrics, 9,* 129–133.

Gabel, S., Hegedus, A. M., Wald, A., Chandra, R., & Chiponis, D. (1986). Prevalence of behavioral problems and mental health utilization among encopretic children: Implications for behavioral pediatrics. *Journal of Developmental and Behavioral Pediatrics, 7,* 293–297.

Geffken, G., Johnson, S. B., & Walker, D. (1986). Behavioral interventions for childhood nocturnal enuresis: The differential effect of bladder capacity on treatment progress and outcome. *Health Psychology, 5,* 261–272.

Glicklich, L. B. (1951). An historical account of enuresis. *Pediatrics, 8,* 859–876.

Haley, J. (1976). *Problem-solving therapy.* San Francisco: Jossey-Bass.

Houts, A. C., Berman, J. S., & Abramson, H. (1994). Effectiveness of psychological and pharmacological treatments for nocturnal enuresis. *Journal of Consulting and Clinical Psychology, 62,* 737–745.

Houts, A. C., Mellon, M. W., & Whelan, J. P. (1988). Use of dietary fiber and stimulus control to treat retentive encopresis: A multiple baseline investigation. *Journal of Pediatric Psychology, 13,* 435–445.

Houts, A. C., Peterson, J. K., & Whelan, J. P. (1986). Prevention of relapse in Full-Spectrum Home Training for primary enuresis: A components analysis. *Behavior Therapy, 17,* 462–469.

Johnston, B. D., & Wright, J. A. (1993). Attentional dysfunction in children with encopresis. *Journal of Developmental and Behavioral Pediatrics, 14,* 381–385.

Kanner, L. (1972). *Child psychiatry.* Springfield, IL: Charles C. Thomas.

Kaplan, B. J. (1985). A clinical demonstration program of a psychobiological approach to childhood encopresis. *Journal of Child Care, 2,* 47–54.

Kaplan, S. L., Breit, M., Gauthier, B., & Busner, J. (1988). A comparison of three nocturnal enuresis treatment methods. *Journal of the American Academy of Child and Adolescent Psychiatry, 28,* 282–286.

Keating, J. C., Butz, R. A., Burke, E., & Heimburg, R. G. (1983). Dry Bed Training without a urine alarm: Lack of effect of setting and therapist contact with child. *Journal of Behavior Therapy and Experimental Psychiatry, 14,* 109–115.

Knell, S. M., & Moore, D. J. (1990). Cognitive-behavioral play therapy in the treatment of encopresis. *Journal of Clinical Child Psychology, 19 ,* 55–60.

Knopf, I. J. (1979). *Childhood psychopathology: A developmental approach.* Englewood Cliffs, NJ: Prentice-Hall.

Kolko, D. J. (1987). Simplified inpatient treatment of nocturnal enuresis in psychiatrically disturbed children. *Behavior Therapy, 2,* 99–112.

Kolko, D. J. (1989). Inpatient intervention for chronic functional encopresis in psychiatrically disturbed children. *Behavioral Residential Treatment, 4,* 231–252.

Levine, M. (1975). Children with encopresis: A descriptive analysis. *Pediatrics, 56,* 412–416

Mesaros, J. D. (1993). Fluoxetine for primary enuresis. *Journal of the American Academy of Child and Adolescent Psychiatry, 32,* 877–878.

Morgan, R. T. T & Young, G. C. (1975). Parental attitudes and the conditioning treatment of childhood enuresis. *Behavior Research and Therapy, 13,* 197–199.

Mountjoy, P. T., Ruben, D. H., & Bradford, T. S. (1984). Recent technological advancements in the treatment of enuresis. *Behavior Modification, 8,* 291–315.

Mowrer, O. H., & Mowrer, W. M. (1938). Enuresis: A method for its study and treatment. *American Journal of Orthopsychiatry, 8,* 436–459.

O'Brien, S., Ross, L. V., & Christophersen, E. R. (1986). Primary encopresis: Evaluation and treatment. *Journal of Applied Behavioral Analysis, 19,* 137–145.

Olness, K. (1975). The use of self-hypnosis in the treatment of childhood nocturnal enuresis: A report on 40 patients. *Clinical Pediatrics, 14,* 273–279.

Owens-Stively, J. A. (1987). Self-esteem and compliance in encopretic children. *Child Psychiatry and Human Development, 18,* 13–21.

Paschalis, A. P., Kimmel, H. D., & Kimmel, E. (1972). Further study of diurnal instrumental conditioning in the treatment of enuresis nocturna. *Journal of Abnormal Child Psychology, 5,* 277–287.

Protinsky, H., & Dillard, C. (1983). Enuresis: A family therapy model. *Psychotherapy: Theory, Research, & Practice, 20,* 81–89.

Protinsky, H., & Kersey, B. (1983). Psychogenic encopresis: A family therapy approach. *Journal of Clinical Child Psychology, 12,* 192–197.

Rockney, R. M., McQuade, W. H., Days, A. L., Linn, H. E., & Alario, A. J. (1996). Encopresis treatment outcome: Long-term follow-up of 45 cases. *Journal of Developmental and Behavioral Pediatrics, 17,* 380–385.

Rushton, H. G. (1993). Evaluation of the enuretic child. *Clinical Pediatrics, 14,* 18.

Scharf, M. B., & Jennings, S. W. (1988). Childhood enuresis: Relationship to sleep, etiology, evaluation, and treatment. *Annals of Behavioral Medicine, 10,* 113–120.

Scharf, M. B., Pravada, M. F., Jennings, S. W., Kauffman, R., & Ringel, J. (1987). Childhood enuresis: A comprehensive treatment program. *Psychiatric Clinics of North America, 10,* 655–667.

Shaffer, D., Gardner, A., & Hedge, B. (1984). Behavior and bladder disturbance of enuretic children: A rational classification of a common disorder. *Developmental Medicine and Child Neurology, 26,* 781–792.

Sprenger, D. (1997). Sertraline for nocturnal enuresis. *Journal of the American Academy of Child and Adolescent Psychiatry, 36,* 304–305.

Stark, L. J., Spirito, A., Lewis, A. V., & Hart, K. J. (1990). Encopresis: Behavioral parameters associated with children who fail medical management. *Child Psychiatry and Human Development, 20,* 169–179.

Steinhausen, H. C., & Gobel, D. (1989). Enuresis in child psychiatric clinic patients. *Journal of the American Academy of Child and Adolescent Psychiatry, 28,* 279–281.

Taylor, P. D., & Turner, R. K. (1975). A clinical trial of continuous, intermittent, and overlearning "bell and pad" treatments for nocturnal enuresis. *Behavior Research and Therapy, 13,* 281–293.

Thompson, S., & Rey, J. M. (1995). Functional enuresis: Is desmopressin the answer? *Journal of the American Academy of Child and Adolescent Psychiatry, 34,* 266–271.

Wagner, W. G. (1987). The behavioral treatment of nocturnal enuresis. *Journal of Counseling and Development, 65,* 262–265.

Wagner, W. G., & Geffken, G. (1986). Enuretic children: How they view their wetting behavior. *Child Study Journal, 16,* 13–18.

Wagner, W. G., & Johnson, J. T. (1988). Childhood nocturnal enuresis: The prediction of premature withdrawal from behavioral conditioning. *Journal of Abnormal Child Psychology, 16,* 687–692.

Wald, A., & Handen, B. L. (1987). Behavioral aspects of disorders of defecation and fecal continence. *Annals of Behavioral Medicine, 9,* 19–23.

Warzak, W. J. (1993). Psychosocial implications of nocturnal enuresis. *Clinical Pediatrics,* 38–40.

Werry, J. S., & Cohrssen, J. (1965). Enuresis—an etiologic and therapeutic study. *Journal of Pediatrics, 67,* 423–431.

Whelan, J. P., & Houts, A. C. (1990). Effects of a waking schedule on primary enuretic children treated with Full-Spectrum Home Training. *Health Psychology, 9,* 164–176.

Wiener, J. M. (1984). Psychopharmacology in childhood disorders. *Psychiatric Clinics of North America, 7,* 831–843.

Young, G. C., & Morgan, R. T. T. (1972a). Overlearning in the conditioning treatment of enuresis: A long-term follow-up study. *Behavior Research and Therapy, 10,* 419–420.

Young, G. C., & Morgan, R. T. T. (1972b). Overlearning in the conditioning treatment of enuresis. *Behavior Research and Therapy, 10,* 147–151.

Young, M. H., Brennen, L. C., Baker, R. D., & Baker, S. S. (1995). Functional encopresis: Symptom reduction and behavioral improvement. *Journal of Developmental and Behavioral Pediatrics, 16,* 226–232.

☐ CHAPTER 5

Mood Disorders

■ **Bipolar Disorder and Cyclothymic Disorder**

☐ CLINICAL DESCRIPTION

Diagnostic Considerations

DSM-IV does not include separate diagnostic criteria for childhood mood disorders. Instead, DSM-IV takes the position that depression is basically the same syndrome in children as in adults, with some developmental considerations. Hence, DSM-IV incorporates developmental considerations into the adult mood disorder diagnoses.

DSM-IV recognizes two broad groups of mood disorders: Bipolar Disorders and Depressive Disorders. Of these two groups the Bipolar Disorders are more rare in preadolescent children, although some clinicians have expressed concern that early-onset Bipolar Disorders may be underdiagnosed (Weller, Weller, & Fristad, 1995). The Bipolar Disorders have as their defining characteristic the presence of Manic, Mixed, or Hypomanic Episodes of behavior. Manic and Hypomanic Episodes involve such symptoms as elevated or irritable mood, grandiose self-image, little need for sleep, being overly talkative, flight of ideas, distractibility, overactivity, and dangerous behavior. Manic and Hypomanic Episodes differ based on duration and severity. A Manic Episode must involve symptom presence for at least one week and marked impairment in daily functioning. A Hypomanic Episode, on the other hand, may last only 4 or more days, and it involves less severe symptoms that are noticeable but do not cause marked problems. Mixed Episodes occur when a child meets the criteria for a Manic Episode and a Major Depressive Episode "nearly every day" for 1 week or more, with marked impairment in functioning (American Psychiatric Association, 1994).

In addition to manic symptoms, Bipolar Disorders are classified based on the presence of depressive symptoms, in the form of a Major Depressive Episode. A Major Depressive Episode involves the presence of five or more depressive symptoms during a 2-week period. At least one of the symptoms must be depressed mood or anhedonia. Other symptoms characteristic of a Major Depressive Episode are weight (or appetite) change, insomnia or hypersomnia, psychomotor agitation or retardation, fatigue, sense of worthlessness, feelings of guilt, concentration problems, and preoccupation with death or suicide. In children, irritable mood may be substituted for depressed mood. A Major Depressive Episode may be diagnosed only if the person has significant distress or problems in daily functioning, without sufficient manic symptoms for a Mixed Episode to be diagnosed.

Based on the number of Major Depressive, Manic, Mixed, and Hypomanic Episodes, a number of variants of Bipolar Disorder can be diagnosed. Bipolar I Disorders are diagnosed when the person has had or is having a Manic or Mixed Episode. Diagnostic qualifiers are added depending on the presence of past or current Manic or Mixed Episodes, current Hypomanic Episodes, past Major Depressive Episodes, and current Major Depressive Episodes (American Psychiatric Association, 1994). Bipolar II Disorder is diagnosed when the person has never had a Manic Episode but has had Hypomanic and Major Depressive Episodes. Cyclothymic Disorder is diagnosed when the child has multiple occurrences of hypomanic symptoms and multiple occurrences of depressed mood/anhedonia during a 1-year period (2 years for adults), without the presence of a Major Depressive Episode or a Manic Episode. Hence, Cyclothymic Disorder has a more chronic but less severe symptom picture.

Bipolar Disorders may be further subtyped based on the speed and timing of cycling. A seasonal pattern is diagnosed when the depressive episodes occur at a particular time of year (usually fall/winter). Rapid cycling is diagnosed when a mood disturbance episode (depression, mania, hypomania, or mixed episode) occurs at least four times in a 1-year period.

The Bipolar Disorders are not commonly seen in prepubertal children, but their incidence jumps in adolescence, with about 20% of all Bipolar Disorders emerging between the ages of 15 and 19 (American Academy of Child and Adolescent Psychiatry, 1997; Keller & Wunder, 1990). Although no large studies report on the incidence of Bipolar Disorder in children under the age of 13, Wozniak et al. (1995) cite three studies showing that 0.3–0.5% of adults with Bipolar Disorder report onset of symptoms prior to age 10. Hence, prepubertal onset of Bipolar Disorder is rare but not unseen (Table 5.1).

The Bipolar Disorders should be diagnosed cautiously in children and adolescents for several reasons: First, the base rate of Bipolar Disorder in preteen children appears to be low (although some authors disagree with this assessment; see Wozniak et al., 1995). Hence, the probability of Bipolar Disorder occurring in any one child, even in a clinical setting, is small. Second, many diagnostic features of other childhood disorders overlap with manic features or could be interpreted as manic features. Hyperactivity, distractibility, and lack of goal direction, for example, could be symptoms of Attention-Deficit Hyperactivity Disorder (ADHD) as opposed to a Bipolar Disorder; dangerous behavior could be symptomatic of Conduct Disorder (CD). Both ADHD and CD occur much more commonly in children than the Bipolar Disorders, making either of these diagnoses more likely in any given child. Third, children and, particularly, adolescents are often prone to greater, more frequent mood swings than are adults. These mood swings may be triggered by apparently minor events (e.g., getting a good grade; having a bad hair day for the prom). Hence, euphoria over minor events may be developmentally normal (or at least not bizarre) for adolescents. To diagnose such mood swings as Cyclothymic Disorder or Bipolar II would result in astronomically high rates of these disorders in adolescents.

In addition to ruling out plausible alternative diagnoses, the clinician must be careful to recognize comorbid diagnoses when they occur. There is evidence that children with Bi-

TABLE 5.1 Epidemiology and Course of Bipolar Disorder

Prevalence: Unknown in children under age 13, but unusual (likely < 0.1%).
0.2–1% in adolescents age 13–18

Sex Ratio (Male:Female): 1:1, with greater male:female ratio at younger ages

Typical Onset Age: 13–30 years of age

Course: Symptoms are cyclic, with multiple episodes (of depression and mania or hypomania) typically occurring in the course of the disorder (treatment reduces the number of episodes). Duration of episodes can vary from several weeks to several months, although very rapid cycling (for periods of hours) is sometimes seen in younger children. Episodes can continue through the lifetime of the individual, although there is no "typical" course. Poorer prognosis and/or treatment resistance associated with earlier onset, psychotic symptoms, substance abuse, and rapid cycling.

Common Comorbid Conditions: 1. Attention-Deficit Hyperactivity Disorder
2. Conduct Disorder
3. Sleep Disorders
4. Substance Abuse

Relevant Subtypes: 1. Bipolar I (manic episodes) vs. Bipolar II (hypomanic episodes only)
2. Seasonal
3. Rapid Cycling

polar Disorder are more prone to have a variety of comorbid diagnoses as compared to children with other psychiatric disorders. Some studies have estimated that 10–20% of children with ADHD may have or develop Bipolar Disorder (Biederman et al., 1996; Wozniak et al., 1995), although these figures require additional research. Hence, the presence of ADHD or another Axis I diagnosis does not necessarily rule out a co-occurring Bipolar Disorder.

Appearance and Features

Classic DSM-IV criteria for manic episodes are most clearly and commonly seen in adolescents and adults. In contrast to adult-onset mania, adolescent-onset Bipolar Disorder tends to be associated with features such as flagrantly psychotic symptoms (hallucinations and disorganization of thought), rapid fluctuations in mood, and/or rapid and significant deterioration in behavior (American Academy of Child and Adolescent Psychiatry, 1997). These features sometimes lead to a misdiagnosis of schizophrenia.

Prior to adolescence, children with Bipolar Disorder or Cyclothymia tend to have less clear cycles of manic behavior. When cycles occur in children under age 13, they tend to be of very brief duration (as short as 4 hours) and may be interpreted as the child's typical style of behavior in the environment (American Academy of Child and Adolescent Psychiatry, 1997; Geller et al., 1995). Very rapid cycling is seen in as many as 81% of children and adolescents with Bipolar Disorder, with cycles longer than 2 weeks being extremely rare (Geller et al., 1995). Instead of displaying clear cycles of manic and depressed behavior, prepubertal children with Bipolar Disorder are often irritable, moody, disruptive, impulsive, energetic, and hyperactive; clear euphoria is present in fewer than 15% of preadolescent children with emerging Bipolar Disorder (Wozniak et al., 1995). They have difficulty sleeping, poor frustration tolerance, and explosive outbursts. Depressive symptoms are common. Because many of these symptoms overlap with depression and ADHD, it can be extremely difficult to differentiate early-onset Manic or Hypomanic Episodes from other diagnoses (American Academy of Child and Adolescent Psychiatry, 1997; Carlson, 1983, 1990; Weller et al., 1995).

A high degree of intensity, characterized by excessive, prolonged responses to mildly arousing stimuli, may be one factor that can differentiate children at risk for Bipolar Disorder from children with other diagnoses; however, clinicians must be careful not to confuse an intense temperament with bipolarity. Another differentiating factor may be the presence of clear depressive episodes combined with or followed by pressured hyperactivity and prolonged irritability. Some children with Bipolar Disorders present as cases of extreme ADHD, with symptoms that are so extreme as to be grandiose, bizarre, or excessively intense. Increased sexual acting-out (in the absence of abuse), grandiosity, and lack of sleep are other symptoms characteristic of preadolescent mania. Onset is often rapid, occurring over a period of under 2–3 months (American Academy of Child and Adolescent Psychiatry, 1997; Carlson, 1983, 1990; Weller et al., 1995).

Bipolar Disorder in children and adolescents is associated with a variety of risky behaviors, which should be routinely monitored. Substance abuse is a common comorbid condition with Bipolar Disorder. Furthermore, the risk of suicidal ideation and attempts is higher than for other disorders. Up to one-third of children under age 13 with Bipolar Disorder have serious suicidal ideation. As many as half of adolescents with Bipolar Disorder have serious suicidal ideation, and as many as 20% make significant suicide attempts (American Academy of Child and Adolescent Psychiatry, 1997; Geller et al., 1995).

In order to avoid the pitfalls of misdiagnosing or failing to diagnose Bipolar Disorders in children and adolescents, the clinician is advised to bear the following features of the disorder in mind (Table 5.2):

1. Familial incidence of Bipolar Disorder is considered a risk factor in the disease (Keller & Wunder, 1990; Strober, 1992). Alcoholism, especially in male relatives, appears to put children with depression at increased risk for development of a Bipolar Disorder (Todd, Geller, Neuman, Fox, & Hickok, 1996).

2. A significant change from previous functioning, involving manic symptoms, may be more symptomatic of a Bipolar Disorder than of ADHD or CD in children (Pataki & Carlson, 1992). However, the presence of an organic factor or a traumatic stressor should also be evaluated to explain such a rapid change in functioning.

3. Consistently bizarre, pressured behavior, regardless of stressors or environmental factors, may suggest Bipolar Disorder, particularly if flight of ideas and pressured speech are consistently seen in an adolescent. Psychotic behaviors are more characteristic of mania than of other childhood disorders, with the exception of schizophrenia (Pataki & Carlson, 1992).

4. Psychotic behaviors seen during Bipolar Disorder are manic mood-congruent (usually related to grandiosity or overactivity), whereas those of other disorders may not be as influenced by mood (Keller & Wunder, 1990).

5. Rule-breaking behavior during a manic episode tends to have more of a grandiose, oblivious, or excitement-seeking quality, as compared to the more malicious, antisocial behavior of children with Conduct Disorders. The presence of true guilt or regret is more characteristic of Bipolar Disorder than of Conduct Disorder (Weller et al., 1995).

TABLE 5.2   Appearance and Features of Bipolar Disorder

COMMON FEATURES

1. Manic or hypomanic behavior: elevated mood, grandiosity, decreased sleep, talkative, flight of ideas, distractibility, overactive
2. Major depressive episodes or depressive symptoms (not required but frequently present)
3. Onset almost always after age 12
4. Cycling presentation of symptoms, especially if onset after age 12
5. Familial incidence of mood disorder
6. Irritability, moodiness, impulsivity (preadolescent onset)
7. Explosive outbursts (preadolescent onset)

OCCASIONAL FEATURES

1. Familial incidence of alcoholism
2. Psychotic symptoms (adolescent onset)
3. Rapid, brief cycles
4. Extremely intense style of response to stimuli (preadolescent onset)
5. Sexual acting-out
6. Substance abuse
7. Suicide attempts

Note: The features listed in the table are often seen but are not universal. Some features may be diagnostically relevant or required, whereas others may not be required for diagnosis.

6. The risk of overdiagnosing Bipolar Disorder in adolescents is high if developmentally appropriate norms for "euphoria," "elevated mood," and "overactivity" are not used. Some mood swings and overactivity are typical of the adolescent phase of life. On the other hand, the incidence of Bipolar Disorder increases markedly in adolescence and young adulthood.

7. Grossly inflated self-esteem is more typical of a Bipolar Disorder in a child or adolescent, whereas most other disorders involve low self-esteem (Keller & Wunder, 1990).

8. Bipolar Disorder in children and adolescents is cyclic, whereas other disorders such as ADHD, CD, and Oppositional-Defiant Disorder more consistently affect the behavior of the child or are affected strongly by environment.

9. The onset of ADHD occurs before the age of 7. Therefore, hypomanic symptoms that emerge after age 10–12, with no evidence of ADHD symptoms prior to age 7, are much more likely to be due to a hypomanic/manic episode (or other disorder) than to ADHD.

10. The presence of a childhood depression, followed by onset of clear hypomanic or manic behavior later in childhood or adolescence, raises the likelihood of Bipolar Disorder or Cyclothymia. This is especially true when the child has no history of ADHD or hyperactive behavior prior to the onset of the manic behavior. About 20–30% of children with Major Depressive Disorders will develop Bipolar Disorder within 5 years (American Academy of Child and Adolescent Psychiatry, 1997; Todd et al., 1996).

11. Significant change in sleep patterns, in the presence of other bipolar symptoms, is more characteristic of Bipolar Disorder than of other diagnoses such as ADHD. Children with ADHD often have consistent sleep problems such as onset insomnia and short duration of sleep. Children with Bipolar Disorder often show a sudden change in sleep patterns, usually sleeping less and staying awake more at night (Weller et al., 1995).

Etiology

Biological Theories

Strong evidence supports a physiological-genetic etiology for Bipolar Disorder. Bipolar Disorder tends to run in families, and children with relatives suffering from Bipolar Disorder are more likely to develop Bipolar Disorder themselves. Additionally, psychostimulant and antidepressant medications can sometimes provoke manic episodes in individuals manifesting depressive symptoms, suggesting a possible biochemical triggering effect. Medication treatments tend to be the most effective interventions for Bipolar Disorder; psychotherapy and environmental modifications can reduce the severity (and possibly the frequency) of some episodes in some individuals, but there is no evidence that psychotherapy alone results in remission of bipolar symptoms (American Academy of Child and Adolescent Psychiatry, 1997). These factors argue strongly for a biologically mediated etiology to the disorder, with some smaller influence of environmental effects.

☐ ASSESSMENT PATTERNS

Because of the rarity of Bipolar Disorder in children, little is known about its assessment in childhood. Certainly, assessment of suspected Bipolar Disorder should include instruments measuring depression (described later in this chapter) and plausible alternative or comorbid disorders such as ADHD and Conduct Disorder (Table 5.3). Of the broad-band behavior checklists, only the ASI-4 has a Bipolar Disorder subscale, which has received little research attention to date. Assessment of adolescents with Bipolar Disorder generally uses

TABLE 5.3 Sample Assessment Battery for Mood Disorders

PERSONALITY

1. Thematic Apperception Test
2. Sentence Completion Test

BEHAVIORAL

1. Behavior Assessment System for Children (Parent, Teacher, and Self)
2. Personality Inventory for Youth

SYNDROME-SPECIFIC

1. Children's Depression Inventory
2. Hopelessness Scale

Note: Assessment instruments are intended to supplement (not substitute for) a good clinical interview and, when possible, a structured diagnostic interview.

adult instruments, such as the MMPI (see Meyer & Deitsch, 1996 for additional discussion of assessment of Bipolar Disorder in adolescents and adults).

Broad Assessment Strategies

Cognitive Assessment

Clinician-Administered.   There is some evidence that children with Bipolar Disorder, as a group, score lower on WISC-III Full Scale IQ, Verbal IQ, and Freedom From Distracti-bility, compared to children with ADHD and other diagnoses (Biederman et al., 1996; Wozniak et al., 1995); however, the majority of children with Bipolar Disorder have IQ in the average range (American Academy of Child and Adolescent Psychiatry, 1997). Children with Bipolar Disorder have also been found to score lower on arithmetic and reading achievement tests and to have higher rates of learning disabilities, compared to psychiatric control groups (Biederman et al., 1996; Wozniak et al., 1995).

Psychological Assessment

Clinician-Administered.   All major semistructured diagnostic interviews (DICA, DISC, K-SADS) screen for manic symptoms and can be very useful if extensive and comprehensive evaluation of symptoms is needed. In some cases, these techniques can produce false positives (children who endorse manic symptoms when they in fact do not have Bipolar Disorder) when a child is overly zealous or histrionic about answering interview questions. This risk is particularly pronounced in adolescents, who will often report wide swings in mood and excitement.

Behavioral Assessment

Parent-Report and Other-Report.   The CBCL, BASC, and CRS-R do not include sub-scales specifically targeting manic symptoms, but children with Bipolar Disorder would be expected to elevate hyperactivity, depression, and related subscales on these question-naires. Elevation of subscales containing unusual or psychotic behaviors (Thought Problems on the CBCL, Atypicality on the BASC, and Psychosis on the PIC) would also be characteristic of a child with severe manic episodes. For example, children with Bipolar Disorder tend to produce extreme elevations (T-scores greater than 70 for group means) of the CBCL Aggressive Behavior, Anxious-Depressed, and Attention Problem subscales. In empirical research, children with Bipolar Disorder have scored significantly higher than children with ADHD on the Delinquent Behavior, Aggresive Behavior, Somatic Complaints, Anxious-Depressed, and Thought Problems subscales, with the largest differences occurring on the Aggressive Behavior, Anxious-Depressed, and Delinquent Behavior sub-scales (Biederman et al., 1995, 1996). On the other hand, Weller et al. (1995) caution that the original versions of the Conners' scales may not discriminate children with Bipolar Disorder from those with ADHD. It is important to obtain both parent-report and teacher-report to evaluate the severity and pervasiveness of symptoms.

□ TREATMENT OPTIONS

Psychotherapy

Psychotherapy for children with Bipolar Disorder is usually seen as an important but not sufficient treatment. When Bipolar Disorder is comorbid with another Axis I disorder (such as Conduct Disorder, Substance Abuse, or Learning Disorder), psychotherapeutic and behavioral interventions are directed at that specific comorbid disorder in addition to other treatments for Bipolar Disorder. Psychotherapy specifically for Bipolar Disorder typically has five main goals:

1. Educate the child and family about the disorder, risks, outcomes, and treatments. A review of information about Bipolar Disorder, along with the identification of household rules to address manic and depressive episodes, are the main parts of a psychoeducational intervention. Medication benefits, side effects, and regimens are also typically discussed. Fears and irrational beliefs about Bipolar Disorder are addressed and corrected.

2. Encourage compliance with medication. Medication is frequently effective in treating Bipolar Disorder, and failure to take medication is often associated with relapse. Relapse rates for adolescents who failed to take their medication (lithium) was 90% in one study, as compared to 37.5% for those who continued to take their medication (Strober, Morrell, Lampert, & Burroughs, 1990).

3. Treat the child during depressive episodes, using depression interventions (described later in this chapter).

4. Provide support and structure for the child and family. Adjusting to Bipolar Disorder is a stressful event for child and family. The therapist should evaluate stress and assist the child and family in implementing structure to provide support when it is needed by family members. Because Bipolar Disorder can affect the child's functioning in other areas, a psychotherapy treatment plan should address adaptive behavior in the social, academic, family, work, and other environments. Family therapy may be needed to assist the family in maintaining stability and support while reducing conflict and stress.

5. Educate the school and collaborate on interventions to monitor and address manic and depressive symptoms at school. It is often helpful for the school to have an understanding of the child's disorder, its treatment, and rules for addressing symptoms when they arise. Children are often reassured by the knowledge that they will be taken care of at school as well as at home and in the therapist's office (Table 5.4).

Medication

Medication is the primary treatment of choice for both children and adults with Bipolar Disorder. Although lithium is a treatment of choice for adults with Bipolar Disorder, its efficacy in children has not been widely investigated. Case reports and open-label studies note improvements in 33–74% of children placed on lithium although, on average, it appears to be a less effective treatment for children and adolescents than for adults (Kafantaris, 1995; Weller et al., 1995). Carbamazepine (Tegretol) and valproate (Depakote) have also been used in some cases with success, although their effectiveness is variable (Bezchlibnyk-Butler & Jeffries, 1997; Weller et al., 1995). Comorbid disorders, early onset, and rapid cy-

TABLE 5.4   Treatment Options for Bipolar Disorder

PSYCHOTHERAPY

1. Psychoeducation
2. Medication compliance encouraged
3. Depression treatments
4. Family and supportive individual psychotherapy
5. Collaboration with school on behavioral plans and expectations

MEDICATION

1. Lithium
2. Carbamazepine
3. Valproate

Note: This outline of options summarizes major treatments covered in the text. Specific treatments are often combined into an intervention package. Refer to the text for additional descriptions of each treatment. This table is not necessarily an exhaustive list of all treatments available.

cling have been associated with poorer response to lithium, and Tegretol is often tried in those cases (Kafantaris, 1995). Other medications that have been tried for childhood-onset Bipolar Disorder include neuroleptics and benzodiazepines; the appropriateness of these medications for most children with Bipolar Disorder is questionable (Kafantaris, 1995).

■ Major Depressive Disorder and Dysthymic Disorder

☐ CLINICAL DESCRIPTION

Diagnostic Considerations

Depressive disorders in children may be classified in one of two categories: Major Depressive Disorder is typically more severe, often recurrent, and of shorter duration; it involves the presence of one or more Major Depressive Episodes with no Manic, Mixed, or Hypomanic Episodes. Dysthymic Disorder, on the other hand, is typically less severe and lasts longer than 1 year in children and adolescents. Depressive disorders that do not fit one of these two categories must be classified as Depressive Disorder, Not Otherwise Specified (NOS), or as Adjustment Disorder with Depressed Mood (which is technically an Adjustment Disorder and not a Mood Disorder). Adjustment Disorder with Depressed Mood is qualitatively different from the depressive disorders, with rapid onset and recovery (unless it develops into a depressive disorder), and a clear link to a stressor (Burgin, 1986).

There are few age-based diagnostic differences in Depressive Disorder criteria. For Dysthymic Disorder the duration of depressed mood is reduced from 2 years for adults to 1 year for children and adolescents. For both Major Depressive Disorder and Dysthymic Disorder, depression in children may be shown by irritable (as opposed to depressed) mood.

Much of the research and clinical literature on childhood depression does not mirror the diagnostic nosology of DSM-IV. Instead, most literature refers to "Childhood Depression" or a "depressed group," using definitions that sometimes fit DSM criteria and sometimes are assigned according to a different set of criteria. The plethora of definitions for *depression* complicates the review of childhood depression literature. To simplify this process, *depression* will be used in this section to describe a syndrome that resembles closely the definitions of Major Depressive Disorder and/or Dysthymic Disorder. Differing definitions of depression will be noted when they stray significantly from the Major Depressive Disorder/Dysthymic Disorder presentation.

The hallmark of depression is depressed mood, although irritable mood has been added for child diagnoses. DSM-IV adds loss of interest or pleasure (anhedonia) as a key symptom for a Major Depressive Episode and then provides a group of vegetative (weight loss or gain, sleep disturbance, fatigue), cognitive (worthlessness, guilt, difficulty concentrating, suicidal ideation), and behavioral (psychomotor agitation, psychomotor retardation) symptoms. Importantly, depression should not be diagnosed within 2 months of the death of a loved one, unless impairment is marked. This latter criterion reflects the belief that depression should not be diagnosed if the symptoms are part of a normal grief reaction.

Differentiating depression from a "normal" grief reaction can be a difficult task. Weller, Weller, Fristad, & Bowes, (1991) compared recently bereaved children with hospitalized children with depression and found some differences that may be of diagnostic assistance. In general, bereaved children commonly (more than 20% of sample) reported depressive symptoms, such as dysphoria, loss of interest, appetite disturbance, sleep disturbance, psychomotor retardation/agitation, guilt, and suicidal ideation. However, bereaved children reported fewer symptoms overall than did children with depression. Large differences were found between the groups on sleep disturbance (74% of depressed vs. 29% of bereaved), psychomotor retardation (66% of depressed vs. 32% of bereaved), fatigue (47% of depressed vs. 8% of bereaved), guilt/worthlessness (76% of depressed vs. 21% of bereaved), and trouble concentrating (47% of depressed vs. 5% of bereaved). Importantly, 26% of the bereaved sample had symptoms of sufficient severity to be diagnosed as having a Major Depressive Episode.

The incidence of Major Depressive Disorder in school-aged children is generally found to be around 1.5–2%, whereas that of Dysthymic Disorder is slightly higher (2–2.5%) (Table 5.5). Depression appears to become more common with age, increasing to 4.7% and 3.3% for adolescents with Major Depressive Disorder or Dysthymic Disorder, respectively (Anderson, Williams, McGee, & Silva, 1987; Birmaher et al., 1996; Kashani et al., 1987; Kashani & Schmid, 1992). In preschoolers, on the other hand, Major Depressive Disorder appears to be uncommon (perhaps less than 1%; Kashani, Holcomb, & Orvaschel, 1986; Kashani & Ray, 1983; Kashani & Schmid, 1992). The prevalence of preadolescent depression is approximately equal in males and females, but in adolescence, females with depression outnumber males by 2–5 to 1 (Birmaher et al., 1996; Kashani & Schmid, 1992).

In contrast to rates for depressive syndromes, the prevalence of single depressive symptoms is quite high in children. Rates of 7% for preschoolers with one or more depressive symptoms and 40% for adolescents with one or more depressive symptoms have been reported (Kashani et al., 1986; Kashani et al., 1987; Pataki & Carlson, 1990). Hence, it is not surprising to find one or two symptoms of depression in a child. Furthermore, the pres-

TABLE 5.5   Epidemiology and Course of Depressive Disorders

Prevalence: 1.5–4% in Preadolescent Children
                       3–8% in Adolescents

Sex Ratio (Male:Female):   1:1 in Preadolescent Children
                                           1:2 in Adolescents

Typical Onset Age: Can be anytime in childhood but usually not later than adolescence

Course: The average Major Depressive Episode lasts 6–9 months; mean length of Dysthymic Disorder episode is 2–4 years. 70% of children with Dysthymic Disorder will go on to have a Major Depressive Episode, typically within 3 years of the onset of dysthymia. 40% of children with a Major Depressive Episode will have a second episode within 2 years; 70% will have a second episode by 5 years. As many as 1 in 5 adolescents with a Major Depressive Disorder will have a manic episode within 5 years. There is increased risk of suicide, chronic low self-esteem, and interpersonal problems.

Common Comorbid Conditions: 1. Anxiety Disorder
                                                    2. Conduct or Oppositional Defiant Disorder
                                                    3. Substance Abuse
                                                    4. Suicidal Ideation, Intent, or Attempt

Relevant Subtypes: 1. Major Depressive Disorder vs. Dysthymic Disorder vs. "Double Depression" (Major Depressive Disorder superimposed on Dysthymic Disorder)
                                                    2. Seasonal Affective Disorder
                                                    3. "Acting-Out" Depression (depression comorbid with disruptive behavior)
                                                    4. Anaclitic Depression (infancy)
                                                    5. Hospitalism

ence of a depressive symptom does not necessarily indicate that the child has a diagnosable depressive syndrome. Symptoms may be isolated or transient, whereas the syndrome will be more pervasive and long-standing.

In DSM-IV, Bipolar I and II Disorders and Major Depressive Disorder can also be specified as having a seasonal pattern if the onset and remission of the Major Depressive Episodes occur at the same time of the year for the last 2 years. During the last 2 years, there cannot have been any affective disorders out of this seasonal pattern, and over the individual's lifetime, seasonal episodes must outnumber nonseasonal episodes. The most typical presentation of this subtype in children (referred to as Seasonal Affective Disorder or SAD) is for depression to occur throughout the winter and to remit in spring (Rosenthal, Sack, Skwerer, Jacobsen, & Wehr, 1989; Sonis, 1992). SAD is more common in adolescents than in children, with mean ages in various studies of children with SAD of between 12 and 16 years (Sonis, 1989; 1992).

Because SAD is hypothesized to be caused by seasonal patterns of light that disrupt biological rhythms (particularly the decreased light of winter), the common treatments for SAD attempt to reorient the person's biological rhythms (Sonis, 1992). Most common is phototherapy, which involves exposure to bright light at a certain time each day (Sonis, 1989). Hypothetically, this mimics summer light and resets biological rhythms. The intensity, wavelength, site, timing, and duration of the light are adjusted to be ideal. For example, ultraviolet light is not necessary, and the eyes should be used as the focus site (Rosenthal et al., 1989; Sonis, 1992). Some success has been reported following the use of phototherapy with small samples of children with SAD (Sonis, 1992). Other treatments sometimes used to treat SAD are sleep deprivation and pharmacotherapy (lithium for SAD-Bipolar).

Appearance and Features

Developmental Appearance

Numerous authors have suggested that the appearance and features of depression differ by age (Birmaher et al., 1996; Shafii & Shafii, 1992). In general, behavioral and attachment symptoms are more common at very young ages, whereas cognitive and emotional symptoms become more common with older age. Suicide attempts, psychosis, and adaptive functioning deficits are more common in adolescents, whereas anxiety, phobias, somatic complaints, and disruptive behavior are more common in younger children with depression (Birmaher et al., 1996).

In infancy and toddlerhood, depressive symptoms and syndromes are manifest predominantly in behavioral flatness and attachment disruption. Cognitive components such as beliefs and pessimism are not present. *Anaclitic (infant) depression* (Spitz, 1945, 1946, 1965) is characterized by whining, withdrawal, weight loss, slowed or stunted growth, susceptibility to infection, dazed and immobile facial expression, intellectual decline, impaired social interaction, and withdrawal (Spitz, 1965). This syndrome occurs in infants who are emotionally deprived, usually because of separation or infrequent contact with a major attachment figure within the first year of life (Burgin, 1986). Separation is usually physical, although extreme emotional unavailability may also lead to an anaclitic depression. Mothers with depression, for example, are at risk for having infants and children with depression (Burgin, 1986). If the separation lasts several weeks or months, whining gives way to withdrawal, expressionless looks, and resisting interaction. Hospitalism (named because it was initially seen in hospitalized or institutionalized infants) is a severe subtype of anaclitic depression typically caused by long periods of separation from an attachment figure within the first year of life (Spitz, 1965). In hospitalism, more severe symptoms of slowed motor responsiveness, expressionless face, bizarre/self-stimulating behaviors (hand waving, rocking), extreme intellectual decline (to the point of mental retardation), unresponsiveness to social interaction, and high mortality rate are superimposed on the anaclitic depression (Spitz, 1965).

Toddler depression affects children in the 1–2 age range. Some age-specific symptoms of toddler depression are irritable mood, delay in developmental challenges of toddlerhood (walking, standing, language, toilet training), nightmares and night terrors, self-stimulating behaviors (rocking, head banging, masturbation), clinginess, oppositional behavior, excessive fears, and decrease in play (Shafii & Shafii, 1992). At younger toddler ages, many of the symptoms of anaclitic depression may emerge or persist. It is important to note that toddlers who have had traumatic experiences may show these symptoms as a part of a Post-Traumatic Stress Disorder or other Anxiety Disorder.

At preschool ages (age 3–5 years), depressive symptoms often take the form of sadness, weight loss, motor retardation, tiredness, suicidal ideation, anger, apathy, illness, irritability, and social withdrawal (Kashani et al., 1986). As a result of these symptoms, preschoolers who are depressed typically play less with other children and verbally express feelings of sadness, worthlessness, and fearfulness (Shafii & Shafii, 1992).

After age 6, depression in children comes to resemble more closely that of adults in terms of cognitive, mood, behavioral, and vegetative symptoms. Often the presence of depression in a school-aged child is first manifest by declining performance, which is more clearly evaluated at school ages than before. Thus, declines in grades, failure to complete chores, or declining performance in sports make the reality of depression more apparent to caretakers. In addition, peer relationships take on greater importance at these ages, and the status of a child as popular, average, rejected, or neglected may have an impact on the development of depressive symptoms. Reciprocally, depression may have a major impact on the child's social standing. School-age children may also show depression through a variety of other symptoms such as oppositionality, anger, delinquency, overactivity, fears, and somatization (Cytryn & McKnew, 1972; Glaser, 1968).

In adolescence, volatile mood, rage, intense self-consciousness, low self-esteem, poor school performance, delinquent behaviors, substance abuse, sexual acting-out, and social withdrawal are common depression symptoms (Shafii & Shafii, 1992). In addition, adolescents may have oversleeping and overeating problems at higher rates than do adults (Simeon, 1989). A significant risk of suicidal behavior also exists in the adolescent group, and any suicidal ideation or threat should be taken seriously.

General Appearance

In addition to developmental variation in depressive symptoms, depressive syndromes in children age 4–12 years share certain similarities. At ages younger than 4, a restricted cognitive capacity limits the presentation of depression to infant/toddler features. After age 12 or 13, depression tends to resemble adult depression, with some developmental variation as described earlier.

Many of the depressive features observed in adults occur in school-age children with depression (Table 5.6). Depressed mood and irritable mood are some of the most common symptoms in children, occurring in approximately 80% and 40% of children with depression, respectively (Stark, Rouse, & Livingston, 1991). This mood disturbance is frequently manifest by flat, sad, angry, or tearful facial expression, although the child may deny a mood problem when directly questioned. Because children tend to act out their mood states, oppositional and hostile behavior may follow from depressed or irritable mood (Burgin, 1986). For example, depression may manifest itself in the previously well-behaved child who suddenly resists all requests and throws temper tantrums for small reasons.

Diminished interest or pleasure occurs in as many as half of children with depression (Stark et al., 1991). Such anhedonia is manifest as complaints of boredom, resistance to take part in any activity, reluctance to leave the room or house, and lack of motivation (Dennison, 1989). This may be particularly noticeable when one attempts to engage the child in play. However, anhedonia in children is rarely total, and the ability of the child to enjoy some activities should not be used to exclude a diagnosis of depression (Pataki &

TABLE 5.6 Appearance and Features of Depression in Early and Middle Childhood

COMMON FEATURES

1. Affective features: Sad or irritable affect
2. Cognitive features: Negative attribution bias, low self-esteem, guilt, worthlessness, helplessness, difficulty concentrating
3. Vegetative features: Sleep and appetite disturbance, fatigue
4. Anhedonia, apathy, repeated claims of being "bored"
5. Anxiety and fears
6. Social withdrawal
7. Decline in academic or social functioning
8. Suicidal ideation
9. Decline in self-care behaviors
10. Physical complaints

OCCASIONAL FEATURES

1. Suicide attempt
2. Oppositionality
3. Poor peer relationships
4. Psychomotor agitation or retardation

Note: The features listed in the table are often seen but are not universal. Some features may be diagnostically relevant or required, whereas others may not be required for diagnosis. "Common" features are typical of the disorder; "occasional" features appear frequently but are not necessarily seen in a majority of cases.

Carlson, 1990). Instead, anhedonia in children is often shown in a diminished pleasure with respect to everyday activity.

Anhedonia frequently combines with fatigue, which affects as many as 50–70% of children with depression (Stark et al., 1991). Children with anhedonic fatigue complain that any adult suggestion requires too much effort. These protests may balloon into temper tantrums or withdrawal. Children with depressive disorders tend to be less active, especially in the daytime, compared to children without depression and compared to children with other psychiatric disorders. Objective measures of lower activity level correlate with clinician ratings of sadness, lack of interest in pleasant activities, and poor self-esteem (Aronen et al., 1996).

In so-called "agitated depression," children with depression show higher rather than lower levels of activity. Psychomotor agitation is manifest in extensive, often purposeless activity. This activity serves the apparent goal of providing distraction from painful cognitions and affects. Anger is often, but not always, associated with agitated states. Agitation occurs in about 35% of children with depression (Stark et al., 1991).

Cognitive symptoms of depression, such as feelings of worthlessness, guilt, and difficulty concentrating, may be difficult for a child to articulate (Burgin, 1986). Behaviorally, feelings of worthlessness may be seen when a child expects to be criticized, ignored, or rejected by other children. Likewise, the way in which the child interprets neutral situations may show underlying thoughts and schemas. Children with depression who have feelings of worthlessness or hopelessness will often enter situations expecting to fail or with a sense of futility; these feelings may be expressed by anxiety, reluctance, or defensive hostility. Ambiguous behaviors of other children are interpreted as reinforcing the child's belief that he or she is worthless, and failure experiences are likely to be catastrophized and overgeneralized. Worthlessness and hopelessness may also be seen in a lack of interest in self-care and appearance behaviors (Dennison, 1989). The child with depression may not show interest in dress or grooming. Feelings of guilt may emerge in defensive or anxious behaviors surrounding a negative situation.

The child's inability to concentrate may be misinterpreted as an attention deficit. However, when it is combined with a sad appearance, anxiety, low self-esteem, fatigue, irritability, and/or a negative outlook, depression should be strongly considered as a diagnosis. "Pure" ADHD children typically do not have the degree of anxiety, low self-esteem, and fatigue shown by children with depression unless depression and ADHD are comorbid.

Depression is also manifest in the social environments of children (Pataki & Carlson, 1990; Simeon, 1989). In school, performance typically declines with the onset of depression (Pataki & Carlson, 1990). Children with depression score lower on reading and mathematics achievement than peers (Edelsohn, Ialongo, Werthamer-Larsson, Crockett, & Kellam, 1992). School problems can grow and have a "domino effect" on other areas of the child's life. For example, school failure is sometimes viewed by parents and teachers as a sign that the child is being lazy or oppositional, leading to conflict between the child and authorities (Simeon, 1989). Peer relationships may be disrupted, especially because children are typically less willing than adults to accept and sympathize with a peer who is depressed and withdrawn. This may result in the loss of friends, loss of popularity within the classroom, and increased isolation. Interestingly, however, research indicates that rejection and poor social competence are far stronger predictors of later depression than depression is a predictor of popularity (Cole, Martin, Powers, & Truglio, 1996).

Almost three-fourths of children with depression may be socially withdrawn, and irritability and fighting with peers may lead to complete isolation and rejection by the group (18% of children with depression; Stark et al., 1991). Children with depression are rated as less likeable by peers (Edelsohn et al., 1992), and children with depression tend to inaccurately interpret social relationships more negatively than other children (Rudolph, Hammen, & Burge, 1997). Children with depression also tend to have poorer social problem-solving skills than their peers, which may make them particularly vulnerable to social stresses (Goodman, Gravitt, & Kaslow, 1995). At home, the child's irritable, moody, and oppositional behavior can be alternately distressing and frustrating to parents. Discipline attempts may be perceived by the child as yet another confirmation of a negative world-view.

Somatic symptoms are common components of depression in children. Trouble going to sleep is relatively frequent, but early awakening is often less of a problem for children than for adults; sleep problems tend to become more pronounced in adolescence (Dahl et al., 1996). Physical complaints are very common in young children who are depressed because these are often used as a way of obtaining help and comfort from parents. Furthermore, young children have less insight and, therefore, less understanding of the nature of depression. Their experiences and vocabulary, thus, lead them to physical complaints as a way of experiencing and expressing their distress. Somatic complaints are also common in adolescents, with 70% of adolescents with depression reporting significant somatic symptomatology (McCauley, Carlson, & Calderon, 1991). Change in appetite is occasionally seen in children and adolescents (one-third to one-half of children; Pataki & Carlson, 1990), although this rarely results in actual weight loss (less than one-third of the time; Pataki & Carlson, 1990; Stark et al., 1991). Psychomotor retardation is also less common in children than adults, occurring in only about 20% of children with depression (Stark et al., 1991).

Another common feature of childhood depression is anxiety, which co-occurs so often with depression that it is often difficult to tease the two apart. Children with depression worry about a multitude of things, from their own self-esteem and performance to disasters that may befall themselves or their family. Hence, separation anxiety is a common associated problem for young children. Comorbid depression and anxiety are generally associated with more negative outcomes than depression alone, including increased duration of depressive symptoms, increased risk of suicidal behavior, and poorer response to psychotherapy (Birmaher et al., 1996).

There is some evidence, particularly in prepubertal children, that symptoms of depression and anxiety frequently co-occur in a depressive-anxious syndrome that does not easily fit into either diagnostic category. This syndrome is characterized by a combination of symptoms of both depression and anxiety, and it has been called names such as *negative affectivity* and *negative affect*. Factor analytic studies have shown that separate syndromes of depression, anxiety, and negative affectivity can be identified in sixth grade children, but negative affectivity alone (and not depression or anxiety) seems to better capture the symptom pattern most typical of third grade children (Cole, Truglio, & Peeke, 1997; Joiner, Catanzaro, & Laurent, 1996). This finding could suggest that most early childhood-onset syndromes of depression or anxiety begin as an undifferentiated syndrome of negative affectivity. Later in childhood, more clear versions of anxiety and depression may be differentiated by the presence of physiological hyperarousal (characteristic of anxiety) or absence of positive affect (characteristic of depression).

In some children, depression is also accompanied by symptoms of disruptive behaviors and oppositionality. Such "acting-out" depressions are doubly stressful for the child's family and environment. When depression and disruptive behavior co-occur, a pattern is sometimes seen between mood and oppositional-aggressive behavior. Such children may also express unhappiness, dissatisfaction, and sadness about their behavior problems. There is some evidence that acting-out depressions are associated with fewer of the "classic" features of depression such as family incidence of depression, vegetative symptoms, and recurrent depressive episodes. However, they have a higher risk of problems often associated with disruptive behavior problems, including criminal behavior and suicide attempts (Birmaher et al., 1996). History of abuse and family violence tend to be associated with comorbid depression and disruptive behavior disorder, whereas symptoms of anxiety are more typical of depression without disruptive behavior disorder (Meller & Borchardt, 1996).

The long-term course of depression typically involves stability of depressive symptoms over a short-term (3–9 month) period (Birmaher et al., 1996; Kaslow & Racusin, 1990). The vast majority (about 90%) of cases of Major Depressive Disorder go into remission within 1.5 years, whereas Dysthymic Disorder takes longer to remit (6 years to reach 89% remission rate). For children, the median duration of an episode of Major Depressive Disorder is 32–40 weeks, while that for Dysthymic Disorder is in the 3–5 year range. Furthermore, Dysthymic Disorder typically has an earlier onset (7–9 years of age) than Major Depressive Disorder (10–11 years of age) (Kovacs, Obrosky, Gatsonis, & Richards, 1997). By comparison, Adjustment Disorder with Depressed Mood typically lasts only 9 months (Kovacs, Feinberg, Crouse-Novak, Paulauskas, & Finkelstein, 1984a). Children with comorbid disruptive behavior disorders tend to have longer duration of dysthymic symptoms, but few variables seem to predict the duration of an episode of Major Depressive Disorder (Kovacs et al., 1997).

Children who have Dysthymic Disorder or Major Depressive Disorder are also at considerable risk for a future Major Depressive Episode. Approximately 70% of children with Dysthymic Disorder develop a Major Depressive Episode within 5 years of diagnosis of their disorder (Kovacs et al., 1984b). There is some disagreement about the percentage of children with depression who later develop Bipolar Disorder, with estimates as high as 20–40%; earlier onset of depression, family history of bipolar disorder, psychotic features, and psychomotor retardation appear to increase the risk of bipolar disorder (Birmaher et al., 1996; Pataki & Carlson, 1990).

Suicide

Perhaps one of the most troublesome and dangerous features of depression is an increased risk of suicidal ideation, suicidal intent, and suicide attempts (Kotsopoulos, 1989). Serious suicidal ideation may be present in as many as 27% of children with depression (Stark et al., 1991) and over 60% of adolescents (Wetzler et al., 1996). Suicidal ideation and attempts follow from the feelings of hopelessness and low self-esteem that are characteristic of depression (Pataki & Carlson, 1990), although some authors emphasize that unbearable psychological pain is the key stimulus in suicide (Leenaars & Wenckstern, 1991). As the pain becomes unbearable, the child increasingly views suicide as a reasonable or exclusive option.

Fortunately, completed suicide rarely occurs before the age of 10, although suicide risk increases dramatically in adolescence (Pataki & Carlson, 1990). Suicide attempts in adolescents may be as high as 8% (Smith & Crawford, 1986) to 30–40% (Lewinsohn, Clarke, Rohde, Hops, & Seeley, 1996). Fortunately, over three-fourths of suicide attempts are not of sufficient severity to merit medical attention (Centers for Disease Control, 1991), and completed suicides are even more rare (Leenaars & Wenckstern, 1991). However, completed suicides in adolescents have increased by 300% over the past 30 years, with prevalence rates of nearly 0.01%. Adolescent girls make more suicide attempts, but adolescent boys complete suicide four to five times as often as girls (Simeon, 1989). This is not the case for children under age 12; preadolescent boys and girls tend to make suicide attempts of equivalent severity, and the rate of completed suicide is roughly equal between the sexes (Leenaars & Wenckstern, 1991). Although many child and adolescent suicides are associated with depressive symptomatology, not all children and adolescents who commit suicide are depressed (Leenaars & Wenckstern, 1991; Simeon, 1989). Three other problems accounting for many suicides are conduct disorders, substance abuse, and withdrawal-anxiety.

Identification of individuals at risk for suicide is obviously of paramount importance, and this identification is particularly relevant in the case of children with depression, who already carry an increased risk for suicidal ideation and behavior; 60–80% of suicide victims have a depressive disorder (Myers et al., 1991a; Pfeffer, 1992). In addition to depression, several authors have suggested the following issues to be considered in assessing suicide risk in children (Leenaars & Wenckstern, 1991; Myers et al., 1991a; Myers, McCauley, Calderon, & Treder, 1991b; Pfeffer, 1992):

1. *Suicidal ideation:* Assessment of suicidal risk begins with an investigation of the presence, frequency, and severity of suicidal ideation. More lifetime suicidal ideation and more specific plans are related to risk of making a suicide attempt (Wetzler et al., 1996). As a general rule, children with specific plans, specific times, and stated intent to carry out plans are considered to be at significant risk for a suicide attempt.

2. *Precipitating events:* Precipitating events are often more of a factor in adolescent suicide than in preteen childhood suicide. For children, cumulative stressful events coupled with vulnerability (unsupportive environment, poor coping skills) are often responsible for a suicide attempt (De Man & Leduc, 1995; Harris & Ammerman, 1986; Myers et al., 1991a). However, certain major stresses, such as death of a parent by suicide or a severe disciplinary crisis, significantly increase the risk of child suicide (Leenaars & Wenckstern, 1991; Pfeffer, 1992). Anticipated painful events may also increase risk if suicide is seen as a way to avoid them.

For adolescents, specific stresses such as termination of an intense romantic relationship can increase risk of suicidality in an already vulnerable adolescent. Stresses related to sexuality (being pressured to have sex; worries about being pregnant) predict suicide attempts independent of ideation (Wagner, Cole, & Schwartzman, 1995).

3. *Poor coping skills:* Some children rapidly exhaust their coping options or do not know how to cope with stressful experiences. For example, if a child feels that he or she cannot talk to parents, cannot change or avoid his or her stressful situation, and is facing a catastrophic stress, he or she may become desperate and resort to maladaptive behavior. To the extent that children consider suicide an option in removing their problems, they will have suicidal ideation and, possibly, attempt suicide. On the other hand, a child who is willing to use other coping behaviors might reduce his or her stress appraisal sufficiently to avoid the desperation and psychological pain that could lead to suicidal behavior.

4. *Maladaptive family environment:* Among the family risk factors for suicide are lack of boundaries, parent-child conflict, inflexibility, severe stress, parental psychopathology, and a suicide attempt in the family. Compared to adolescents with suicidal ideation, adolescents who attempt suicide report that their parents do not spend enough time with them, that their parents do not understand them, and that their parents are overly critical or strict (Wagner et al., 1995). Furthermore, suicide attempts in the family increase family stress and provide a dangerous model of maladaptive behavior (Harris & Ammerman, 1986; Myers et al., 1991a; Pfeffer, 1992).

5. *Previous attempts:* The best predictor of future behavior is past behavior, particularly when the environmental and precipitating circumstances are similar. Hence, a child who has attempted suicide once is more likely to do so again than is a child who has never attempted suicide. Furthermore, children who have attempted suicide are more likely to engage in a future attempt compared to children with suicidal ideation who have not attempted suicide in the past (Wetzler et al., 1996). The ratio of attempts to completed suicides is somewhere between 8:1 and 100:1 (Leenaars & Wenckstern, 1991), indicating that most attempts are not successful. However, the fact that previous suicide attempts have failed is not a good reason to take future attempts lightly. The rate of completed suicide is much higher for those who have attempted before than for the general population (Myers et al., 1991b; Pfeffer, 1992).

There is some evidence that the method used for an initial suicide attempt can predict the risk of a serious (e.g., medically dangerous) future attempt. Wetzler et al. (1996) found that adolescents who made serious repeat suicide attempts tended to have used overdoses as the method for their first suicide attempt. Adolescents who made less serious repeat suicide attempts tended to have used cutting themselves as the method for their first suicide attempts. Number of prior attempts and age at first attempt did not predict the medical seriousness of future suicide attempts (Wetzler et al., 1996).

6. *Threats:* As with attempts, many more threats (which may be verbal or in the form of a note) occur than do actual suicides. Because of this, threats are sometimes downplayed or even replied to with taunts by angry family members. The risk involved in missing even one serious threat, however, is sufficiently great that any threat should be taken seriously. Most threats occur in verbal or written form, although a child will occasionally threaten by using nonverbal behavior (e.g., looking for a gun). The fact that the child is communicating the threat suggests the belief that something can be done to redress the situation. Although the parent or clinician does not want to reward suicidal threats, provision of support, understanding, or restraint can buy valuable time to enhance the child's coping skills and reduce future threats. Communication of suicidal ideation or oblique references to suicide should be managed in the same way as direct threats.

7. *Cognitive constriction:* Children who are seriously considering suicide often acquire a narrow and inflexible view of their problems. Suicidal ideation, for example, is more prevalent in adolescents who select fewer positive and more negative problem-solving strategies to common stressful situations faced by adolescents (Adams & Adams, 1996).

8. *Emotional turmoil:* Suicide is rarely considered by a calm, rational child or adolescent. Rather, suicidal children are typically in great emotional distress. They are extremely anxious, distraught, agitated, and desperate. Anger and hostility are often present, particularly in "angry" suicides in which the child views suicide as a way to punish another person.

9. *Cognitive desperation:* Cognitive desperation is usually manifest as thoughts of hopelessness and helplessness toward the environment and the future. Things will not change or improve; often the expectation is that they will get worse. Cognitive constriction contributes to the feeling of desperation and hopelessness. Hopelessness, low self-esteem, and external locus of control have been shown to be empirically related to suicidality (De Man & Leduc, 1995; Myers et al., 1991a).

10. *Sudden behavioral changes:* A dramatic increase in risky or life-threatening behavior may indicate impulsivity or self-hate and may portend a suicide attempt. Likewise, sudden "completion" behaviors, which involve finishing things and getting one's affairs in order, suggest some motive such as suicide.

11. *Preoccupation with death:* Children are inherently curious about a number of things, including death, but repeated focus on death in the absence of other interests suggests a problem (Harris & Ammerman, 1986). Adolescents may adopt a preoccupation with death by identifying with a model who embraces death or by becoming fascinated with the existential questions of life and death.

12. *Lack of perceived support:* Adolescents who have fewer social supports and who are less satisfied with their social support have more suicidal ideation (De Man & Leduc, 1995). Compared to adolescents with ideation alone, adolescents who attempt suicide report feeling less supported by teachers, school counselors, and the police (Wagner et al., 1995).

13. *Conduct problems/antisocial behavior:* The combination of antisocial behavior, anger, impulsivity, risk taking, and disrespect for rules seen in children with conduct problems is a risky combination that sometimes leads to suicide attempts or ideation (Myers et al., 1991; Pfeffer, 1992). Conduct problems combined with depression are particularly risky features.

14. *Use of drugs and/or alcohol:* Substance abuse both dulls inhibition and impairs judgment, increasing the risk of suicide. Alcohol and drug abuse are two of the only factors that appear to predict suicidal ideation independent of the predictive effect of depression (De Man & Leduc, 1995; Wagner et al., 1995).

15. *Psychomotor agitation/poor impulse control:* Psychomotor agitation increases the risk for suicide by creating impulsivity and a press for action within the person (Pfeffer, 1992). Children who are hyperactive and feel that they must act immediately are at greater risk for suicide because of their inclination to act without thinking. Although children with poor impulse control are more likely to engage in drastic or irresponsible behavior, studies are mixed as to the relationship between poor impulse control and suicide (Harris & Ammerman, 1986).

Etiology

Biological Theories

Family, genetic, and biochemical studies provide some support for a biological predisposition or vulnerability to depression. Children of depressed parents are three times more likely to have a Major Depressive Episode, and lifetime risk of developing depression if one has a depressed parent is in the 15% to 45% range. Children who have two depressed parents are at even higher risk (Beardslee, Bemporad, Keller, & Klerman, 1983; Birmaher et al., 1996). Results from twin studies suggest that as much as 35–45% of the variance in depression diagnoses may be explained by genetic influences. The concordance rates for depression in monozygotic twins exceed 50% (even when the twins are reared apart), whereas those for dizygotic twins are under 20% (Gershon, Targum, Kessler, Mazure, & Bunney, 1977; Kashani & Sherman, 1988). Over all, considerable evidence exists supporting a genetic role in depression, with estimates as high as 50% of the variance in depression explained by genetic factors (Birmaher et al., 1996). It appears based on present data that genetics may create a predisposition for depression but that other environmental and biological factors are often necessary for its full development. Genetic factors appear to have much more impact on depressive symptoms following age 12, whereas earlier depressions may be more environmentally mediated (Murray & Sines, 1996).

The possibility of genetic transmission of depression suggests some mechanism of biological development of the disorder. Research in this area has focused on the neurochemical effects of antidepressant medications and the identification of biological markers for depression. Several neurotransmitters have been associated with the regulation of mood by the hypothalamus and limbic system: acetylcholine (ACH), norepinephrine (NE), and serotonin (5-HT). Because of the importance of these neurotransmitters for mood, imbalances in their production, secretion, or reuptake have been suggested as potential causes for depression. The catecholamine hypothesis, for example, focuses on disturbances of the catecholamine neurotransmitters, particularly NE. Similar theories have been posited for 5-HT, ACH, and a combination of neurotransmitters, although no single theory has yet been affirmed (Kashani & Schmid, 1992). Additional support for the importance of NE and 5-HT in the development of depression comes from evidence that their levels are affected by medications that have antidepressant effects. Amitriptyline (Elavil) and imipramine (Tofranil), for example, block reuptake of NE and 5-HT, whereas nortriptyline (Pamelor) and desipramine (Norpramin) affect NE (Finch, Casat, & Carey, 1990; Kashani & Schmid, 1992). Selective serotonin reuptake inhibitors (SSRIs), such as fluoxetine (Prozac) and sertraline

(Zoloft), are some of the newest and most widely used antidepressant medications. These medications block the reuptake of 5-HT (serotonin), causing more 5-HT to be available in the synaptic cleft. Because of the selective effectiveness of the SSRIs, hypotheses that depression results from an undersupply of serotonin are currently the most widely held.

A second direction of biological research on depression is the identification of biochemical markers for depression. Most of these biochemical markers are the result of presumed neuroendocrine abnormalities that may cause or result from depression. Perhaps the most well-known marker of depression in adults is the dexamethasone suppression test (DST). The DST consists of oral administration of dexamethasone followed by repeated blood sampling over the next day. In 85–90% of people who are not depressed, the production of cortisol is suppressed following administration of a dose of dexamethasone. However, 40–50% of adults with depression fail to suppress cortisol following administration of dexamethasone (Arana, Baldessarini, & Ornsteen, 1985; Yaylayan, Weller, & Weller, 1992). Hence, the nonsuppression of cortisol following a dose of dexamethasone has been hypothesized to be a biological marker for depression. This effect may be a result of disregulation of NE and 5-HT, which control the inhibition and release of cortisol, respectively. The results of child DST studies have yielded poor sensitivity (at best, 50–80% probability of labeling a child as depressed when he or she is actually depressed; 20–50% miss rate) and specificity (at best, 60–90% probability of labeling a child as *not* depressed when he or she is actually *not* depressed; 10–40% false positive diagnoses), and adolescent studies have shown similar or worse figures (at best, 30–70% sensitivity and 80–90% specificity; Casat, Arana, & Powell, 1989; Finch et al., 1990; Kashani & Schmid, 1992; Yaylayan et al., 1992).

Other tests of biological markers measure the levels of growth hormone (GH) and melatonin, and production of thyroid-stimulating hormone (TSH) (Kashani & Schmid, 1992). Levels of GH are reported to be elevated in adults and adolescents who have depression. This group shows blunted GH increases in response to doses of imipramine, desipramine, clonidine, and insulin (Finch et al., 1990; Yaylayan et al., 1992). Children with depression show hypersecretion of GH during sleep (Yaylayan et al., 1992). It has been suggested that these abnormal GH levels could reflect a disruption in the norepinephrine or serotonin neurotransmitter systems. Melatonin levels show less of a nighttime rise in children and adults with Major Depressive Disorder, compared to controls (Brown et al., 1985; Cavallo, Holt, Hejazi, Richards, & Myer, 1987). Although there may be a small subgroup of adolescents with depression who show a disruption in thyroid hormone function (functional hypothyroidism; Dorn et al., 1996), convincing evidence has yet to be found for a role of TSH or thyroid functioning in the majority of adolescents with depressive disorders. In general, then, these other biological tests should be considered experimental and as providing only preliminary evidence for a biological theory of depression.

Psychological Theories

Cognitive-Behavioral Theories.   The most widely accepted psychological theories of the etiology of depression use a cognitive-behavioral approach. Cognitive-behavioral theory emphasizes the role of the child's beliefs and behavioral contingencies in causing depression (Stark et al., 1991). One cognitive-behavioral model (Beck, 1976), for example, states that children with depression hold maladaptive thoughts and beliefs that distort the way in which they process information. These maladaptive beliefs consist of negative views of themselves, their world, and their future. Incoming information is interpreted based on their beliefs that they are incompetent, that their world is threatening, and that their future is hopeless. Hence, they see everyday events as hopeless, sad, and aversive, leading predictably to unhappiness. Cognitive errors such as overgeneralization (applying a specific event to all events) and minimization (trivializing the meaning of a positive event) result from this thinking style. Evidence exists, for example, that children with depression evaluate their performance on a task more negatively than do controls, even when the groups show no difference on performance (Kendall, Stark, & Adam, 1990). Furthermore, studies indicate that children with depression have poorer self-concepts than do controls and that changes in cognitions cause changes in mood (Kashani & Sherman, 1988).

A second cognitive-behavioral model is the Seligman (1975) learned helplessness model. This model posits that depression results when children, through repeated experience with uncontrollable events, come to believe that they have no control over events in their lives. This leads to apathy and lack of motivation to modify aversive events (Kashani & Sherman, 1988). Seligman and colleagues (Abramson, Seligman, & Teasdale, 1978) have extended this original model to include the faulty attributions typically made by people with depression. These maladaptive attributions focus on internal, stable, and global attributions for negative life events. Hence, children with depression see themselves as responsible (internal); little can be done to change the situation (stable); and the situation is pervasive (global). Depressive attributional styles have been found to be related to depressive symptoms in children over a relatively long period of time (6 months) (Seligman et al., 1984).

Other cognitive-behavioral models resemble the Beck and Seligman models, with differences in the emphasized maladaptive thoughts and beliefs. Rehm's (1977) self-control model, for example, states that depressive symptoms occur when self-monitoring, self-evaluation, and self-reinforcement are deficient or distorted. When these distortions occur, the person overemphasizes negative events (distorted self-monitoring), sets unreachable self-standards (distorted self-evaluation), and fails to reward good performance (distorted self-reinforcement). Lewinsohn (1974), on the other hand, attributes depression to a reduction in reinforcement from the environment, with particular emphasis given to social reinforcement. Often, social skills deficits cause the child with depression to elicit negative responses (or few positive responses) from others. A lack of positive responses from the environment causes the child with depression to view the world negatively and withdraw, leading to depressive cognitions and maladaptive social behaviors. This cycle creates a continuing lack of environmental reinforcement and additional feelings of unhappiness. Research supporting Lewinsohn's theory has shown that children with depression hold more negative beliefs about interpersonal relationships, that children with depression have weaker social problem-solving skills, and that social competence at the beginning of the school year predicts depressive symptoms at the end of the school year (Cole et al., 1996; Goodman et al., 1995; Rudolph et al., 1997).

Stress and Coping Theories. In addition to cognitive-behavioral theories, another group of etiological theories of depression emphasizes stress, coping, and social support in the etiology of depression. These theories hold that stress renders individuals vulnerable to negative interpretations and emotions regarding themselves and their environment. If the individual feels overwhelmed by stress, he or she may become unhappy, hopeless, and desperate, resulting in the development of depressive symptoms. Factors that buffer individuals from stress, such as adaptive coping and social support, attenuate the effects of the stress and reduce risk of depression. Evidence exists, for example, that children with depression have experienced more stressful life events than controls and that stressful events often immediately precede the development of depression (Birmaher et al., 1996). Furthermore, people with depression tend to appraise stresses more negatively than do others, creating additional feelings of being overwhelmed or stressed.

Stress, coping, and social support within the family may be especially important in the etiology of depression. Family stresses can contribute to the development of depressive symptoms, and the family can be a source of support to buffer its members from the negative effects of stress (Kashani, Allan, Dahlmeier, Rezvani, & Reid, 1995; Kronenberger, 1990). These effects may be particularly pronounced for children, who are emotionally and physically dependent on the family. Furthermore, modeling of affective responses to situations and of coping behaviors can have a profound effect on child behavior. Hence, the presence of a parent with depression in the household provides both a family stress and a maladaptive model for the children. Children with depression perceive their family more negatively than do children without depression, and children with depression are likely to have families with more psychopathology (Kaslow, Rehm, Pollack, & Siegel, 1990). In addition, referred children with depression are more likely to have a mother with depression than are referred children who are not depressed (Kaslow et al., 1990), and the timing of child depression is closely related to the manifestation of maternal depression (Hammen, Burge, & Adrian, 1991). This latter finding argues against the mother-child concordance rate for depression being merely a result of genetic influence. It appears that high stress and the presence of a maternal model of depression puts children at substantially greater risk than stress alone. Such depression evolves from the interpersonal relationship with a currently depressed parent as opposed to a purely genetic influence (Hammen et al., 1991).

Psychoanalytic Theories.   Psychoanalytic theories of adult depression attribute the low self-esteem, hopelessness, unhappiness, and other symptoms of the disorder to situations involving loss. A person who experiences the loss of a loved object may feel anger at being abandoned or at having some issues unresolved. This anger, however, is threatening because it is directed at the one who is loved and lost. To repress the feelings of anxiety and shame related to having this anger, the person represses the anger or unconsciously turns it on the self. This "anger turned inward" is then manifest on the surface in the form of depressive symptoms: negative cognitions, low self-esteem, hopelessness, guilt, and unhappiness. Other analytic theorists have taken somewhat different points of view from the starting point of loss. For example, the loss may be seen as creating feelings of anxiety about one's ability to continue effectively in the world, or the loss may remove an object/person who was the target of strong identification (Kashani & Schmid, 1992).

□   ASSESSMENT PATTERNS

Broad Assessment Strategies

Cognitive Assessment

Clinician-Administered.   At least one study (Kendall et al., 1990) suggests that children with depression do not have a cognitive ability deficit (not to be confused with the cognitive distortions seen in these children). Severe depression may affect a child's performance on cognitive testing if it results in deficits in concentration or in psychomotor retardation. Either of these deficits would result in substantially lower WISC-III Freedom from Distractibility/Working Memory (FFD/WM) and Processing Speed (PS) scores, and, to a lesser extent, lower Perceptual Organization scores (because these subtests are timed). Rispens et al. (1997), for example, found group mean FFD scores for children with mood disorders to be lower than FFD scores for all other clinical groups except ADHD. Verbal Comprehension scores are less likely to be affected by depression, because the tests are not timed, do not require extensive concentration, and involve material that is typically overlearned.

Psychological Assessment

Clinician-Administered. Perhaps the most common clinician-interpreted test for depression in adults is the MMPI. Although the MMPI and MMPI-A may be administered to adolescents, their lower age range of 14 years severely limits their utility in the diagnosis of child depression. Adolescents with depression who can complete the MMPI-A typically produce elevations of scales 2 (Carter & Dacey, 1996) and 7, reflecting depressive symptoms, concentration problems, and anxiety that typically accompany a diagnosis of depression. Elevation of scales 1 and 3 suggests a somatic component to the depression or that the depression is secondary to illness issues. Elevations of scales 4 and/or 6 indicate an angry, cynical, alienated, and/or rebellious tone to the depressive symptomatology. Elevation of scale 9 can suggest an agitated depression or possible emerging manic-depressive disorder, whereas elevation of scale 8 can indicate a lack of control and alienation associated with the depression. Adolescents who show significant elevations of scales 2 and 9 (especially if scale 8 is also elevated) should be screened carefully for dangerous or suicidal behavior or ideation.

Projective testing can also be useful in the assessment of children with depression, particularly if they lack insight or deny symptoms. A variety of techniques can be used in this endeavor, ranging from sentence completion tests to storytelling tests to the Rorschach. All of these assessment instruments are based on the assumptions that children with depression see the world in ways that differ from those of children who do not have depression, and that the child will project this distorted perception onto an ambiguous stimulus. This projected perception should provide the clinician with some insight into the child's perceptual biases and cognitive processing.

On the TAT and other storytelling tests, many children with depression tell one of two types of stories. The first type is the brief, unelaborated story, with little plot, excitement, or emotion. This story type often reflects the child's cognitive fatigue, hopelessness, lack of motivation, negative outlook, and/or passive resistance to change. Such children do not want to try anything, including a projective test. Hence, they provide the minimum amount of effort needed to overtly comply with the task, hoping to bring it to an end.

The second type of TAT story often told by children with depression reflects their cognitive errors and negative affective state. These stories are dominated by negative themes and affects of sadness, anger, relationship problems (including distant or detached relationships, or loneliness), anxiety, and hopelessness. Main characters are often unhappy, malicious, lonely, helpless, or victims of negative circumstances. Plots are dominated by death, separation, conflicts, isolation, or unhappiness, and story endings are either negative or miraculously, stereotypically positive. Careful analysis of the stories can provide the clinician with insight into the child's cognitive errors, fears, and current stresses. Particular attention should be paid to themes that are repeated across stories, strong affects within stories, unique story lines, and omissions of major card features.

The Rorschach also has several indicators of depression, most of which involve responses to achromatic or shading features of the card. Achromatic color responses presumably reflect depressive affects, whereas the shading responses may reflect psychic pain, stress, or negative self-views. Rorschach responses should not be analyzed individually but need to be viewed in the context of the content and other determinants of the response. In addition to the determinants of the response, the content can be helpful in understanding the child with depression. Malicious or morbid contents, such as bugs, dead or injured animals or people, and blood, can be indicators of depression. As with the TAT, repeated content and unique answers may reflect salient features of the depression.

Several authors have expressed significant reservations about the use of projective tests in the assessment of children with depression. Kazdin (1987, 1990) notes that differences between children with and without depression are often not found in research using projective tests. In empirical studies, Rorschach indices of depression generally do not differentiate between children with and without depression (Ball, Archer, Gordon, & French, 1991; Carter & Dacey, 1996). Over all, little research has been done to validate projective instruments in the diagnosis of childhood depression. This does not, however, mean that projective instruments will not be helpful in individual cases. However, given these caveats, it appears that the wisest use of projective tests for the evaluation of depression is to generate hypotheses, which may then be followed up with interviews, other testing, or interventions.

Behavioral Assessment

Parent-Report and Other-Report.   Most broad-band measures of child behavior problems and psychopathology include a measure of depression. The Achenbach scales, for example, have several subscales measuring depressive symptoms: Anxious-Depressed, Withdrawn, and Social Problems. Children with depression would likely elevate these subscales into the 70–90 T-score range. A disadvantage in the use of the Achenbach scales with children with depression is that they do not include a "pure" depression subscale (because depression items are combined with anxiety items in the Depressed-Anxious subscale); they also do not mirror DSM-IV criteria for depression. Hence, the Achenbach subscales should not be used for diagnostic purposes, although they may provide insight into broad-band problems and respondent disagreement over symptoms.

On the BASC-PRS and BASC-TRS, responses of parents and teachers of children with depression produce significant elevations of the Depression subscale. Typically, subscales with related internalizing items, such as Withdrawal, Somatization, and Anxiety, show elevations as well. Elevations of the Aggression and Conduct Problems subscales suggest a comorbid Disruptive Behavior Disorder or an angry-agitated depression. It is often very helpful to examine the BASC-PRS positive behavior subscales, which indicate the quality of the child's social functioning (Leadership and Social Skills subscales) and coping (Adaptability). It is notable that a depressed sample produced some of the most significant elevations across all of the BASC subscales (Reynolds & Kamphaus, 1992).

The ECI-4, CSI-4, and ASI-4 include questions about specific DSM-IV criteria for Major Depressive Disorder and Dysthymic Disorder. However, duration of symptoms, which is a critical component of depression diagnoses, is not specifically questioned in the SI-4. Additionally, SI-4 questions about depression do not ask about the exact frequency of symptoms, instead using a scale ranging from "never" to "sometimes" to "often" to "very often." Answers of "often" or "very often" are taken to indicate symptom presence, but follow-up interview questions must clarify which response choice meant "more days than not" or "most of the time" to the respondent.

Child-Report. In addition to the YSR, the BASC-SRP and PIY are excellent self-report measures for depression in children as young as 8 years old. The BASC-SRP includes a Depression subscale and subscales measuring feelings of inadequacy (Sense of Inadequacy), positive self-esteem (Self-Esteem), self-confidence (Self-Reliance), and quality of social interaction (Social Stress, Relations with Parents, Interpersonal Relations). These scales can collectively provide a rich picture of the severity and nature of the child's depressed symptoms.

The Psychological Discomfort scale of the PIY is an excellent measure of depression, which has received empirical support (Lachar & Gruber, 1995). The pattern of elevation on PIY subscales measuring Social Skills Deficits, Somatic Concern, and Social Withdrawal can provide additional information about associated depressive features. The extensive validity subscales of the PIY also assist with the assessment of children whose quality of self-report is in question.

The PHSCS can be useful in the assessment of self-esteem strengths and weaknesses of children with depression. Although children with severe depression may produce low scores on all PHSCS subscales and total score, other children with depression will give a pattern of subscale scores that can suggest areas of vulnerability to target for intervention. In other cases, children may deny feeling sad but endorse significant self-esteem problems that are suggestive of a depressive syndrome. In addition to the PHSCS, self-esteem scales such as the Multidimensional Self Concept Scale (for ages 9–19 years; Bracken, 1992), the Culture-Free Self-Esteem Inventories (Battle, 1992), and the Coopersmith Self Esteem Inventory (Coopersmith, 1981) may also be useful in identifying self-esteem problems in children with depression.

Syndrome-Specific Tests

Clinician-Administered

Children's Depression Rating Scale—Revised. The Children's Depression Rating Scale—Revised (CDRS-R; Poznanski & Mokros, 1996), for children age 6–12, is a 17-item, clinician-completed rating scale. Each item is a symptom area that is rated by the clinician based on data gathered from multiple interview sources (usually parents and child) and observation of the child's behavior. The 17 item areas are Impaired Schoolwork, Difficulty Having Fun, Social Withdrawal, Appetite Disturbance, Sleep Disturbance, Excessive Fatigue, Physical Complaints, Irritability, Excessive Guilt, Low Self-Esteem, Depressed Feelings, Morbid Ideation, Suicidal Ideation, Excessive Weeping, Depressed Facial Affect, Listless Speech, and Hypoactivity. A total score based on the items can be used as a summary measure of depression symptoms, with T-scores based on a nonrepresentative normative sample. CDRS-R scores correlate with objective measures of reduced daytime activity in children, providing good construct validity support (Aronen et al., 1996).

Child Report

Children's Depression Inventory. The Children's Depression Inventory (CDI; Kovacs, 1992), a downward extension of the Beck Depression Inventory, contains 27 items measuring cognitive, affective, behavioral, and social symptoms of depression in children age 6–17. Each item consists of three statements, one of which represents nondepressed symptomatology, one of which represents moderately depressed symptomatology, and one of which represents severely depressed symptomatology. The child chooses the one of the three statements that best describes him or her during the past 2 weeks. Endorsing the nondepressed statement receives a score of 0; the moderately depressed statement is scored 1; the severely depressed statement is scored 2.

Items are added to give a total score and five subscale scores (Negative Mood, Interpersonal Problems, Ineffectiveness, Anhedonia, Negative Self-Esteem). Raw scores can be converted to T-scores based on normative samples divided by age and sex (Kovacs, 1992). Although T-scores are now available to assist with CDI interpretation, in the past interpretation has often been done based on cutoff raw scores of 12 to 19 (Fristad, Weller, Weller, Teare, & Preskorn, 1991). Scores at or above the cutoff presumably indicate clinical levels of depression. The most commonly used cutoff score is probably 19, with children scoring at or above this level classified as clinically depressed (Smucker, Craighead, Craighead, & Green, 1986). Lower cutoff scores provide greater sensitivity but lower specificity. Answers to individual items may also be clinically relevant, such as item 9, which asks about suicidal ideation and intent.

More recent factor analyses of CDI scores in child and adolescent samples have supported the presence and content of four of the five subscales. Little support was found for the Anhedonia subscale, however. Furthermore, a factor consisting of the sleep disturbance, fatigue, and loss of appetite items was found in the adolescent sample. This Biological Dysregulation factor may be a component of self-reported depressive symptoms that does not appear until adolescence (Craighead, Smucker, Craighead, & Ilardi, 1998).

The CDI has good psychometric properties, with the possible exception of discriminant validity in clinical samples. Internal consistency is high, and test-retest reliability is moderate. Construct and criterion validity studies show that the CDI relates to self-esteem, hopelessness, cognitive processing, and depression as measured by other instruments (Kazdin, 1989b, 1990; Kovacs, 1992). However, it does not typically differentiate clinically referred children with depression from other clinical subgroups, especially anxious children (Kazdin, 1990; Kovacs, 1992), and CDI scores do not correlate with objective measures of low activity level, a common symptom of depression (Aronen et al., 1996). In addition, the CDI was not designed to reflect DSM-IV symptomatology, and hence, may not have acceptable power in identifying children with DSM-IV-defined depression. In one study, only 31.6% of children with a Major Depressive Disorder diagnosis scored at or above the CDI cutoff of 19 (Kazdin, 1989b). Therefore, the CDI should be considered as a self-report measure of depression-anxiety, with most items being face-valid for depression. Combined with other scales from multiple informants, it can contribute significantly to the assessment of a child's depression-related distress.

A parent-completed version of the CDI has been used in research, with relatively low agreement between child and parent CDI scores. As with child scores, parent CDI scores do not identify children with DSM-IV diagnosed depression very well (Fristad et al., 1991; Kazdin, 1989b). In fact, child CDI scores may be more predictive of depression than parent CDI scores (Fristad et al., 1991).

Children's Depression Scale. The Children's Depression Scale (CDS; Lang & Tisher, 1978; Tisher, Lang-Takac, & Lang, 1992) is a 66-item measure of depressive symptoms and positive affects in children age 9–16. For the original use of the CDS, each item was printed on a card (a questionnaire-based version now exists as well). The cards are read to the child and placed by the child into one of five categories ranging from very wrong (assigned a value of 1) to very right (assigned a value of 5). The card response format presumably encourages accurate responding on the part of the child, although the paper and pencil form is now more widely used.

CDS items cluster into two broad scales (48-item Depression scale and 18-item Positive Affective Experience scale) and six specific subscales (Affective Response, Social Problems, Self-Esteem, Preoccupation with Own Sickness or Death, Guilt, and Pleasure/ Enjoyment). Scale and subscale scores are sums of item scores, with higher scores reflecting more depression. Clinically depressed samples score in the 165 to 190 range on the Depression scale, whereas nondepressed controls score in the 120 to 140 range (Tisher et al., 1992). Other clinical groups score between these ranges (Tisher et al., 1992). Like the CDI, there is a parent version of the CDS, with similar weak correspondence between parent-report and child-report (Mokros & Poznanski, 1992; Tisher et al., 1992).

Psychometric properties of the CDS appear to be good, and norms are reported for several nonclinical samples in various studies (Tisher et al., 1992). Factor analysis has not supported the subscales, which were derived on an a priori basis, but some evidence does exist that the Depression scale and Positive Affective Experience scale are not simply opposites of each other (Kazdin, 1990; Tisher et al., 1992). Studies have also found a significant relationship between CDS scores and other measures of depression (Kazdin, 1989b; Tisher et al., 1992). Discriminant validity (ability to differentiate between depressed and other groups) is reported to be better than that of the CDI (Tisher et al., 1992). The CDS is useful because of its broad range of items and its inclusion of a positive experience scale. Finch et al. (1990) suggest that the CDS is more a measure of negative affect in general than of depressive symptomatology in particular. In this respect, CDS scores may be interpreted in the same manner as CDI scores—as a measure of anxiety-depression and general upset (Kazdin, 1990).

Depression Self-Rating Scale. The Depression Self-Rating Scale (DSRS; Birleson, 1981; Birleson, Hudson, Gray-Buchanan, & Wolff, 1987) is an 18-item self-report measure of depression for children age 7–14. Each item is a depressive symptom that the child rates on a 0–2 scale of frequency (most of the time, sometimes, never) based on the experiences of the past week (sometimes the past 2 weeks are used; Asarnow, Carlson, & Guthrie, 1987). Item scores are added to give a total depression score, with scores of 13 or 14 and higher indicating depression (Birleson, 1981; Birleson et al., 1987). Reliability and validity for the DSRS are reported to be adequate (Birleson, 1981; Finch et al., 1990; Kaslow &

Racusin, 1990), although little research has been done on other psychometric properties. This fact, combined with the lack of norms, limits the scale's clinical utility. Modified versions of the DSRS with additional items have been used but have not been adequately studied (Asarnow & Carlson, 1985; Kaslow & Racusin, 1990).

Reynolds Adolescent Depression Scale. The Reynolds Adolescent Depression Scale (RADS; Reynolds, 1987a; Reynolds & Coats, 1986) is a 30-item measure of depression in adolescents. Each item is rated on a four-point scale, and item scores are summed to give a total score. Normative data are available for a large sample of adolescents between ages 13 and 18 (Reynolds, 1987a). Psychometric properties are quite good (Finch et al., 1990), with good test-retest reliability and excellent internal consistency. RADS scores correlate highly with other measures of depression and related constructs (Finch et al., 1990; Reynolds, 1987a).

Reynolds Child Depression Scale. The Reynolds Child Depression Scale (RCDS; Reynolds, 1989; Reynolds & Graves, 1989) is a 30-item measure of depression in children in grades 3–6, similar to the RADS. Items are intended to correspond roughly to DSM-III-R criteria for Major Depressive Disorder and Dysthymic Disorder. The first 29 items are scored on a four-point frequency ("almost never" to "all the time") scale, whereas the thirtieth item is a list of five faces ranging from sad to happy (scored on a one- to five-point scale). The sum of the items gives a depression score. Internal consistency, test-retest reliability, and criterion validity are reported to be good, and norms exist based on a relatively large normative sample (Reynolds, 1989; Reynolds & Graves, 1989).

Multiscore Depression Inventory for Children. The Multiscore Depression Inventory for Children (MDI-C; Berndt & Kaiser, 1996) is a 79-item, true-false measure of depressive symptoms in children age 8–17. Because items are written at a second-grade reading level, the MDI-C can be used with relatively young children. The MDI-C yields a total score, a validity subscale (measuring careless or erratic responding), and eight clinical subscales: Anxiety, Self-Esteem, Social Introversion, Instrumental Helplessness, Sad Mood, Pessimism, Low Energy, and Defiance. Norms, based on a large national sample, allow conversion of subscale scores to T-scores.

Depression Adjective Checklist. Forms H and I of the Children's Version of the Depression Adjective Checklist (C-DACL; Sokoloff & Lubin, 1983) are 34-item lists of adjectives that pertain to depressed mood or its absence. Internal consistency reliability and validity are reported to be good (Sokoloff & Lubin, 1983). The C-DACL has low test-retest reliability, which is consistent with the authors' contention that the version used in their study is a state measure as opposed to a trait measure. A trait measure of the C-DACL also exists (differing from the state measure only by changing the time frame from "how you feel today" to "how you generally feel"). Over all, the C-DACL has received relatively little research or clinical attention.

Preschool Symptoms Self-Report. The Preschool Symptoms Self-Report (PRESS; Martini, Strayhorn, & Puig-Antich, 1990), a 25-item, self-report measure of depression in children age 3–5, has the youngest age range for a self-report measure of depression. Each PRESS item consists of two pictures, one illustrating a symptom of depression, and the other showing the absence of the symptom. Each picture is described by a caption that is read aloud by the examiner, followed by the question, "Which one is most like you?" The total PRESS score is the number of symptom pictures (e.g., depicting a depressive symptom) chosen by the child. Separate male and female forms exist, differing only in the sex of the main character in the pictures. A parent/teacher version of the PRESS exists as well (Martini et al., 1990). The psychometric properties of the PRESS have received relatively little attention, with one study finding adequate test-retest and internal consistency reliability (Martini et al., 1990). Correlations between child, parent, and teacher ratings on the PRESS were essentially zero (Martini et al., 1990).

Children's Attributional Style Questionnaire. The Children's Attributional Style Questionnaire (CASQ or KASTAN; Benfield, Palmer, Pfefferbaum, & Stowe, 1988; Bodiford, Eisenstadt, Johnson, & Bradlyn, 1988; Kaslow, Tannenbaum, & Seligman, 1978; Seligman & Peterson, 1986) is a 48-item measure of the attributional style of children in grades 3–6; a short version of the CASQ (the CASQ-R, which consists of a 24-item subset of the complete CASQ) also exists (Thompson, Kaslow, Weiss, & Nolen-Hoeksema, 1998). Based on learned helplessness theory, the CASQ does not assess depression directly but rather focuses on attributional biases thought to be related to the development of depressive symptoms. The CASQ consists of a number of descriptions of positive or negative events. For each event, the child chooses one of two possible causes. The causes vary on three attributional dimensions: internal-external, global-specific, and stable-unstable. The CASQ yields six subscales (Good Internality, Good Stability, Good Globality, Bad Internality, Bad Stability, and Bad Globality), two composites (Positive and Negative), and a Depressive Attribution score (Positive minus Negative) (Kaslow et al., 1978; Bodiford et al., 1988). Internal, global, and stable attributions are believed to be related to the development of depressive symptoms in the case of bad event outcomes (Abramson et al., 1978). The CASQ has been predominantly used as a research instrument, although it could be clinically useful in identifying target attributions for cognitive-behavioral therapy.

Hopelessness Scale for Children. The Hopelessness Scale for Children (Kazdin, Rodgers, & Colbus, 1986) is a 17-item, true-false scale measuring negative future expectations in children age 6–13. Children receive one point for each item they endorse in the "hopeless" direction. Items appear to cluster into two factors: negative expectations/giving up and unhappiness/negative expectations. Like the CASQ, the Hopelessness Scale does not measure depression but rather measures future expectations and hopelessness. Higher scores reflect greater hopelessness and correlate with depression, suicidal ideation, low self-esteem, poor social skills, poor school performance, and CDI scores (Kazdin, 1989a; Kazdin, 1989b; Kazdin et al., 1986).

Children's Negative Cognitive Error Questionnaire. The Children's Negative Cognitive Error Questionnaire (CNCEQ; Leitenberg, Yost, & Carroll-Wilson, 1986) is a 24-item measure of cognitive processing errors based on Beck's (1976) theory of depression. For each item, the child is presented with a situation and a statement about the situation that reflects one of Beck's cognitive errors. Using a 1–5 scale, the child rates the degree to which the statement reflects his or her thoughts about or perceptions of the situation. The scale is designed to be completed by children in grades 4–8 (Leitenberg et al., 1986). The psychometric properties of the scale appear to be adequate, and data based on a large sample of fourth, sixth, and eighth graders have been published (Leitenberg et al., 1986).

Loneliness Questionnaire.   The Loneliness Questionnaire (Asher, Hymel, & Renshaw, 1984; Asher & Wheeler, 1985) is a 24-item measure of loneliness at school for children in grades 3–6. Items assess popularity, difficulty making friends, and social isolation at school. Children rate each item on a five-point scale of degree to which the item is true of them. Eight of the items are "filler" items and are not used in scoring.

Inventory of Suicide Orientation-30.   The Inventory of Suicide Orientation-30 (ISO-30; King & Kowalchuk, 1994) is a 30-item, self-report measure of suicidal ideation and other constructs related to having suicidal ideation or intent. Adolescents age 13–18 answer each item on a four-point scale of agreement with item content. Items fall into five constructs: Hopelessness, Low Self-Esteem, Inability to Cope with Emotions, Social Isolation and Withdrawal, and Suicidal Ideation. Two scores are obtained from ISO-30 responses: A total raw score (based on all items) is compared to cutoff scores for risk of orientation toward suicide, and a critical item score is based on strong endorsement of items reflecting suicidal ideation. There are no formal norms or standard scores. ISO-30 scores correlate significantly with measures of hopelessness and suicidal ideation (King & Kowalchuk, 1994). In addition to the ISO-30, several other tests measure suicidality, such as the Suicidal Ideation Questionnaire (Reynolds, 1987b).

Other Measures.   Many other instruments are potentially useful in the measurement of depressive symptoms and associated features (Kazdin, 1990). A multitude of additional specific depression measures exist, for example, but many of these have been inadequately researched and have unknown psychometric properties or are used exclusively in the context of a therapeutic intervention (see Kaslow & Racusin, 1990, and Kazdin, 1990, for reviews). In addition, scales measuring features associated with depression may also be helpful, such as measures of stress (e.g., Life Events Checklist; Johnson & McCutcheon, 1980), reinforcement (e.g., Adolescent Reinforcement Survey Schedule; Holmes, Heckel, Chestnut, Harris, & Cautela, 1987), social support (e.g., the Social Support Questionnaire; Sarason, Levine, Basham, & Sarason, 1983), social skills (e.g., Matson Evaluation of Social Skills with Youngsters; Matson, Rotatori, & Helsel, 1983), maladaptive thoughts (e.g., Automatic Thoughts Questionnaire; Hollon & Kendall, 1980), and adaptive thoughts (e.g., Automatic Thoughts Questionnaire-Positive; Jolly & Wiesner, 1996). Other measures are intended to facilitate cognitive-behavioral and family psychotherapy interventions (e.g., Stark, Raffaelle, & Reysa, 1994; some of these are described in the Treatment Options section of this chapter). Ultimately, the decision whether to administer these additional instruments will depend on the characteristics of the child, the etiology of the depression, and the orientation of therapy.

Parent Report

As noted earlier, the CDI, CDS, and PRESS have parent forms that are identical to the child forms but use parental response instead of self-report. These forms have not been extensively studied (see Table 5.3 for an example of a prototypic assessment battery for mood disorders).

☐   TREATMENT OPTIONS

Medication

Treatment options for depression in early and middle childhood are outlined in Table 5.7. The effects of medication on childhood depression are variable. Furthermore, studies of antidepressant treatment effects in children tend to produce much weaker results than do studies of adults.

    The most obvious potential medications for the treatment of childhood depression are the selective serotonin reuptake inhibitors (SSRIs) and tricyclic antidepressants. Of the SSRIs, fluoxetine (Prozac), sertraline (Zoloft), and paroxetine (Paxil) have seen the most widespread clinical use, with positive effects reported in many individual cases, especially

TABLE 5.7   Treatment Options for Depression in Early and Middle Childhood

1. Medication
   a. Tricyclic antidepressants
   b. Selective serotonin reuptake inhibitors
2. Psychotherapy
   a. Cognitive-behavioral interventions
      (1) Psychoeducation
      (2) Self-monitoring
      (3) Challenging automatic thoughts
      (4) Cognitive restructuring
      (5) Self-reinforcement
      (6) Activity scheduling
      (7) Realistic goal setting
      (8) Behavioral exposure
      (9) Relaxation training
      (10) Social skills training
      (11) Cognitive-affective modeling
      (12) Anticipatory coping
      (13) Problem solving
      (14) Self-talk
   b. Play therapy
   c. Group therapy
3. Family Interventions
   a. Family therapy
   b. Parent psychotherapy
   c. Parent-child psychotherapy

Note: This outline of options summarizes major treatments covered in the text. Specific treatments are often combined into an intervention package. Refer to the text for additional descriptions of each treatment. This table is not necessarily an exhaustive list of all treatments available.

for older children and adolescents. Of the tricyclic antidepressants, imipramine (Tofranil), desipramine (Norpramin), amitriptyline (Elavil), and nortriptyline (Pamelor) are the most commonly used. Other antidepressants that have seen clinical use in child populations include bupropion (Wellbutrin) and trazodone (Desyrel).

Use of the SSRIs with children has produced positive results in case studies and clinical settings, and more recent controlled studies are lending further support to the efficacy of the SSRIs. Results for tricyclics, on the other hand, are generally less positive. In open, uncontrolled trials, 50–100% of children and 30–40% of adolescents were reported to respond positively to tricyclics (Pliszka, 1991; Rancurello, 1985), although the results of controlled, blind treatment studies are more negative (Campbell & Cueva, 1995; Ryan, 1992). This discrepancy in findings may be the result of as many as 20–60% of children and adolescents improving on placebo (Campbell & Cueva, 1995; Pliszka, 1991). Over all, antidepressant medication does result in a decline in depressive symptoms for the majority of children, but the effectiveness of many antidepressants (especially tricyclics) may be no more impressive than placebo.

Other than SSRIs and tricyclics, monoamine oxidase inhibitors (MAOIs) have been used with children with depression, but their efficacy is unestablished, and their side effects can be a significant problem (Rancurello, 1985). Use of the MAOIs requires dietary restrictions, which may not be taken seriously by children. Hence, use of the MAOIs with children is relatively rare.

Psychotherapy

Cognitive-Behavioral Interventions

Cognitive-behavioral interventions for depression in children are based on theories of the cognitive-behavioral etiology of depression. They, therefore, seek to change the child's distorted cognitions and lack of pleasant activities. At the initiation of treatment, a firm therapeutic alliance must be established, because the remainder of therapy will involve challenges to the child's way of thinking. If the child does not accept the therapist, the child is very unlikely to accept the therapist's challenges to cognitions, particularly because many children do not want to be in therapy in the first place. During this initial period, problems, goals, and a therapeutic contract are agreed upon, giving the child a sense of what will happen in therapy and when. Often cognitive-behavioral therapy is time limited, intensifying the need for a clear sense of agenda. Following these preliminary tasks, cognitive-behavioral interventions are undertaken in therapy. These interventions take many forms, but the most common ones are psychoeducation, self-monitoring, challenging automatic thoughts, cognitive restructuring, self-reinforcement, activity scheduling, realistic goal setting, behavioral exposure, relaxation training, social skills training, cognitive-affective modeling, anticipatory coping, problem solving, and self-talk (Lewinsohn et al., 1996; Schrodt, 1992; Stark et al., 1991).

Psychoeducational interventions involve teaching the child and family about depression and its treatment. Background information about symptoms, prevalence, prognosis, and comorbid disorders is given. Regarding treatment, the child and family are taught the tenets of the cognitive-behavioral theories of depression. Specifically, the child learns that distorting incoming information can lead to the thoughts and feelings characteristic of depression. This can be particularly difficult to explain to young children, who may have problems monitoring what they are thinking. Furthermore, young children tend to find lengthy psychological explanations boring and fail to attend to them. Hence, cognitive-behavioral principles usually must be acted out for younger children, for example, in doll/puppet play, role playing, game, or story form.

Many children respond to gamelike ways of teaching the premises of cognitive-behavioral therapy (Dennison, 1989). Stark et al. (1991), for example, suggest several games to teach children how thoughts and affects are related. In Emotional Vocabulary, the players pick cards with names of emotions. The players describe how the emotion feels, state the situation in which they last felt the emotion, and then state what a person who is experiencing the emotion might be thinking or doing. In Emotional Charades, one player acts out an emotion while another player tries to guess what the emotion is. When the emotion is correctly named, the second player states the situation in which he or she last felt the emotion and what his or her thoughts were at that time. Stark et al. (1992) and Dennison (1989) suggest other games, all of which have as their goal increasing children's awareness of what they are thinking and feeling.

For older children, psychoeducation may be more direct. Depression theories and treatment rationales may be spelled out more clearly to these children. Examples may be provided, such as pointing out the child's cognitive errors and showing how they lead to depressive symptoms. Defining such cognitive distortions as personalization, catastrophizing, overgeneralization, and minimization (Beck, 1976; Schrodt, 1992) also enhances the process of monitoring and correcting thoughts. Books may also be used to assist with psychoeducation related to depression (Dennison, 1989).

Parents are involved in psychoeducation by learning the same concepts about depression and treatment that are taught to children. Parents are also taught to encourage the child to complete therapy homework assignments, and they may also help to point out cognitive distortions to the child, provided that this does not create problems for the child or the family. Parents also may be taught to monitor their child's depressive symptoms and to take protective measures if necessary.

Psychoeducation is often combined with homework assignments to apply what is learned in therapy. One such intervention is *self-monitoring* of depressive symptoms, negative thoughts and emotions, and therapy goals (Stark et al., 1996a; Stark, Swearer, Kurowski, Sommer, & Bowen, 1996b). Initially, the child is asked to track simple behaviors and emotions, such as happiness or sadness. The target thought/emotion is then attached to the monitoring of other related phenomena, such as the situation in which the emotion occurred and the thoughts that accompanied the emotion (Kazdin, 1989a). Situation, thought, and emotion are then recorded for discussion at the next therapy session. This may be done using a three-column worksheet, with the situation in the first column, the emotion in the second column, and the thought in the third column. In cases in which the child does not have time to write in narrative form, tick marks can be used to track the occurrence and timing of thoughts, feelings, and situations.

Monitoring thoughts and emotions may initially occur during the therapy session. The therapist helps the child to trace the automatic thoughts underlying feelings such as frustration, sadness, and inadequacy. These thoughts and feelings are then recorded, during the therapy session, just as they would be at home. The use of self-monitoring in therapy gives the therapist a chance to observe the child and make corrections or changes in the procedure. The child may then implement self-monitoring at home, with instructions to record the self-monitoring data as soon as possible after the target thought/emotion.

Self-monitoring encourages the child to gain insight into feelings and the thoughts that underlie them. In some cases, this insight alone and the increased feeling of self-control are beneficial. In other cases, this information must be used in therapy to challenge maladaptive thoughts and to show how these thoughts lead to negative affect. Based on the self-monitoring diary, the child is encouraged to change behavior to maximize situations and thoughts leading to positive affect.

Much of the focus in cognitive-behavioral therapy is on the identification and *challenging of automatic negative thoughts* that underlie negative emotion (Schrodt, 1992). Children with depression focus on problems or excuses, and it is the task of the therapist to redirect the child to the thoughts that underlie negative feelings. Identifying thoughts, however, is not sufficient. The child must be shown how these thoughts lead to unhappiness and behavior problems. Taking the child slowly through a specific scenario that happened in the past week can be particularly instructive.

After the child sees how negative thoughts lead to unhappiness, the task turns to changing the thoughts. Schrodt (1992) suggests that the child initially be encouraged to regard thoughts as hypotheses, not as conclusions. Another alternative is to show the child that thoughts are chosen freely and are a matter of interpretation, not fact. Both of these strategies loosen the child's allegiance to negative thought patterns by allowing at least the acknowledgment of alternative thoughts. Early in therapy, the goal is not to abandon the automatic thoughts but rather to admit that other thoughts are possible.

Once the child is willing to accept the possibility of alternative thoughts, techniques may be employed to test the reality of the automatic thoughts. First, the child can learn to use evidence to discount negative automatic thoughts. The therapist begins this process by asking the child for evidence that the automatic thought is true (Stark et al., 1991). Then the child is asked to provide evidence that the thought is not true. If the child is unable to give disconfirming evidence, the therapist does it for the child. An example is the thought that "I can never pass a spelling test, no matter how hard I try." The child might provide evidence in favor of this, such as times when he or she has studied and still failed. Then the child is asked to provide disconfirming evidence. Perhaps the child did not really study very hard, or perhaps studying has helped on other spelling tests.

Next, therapist and child test the evidence for alternative thoughts. For example, if the automatic thought is "If I don't pass the spelling test, I'm a complete failure," then an alternative could be "If I don't pass the spelling test, I can try harder the next time and improve my grade" or "If I don't pass the spelling test, I'll have to try harder, but I can still be good at other things." The generation of alternative thoughts may be difficult for children with depression because it violates their world-view and introduces an unfamiliar world-view into their life. The therapist may initially provide extensive assistance in this process. Later, the child gradually assumes responsibility for generating alternative explanations and thoughts.

Cognitive restructuring techniques encourage children with depression to interpret situations in alternative ways (Meichenbaum, 1977). Reframing, for example, involves taking a different point of view to make a situation seem less catastrophic, less significant, or even positive. A child may reframe an upcoming difficult experience not as a threat of failure but as a challenge to succeed. Taking the SAT test, for instance, could be seen as an opportunity to gain experience with standardized tests as opposed to the only chance for a college education. Likewise, children may be taught to see past negative experiences as less significant. For example, losing a tennis match may be seen as an opportunity to identify weaknesses. Reframing can work well even with young children, because the therapist can suggest the reframe and all that the child must do is accept it.

Another variant of cognitive restructuring is decatastrophizing. Decatastrophizing encourages the child to perceive a negative event accurately as opposed to magnifying the threat and significance of it. For example, a child who loses a tennis match may catastrophize the experience by assuming that he or she will be kicked off the team for the loss and will be abandoned by friends. Decatastrophizing this situation would involve noting that it is unlikely that either of these scenarios would happen. Related to decatastrophizing is the "What If?" intervention described by Stark et al. (1991). This intervention accepts that the event feared by the child will occur and asks what the aftermath will be. Children with depression often overestimate the extent to which a negative event will lead to catastrophe. Realistic discussion of the aftermath often reveals that the outcome is not likely to be as negative as the child feared and that the child's emotional response is exaggerated.

Self-reinforcement involves rewarding oneself for successful completion of a goal or task (Stark et al., 1991, 1996a). The therapist and child identify possible rewards and target behaviors for the child. Then a single target behavior and a single reward are chosen and paired in a contingency. When the child completes the target behavior, the child gives himself or herself the reward. For example, the child may reward himself or herself with a half hour of video games for completing homework.

Although self-reinforcement is straightforward, children with depression are at risk to fail at almost every stage of the self-reinforcement procedure. As a result of their anhedonia, children with depression often have considerable trouble identifying rewards or fun activities. The therapist may circumvent this problem by asking the parent which activities the child seems to prefer. Alternatively, the therapist may create a hierarchy of events in the order of liked least to liked most. Even if the child with depression believes that everything is bad, he or she is likely to believe that some things are worse than others. The ordering of things along this parameter shows that some things are desired relative to others. Once a reward is chosen, the therapist must ensure that the child has access to it when a goal is met. The system should involve rewards that are immediate, contingent only on the target behavior, and meaningful to the child. In general, involving the parents at this stage is important in the selection of rewards and in the implementation of a realistic plan (Stark et al., 1991).

In addition to having problems identifying rewards, children with depression may choose unrealistic target behaviors. Essentially, they set themselves up to fail. In such a case, the therapist should encourage the child to select behaviors that are relatively objective and, at first, easily attainable.

After target behaviors and rewards are identified, the therapist and child should practice the self-reinforcement system in therapy (Stark et al., 1991). Following external success with a simple target behavior and a simple reinforcer, the self-reinforcement system may be modified to include more difficult behaviors and more potent reinforcers. As with other interventions, monitoring is integral to self-reinforcement, and the child should be encouraged to use some record-keeping system that can be brought into therapy for discussion and modification.

Activity scheduling (Appendix C) requires the structuring of the child's day so that purposeful or pleasant activity is built into each day (Kazdin, 1989a; Lewinsohn & Rohde, 1993; Stark et al., 1991). Planned activities should involve interesting stimuli, active behavior, and removal from social withdrawal. The child's daily schedule is altered to reduce the frequency of "empty time" and to increase the frequency of pleasant or productive activities. Examples of scheduled activities are going to the zoo, getting a book from the library, going to the museum, attending a movie, fishing, taking a walk, or sitting on the porch. Initially, the child may resist this intervention and complain that the activity is aversive. This response is typical and reflects the hopeless resistance characteristic of depression. However, if the activity is inherently purposeful, interesting, or pleasant, the child usually comes to a positive acceptance and anticipation of it. A scale such as the Pleasant Events Schedule (MacPhillamy & Lewinsohn, 1982) or the Forty No-Cost/Low-Cost Family Activities sheet (Stark, Raffaelle, & Reysa, 1994) may be helpful in the selection of activities to schedule.

Activity scheduling injects structure into the child's life and gives the child a sense of anticipating positive events. Furthermore, activities increase the chance of reinforcement and pleasant experiences. Activity scheduling is an excellent intervention for the severely impaired child who resists or does not respond to any other intervention.

Realistic goal setting is an effective intervention for children with depression who experience multiple failures because of unachievable goals and ideals. If unrealistic goals are contributing to negative self-evaluation and negative affect, altering the child's goals and ideals may result in improved affect. This may be accomplished by encouraging the child to engage in activities that are nonevaluative, amenable to internally set goals, or unique (e.g., not engaged in by a sibling and, thus, not allowing social comparison). Alternatively, clear, realistic goals may be imposed by powerful adults in the child's environment with overt rewards for meeting goals. Tasks that are too difficult for the child should be discouraged or broken down into manageable steps, with each step existing as its own goal and with its own reward (Schrodt, 1992). In some cases, parents initiate or encourage unrealistic goals and expectations. When this is the case, the therapist and parents should first work on making parental goals and expectations realistic.

Behavioral exposure is a technique that can be used with children with depression who refrain from engaging in numerous behaviors because of their fear of failure. Behavioral exposure involves prescribing homework assignments in which the child engages in progressively increasing amounts of the feared behavior. For example, a child with depression who feels inferior and will not play with peers may be given an initial homework assignment to say "hi" to one peer each day of the week. The next week, the assignment may be increased to saying one sentence to one peer each day. The assignments could progress until the child is playing with peers.

In addition to reducing the self-defeating withdrawal and paralysis of depression, behavioral exposure gives the child a chance to try out techniques practiced in therapy. Furthermore, the results of the behavioral exposure are often discrepant with the child's catastrophic expectations. They can then be used to assist with cognitive restructuring. Finally, as the child engages the feared situation without catastrophe, confidence grows and self-esteem improves.

The obvious risk with behavioral exposure is the failure of the child in the task or an extremely aversive environmental response. To reduce this risk, the child may be coached in therapy, with role playing and reinforcement for desired behavior. In addition, the behavioral task should initially be as innocuous and nonthreatening as possible, with supportive encouragement and oversight from adults.

Relaxation training teaches the child to use imagery and concentration to achieve somatic and cognitive relaxation. The relaxation increases the child's sense of control and well-being, resulting in affective improvement. Relaxation may also counter some of the negative somatic symptoms characteristic of depression, giving the child a feeling of control over bodily sensations. Studies of the efficacy of relaxation training in reducing depressive symptoms have been promising (Field et al., 1992).

Social skills training aims to increase the frequency of positive social interactions for the child with depression because social withdrawal and lack of social reinforcement are two features commonly associated with depression (Kazdin, 1989a). Most social skills training programs teach basic cognitive restructuring, social skills, and interpersonal problem solving in order to increase the child's ability to interact positively with peers (Kazdin, 1989a; Lewinsohn & Rohde, 1993; Liddle & Spence, 1990).

A typical social skills training program for children with depression consists of psychoeducation (about social skills and depression), self-talk and self-praise, challenging negative thoughts (such as the belief that others do not or will not like them), problem solving, nonverbal communication, group entry behavior (beginning and joining conversations with peers), requests and assertiveness, self-expression, disagreeing with others and setting limits, learning empathy, ending social interactions, and conflict resolution (LeCroy, 1994; Liddle & Spence, 1990). Modeling, rehearsal, discussion of specific examples, solving social problems on paper, and homework assignments to practice skills are used to hone and practice the new skills. Empirical findings on the efficacy of social skills training for children with depression are equivocal, although they almost certainly receive some benefit in the form of improved knowledge (LeCroy, 1994; Liddle & Spence, 1990). Manualized forms of social skills training groups (LeCroy, 1994) should allow for more careful analysis of the empirical results of social skills training.

In *cognitive-affective modeling,* the therapist models positive, adaptive thoughts and emotions in the context of therapy, and parents are encouraged to do the same at home. Stark et al. (1991), for example, suggest that the therapist verbalize adaptive thoughts related to problematic situations that the child may face. This may take the form of telling a story about a similar event that happened to the therapist (understanding that self-disclosure should be cautiously used in therapy) and how the therapist dealt adaptively with the event. Showing positive emotion, enthusiasm, and optimism are other positive-adaptive behaviors that can be modeled by the therapist in routine interaction with the child and family. The modeling of hope and confidence by the therapist offers the child an initial confidence and an eventual example of adaptive thinking.

Parents can also be coached to use cognitive-affective modeling at home, by showing a positive outlook and positive emotions about their environment. Sarcastic and negative comments are replaced with optimistic comments and pleasant emotions. By observing the positive thoughts and emotions of those around them, children with depression may improve their own outlook, as predicted by social learning theory.

Anticipatory coping is an important tool in assisting children with depression who are facing or reacting to severe stresses. Many children anticipate stresses with denial and avoidance, resulting in shock and a lack of preparation when the stress occurs. With no preparation for the stress, the chances of the child responding maladaptively to it are very high. Such maladaptive responses include decompensation, inappropriate behavior, emotional upset, and additional depression. Some preparation may assist the child in understanding the stress when it occurs, in reducing false beliefs about the stressor, and in adopting coping strategies for minimizing the effects of the stress.

Anticipatory coping usually consists of exposure to a lower level of the feared situation or the development of a plan for coping with the stress. The former intervention is typically administered in the form of systematic or *in vivo* desensitization. The latter intervention usually takes the form of talking about the future stressor and developing coping strategies for dealing with the stressor. The strategies are then practiced extensively and used when the stressor occurs. Anticipatory coping may be done more subtly by talking with the child about his or her expectations for a stressful situation and plans for dealing with the situation. When the stress occurs, the child is then more prepared to understand and respond to it.

An example of anticipatory coping occurs frequently in therapeutic interventions with children who are both chronically ill and depressed. These children face major stresses on a daily basis, including physical exams, IVs, surgery, separation from parents, and adapting to a new environment. Exposing the child to these situations prior to their occurrence reduces the child's unrealistic beliefs and catastrophic fears about them. Likewise, talking to an older child about the process of recovering from a surgical procedure may reduce shock or uncertainty.

Problem solving is the teaching of a semistructured procedure for managing problems when they arise. Children with depression often rigidly adopt a defeatist attitude with regard to problems or respond to problems without thinking. Either strategy is likely to lead to failure and a confirmation of the child's depressive belief system, creating a self-fulfilling prophecy. Despite some differences, most problem-solving interventions teach a variant of a five-step package including identification of the problem, generation of alternative solutions, evaluation of outcomes for each solution, choice of a solution, and evaluation of the outcome. In therapy, direct teaching, modeling, coaching, role playing, and practice in situations of increasing difficulty are used to teach the problem-solving package. Reinforcement and self-monitoring are used to motivate the child with depression.

Self-talk techniques are incorporated in most of the cognitive-behavioral interventions described earlier. These interventions train the child to internally say certain words or phrases. These self-talk phrases assist the child in identifying maladaptive cognitions and in implementing cognitive-behavioral techniques. For example, the child may mentally recite the steps of problem solving when faced with a difficult problem. At another time, the child may say a phrase such as "I can get over this just fine" at a time when the child feels like he or she is facing a catastrophe.

Most cognitive-behavioral techniques share some overlap and are incorporated into treatment packages. Lewinsohn et al. (1996), for example, combine most of the previously described cognitive-behavioral components into a group treatment program for adolescents called Adolescent Coping with Depression (CWD-A). The CWD-A has been shown to be superior to wait-list control, with two-thirds of adolescents showing remission of Major Depressive Disorder at the end of treatment versus 48% of wait-list controls. Stark et al. (1996a) also provide a structured treatment protocol that can be tailored somewhat for each child's individual symptoms. Their protocol includes several examples of each of the cognitive-behavioral techniques described earlier, with appropriate modifications to make them developmentally appropriate for preadolescent children. Research on Stark et al.'s (1996b) techniques has shown them to be effective in producing positive change in depressive symptoms in children.

Interpersonal Psychotherapy

Interpersonal psychotherapy techniques place their emphasis on the role of social relationships in the development, maintenance, and treatment of depressive symptoms. Treatment is directed toward discussion of key relationships or disruptions in significant relationships that contribute to negative mood. Conversely, improvement in interpersonal functioning is expected to result in more rewarding social interactions and in improved mood (Lewinsohn et al., 1996).

Major issues discussed in interpersonal psychotherapy for children and adolescents with depression include losses of important relationships, conflict in important relationships, role expectations at home, role expectations at school, peer group interactions, social skills challenges, and social self-esteem. For each patient, a unique set of interpersonal issues are identified and become the content to be covered in treatment. Goals are set based on these interpersonal issues. The process of treatment involves using techniques such as promoting insight into the problem, role playing, self-monitoring, psychoeducation, process interpretation (immediate feedback about the adolescent's relationship with and behavior toward the therapist), involvement of parents, problem solving, reexperiencing (and reprocessing) traumatic events, and social skills training to promote better interpersonal functioning for the adolescent and to promote better psychological functioning where social issues are concerned. Cognitive-behavioral techniques are often integrated into the treatment.

Mufson, Moreau, and Weissman (1996) describe a specific 12-week interpersonal psychotherapy treatment protocol that they applied to a group of adolescents with depression. Their patients improved significantly over the treatment period. At termination, all patients no longer met criteria for a diagnosis of depression.

Play Therapy

Psychodynamic play therapy for depression is based on the assumption that the depression is the result of an internal conflict of which the child is unaware, probably related to parenting and attachment. Impaired parent-child interactions can communicate a sense of nonacceptance and worthlessness to the child, particularly when these interactions involve neglect or abuse. Many children with depression have internalized a view of themselves as unworthy of nurturance and inferior to others. Other children may harbor a latent anger toward the parent, which is threatening and turned inward.

Psychodynamic play therapy aims to elicit these conflicts and emotions in the relatively nondirective, accepting, interpretive world of play therapy. By playing out conflicts and emotions, the child can relieve the stress of having them unresolved and avoided. Dealing with the conflicts also allows the child to gain insight into how the conflicts affect behavior (Kaslow &

Racusin, 1990). The acceptance and warmth communicated by the therapist allow the child to adopt an attitude of self-acceptance that is needed to combat the negative self-view characteristic of depression, particularly as painful conflicts and emotions emerge.

Typically, play therapy with a child with depression is initially nondirective, although the therapist may need to engage an extremely withdrawn child. As the child plays, themes emerge, particularly in play involving interaction between characters. The therapist can facilitate the emergence of conflicts, emotions, and maladaptive cognitions by playing along with the child and conveying acceptance of what the child is doing. Eventually, interpretive statements describing the child's feelings and thoughts in play therapy will assist the child in understanding and accepting the issues driving behavior. Maladaptive thoughts, negative affects, and interpersonal (particularly nurturing) relationships are key targets for interpretation. The delivery of these interpretations while maintaining a warm, accepting, and nondirective attitude is vital in helping the child to develop a healthy self-concept.

No controlled studies have systematically evaluated the efficacy of play therapy for depression. It is sometimes combined with behavioral and cognitive-behavioral techniques to add a psychodynamic component, as well as to assist in evaluating the child's cognitive-affective status. For preschool children and toddlers, play therapy is often the modality of choice because very young children often do not respond to cognitive-behavioral techniques.

Group Therapy

Many cognitive-behavioral interventions are delivered completely or partially in group settings because the structured, didactic presentation of cognitive-behavioral interventions is amenable to groups. Groups also give children the chance to practice new behaviors and thoughts with peers. Social skills training, for example, is well-suited to groups, and the interactions of group members are used to train skills.

More eclectic forms of group therapy are designed specifically to focus on the interaction of group members, as opposed to being exclusively a by-product of a cognitive-behavioral intervention. Such groups allow children to see that some of their peers have the same feelings that they do, reducing feelings of being strange, isolated, or inferior. Most eclectic groups also encourage expression of feelings and thoughts because group members model expression for each other, because there is some group peer pressure to express, and because group members can express feelings as a way of eliciting support from other group members. The group setting also allows children with depression to see the impact of their depressive behavior on others. This experience increases insight and may improve social skills (Baxter & Kennedy, 1992).

Family Interventions

The inclusion of the family in the treatment of a child with depression may occur to facilitate a behavioral or cognitive-behavioral intervention (Stark et al., 1994). Alternatively, family therapy may be the major treatment modality. Parents have a significant impact on the child's behavior by virtue of their role as caretaking figures, providers of reinforcement and punishment, and models of adaptive behavior. Hence, enlisting the parents' aid is vital to the success of intervention for childhood depression.

Unfortunately, many parents of children with depression have substantial problems themselves, which may in part be responsible for the development of the child's depression in the first place. In these cases, the parents are often well-intentioned but imperfect therapy partners. In some cases, parents can be saboteurs of therapeutic progress. In cases in which the parents have significant problems, family therapy and/or individual therapy for one or both parents may be warranted. Hence, the therapist should be alert for significant problems in the family of the child with depression.

Family therapy for depression in a child often includes components of structural family therapy and behavioral modification (see Brent et al., 1996, for example). Structural techniques involve joining with the family system, analyzing the subsystems and boundaries in the family, and strengthening appropriate boundaries (such as between parents and children) while weakening inappropriate boundaries (such as an enmeshed parent-child subsystem). Behavioral techniques typically require the identification of goals, rewards, and daily expectations (e.g., schedules) that aim to reduce depressive and withdrawn behaviors. The behavioral expectations and contingencies are delivered in the family context with communication, problem solving, and homework assignments used to facilitate positive family relationships and change in the adolescent's mood and behavior.

For infants who are showing anaclitic depression, parent (or other caretaker)-child psychotherapy is necessary to promote attachment. As a part of such therapy, the therapist models attachment-eliciting behaviors such as talking, eye contact, holding the child in a face-to-face position, holding the child in a comfortable and warm position, smiling, and play. Parent behavior is then shaped to encourage these important social-attachment interactions. Issues of parenting stress, self-esteem, and parental depression are discussed in the context of the parent's learning the attachment-eliciting behaviors, as these factors can interfere with the parent-child relationship. Regular, exclusive interaction between the parent and child is encouraged, and separations and multiple caretakers are discouraged.

■ References

Abramson, L. Y., Seligman, M. E. P., & Teasdale, J. D. (1978). Learned helplessness in humans: Critique and reformulation. *Journal of Abnormal Psychology, 87,* 49–74.

Adams, J., & Adams, M. (1996). The association among negative life events, perceived problem solving alternatives, depression, and suicidal ideation in adolescent psychiatric patients. *Journal of Child Psychology and Psychiatry, 37,* 715–720.

American Academy of Child and Adolescent Psychiatry. (1997). Practice parameters for the assessment and treatment of children and adolescents with Bipolar Disorder. *Journal of the American Academy of Child and Adolescent Psychiatry, 36,* 138–157.

American Psychiatric Association. (1994). *Diagnostic and statistical manual of mental disorders, fourth edition.* Washington, DC: Author.

Anderson, J. C., Williams, S., McGee, R., & Silva, P. A. (1987). DSM-III disorders in preadolescent children:

Prevalence in a large sample from the general population. *Archives of General Psychiatry, 44,* 69–76.

Arana, G. W., Baldessarini, R. J., & Ornsteen, M. (1985). The dexamethasone suppression test for diagnosis and prognosis in psychiatry: Commentary and review. *Archives of general Psychiatry, 42,* 1193–1204.

Aronen, E. T., Teicher, M. H., Geenens, D., Curtin, S., Glod, C. A., & Pahlavan, K. (1996). Motor activity and severity of depression in hospitalized prepubertal children. *Journal of the American Academy of Child and Adolescent Psychiatry, 35,* 752–763.

Asarnow, J. R., & Carlson, G. A. (1985). Depression self-rating scale: Utility with child psychiatric inpatients. *Journal of Consulting and Clinical Psychology, 53,* 491–499.

Asarnow, J. R., Carlson, G. A., & Guthrie, D. (1987). Coping strategies, self-perceptions, hopelessness, and perceived family environments in depressed and suicidal children. *Journal of Consulting and Clinical Psychology, 55,* 361–366.

Asher, S. R., Hymel, S., & Renshaw, P. D. (1984). Loneliness in children. *Child Development, 55,* 1456–1464.

Asher, S. R., & Wheeler, V. A. (1985). Children's loneliness: A comparison of rejected and neglected peer status. *Journal of Consulting and Clinical Psychology, 53,* 500–505.

Ball, J. D., Archer, R. P., Gordon, R. A., & French, J. (1991). Rorschach depression indices with children and adolescents: Concurrent validity findings. *Journal of Personality Assessment, 57,* 465–476.

Battle, J. (1992). *Culture-Free Self-Esteem Inventories, Forms A and B, Second Edition.* Austin, TX: Pro-Ed.

Baxter, R. F., & Kennedy, J. F. (1992). Group therapy of depression. In M. Shafii & S. L. Shafii (Eds.), *Clinical guide to depression in children and adolescents* (pp. 177–195). Washington, DC: American Psychiatric Press.

Beardslee, W. R., Bemporad, J., Keller, M. B., & Klerman, G. L. (1983). Children of parents with major affective disorder: A review. *American Journal of Psychiatry, 140,* 825–832.

Beck, A. T. (1976). Cognitive therapy and the emotional disorders. New York: International Universities Press.

Benfield, C. Y., Palmer, D. J., Pfefferbaum, B., & Stowe, M. L. (1988). A comparison of depressed and nondepressed disturbed children on measures of attributional style, hopelessness, life stress, and temperament. *Journal of Abnormal Child Psychology, 16,* 397–410.

Berndt, D. J., & Kaiser, C. F. (1996). *Multiscore Depression Inventory for Children.* Los Angeles: Western Psychological Services.

Bezchlibnyk-Butler, K. Z., & Jeffries, J. J. (1997). *Clinical handbook of psychotropic drugs.* Toronto: Hogrefe & Huber Publishers.

Biederman, J., Faraone, S., Mick, E., Wozniak, J., Chen, L., Ouellette, C., Marrs, A., Moore, P., Garcia, J., Mennin, D., & Lelon, E. (1996). Attention-Deficit Hyperactivity Disorder and juvenile mania: An overlooked comorbidity? *Journal of the American Academy of Child and Adolescent Psychiatry, 35,* 997–1008.

Biederman, J., Wozniak, J., Kiely, K., Ablon, S., Faraone, S., Mick, E., Mundy, E., Kraus, I. (1995). CBCL clinical scales discriminate prepubertal children with structured interview-derived diagnosis of mania from those with ADHD. *Journal of the American Academy of Child and Adolescent Psychiatry, 34,* 464–471.

Birleson, P. (1981). The validity of depressive disorder in childhood and the development of a self-rating scale: A research project. *Journal of Child Psychology and Psychiatry, 22,* 73–88.

Birleson, P., Hudson, I., Gray-Buchanan, D., & Wolff, S. (1987). Clinical evaluation of a self-rating scale for depressive disorder in childhood (Depression Self-Rating Scale). *Journal of Child Psychology and Psychiatry, 28,* 43–60.

Birmaher, B., Ryan, N. D., Williamson, D. E., Brent, D. A., Kaufman, J., Dahl, R. E., Perel, J., & Nelson, B. (1996). Childhood an.d adolescent depression: A review of the past 10 years. Part I. *Journal of the American Academy of Child and Adolescent Psychiatry, 35,* 1427–1439.

Bodiford, C. A., Eisenstadt, T. H., Johnson, J. H., & Bradlyn, A. S. (1988). Comparison of learned helpless cognitions and behavior in children with high and low scores on the Children's Depression Inventory. *Journal of Clinical Child Psychology, 17,* 152–158.

Bracken, B. A. (1992). *Multidimensional Self Concept Scale.* Austin, TX: Pro-Ed.

Brent, D. A., Roth, C. M., Holder, D. P., Kolko, D. J., Birmaher, B., Johnson, B. A., & Schweers, J. A. (1996). Psychosocial interventions for treating adolescent suicidal depression: A comparison of three psychosocial interventions. In E. D. Hibbs & P. S. Jensen (Eds.), *Psychosocial treatments for child and adolescent disorders: Empirically based strategies for clinical practice.* (pp. 187–206). Washington, DC: American Psychological Association.

Brown, R., Kocsis, J. H., Caroff, S., Amsterdam, J., Winokur, A., Stokes, P. E., & Frazer, A. (1985). Differences in nocturnal melatonin secretion between melancholic depressed patients and control subjects. *American Journal of Psychiatry, 142,* 811–816.

Burgin, D. (1986). Depression in children and adolescents. *Psychopathology, 19* (Supplement 2), 148–155.

Campbell, M., & Cuevu, J. E. (1995). Psychopharmacology in child and adolescent psychiatry: A review of the past seven years: II. *Journal of the American Academy of Child and Adolescent Psychiatry, 34,* 1262–1272.

Carlson, G. A. (1983). Bipolar affective disorders in childhood and adolescence. In D. P. Cantwell & G. A. Carlson (Eds.), *Affective disorders in childhood and adolescence: An update.* New York: Spectrum Publications.

Carlson, G. A. (1990). Annotation: Child and adolescent mania—diagnostic considerations. *Journal of Child Psychology and Psychiatry and Allied Disciplines, 31,* 331–341.

Carter, C. L., & Dacey, C. M. (1996). Validity of the Beck Depression Inventory, MMPI, and Rorschach in assessing adolescent depression. *Journal of Adolescence, 19,* 223–231.

Casat, C. D., Arana, G. W., & Powell, K. (1989). The DST in children and adolescents with major depressive disorder. *American Journal of Psychiatry, 146,* 503–507.

Cavallo, A., Holt, K. G., Hejazi, M. S., Richards, G. E., & Myer, W. J. (1987). Melatonin circadian rhythm in childhood depression. *Journal of the American Academy of Child and Adolescent Psychiatry, 26,* 395–399.

Centers for Disease Control (1991). Attempted suicide among high school students—United States, 1990. *Morbidity and Mortality Weekly Report, 40,* 633–635.

Cole, D. A., Martin, J. M., Powers, B., & Truglio, R. (1996). Modeling causal relations between academic and social competence and depression: A multitrait-multimethod longitudinal study of children. *Journal of Abnormal Psychology, 105,* 258–270.

Cole, D. A., Truglio, R., & Peeke, L. (1997). Relation between symptoms of anxiety and depression in children: A multitrait-multimethod-multigroup assessment. *Journal of Consulting and Clinical Psychology, 65,* 110–119.

Coopersmith, S. (1981). *Coopersmith Self Esteem Inventory: School Form.* Palo Alto, CA: Consulting Psychologists Press.

Craighead, W. E., Smucker, M. R., Craighead, L. W., & Ilardi, S. S. (1998). Factor analysis of the Children's Depression Inventory in a community sample. *Psychological Assessment, 10,* 156–165.

Cytryn, L., & McKnew, D. H. (1972). Proposed classification of childhood depression. *American Journal of Psychiatry, 129,* 149–155.

Dahl, R. E., Ryan, N. D., Matty, M. K., Birmaher, B., Al-Shabbout, M., Williamson, D. E., & Kupfer, D. J. (1996). Sleep onset abnormalities in depressed adolescents. *Biological Psychiatry, 39,* 400–410.

De Man, A. F., & Leduc, C. P. (1995). Suicidal ideation in high school students: Depression and other correlates. *Journal of Clinical Psychology, 51,* 173–180.

Dennison, S. T. (1989). *Twelve counseling programs for children at risk.* Springfield, IL: Charles C. Thomas.

Dorn, L. D., Burgess, E. S., Dichek, H. L., Putnam, F. W., Chrousos, G. P., & Gold, P. W. (1996). Thyroid hormone concentrations in depressed and nondepressed adolescents: Group differences and behavioral relations. *Journal of the American Academy of Child and Adolescent Psychiatry, 35,* 299–306.

Edelsohn, G., Ialongo, N., Werthamer-Larsson, L., Crockett, L., & Kellam, S. (1992). Self-reported depressive symptoms in first-grade children: Developmentally transient phenomena? *Journal of the American Academy of Child and Adolescent Psychiatry, 31,* 282–290.

Field, T., Morrow, C., Valdeon, C., Larson, S., Kuhn, C., & Schanberg, S. (1992). Massage reduces anxiety in child and adolescent psychiatric patients. *Journal of the American Academy of Child and Adolescent Psychiatry, 31,* 125–131.

Finch, A. J., Jr., Casat, C. D., & Carey, M. P. (1990). Depression in children and adolescents. In S. B. Morgan & T. M. Okwumabua (Eds.), *Child and adolescent disorders: Developmental and health psychology perspectives* (pp. 135–173). Hillsdale, NJ: Lawrence Erlbaum Associates.

Fristad, M. A., Weller, R. A., Weller, E. B., Teare, M., & Preskorn, S. H. (1991). Comparison of the parent and child versions of the Children's Depression Inventory (CDI). *Annals of Clinical Psychiatry, 3,* 341–346.

Geller, B., Sun, K., Zimerman, B., Luby, J., Frazier, J., & Williams, M. (1995). Complex and rapid-cycling in bipolar children and adolescents: A preliminary study. *Journal of Affective Disorders, 34,* 259–268.

Gershon, E. S., Targum, S. D., Kessler, L. R., Mazure, C. M., & Bunney, W. E., Jr. (1977). Genetic studies and biologic strategies in the affective disorders. *Progress in Medical Genetics, 2,* 101–164.

Glaser, K. (1968). Masked depression in children and adolescents. In S. Chess & A. Thomas (Eds.), *Annual progress in child psychiatry and child development* (Vol. 1, pp. 345–355). New York: Brunner/Mazel.

Goodman, S. H., Gravitt, G. W., & Kaslow, N. J. (1995). Social problem solving: A moderator of the relation between negative life stress and depression symptoms in children. *Journal of Abnormal Child Psychology, 23,* 473–485.

Hammen, C., Burge, D., & Adrian, C. (1991). Timing of mother and child depression in a longitudinal study of children at risk. *Journal of Consulting and Clinical Psychology, 59,* 341–345.

Harris, F. C., & Ammerman, R. T. (1986). Depression and suicide in children and adolescents. *Education and Treatment of Children, 9,* 334–343.

Hollon, S. P., & Kendall, P. C. (1980). Cognitive self-statements in depression: Development of an automatic thoughts questionnaire. *Cognitive Therapy and Research, 4,* 383–395.

Holmes, G. R., Heckel, R. V., Chestnut, E., Harris, N., & Cautela, J. (1987). Factor analysis of the Adolescent Reinforcement Survey Schedule (ARSS) with college freshmen. *Journal of Clinical Psychology, 43,* 386–390.

Johnson, J. H., & McCutcheon, S. M. (1980). Assessing life stress in older children and adolescents: Preliminary findings with the Life Events Checklist. In I. G. Sarason & C. D. Spielberger (Eds.), *Stress and anxiety* (Vol. 7, pp. 111–125). Washington, DC: Hemisphere.

Joiner, T. E., Catanzaro, S. J., & Laurent, J. (1996). Tripartite structure of positive and negative affect, depression, and anxiety in child and adolescent psychiatric inpatients. *Journal of Abnormal Psychology, 105,* 401–409.

Jolly, J. B., & Wiesner, D.C. (1996). Psychometric properties of the Automatic Thoughts Questionnaire-Positive with inpatient adolescents. *Cognitive Therapy and Research, 20,* 481–498.

Kafantaris, V. (1995). Treatment of Bipolar Disorder in children and adolescents. *Journal of the American Academy of Child and Adolescent Psychiatry, 34,* 732–741.

Kashani, J. H., Allan, W. D., Dahlmeier, J. M., Rezvani, M., & Reid, J. C. (1995). An examination of family functioning utilizing the circumplex model in psychiatrically hospitalized children with depression. *Journal of Affective Disorders, 35,* 65–73.

Kashani, J. H., Carlson, G. A., Beck, N. C., Hoeper, E. W., Corcoran, C. M., McAllister, J. A., Fallahi, C., Rosenberg, T. K., & Reid, J. C. (1987). Depression, depressive symptoms, and depressed mood among a community sample of adolescents. *American Journal of Psychiatry, 144,* 931–934.

Kashani, J. H., Holcomb, W. R., & Orvaschel, H. (1986). Depression and depressive symptomatology in preschool children from the general population. *American Journal of Psychiatry, 143,* 1138–1143.

Kashani, J. H., & Ray, J. S. (1983). Depressive symptoms among preschool-age children. *Child Psychiatry and Human Development, 13,* 233–238.

Kashani, J. H., & Schmid, L. S. (1992). Epidemiology and etiology of depressive disorders. In M. Shafii & S. L. Shafii (Eds.), *Clinical guide to depression in children and adolescents* (pp. 43–64). Washington, DC: American Psychiatric Press.

Kashani, J. H., & Sherman, D. D. (1988). Childhood depression: Epidemiology, etiological models, and treatment implications. *Integrative Psychiatry, 6,* 1–21.

Kaslow, N. J., & Racusin, G. R. (1990). Childhood depression: Current status and future directions. In A. S. Bellack, M. Hersen, & A. E. Kazdin (Eds.), *International Handbook of Behavior Modification and Therapy* (2nd ed., pp. 223–243). New York: Plenum.

Kaslow, N.J., Rehm, L. P., Pollack, S. L., & Siegel, A. W. (1990). Depression and perception of family functioning in children and their parents. *The American Journal of Family Therapy, 18,* 227–235.

Kaslow, N. J., Tannenbaum, R. L., & Seligman, M. E. P. (1978). *The KASTAN: A children's attributional style questionnaire.* Unpublished manuscript, University of Pennsylvania.

Kazdin, A. E. (1987). Assessment of childhood depression: Current issues and strategies. *Behavioral Assessment, 9,* 291–319.

Kazdin, A. E. (1989a). Childhood depression. In E. J. Mash & R. A. Barkley (Eds.), *Treatment of childhood disorders* (pp. 135–166). New York: Guilford.

Kazdin, A. E. (1989b). Identifying depression in children: A comparison of alternative selection criteria. *Journal of Abnormal Child Psychology, 17,* 437–454.

Kazdin, A. E. (1990). Assessment of childhood depression. In A. M. LaGreca (Ed.), *Through the eyes of the child: Obtaining self-reports from children and adolescents* (pp. 189–233). Boston: Allyn & Bacon.

Kazdin, A. E., Rodgers, A., & Colbus, D. (1986). The Hopelessness Scale for Children: Psychometric characteristics and concurrent validity. *Journal of Consulting and Clinical Psychology, 54,* 241–245.

Keller, M. B., & Wunder, J. (1990). Bipolar disorder in childhood. In M. Hersen & C. G. Last (Eds.), *Handbook of child and adult psychopathology* (pp. 69–81). New York: Pergamon.

Kendall, P. C., Stark, K. D., & Adam, T. (1990). Cognitive deficit or cognitive distortion in childhood depression. *Journal of Abnormal Child Psychology, 18,* 255–270.

King, J. D., & Kowalchuk, B. (1994). *Inventory of Suicide Orientation-30 (ISO-30).* Minneapolis, MN: NCS.

Kotsopoulos, S. (1989). Phenomenology of anxiety and depressive disorders in children and adolescents. *Psychiatric Clinics of North America, 12,* 803–814.

Kovacs, M. (1992). *Children's Depression Inventory (CDI) manual.* North Tonawanda, NY: Multi-Health Systems.

Kovacs, M., Feinberg, T. L., Crouse-Novak, M. A., Paulauskas, S. L., & Finkelstein, R. (1984a). Depressive disorders in childhood: I. A longitudinal prospective study of characteristics and recovery. *Archives of General Psychiatry, 41,* 229–237.

Kovacs, M., Feinberg, T. L., Crouse-Novak, M. A., Paulauskas, S. L. Pollock, M., & Finkelstein, R. (1984b). Depressive disorders in childhood: II. A longitudinal study of the risk for a subsequent major depression. *Archives of General Psychiatry, 41,* 643–649.

Kovacs, M., Obrosky, S., Gatsonis, C., & Richards, C. (1997). First-episode major depressive and dysthymic disorder in childhood: Clinical and sociodemographic factors in recovery. *Journal of the American Academy of Child and Adolescent Psychiatry, 36,* 777–784.

Kronenberger, W. G. (1990). The effects of perceived social, marital, and familial environments on the psychological adjustment of mothers of children with spina bifida. Doctoral Dissertation, Duke University.

Lachar, D., & Gruber, C. P. (1995). *Personality Inventory for Youth (PIY) manual.* Los Angeles: Western Psychological Services.

Lang, M., & Tisher, M. (1978). *Children's Depression Scale.* Victoria, Australia: Australian Council for Educational Research.

LeCroy, C. W. (1994). Social skills training. In C. W. LeCroy (Ed.), *Handbook of child and adolescent treatment manuals.* New York: Lexington.

Leenaars, A. A., & Wenckstern, S. (1991). Suicide in the school-age child and adolescent. In A. A. Leenaars (Ed.), *Life span perspectives of suicide* (pp. 95–107). New York: Plenum.

Leitenberg, H., Yost, L. W., & Carroll-Wilson, M. (1986). Negative cognitive errors in children: Questionnaire development, normative data, and comparisons between children with and without self-reported symptoms of depression, low self-esteem, and evaluation anxiety. *Journal of Consulting and Clinical Psychology, 54,* 528–536.

Lewinsohn, P. M. (1974). Clinical and theoretical aspects of depression. In K. S. Calhoun, H. E. Adams, & K. M. Mitchell (Eds.), *Innovative treatment methods of psychopathology* (pp. 63–120). New York: Wiley.

Lewinsohn, P. M., Clarke, G. N., Hops, H., & Andrews, J. (1990). Cognitive-behavioral treatment for depressed adolescents. *Behavior Therapy, 25,* 385–401.

Lewinsohn, P. M., Clarke, G. N., Rohde, P., Hops, H., & Seeley, J. R. (1996). A course in coping: A cognitive-behavioral approach to the treatment of adolescent depression. In E. D. Hibbs & P. S. Jensen (Eds.), *Psychosocial treatments for child and adolescent disorders: Empirically based strategies for clinical practice* (pp. 109–136). Washington, DC: American Psychological Association.

Lewinsohn, P. M., & Rohde, P. (1993). The cognitive-behavioral treatment of depression in adolescents: Research and suggestions. *The Clinical Psychologist, 46,* 177–183.

Liddle, B., & Spence, S. H. (1990). Cognitive-behaviour therapy with depressed primary school children: A cautionary note. *Behavioural Psychotherapy, 18,* 85–102.

MacPhillamy, D. J., & Lewinsohn, P. M. (1982). The Pleasant Events Schedule: Studies on reliability, validity, and scale intercorrelation. *Journal of Consulting and Clinical Psychology, 50,* 363–380.

Martini, D. R., Strayhorn, J. M., & Puig-Antich, J. (1990). A symptom self-report measure for preschool children. *Journal of the American Academy of Child and Adolescent Psychiatry, 29,* 594–600.

Matson, J. L., Rotatori, A. F., & Helsel, W. J. (1983). Development of a rating scale to measure social skills in children: The Matson Evaluation of Social Skills with Youngsters (MESSY). *Behavior Research and Therapy, 21,* 335–340.

McCauley, E., Carlson, G. A., & Calderon, R. (1991). The role of somatic complaints in the diagnosis of depression in children and adolescents. *Journal of the American Academy of Child and Adolescent Psychiatry, 30,* 631–635.

Meichenbaum, D. (1977). *Cognitive-behavior modification: An integrative approach.* New York: Plenum.

Meller, W. H., & Borchardt, C. M. (1996). Comorbidity of major depression and conduct disorder. *Journal of Affective Disorders, 39,* 123–126.

Meyer, R. G. & Deitsch, S. (1996). *The clinician's handbook* (4th ed.). Boston: Allyn & Bacon.

Mokros, H. B., & Poznanski, E. O. (1992). Standardized approaches to clinical assessment of depression. In M. Shafii & S. L. Shafii (Eds.), *Clinical guide to depression in children and adolescents* (pp. 129–155). Washington, DC: American Psychiatric Press.

Mufson, L., Moreau, D., & Weissman, M. M. (1996). Focus on relationships: Interpersonal psychotherapy for adolescent depression. In E. D. Hibbs & P. S. Jensen (Eds.), *Psychosocial treatments for child and adolescent disorders: Empirically based strategies for clinical practice* (pp. 137–156). Washington, DC: American Psychological Association.

Murray, K. T., & Sines, J. O. (1996). Parsing the genetic and nongenetic variance in children's depressive behavior. *Journal of Affective Disorders, 38,* 23–34.

Myers, K., McCauley, E., Calderon, R., Mitchell, J., Burke, P., & Schloredt, K. (1991a). Risks for suicidality in major depressive disorder. *Journal of the American Academy of Child and Adolescent Psychiatry, 30,* 86–94.

Myers, K., McCauley, E., Calderon, R., & Treder, R. (1991b). The 3-year longitudinal course of suicidality and predictive factors for subsequent suicidality in youths with major depressive disorder. *Journal of the American Academy of Child and Adolescent Psychiatry, 30,* 804–810.

Pataki, C. S., & Carlson, G. A. (1990). Major depression in childhood. In M. Hersen & C. G. Last (Eds.), *Handbook of child and adult psychopathology* (pp. 35–50). New York: Pergamon.

Pataki, C. S., & Carlson, G. A. (1992). Bipolar disorders: Clinical manifestations, differential diagnosis, and treatment. In M. Shafii & S. L. Shafii (Eds.), *Clinical guide to depression in children and adolescents* (pp. 269–294). Washington, DC: American Psychiatric Press.

Pfeffer, C. R. (1992). Relationship between depression and suicidal behavior. In M. Shafii & S. L. Shafii (Eds.), *Clinical guide to depression in children and adolescents* (pp. 115–127). Washington, DC: American Psychiatric Press.

Pliszka, S. R. (1991). Antidepressants in the treatment of child and adolescent psychopathology. *Journal of Clinical Child Psychology, 20,* 313–320.

Poznanski, E. O., & Mokros, H. B. (1996). *Children's Depression Rating Scale—Revised.* Los Angeles: Western Psychological Services.

Rancurello, M. D. (1985). Clinical applications of antidepressant drugs in childhood behavioral and emotional disorders. *Psychiatric Annals, 15,* 88–100.

Rehm, L. P. (1977). A self-control model of depression. *Behavior Therapy, 8,* 787–804.

Reynolds, C. R., & Kamphaus, R. W. (1992). *Behavior Assessment System for Children manual.* Circle Pines, MN: American Guidance Service.

Reynolds, W. M. (1987a). *Assessment of depression in adolescents: Manual for the Reynolds Adolescent Depression Scale (RADS).* Odessa, FL: Psychological Assessment Resources, Inc.

Reynolds, W. M. (1987b). *Suicidal Ideation Questionnaire.* Odessa, FL: Psychological Assessment Resources.

Reynolds, W. M. (1989). *Reynolds Child Depression Scale: Professional manual.* Odessa, FL: Psychological Assessment Resources.

Reynolds, W. M., & Coats, K. I. (1986). A comparison of cognitive-behavioral therapy and relaxation training for the treatment of depression in adolescents. *Journal of Consulting and Clinical Psychology, 54,* 653–660.

Reynolds, W. M., & Graves, A. (1989). Reliability of children's reports of depressive symptomatology. *Journal of Abnormal Child Psychology, 17,* 647–655.

Rispens, J., Swaab, H., Van Den Oord, E. J. C. G., Cohen-Kettenis, P., Van Engeland, H., & Van Yperen, T. (1997). WISC profiles in child psychiatric diagnosis: Sense or nonsense? *Journal of the American Academy of Child and Adolescent Psychiatry, 36,* 1587–1594.

Rosenthal, N. E., Sack, D. A., Skwerer, R. G., Jacobsen, F. M., & Wehr, T. A. (1989). Phototherapy for seasonal affective disorder. In N. E. Rosenthal & M. C. Blehar (Eds.), *Seasonal affective disorders and phototherapy* (pp. 273–294). New York: Guilford.

Rudolph, K. D., Hammen, C., & Burge, D. (1997). A cognitive-interpersonal approach to depressive symptoms in preadolescent children. *Journal of Abnormal Child Psychology, 25,* 33–45.

Ryan, N. D. (1992). The pharmacologic treatment of child and adolescent depression. *Pediatric Psychopharmacology, 15,* 29–40.

Sarason, I. G., Levine, H. M., Basham, R. B., & Sarason, B. R. (1983). Assessing social support: The Social Support Questionnaire. *Journal of Personality and Social Psychology, 44,* 127–139.

Schrodt, G. R. (1992). Cognitive therapy of depression. In M. Shafii & S. L. Shafii (Eds.), *Clinical guide to depression in children and adolescents* (pp. 197–217). Washington, DC: American Psychiatric Press.

Seligman, M. E. P. (1975). *Helplessness: On depression, development and death.* San Francisco: W. H. Freeman.

Seligman, M., Kaslow, N., Alloy, L., Peterson, C., Tannenbaum, R., & Abramson, L. (1984). Attributional style and depressive symptoms among children. *Journal of Abnormal Psychology, 93,* 235–238.

Shafii, M., & Shafii, S. L. (1992). Clinical manifestations and developmental psychopathology of depression. In M. Shafii & S. L. Shafii (Eds.), *Clinical guide to depression in children and adolescents* (pp. 3–42). Washington, DC: American Psychiatric Press.

Simeon, J. G. (1989). Depressive disorders in children and adolescents. *Psychiatric Journal of the University of Ottawa, 14,* 356–361.

Smith, K., & Crawford, S. (1986). Suicidal behavior among "normal" high school students. *Suicide and Life-Threatening Behavior, 16,* 313–325.

Smucker, M. R., Craighead, W. E., Craighead, L. W., & Green, B. J. (1986). Normative and reliability data for the Children's Depression Inventory. *Journal of Abnormal Child Psychology, 14,* 25–39.

Sokoloff, M. R., & Lubin, B. (1983). Depressive mood in adolescent, emotionally disturbed females: Reliability and validity of an adjective checklist (C-DACL). *Journal of Abnormal Child Psychology, 11,* 531–536.

Sonis, W. A. (1989). Seasonal affective disorder of childhood and adolescence: A review. In N. E. Rosenthal & M. C. Blehar (Eds.), *Seasonal affective disorders and phototherapy* (pp. 46–84). New York: Guilford.

Sonis, W. A. (1992). Chronobiology of seasonal mood disorders. In M. Shafii & S. L. Shafii (Eds.), *Clinical guide to depression in children and adolescents* (pp. 89–114). Washington, DC: American Psychiatric Press.

Spitz, R. A. (1945). Hospitalism. *Psychoanalytic Study of the Child, 1,* 53–74.

Spitz, R. A. (1946). Anaclitic depression: An inquiry into the genesis of psychiatric conditions in early childhood, II. *Psychoanalytic Study of the Child, 2,* 313–342.

Spitz, R. A. (1965). *The first year of life.* New York: International Universities Press.

Stark, K. D., Kendall, P. C., McCarthy, M., Stafford, M., Barron, R., & Thomeer, M. (1996a). *Taking ACTION: A workbook for overcoming depression.* Ardmore, PA: Workbook Publishing.

Stark, K. D., Raffaelle, L., & Reysa, A. (1994). The treatment of depressed children: A skills training approach to working with children and families. In C. W. LeCroy (Ed.), *Handbook of child and adolescent treatment manuals* (pp. 343–397). New York: Lexington.

Stark, K. D., Swearer, S., Kurowski, C., Sommer, D., & Bowen, B. (1996b). Targeting the child and the family: A holistic approach to treating child and adolescent depressive disorders. In E. D. Hibbs & P. S. Jensen (Eds.), *Psychosocial treatments for child and adolescent disorders: Empirically based strategies for clinical practice* (pp. 207–238). Washington, DC: American Psychological Association.

Stark, K. D., Rouse, L. W., & Livingston, R. (1991). Treatment of depression during childhood and adolescence: Cognitive-behavioral procedures for the individual and family. In P. C. Kendall (Ed.), *Child and adolescent therapy: Cognitive-behavioral procedures* (pp. 165–206). New York: Guilford.

Strober, M. (1992). Bipolar disorders: Natural history, genetic studies, and follow-up. In M. Shafii & S. L. Shafii (Eds.), *Clinical guide to depression in children and adolescents* (pp. 251–268). Washington, DC: American Psychiatric Press.

Strober, M., Morrell, W., Lampert, C., & Burroughs, J. (1990). Relapse following discontinuation of lithium maintenance therapy in adolescents with bipolar illness: A naturalistic study. *American Journal of Psychiatry, 147,* 457–461.

Thompson, M., Kaslow, N. J., Weiss, B., & Nolen-Hoeksema, S. (1998). Children's Attributional Style Questionnaire–Revised: Psychometric examination. *Psychological Assessment, 10,* 166–170.

Tisher, M., Lang-Takac, E., & Lang, M. (1992). The Children's Depression Scale: Review of Australian and overseas experience. *Australian Journal of Psychology, 44,* 27–35.

Todd, R. D., Geller, B., Neuman, R., Fox, L. W., & Hickok, J. (1996). Increased prevalence of alcoholism in relatives of depressed and bipolar children. *Journal of the American Academy of Child and Adolescent Psychiatry, 35,* 716–724.

Wagner, B. M., Cole, R. E., & Schwartzman, P. (1995). Psychosocial correlates of suicide attempts among junior and senior high school youth. *Suicide and Life-Threatening Behavior, 25,* 358–372.

Weller, E. B., Weller, R. A., & Fristad, M. A. (1995). Bipolar Disorder in children: Misdiagnosis, underdiagnosis, and future directions. *Journal of the American Academy of Child and Adolescent Psychiatry, 34,* 709–715.

Weller, R. A., Weller, E. B., Fristad, M. A., & Bowes, J. M. (1991). Depression in recently bereaved prepubertal children. *American Journal of Psychiatry, 148,* 1536–1541.

Wetzler, S., Asnis, G. M., Hyman, R. B., Virtue, C., Zimmerman, J., & Rathus, J. H. (1996). Characteristics of suicidality among adolescents. *Suicide and Life-Threatening Behavior, 26,* 37–45.

Wozniak, J., Biederman, J., Kiely, K., Ablon, S., Fara-sone, S. V., Mundy, E., & Mennin, D. (1995). Mania-like symptoms suggestive of childhood-onset Bipolar Disorder in clinically referred children. *Journal of the American Academy of Child and Adolescent Psychiatry, 34,* 867–876.

Yaylayan, S., Weller, E. B., & Weller, R. A. (1992). Neurobiology of depression. In M. Shafii & S. L. Shafii (Eds.), *Clinical guide to depression in children and adolescents* (pp. 65–88). Washington, DC: American Psychiatric Press.

CHAPTER 6

Anxiety Disorders

Anxiety disorders of childhood and adolescence appear under two sections of DSM-IV: "Disorders Usually First Diagnosed in Infancy, Childhood, or Adolescence" and "Anxiety Disorders." Only Separation Anxiety Disorder (SAD) appears in the childhood disorders section, where it is grouped with the "Other Disorders of Infancy, Childhood, or Adolescence." The other anxiety disorders may be diagnosed in adults as well as in children; they fall in the "Anxiety Disorders" section of DSM-IV.

Panic Disorder (PD) is one anxiety disorder that is far more common in adolescents and adults than in children. Research has shed light on some unique aspects of PD in children (Ollendick, 1998), but PD in children, independent of significant symptoms of SAD, Social Phobia, or GAD, appears to be relatively rare. Most current knowledge of evaluation and treatment of PD is directed at the adolescent and adult population, with childhood treatments mirroring treatments for adults. Readers interested in treating PD in adolescents and adults are referred to Meyer and Deitsch (1996).

■ Separation Anxiety Disorder

□ CLINICAL DESCRIPTION

Diagnostic Considerations

Anxiety over separation from primary caregivers is a normal phenomenon, especially from the ages of 6 months through 5 years. However, when anxiety over separation is excessive and causes significant problems in daily functioning, the presence of Separation Anxiety Disorder (SAD) should be evaluated. The essential feature of SAD is excessive anxiety when the child is separated from a major attachment figure. This anxiety may approach a panic level and impairment may be severe if the child refuses to engage in independent functioning. Anxiety is relieved when the child is in the presence of attachment figures.

While separated, the child may experience worries about injury, illness, harm, or other circumstances preventing reunion. He or she may resist engagement in other activities, such as school, social interaction, play, or even sleep. Nightmares and somatic complaints are other commonly seen diagnostic criteria. Onset is required before age 18, but onset after age 10 is unusual (Table 6.1).

Normal childhood development includes a period when separation from attachment figures causes an anxiety reaction. In fact, lack of any reaction at separation from a caretaker could indicate a Reactive Attachment Disorder (Chapter 16). Diagnosis of SAD, therefore, requires consideration of the child's age and developmental level.

The terms *school phobia* and *school refusal* are often used to indicate the school avoidance feature of SAD, but they do not exist as independent diagnoses. Rather, school refusal is usually an associated feature of a constellation of anxiety problems as opposed to a stand-alone problem. Although school refusal is the most common problem prompting referral of children for SAD (present in as many as three-fourths of SAD cases), school refusal is not necessarily synonymous with SAD. In as many as two-thirds of cases of school refusal, SAD is not the primary diagnosis. Rather, school refusal may be diagnosed separately as Specific Phobia, Social Phobia, or Generalized Anxiety Disorder (Black, 1995).

School refusal appears to be of two types: young children with a rapid onset of refusal to attend school and older children with recurrent school refusal that occurs after a more gradual onset. The former type tends to occur in more well-adjusted families and to respond well to treatment, whereas the latter type is associated with family pathology and treatment resistance (Kennedy, 1965).

SAD is probably the most common childhood anxiety disorder, with a prevalence as high as 4% (American Psychiatric Association, 1994). SAD is more unusual in adolescents. Bowen, Offord, and Boyle (1990) found that 2.4% of Canadian adolescents in an epidemiological study were diagnosable with SAD. In their community adolescent sample, Kashani and Orvaschel (1988) found SAD to be the least common anxiety disorder. Among children and adolescents presenting for treatment at an outpatient anxiety disorders clinic, SAD was the most common primary diagnosis, comprising 33% of the sample (Last, Strauss, & Francis, 1987). Cantwell and Baker (1987) report a high prevalence of SAD and Social Phobia (10%) in children receiving treatment for communication disorders.

TABLE 6.1   Epidemiology and Course of Separation Anxiety Disorder

Prevalence: 3–5%, declining with age to under 2% in adolescence

Sex Ratio (Male:Female):   More prevalent in females

Typical Onset Age: 5–9 years old

Course: Variable, usually remitting if onset is acute and immediately addressed with structure and limits. More chronic if reinforced or allowed to occur without intervention.

Common Comorbid Conditions: 1. Generalized Anxiety Disorder
2. Social Phobia
3. Specific Phobia
4. Depressive Disorders

Relevant Subtypes: 1. With Associated School Avoidance

SAD usually co-occurs with another anxiety or mood disorder diagnosis. Over half of children with SAD will have another anxiety disorder diagnosis (typically Generalized Anxiety Disorder or Specific Phobia), and as many as one-third may receive a diagnosis of depression (American Psychiatric Association, 1994; Black, 1995).

Appearance and Features

The appearance of SAD (see Table 6.2) varies by age (Francis, Last & Strauss, 1987). Preschool children often express vague fears and general distress upon separation from caretakers. Because some separation distress is normal at the preschool age, distress qualifying for SAD diagnosis must be profound. A typical preschool response to parental separation may include some crying, social withdrawal, and attempt to follow the parent. However, the preschooler can often eventually be engaged (usually within 10 minutes or less but almost always within an hour or two) in an appealing activity with appropriate support. On the other hand, extremely long or severe temper tantrums, excessive crying and sobbing, persistent social withdrawal, and paralyzing fear responses are typical of the preschool child with SAD. At home, the preschool child with SAD may resist sleeping alone in bed or in a room.

At early school ages, children with SAD experience more defined separation fears. Themes of getting lost are typical, and fears of specific dangers such as illness, death, kidnapping, and assault are common. School-aged children with SAD frequently worry about unrealistic harm to attachment figures. If separation anxiety has not been noticed prior to school ages, it is almost always noticed at entry to school at age 5 or 6. Frequent illness complaints, missed school days, visits to the school nurse, calls home during the school day, crying in class, social withdrawal, and manipulative behavior to avoid school are all

TABLE 6.2   Appearance and Features of Separation Anxiety Disorder

COMMON FEATURES

1. Extended show of distress upon real or threatened separation from primary caregivers (tantrums, crying, freezing, somatic complaints, social withdrawal)
2. Fear of harm or permanent separation from caretaker
3. Fear of getting lost, death, kidnapping, assault
4. Lower socioeconomic status
5. School refusal

OCCASIONAL FEATURES

1. Somatic symptoms of distress
2. Nightmares with separation theme
3. Refusal to sleep alone
4. Whiny, clinging, or demanding behavior when not receiving caretaker attention

Note: The features listed in the table are often seen but are not universal. Some features may be diagnostically relevant or required, whereas others may not be required for diagnosis. "Common" features are typical of the disorder; "occasional" features appear frequently but are not necessarily seen in a majority of cases.

suggestive of SAD. Approximately 75% of children with SAD exhibit school refusal or avoidance (Last, Francis, Hersen, Kazdin, & Strauss, 1987).

Families of children with SAD are often described as close-knit and caring (Kaplan & Sadock, 1988), but these adjectives often suggest enmeshed relationships. In many cases, children with SAD appear to be overly attached to their caretakers. Whiny, demanding behavior is common, particularly when the caretaker's attention is diverted from the child. Often, however, children with SAD appear shy and compliant at home.

In some cases, a child with SAD perceives stress or distress in the parent and tries to support the parent with the child's presence and dependency. Parents who are experiencing extreme stress may inadvertently encourage separation anxiety by leaning on children too strongly for support.

Symptoms of SAD vary considerably with time, and there is no typical course of SAD. In the case of acute onset in a young child, SAD often remits with the imposition of rules that require the child to learn to tolerate separation. In other cases, children with early onset of SAD continue to have problems with anxiety and high sensitivity level throughout their lives; in such cases, anxiety appears to be temperamental. SAD can be long-lasting and difficult to treat when the child is reinforced for the symptoms or when avoidance is allowed for an extended period of time (e.g., by sleeping in the parental bed). Cantwell and Baker (1990) observed a high rate of recovery and a low rate of stability of SAD over a 4- to 5-year period for children receiving treatment at a speech and language clinic.

Etiology

Biological contributions to the development of SAD include anxious temperament and possible genetic propensity for the disorder. Children with SAD may have a temperamental disposition to be anxious and fearful, which becomes focused on the presence of the parent for security; this theory is in need of more research support. Support for a genetic basis of SAD has yielded equivocal results. Mothers of children with separation anxiety did not have an increased history of the disorder, but 83% of mothers of children with SAD or GAD had a lifetime history of anxiety disorders (Last, Phillips, & Statfeld, 1987). Additionally, families of children with SAD show a higher than average prevalence of anxiety and mood disorders (Black, 1995). Furthermore, it has been suggested that there may be a similar genetic etiology for SAD and Panic Disorder (see Casat, 1988 for review).

Given a biological vulnerability for the disorder, SAD can develop in a number of ways. In some cases, stressors involving separation or danger are responsible for onset of SAD. The child seeks proximity to the caretaker in order to prevent a recurrence of the stressor and to decrease feelings of anxiety. In other cases, familial and behavioral causes appear to be responsible for SAD. Attachment theorists suggest that SAD may develop because of a child's insecure attachment with the primary caretaker. The child feels that he or she must constantly be vigilant or else the fragile attachment will be broken, resulting in loss of the caretaker. Bowlby's (1973) attachment theory strongly influences this etiological hypothesis. Infants who do not experience a sensitive, responsive, and available mother fail to develop a firm base of security and trust, leading to anxiety and SAD.

Other family-based etiological theories suggest that SAD develops out of enmeshed relationships between parent and child. Enmeshment prevents children from developing an independent, confident view of themselves, fostering excessive dependence on the parent.

Such children feel disloyal and vulnerable without the presence of the parent. Often, the parent or the family system derives some benefit from the enmeshed relationship as well. For example, a depressed parent may rely on the constant presence of the child for social support. Alternatively, the child's "disorder" may deflect attention from problems in the relationship between the parents.

Behavioral theories focus on the reinforcing effects of SAD. SAD may gain the child increased access to the parent and allow the child to avoid situations of stress and failure, such as school and social relationships. Hence, children develop separation anxiety because reinforcements associated with the presence of the parent outweigh the reinforcements associated with the absence of the parent. This presence/absence reinforcement ratio is sufficiently large that the child with SAD will engage in extreme behaviors and psychological reactions in order to retain it. Attention to secondary gain for SAD symptoms is important in understanding the underlying behavioral etiology of SAD.

Negative reinforcement theories of SAD hold that the child maintains proximity to the parent in order to relieve the unpleasant anxious state of being out of the parent's presence. When not in the presence of the parent, the child feels distressed, ill, and/or vulnerable. Remaining in the presence of the parent, then, allows the child to escape the noxious effects of being alone. Negative reinforcement theories do not explain why the child would be anxious when separated in the first place.

Cognitive and social learning theories of SAD explain the disorder based on the child's observations of an anxious or needy parent. Some parents unwittingly model separation anxiety by appearing anxious or concerned when their child is separated from them. This scenario is likely to emerge if the parent has experienced a stressful situation involving potential separation from their child, such as childhood chronic illness or loss of the child in a divorce. The child notices the parent's anxiety and becomes anxious as well.

☐ ASSESSMENT PATTERNS

A sample assessment battery for childhood anxiety disorders (including SAD) is shown in Table 6.3.

Broad Assessment Strategies

Behavioral Assessment

Parent- and Teacher-Report. The value of observer-report checklists for evaluating what amounts to an internal, experiential state such as anxiety has been questioned. Nevertheless, internal states are frequently reflected in external behaviors that are observed by parents. Hence, parent-report checklists can provide insight into the effects of anxiety on the external behavior of the child.

Children with SAD can be expected to elevate the Anxious-Depressed, Somatic Complaints, Withdrawn, Social Problems, and Internalizing scales of the CBCL and TRF. Because the Anxious-Depressed subscale includes a mix of anxiety and depression items, individual items should be examined to see if the child is showing primarily anxious or primarily depressed symptoms. Higher scores on the Somatic Complaints scale often indicate

TABLE 6.3   Sample Assessment Battery for Anxiety Disorders

BEHAVIORAL

1. Child Symptom Inventory—4 (Parent-Report and Teacher-Report)
2. Behavior Assessment System for Children (Parent-Report and Teacher-Report)
3. Personality Inventory for Youth (if 8 years or older)

FAMILY

1. Family Environment Scale

SYNDROME-SPECIFIC

1. Multidimensional Anxiety Scale for Children
2. Fear Survey Schedule for Children—Revised
3. Social Anxiety Scale for Children (especially for Social Phobia)
4. Maudsley Obsessional-Compulsive Inventory (especially for Obsessive-Compulsive Disorder)
5. Children's Yale-Brown Obsessive-Compulsive Scale (especially for Obsessive-Compulsive Disorder)
6. Trauma Symptom Checklist for Children (especially for Posttraumatic Stress Disorder)

Note: Assessment instruments are intended to supplement (not substitute for) a good clinical interview and, when possible, a structured diagnostic interview.

the use of somatic problems to maintain proximity to the parent, whereas the Withdrawn and Social Problems scales can indicate the extent to which SAD is harming social relationships. Elevations of the Thought Problems scale typically indicate the presence of obsessional thought processes, possibly surrounding separation fears. Elevations of the Externalizing subscales are less common in children with SAD; if these are seen, they could indicate the presence of aggressive or coercive behavior to maintain proximity to the parent. One CBCL/TRF item pertains specifically to school avoidance, whereas several other items describe shyness/withdrawal that could indicate separation anxiety.

On the BASC, children with SAD would be expected to elevate the Anxiety, Somatization, and Withdrawal subscales, reflecting general anxiety, physical complaints, and social withdrawal, respectively. Conversely, low scores would be expected on several adaptive subscales such as Adaptability (indicating that the child adapts poorly to new situations) and Leadership (suggesting lack of confidence and lack of participation in activities). Failure to find extreme scores on the Withdrawal and Leadership scales may indicate that the child does well with peers in the presence of the parent or in the classroom.

The parent versions of the ECI-4, CSI-4, and ASI-4 include one subscale (Separation Anxiety Disorder) that consists exclusively of the eight "Category A" (behavioral-emotional) symptoms of SAD. Hence, SI-4 results can be used to directly evaluate and quantify these symptoms by parent-report. The teacher version of the CSI-4 does not contain that subscale, presumably because teachers have less exposure to SAD symptomatology. In interpreting SI-4 results, it is important to remember that the duration (at least 4 weeks) and onset (prior to age 18) criteria of SAD are not covered by the SI-4.

On the Conners' scales, elevations of the Anxious-Shy, Perfectionism, Social Problems, and Psychosomatic scales would be expected for a child with SAD. Scores on the Perfectionism scale may also indicate the presence of obsessive thought processes and difficulty tolerating change, which could further contribute to separation anxiety.

In some cases, the parent-report of the BASC, CBCL, CPRS, and SI-4 will elevate subscales characteristic of SAD, whereas the teacher-report shows less significant elevations. When this happens, the child may adjust well, once separation from the parent is accomplished (e.g., once the child is in the classroom), with more severe SAD symptoms in the presence of the parent.

Self-Report. Because SAD becomes less common with age, self-report questionnaires for teenagers and older children (including the MMPI-A and YSR) are often too advanced for use at more common (younger) ages. The PIY and self-report version of the BASC, on the other hand, can be completed by children as young as 8 or 9 years old. These latter two scales may, therefore, be more useful for children with SAD.

Neither the PIY nor the BASC contains a focused separation anxiety subscale. However, both questionnaires include subscales measuring distress, anxiety, social adjustment, and somatic complaints. The Psychological Discomfort scale of the PIY contains items measuring anxiety, depression, and sleep disturbance; the Fear and Worry subscale of the Psychological Discomfort scale is a more specific measure of anxiety on the PIY. The PIY also contains several scales and subscales measuring social adjustment (Social Withdrawal scale, Social Introversion subscale, Isolation subscale, Social Skills Deficits scale, Limited Peer Status subscale, Conflict with Peers subscale) and somatization (Somatic Complaints scale, Psychosomatic Syndrome subscale, Muscular Tension and Anxiety subscale, Preoccupation with Disease subscale). These PIY scales and subscales can provide considerable insight into the child's self-reported anxiety, social adjustment, and somatization. Children with SAD may elevate any of these subscales, but the Fear and Worry subscale, Psychosomatic Syndrome subscale, and Social Introversion subscale best capture the anxiety, somatization, and shyness characteristic of many children with SAD. In addition, very low scores on the Family Dysfunction scale may be consistent with strong or enmeshed family relationships that have been described as characteristic of SAD.

On the BASC-SRP, children with SAD would be expected to elevate the Anxiety and Somatization subscales. Elevated scores on the Social Stress subscale and Sense of Inadequacy subscale would indicate that fears of isolation/alienation and feelings of inferiority/failure, respectively, are also problems for the child. The Attitude to School subscale and Attitude to Teachers subscale can be used to investigate the degree to which the child is alienated from school and teachers. Significant elevations on the Relations with Parents subscale (an adaptive subscale, for which higher scores mean better relationship with parents), combined with Anxiety and Somatization elevations, would imply that strong or enmeshed family relationships are concurrent with the separation anxiety features.

When using a self-report scale, there is always the danger of distorted responding. For children who want to hide their SAD by denying symptoms, PIY and BASC clinical subscale scores would fall in average ranges. In such cases, however, inspection of the L validity scale on the BASC and/or the Defensiveness validity scale on the PIY may provide evidence that the child adopted a defensive or denying response set with regard to psychological and behavioral symptoms.

Family Assessment

Parent-Report.   Separation anxiety frequently occurs in close-knit, caring, and/or enmeshed families. The FES may provide an evaluation of these and other aspects of family functioning. Typical SAD families would likely show a pattern of relatively high scores on the Cohesion and Control scales and comparatively low scores on the Independence and Active-Recreational Orientation scales. High Supportive factor scores might indicate that the family wishes to portray themselves as "perfect" and free of problems in interpersonal functioning. Typically, the FES must be completed by a parent because the child is too young to complete the scale. Child-report on the FES can be useful with children over the age of 13.

Syndrome-Specific Tests

Clinician-Administered

A useful anxiety-focused, semistructured clinical interview is the Anxiety Disorders Interview Schedule for Children—Child and Parent versions (ADIS-IV-C and ADIS-IV-P) (Silverman & Albano, 1996). The ADIS-IV-C and ADIS-IV-P allow for systematic data collection and assessment of DSM-IV anxiety diagnoses in children age 7–17. ADIS-IV-C/P items ask about anxiety symptoms, cues, intensity, avoidance, and precipitating events. In addition to the DSM-IV diagnosis, ADIS-IV-C/P data provide an extensive overview of the child's symptoms, and possible comorbid or alternative diagnoses (such as mood disorders and ADHD) are screened with interview questions. Reliability of the interview appears to be good (Silverman & Albano, 1996).

Child-Report

Several well-known, broad anxiety scales can provide valuable information about the extent and types of fears and anxieties being experienced by the child with SAD, although only a couple of the scales contain separation anxiety subscales. In using these scales, it is important to remember that high scores on any of the scales (with the exception of the SAD subscales) are as likely to be indicative of another anxiety disorder as they are to be indicative of SAD.

Revised Children's Manifest Anxiety Scale.   The RCMAS (Reynolds & Richmond, 1978) is a 37-item (8 of which form a lie scale) yes-no scale that assesses anxious thoughts, behaviors, physiological responses, and emotions across a variety of situations. It produces a total score and three factor-analytically derived subscales: Worry/oversensitivity, Physiological, and Concentration. The Worry/sensitivity factor appears best able to discriminate children with and without anxiety, using a cutting T-score of 60 (Mattison, 1992). Psychometric properties are reported to be good (Mattison, 1992; Reynolds & Richmond, 1978), although some items overlap with symptoms of depression. Hence, the degree to which the RCMAS discriminates between anxiety and depression is suspect, particularly given the strong co-occurrence of anxious and depressive symptoms in children. Nonetheless, it has seen wide use in assessing anxiety in children and adolescents.

State-Trait Anxiety Inventory for Children.   The State-Trait Anxiety Inventory for Children (STAIC; Spielberger, Edwards, Lushene, Montouri, & Platzek, 1973) is composed of two 20-item subscales that assess anxiety-state (situational symptoms or transitory anxiety) and anxiety-trait (generalized anxiety across a variety of situations). The extent to which young children can successfully differentiate between transitory and stable anxiety, however, is suspect (Johnson & Melamed, 1979). The STAIC has been shown to successfully discriminate anxiety-disordered children with and without major depression from each other and from children free of anxiety. It does not appear useful, however, in discriminating among anxiety disorders (Mattison, 1992).

Fear Survey Schedule for Children—Revised.   The Fear Survey Schedule for Children—Revised (FSSC-R; Ollendick, 1983) is an 80-item scale that asks children age 7–18 to rate their fear of a variety of objects and events on a three-point scale. Factor analyses of the FSSC-R indicate five item clusters (Fear of Failure/Criticism, Fear of the Unknown, Fear of Injury and Small Animals, Fear of Danger/Death, and Fear of Medical Situations), and extensive normative data are available (Ollendick, Matson, & Helsel, 1985). The FSSC-R can provide data concerning not only the types of fears that the child has but also the degree of fear relative to comparison samples.

Multidimensional Anxiety Scale for Children.   The Multidimensional Anxiety Scale for Children (MASC; March, 1997) is a 39-item questionnaire measuring self-reported anxiety symptoms in children and adolescents. Items fall into four factor-analytically derived scales: Physical Symptoms (with two subscales: Tense Symptoms and Somatic Symptoms), Harm Avoidance (Perfectionism subscale and Anxious Coping subscale), Social Anxiety (Humiliation Fears subscale and Performance Anxiety subscale), and Separation/Panic (no subscales). A total MASC score is obtained by adding the four scale scores. Finally, an Anxiety Disorders Index consists of items found to differentiate between children with an anxiety disorder diagnosis and children with no psychiatric diagnosis. Preliminary research with the MASC has produced promising psychometric results (March, 1997).

Children with SAD would be expected to elevate the MASC Separation/Panic scale, which measures fear of being alone and desire to stay close to home or family. Elevation of the Social Anxiety scale would also be common for a child with SAD, indicating some concerns about performing in front of groups or of being ridiculed and embarrassed by others. An elevation of the Harm Avoidance scale, on the other hand, may indicate that the child has fears of failing or being hurt, which are contributing to the separation anxiety.

Screen for Child Anxiety Related Emotional Disorders.   The Screen for Child Anxiety Related Emotional Disorders (SCARED; Birmaher et al., 1997) is a 38-item child- or parent-report questionnaire of anxiety in five areas (factor-derived subscales): Panic/Somatic, Separation Anxiety, Social Phobia, General Anxiety, and School Phobia. Children age 9–18 answer questions about anxiety symptoms on a 0 (not true) to 2 (often true) frequency scale. Psychometric analyses have shown good interrater reliability, internal consistency, and test-retest reliability. The SCARED also appears to have some validity for discriminating among anxiety disorders (Birmaher et al., 1997). Children with SAD would be expected to elevate the Separation Anxiety subscale of the SCARED.

Visual Analogue Scale for Anxiety—Revised.   The Visual Analogue Scale for Anxiety—Revised (Bernstein, Garfinkel, & August, 1986) is a self-report instrument on which appear sets of faces ranging from "steady" to "jittery/nervous." Each set of faces is accompanied by a phrase describing various situations that may prove anxiety provoking. Children are instructed to indicate their experience of anxiety in that situation by choosing a descriptive image. Construct validity for this instrument is based on correlations with similar tests (Bernstein, 1990).

□ TREATMENT OPTIONS

Behavioral Interventions

Several behavior therapy methods can be used to treat SAD (Werry & Wollersheim, 1991), including *in vivo* desensitization, flooding, contingency management, and modeling (Table 6.4). Research suggests that all of these techniques are effective in treating SAD and related anxiety problems (Ollendick & King, 1998). For acute onset, first episode SAD cases (duration less than 2–4 months), behavioral suggestions to firmly impose rules about separation behavior, while rewarding appropriate separation behavior and removing rewards for avoidance, are often sufficient to eliminate SAD symptoms (Black, 1995). However, more severe or long-lasting cases may require a more programmatic behavioral intervention.

In vivo desensitization/exposure is probably the most commonly used (and possibly most effective) treatment for SAD. This treatment consists of graduated exposure of the

TABLE 6.4 Treatment Options for Separation Anxiety Disorder

1. Behavioral Interventions
    a. *In vivo* desensitization/exposure
    b. Flooding/implosive therapy
    c. Contingency management (operant conditioning)
    d. Modeling techniques
2. Psychotherapy
    a. Cognitive-behavioral interventions
        (1) Self-monitoring
        (2) Self-talk
        (3) Distraction
        (4) Self-reinforcement
        (5) Relaxation techniques
3. Family Interventions
    a. Parent education and support
    b. Family therapy
4. Medication
    a. Selective serotonin reuptake inhibitors
    b. Tricyclic antidepressants
5. Referral to Authorities

Note: This outline of options summarizes major treatments covered in the text. Specific treatments are often combined into an intervention package. Refer to the text for additional descriptions of each treatment. This table is not necessarily an exhaustive list of all treatments available.

child to actual separation from the parent. Ideally, the child maintains a response incompatible with anxiety (such as relaxation, distraction, or engagement in activity) during *in vivo* desensitization, but mere exposure to the separation situation typically is sufficient to cause eventual reduction in anxiety symptoms. Progression through a hierarchy of anxiety-producing situations is used to gradually expose the child to increasingly threatening separation experiences.

For example, in the case of SAD in which school avoidance is the major problem, the initial goal may be for the child to visit the school after hours, with the parent in another room or out of the building. Next, the child may be driven by the parent to attend a half day of school. A third step could be attending a full day of school with a phone call home allowed at lunchtime. Final steps would involve the elimination of the phone call and riding the bus to school. Throughout the process, the child and teacher are given strategies to reduce anxiety. For example, the child may be taught relaxation strategies, and problem situations may be anticipated and practiced.

Success of an *in vivo* desensitization plan often depends on a firm set of rules: The child may go to the nurse's office if feeling faint, upset, or sick. The child may not call the parent or have any parental contact during the day (except for that allowed by the treatment plan). The child may not engage in social interaction or favored activity while in the nurse's office. Complaining and whining are ignored at school and at home. The child is dropped off at school every morning regardless of manipulation or complaints.

Flooding and *implosive therapy* involve continuous, actual or imagined exposure to the object or situation that elicits anxiety (e.g., attendance at school and separation from caretaker) until the child's anxiety level decreases. Flooding, which is more often used with children, involves actual or imagined exposure to the anxiety-provoking situation. Implosive therapy uses only imagined exposure to the situation. For example, a common flooding treatment for the child with SAD is to force the child to go to school for a full day regardless of complaints or attempts to resist separation from the parent. Unlike desensitization, there is no gradual exposure to separation; separation from the caretaker is sudden and complete.

Flooding is very effective in school avoidance situations because most schools have resources (e.g., nurse's office, ability to contact parent) to accommodate the child if an adverse reaction should occur. Although implosion and flooding can be effective treatments, they should be used cautiously with children, who may have a more limited ability than do adults to tolerate extreme anxiety. Flooding may be most appropriate for SAD cases that have acute and recent onset and when the child does not seem to have extreme, debilitating anxiety.

Operant conditioning or contingency management methods identify and modify the rewards and secondary gain that maintain SAD. Such interventions begin with a thorough evaluation of the positive reinforcement and negative reinforcement the child receives for displaying separation anxiety. Common positive reinforcers are increased access to pleasant activities with the parent (e.g., staying home from school and playing games with mom), increased control over environment (e.g., access to preferred foods because the child is "sick"), and parental attention and positive interaction with the parent (e.g., the message that the child is "a good little girl" who stays with her parent). Common negative reinforcers are avoidance of negative peer interactions, avoidance of the fear that something will happen to the parent, avoidance of failure and work at school, avoidance of having to achieve independence and separation, and avoidance of general anxiety at being separated from the parent. Existing reinforcers of the SAD behavior must be eliminated, and new reinforcers of behavior that is incompatible with SAD are identified and implemented. For example, if the child stays home from school, the parent might be instructed to confine the child to his or her room with only schoolwork (no TV or other social interaction with the parent). Rewards may be set up for each day that the child attends school. The efficacy of contingency management is often enhanced when it is combined with desensitization.

Social learning treatments, such as *modeling,* may also be effective components in the management of SAD. Typical modeling techniques used for SAD are participant modeling (usually most effective), use of live models, and filmed modeling (Husain & Kashani, 1992). In live model and participant modeling techniques, another person demonstrates successful separation from the caretaker. The model should show initial difficulty with separation, followed by gradual mastery. With participant modeling, the child repeats the modeled behavior after the model has demonstrated it. In filmed modeling, the child watches a videotape of another child successfully performing the desired separation. Alternatively, the therapist may describe the child successfully separating from the caretaker. In general, greater similarity between the model, the situation, and the child produces better results.

Behavioral interventions have produced generally positive results for SAD (Ollendick & King, 1998; Thyer, 1991). However, the choice of which behavioral treatment is most effective or appropriate for a particular child remains up to the clinical decision of the therapist. A multimodal approach involving modeling, contingency management, and *in vivo* desensitization is likely to be effective for most children.

Psychotherapy

Cognitive-behavioral treatment methods, which teach the child to identify anxiety cues and to apply specific coping responses, are used with older children with SAD, as well as in other anxiety disorders (Werry & Wollersheim, 1991). These treatments begin with self-monitoring tasks, such as keeping a diary of anxiety-provoking situations and cues. Based on self-monitoring, the child learns to identify cues that lead to anxiety in future situations, such as separation from the caretaker. Next, the child is taught coping skills to use in separation situations. Examples of coping skills include positive self-talk, distraction, self-reinforcement, and progressive muscle relaxation. Finally, the child applies the coping skills to the separation event. This general approach has received both clinical and research support (Ollendick & King, 1998).

Kendall (1994) applied a 16-week cognitive-behavioral regimen to children diagnosed with primary SAD, Generalized Anxiety Disorder, or Social Phobia. The intervention included several components: recognizing somatic reactions and anxious feelings, becoming aware of anxiety-related cognitions, developing a coping plan (self-talk and problem solving), evaluating coping responses, and applying self-reinforcement for adaptive behavior. Measurements taken at completion and at 1-year follow-up indicated that treatment was beneficial compared to controls.

Family Interventions

Parent Intervention

Because the child's anxiety is centered on the relationship with the primary caretaker, education of the parents about the etiology, symptoms, and treatment of SAD is often a good introduction to any intervention. This education can motivate parents to change their behaviors and to support behavioral and family interventions. Parents should also be educated about the role of their behaviors and environmental stresses in evoking SAD symptoms in their child.

Behavioral interventions are also more effective when they include a component of support for the parents. Parents often feel guilty and doubtful about the limits that they are imposing on the child with SAD during behavioral treatment. Education and reassurance can allay parental concerns and provide information to encourage the parent to adhere to the ongoing behavioral intervention.

Family Therapy

In some cases of SAD, the parent interview may indicate that the parent is overreliant on the child and is reinforcing the child for the clinging behavior. In such cases, the parent may have difficulty implementing a behavioral intervention, or the parent may sabotage such an intervention. A focus in family therapy on boundaries and roles of family members may address systemic characteristics that are maintaining SAD (Bernstein, 1990). Restoration of appropriate family roles, reinforcement of child-parent boundaries, and reinstatement of the proper family hierarchy may then become targets of therapy (Meyer & Deitsch, 1996).

Medication

Differing opinions exist about the appropriateness and efficacy of psychopharmacological treatments for SAD. One view is that, due to lack of systematic study with children, pharmacotherapy is not recommended as a first-choice intervention. Rather, it may prove a useful adjunct to behavioral therapy when the child's experience of anxiety prevents engagement in other treatments (Thyer, 1991). Another view is that pharmacotherapy should be immediately initiated in order to facilitate achievement of normal separation behavior (Kaplan & Sadock, 1988). Later, medication may be reduced once the adaptive separation behavior is in place. This latter view has particular merit in cases when the anxiety is so severe that the child cannot engage in even basic therapeutic techniques.

Some tricyclic antidepressants and benzodiazepines have been used with children with SAD (Sylvester & Kruesi, 1994). In particular, imipramine has shown promising results, although it may not be as widely effective as once thought (Klein, Koplewicz, & Kanner, 1992). Alprazolam and imipramine have been used for children with anxiety-related school refusal, and a host of other benzodiazepines have seen use for general anxiety as a result of caretaker separation (Sylvester & Kruesi, 1994). In some individual cases, selective serotonin reuptake inhibitors (SSRIs; e.g., fluoxetine) have been used to treat children with SAD.

Referral to Authorities

Although it is unlikely that children with SAD will need a referral to legal authorities, excessive school refusal will sometimes result in legal action taken by the school. In these cases, coordination of the efforts of clinician and school are even more important than usual. Direct communication between the clinician and school is important in cases of parent or family pathology, because the parent may distort information in such cases (Bernstein, 1990).

■ Specific Phobia

☐ CLINICAL DESCRIPTION

Diagnostic Considerations

The essential feature of Specific Phobia is an irrational fear of an object or situation that produces an anxiety or avoidance response. In children, this response may be expressed by crying, immobilization, clinging to an adult, aggressive avoidance, or tantrums. In order to reduce anxiety, the phobic stimulus is either avoided or endured with intense upset, resulting in significant interference with normal routine or with social activities or relationships. The child may not be aware that this phobic reaction is a problem or is out of normal proportion to the stimulus, although such awareness is typical of adolescents. Specific Phobia does not include fears better accounted for by Panic Disorder or Social Phobia.

Phobic anxiety differs from normal fear responses in a number of ways: First, the child's fear is far out of proportion to the actual danger posed by the object. Second, the child's fear is extreme, sometimes resulting in an anxious outburst or excessive avoidance of certain situations. Third, the child's fear has a significant negative impact on daily functioning. Fourth, the child's fear is resistant to attempts to extinguish it. Although these characteristics may apply, to a certain extent, to many childhood fears, when they are severe and occur together, a specific phobia is likely.

Typically, physiological, psychological, and behavioral signs of anxiety occur in the presence of the phobic stimulus. Anticipatory anxiety is likely if children expect to confront the phobic stimulus, and children soon learn to avoid the source of their fear. The impact of such avoidance on daily life will depend on the rate of normal contact with the phobic stimulus, but some functional impairment is necessary for a diagnosis. Obviously, uncommon contact will result in relatively little impairment (e.g., fear of elephants will not impair a city-dwelling child except in zoo or circus environments), but fear of an object or situation with which there is much contact can become quite debilitating.

Phobias are a common anxiety disorder in children. However, they generally go untreated due to the ease with which the phobic stimulus may be avoided (American Psychiatric Association, 1994). Using a 6-month duration criterion, prevalence estimates of 5–12% have been found in various studies that cross all age levels (Kaplan & Sadock 1988) (Table 6.5). Prevalence studies of Specific Phobia in child populations, however, are sparse and produce estimates of 0.7% to 2.4% in school-age children (Anderson, Williams, McGee, & Silva, 1987; Rutter, Tizard, & Whitmore, 1970).

Appearance and Features

Typical phobic stimuli vary by age. Animal phobias are most common in childhood, whereas blood-injury phobias emerge as most common in adolescence. Children with phobias show varying responses when confronted with the phobic object. Most children cringe, grimace, and attempt to distance themselves from the object. Persistence of the presence of the phobic object may cause crying, shaking, immobilization, and an attempt to get caretakers to intervene. If those efforts do not work, the child may try to physically escape the situation (at

TABLE 6.5   Epidemiology and Course of Specific and Social Phobia

Prevalence: 1–3% (for each disorder)

Sex Ratio (Male:Female):   1:2

Typical Onset Age: Early to middle childhood (4–12 years of age) for Specific Phobia
12–15 years of age for Social Phobia

Course of Specific Phobia: Symptoms often improve with time, and spontaneously remit (or decline to manageable levels) in a majority of children. A significant minority, however, have persistent symptoms that can evolve into or co-occur with generalized anxiety.

Course of Social Phobia: Variable; some (probably a minority) children experience spontaneous remission of symptoms, but most have some residual symptoms into adulthood. Often, a sensitive, anxious, or withdrawn style or preference persists.

Common Comorbid Conditions: 1. Generalized Anxiety Disorder
2. Obsessive-Compulsive Disorder
3. Separation Anxiety Disorder
4. Depressive Disorders
5. Communication Disorders (Social Phobia)

Relevant Subtypes (Social Phobia):   1. Generalized vs. Specific

---

times using aggressive behavior) or may decompensate further. Symptoms similar to those of a panic attack may be seen in response to exposure to the phobic stimulus. Internally, children with phobias tend to make negative self-statements and to have catastrophizing ideas and images about the phobic stimulus (Nelson, 1981) (Table 6.6).

Etiology

Biological factors are not significantly supported in the development of phobias, although a predisposition to be anxious or fearful may be present. Relatives of children with phobias have a greater likelihood of having phobias themselves. Furthermore, the type of feared stimulus may run in families. For example, if one member of a family has an animal pho-

---

TABLE 6.6   Appearance and Features of Specific Phobia

COMMON FEATURES

1. Intense anxiety in presence of feared object or situation manifest as crying, immobilization, clinging, aggressive avoidance, tantrums, or panic attacks
2. Avoidance of feared object or situation

OCCASIONAL FEATURES

1. Denial of phobia

Note: The features listed in the table are often seen but are not universal. Some features may be diagnostically relevant or required, whereas others may not be required for diagnosis. "Common" features are typical of the disorder; "occasional" features appear frequently but are not necessarily seen in a majority of cases.

bia, the other family members are more likely to have animal phobias than other phobias (American Psychiatric Association, 1994). On the other hand, this familial concordance could reflect the impact of learning and observing that some stimuli are to be feared.

Behavioral theories of phobias currently have the most research and clinical support. Both classical conditioning and operant conditioning provide explanations for the development of phobias. In classical (Pavlovian) conditioning of a phobia, a natural fear response (unconditioned response) to a natural fear elicitor (unconditioned stimulus) is paired with a formerly neutral situation or object (conditioned stimulus). For example, a child who is painfully bitten (natural fear elicitor or unconditioned stimulus) has a reflexive fear response (natural fear response or unconditioned response) to the presence of a dog (formerly neutral, conditioned stimulus) that bit him. The next time that the child encounters a dog, the pairing of dog—bite/pain—fear is shortened to dog—fear, and the child shows a fear response to the dog even though there is no bite. The fear response persists across time and different dogs, and in the absence of the natural fear elicitor (bite). Actual experience may not be necessary for this conditioning if the child has the opportunity to observe another person receiving negative consequences from a stimulus object. In other words, a phobia may be conditioned by observation as opposed to personal experience.

In operant conditioning, environmental contingencies account for the development and maintenance of a phobic reaction. Simply stated, the child is rewarded for the phobic behavior. Rewards may take the form of social attention, avoidance of an unpleasant activity, or caretaking behavior. For example, a child who expresses a fear of dogs may be rewarded by the elimination of a chore (e.g., taking out the trash, which the child fears will put him in proximity to a dog) and the sympathy of his or her parents. The phobia persists because it is rewarded.

Mowrer's (1939) two-factor theory joins the two conditioning paradigms (classical and operant) and attempts to explain acquisition of the phobic avoidance behavior. Phobic behavior is rewarded because it allows the child to avoid exposure to the feared stimulus and to prevent a classically conditioned anxiety response to the phobic stimulus. Hence, the reward (operant conditioning) is avoidance of unpleasant anxiety. The phobic stimulus produces anxiety because it has been associated, through classical conditioning, with the anxiety response. Mowrer's theory explains why individuals do not give up their phobias after repeated evidence that no harm comes to them when they are in the presence of the phobic object. They are constantly reinforced for the phobia by avoiding the anxiety associated with the phobic object. Because of this constant reinforcement, the behavior persists. Hence, phobias persist because they reduce anxiety, regardless of whether the anxiety is justified based on the person's experience.

Cognitive theories provide an explanation for the intensity and persistence of phobias by emphasizing the internal thoughts and images of the child with specific phobia. Children with phobic anxiety tend to make more negative self-statements and to have more catastrophizing thoughts and images about the phobic stimulus compared to children without anxiety problems. As a result, their expectations are strongly negative, and their fear is maintained by these negative expectations (Silverman & Ginsburg, 1995).

ASSESSMENT PATTERNS

A sample assessment battery for childhood anxiety disorders (including Specific Phobia) is shown in Table 6.3.

Broad Assessment Strategies

Behavioral Assessment

Parent-Report. Parents are often excellent sources of information about the child's phobia and the circumstances surrounding it. Psychological testing for Specific Phobia, however, is often difficult because the child's symptom may be quite specific (e.g., a fear of spiders, but otherwise no symptoms) even if it is very severe. In addition, the phobic stimulus can vary widely from child to child. One child may be afraid of spiders while another fears dogs. Hence, most of the broad-band parent-report questionnaires include one or two items about severe, irrational fears, but they do not have subscales or norms for Specific Phobia symptoms.

Subscale scores on the CBCL can be deceptive for children with specific phobia because the CBCL's one phobia item alone will not cause a major elevation on any subscale. Hence, a child with a circumscribed Specific Phobia would not show elevations on CBCL scales. However, the CBCL can be an important instrument for detecting the child's other behavioral problems. Children with specific phobia may elevate the Anxious/Depressed scale if they have additional anxiety symptoms. Other CBCL configurations may suggest additional behavioral problems in the child. Analysis of the single phobia item on the CBCL can indicate the intensity and stimulus of the phobia. Similar issues apply to the TRF and YSR.

The ECI-4, CSI-4, and ASI-4 also include one item about Specific Phobia but (like other questionnaires) leave the parent to interpret the meaning of "excessive fear." In addition, the SI-4 item suggests some possible phobic stimuli, but parents can apply the "excessive fear" criterion to any situation that they believe is appropriate. As a result, endorsement of the Specific Phobia item on the SI-4 may or may not indicate the Specific Phobia diagnosis. Other syndromes that commonly cause endorsement of this item are Post-Traumatic Stress Disorder (when the parent describes the feared situation as the revisiting of an association with the traumatic stressor), Social Phobia (when the parent describes the feared situation as humiliation or performance concerns), Adjustment Disorders, and Generalized Anxiety Disorder (when the parent means that the child is afraid of many specific things and situations).

The CPRS has one item about fearfulness and another item about specific fears of the dark, animals, and bugs. Although both of these items are on the Anxious-Shy subscale, elevation of the Anxious-Shy subscale would also require the presence of general fearfulness and/or social anxiety. The CTRS Anxious-Shy subscale, on the other hand, does not include items about specific fears; children who elevate the CTRS Anxious-Shy subscale are more sensitive and emotional than fearful of specific things.

Unlike the Achenbach and Conners' subscales, the BASC Anxiety subscale includes several specific fears about subjects such as dying, schoolwork, making mistakes, test anxiety, fear of failure, and fear of negative evaluation. However, other, more classic phobic stimuli, such as animals, storms, and the dark, are not subjects of BASC Anxiety subscale questions. Children with many phobic fears or with phobia and generalized anxiety would be expected to elevate the Anxiety and Somatization subscales. However, it is possible for a child with a well-encapsulated phobia to produce no BASC subscale elevations.

Child-Report. Obtaining structured self-report data on the PIY and/or BASC can be helpful in understanding the overall symptom picture and personality of the child with a

Specific Phobia. On the PIY, children with phobias about disease tend to elevate the Somatic Concern scale. Within the Somatic Concern scale, the Preoccupation with Disease subscale has several items that measure worrying and talking about disease, whereas the Muscular Tension and Anxiety subscale has several questions that overlap with symptoms of a panic attack. The Fear and Worry subscale of the PIY Psychological Discomfort scale, on the other hand, includes questions about generalized worries and specific phobic symptoms (thunder, lightning, blood). Hence, elevation of the Psychological Discomfort scale and/or Somatic Concerns scale would be most characteristic of a child with Specific Phobia. Other PIY scale scores may provide additional information about the child's personality and additional symptoms.

On the self-report BASC, children with Specific Phobia would be expected to elevate the Anxiety scale, which includes questions about both generalized anxiety and specific fears. Elevation of the Atypicality scale often indicates that the fears have an associated obsessive-compulsive quality, whereas elevation of the Somatization scale may be found in a child whose phobia concerns physical health or disease. Like the PIY, the BASC has other subscales that are useful in assessing associated symptoms and general personality of the child.

In some cases, children with Specific Phobias will not elevate BASC or PIY scales. This could be a result of a very encapsulated, specific fear without the associated other fears and generalized anxiety needed to produce elevation of an entire subscale. Alternatively, the child may be denying or minimizing problems, in which case the BASC L validity scale and the PIY DEF validity scales (both of which are sensitive to denial or minimization) would be expected to show some elevation.

Syndrome-Specific Tests

Clinician-Administered

Semistructured Interviews and Behavioral Observation. Semistructured interviews such as the ADIS-IV-C/P can be useful if a structured, comprehensive review of symptoms is desired in assessing the child with Specific Phobia. These interviews were described in the section on SAD earlier in this chapter, and more general semistructured interviews are reviewed in Chapter 1. In addition to interview techniques, the child's fear can sometimes be evaluated by behavioral observation. Occasionally, the child will demonstrate the fear response when the feared object is mentioned by the clinician. In other cases, the child's response may be elicited by pictures or by the actual presence of the feared object. Observation of the child's behavior in the presence of the feared object can be a useful way to document the severity, characteristics, and elicitors of the child's phobic response.

Child-Report

General Anxiety Self-Report Questionnaires. The Revised Children's Manifest Anxiety Scale (RCMAS), State-Trait Anxiety Inventory for Children (STAIC), Multidimensional Anxiety Scale for Children (MASC), and Screen for Child Anxiety Related Emotional Disorders (SCARED) (described in the SAD section of this chapter) can be useful for measuring general anxiety and distress in the child with specific phobia. Children with specific phobia who are in little distress (usually because they can avoid the phobic stimulus) may not give high scores on these scales. As a group, however, children with specific phobia give higher RCMAS scores than do normal controls, although their scores are lower than those of children with Post-Traumatic Stress Disorder (Saigh, 1989a). A high Lie scale on the RCMAS may indicate the child's reluctance to admit faults and, therefore, a tendency to minimize phobic symptoms. The RCMAS includes several items about specific fears, whereas the MASC includes one item about specific fears; inspection of these individual items may give some information about phobic fears. The Fear Survey Schedule for Children—Revised (FSSC—R) may also assist with the identification of the type and variety of objects feared by the child with specific phobia.

Subjective Units of Distress (SUDS) Scales. SUDS scales are simple ratings of the fear or distress associated with contact with a specific stimulus. Ratings are made on a 1 (no distress) to 10 or 100 (worst distress possible) scale, typically with no intermediate anchoring values. SUDS scales are used to assist with constructing a hierarchy of feared situations associated with the phobic stimulus or situation (e.g., Albano, March, & Piacentini, 1999). The hierarchy then becomes the basis for an exposure/response prevention intervention.

Children's Anxious Self-Statement Questionnaire. Evaluation of the cognitive underpinnings of the phobic behavior may be assisted by the use of the Children's Anxious Self-Statement Questionnaire (CASSQ; Kendall & Ronan, 1989). The CASSQ asks about the child's anxiety-related self-statements. It yields two subscales: Negative Self-Focused Attention and Positive Self-Concept and Expectations.

☐   TREATMENT OPTIONS

Behavioral Interventions

Behavior therapies are the most effective and most researched treatment approaches for Specific Phobia (Husain & Kashani, 1992; Strauss & Francis, 1989). Specifically, exposure and desensitization appear to be the treatment of choice for most childhood phobias (Table 6.7). Desensitization pairs gradual exposure to the phobic stimulus with a relaxed internal state. Systematic desensitization exposes the child to *imagined* stimuli, whereas *in vivo* desensitization exposes the child to *actual* stimuli. In most cases with children, *in vivo* desensitization is preferred because less cognitive effort is required and because the situation more closely approximates reality. A typical *in vivo* desensitization plan includes components of contingency management and modeling, proceeding as follows:

1. Assess the child's phobia and associated symptoms.
2. Identify a hierarchy of anxiety-provoking situations related to the phobic stimulus (fear hierarchy). For example, if a child or adolescent is afraid of dogs, such a hierarchy might include (in order of increasing anxiety) looking at a picture of a dog, walking down a street where dogs may be seen behind fences, approaching a dog who is on a leash, and petting a dog.

TABLE 6.7   Treatment Options for Specific Phobia

1. Behavioral Interventions
    a. *In vivo* desensitization
    b. Systematic desensitization
    c. Flooding/implosive therapy
    d. Modeling
2. Psychotherapy
    a. Cognitive-behavioral interventions
3. Medication

Note: This outline of options summarizes major treatments covered in the text. Specific treatments are often combined into an intervention package. Refer to the text for additional descriptions of each treatment. This table is not necessarily an exhaustive list of all treatments available.

3. Teach the child strategies for coping with exposure to the phobic stimulus. Commonly used strategies are relaxation training, soothing self-talk, and distraction. Examples of relaxation training include progressive muscle relaxation, hypnosis, or even tranquilizing drugs in difficult cases.

4. Use contingency management techniques to give reward the child for successful attainment of exposure to different levels of the fear hierarchy. Social reinforcement can also be used as a reward for attaining therapy goals. In addition to providing rewards for goal attainment, it is essential to identify and remove any factors that are reinforcing or maintaining the phobic behavior. Typically, these factors involve increased attention, avoidance of a negative event, or changes in family structure. Attention must be given to these potentially interfering factors in the initial assessment, with appropriate steps taken prior to intervention.

5. Set a plan for gradual exposure of the child to the levels of the hierarchy. Included in the plan should be the presence of a trusted other person (usually a parent or the therapist), who coaches the child and ensures that the child does not escape or inappropriately avoid the exposure. The timing and setting of the exposure events should be a part of the plan.

6. Expose the child to increasingly intense levels of the phobic situation, consistent with the hierarchy and plan. During exposure, the child should be encouraged to use coping techniques.

7. Monitor the child's response and modify the plan if problems occur. Although the child should be strongly encouraged during exposure to stay in the feared situations and tolerate the associated fear, children sometimes need more gradual exposure to phobic stimuli than originally planned. In such cases, the hierarchy and plan may need to be revised. Monitoring is also necessary for dispensing of reinforcement and for tracking the child's progress toward therapy goals.

8. Use modeling components. Many exposure interventions include a modeling component (Strauss & Francis, 1989), in which another person demonstrates achievement of each treatment goal. Modeling techniques have the greatest effectiveness when live models similar to the child are used. Another common modeling technique is for the therapist to model exposure to the feared stimulus, with the child initially watching the therapist and later joining the therapist in exposure (Ollendick & Cerny, 1981).

Two additional behavioral methods that employ more intensive exposure to the phobic stimulus are flooding and implosive therapy. These therapy techniques expose the child to the full intensity of the feared stimulus until the fear diminishes. The exposure may be carried out *in vivo* or it may be accomplished imaginally (implosive therapy). *In vivo* flooding is the preferred method, as the impact of implosive therapy will necessarily depend on such variables as capacity for imagination and willingness to comply with an anxiety-provoking technique (Meyer & Deitsch, 1996).

Although modeling is frequently combined with desensitization procedures, modeling techniques are also used in isolation. Modeling can either be done with a videotaped (filmed modeling) or live (live modeling) demonstration, both of which have been shown to be effective in improving phobic symptoms. In addition, modeling may include the child as an observer (observation modeling) or as a participant with the models during the modeling demonstration (participant modeling). Participant modeling appears to be the most effective modeling intervention (Ollendick & King, 1998).

Overall, *in vivo* desensitization and participant modeling appear to be the most effective treatments for phobias in children, although systematic desensitization is also an effective treatment (Ollendick & King, 1998). Furthermore, several things can be done to increase the probability of success of a desensitization intervention. First, the use of cognitive-behavioral components such as self-talk and relaxation can be quite helpful during the desensitization process. Second, use of modeling can also enhance desensitization therapy. Finally, it is important to build in rewards for attainment of goals and to remove any secondary gain for the phobia (Silverman & Ginsburg, 1995).

Psychotherapy

Cognitive-behavioral approaches have been used to reduce anxiety and avoidance in some children with specific phobia. The most promising of these include the use of three types of self-statements: positive attributes ("I am a brave boy"), coping commands ("I should just think about something else and stay in this dark room"), and competency statements ("I have done this before") (Ollendick & King, 1998; Strauss & Francis, 1989).

Nelson (1981) describes a cognitive-behavioral intervention for a child with a dental phobia. An examination of the child's thoughts, feelings, and behavior while she imagined a dental visit revealed that her negative self-statements and images were contributing to her high level of anxiety and avoidant behavior. Based on these results, a four-step, self-statement treatment program was designed. First, the therapist modeled coping statements to reduce fear and increase self-efficacy (cognitive modeling). Second, the child verbalized the statements under the therapist's guidance (external guidance). Third, the child verbalized them by herself (overt self-guidance). Finally, the child role played the target scenario while verbalizing the coping statements to herself (covert self-guidance).

Cognitive-behavioral techniques can provide children with coping strategies to use when confronting a phobic stimulus. Furthermore, they can help children to understand their cognitive responses and the contribution of thoughts to the anxiety problem. However, purely cognitive methods are rarely used for the treatment of Specific Phobia in children. Rather, cognitive techniques are often used to augment desensitization interventions. Research has shown cognitive techniques to assist in decreasing phobic symptoms (Ollendick & King, 1998).

Medication

Treating Specific Phobias with the use of medications is not well documented in the literature, but severe cases may warrant therapeutic drug trials in conjunction with behavior therapy (Kaplan & Sadock, 1988). Antianxiety agents may reduce the child's anxious mood, but they are not curative for phobia. Diazepam, clonazepam, and alprazolam, for example, may be used for general anxiety symptoms, such as those resulting from a Specific Phobia (Sylvester & Kruesi, 1994).

■ Social Phobia

□ CLINICAL DESCRIPTION

Diagnostic Considerations

Prior to DSM-IV, fears leading to avoidance in social situations were diagnosed in two categories based on age: Social Phobia (adults) and Avoidant Disorder of Childhood or Adolescence (children). The DSM-IV Social Phobia diagnosis combined these prior diagnoses across the age span. In Social Phobia, anxiety is focused on a specific type of situation: contact with unfamiliar people or negative social appraisal. Because of this anxiety, there is excessive shrinking from unfamiliar social contact, which is sufficiently severe to interfere with social relationships. Children with Social Phobia may seem socially withdrawn, embarrassed, and timid in the company of unfamiliar people, but they may not realize that their fear is unreasonable. Requests to interact in even a minor way with strangers bring on anxiety in the form of avoidance, shaking, hiding, immobilization, or clinging to familiar others. If social anxiety is severe, the child may become inarticulate and even mute. Anxious-somatic and panic symptoms are frequently reported, including heart palpitations, shakiness, chills, nausea, and sweating (Beidel & Morris, 1995). In contrast, contact with familiar people is welcome and desired, indicating that the child can achieve normal social relationships. To warrant the diagnosis of Social Phobia, the avoidant behavior must have been present for at least 6 months.

Social Phobia differs from normal quietness and separation anxiety. Children or adolescents who are socially reticent but not socially phobic are slow to warm up to strangers but eventually do respond. Shy or quiet children do not suffer severe impairment in peer interaction; children with Social Phobia, on the other hand, take an excessive amount of time to "warm up." In addition, Social Phobia differs from SAD because SAD-based anxiety is experienced as a result of separation from caretakers, regardless of the presence of others. The child clearly identifies (verbally or behaviorally) the loss of the caretaker as the anxiety-provoking event. In Social Phobia, anxiety results from contact with people who are unfamiliar, and the child identifies the presence of unfamiliar people as the anxiety-provoking event. Hence, children with SAD are often comfortable in social situations at home with their parents, whereas children with Social Phobia usually fear and avoid social situations in their home.

Across the life span, prevalence rates for Social Phobia are estimated at 3–13% (American Psychiatric Association, 1994), but child studies have yielded prevalence estimates closer to 1–2% (Beidel & Morris, 1995). Social Phobia rarely occurs alone and frequently coexists with another anxiety disorder (American Psychiatric Association, 1994; Kashani & Orvaschel, 1988). In a clinical sample of children and adolescents, for example, 27.3% of those diagnosed with GAD and 4.5% of those having SAD also received a Social Phobia diagnosis (Bernstein & Borchardt, 1991); overlap with Major Depressive Disorder is also common (Last, Francis, et al., 1987). It is not clear whether Social Phobia is more prevalent in children or adults, but onset is usually in childhood or adolescence.

Appearance and Features

Appearance and features of Social Phobia are listed in Table 6.8. At a subclinical level, the hallmark of Social Phobia—social withdrawal resulting in little interaction with peers and possible refusal to speak in school—has been found in 2–10% of the normal school-age population and in 10–20% of the normal preschool population (Morris, Kratochwill, & Aldridge, 1988). Hence, some degree of shyness in children is common, and even symptoms of excessive shyness are not unusual.

Because social contact and the emergence of evaluation fears increase dramatically in the early school years, the onset of Social Phobia in children can be as early as age 5–7, although mean ages of onset in early to middle adolescence are more often reported (Albano & Barlow, 1996; Beidel & Morris, 1995). Unlike developmentally normal social anxiety, the intensity and persistence of Social Phobia symptoms are markedly greater than the develop-

TABLE 6.8   Appearance and Features of Social Phobia

COMMON FEATURES

1. Anxiety at contact with unfamiliar people
2. Fear of negative social appraisal
3. Social withdrawal, embarrassment, or timid appearance
4. Social skills deficits
5. Attempt to avoid or escape social situations
6. Attachment to a few familiar people
7. Easily embarrassed
8. Unassertive

OCCASIONAL FEATURES

1. Refusal to speak in social situations
2. School avoidance
3. Somatic complaints
4. Low self-esteem, lack of self-confidence
5. Perfectionism
6. Hypersensitivity to criticism

Note: The features listed in the table are often seen but are not universal. Some features may be diagnostically relevant or required, whereas others may not be required for diagnosis. "Common" features are typical of the disorder; "occasional" features appear frequently but are not necessarily seen in a majority of cases.

mental norm. Toddlers and preschool children may hide behind adults or may attempt to physically leave social situations. Older children may remain in the social situation but are silent and removed. Frequently, some school avoidance or anxiety is present, and a number of children who present with school avoidance will be found to suffer from Social Phobia.

Children with Social Phobia frequently appear unassertive, withdrawn, anxious, and lacking in self-confidence (Last, 1989a). They demonstrate a high degree of inhibition in social or recreational activities, preventing the experience of normal social interaction. In school-age children and adolescents, social inhibition is often the result of fears of embarrassment or rejection. Frequently children with Social Phobia are perfectionistic, overly sensitive, and self-condemning (Bernstein, 1990; Husain & Cantwell, 1991). Low self-esteem and feelings of alienation and inferiority are common. Because of their lack of social experience, impairment in social functioning and social skills can be severe. Children with Social Phobia typically have only one friend or no close friends, although in some cases they may interact comfortably with extended family members. They generally will say that they want to be liked by others. Commonly feared situations for children with social phobia include speaking or eating in front of others, attending social group functions, writing in front of others, using public restrooms, talking with other people, and attending school. Most children with social phobia report fearing more than one type of social situation. A distinction can be made between children who fear only one type of social situation (specific subtype) and those who fear many social situations (generalized subtype) (Beidel & Morris, 1995).

Coaxing the child with social phobia to engage in social interaction is typically unsuccessful. Young children may respond to such coaxing with increased anxiety, crying, and additional withdrawal. Older children may become oppositional, embarrassed, or silent, appearing to resent the intrusion on their withdrawal. When a child with Social Phobia is forced or coaxed to engage in social activity, he or she is clearly anxious and unhappy throughout the interaction, failing to experience the sense of involvement with the other children.

The clinical course of social phobia is variable. Some children (probably a minority) enjoy spontaneous recovery, which is more likely to occur after a positive social experience with peers (Husain & Cantwell, 1991). Other children experience ongoing feelings of isolation and depression due to their failure to form friendships and social bonds outside the family (American Psychiatric Association, 1994). Some residual or full-blown symptoms of the disorder often persist into adulthood, with exacerbations or remissions based on the degree and type of stress in the environment (American Psychiatric Association, 1994; Last, 1989a).

Etiology

One potential pathway for development of Social Phobia is lack of early experience in developing social relationships, leading to poor social skills and social failures. Out of these difficulties, anxiety develops. This anxiety is perpetuated when the child with poor social skills and negative social expectations behaves in ways that elicit negative responses from peers. Several conditions could act as catalysts in preventing crucial early social experiences: isolated family, losses of significant others, chronic medical illness, family moves, insecure attachments, and profound differences from the majority culture (e.g., speaking a foreign language).

Temperamental differences such as shyness or timidity are also probable contributing factors in the development of Social Phobia (Husain & Cantwell, 1991). Therefore, it is usually wise to ask the parent questions about the child's early temperament. Children with Social Phobia are sometimes described as having been hypersensitive or withdrawn as infants. When this is the case, a temperamental-biological explanation should be considered. In addition to causing a tendency toward hypersensitivity, a difficult temperament may also elicit negative responses from caretakers, causing the child to develop social anxiety and ambivalence during the critical attachment period (Beidel & Morris, 1995).

In addition to temperamental features, developmental disorders may predispose a child to the emergence of Social Phobia by interfering with language and speech development (American Psychiatric Association, 1994). Because speech is a critical social-communication modality, children who fail to develop adequate speech are at risk for social stresses and resulting anxiety. Furthermore, such children may have a more difficult time learning social skills and tracking social interactions, leading to frustration in social interactions and rejection by peers.

Behaviorally, parents may intentionally or unwittingly reinforce socially phobic behavior by giving it attention or other secondary gain. For example, the child with Social Phobia may be perceived by the parent as vulnerable, leading to increased nurturant behavior. Alternatively, a parent who overdoes the (usually appropriate) "don't talk to strangers" rule may scare the child or communicate that avoidant behavior will be rewarded. Notably, parents of children suspected of having Social Phobia are less likely to refer them for clinical attention than are teachers, who can observe their discomfort among peers in the school setting (Last, 1989a).

A second behavioral explanation for the development of Social Phobia cites the role of internal reinforcement for withdrawn behavior. Internally, the child's experience of anxiety is paired with the presence of unfamiliar people, perhaps as a result of early negative experiences or a lack of social confidence. The child feels inferior or threatened by the presence of others and avoids interaction in order to reduce anxiety. Withdrawal, then, is negatively reinforced by a reduction in feelings of anxiety, insecurity, and inferiority.

Cognitively, Social Phobia may be driven by negative expectations of social interaction and a tendency to pay excessive attention to one's behavior in social situations. Early negative social experiences, combined with a temperamental tendency to be anxious about performance, may cause these expectations and excessive self-focus to develop. This cognitive explanation may explain the relatively high comorbidity of Social Phobia, Generalized Anxiety Disorder, and depressive disorders.

Biological theories of Social Phobia have received some attention, but empirical data are preliminary. Support for the presence of familial patterns is accumulating (American Psychiatric Association, 1994), although the extent to which this reflects genetic or environmental influences has yet to be determined. There is some evidence that mothers of children with anxiety disorders such as Social Phobia experience anxiety disorders at a rate higher than the general population (Bernstein & Borchardt, 1991).

☐   ASSESSMENT PATTERNS

A sample assessment battery for childhood anxiety disorders (including Social Phobia) is shown in Table 6.3.

Broad Assessment Strategies

Cognitive Assessment

Clinician-Administered.   Cantwell and Baker (1987) have found that communication skills are frequently impaired in the presence of Social Phobia. Cognitive testing that evaluates various aspects of communication skills may be warranted given the relationship of Social Phobia and communication difficulties. Children with co-occurring communication problems and Social Phobia show deficits on WISC-III Verbal Comprehension factor and subscale (Vocabulary, Comprehension, Information, Similarities) scores. On the WJ-R and WIAT, such children may have difficulty with reading and written language subtests.

Psychological Assessment

Child-Report.   In some cases, Social Phobia can be linked to feelings of low self-esteem. Whether such self-esteem problems are a cause or a result of Social Phobia, they are important to consider in designing a treatment plan. Administration of the PHSCS may indicate self-esteem problems that are contributing to the anxiety, withdrawal, and evaluation fears common in Social Phobia. On this instrument, children with Social Phobia may show particularly low scores on the Anxiety and Popularity scales, reflecting the lack of social self-esteem and dissatisfaction over social anxiety. A general depression of all scales and the total score is not unexpected.

Behavioral Assessment

Parent- and Teacher-Report.   The CBCL and TRF include several items that relate to the Social Phobia diagnosis. For the most part, these items fall into two groups: those that ask about shyness and withdrawal and those that ask about attachment behavior toward familiar and unfamiliar people. On the CBCL and TRF, children with Social Phobia elevate the Withdrawn and Social Problems scales, with possible secondary elevations of the Anxious/ Depressed and Somatic Complaints scales. More unusual are elevations of the Externalizing factor and subscales.

When interpreting CBCL and TRF results, it is especially important to keep in mind the respondent for these scales. Because parents are the respondents for the CBCL, CBCL scores may reflect the greater warmth and social competence that the child shows around the parents, who are familiar to the child. The teacher, however, may see more of the shyness, withdrawal, and lack of social competence typical of the child with Social Phobia in less familiar, more social situations. This discrepancy may be particularly pronounced for the CBCL and TRF social competence scales, which are most likely to be affected by the environmental context of the child.

Like the CBCL and TRF, the BASC parent and teacher versions include items measuring shyness, withdrawal, anxiety, and social competence. Different BASC subscales capture different dimensions of Social Phobia. Elevations of the Anxiety and Somatization subscales are consistent with the anxiety component of Social Phobia, whereas the Withdrawal and Leadership (low scores on the Leadership subscale) subscales reflect the shyness, social avoidance, and social fearfulness typical of Social Phobia. The Social Skills subscale can provide some insight into the child's display of manners, helpfulness, and other appealing social behaviors. As with the CBCL, parents and teacher may provide discrepant reports because of the child's differing behavior around familiar versus unfamiliar others. This may be especially evident on the Withdrawal and Leadership subscales.

Although both the CBCL and BASC provide excellent information about the social and anxiety behavior of the child with Social Phobia, the BASC appears to give more information about specific subsets of core and associated symptoms. Multiple BASC subscales provide information about anxiety, shyness, self-confidence, and social skills. Additionally, like the CBCL, the BASC has parent and teacher forms with corresponding subscales.

Child-Report.   Both the BASC-SRP and the PIY are excellent self-report measures for the assessment of Social Phobia. On the PIY, children with Social Phobia tend to show elevations of the Social Withdrawal scale. The Social Introversion subscale of the Social Withdrawal scale is an excellent measure of social anxiety, shyness, and fear of embarrassment, whereas the Isolation subscale of the Social Withdrawal scale is a good measure of preference or tendency to be alone. Other PIY scales may indicate the presence of associated generalized anxiety (Psychological Discomfort scale, Fear and Worry subscale) and social rejection or neglect (Social Skills Deficits scale).

On the self-report version of the BASC, children with Social Phobia tend to elevate the Anxiety, Social Stress, and Sense of Inadequacy scales, reflecting generalized anxiety, social worries and isolation, and feelings of social inferiority, respectively. Low scores on the Interpersonal Relations and Self-Reliance scales would also show the lack of good peer relationships and lack of self-confidence and independence typical of children with Social Phobia. Conversely, high scores would be expected on the Relations with Parents scale, consistent with the open and warm relationships that children with Social Phobia tend to have with their parents.

As with other diagnoses, there is a significant risk that social desirability, denial, or low insight will interfere with the child's accurate self-report of symptoms on the BASC and PIY. Elevations of the validity scales, especially those reflecting denial or minimization of symptoms, should be checked if no clinical scale elevations are found. Specifically, the BASC L scale and the PIY DEF scale warrant inspection in such cases.

Family Assessment

Parent-Report.   Children with Social Phobia show dramatically different behaviors depending on whether they are in the peer or family environment. The FES can provide structured information about the family environment to assist with the understanding of the child's differing peer and family behaviors. Families with relatively high scores on the Cohesion and Control scales and comparatively low scores on the Independence and Active-Recreational Orientation scales may have problems with enmeshment and a lack of independence of family members. When this is the case, the child may fear separation from the family and see the peer situation as threatening relative to the overprotective family.

Syndrome-Specific Tests

Child-Report

Multidimensional Anxiety Scale for Children. The Multidimensional Anxiety Scale for Children (MASC; March, 1997) was described earlier in this chapter. Children who elevate the Social Anxiety scale of the MASC tend to have many of the characteristics of Social Phobia. They fear being made fun of or embarrassed; they are anxious about having social attention drawn to them; and they intensely dislike performing in public. Items on the Social Anxiety scale fall into two subscales that reflect expectations and fears of embarrassment and rejection (Humiliation/Rejection subscale) and anxiety about performing in front of others (Performing in Public subscale). Overall, the MASC appears to be an excellent measure for use in evaluating children with suspected Social Phobia.

Screen for Child Anxiety Related Emotional Disorders. On the SCARED (see description under SAD earlier in this chapter), children with Social Phobia elevate the Social Phobia scale. Depending on specific symptoms, the School Phobia and General Anxiety scales may also be elevated. The SCARED has shown good discriminant validity within anxiety disorder samples (Birmaher et al., 1997).

Social Anxiety Scale for Children. The Social Anxiety Scale for Children (SASC; LaGreca, Dandes, Wick, Shaw, & Stone, 1988; LaGreca & Stone, 1993) is a 22-item scale measuring three factor-analytically derived areas: avoidance/distress in new social situations, fear of evaluation, and general social distress. Hence, it may be helpful in evaluating these components of Social Phobia in school-aged children.

Social Phobia and Anxiety Inventory for Children. The Social Phobia and Anxiety Inventory for Children (SPAI-C; Beidel, Turner, & Fink, 1996) is a 26-item measure of social anxiety and distress in children age 8–17. Items on the SPAI-C measure anxiety related to five factor-analytically derived areas: Assertiveness, General Conversation, Physical and Cognitive Symptoms, Avoidance, and Public Performance. Psychometric properties and validity of this scale appear to be strong (Beidel et al., 1996).

□   ## TREATMENT OPTIONS

Behavioral Interventions

Behavioral strategies dominate the treatment of children with Social Phobia (see Table 6.9). Furthermore, in light of the interpersonal nature of Social Phobia, social experience and social skills building are often important components of behavioral and cognitive-behavioral treatments. The most commonly used and most effective behavioral treatments include contingency management, modeling-shaping techniques, systematic desensitization, *in vivo* exposure, and social skills training (Beidel & Morris, 1995; LeCroy, 1994; Morris et al., 1988).

TABLE 6.9   Treatment Options for Social Phobia

1. Behavioral Interventions
   a. Contingency management
   b. Modeling-shaping techniques
   c. Systematic desensitization
   d. *In vivo* desensitization/exposure
   e. Social skills
   f. School-based interventions
2. Psychotherapy
   a. Cognitive-behavioral interventions
      (1) Self-monitoring
      (2) Self-talk
   b. Play therapy
3. Family Interventions
   a. Family therapy
4. Medication
   a. Alprazolam
   b. Imipramine
   c. Buspirone
   d. Fluoxetine

Note: This outline of options summarizes major treatments covered in the text. Specific treatments are often combined into an intervention package. Refer to the text for additional descriptions of each treatment. This table is not necessarily an exhaustive list of all treatments available.

Contingency Management

Contingency management techniques reward the child for increased interactions with peers while making avoidance and withdrawal less rewarding. Typically, a hierarchy of social goals is developed, beginning with very modest goals (e.g., stand or sit next to another child) and moving to more complex ones (start a conversation, play a game). Reinforcers are identified and paired with goal attainment. A monitor in the child's environment (usually a parent or teacher) records attainment of each goal and dispenses rewards. Conversely, withdrawal and avoidance are discouraged by restricting the child's access to preferred activities when these behaviors occur. For example, if the child refuses to go to a social event, he or she might not be permitted to watch TV or use the computer at those times.

Contingency management techniques assume that the child has the social skills to engage in rewarding social interaction. If the child does not have such skills, encouraging social interaction may only lead to failure and confirmation of the child's negative expectations. Hence, an assessment of social skills and, if needed, social skills training may have to precede contingency management interventions.

Modeling-Shaping Techniques

In a modeling-shaping intervention, the child watches another person demonstrating adaptive social behavior in a situation that would produce social anxiety in the child. The modeling may be done "live" in front of the child (live modeling), or videotapes may be used (filmed modeling). Review or discussion may follow the demonstration to clarify the expected behaviors or to anticipate potential problems. Shaping techniques are then added to have the child practice and gradually approximate the desired behavior of the model. Role-playing techniques are usually used to facilitate the shaping process, allowing the child to practice the modeled behavior in a safe situation with the therapist.

Systematic Desensitization

Desensitization techniques (described at length in the Specific Phobia section earlier in this chapter) help the child to associate situations that produce social anxiety with a response that is incompatible with anxiety (usually relaxation). In systematic desensitization, the child develops a hierarchy of feared situations and learns relaxation techniques. Once the child has learned the relaxation techniques, he or she is instructed to vividly imagine the feared situations (progressing in the hierarchy from least anxiety provoking to most anxiety provoking) while remaining in the relaxed state. The child gradually proceeds through the hierarchy of feared situations, moving up on the hierarchy only when he or she is able to completely relax while imagining the feared situation.

In Vivo Desensitization/Exposure

Because children frequently have difficulty with imaginal techniques such as systematic desensitization, use of actual anxiety-producing situations is often preferred for a desensitization intervention. As with systematic desensitization, the child uses relaxation, social skills, and other coping techniques (see the section on Specific Phobia for additional details) to maintain a calm state while exposed to social situations based on a fear hierarchy. Often, a familiar other person accompanies the child during the early stages of the desensitization hierarchy, but the presence of that person is faded as the child progresses in the hierarchy.

Social Skills Interventions

To address potential social skills deficits in children with Social Phobia, a variety of modified social skills training interventions have been developed (e.g., Francis & Ollendick, 1988; LeCroy, 1994). These typically involve education and practice to teach children social skills in a structured way. A typical social skills intervention program involves five major steps. First, children learn the content and principle behind a social skill. Second, children learn to identify situations in which the skill may be applied. Third, children learn to perform the skill and watch others demonstrating the skill. Fourth, children practice the skill in a mock social situation. Finally, children implement the skill *in vivo* and notice the response of the social environment. Social skills that are typically taught include smiling, starting a conversation, giving compliments, receiving compliments, saying hi, saying goodbye, asking questions and making requests, seeking out proximity to others, reading social cues to approach or end interaction, being assertive, expressing feelings, setting limits on others, learning empathy, resolving conflicts, and entering unfamiliar groups.

Because social skills training provides both education and practice, it overcomes deficits in both knowledge and implementation of social skills. Koplewicz (1989) recommends group social skills therapy as the treatment of choice for children with Social Phobia. The group situation facilitates learning by providing immediate opportunity for social interaction and by allowing the children to learn from the behavior of others in the group.

School-Based Behavioral Interventions

In addition to home- and office-based interventions, the school setting offers numerous opportunities for the application of behavioral techniques to promote the child's social interaction and engagement. Therapist enlistment of teachers' cooperation opens up avenues for using teacher-child interaction and child-peer interaction that will improve social skills and provide the basis for positive learning experiences. Among the types of strategies that might be employed are reinforcement of social interaction during classroom instruction, development with the child of a hierarchical list of preferred reinforcers that can be earned through specific social behaviors in the school setting, seating placement near others whom the child likes and away from anyone who may tease or bully the child, assignment of a more socially skilled "buddy" who will engage the child and involve him or her in group activities, and avoidance of placing the child in socially embarrassing or frightening situations (Blanco & Bogacki, 1988).

Outcomes of Multifactorial Behavioral Interventions

Research has shown behavioral and cognitive-behavioral interventions for Social Phobia to have positive results. Albano and Barlow (1996), for example, describe a 16-session manualized intervention for Social Phobia that combines elements of psychoeducation, modeling-shaping, *in vivo* desensitization, and social skills training. They report positive improvements in adolescents completing their protocol, and they note that similar techniques can be applied to preadolescent children.

Psychotherapy

Cognitive-Behavioral Techniques

Treatment that combines behavioral training with cognitive psychotherapy techniques can be especially helpful for avoidant children who experience high levels of anticipatory anxiety. Cognitive-behavioral intervention may be essential if the child's anxiety precludes the implementation of even the simplest behavioral goals. In these cases, the child must gain some control over anxiety before adequate performance of behavioral homework assignments can be expected.

Some of the most promising of the cognitive-behavioral interventions for social anxiety involve the use of self-monitoring and self-statements that reflect coping and competency (Strauss & Francis, 1989). Cognitive-behavioral interventions begin with assessment and self-monitoring techniques. For example, the therapist might sample the child's thoughts, feelings, and behavior at intervals while the child imagines a recent unsuccessful social interaction. Alternatively, the child might record an actual experience in a diary. Underlying beliefs and self-statements are identified and linked to feelings and behaviors. The child's negative beliefs are then challenged, and alternative beliefs are suggested. The alternative beliefs are then tested with *in vivo* homework assignments. To reduce the stress of *in vivo* experiences, the child is taught alternative self-statements that are related to positive thoughts and less anxiety. In some cases, additional skills, such as relaxation and written plans for coping with social stress, are used.

Play Therapy

Nondirective (Axlinian) play therapy may be effective for younger children with Social Phobia whose home environments are fairly restrictive. The success of developing a relationship with the therapist gives the child a positive social experience. Based on this experience, the child may overcome social inhibition and increase self-confidence and assertiveness in other social situations (Husain & Cantwell, 1991; Husain & Kashani, 1992). Furthermore, the development of independent, self-directed behavior emerges from the nondirective environment, which requires that the child take the lead in social interaction.

Family Therapy

When parents or other family members consciously or unconsciously reinforce the child's dependence and isolation, family therapy may be indicated (Husain & Cantwell, 1991). In addition, if the child's avoidant symptoms seem to be serving a role in the family environment, structural family issues may need to be addressed prior to behavioral interventions. If such family influences are ignored, the family may be subtly resistant to behavioral interventions.

Medication

Alprazolam (Xanax) and imipramine (Tofranil) have received some research support in the treatment of Social Phobia (Beidel & Morris, 1995; Simeon & Ferguson, 1987). There are anecdotal and case reports of buspirone (Buspar) helping with symptoms of social anxiety as well (Beidel & Morris, 1995). Fluoxetine (Prozac) has been found to be effective in the treatment of a group of children with anxiety disorders, including Social Phobia (Birmaher et al., 1994).

■ Obsessive-Compulsive Disorder

□ CLINICAL DESCRIPTION

Diagnostic Considerations

The symptoms and appearance of Obsessive-Compulsive Disorder (OCD) in children closely resemble those for adults. Either obsessions, compulsions, or both must be present for diagnosis. *Obsessions* are defined as persistent thoughts, ideas, images, or impulses that are considered inappropriate and intrusive and create marked distress or anxiety. *Compulsions* are repetitive behaviors or mental acts engaged in for the purpose of reducing or preventing distress or anxiety. These behaviors are not engaged in for any pleasurable or satisfying benefits they may produce. The requirement that the obsessions and compulsions be ego-dystonic is relaxed for children, but children often recognize their excessive nature. In many cases, the child is able to suppress symptoms when away from the home, only to experience their recurrence after returning home. The symptoms of OCD must significantly interfere with normal functioning due to either the distress experienced, interference with thought processing, or the time involved in completing compulsive acts (American Psychiatric Association, 1994).

Repetitive thoughts are characteristic of numerous disorders in addition to OCD, and the presence of such thoughts during the course of another mental disorder does not necessarily indicate that a diagnosis of OCD is warranted. For example, the other anxiety disorders, mood disorders, phobias, eating disorders, Tourette's syndrome, mental retardation, pervasive developmental disorders, brain damage syndromes, and schizophrenia share features with OCD that must be carefully considered in diagnosis (Leonard, Swedo, & Rapoport, 1991; Swedo & Rapoport, 1988). In general, OCD differs from other mental disorders in several ways:

1. The obsessions or compulsions are ego-dystonic (unlike repeated thoughts in the mood or eating disorders), although this requirement is relaxed for children.

2. The obsessions or compulsions are not specific to the content of another anxiety disorder (e.g., separation, phobia).

3. The obsessions or compulsions are understood to be excessive or unrealistic (unlike delusions or psychosis), although this may not be true for children.

4. The obsessions or compulsions are not rigidly tied to a single feared stimulus (unlike a phobia).

5. The obsessions or compulsions are related to beliefs and do not appear to offer anxiety relief (unlike the stereotypical behaviors seen in mental retardation and the pervasive developmental disorders; also unlike the reflexive behaviors of tics).

It should be noted, however, that Major Depressive Disorders, other anxiety disorders, eating disorders, and Tourette's syndrome often co-occur with OCD (King, Leonard, & March, 1998; Swedo et al., 1989). In fact, OCD may co-occur with other psychological disorders more often than it occurs alone. In a large prospective study of childhood OCD, 74% of 70 children and adolescents presenting with a primary diagnosis of OCD met criteria for other psychiatric diagnoses as well (Leonard et al., 1991). Diagnoses most frequently comorbid with OCD are depression (20–70%), mild/transient to severe tics (30–60%), developmental disabilities (24%), Specific Phobia (17%), GAD (16%), Oppositional-Defiant Disorder (11%), and Attention-Deficit/Hyperactivity Disorder (10–30%) (King et al., 1998; Leonard et al., 1991; Swedo et al., 1989).

The comorbid presentation of a Tic Disorder and OCD (OCD-Tic subtype) may constitute a specific subtype of OCD that has implications for course, treatment, and prognosis. The OCD-Tic subtype tends to occur at earlier ages and to have symptoms of symmetry, hoarding, touching, and aggressive thoughts and compulsions; there appears to be more of a compulsive and less of a worried component to this subtype. The non–OCD-Tic subtype, on the other hand, tends to be associated with cleaning impulses and contamination obsessions, with more anxiety and worry involved (Holzer et al., 1994). The OCD-Tic subtype may be more resistant to treatment with a selective serotonin reuptake inhibitor medication alone, requiring the addition of a neuroleptic medication for adequate treatment of symptoms (Mc-Dougle et al., 1994).

One-third to one-half of adult OCD cases experience onset by age 15 (Rapoport, 1988). The prevalence of OCD in preadolescent children is probably in the 0.5–1.0% range, increasing into the 1.0–3.5% range in adolescence (American Psychiatric Association, 1994; Flament et al., 1990; King et al., 1998; Rapoport, 1988) (Table 6.10). Onset age for OCD may be earlier for males than females, with a typical male onset age in the 6–15-year-old range and a typical female onset age in the 20–29-year-old range (American Psychiatric Association, 1994). Onset age for childhood OCD also shows the pattern of earlier onset for boys (age 9) than girls (age 12), with 1.5–2 boys with OCD for every girl with OCD during childhood (Leonard et al., 1991).

Appearance and Features

Transient, minor obsessions and compulsions are not unusual for children and adolescents, with up to one-fifth of children reporting obsessive thoughts or impulses that they consider senseless. Common topics are neatness, hoarding, repetitive urges or actions, and routines, all of which may be found in one-fourth or greater of the adolescent population (King et al., 1998). However, these obsessive thoughts and compulsions do not cause significant distress or debilitation to the child without OCD. OCD is diagnosed when these symptoms are debilitating and/or very distressing to the child.

TABLE 6.10 Epidemiology and Course of Obsessive-Compulsive Disorder

Prevalence: 1.0–3.5% in adolescents

Sex Ratio (Male:Female):   3:2 in childhood, approaching 1:1 in adolescence and early adulthood

Typical Onset Age: Mean age of onset in childhood is around 10 years, usually earlier in boys (age 9) than girls (age 12).

Course: Variable. Symptoms often subside during periods of distraction and lower stress but are exacerbated by boredom or stress. At follow-up intervals of from 2–7 years, about two-thirds will have ongoing symptoms of moderate or greater severity; fewer than one-fifth show total symptom remission. About 15% of people show a progressively declining course. Outcome tends to be worse when OCD is comorbid with a Tic Disorder.

Common Comorbid Conditions:
1. Depressive Disorders
2. Specific Phobia
3. Generalized Anxiety Disorder
4. Tic Disorders
5. Oppositional-Defiant Disorder
6. Attention-Deficit/Hyperactivity Disorder

Relevant Subtypes:
1. With Poor Insight
2. OCD with Tic Disorder or Family History of Tics

Many children with OCD hide their obsessive-compulsive symptoms (see Table 6.11) because the symptoms frequently involve "internal," thought-based activity. There is sometimes indirect evidence for OCD when the child seems distracted, has difficulty concentrating, and has difficulty with activities because of a lack of task focus. Symptoms may reach dramatic proportions before coming to the attention of parents (e.g., skin breakdown from a handwashing ritual). Signs that OCD should be considered include repeated touching of objects, unproductive hours spent on homework, retracing over words, excessive erasures, unexplained increases in utility bills or laundry, very fast depletion of cleaning supplies, stopped-up toilets, requests that family members repeat phrases, unreasonably high numbers of requests for reassurance, a preoccupying fear of harm coming to the child or to others, long bedtime rituals, fear of leaving the home, hoarding of useless objects, or peculiar patterns of sitting or walking (Leonard et al., 1991).

The most frequent compulsions seen in children and adolescents with OCD are washing, repeating, checking, touching, counting, arranging, hoarding, and scrupulosity. Common obsessions are contamination, danger, doubts, disorder, guilt for imagined negligence, aggressive thoughts, and sexual thoughts (King et al., 1998; Leonard et al., 1991). Onset of OCD is sometimes acute and children can occasionally recall when they first began to experience OCD symptoms (Rapoport, 1988). Symptoms commonly change over time, such as when cleaning rituals give way to repeating or checking (Leonard et al., 1991; Swedo & Rapoport, 1988).

The course of OCD is variable. Some children report that their obsessions and compulsions subside during certain periods of time, whereas others report that they are continuous. Stress or boredom may be related to exacerbation of symptoms; distraction is sometimes effective in preventing obsessions and compulsions. About 15% of people with OCD show a progressively declining course (American Psychiatric Association, 1994). Suicide is a risk for children with OCD and should be investigated in interview (Kaplan & Sadock, 1988).

TABLE 6.11   Appearance and Features of Obsessive-Compulsive Disorder

---

COMMON FEATURES

1. Persistent, automatic, intrusive thoughts, images, or impulses
2. Repetitive behaviors
3. Cleaning, repeating, checking
4. Hiding of disorder as long as possible

OCCASIONAL FEATURES

1. Difficulty concentrating
2. Lack of productive or purposeful activity
3. Sudden onset
4. Missing household items, rearranged items, or overuse of items

---

Note: The features listed in the table are often seen but are not universal. Some features may be diagnostically relevant or required, whereas others may not be required for diagnosis. "Common" features are typical of the disorder; "occasional" whereas features appear frequently but are not necessarily seen in a majority of cases.

Etiology

Three groups of theories have received the most attention in OCD etiology: biological, behavioral, and psychodynamic. Biological theories identify neurotransmitters and genetics as primary in the explanation of OCD; these theories have received the most attention to date. A serotonin hypothesis of OCD is based on clinical response to the serotonin reuptake inhibitors; dopamine has also been suggested as an important neurotransmitter in development of OCD, but dopaminergic hypotheses are less well accepted than serotinergic ones.

Neuroanatomical studies using CAT and PET scans have found some abnormalities in some patients with OCD. The involvement of abnormalities of basal ganglia is supported by the association of OCD and Sydenham's chorea in some children, the presence of obsessive-compulsive symptoms in Tourette's syndrome, and OCD's association with postencephalitic Parkinson's disease. In some cases, OCD symptoms can be caused by certain infections or autoimmune responses, but this does not explain the vast majority of OCD cases (King et al., 1998). The frontal lobe cortex area has also been implicated in the development of OCD. In addition to neuroanatomical studies, family and twin studies support a genetic hypothesis, with approximately 20% of first-degree relatives of OCD patients meeting OCD diagnostic criteria (American Psychiatric Association, 1994; Insel, 1992; Leonard et al., 1991).

Psychodynamic theories emphasize the role of obsessions and compulsions as defenses to deflect anxiety arising from internal conflicts. Because the conflicts are too threatening to experience directly, the child represses the actual content of the internal conflict. In its place emerge obsessive thoughts and compulsive behavior that may be symbolically related to the original intrapsychic conflict but deflect attention from the original conflict. For example, a child with Oedipal urges toward his mother may develop obsessions of sex with a girl next door. Ultimately, psychodynamic theories stress the importance of uncovering the underlying conflict and resolving it. Without the repressed conflict, the obsessions and compulsions have no reason to continue.

Behavioral theories explain the presence of obsessions and compulsions by stressing the anxiety relief that the person gets from engaging in them. Holding back an obsession, for example, creates feelings of anxiety and stress in the child. The anxiety relief from giving in to the obsession is reinforcing, causing the child to give in to the obsession at a later time for anxiety relief. Although this model explains the maintenance of OCD, it does not address questions about its emergence.

ASSESSMENT PATTERNS

A sample assessment battery for childhood anxiety disorders (including OCD) is shown in Table 6.3.

Broad Assessment Strategies

Cognitive Assessment

OCD does not seem to cluster in the upper ranges of intellectual functioning, as was previously widely believed. Rather, OCD has been found in persons of varying intellectual abilities (American Psychiatric Association, 1994), and children with OCD tend to have an average distribution of intelligence (Husain & Kashani, 1992). Consequently, intelligence and achievement testing scores do not provide material that can be used to support or rule out an OCD diagnosis. Occasionally, severe OCD symptoms can interfere with processing speed, attention, and concentration on intelligence tests. This interference is usually easily observed behaviorally, and it may result in lower scores on the Wechsler Arithmetic, Digit Span, Coding, and Symbol Search tests. Interference with motor speed may also affect any timed cognitive test, such as the Wechsler performance subtests.

OCD has been found to be associated with lower scores on neuropsychological tests of frontal lobe functioning, including executive functioning, cognitive flexibility, use of feedback, and abstract learning. Tests such as the Stroop Color and Word Test (Golden, 1978), Wisconsin Card Sorting Test (Heaton, Chelune, Talley, Kay, & Curtis, 1993), Children's Category Test (Boll, 1993), and Tower of Hanoi (Welsh, Pennington, & Groisser, 1991) are commonly used to assess these neuropsychological areas. There is relatively little evidence that these tests will yield data directly relevant to an OCD diagnosis in children, but they may provide additional insight into executive functioning deficits in a child with known OCD and concurrent ability or achievement difficulties.

Psychological Assessment

Clinician-Administered. On projective tests, OCD symptoms are usually manifest in overelaborated, perfectionistic, minute, detailed, or repetitive responses. On the TAT, children with OCD often tell elaborate, detailed stories, giving names to characters and providing detailed descriptions of irrelevant story details. Some hesitation or lack of coherence in the story lines could indicate that the obsessions are interfering with the child's storytelling thought process. Repetitive themes may be present and should be analyzed for connections with the reported obsessions or compulsions. Perfectionistic tendencies characterized by minute changes in story detail or difficulty settling on a story line are frequently seen. In other cases, the stories may be stereotypical and devoid of emotion. For many children with OCD, the "tired hand" rule applies to the TAT: If the clinician's hand is tired of writing down all of the child's story details and elaborate themes, consider the OCD diagnosis (this is not entirely facetious, although it has not been empirically studied).

The Rorschach responses of children with OCD may indicate doubt as to the content of percepts, with modification of responses immediately or during the inquiry. Small details of the blots may be used for responses, with the whole ignored. Alternatively, children with OCD may exclude small details of the blots in an attempt to have the blots more closely fit their responses. Descriptions of blots may be elaborate and detailed, although this detail may not result in increased determinant complexity. A large number of responses is typical, with many W or Dd responses, a high F+ percentage, and many edge details (Meyer & Deitsch, 1996).

Behavioral Assessment

Parent-Report and Teacher-Report. The Achenbach scales include several items relevant for the assessment of OCD. For the most part, these items cluster on the Thought Problems subscale. Hence, children with OCD almost always have elevated Thought Problems scores on the CBCL or TRF. When interpreting the CBCL/TRF profile, it is important to remember that the elevated Thought Problems score does not always refer to thought problems in the psychotic sense. Rather, the Thought Problems subscale tends to be more of an obsessive-compulsive-unconventional thought scale. In addition to the Thought Problems scale, the Attention Problems scale includes several items (e.g., poor concentration) that are either directly or tangentially related to OCD symptoms. Hence, this scale is also often elevated in children with OCD. Again, it is important to be clear as to the meaning of an elevated Attention Problems scale for a child with OCD. In such an instance, the Attention Problems scale probably reflects obsessive-compulsive thought processes as opposed to a fundamental attention deficit. The pattern of elevations of the other CBCL subscales may indicate characteristics of the OCD and related problems.

The ECI-4, CSI-4, and ASI-4 each contain items about obsessions and compulsions. These are general screening items that do not combine to yield a subscale score. Rather, they are intended to prompt the clinician to further evaluate parent- or teacher-report of these symptoms.

The Anxiety scale of the BASC contains several items that can reflect perfectionistic, repetitive worries about mistakes, dying, and achievement. However, items that correspond most directly to the symptoms of OCD fall on the BASC Atypicality scale. On the BASC-PRS for 8–11-year-old children, one such item asks about compulsive behaviors in general (repeating behaviors many times), whereas another item reflects obsessions in general (unable to stop unwanted thoughts). However, because Atypicality scale items cover other diverse symptoms (including symptoms of Schizophrenia, Pervasive Developmental Disorder, Pica, and self-harm), OCD alone is usually not enough to produce a severe elevation of this scale. The Adaptability scale is frequently depressed (reflecting poor adaptability) in children with OCD who do not adjust well to change or ambiguity.

On the Conners' scales, OCD symptoms are contained on the Perfectionism subscale. This subscale is a measure of the child's need to have his or her behavior and environment clean, exact, and unchanging. The Perfectionism subscale also includes an item asking about repeated checking behaviors (a common compulsion symptom). On the parent version (not the teacher version), an item about rituals also falls on the Perfectionism subscale. Although the Anxious-Shy subscale should show some elevation for many children with OCD, it does not include items about specific OCD symptoms. Rather, the Anxious-Shy subscale tends to measure generalized anxiety and social fears (parent version) or sensitive-emotional personality and behavior (teacher version).

Self-Report

Like the CBCL, the YSR contains several items measuring OCD symptoms and related problems. Furthermore, administration of the YSR may identify symptoms of which the parent is unaware because the self-report YSR taps internal experience and personal appraisal of the symptoms. Because of the internal nature of obsessions, the YSR can be a valuable component of assessment, although its utility is diminished because it cannot be administered to children less than 11 years of age. Profile patterns and interpretation of the YSR mirror those for the CBCL.

Like the parent and teacher versions of the BASC, the self-report version of the BASC includes several items about specific OCD symptoms. These items (along with an array of other odd and atypical symptoms) fall on the Atypicality scale. Interpretation of other

BASC self-report subscales mirrors that for the parent- and teacher-report scales for children with OCD.

On the PIY, items about repetitive or distressing thoughts and behaviors tend to fall on the Feelings of Alienation subscale of the Reality Distortion scale. Like the BASC Atypicality scale, however, the Reality Distortion scale and Feelings of Alienation subscale also include other types of items, ranging from hallucinations and delusions (Reality Distortion scale) to lack of trust or social connection (Feelings of Alienation subscale). Obsessions and compulsions related to cleanliness or disease will also cause the Somatic Concern scale (especially the Preoccupation with Disease subscale of this scale) to be elevated. Generalized anxiety or distress will be reflected in scores on the Psychological Discomfort scale and on the Fear and Worry subscale of this scale. Like the BASC and YSR, the PIY does not include a single, focused subscale exclusively for OCD symptoms.

Syndrome-Specific Tests

Clinician-Administered

Children's Yale-Brown Obsessive-Compulsive Scale. In addition to structured interview information gathered with interviews such as the ADIS-IV-C/P (see description in SAD section of this chapter), a clinician rating scale may be used to document the child's OCD symptoms. The Children's Yale-Brown Obsessive-Compulsive Scale (CY-BOCS; Goodman, Price, & Rasmussen, 1989a, 1989b) is a clinician rating scale that assesses the severity of both obsessive and compulsive symptoms. The CY-BOCS consists of an extensive list of specific obsessive thoughts and compulsive rituals. For each obsession and compulsion, the following categories are assessed: amount of time consumed per day, amount of distress, interference with normal functioning, effort required to resist the symptom, and the amount of control the individual has over symptoms. A total severity score is obtained by summing individual symptom scores.

Child-Report

Multidimensional Anxiety Scale for Children. Although the MASC (March, 1997) does not include a specific OCD subscale, items reflecting perfectionism and checking are covered on the Harm Avoidance scale. As the scale name indicates, these items tend to be slanted toward avoidance of physical and/or psychological danger and mistakes. Fears of harm and threats to personal integrity have a major impact on this scale score, in addition to OCD tendencies.

SUDS Scales. SUDS scales (see description under Specific Phobia) are used to quantify the level of distress associated with exposure to the content of target obsessions or compulsions. They are frequently used to assist with the construction of an exposure hierarchy for an exposure-response prevention intervention.

Maudsley Obsessional-Compulsive Inventory. The Maudsley Obsessional-Compulsive Inventory (MOCI; Hodgson & Rachman, 1977) is specifically designed for use in evaluating the cognitive and behavioral aspects of OCD. It is made up of 30 true-false items that yield a total score as well as scores for Washing, Checking, Slowness, and Doubting. The MOCI has been found to be useful both in assessing treatment effects and in discriminating between OCD-disordered individuals and those not having the disorder (McCarthy & Foa, 1988; Rachman & Hodgson, 1980).

Leyton Obsessional Inventory—Child Version. The Leyton Obsessional Inventory— Child Version (LOI-CV) is a downward age extension of the adult version of the scale. The LOI-CV consists of 44 OCD symptoms that are rated for presence/absence and degree of interference with functioning. It yields four factor-analytically derived item groups that may be evaluated as subscales: general obsessive, dirt-contamination, numbers-luck, and school-related symptoms (Berg, Rapoport, & Flament, 1986; Berg, Whitaker, Davies, Flament, & Rapoport, 1988). A variety of other checklists for OCD exist, such as the Compulsive Activity Checklist and various global rating scales (Albano et al., 1999; McCarthy & Foa, 1988).

□   TREATMENT OPTIONS

Behavioral Interventions

The child's cooperation is often very important for conducting effective behavior therapy for OCD. Eliciting anxiety-provoking private events is sometimes required for treatment to be effective, and such private behavior cannot easily be externally verified. Thus, the child's accurate self-report of internal events is important for success. These requirements are less crucial for external compulsive behavior and avoidance based on obsessions, which can be monitored by observation. However, even external exposure to anxiety-provoking stimuli is most easily done when at least some cooperation is provided by the child.

Two behavioral approaches (that are often combined) dominate OCD treatment for children and adolescents: exposure procedures and response prevention (Table 6.12). *Exposure procedures,* such as desensitization, flooding, and satiation, expose the child gradually or completely/rapidly to obsessions, to compulsions, or to situations that evoke the obsessions or compulsions. This exposure presumably reduces the anxiety associated with the obsession, compulsion, or trigger situation by pairing a lack of avoidance and reduced anxiety state (or relaxation) with the anxiety-provoking symptom or situation. For example, a child with cleanliness obsessions may be asked to cover himself or herself with dirt. In children, desensitization techniques, which involve gradual exposure, are most often used. Flooding techniques, which involve full exposure to the stimulus without gradual introduction, can lead to states of severe anxiety and panic in children and should be carefully used.

Satiation techniques expose the child to high levels of the obsessive-compulsive behavior in an attempt to make the behavior aversive or to tire the processes driving the behavior. They also bring the "uncontrollable" urges under control by "prescribing the symptom." For example, a child may be asked to perform the obsession or compulsion repeatedly until he or she can do so no more because of boredom or fatigue. The pairing of the symptom with control, monotony, and fatigue encourages the child to discontinue it.

Some individuals can be exposed to their obsessions only in fantasy, such as committing murder or arson. Nonetheless, where possible the actual anxiety-provoking stimulus should be used in treatment as this produces better results than imaginal exposure (Foa &

TABLE 6.12   Treatment Options for Obsessive-Compulsive Disorder

1. Behavioral Interventions
   a. Exposure therapies
      (1) Desensitization
      (2) Flooding
      (3) Satiation
   b. Response prevention
   c. Reinforcement
2. Psychotherapy
   a. Cognitive-behavioral interventions
      (1) Cognitive restructuring
      (2) Psychoeducation
      (3) Distraction
      (4) Relaxation techniques
      (5) Modeling
3. Medication
   a. Clomipramine
   b. Selective serotonin reuptake inhibitors (fluoxetine)

Note: This outline of options summarizes major treatments covered in the text. Specific treatments are often combined into an intervention package. Refer to the text for additional descriptions of each treatment. This table is not necessarily an exhaustive list of all treatments available.

Steketee, 1989). Additionally, exposure must take place until habituation has occurred and OCD symptoms have diminished.

Response prevention, which involves preventing rituals, thoughts, or avoidance behaviors, is also effective in reducing the number of obsessive thoughts or the performance of compulsive behaviors. Response prevention removes the rewarding feeling of a reduction in anxiety following avoidance or ritualistic behaviors. Removal of the reinforcement results in the response being extinguished.

Response prevention typically begins by limiting the child to a single performance of a compulsive act or obsessive thought, and then eventually completely extinguishing its performance. The limiting may be done by the self-control of the patient, alteration of the environment (e.g., not giving a hand-washer private access to the bathroom), physical restraint (having a hand-washer wear gloves or restraints to prevent washing), or administration of a punishment whenever the event occurs.

Exposure and response prevention have been employed singly with some success. However, when used in combination the results have proven superior to either single method (Foa & Steketee, 1989). Hence, exposure/response prevention (E/RP) plans are generally considered to be standard effective treatments for OCD in children.

E/RP techniques are often implemented with psychoeducation and reinforcement components. The *psychoeducation* component involves teaching the child about the cognitive (thoughts and beliefs), physiological, and emotional components of OCD specifically and anxiety in general. The *reinforcement* component of treatment encourages the child to participate by providing rewards for completion of homework assignments and goal attainment (March & Mulle, 1996). Descriptions of combined behavioral treatments for OCD are presented in March and Mulle (1996) and Emmelkamp, Kloek, and Blaauw (1992).

Psychotherapy

Cognitive-Behavioral Interventions

Cognitive-behavioral techniques have been incorporated successfully into behavioral programs, sometimes resulting in faster responses with less emotional distress. Commonly used cognitive-behavioral techniques with children include cognitive restructuring, psychoeducation, distraction, relaxation techniques, and modeling (King et al., 1998; March & Mulle, 1996). Cognitive restructuring techniques involve challenging children to see their obsessive-compulsive symptoms from a different point of view. Psychoeducation is often used to assist in cognitive restructuring by providing children with accurate information about the situation or behaviors that are associated with symptomatology. For example, a child with fears of contamination may be taught that dirt does not inevitably lead to disease, and that the body has effective natural barriers (skin, immune system) to contamination. Distraction and relaxation techniques are taught to children as ways of reducing their anxious responses during E/RP. Finally, modeling is used to show children examples of exposure and response prevention with concurrent use of cognitive coping techniques (relaxation, cognitive restructuring). The model demonstrates the treatment while also noting the cognitive strategies that he or she is using. Participant modeling, in which the child accompanies the model through the treatment, can also be used to assist the child in completing an OCD treatment plan.

Cognitive-behavioral therapy techniques are rarely used alone in the treatment of OCD because some exposure to the anxiety associated with the symptoms appears to be crucial for success. Combined with E/RP methods, however, cognitive-behavioral techniques can give the child ways to cope with anxiety and negative thoughts during exposure. March and Mulle (1993, 1996), for example, have developed a manualized treatment program for OCD that integrates exposure, response prevention, psychoeducation, cognitive restructuring, and relaxation techniques. Storytelling is used to bring these components to a level that the child can understand, remember, and use. Cognitive-behavioral therapy with an E/RP component is currently considered the treatment of choice for childhood OCD, with medication added for older children with more severe symptoms (Albano et al., 1999).

Psychodynamic Psychotherapy

Insight therapies do not appear to be as successful as other interventions for OCD (Husain & Kashani, 1992; Rapoport, 1988), although success in individual cases does occur. As a result, psychodynamic treatment is not seen as a common or first-line treatment for OCD in adults or children. When OCD is associated with a constellation of other maladaptive personality traits, Axis I disorders, and historical stresses, insight-oriented psychotherapies may be more appropriate, although this assumption remains to be tested by outcome research.

Family Interventions

If a child's OCD has a major impact on family life, the family may also require treatment to adapt to the stress of the child's symptoms or to the changes as the child's symptoms abate. Alternatively, family members may act as cotherapists in the implementation of behavioral techniques at home. Finally, families may benefit from education about the nature and treatment of OCD in children. The overriding consideration in these family scenarios is the importance of the family in changing and/or maintaining the behavior of the child. To the extent that this family power can be harnessed and channeled in a positive (e.g., discouraging symptoms) direction by the therapist, therapy is more likely to be effective.

In some cases, formal family therapy may be required to intervene in maladaptive family dynamics that have evolved in response to the aberrant behavior on the part of the child. Family members' overinvolvement with the child with OCD and a reluctance to change family structure to accommodate symptom change can interfere with treatment (Leonard et al., 1991).

Medication

Pharmacological Interventions

A number of pharmacological interventions have been tried with OCD with varying success. Benzodiazepines are seeing less use as the selective serotonin reuptake inhibitors (SSRIs) are found to be more effective in the treatment of OCD with fewer side effects. Given their demonstrated clinical benefit and milder side effect profile, the SSRIs have become the medication treatment of choice for OCD, with 60–70% of children responding to SSRI treatment. Within the group of SSRIs, most attention has focused on fluoxetine (Prozac), fluvoxamine (Luvox), and sertraline (Zoloft). Fluoxetine appears to improve symptoms in 50% or more of children with OCD with evidence that it is superior to placebo in double-blind studies (Albano et al., 1999; Bezchlibnyk-Butler & Jeffries, 1997; Popper, 1993). However, there is no evidence supporting the use of one SSRI over another.

Clomipramine (Anafranil), a cyclic antidepressant and serotonin reuptake inhibitor, has shown to produce improvement in OCD symptoms in one-half to three-fourths of children and adolescents with support coming from well-designed, double-blind studies. However, even following treatment with clomipramine, most children have some continuing OCD symptoms (Popper, 1993). Additionally, clomipramine's effectiveness has in some cases "worn off" over time so that it should not be considered a complete solution for child OCD (Rapoport, 1988). Concern about cardiac side effects has also reduced the frequency with which clomipramine is used to treat OCD in children.

Children with the OCD-Tic subtype of OCD may not show a typical response to medications, particularly the SSRIs. For such children, addition of a neuroleptic is sometimes considered, or different medication regimens may have to be tried (King et al., 1998; McDougle et al., 1994).

Combination Treatments

The most efficacious treatment for OCD may be a combination of exposure with response prevention and pharmacotherapy (Abel, 1993). Each of these two OCD treatments affects different symptomatology. Exposure with response prevention is more efficacious over all and seems to have the greatest effect on alleviating compulsive rituals. Medication (especially clomipramine), on the other hand, has greater overall effect among individuals experiencing obsessions only and among those with comorbid depression. Used in combination, then, there is the opportunity for a greater reduction in both obsessive and compulsive symptoms. Additionally, such combination might also serve to increase compliance by providing quicker symptom relief.

Inpatient Hospitalization

In extreme or dangerous cases of OCD, therapy is conducted on an inpatient basis. The inpatient setting provides a structured environment in which the child receives constant monitoring and consistent behavior management by staff. At times such close supervision and constant monitoring cannot be carried out in the home, particularly if the home environment is chaotic, the child's symptoms are functionally debilitating, and the child resists outpatient treatment. When these characteristics occur in the child's OCD, inpatient hospitalization may be appropriate. Inpatient treatment of OCD usually involves a more intensive implementation of the traditional behavioral and medical therapies.

■ Posttraumatic Stress Disorder

☐ CLINICAL DESCRIPTION

Diagnostic Considerations

The essential feature of Posttraumatic Stress Disorder (PTSD) is development of intrusive and avoidant symptoms following exposure to a traumatic event. A traumatic event is defined by two criteria: First, the event involves a threat to the physical integrity (including death, injury, or other physical harm) of self or others. The person need not be present at the event if it involved a family member or close friend, although some personal experience (at least witnessing the event) appears to be required if the event involved a less familiar person. Second, the experience of the event includes intense fear, terror, helplessness, disorganized behavior, or agitated behavior (the latter two criteria apply only to children).

PTSD's characteristic symptoms fall into three categories: intrusive reexperiences of the event, avoidance of experiences related to the event, and physiological arousal. Intrusive reexperiences include memories of the event (in children this may be through repetitive play or reenactment), dreams or nightmares related to the event, reliving part or all of the experience, and psychological or physiological upset in response to cues related to the event. Avoidance symptoms include avoidance of thoughts connected with the experience, avoidance of activities and social interaction connected with the experience, amnesia for part of the trauma, reduced interest in activities, numbness, feeling of detachment, flat or constricted affect, and sense of shortened future. Physiological arousal symptoms include difficulty sleeping, irritability, diminished concentration, hypervigilance, and exaggerated startle response.

PTSD symptoms are essentially the same for children and adults, with some provisions for children to have less defined cognitive symptoms and more behavioral symptoms. For example, children's memories may be expressed in play. PTSD has been established to occur in children at various ages from preschool through adolescence (Saigh, 1988, 1989a, 1989b).

PTSD symptomatology must have been present for at least one month for the PTSD diagnosis to be made (American Psychiatric Association, 1994). If the event is more recent than one month or the duration of symptoms is less than one month, a diagnosis of Acute Stress Disorder should be considered. The Acute Stress Disorder diagnosis requires fewer intrusive and avoidant symptoms, and it must be of 2 days to 4 weeks duration; symptoms must develop within 4 weeks of the traumatic event.

Lifetime prevalence of PTSD is estimated at 1.2% for women and 0.5% for men (Kaplan & Sadock, 1988), or approximately 1% for adults (Pynoos, 1990). Although no such data are available for children, children are exposed to traumatic situations, such as natural disasters, domestic violence, abuse, neglect, gunshot injury, war, death of a loved one, and chronic illness. In a psychiatric inpatient sample, 20.7% of sexually abused, 6.9% of physically abused and 10.3% of nonabused psychiatric cases met criteria for PTSD (Deblinger, McLeer, Atkins, Ralphe, & Foa, 1989).

Appearance and Features

Children with PTSD typically present with a mix of intrusive and avoidant symptoms (see Table 6.13). Perhaps the most common intrusive symptom seen is nightmares, the content of which the child sometimes cannot remember. However, avoidant symptoms are more prominently seen in the clinic or hospital situation, probably because the clinic environment is safe and different from the environment in which the traumatic event occurred. Often, children with PTSD resist attempts to talk about the situation, or they give a flat, "newspaper" account of what happened. They may appear withdrawn and cautious, and obvious signs of adult-type grief (e.g., crying) may be infrequent. Very young children

---

TABLE 6.13   Appearance and Features of Posttraumatic Stress Disorder

COMMON FEATURES

1. Intrusions: nightmares, unbidden thoughts, intrusive emotions, tenseness, exaggerated startle, agitation, disorganized behavior
2. Avoidance/denial: avoidance of stimuli associated with the event, emotional numbness, flat appearance, refusal to discuss event
3. Occurrence of traumatic event that caused the symptoms

OCCASIONAL FEATURES

1. Calm, avoidant presentation when in a safe environment that allows cognitive avoidance
2. Self-destructive behavior
3. Dissociation
4. Feelings of guilt or shame
5. Anger

Note: The features listed in the table are often seen but are not universal. Some features may be diagnostically relevant or required, whereas others may not be required for diagnosis. "Common" features are typical of the disorder; "occasional" features appear frequently but are not necessarily seen in a majority of cases.

may show no reaction or a muted reaction to the death of a loved one because of their limited comprehension. They often have limited understanding of the permanence of death, believing that the loved one has gone bodily to a different place and may return.

Some children are overwhelmed by intrusive symptoms, which are frequently acted out in behavior. Sexual acting-out, aggressive behavior, tantruming, and escape behaviors are common intrusive behaviors seen in children with PTSD. At times, these can be mistaken for oppositionality, but their temporal association and appearance suggest their correspondence to the traumatic event.

Although emotional upset, anhedonia, sleep problems, memory problems, attention problems, fear of recurrence, and guilt tend to be the most commonly seen symptoms in all children following a severe traumatic event, these symptoms tend to affect children in general and not specifically those with PTSD. Rather, symptoms of numbing and avoidance appear to be the most diagnostically specific symptoms of PTSD in children following a traumatic event (Lonigan, Anthony, & Shannon, 1998). Hence, flatness, avoidance, and withdrawal may be the key symptoms in identifying PTSD in children.

Although children with PTSD show many similarities in behavior, there are some differences in presentation based on the child's premorbid personality and the type of trauma experienced. For children exposed to a single violent event, temporal proximity to the event is correlated with severity of symptoms. Disturbances of concentration and sleep are typical of severe reactions to the single traumatic event, whereas moderate reactions to the event are characterized by emotional constriction and avoidance of reminders of the trauma. Exposure to multiple or chronic traumatic experiences (e.g., childhood physical and sexual abuse) causes greater disruption of normal development, adoption of a guarded attitude, and more profound effects on self-esteem and long-term emotional stability (Bernstein & Borchardt, 1991).

Symptom differences have also been observed among children and adolescents having acute (4 months or less) versus chronic (8 months or more) duration of PTSD symptoms (Famularo, Kinscherff, & Fenton, 1990). Those in the acute duration group primarily experience nightmares, distress upon real or symbolic exposure to the trauma situation, difficulty falling asleep, an exaggerated startle response, hypervigilance, agitation, and generalized anxiety. The chronic duration group, on the other hand, experiences detachment, estrangement from others, restricted range of affect, sadness, thinking that life would be hard, and dissociative episodes (Famularo et al., 1990).

Deblinger et al. (1989) found that the symptom pictures of PTSD in sexually, physically, and nonabused individuals differed across subject categories. Reexperiencing phenomena and inappropriate sexual behaviors were significantly more prevalent among the sexually abused children than in the other two groups. Also, sexually and physically abused individuals exhibited more symptoms of avoidance/dissociation than did the nonabused children.

Etiology

PTSD and Acute Stress Disorder are unique among the anxiety disorders in that they require the occurrence of a specific type of external event (an abnormal and serious stressor) for diagnosis. Therefore, all etiological theories aim to explain the effects of a traumatic stressor. The theories differ in the role of predisposing factors and in the explanation of how the traumatic event causes PTSD.

Biological theories posit that a premorbid tendency to excessive autonomic reaction exists in those who eventually develop PTSD. Biological theories also hypothesize that PTSD symptoms are reflections of biological changes caused by the traumatic experience. One hypothesis suggests that endogenous opioids are released when the trauma is relived and intervening symptoms are the result of opioid withdrawal. Another hypothesis suggests that PTSD patients demonstrate increased release of catecholamine neurotransmitters while reexperiencing the traumatic event. Sleep EEG studies point to similarities between PTSD and Major Depressive Disorder because there is increased REM latency and stage 4 sleep in many cases of both disorders (Kaplan & Sadock, 1988).

Several theorists have proposed cognitive-psychodynamic models for the development of PTSD in response to a traumatic stressor (e.g., Horowitz, 1986; Roth & Lebowitz, 1988; Straker, Moosa, & Sanctuaries Counselling Team, 1988; Watson, Kucala, Manifold, Juba, & Vassar, 1988). These models suggest that people have mental structures, called schemas, that allow them to make sense of incoming information in their daily experiences. A schema is a structure that anticipates relationships or rules involving life experiences. Stated differently, a schema is a belief about the way the person and the world operate. Although some of these schemas are value neutral (e.g., how to behave in an unfamiliar restaurant), others are extremely important and form the core of an individual's identity (e.g., the sense of a just world; the sense that one has reasonable control over what happens to oneself).

Traumatic experiences are so damaging and out of the normal sphere of human experience that they are incompatible with key schemas. Thus, the individual who experiences a traumatic event is faced with discrepant cognitive structures: the memory of the event and the schemas that the event violated. In order to achieve cognitive stability, the discrepancy between the memories and the schemas must be resolved. This resolution can happen only by processing the memory of the traumatic event and modifying the schemas, so that the traumatic memory can be incorporated into the individual's core schemas. The ultimate goal is to change the schemas so that they account for the event while still making sense based on the remainder of the individual's experience. Essentially, the individual is trying to understand the meaning of the event, but meaning can only be achieved with a modification of basic core schemas that the traumatic event has violated. This is done by "dosing" with the traumatic memory so that the memory is processed on the one hand, but the emotional upset caused by constantly dwelling on the memory is avoided.

The initial processing of a traumatic memory is painful and difficult because it causes a questioning of basic schemas; if this initial processing reaches a certain level of difficulty, it takes the form of intrusive symptoms of PTSD. Likewise, the individual attempts to contain the effects of the memory so as to not become overwhelmed with upset; this containment of memory comes in the form of avoidance and denial. The person cycles between avoidance/denial and intrusion as a way of processing the memory while maintaining adequate stability and functioning (this process is referred to as "working through" the trauma). This processing continues until the memory and the core schemas are reconciled. Ideally, the memory and the schema become integrated so that the individual can access both without feeling that there is a discrepancy between them. Until this happens, however, the traumatic event remains in "active memory," threatening to emerge and affect the individual's thoughts or behaviors without warning (Horowitz, 1986). PTSD occurs when the amplitude of the swings between intrusion and denial becomes excessive and significantly interferes with functioning over a relatively long and consistent period of time.

☐   ASSESSMENT PATTERNS

A sample assessment battery for childhood anxiety disorders (including PTSD) is shown in Table 6.3.

Broad Assessment Strategies

Cognitive Assessment

Clinician-Administered.   PTSD presumably affects concentration more than it affects "crystallized" intelligence tasks (e.g., vocabulary, basic knowledge). Thus, administration of a Wechsler scale may indicate the extent to which certain abilities have been temporarily affected by PTSD symptoms. Low scores on Digit Span, Arithmetic, Coding, and Symbol Search could indicate attention, concentration, and processing speed deficits secondary to PTSD symptoms.

Psychological Assessment

Clinician-Administered.   Several MMPI/MMPI-A code types may be expected in adolescents with PTSD, with the F-2-8 code type probably the most common. This code type indicates a feeling of dissatisfaction, alienation, loss of control, and unique experiences. Another expected code type is the 7-2, which may indicate social distancing and distress (Meyer & Deitsch, 1996). An elevation on scale 9 can indicate that the PTSD is characterized by components of agitation, pressure for action, and avoidance of introspection. Elevations of scales 4 and 6 are present in individuals who are angry, alienated, and suspicious as a result of their traumatic experience.

Projective personality tests such as the TAT and Rorschach may reveal intrusive themes or rigid denial structures. Intrusive themes may be represented by violent content and many color and shading responses on the Rorschach. Denial structures will be manifest in brief, unelaborated TAT stories and Rorschach protocols with high lambda and low R scores. The plot of TAT stories may be analyzed to see the schemas of the child. For example, the child who consistently has authority figures behaving illegally and immorally may hold a schema that authorities are untrustworthy and dangerous.

Behavioral Assessment

Parent-Report and Teacher-Report.   Most broad-band behavior checklists are of limited use in assessing the symptomatology of PTSD, but they may be helpful in identifying associated features or co-occurring problems. On the CBCL and TRF, children with PTSD typically elevate the Anxious/Depressed, Thought Problems, and Attention Problems scales. Social withdrawal is often present in PTSD, leading to elevation of the Withdrawal scale.

Like the Achenbach scales, the BASC does not contain a set of items that overlaps with PTSD symptomatology. Items about anxiety and intrusive thoughts and behaviors are contained on the Anxiety and Atypicality scales, which would be expected to show elevations for a child with PTSD. Other scales likely to show elevations for a child with PTSD are the Somatization scale (reflecting the physiological hyperarousal symptoms of PTSD), the Attention Problems Scale (reflecting symptoms of cognitive avoidance), and the Depression scale. For children showing agitation, the Hyperactivity scale would show an elevation.

The CSI-4 includes one screening item for PTSD, which asks about the child's experiencing of an extremely upsetting event. The ECI-4 contains most symptoms of PTSD, reworded as questionnaire items; the ASI-4 contains two PTSD symptom items. The Conners' scales include less content relevant to PTSD because of their focus on externalizing behaviors, social problems, and attention problems. However, the CTRS Anxious-Shy subscale may be elevated, reflecting increased sensitivity of the child. The CPRS Anxious-Shy subscale may be elevated if the child is showing many fears and some shyness.

Child-Report. Like the adult versions of the broad-band behavior questionnaires, most broad-band child self-report questionnaires do not include specific subscales for PTSD. On the BASC, children with PTSD would be expected to elevate the Anxiety scale, which measures worries, fears, and feeling overwhelmed. Elevations of the Atypicality scale (odd thoughts and behaviors; dyscontrol of thought processes), Locus of Control scale (feeling that one has little control over the world and future), and Somatization scale (physical complaints that may be consistent with hyperarousal) would also be commonly seen. For children with comorbid depressive symptoms, elevations of the Depression and Sense of Inadequacy scale, combined with depressed scores on the Interpersonal Relations, Self-Esteem, and Self-Reliance scales, would be expected.

Although the PIY does not have a PTSD subscale, several scales of the PIY overlap substantially with PTSD symptom areas. The Muscular Tension and Anxiety subscale of the Somatic Concern scale reflects physiological hyperarousal consistent with panic or PTSD. The Sleep Disturbance subscale of the Psychological Discomfort scale indicates problems with sleep that could be characteristic of intrusive experiences of PTSD (nightmares, insomnia). The Fear and Worry subscale of the Psychological Discomfort scale measures generalized anxiety and specific fears. The Feelings of Alienation subscale of the Reality Distortion scale reflects symptoms of intrusive and/or unusual thoughts, behaviors, and feelings, along with feelings of disconnection from others or from reality. These symptoms overlap fairly well with PTSD symptom clusters of intrusion and avoidance. Elevations of all of these subscales would be expected for a child with PTSD, and analysis of the specific subscales could give a good idea of what types of symptoms the child is experiencing most intensely.

Syndrome-Specific Tests

Clinician-Administered

As a starting point in PTSD assessment, the ADIS-IV-C/P (see description in the SAD section of this chapter) may be helpful in documenting the child's anxiety symptomatology. Alternatively, the clinician-rated Children's PTSD Inventory can be used to assist with PTSD diagnosis using DSM-III criteria (Saigh, 1987). It is made up of four groups of items dichotomously scored according to presence or absence of symptoms. Field trials demonstrated an 85% classification rate of children diagnosed with PTSD.

Child-Report

General Anxiety Tests.   Revised Children's Manifest Anxiety Scale (RCMAS) scores are elevated in children with PTSD (Saigh, 1988; 1989a; 1989b) and may provide information about general levels of anxiety. On the MASC, children with PTSD show significant elevations of most scales. Typically, the highest elevations occur on the Separation/Panic scale, Physical Symptoms scale, and Anxious Coping subscale (repeatedly checking to see if one is safe) of the Harm Avoidance scale. The Social Anxiety scale and subscales may or may not be elevated, depending on the social nature of the traumatic event.

Post-Traumatic Disorder Symptom Rating Scales.   Many practitioners and researchers develop these rating scales by paraphrasing DSM-IV items in questionnaire form. Children or parents rate each item (symptom) based on its frequency or severity. A four-point scale (e.g., never, sometimes, often, almost always) is usually used for rating. There is no single well-researched, well-normed version of these scales for DSM-IV symptoms in children. Nevertheless, clinicians often find them helpful for quantifying the child's experience and the parent's observations.

Trauma Symptom Checklist for Children.   The Trauma Symptom Checklist for Children (TSCC; Briere, 1996) is a 54-item measure of common symptoms reported by children (age 8–16 years) who have experienced traumatic events. Items are rated on a 4-point scale. The TSCC yields 6 clinical subscales: Anxiety, Depression, Anger, Post-traumatic Stress, Dissociation, and Sexual Concerns (an alternative version of the TSCC does not include the Sexual Concerns scale). Norms are available based on a nonreferred (but nonrandom) sample, and comparison values based on clinical samples are also available. In addition to the clinical scales, the TSCC includes two validity scales measuring avoidance/denial of symptoms (Underresponse) and exaggeration of symptoms (Hyperresponse) (Briere, 1996).

☐   TREATMENT OPTIONS

Overview

PTSD can have a long-term impact on functioning, so early treatment is important (Eth, 1990). Generally, the principal aims in PTSD treatment techniques are to desensitize the individual to the memories of the event and to integrate the trauma into the individual's enduring schema of the world (Straker et al., 1988). Reenactment or exposure of some type in a safe environment is typically a necessary part of this process (Cantwell & Baker, 1989a). Additional goals for treatment are desensitization of the individual to environmental stimuli that are associated with the traumatic experience (Table 6.14).

In many cases, preventive intervention programs can be used to reduce the incidence of PTSD in a population of children who have been exposed to a traumatic stressor. Talking with a counselor about the event and related concerns in a supportive and safe atmosphere (debriefing) is a common component of prevention programs. Giving children a helping role and providing structure are additional elements of prevention programs.

TABLE 6.14   Treatment Options for Posttraumatic Stress Disorder

1. Behavioral Interventions
   a. Exposure treatments
   b. Provision of structure, predictability, and control
2. Psychotherapy
   a. Cognitive-psychodynamic psychotherapy
      (1) Psychoeducation about PTSD and stress recovery process
      (2) Management and reduction of stress
      (3) Articulation of affect
      (4) Processing the traumatic experience
      (5) Cognitive transformation
      (6) Mastery
      (7) Integration of the experience
3. Medication
   a. Tricyclic antidepressants and antihistamines for sleep and depressive symptoms
   b. Fluoxetine

Note: This outline of options summarizes major treatments covered in the text. Specific treatments are often combined into an intervention package. Refer to the text for additional descriptions of each treatment. This table is not necessarily an exhaustive list of all treatments available.

Behavioral Interventions

Exposure to stimuli associated with the traumatic event, usually by gradual desensitization, is a common behavioral method used to treat children and adolescents suffering from PTSD (Cantwell & Baker, 1989a; see description under Specific Phobia). Without exposure, the individual continues to receive reinforcement from the anxiety relief of avoiding stimuli associated with the trauma. In addition to exposure to environmental stimuli associated with the event, exposure therapies may also use memories or imagined scenes as stimuli.

Provision of structure, predictability, and control are used to stabilize the child and to restore a sense of normalcy to the child's experience. Parents and other caretakers are encouraged to keep to a regular schedule and to inform the child of upcoming events. Whenever possible, the child is given choices about the schedule or events. Caretakers are encouraged to give the child a clearly defined role to provide additional structure. Often, helping roles make children feel more competent and powerful. Affective modeling is a technique in which caretakers model calmness and control to the child; the child infers from this appearance of calmness and control that the environment is safe, predictable, and under control.

Psychotherapy

Cognitive-Behavioral Interventions

Cognitive-behavioral interventions teach the child coping techniques and strategies for dealing with intrusive thoughts and emotional states. Relaxation techniques, distraction, seeking social support, and cognitive restructuring are commonly used. Children and adolescents may also be encouraged to develop and keep to an activity schedule, in order to promote adequate functioning while also helping to distract them from memories of the trauma.

Another valuable component of cognitive-behavioral interventions for PTSD is psychoeducation. Children and parents are frequently relieved to hear that the child's nightmares, flat affect, emotional lability, and other symptoms are not unexpected after a traumatic event. Explanations of the etiology and treatment of PTSD give both child and parent a sense of predictability and control in the face of symptoms that are puzzling and overwhelming.

Cognitive-Psychodynamic Interventions

As noted earlier, a common goal of psychotherapy for PTSD is to achieve an integration of the memory of the traumatic event with the individual's existing schemas. Psychotherapy methods designed to achieve this goal have several components in common. First, they involve the systematic alternation of opening up (e.g., remembering) traumatic memories and then closing (e.g., removing from the individual's immediate awareness) the memories. "Opening" and "closing" occur based on the degree to which the individual is capable of reexperiencing the memories without being overwhelmed. Second, memories of the trauma are processed in detail. Often, individuals with PTSD will tell quick, unelaborated stories of their traumatic experience. PTSD-focused psychotherapy asks for detailed explanations of what happened, how the person felt, what he or she was thinking, and what he or she expected to happen next. To facilitate this recounting of the event, individuals are sometimes told to describe it in detail as though the therapist were watching it on a movie or reading it in a book. Detailed accounts assist with the reexperiencing of the trauma, although the psychotherapist must be sensitive to signs that the individual is becoming overwhelmed. At those times, avoidance and "closing" techniques (distraction, redirection, reframing, changing the topic of conversation, using relaxation techniques, physically leaving a situation) are used to prevent the overwhelmed state. Because of the higher risk of younger children becoming overwhelmed when remembering traumatic events, reexperiencing is frequently done in a much more permissive, less directive way, often using toys. Third, PTSD-focused therapies attempt to change the individual's cognitive-affective interpretation of the memories based on careful processing in the safe therapeutic environment. The person is able to change from being a participant in the memories to also being an observer of the memories. The observer role allows the person to control and access the memory without being overwhelmed. Finally, PTSD-focused therapies help the person to make sense out of the memory and to integrate it into his or her world-view.

Play Therapy

Nondirective or minimally directive play therapy is frequently used with younger children with PTSD. The establishment of a safe, structured (in the sense of having well-defined boundaries), but permissive environment frees the child to show his or her most influential thoughts, feelings, and schemas. In many cases, these will include issues related to the traumatic event. Common feelings and behaviors are aggression, anger, destructive impulses (although destruction of the therapy room or toys is not permitted), detachment, and injury/

illness. As the child plays out themes related to the traumatic event, he or she is better able to observe and work with them. The therapist facilitates by providing support and by acting as a safe person during the child's acting-out of the threatening thoughts, emotions, and beliefs. In many cases, after repetitive playing out of the themes related to the traumatic event, the child is able to change play to other topics, signaling that the trauma has less of an effect on his or her immediate thoughts and feelings. Although significant repetition in play should be expected (and usually not interfered with), some children become overly upset or fixed on a theme. In those cases, the therapist may want to model alternative behaviors, beliefs, and emotions, praising the child for imitating them.

Medication

Tricyclic antidepressants (imipramine) and antihistamines (diphenhydramine, hydroxyzine) have been used to manage some of the depressive and sleep symptoms arising from PTSD. Benzodiazepines such as diazepam, lorazepam, and alprazolam, on the other hand, may be used to treat severe hyperarousal and anxiety. Propranolol and clonadine have also shown promise in PTSD treatment, although cardiovascular side effects must be monitored (Sylvester & Kruesi, 1994). The most recent interest, however, has been in treatment with the selective serotonin reuptake inhibitors (SSRIs), especially fluoxetine (Prozac). Fluoxetine may help with the denial/avoidance symptoms of PTSD as well as with comorbid depressive symptoms (Amaya-Jackson & March, 1995).

■ Generalized Anxiety Disorder

☐ CLINICAL DESCRIPTION

Diagnostic Considerations

Criteria for childhood GAD include excessive worry and anxiety about a number of activities or events, difficulty controlling the worry, and a variety of worry-related symptoms such as restlessness, tiring easily, difficulty in maintaining concentration, irritability, body tension, and disturbed sleep. The frequency, intensity, and duration of GAD worries sets them apart from normal levels of anxiety. Children with GAD report experiencing multiple worries in numerous situations, without precipitating circumstances. In addition, they report difficulties controlling their worries and that their worries interfere with daily activity. GAD differs from other anxiety disorders because it involves multiple topics of worry that cannot be traced to a single issue (such as separation from parent or an acute stressor) or other disorder (such as depression). Furthermore, GAD worries tend to be about everyday or real-world problems as opposed to obsessions or delusional worries.

Strauss, Lease, Last, & Francis, (1988) found that other disorders often co-occur with GAD. In a 5–11-year-old group, SAD was found in 70% of GAD-diagnosed children, and Attention-Deficit/Hyperactivity Disorder had an occurrence rate of 35%. Among adolescents with GAD, a major depressive episode was found 47% of the time, and Specific Phobia was present in 41% of the sample. These percentages, however, may be inflated somewhat by failure to apply the exclusionary criteria of DSM-IV.

In preadolescent children, symptoms of anxiety and depression occur together more often than they do independently. This combined anxious-depressed syndrome is often referred to as "negative affectivity," and it may be a precursor to a later, more well-defined GAD or mood disorder. Hence, clinicians should expect to find some depressive symptoms in preadolescent children with GAD.

Lifetime prevalence of GAD is estimated to be 2–5% (American Psychiatric Association, 1994; Silverman & Ginsburg, 1995), and it is one of the more common anxiety disorders. At one anxiety disorders clinic, GAD was diagnosed in 52% of all children and adolescents presenting for treatment (Husain & Cantwell, 1991). The mean age of presentation for children with a GAD diagnosis is in early adolescence (12–14 years), with GAD occurring more frequently in adolescent than in preadolescent children. Boys and girls appear to be equivalently represented in the diagnosis, although GAD is more prevalent in females in adulthood (American Psychiatric Association, 1994; Last, Hersen, Kazdin, Finkelstein, & Strauss, 1987; Silverman & Ginsburg, 1995).

Appearance and Features

Appearance and features of GAD are listed in Table 6.15. Younger children commonly report anxiety in more circumscribed situations than do older children (e.g., in the presence of a particular person). Anxiety topics appear to generalize to more people and situations with increasing age, perhaps reflecting children's growing social sphere and cognitive ability. Typical topics of GAD worries range from the mundane (school performance, performance

---

TABLE 6.15 Appearance and Features of Generalized Anxiety Disorder

COMMON FEATURES

1. Excessive worry about multiple topics
2. Worry is not cued by specific stimuli
3. Restlessness, irritability, difficulty concentrating, tension, sleep problems, and hyperarousal
4. Overly serious presentation
5. Perfectionism/overachievement
6. Constant seeking of reassurance

OCCASIONAL FEATURES

1. Somatic complaints
2. Self-consciousness
3. School avoidance

Note: The features listed in the table are often seen but are not universal. Some features may be diagnostically relevant or required, whereas others may not be required for diagnosis. "Common" features are typical of the disorder; "occasional" features appear frequently but are not necessarily seen in a majority of cases.

in sports or the arts, being on time, animals, the environment, rejection by peers) to the unusual (nuclear war, natural disasters, being condemned for sins, being raped or killed).

Children with GAD seem unable to relax. They carry around a constant level of generalized tension, which is sometimes apparent in motor restlessness (e.g., constant movement, nail biting, or knuckle popping), emotional reactivity (crying), hypersensitivity, and vulnerability to stress. They may exhibit an exaggerated emotional response to stressors, and their coping skills are often poor. Somatic complaints are frequently present in the form of stomachaches, headaches, or a general malaise (Last, 1989b), but these decrease with increasing age.

Parents often describe their child with GAD as "a worrier." Many children with GAD have a pseudomature appearance, with a speaking style and interests that better fit adults. Often they experience greater comfort in the company of adults than peers. Perfectionistic tendencies, conformity, and self-consciousness are commonly present. To counter self-doubts, children with GAD may repeatedly seek reassurances and approval. Because they tend to be hard-working and conforming, children with GAD rarely come to clinical attention at the request of school personnel (American Psychiatric Association, 1994; Last, 1989a, 1989b).

Children having mild GAD may continue to function at a fairly high level while enduring symptoms such as difficulty falling asleep due to worries, problems interacting with peers, withdrawal, avoidance of anxiety-provoking situations, hypersensitivity, and some interference with academic performance. Those with severe GAD, on the other hand, may experience heightened anxiety in most areas of functioning, with associated major depression and suicidal ideation. GAD may persist through the life cycle if left untreated, but its course appears to be quite variable (American Psychiatric Association, 1994; Silverman & Ginsberg, 1995). At least one study (Cantwell & Baker, 1989b) found remission of symptoms in about one in four children with GAD over a 4- to 5-year follow-up period.

Etiology

GAD shows some familial association and responds to anxiolytic medication, suggesting a biological component such as physiological tenseness or hypersensitivity (American Psychiatric Association, 1994; Last, 1989a). In addition, several components of early temperament (reactivity, intensity, adaptability) appear to bear some resemblance to GAD symptoms.

Behavioral theories suggest that GAD may develop out of experiences in which the child was surprised (punished) by unexpected occurrences. Expected worries, on the other hand, did not occur and were, therefore, reinforced (e.g., the feared situation did not come to pass if the child worried). Hence, the child learned that worry was related to a lack of negative outcomes, whereas avoidance or lack of worry was related to unexpected negative outcomes.

Cognitive theories of the etiology of GAD suggest that GAD develops out of multiple negative experiences that are internalized by the child into a view of the world as an unfriendly, worrisome place. Studies show that, compared to nonanxious peers, anxious children engage in more negative interpretations of events, blame themselves more for negative events, and pay more attention to negative than positive aspects of events (Silverman & Ginsberg, 1995). As a result, they expect more problems to emerge from everyday events, and they feel threatened by neutral stimuli. These expectations and thoughts lead to anxiety about their environment.

Social learning theories of the development of GAD hold that anxious children learn their anxious behavior and thoughts by observing and modeling their anxious parents. As noted earlier, anxiety disorders tend to run in families. Therefore, children at risk for GAD or other anxiety disorders are often exposed to anxious parents. It does appear that children with GAD have a higher risk of family dysfunction, but there is no clear pattern that distinguishes families of children with GAD from families of children with other psychiatric disorders (Silverman & Ginsberg, 1995).

☐   ASSESSMENT PATTERNS

Broad Assessment Strategies

A sample assessment battery for childhood anxiety disorders (including GAD) is shown in Table 6.3.

Psychological Assessment

Clinician-Administered.   MMPI/MMPI-A scores for adolescents with GAD are likely to show elevations on scales 2, 3, and 7. These scales reflect the anxiety, somatization, and dissatisfaction typical of adolescents with GAD. Given the potential for chronic hyperarousal, scale 9 is sometimes relatively high. A high F scale is expected if GAD worries and somatic complaints are unusual or lead to unusual ideas and sensations (Meyer & Deitsch, 1996). High scale 0 may reflect social anxiety and social withdrawal as a result of performance fears. Scales 4 and 6 are likely to be moderate to low because of the perfectionism and conformity common in GAD adolescents.

The worries and concerns of children with GAD will often affect their projective testing results. Negative outcomes and worried characters, for example, are often seen on the TAT, reflecting the child's generalized worries. Defensive children with GAD may tell overly rosy or unelaborated stories on the TAT. The progression of the plots in the TAT stories may be helpful in understanding the child's expectations about the progression of social interactions and life events. Children with GAD will often be overly exact, elaborate, and perfectionistic in their TAT and Rorschach responses.

Behavioral Assessment

Parent- and Teacher-Report.   The CBCL and TRF include numerous items relating to fears and worries. Parent and teacher response to these items may indicate the extent to which a child suffers from GAD and the content of GAD worries. The fears and worries of GAD tend to elevate the Anxious/Depressed and Thought Problems subscales of the CBCL and TRF. The Somatic Complaints score can be used to assess the degree to which GAD symptoms are associated with somatization. Additional elevations on the Withdrawal and Social Problems subscales could indicate difficulties with social interaction, which may result from

GAD. Elevations on the Attention Problems subscale suggest that GAD is interfering with concentration and task focus or that the child's presentation is quite immature. Alternatively, such an elevation could indicate the presence of a co-occurring attention deficit. In some cases, children attempt to hide their GAD symptoms at school, fearing the negative stigma that would occur if they were identified as a worrier. Children who are successful in this concealment may only show an elevation of the Withdrawal and/or Attention Problems subscales on the TRF.

The ECI-4, CSI-4, and ASI-4 include questions measuring the "Category A" (excessive worry), "Category B" (difficult to control worry), and "Category C" (specific anxiety symptoms) symptoms of the GAD diagnosis. Because these symptoms overlap with other diagnoses (especially anxiety and mood disorders), endorsement of these items is not necessarily consistent with the GAD diagnosis. However, endorsement of the full range of items on an SI-4 GAD subscale strongly indicates that GAD should be further investigated as a potential diagnosis.

On the BASC, children with GAD significantly elevate the Anxiety subscale, which includes items about general worries, worries about what others think, performance fears, and specific worries. Elevation of the Depression subscale is also common, reflecting self-doubt, hypersensitivity, and poor coping skills. Elevation of the Withdrawal subscale can indicate that a child with GAD is withdrawing from social interaction as a way of managing or avoiding worry. A low score on the Adaptability subscale is also typical of GAD and indicates hyperreactivity and difficulty adjusting to changes.

The CPRS Anxious-Shy subscale includes three items suggestive of general fearfulness, but these are combined with items that are more typical of social phobia, separation anxiety, and specific phobia. Hence, a child with GAD and associated symptoms in these other areas (this is the most common presentation of GAD) would show the highest elevation of this subscale. The CTRS Anxious-Shy subscale, on the other hand, includes more items reflecting sensitivity and only one item pertaining to general fearfulness. Nevertheless, children with GAD generally show the sensitivity symptoms that result in elevation of this CTRS subscale.

Child-Report. On the self-report versions of the BASC and Achenbach scales (YSR), children with GAD show generally the same profile pattern as for the parent and teacher versions of these scales. Exceptions to this rule occur on the BASC, which has some different subscales for the self-report version as compared to the parent- and teacher-report versions. The BASC-SRP does not contain Withdrawal and Adaptability subscales. Rather, children with GAD tend to elevate the Sense of Inadequacy subscale while showing low scores on the Self-Reliance subscale (reflecting self-doubt, fears of failure, and difficulty making decisions).

On the PIY, children with GAD often elevate the Psychological Discomfort scale. Of the three subscales comprising the Psychological Discomfort scale, the Fear and Worry subscale contains the most items pertaining to general worries and sensitivity (6 out of 15 total items on the subscale). An additional five items on the Fear and Worry subscale ask about loneliness, crying, and moodiness, which are also somewhat characteristic of childhood GAD. The Sleep Disturbance subscale of the Psychological Discomfort scale provides additional information relevant to the sleep problems symptom of GAD.

Syndrome-Specific Tests

Clinician-Administered

Because children with GAD report a variety of worries, they may appear to qualify for one of several anxiety disorder diagnoses. Use of the ADIS-IV-C/P (see description in the SAD section of this chapter) may assist with differential diagnosis and identification of comorbid Anxiety Disorders. Furthermore, the ADIS-IV-C/P allows systematic evaluation of a variety of anxiety symptoms that may be creating problems for the child.

Child-Report

General Anxiety Tests.   Although most of the general anxiety tests (described earlier in this chapter) lack a specific subscale that corresponds specifically to GAD, high scores on several subscales would be characteristic of (although not specific to) GAD. The SCARED has a General Anxiety subscale that would be expected to be elevated by most children with GAD. For children with comorbid somatic symptoms, the SCARED Panic/Somatic subscale may also be elevated. Other SCARED subscales may also show elevations, depending on the child's specific symptoms (Birmaher et al., 1997). The FSSC-R has been found to reliably discriminate among GAD, SAD, and Social Phobia in children and adolescents in an anxiety disorders clinic (Last et al., 1989). One of its factors, Fear of Failure and Criticism, is particularly likely to be elevated in children with GAD.

☐   TREATMENT OPTIONS

Behavioral Interventions and Cognitive-Behavioral Psychotherapy

A typical treatment package for GAD combines behavioral and cognitive components in such a way as to treat the behavioral, physiological, and cognitive aspects of the disorder, using the following components (Husain & Kashani, 1992; Kendall & Treadwell, 1996; Silverman & Ginsburg, 1995; Thyer, 1991) (Table 6.16):

1. Psychoeducation about symptoms, causes, and treatments (especially cognitive and behavioral) of anxiety disorders. Identification of physiological, cognitive, situational, and behavioral cues of anxiety is learned. This education often also includes family members.
2. Graduated exposure to feared situations (desensitization).
3. Reinforcement for the absence of worrying or anxious behavior.
4. Modeling by parents and therapist of adaptive coping skills and calm, rational responses to threats.
5. Relaxation techniques (e.g., progressive muscle relaxation, visual imagery).
6. Positive self-statements and self-instructional training for problem solving and self-control in threatening situations.

7. Cognitive control strategies in which coping strategies are employed in order to achieve a state of relaxation and a more positive appraisal of anxiety-provoking situations. These include strategies such as self-talk and cognitive restructuring.

8. Social skills training, if needed to address social performance fears.

Clearly, there is substantial overlap between these treatment strategies and the strategies commonly used for other anxiety disorders (each of these treatment components was described at length in earlier sections of this chapter). In part, this reflects the overlap of GAD characteristics, etiology, and symptomatology with symptoms of other anxiety disorders. The overlapping treatments also show the common cognitive-behavioral phenomonology that crosses most of the anxiety disorders. Treatment programs based on these components have been shown to be effective in reducing GAD symptomatology (Eisen & Silverman, 1993; Kendall & Treadwell, 1996).

Kendall (1992) has developed a manualized treatment entitled Coping Cat for GAD and similar disorders. The Coping Cat program incorporates all of the major elements of treatment for GAD described previously in an attractive and structured format for children. Education, problem-solving/coping training, and exposure are the core interventions in the Coping Cat treatment, with repeated practice in a 16-session format. Research on the Coping Cat treatment and its components has yielded very promising results, and the Coping Cat program is probably the most well developed and validated of the cognitive-behavioral treatments for GAD (Ollendick & King, 1998).

The use of psychodynamic or nonspecific therapies in isolation (e.g., play or supportive treatment without concomitant behavior therapy) does not seem indicated for children

---

TABLE 6.16   Treatment Options for Generalized Anxiety Disorder

1. Cognitive-Behavioral Interventions
   a. Psychoeducation
   b. Exposure
   c. Reinforcement strategies
   d. Modeling
   e. Relaxation
   f. Coping strategies
   g. Social skills training
2. Family Interventions
   a. Family behavioral interventions
   b. Family psychoeducation
   c. Family therapy
3. Medication
   a. Selective serotonin reuptake inhibitors
   b. Tricyclic antidepressants

Note: This outline of options summarizes major treatments covered in the text. Specific treatments are often combined into an intervention package. Refer to the text for additional descriptions of each treatment. This table is not necessarily an exhaustive list of all treatments available.

with GAD because there is little research to support their efficacy (Ollendick & King, 1998).

Family Interventions

Involvement of the family in behavioral and cognitive treatments appears to improve the effectiveness of these interventions (Ollendick & King, 1998). Family members can be trained to deliver reinforcement (praise and tangible reinforcers) for goal attainment and to ignore overanxious behavior. Parents also serve as models of effective coping and management of anxiety-producing situations. Affective modeling, in which parents use their own calm emotional states to promote calmness in the child, is another common component of family involvement in cognitive-behavioral treatment.

Medication

The selective serotonin reuptake inhibitors (fluoxetine [Prozac], sertraline [Zoloft], etc.) and venlafaxine (Effexor) are among the newer medications to be used in individual cases of GAD in children and adolescents. Benzodiazepines and tricyclic antidepressants have also proven useful in the treatment of anxiety symptoms such as those experienced in GAD. Sedating medications such as antihistamines (diphenhydramine, hydroxyzine) may be effective in short-term treatment of GAD anxiety occurring with insomnia (Sylvester & Kruesi, 1994). Although successfully used in adults with GAD, long-term use of benzodiazepines in children and adolescents is not recommended due to inhibition of the secretion of growth hormone and problematic side effects (Thyer, 1991). Medication is probably best used for GAD when it is combined with cognitive-behavioral therapy.

■ References

Abel, J. L. (1993). Exposure with response prevention and serotonergic antidepressants in the treatment of obsessive compulsive disorder: A review and implications for interdisciplinary treatment. *Behavior Research and Therapy, 31,* 463–478.

Albano, A. M., & Barlow, D. H. (1996). Breaking the vicious cycle: Cognitive-behavioral group treatment for socially anxious youth. In E. D. Hibbs & P. S. Jensen (Eds.), *Psychosocial treatments for child and adolescent disorders: Empirically based strategies for clinical practice.* Washington, DC: American Psychological Association.

Albano, A. M., March, J. S., & Piacentini, J. (1999). Obsessive-compulsive disorder. In R. T. Ammerman, M. Hersen & C. G. Last (Eds.), *Handbook of prescriptive treatments for children and adolescents* (2nd ed.). Boston: Allyn & Bacon.

Amaya-Jacksoln, L., & March, J. S. (1995). Posttraumatic stress disorder. In J. S. March (Ed.), *Anxiety disorders in children and adolescents.* New York: Guilford.

American Psychiatric Association. (1994). *Diagnostic and statistical manual of mental disorders, fourth edition.* Washington, DC: Author.

Anderson, J. C., Williams, S., McGee, R., & Silva, P. A. (1987). DSM-III disorders in pre-adolescent children. *Archives of General Psychiatry, 44,* 69–76.

Beidel, D., & Morris, T. L. (1995). Social phobia. In J. March (Ed.), *Anxiety disorders in children and adolescents.* New York: Guilford.

Beidel, D. C., Turner, S. M., & Fink, C. M. (1996). Assessment of childhood social phobia: Construct, convergent, and discriminative validity of the Social Phobia and Anxiety Inventory for Children (SPAI-C). *Psychological Assessment, 8,* 235–240.

Berg, C. J., Rapoport, J. L., & Flament, M. (1986). The Leyton Obsessional Inventory—Child Version. *Journal of the American Academy of Child Psychiatry, 25,* 85–91.

Berg, C. J., Whitaker, A., Davies, M., Flament, M. F., & Rapoport, J. L. (1988). The survey form of the Leyton Obsessional Inventory—Child Version: Norms from an epidemiological study. *Journal of the American Academy of Child and Adolescent Psychiatry, 27,* 759–763.

Bernstein, G. A. (1990). Anxiety disorders. In B. D. Garfinkel, G. A. Carlson, & E. B. Weller (Eds.), *Psychiatric disorders in children and adolescents* (pp. 64–83). Philadelphia, PA: W. B. Saunders Company.

Bernstein, G. A., & Borchardt, C. M. (1991). Anxiety disorders of childhood and adolescence: A critical review. *Journal of the American Academy of Child and Adolescent Psychiatry, 30,* 519–532.

Bernstein, G. A., Garfinkel, B. D., & August, G. J. (1986). Visual analogue scale for anxiety, revised. *Scientific proceedings for the annual meeting* (Vol. 2). American Academy of Child and Adolescent Psychiatry.

Bezchlibnyk-Butler, K. Z., & Jeffries, J. J. (1997). *Clinical handbook of psychotropic drugs* (7th ed.). Toronto: Hogrefe & Huber.

Birmaher, B., Khetarpal, S., Brent, D., Cully, M., Balach, L., Kaufman, J., & Neer, S. M. (1997). The Screen for Child Anxiety Related Emotional Disorders (SCARED): Scale construction and psychometric characteristics. *Journal of the American Academy of Child and Adolescent Psychiatry, 36,* 545–553.

Birmaher, B., Waterman, S., Ryan, N., Cully, M., Balach, L., Ingram, J., & Brodsky, M. (1994). Fluoxetine for childhood anxiety disorders. *Journal of the American Academy of Child and Adolescent Psychiatry, 33,* 993–999.

Black, B. (1995). Separation anxiety disorder and panic disorder. In J. S. March (Ed.), *Anxiety disorders in children and adolescents.* New York: Guilford

Blanco, R. F., & Bogacki, D. F. (1988). *Prescriptions for children with learning and adjustment problems: A consultant's desk reference* (3rd ed.). Springfield, IL: Charles C. Thomas.

Boll, T. (1993). *Children's Category Test.* San Antonio, TX: Psychological Corporation.

Bowen, R. C., Offord, D. R., & Boyle, M. H. (1990). The prevalence of overanxious disorder and separation anxiety disorder: Results from the Ontario Child Health

Study. *Journal of the American Academy of Child and Adolescent Psychiatry, 29,* 753–758.

Bowlby, J. (1973). *Attachment and loss: Vol. 2. Separation.* New York: Basic Books.

Briere, J. N. (1996). *Trauma Symptom Checklist for Children* professional manual. Odessa, FL: Psychological Assessment Resources.

Cantwell, D. P., & Baker, L. (1987). The prevalence of anxiety in children with communication disorders. *Journal of Anxiety Disorders, 1,* 239–248.

Cantwell, D. P., & Baker, L. (1989a). Anxiety disorders. In L. K. G. Hsu & M. Hersen (Eds.), *Recent developments in adolescent psychiatry* (pp. 162–199). New York: John Wiley & Sons.

Cantwell, D. P., & Baker, L. (1989b). Stability and natural history of DSM-III childhood diagnoses. *Journal of the American Academy of Child and Adolescent Psychiatry, 29,* 691–700.

Cantwell, D. P., & Baker, L. (1990). Stability and natural history of DSM-III childhood diagnoses. In S. Chess & M. E. Hertzig (Eds.), *Annual progress in child psychiatry and child development, 1990* (pp. 311–332). New York: Brunner/Mazel Publishers.

Casat, C. D. (1988). Childhood anxiety disorders: A review of the possible relationship to adult panic disorder and agoraphobia. *Journal of Anxiety Disorders, 2,* 51–60.

Deblinger, E., McLeer, S. V., Atkins, M. S., Ralphe, D., & Foa, E. (1989). Posttraumatic stress in sexually abused, physically abused, and nonabused children. *Child Abuse and Neglect, 13,* 403–408.

Eisen, A. R., & Silverman, W. K. (1993). Should I relax or change my thoughts?: A preliminary examination of cognitive therapy, relaxation training, and their combination with overanxious children. *Journal of Cognitive Psychotherapy: An International Quarterly, 7,* 265–280.

Emmelkamp, P. M. G., Kloek, J., & Blaauw, E. (1992). Obsessive-compulsive disorders. In P. H. Wilson (Ed.), *Principles and practice of relapse prevention* (pp. 213–234). New York: Guilford.

Eth, S. (1990). Posttraumatic stress disorder in childhood. In M. Hersen & C. G. Last (Eds.), *Handbook of child and adult psychopathology: A longitudinal perspective* (pp. 263–274). New York: Pergamon.

Famularo, R., Kinscherff, R., & Fenton, T. (1990). Symptom differences in acute and chronic presentation of childhood posttraumatic stress disorder. *Child Abuse & Neglect, 14,* 439–444.

Foa, E., & Steketee, G. (1989). Obsessive-compulsive disorder. In C. Lindemann (Ed.), *Handbook of phobia therapy* (pp. 181–206). Northvale, NJ: Jason Aronson.

Francis, G., Last, C. G., & Strauss, C. C. (1987). Expression of separation anxiety disorder: The roles of age and gender. *Child Psychiatry and Human Development, 18,* 82–89.

Francis, G., Last, C. G., & Strauss, C. C. (1992). Avoidant disorder and social phobia in children and adolescents. *Journal of the American Academy of Child and Adolescent Psychiatry, 31,* 1086–1089.

Francis, G., & Ollendick, T. H. (1988). Social withdrawal. In M. Hersen & C. G. Last (Eds.), *Child behavior therapy casebook* (pp. 31–41). New York: Plenum.

Golden, J. C. (1978). *Stroop Color and Word Test.* Chicago, IL: Stoelting Co.

Goodman, W. K., Price, L. H., & Rasmussen, S. A. (1989a). The Yale-Brown Obsessive Compulsive Scale, I: Development, use, and reliability. *Archives of General Psychiatry, 46,* 1006–1011.

Goodman, W. K., Price, L. H., & Rasmussen, S. A. (1989b). The Yale-Brown Obsessive Compulsive Scale, II: Validity. *Archives of General Psychiatry, 46,* 1012–1016.

Heaton, R. K., Chelune, G. J., Talley, J. L., Kay, G. G., & Curtis, G. (1993). *Wisconsin Card Sorting Test (WCST) Manual Revised and Expanded.* Odessa, FL: Psychological Assessment Resources.

Hodgson, R. J., & Rachman, S. (1977). Obsessive compulsive complaints. *Behavior Research and Therapy, 15,* 389–395.

Holzer, J. C., Goodman, W. K., McDougle, C. J., Boyarsky, B. K., Leckman, J. F., & Price, L. H. (1994). Differential symptoms in obsessive compulsive disorder with and without a chronic tic disorder. *British Journal of Psychiatry, 164,* 469–473.

Horowitz, M. J. (1986). *Stress response syndromes.* New York: Jason Aronson.

Husain, S. A., & Cantwell, D. P. (1991). *Fundamentals of child and adolescent psychopathology.* Washington, DC: American Psychiatric Press.

Husain, S. A., & Kashani, J. H. (1992). *Anxiety disorders in children and adolescents.* Washington, DC: American Psychiatric Press.

Insel, T. R. (1992). Toward a neuroanatomy of obsessive-compulsive disorder. *Archives of General Psychiatry, 49,* 739–744.

Jensen, J. B. (1990). Obsessive-compulsive disorder in children and adolescents. In B. D. Garfinkel, G. A. Carlson, & E. B. Weller (Eds.), *Psychiatric disorders in children and adolescents* (pp. 84–105). Philadelphia, PA: W. B. Saunders.

Johnson, S. B., & Melamed, B. G. (1979). Assessment and treatment of children's fears. In B. B. Lahey & A. E. Kazdin (Eds.), *Advances in clinical child psychology* (Vol. 2, pp. 108–139). New York: Plenum.

Kane, M. T., & Kendall, P. C. (1989). Anxiety disorders in children: A multiple-baseline evaluations of a cognitive-behavioral treatment. *Behavior Therapy, 20,* 499–508.

Kaplan, H. I., & Sadock, B. J. (1988). *Synopsis of psychiatry: Behavioral sciences clinical psychiatry* (5th ed.). Baltimore: Williams & Wilkins.

Kashani, J. H., & Orvaschel, H. (1988). Anxiety disorders in mid-adolescence: A community sample. *American Journal of Psychiatry, 145,* 960–964.

Kaufman, A. S., & Kaufman, N. L. (1990). *Kaufman Brief Intelligence Test.* Circle Pines, MN: American Guidance Service.

Kendall, P. C. (1992). *Coping cat.* Available from the author.

Kendall, P. C. (1994). Treating anxiety disorders in children: Results of a randomized clinical trial. *Journal of Consulting and Clinical Psychology, 62,* 100–110.

Kendall, P. C., & Ronan, K. R. (1989). *The Children's Anxious Self-Statement Questionnaire (CASSQ).* Available from the first author, Psychology Department, Temple University, Philadelphia, PA 19122.

Kendall, P. C., & Treadwell, K. R. H. (1996). Cognitive-behavioral treatment for childhood anxiety disorders. In E. D. Hibbs & P. S. Jensen (Eds.), *Psychosocial treatments for child and adolescent disorders: Empirically-based strategies for clinical practice.* Washington, DC: American Psychological Association.

Kennedy, W. A. (1965). School phobia: Rapid treatment of fifty cases. *Journal of Abnormal Psychology, 70,* 285–289.

King, N. J., Gullone, E., & Tonge, B. J. (1991). Childhood fears and anxiety disorders. *Behaviour-Change, 8,* 124–135.

King, R. A., Leonard, H., & March, J. (1998). Practice parameters for the assessment and treatment of children and adolescents with Obsessive-Compulsive Disorder. *Journal of the American Academy of Child and Adolescent Psychiatry, 37* (Supplement), 27–45.

Klein, R. G., Koplewicz, H. S., & Kanner, A. (1992). Imipramine treatment of children with separation anxiety disorder. *Journal of the American Academy of Child and Adolescent Psychiatry, 31,* 21–28.

Koplewicz, H. S. (1989). Childhood phobias. In C. Lindemann (Ed.), *Handbook of phobia therapy* (pp. 147–151). Northvale, NJ: Jason Aronson, Inc.

LaGreca, A. M., Dandes, S. K., Wick, P., Shaw, K., & Stone, W. L. (1988). Development of the Social Anxiety Scale for Children: Reliability and current validity. *Journal of Clinical Child Psychology, 17,* 84–91.

LaGreca, A. M., & Stone, W. L. (1993). Social Anxiety Scale for Children—Revised: Factor structure and concurrent validity. *Journal of Clinical Child Psychology, 22,* 17–27.

Last, C. G. (1988). Separation anxiety. In M. Hersen & C. G. Last (Eds.), *Child behavior therapy casebook,* (pp. 11–17). New York: Plenum Press.

Last, C. G. (1989a). Anxiety disorders. In T. H. Ollendick & M. Hersen (Eds.), *Handbook of child psychopathology* (2nd ed., pp. 219–227). New York: Plenum Press.

Last, C. G. (1989b). Anxiety disorders of childhood or adolescence. In C. G. Last & M. Hersen (Eds.), *Handbook of child psychiatric diagnosis* (pp. 156–169). New York: John Wiley & Sons.

Last, C. G., Francis, G., Hersen, M., Kazdin, A. E., & Strauss, C. C. (1987). Separation anxiety and school phobia: A comparison using DSM-III criteria. *American Journal of Psychiatry, 144,* 653–657.

Last, C. G., Francis, G., & Strauss, C. C. (1989). Assessing fears in anxiety-disordered children with the Revised Fear Survey Schedule for Children (FSSC-R). *Journal of Clinical Child Psychology, 18,* 137–141.

Last, C. G., Hersen, M., Kazdin, A. E., Finkelstein, R., & Strauss, C. C. (1987). Comparison of DSM-III separation anxiety and overanxious disorders: Demographic characteristics and patterns of comorbidity. *Journal of the American Academy of Child and Adolescent Psychiatry, 26,* 527–531.

Last, C. G., Hersen, M., Kazdin, A. E., Francis, G., & Grubb, H. J. (1987). Psychiatric illness in the mothers of anxious children. *American Journal of Psychiatry, 144,* 1580–1583.

Last, C. G., Phillips, J. E., & Statfeld, A. (1987). Childhood anxiety disorders in mothers and their children. *Child Psychiatry and Human Development, 18,* 103–112.

Last, C. G., Strauss, C. C., & Francis, G. (1987). Comorbidity among childhood anxiety disorders. *Journal of Nervous and Mental Diseases, 175,* 726–730.

LeCroy, C. W. (1994). Social skills training. In C. W. LeCroy (Ed.), *Handbook of child and adolescent treatment manuals.* New York: Lexington.

Leonard, H. L., Swedo, S. E., & Rapoport, J. L. (1991). Diagnosis and treatment of obsessive-compulsive disorder in children and adolescents. In M. T. Pato & J. Zohar (Eds.), *Current treatments of obsessive-compulsive disorder* (pp. 87–102). Washington, DC: American Psychiatric Press, Inc.

Lonigan, C. J., Anthony, J. L., & Shannon, M. P. (1998). Diagnostic efficacy of posttraumatic symptoms in children exposed to disaster. *Journal of Clinical Child Psychology, 27,* 255–267.

March, J. (1997). *Multidimensional Anxiety Scale for Children technical manual.* North Tonawanda, NY: MHS.

March, J. S., & Mulle, K. (1993). *How I ran OCD off my land.* Unpublished manuscript, Duke University Medical Center, Durham, NC.

March, J. S., & Mulle, K. (1996). Banishing OCD: Cognitive-behavioral psychotherapy for Obsessive-Compulsive Disorders. In E. D. Hibbs & P. S. Jensen (Eds.), *Psychosocial treatments for child and adolescent disorders: Empirically-based strategies for clinical practice.* Washington, DC: American Psychological Association.

Mattison, R. E. (1992). Anxiety disorders. In S. R. Hooper, G. W. Hynd, & R. E. Mattison (Eds.), *Child psychopathology: Diagnostic criteria and clinical assessment* (pp. 179–202). Hillsdale, NJ: Lawrence Erlbaum Associates, Publishers.

McCarthy, P. R., & Foa, E. B. (1988). Obsessive-compulsive disorder. In M. Hersen & C. G. Last (Eds.), *Child behavior therapy casebook* (pp. 55–69). New York: Plenum Press.

McDougle, C. J., Goodman, W. K., Leckman, J. F., Lee, N. C., Heninger, G. R., & Price, L. H. (1994). Haloperidol addition in fluvoxamine refractory obsessive compulsive disorder: A double-blind, placebo-controlled study in patients with and without tics. *Archives of General Psychiatry, 51,* 302–308.

Meyer, R. G., & Deitsch, S. E. (1996). *The clinician's handbook* (4th ed.). Boston: Allyn & Bacon.

Morris, R. J., Kratochwill, T. R., & Aldridge, K. (1988). Fears and phobias. In J. C. Witt, S. N. Elliott, & F. M.

Gresham (Eds.), *Handbook of behavior therapy in education* (pp. 679–717). New York: Plenum Press.

Mowrer, O. H. (1939). A stimulus-response analysis of anxiety and its role as a reinforcing agent. *Psychological Review, 46,* 553–565.

Nelson, W. M., III (1981). A cognitive-behavioral treatment for disproportionate dental anxiety and pain: A case study. *Journal of Clinical Child Psychology, 10,* 79–82.

Ollendick, T. H. (1983). Reliability and validity of the Revised Fear Survey Schedule for Children (FSSC-R). *Behavior Research and Therapy, 21,* 685–692.

Ollendick, T. H. (1998). Panic disorder in children and adolescents: New developments, new directions. *Journal of Clinical Child Psychology, 27,* 234–245.

Ollendick, T. H., & Cerny, J. A. (1981). *Clinical behavior therapy with children.* New York: Plenum Press.

Ollendick, T. H., & King, N. J. (1998). Empirically supported treatments for children with phobic and anxiety disorders. *Journal of Clinical Child Psychology, 27,* 156–167.

Ollendick, T. H., Matson, J. L., & Helsel, W. J. (1985). Fears in children and adolescents: Normative data. *Behavior Research and Therapy, 4,* 465–467.

Popper, C. W. (1993). Psychopharmacologic treatment of anxiety disorders in adolescents and children. *Journal of Clinical Psychiatry, 54,* 52–63.

Pynoos, R. S. (1990). Posttraumatic stress disorder in children and adolescents. In B. D. Garfinkel, G. A. Carlson, & E. B. Weller (Eds.), *Psychiatric disorders in children and adolescents* (pp. 48–63). Philadelphia, PA: W. B. Saunders.

Rachman, S. & Hodgson, R. J. (1980). *Obsessions and compulsions.* Englewood Cliffs, NJ: Prentice-Hall.

Rapoport, J. L. (1988). Childhood obsessive-compulsive disorder. In S. Chess, A. Thomas, & M. E. Hertzig (Eds.), *Annual progress in child psychiatry and child development, 1987* (pp. 437–445). New York: Brunner/Mazel Publishers.

Reynolds, C. R., & Richmond, B. O. (1978). What I think and feel: A revised measure of children's manifest anxiety. *Journal of Abnormal Child Psychology, 6,* 271–280.

Roth, S., & Lebowitz, L. (1988). The experience of sexual trauma. *Journal of Traumatic Stress, 1,* 79–105.

Rutter, M., Tizard, J., & Whitmore, S. (1970). *Education, Health and Behavior.* London: Longman.

Saigh, P. A. (1987). The development and validation of the Children's Posttraumatic Stress Disorders Inventory.

Paper presented at the meeting of the Association for the Advancement of Behavior Therapy, Boston, MA.

Saigh, P. A. (1988). The validity of the DSM-III posttraumatic stress disorder classification as applied to adolescents. *Professional School Psychology, 3,* 283–290.

Saigh, P. A. (1989a). A comparative analysis of the affective and behavioral symptomology of traumatized and nontraumatized children. *Journal of School Psychology, 27,* 247–255.

Saigh, P. A. (1989b). The validity of the DSM-III posttraumatic stress disorder classification as applied to children. *Journal of Abnormal Psychology, 98,* 189–192.

Silverman, W. K., & Albano, A. M. (1996). *The Anxiety Disorders Interview Schedule for DSM-IV, Child and Parent Versions.* Albany, NY: Graywind Publications.

Silverman, W. K., & Ginsburg, G. (1995). Specific phobias and generalized anxiety disorder. In J. March (Ed.), *Anxiety disorders in children and adolescents.* New York: Guilford.

Simeon, J. G., & Ferguson, H. B. (1987). Alprazolam effects in children with anxiety disorders. *Canadian Journal of Psychiatry, 32,* 570–574.

Spielberger, C. D., Edwards, C. D., Lushene, R. E., Montouri, J., & Platzek, D. (1973). *Preliminary manual for the State-Trait Anxiety Inventory for Children.* Palo Alto, CA: Consulting Psychologists Press.

Straker, G., Moosa, F., & Sanctuaries Counselling Team. (1988). Posttraumatic stress disorder: A reaction to state-supported child abuse and neglect. *Child Abuse & Neglect, 12,* 383–395.

Strauss, C. C., & Francis, G. (1989). Phobic disorders. In C. G. Last & M. Hersen (Eds.), *Handbook of child psychiatric diagnosis* (pp. 170–190). New York: John Wiley & Sons.

Strauss, C. C., Lease, C. A., Last, C. G., & Francis, G. (1988). Overanxious disorder: An examination of developmental differences. *Journal of Abnormal Child Psychology, 16,* 433–443.

Swedo, S. E., & Rapoport, J. L. (1988). Obsessive compulsive disorder in childhood. In M. Hersen & C. G. Last (Eds.), *Handbook of child and adult psychopathology: A longitudinal perspective* (pp. 211–219). New York: Pergamon Press.

Swedo, S. E., Rapoport, J. L., Cheslow, D. L., Leonard, H. L., Ayoub, E. M., Hosier, D. M., & Wald, E. R. (1989). High prevalence of obsessive-compulsive symptoms in patients with Sydenham's chorea. *American Journal of Psychiatry, 146,* 246–249.

Sylvester, C. E., & Kruesi, M. J. P. (1994). Child and adolescent psychopharmacotherapy: Progress and pitfalls. *Psychiatric Annals, 24,* 83–90.

Thyer, B. A. (1991). Diagnosis and treatment of child and adolescent anxiety disorders. *Behavior Modification, 15,* 310–325.

Watson, C. G., Kucala, T., Manifold, V., Juba, M., & Vassar, P. (1988). The relationship of posttraumatic stress disorder to adolescent illegal activities, drinking, and employment. *Journal of Clinical Psychology, 44,* 592–598.

Welsh, M., Pennington, B., & Groisser, D. (1991). A normative-developmental study of executive function: A window on prefrontal function in children. *Developmental Neuropsychology, 7,* 131–149.

Werry, J. S., & Wollersheim, J. P. (1991). Behavior therapy with children and adolescents: A twenty-year overview. In S. Chess & M. E. Hertzig (Eds.), *Annual progress in child psychiatry and child development, 1990* (pp. 413–447). New York: Brunner/Mazel Publishers.

CHAPTER 7

Eating Disorders

Eating disorders are classified in two areas in DSM-IV based on age of onset. Pica, Rumination Disorder, and Feeding Disorder of Infancy or Early Childhood are grouped with other child disorders under the subcategory "Feeding and Eating Disorders of Infancy or Early Childhood." Anorexia Nervosa and Bulimia Nervosa fall under the title "Eating Disorders." The separation of anorexia and bulimia from the other eating disorders reflects differences in fundamental symptoms and onset age between anorexia/bulimia and the other eating disorders. Obesity, which is frequently treated with psychological and behavioral interventions, is not classified as a mental disorder in DSM-IV because "it has not been established that it is consistently associated with a psychological or behavioral syndrome" (American Psychiatric Association, 1994, p. 539).

Many children with eating disorders come first to pediatricians because of the adverse medical effects of these disorders. Very few of these children (less than 10% of children and adolescents with anorexia) are self-referred to psychology clinics; most are referred by pediatricians (Mickalide & Anderson, 1985). In the unlikely event that a child presents for therapy and has not been evaluated by a pediatrician for medical effects of the eating disorder, such an evaluation is essential.

■ Anorexia Nervosa

☐ CLINICAL DESCRIPTION

Diagnostic Considerations

The essential features of Anorexia Nervosa are a failure to maintain body weight at or above the minimal level for age and height, fear of weight gain or being overweight, disturbance of body image, and, in females, absence of at least three consecutive expected menstrual cycles (amenorrhea). Anorexia occurs in 0.5% to 1% of females, with the highest prevalence between ages 14 and 19 (American Psychiatric Association, 1994; Weltzin, Starzynski, Santelli, & Kaye, 1993). Although it is extremely rare before age 8, anorexia does occur in preteen children with approximately the same appearance and diagnostic features (Lask & Bryant-Waugh, 1997).

Anorexia is considerably more rare in adolescent boys, with an estimated 10–20 girls for every boy and an estimated incidence rate of 0.02% for males (American Psychiatric Association, 1994; Weltzin et al., 1993) (Table 7.1). Anorexia is more prevalent in preteen boys than in older boys (Lask & Bryant-Waugh, 1997). There is disagreement over whether males with anorexia differ significantly from females with anorexia. Three research reports of males with anorexia (Burns & Crisp, 1984; Oyebode, Boodhoo, & Schapira, 1988; Robinson & Holden, 1986) conclude that many of the clinical features and outcomes of males resemble those of females, although mortality may be greater for females.

Anorexia occurs primarily in middle and upper socioeconomic class women during early to middle adolescence (Agras, 1987; Bruch, Czyzewski, & Suhr, 1988). Onset before age 11 and after age 22 is unusual. Anorexia is physically dangerous, with mortality rates of 5 to 15%.

Diagnostically, Anorexia Nervosa differs from Bulimia Nervosa in several ways: First, bulimia always involves binge eating, whereas one major subtype of anorexia does not involve this feature. Second, bulimia involves clear attempts to prevent weight gain, usually purging, in which the person uses vomiting or laxatives to remove food from the digestive tract before it can be absorbed into the bloodstream. No such provision is necessary for the anorexia diagnosis. In DSM-IV, the Anorexia Nervosa diagnosis precludes the Bulimia Nervosa diagnosis, unless the bulimia occurs outside of episodes of anorexia. For example, an adolescent who was diagnosed with and subsequently recovered from anorexia may later be diagnosed with bulimia.

Two major subgroups of anorexia can be identified based on the presence of associated binge eating or purging behavior: "Restricting type" (or "restricting anorexia": no binge or

---

TABLE 7.1   Epidemiology and Course of Anorexia Nervosa and Bulimia Nervosa

---

Prevalence (Anorexia):   0.5–1% in females; 0.02% in males
(Bulimia):   1–3% in females; less than 1% in males

Sex Ratio (Male:Female):   1:20 (Anorexia); 1:7 (Bulimia)

Typical Onset Age: 11–22 years of age

Course (Anorexia):   Unlikely to change without treatment and/or environmental changes. About 1 in 5 is likely to be treatment resistant, with continued symptoms 5–7 years after treatment. Mortality rate is 5–15%.

Course (Bulimia):   Not often life threatening, unless associated with anorexia or unless so severe that electrolytes are significantly affected. Can cause dental erosion, electrolyte imbalance, scarring of esophagus, and dehydration. Up to 50% of patients may be symptomatic five years after diagnosis.

Common Comorbid Conditions: 1. Mood Disorders

Relevant Subtypes (Anorexia):   1. Restricting vs. Binge-Eating/Purging

Relevant Subtypes (Bulimia):   1. Purging vs. Nonpurging (Fasting or Exercising) Type

purge episodes; only restricted food intake) and "Binge-Eating/Purging type" (or "bulimic anorexia": associated binge or purge behavior [American Psychiatric Association, 1994; Mickalide & Andersen, 1985]). In the past, adolescents with bulimic anorexia typically received both the anorexia and the bulimia diagnoses. However, in DSM-IV, they receive only the Anorexia Nervosa, Binge-Eating/Purging type diagnosis, unless they develop bulimia outside of the anorexic episodes.

Some evidence exists that adolescents with anorexia of the binge/purge subtype have higher rates of outpatient therapy utilization, impulsivity, premorbid behavior problems, family dysfunction, and psychopathology than those of the restricting subtype (Dancyger, Sunday, & Halmi, 1997; Mickalide & Andersen, 1985; Weltzin et al., 1993). There is disagreement over whether the binge/purge subtype or the restricting subtype is associated with more rapid recovery (Herzog et al., 1996; Herzog, Schellberg, & Deter, 1997).

Appearance and Features

The most obvious feature of anorexia (and the reason for most anorexia referrals) is low body weight. During a clinical interview, however, intense fear of gaining weight and distorted body image generally become apparent. Children and adolescents with anorexia frequently harbor the fear that if they lose control of their hunger they will eat until they are fat. Intensifying this fear is the fact that their "comfort zone" of body size is in the extremely thin range. Hence, they may regard even normal weights as "fat" (appearance and features of anorexia are listed in Table 7.2). Denial of the illness and enjoyment in losing weight are commonly seen.

Adolescents with anorexia typically achieve their weight loss with a combination of reduction in total food intake, ingestion of low-calorie foods, and excessive exercising. Most patients experience intense feelings of hunger that they must keep in check with their exercise regimen or abnormal eating habits. When they do eat, they restrict themselves to foods such as vegetables and diet cola. Exercise such as walking or running may take place several times a day, and some adolescents work out on machines that increase upper body strength. Thus, despite their appearance of frailty, they can be surprisingly strong. They may resort to laxatives and vomiting to maintain their low body weight in the face of food consumption, in which case they receive the Binge-Eating/Purging specification.

Because of its rarity in males, anorexia has been studied almost exclusively in females. Girls with anorexia are often perfectionistic achievers (Hewitt, Flett, & Ediger, 1995), usually reflected in excellent school achievement and high IQ scores. Hence, they frequently present as verbally skilled, insightful, and competent. This verbal skill and insight appear incongruous in the context of their self-starvation. Intent on fulfilling their perfectionistic tendencies, girls with anorexia are often passively controlling and stubborn. Their shy, introverted presentation belies their strength of will to maintain their maladaptive behaviors. When presented with a treatment plan, for example, they typically react in one of two ways: (1) superficial acceptance and openness, coupled with passive resistance and oppositionality or (2) stubborn rejection of the plan as unnecessary and unreasonable.

Underlying the perfectionistic and controlling behavior is often a combination of depressive symptoms and low self-esteem; 20–90% of girls with anorexia also show symptoms of depression (Deep, Nagy, Weltzin, Rao, & Kaye, 1995; Weltzin et al., 1993). In 30–50% of cases, the onset of depression may predate the onset of the eating disorder by 1–2 years. Because of the frequency of underlying depression, adolescents with anorexia may be at risk for

TABLE 7.2   Appearance and Features of Anorexia Nervosa

COMMON FEATURES

1. Low body weight
2. Weight loss
3. Distorted body image
4. Fear of weight gain
5. Preoccupation with weight and food
6. Fear of loss of control
7. Knowledge of food and nutritional principles
8. Excessive exercising
9. Perfectionism
10. Family enmeshment
11. Onset between age 11–22
12. Female

OCCASIONAL FEATURES

1. Mid-upper socioeconomic status
2. Good achievement/high IQ
3. Good verbal skills
4. Depression/low self-esteem
5. Anxiety

Note: The features listed in the table are often seen but are not universal. Some features may be diagnostically relevant or required, whereas others may not be required for diagnosis. "Common" features are typical of the disorder; "occasional" features appear frequently but are not necessarily seen in a majority of cases.

a major depressive episode or, in severe cases, self-injurious behavior, when their fasting defenses are removed in hospitalization or therapy.

Anxiety is also often present with anorexia, either as a component of fear of weight gain or as a comorbid anxiety disorder diagnosis. Anxiety disorders have been found in as many as 75% of anorexic samples, with onset of the anxiety disorder typically occurring several years before onset of the eating disorder (Deep et al., 1995). Although dissociative episodes were initially thought to be associated with anorexia and bulimia, recent research has shown that dissociative symptoms are associated with comorbid anxiety/depression and probably not directly with eating disorder symptomatology (Gleaves & Eberenz, 1995).

Within the family, the child or adolescent with anorexia may be a model child in all areas but eating, which may generate considerable family concern. This concern may be extreme, with family members carefully tracking the adolescent's every bite of food and loss of weight. Many families of children and adolescents with anorexia have been described as overly "enmeshed," with weak boundaries between members who speak, feel, and think for each other. In such families, the parents may be very controlling individuals who use a mixture of control and caring to bind the family together (Golden & Sacker, 1984). Struggling for independence from the family, the patient may use the disorder as the only independent statement that can be made within the family's enmeshed confines. Hence, control is often an issue in these families.

Anorexia can have a persistent and chronic course. In the case of severe anorexia, the median time to achieving significant improvement was found to be 6 years in one study (Herzog et al., 1997). Other research has shown that over 20% of adolescents with anorexia may continue to experience poor outcome at 7-year follow-up, and almost half will continue to qualify for an eating disorder diagnosis at 7-year follow-up (Herpertz-Dahlmann, Wewetzer, Schulz, & Remschmidt, 1996). In general, approximately an additional 5–20% of an anorexic sample will show moderate to significant improvement for each year of follow-up. The most rapid rates of improvement appear to occur in the first three years after diagnosis, with less improvement seen following 3–7 years or more after diagnosis. Mood and anxiety disorders often persist for years after initial treatment for anorexia (Herpertz-Dahlmann et al., 1996; Herzog et al., 1997). Mortality is a significant risk associated with anorexia; mortality rates of 5–6% in the first 5 years after diagnosis and 15–20% in the 20–30 years after diagnosis have been reported (Neumarker, 1997). Although mortality is typically due to medical complications of malnutrition, self-destructive behavior (including suicide) is also responsible for many deaths.

Low body weight, calculated as a body mass index (BMI) based on height and weight, is associated with both slow recovery and with increased mortality risk; girls in their late teens with a BMI less than 13 kg/m^2 are at particular risk (Hebebrand et al., 1997). Long duration of symptomatology and presence of family pathology are also negative prognostic indicators.

Etiology

Anorexia results from different causes for different children, and a combination of biological, psychological, and environmental factors appears to be responsible for its emergence. Biological theories of the etiology of anorexia have focused on the role of serotonin, a neurotransmitter, in regulating food intake. Because serotonin levels affect such functions as appetite and mood, it has been hypothesized that dysfunctions in the brain serotonergic system could disrupt eating behavior and cause anorexia. Specifically, increased levels of serotonin in certain brain pathways inhibit eating behavior and may result in behavioral symptoms (compulsive behavior, inhibition, rigidity) that are associated with anorexia. In support of this theory, anorexic samples have been found to have increased levels of a serotonin metabolite in their cerebrospinal fluid (Weltzin et al., 1993). However, elevated serotonin levels could be either a cause or an effect of anorexia, and no direct serotonin-anorexia causal link has yet been established.

Psychological theories of anorexia have centered on family dysfunction as causally significant in the development and maintenance of anorexia. Family theorists (i.e., Minuchin, 1974) have hypothesized that one role of anorexia is to deflect attention and pressure from a conflicted marital subsystem by making eating behavior the focus of family interaction. As the family channels its attention and energy into concern and monitoring of the child, issues of conflict, unhappiness, and division are less apparent. Furthermore, family agreement emerges from the drama and importance of "helping" the child with anorexia. The resulting appearance of solidarity takes the form of interaction that is fixated on the child with anorexia. Relationships between other family members, especially within the parental subsystem, are minimized, which can be a relief for a tense, conflicted family.

Other family theories focus on overprotectiveness, perfectionism, and rigidity as the cause of anorexic behavior. In one scenario, the child with anorexia is burdened and controlled by family expectations and parental pressures (Horesh et al., 1996), causing rebellion in the specific area of food and eating. In another case, the rigid control over eating may reflect rigid control in all areas of life, which is in turn taught by a family that demands complete compliance and perfection. A third dynamic may occur in a child who fears maturity and independence from an enmeshed family system. The child avoids the pressures of growing up by refusing to eat, and thus (presumably) remaining small and dependent on parents. For girls in particular, anorexia slows (or halts) the development of sex characteristics such as breast development, pubic hair, and the menstrual cycle. These sex characteristics, which reflect the maturing process of adolescence, may be threatening to an adolescent who wishes to remain in a childlike role. Although sexual abuse has been proposed as a possible cause or exacerbating factor for anorexia, recent literature reviews have convincingly shown that sexual abuse is either not associated with restricting anorexia or, when association is found, that sexual abuse is related to psychiatric disorders in general, and not specifically to eating disorders (Horesh et al., 1996; Wonderlich, Brewerton, Jocic, Dansky, & Abbott, 1997).

Recently, the role of societal and environmental factors in the development of anorexia has been more apparent. Obesity is often a source of prejudice and derision in U.S. society, and thinness is particularly valued in adolescent girls and young women. Models and dancers, who depend on a lithe, delicate appearance, may be most at risk for these pressures, but the pressure of social acceptance is profound for all adolescents. A child who suddenly receives complements for weight loss and constantly discusses dieting with friends is given the message that "thin is in." When this message is taken to the extreme, anorexia becomes a risk.

☐　　ASSESSMENT PATTERNS

A sample assessment battery for Anorexia Nervosa is shown in Table 7.3. Other relevant tests for assessing eating behaviors and symptoms are described in the Assessment Patterns section for Bulimia Nervosa later in this chapter.

Broad Assessment Strategies

Cognitive Assessment

Clinician-Administered. WISC-III IQ scores of adolescents with anorexia are often above average, with Verbal IQ (VIQ) scores generally exceeding Performance IQ (PIQ) scores. This verbal-performance difference often reflects overachievement in school-based tasks, especially when elevations are seen on Information, Vocabulary, and Arithmetic subtests. Particularly capable, rigid, controlled adolescents with anorexia will elevate scales on the Freedom from Distractibility index (Arithmetic and Digit Span), reflecting their ability to focus and concentrate. Freedom from Distractibility and Processing Speed scores may decline in those who are experiencing severe malnutrition that affects mental processing. Observation of test-taking behavior and verbal responses may reveal obsessive and/or perfectionistic tendencies.

As with IQ testing, children and adolescents with anorexia frequently meet or exceed expected scores on achievement testing, consistent with achievement-orientation and perfectionism. Although no achievement test score pattern is typical of anorexia, scales that tap achievement in more basic achievement areas (such as reading, spelling, and science)

TABLE 7.3   Sample Assessment Battery for Anorexia Nervosa and Bulimia Nervosa

PSYCHOLOGICAL

1. MMPI/MMPI-A
2. SCL-90-R

BEHAVIORAL

1. Behavioral Assessment System for Children (Parent-Report, Teacher-Report, and Child-Report)
2. Adolescent Symptom Inventory-4 (Parent-Report and Teacher-Report)

FAMILY

1. Family Environment Scale

SYNDROME-SPECIFIC

1. Body Mass Index
2. Eating Disorder Inventory-2
3. Body Image Test
4. Compulsive Eating Scale
5. Bulimic Thoughts Questionnaire

Note: Assessment instruments are intended to supplement (not substitute for) a good clinical interview and, when possible, a structured diagnostic interview.

are more likely to be elevated than those that measure more applied achievement areas (such as oral expression or listening comprehension).

Psychological Assessment

Clinician-Administered.   The perfectionism and denial characteristics of anorexia are sometimes shown by a low number of Rorschach responses (Wagner & Wagner, 1978). Likewise, a low number of human movement (M) responses could reflect a striving beyond resources, whereas a high proportion of major detail responses (D) to M responses may indicate a cognitive defensiveness or cautiousness. A large number of Dd responses, on the other hand, could be consistent with cognitive constriction and perfectionistic attention to detail. Defensiveness and cautiousness are also represented by high F and F+% records. Less common are color responses and sexual responses, which may be indicators of emotional undercontrol, immaturity, and fears of sexual maturity. Anatomical responses may indicate problems with body image and a sense of vulnerability of self-esteem.

Because most people with anorexia are of adolescent age or older, they may be administered adult tests of personality, such as the MMPI/MMPI-A. On the MMPI, adolescents with anorexia may be expected to show the 2–4 pattern typical of adolescent rebelliousness, depression, anger, and family discord (Dancyger et al., 1997). The perfectionism and obsessive features of anorexia will likely elevate scale 7. Scales 6 and 8 may be elevated by general psychopathology and character pathology as well (Small et al., 1981). To the extent that bodily concern, self-centeredness, and egocentricity are present, scales 1 and 3 will be elevated. Denial of pathology, a common associated feature of anorexia, may be manifest as elevations on scales L and K with a depression on the F scale, especially when adolescent norms are used (Gallucci, 1987). Elevations of the L scale also indicate cognitive rigidity, perfectionism, and low insight.

Adolescents with the binge/purge features of anorexia typically produce more elevated MMPI profiles compared to those with restricting features. Elevations on scale 9 are more typical of the binge/purge subtype than of the restricting subtype (Piran, Lerner, Garfinkel, Kennedy, & Brouillette, 1988). Patients with restricting anorexia may be more likely to elevate the L scale, reflecting their greater rigidity and perfectionism (Dancyger et al., 1997).

Behavioral Assessment

Parent-Report, Teacher-Report, and Child-Report. Most broad-band observer (parent or teacher) report behavioral questionnaires include a few items about eating, but few of these questionnaires yield eating disorder subscales. The Achenbach and BASC scales do not contain enough eating-related items to assist with identification of specific symptoms of eating disorder, and these scales do not include anorexia or eating disorder subscales. These behavioral questionnaires may, on the other hand, assist in the identification of co-occurring mood and other symptoms. The ASI-4 contains an Anorexia Nervosa subscale with the major DSM-IV symptoms of the disorder, but this subscale has been the subject of relatively little research.

Child-report behavioral questionnaires also do not typically include subscales specific to eating disorders. The PIY and BASC-SRP, for example, include subscales measuring somatization and self-esteem, but they do not directly measure eating disorder symptomatology. Like the observer-report questionnaires, these self-report scales can be useful in probing for associated or comorbid mood, anxiety, and other symptoms.

Family Assessment

Child-Report. The enmeshment characteristic of families of children with anorexia would likely be shown by elevated scores on the Cohesion, Moral-Religious Emphasis, Organization, and Control scales of the FES and depressed scores on the Independence and Active-Recreational Orientation scales. Repressed emotion may result in low Conflict and Expressiveness scores. Controlling factor scores are likely to be high, whereas scores on the Conflicted factor are usually low. Very high Supportive factor scores (over 280) could reflect denial of problems, social desirability, and tendency to portray the family as perfect.

Syndrome-Specific Tests

Clinician-Administered

Body Mass Index. (BMI; Keyes, Fidanza, Karvonen, Kimura, & Taylor, 1972). The BMI is a simple weight-to-height ratio that gives an estimate of thinness or obesity. The

BMI may be calculated by dividing the child's weight (in kilograms) by the square of the child's height (in meters); hence, BMI is expressed in increments of kg/m^2. BMI values of 13 and lower are considered very thin for girls in their late teens; BMI values for other ages and for boys must be compared to other norm scores.

Eating Disorder Examination. (EDE; Wilson & Smith, 1989). The EDE is a semistructured interview consisting of questions about the frequency and severity of eating disorder symptoms and related beliefs and behaviors. It yields five subscales (Restraint, Shape Concern, Weight Concern, Bulimia, and Eating Concern) and a global eating disorder score. A self-report questionnaire, the Eating Disorder Examination-Questionnaire (EDE-Q; Fairburn & Beglin, 1995), has also been developed based on the EDE but may not be as valid as the interview measure.

Child-Report

Eating Disorder Inventory-2. (EDI-2; Garner, 1991). The EDI-2 is a 91-item self-report measure of psychological and behavioral traits common to anorexia and bulimia. Items are rated on a 6-point scale (always to never) of frequency or agreement. The first 64 items of the EDI-2 yield the 8 basic subscales: Drive for Thinness (DT), Bulimia (B), Body Dissatisfaction (BD), Ineffectiveness (I), Perfectionism (P), Interpersonal Distrust (ID), Interoceptive Awareness (IA), and Maturity Fears (MF). The final 27 items provide three provisional subscales: Asceticism (A), Impulse Regulation (IR), and Social Insecurity (SI). Adolescents with anorexia generally score higher than nonclinical samples on all scales of the EDI-2, although DT and BD are typically the most elevated. Scores on the B scale may indicate whether the anorexia is of the Restricting or of the Binge Eating/Purging type; the latter type generally elevates the B scale.

Eating Attitudes Test. (EAT; Garner & Garfinkel, 1979). The EAT is a 40-item inventory that gives a total score and three subscale scores: Dieting, Bulimia/Food Preoccupation, and Oral Control. Items, which are rated on a 1–6 scale of frequency, reflect anorexic thoughts and behaviors. Scoring is not a matter of simply summing items; certain items and ratings are weighted differently. Total scores of 59 are typical of patients with anorexia, whereas scores of 16 are average for controls; a cutting score of 30 may be used to identify eating concerns typical of patients with anorexia (Garner & Garfinkel, 1979). Adolescents with anorexia elevate all subscales of the EAT, and those with the binge/purge subtype endorse many of the "bulimia" items. The EAT includes fewer cognitive and affective items than the EDI-2. Hence, although both the EAT and EDI-2 provide diagnostically useful information, the EDI-2 is preferable in cases with a significant cognitive/affective component.

Modified, shorter versions of the EAT (Children's Eating Attitude Test [ChEAT; Maloney, McGuire, & Daniels, 1988] and Adapted Eating Attitudes Test [A-EAT; Vacc & Rhyne, 1987]) have been developed for preadolescent children in grades 3 and older. Although these versions have demonstrated adequate psychometrics, they have been criticized for having adult-level content (Candy & Fee, 1998).

Eating Behaviors and Body Image Test. (EBBIT; Candy & Fee, 1998). The EBBIT is a 38-item measure of body image dissatisfaction, restricted eating behavior, and binge eating behaviors in preadolescent girls; it has been studied in girls as young as fourth grade. EBBIT scores fall into two factor-analytically derived subscales: Body Image Dissatisfaction/ Restrictive Eating and Binge Eating. The EBBIT appears to be more appropriate for preadolescent children than the EAT or EDI-2, but it has received less research or clinical attention.

Body Attitude Test. (BAT; Probst, Vandereycken, Van Coppenolle, & Vanderlinden, 1995). The BAT is a 20-item self-report measure of dissatisfaction with body size, shape, and appearance. Factor analyses of the BAT have shown three multi-item factors, which may be used as subscales: Negative Appreciation of Body Size, Lack of Familiarity with One's Own Body, and General Body Dissatisfaction. The BAT appears to have good psychometric properties, including approximately 75% sensitivity and specificity in identifying eating-disordered from nonreferred subjects. Patients with bulimia tend to score highest on the BAT, followed by patients with the binge-purge subtype of anorexia; patients with restricting symptoms have the lowest scores, which are still elevated relative to nonreferred subjects. BAT scores correspond closely to EDI-2 Total and Body Dissatisfaction subscale scores (Probst et al., 1995). Although the BAT has not received extensive clinical use, its brevity and relevance for measuring body image issues make it a potentially valuable clinical instrument.

☐ ■ TREATMENT OPTIONS

Treatment options for Anorexia Nervosa are outlined in Table 7.4.

Medical Evaluation/Hospitalization

First and foremost, patients with anorexia must be closely evaluated and followed medically. Because many organic conditions may lead to weight loss, organic causes must be first ruled out before the Anorexia Nervosa diagnosis is made and psychological treatments are deemed appropriate. Once the Anorexia Nervosa diagnosis is made, treatment generally involves three components: (1) weight gain; (2) resolution of psychological, social, and behavioral abnormalities; and (3) weight maintenance.

Because of the potentially life-threatening weight loss and accompanying physical symptoms, hospitalization is often necessary to facilitate the attainment of the first two treatment goals (weight gain and psychotherapy). Medically, the hospitalized child should be evaluated for weight gain, food intake, electrolyte balance, output, and complications. Weight gain is usually targeted at ¼ to ½ pound per day (Golden & Sacker, 1984), and a target weight is set as a criterion for hospital discharge. Meals in the hospital are based on calorie intake goals, with gradual increases of relatively modest initial calorie goals. The child is usually allowed to choose specific food and drinks, as long as the ultimate intake goals are met.

The hospital provides a tightly controlled environment that allows the management team to remove the child from the home/family environment, set behavioral contingencies, and restrict access to laxatives and exercise equipment. Psychopharmacological interventions may be tried during hospitalization to address the anorexia or associated psychological features (i.e., depression, anxiety). It is unusual, however, for medications to cause a significant behavioral response in the absence of other intervention.

Commerford, Licinio, & Halmi, (1997) proposed six goals to be met by patients with anorexia during hospitalization: achievement of a target weight, maintenance of target weight

TABLE 7.4   Treatment Options for Anorexia Nervosa

1. Medical Evaluation/Hospitalization
   a. Physical exam
   b. Tests to rule out other conditions
   c. Enforced, monitored weight gain (¼ to ½ pound/day)
      (1) Enforced, monitored food intake
      (2) Monitored electrolyte balance
      (3) Monitored output
   d. Restricted access to laxatives
   e. Restricted access to exercise
2. Behavioral Interventions
   a. Reinforcers tied to weight gain
3. Psychotherapy
   a. Psychodynamic psychotherapy
   b. Cognitive-behavioral interventions
      (1) Assessment and joining
      (2) Psychoeducation
      (3) Goal setting
      (4) Identification of logical consequences for goal attainment
      (5) Monitoring and enforcement of eating rules by adults
      (6) Stimulus control strategies
      (7) Identification and restructuring of negative automatic thoughts
      (8) Relaxation techniques
      (9) Addressing of family stresses
      (10) Identification and treatment of comorbid problems
      (11) Relapse prevention
   c. Group therapy
4. Family Interventions
   a. Family therapy (typically with systemic approach focused on boundaries within the family)
5. Medications (usually for co-occurring diagnoses such as depression)
   a. Antidepressant medications

Note: This outline of options summarizes major treatments covered in the text. Specific treatments are often combined into an intervention package. Refer to the text for additional descriptions of each treatment. This table is not necessarily an exhaustive list of all treatments available.

for two weeks, independent selection of a balanced diet, eating without difficulty in real-world settings (home, restaurants), lack of purging behavior for two weeks, and no self-harming behaviors for two weeks. Attainment of these goals was related to better status at 5-year follow-up.

Behavioral Interventions

Behavioral modification is the cornerstone of intervention to correct anorexia. Once reinforcers and punishers are identified, these are tied to weight gain. A common strategy is to allow the child initial access to basic hospital amenities (TV, bathroom privileges, books, freedom to leave room, makeup, toiletries, telephone, and clothes) with the understanding these privileges will be present for as long as the child meets weight goals. An alternative strategy is to start with no amenities, with the child required to earn access to them when goals are met.

Weight goals should be explicit and time of day for weighing should be constant from day to day. If the patient fails to meet weight goals, privileges are progressively removed with the understanding that they will be returned progressively on the first day of weight gain. It is possible in the first few days of hospitalization to find a girl with anorexia in her room with no phone, no TV, only a hospital gown to wear, no makeup, and restricted access to the bathroom or to the unit outside the room. If behavioral interventions fail (which is rare) or the patient is too weak to respond, intravenous feeding may be necessary.

Psychotherapy

Psychodynamic Psychotherapy

Although behavioral treatment often results in weight gain, in many cases changes in thoughts and feelings must accompany the behavioral change to prevent a relapse of weight loss and adjustment problems. Individual psychodynamic psychotherapy generally addresses common anorexia and eating issues such as ambivalence over dependency, denial of illness, fear of being overweight, need for perfectionism, and anger at family (Bruch, 1978). More psychodynamic approaches stress the need to access fears and emotions tied to these issues and to achieve resolution through insight.

Cognitive-Behavioral Interventions

Cognitive-behavioral approaches, on the other hand, take a systematic approach by building a therapeutic relationship; identifying maladaptive thoughts, feelings, and behaviors; correcting maladaptive thoughts; practicing coping; boosting self-esteem with self-monitoring and self-statements; and teaching relaxation techniques (Sagardoy, Ashton, Mateos, Perez, & Carrasco, 1989). Cognitive-behavioral interventions for anorexia nervosa typically integrate behavioral, family, and cognitive components into a structured treatment plan with clear goals and expectations. Robin, Bedway, Siegel, and Gilroy, (1996) and Peterson and Mitchell (1996) provide specific examples of cognitive-behavioral treatment plans for anorexia. The major components of cognitive-behavioral psychotherapy for anorexia nervosa are the following (in approximate order of their introduction in the psychotherapy process):

1. *Assessment and Joining.* Initial evaluation includes medical, psychological, and social components. During the assessment phase, it is essential to establish rapport and to adopt a supportive and nonthreatening role toward the family. The family should be told that this initial session or two will not include any psychological interventions, so that the therapist can get to know the child and family and so that the therapist and family can develop a relationship without the pressure of change.

2. *Psychoeducation.* Psychoeducation about eating disorder symptoms, associated features, etiology, and treatment provides the family with a foundation of information and

a sense of what to expect in treatment. Societal pressures and expectations for thinness are also discussed in this phase of treatment. The impact of these sociocultural influences and peer/family expectations for body size and appearance is important to establish as a means of understanding why eating disorders may emerge.

3. *Goal Setting.* Goals are set in several areas: balanced food menus, calorie intake, weight goals, and activity goals. Balanced menus and calorie intake goals (usually in the range of 1,500 calories initially) are typically developed in conjunction with a dietician, based on the child's food preferences and nutritional status. Weekly expectations for weight gain (typically in the 1 pound per week range for outpatients; inpatient weight goals are often in the range of about ¼ pound per day) are set in consultation with the pediatrician and dietician. If the child is hospitalized, weight goals are set and monitored daily. Activity goals are based on the child's daily schedule and involve expectations for exercise, social interaction, school, and chores. In most cases, activities will be cut back (in order to reduce the child's burning of calories), and the child is restricted from social situations that encourage problem eating behavior. Activity goals also involve agreement on where eating occurs.

4. *Identification of Logical Consequences for Goal Attainment.* Early in treatment, typical adolescent privileges, such as control over one's schedule, going out with friends, and other freedoms, are restricted as there is a need for monitoring the adolescent's eating and other behaviors. In more severe cases, more significant restrictions (such as confinement to the hospital room unless accompanied by medical personnel) may need to be put in place. It is important in the early stages of treatment to emphasize that these privileges and freedoms will be returned when the situation no longer requires their restriction. Specific privileges that are returned contingent on specific (usually weight) goals can be identified, so that the adolescent sees some benefit in achieving goals.

5. *Monitoring and Enforcement of Eating Rules by Adults.* Adults (typically parents for an outpatient intervention) in the environment must initially take the responsibility for making sure that the adolescent with anorexia is actually following through on the rules and goals set earlier in the program. Parents set the menu and timing of meals, eat with the child, record the child's food intake and daily weight, and sit with the child for 60–90 minutes after meals to ensure that there is no purging behavior. The therapist reviews the food intake and daily record with the family on a regular basis (typically weekly in an outpatient setting and every 1–2 days in an inpatient setting).

6. *Stimulus Control Strategies.* Stimulus control strategies involve the identification and manipulation of cues or sources of negative association in the environment. The patient learns which stimuli lead to exacerbation of eating disorder symptoms, and a plan is developed to avoid such stimuli and to deal effectively with them when they are present. Typical cues or stimuli are workout equipment, TV shows that emphasize thinness, and presence of low-calorie foods.

7. *Identification and Modification of Perfectionism, Negative Thoughts and Beliefs, and Low Self-Esteem.* Adolescents with anorexia frequently experience negative or catastrophic thoughts about their body size, their self-esteem, the need to be perfect, eating problems, and getting fat. Initially, one goal is to discuss the concepts of perfectionism, self-esteem, and body image. These concepts are presented in a didactic manner at first, leading to a discussion of how the patient's belief system reflects these problems. Once adolescents with anorexia have learned these concepts, they are then taught how their thoughts and beliefs cause them to be anxious and depressed about body image and eating behavior. Those negative thoughts and beliefs are then targeted as the cause of their depression, perfectionism, problematic eating behavior, and weight loss. Adolescents with anorexia learn to identify the negative thoughts first, and then to change them once they have been identified. Techniques to change negative self-esteem, perfectionism, and distorted thoughts and beliefs include hypothesis testing (testing whether the thought is accurate), generating plausible alternative thoughts and beliefs, identifying positive things about the self, and demonstrating typical cognitive errors that people make in their negative thought processes (overgeneralizing, catastrophizing, and dichotomous thinking).

8. *Relaxation Techniques.* Breathing and imagery-based relaxation techniques are taught to the adolescent as ways of reducing the worry and tension that are associated with eating and weight gain. Many patients with anorexia will describe a feeling of physiological tension or psychological worry that accompanies any improvement in weight status. In some cases, this tension and worry interfere with the drive to eat and can cause nausea. Relaxation techniques produce a state that is incompatible with tension and, thus, reduces these unpleasant psychological and physical symptoms of anxiety.

9. *Addressing of Family Stresses.* Throughout cognitive-behavioral psychotherapy, the family experiences considerable strain as typical patterns and roles are changed in order to promote and monitor change. Initially, adolescents lose a measure of independence as the parent assumes responsibility for their child's eating behavior. Parents face more frequent conflict with the adolescent and have the challenge of coordinating their own busy schedule with monitoring the adolescent. The therapist must elicit conversation about these topics, be supportive, identify maladaptive family interactions, prevent sabotage of the plan, and promote the psychological well-being of all family members. Above all, the therapist must adopt a supportive and empathetic demeanor toward the adolescent's distress while also remaining firm about the need to continue the intervention plan. Robin et al. (1996) demonstrate the integration of these techniques into a cognitive-behavioral plan.

10. *Identification and Treatment of Comorbid Problems.* During the course of treatment, comorbid problems such as depression, family problems, anxiety, and negative personality traits may emerge. Frequently, there is a need for assertiveness training and learning to express emotions adaptively. These problems should be treated concurrently with the anorexia, and separate goals may need to be set for the resolution of comorbid problems.

11. *Relapse Prevention.* Once goals are achieved, the focus of treatment turns to the prevention of excessive weight loss in the future. Therapy sessions become less frequent at this time, as parents take on more of the role of monitoring and intervening if problems arise. The child takes more responsibility for diet, eating, and maintenance of weight, as parents reduce the intensity of monitoring. Regular weight checks by parents are usually built into this stage of treatment, and significant decrease in weight requires a return to an earlier stage of the treatment plan. Therapy ends when weight has been maintained at a goal level for several months and when the family and therapist have agreed to a set of rules for periodic monitoring and responses to weight loss (including a restarting of treatment).

Using a combination of cognitive-behavioral and family therapy techniques, Robin et al. (1996) found that 64% of their anorexic sample reached their goal weight by the end of the 16-month treatment period. At a 1-year follow-up, 82% were at goal weight. Similar percentages were found in a more traditional, largely individual/psychodynamic, psychotherapy intervention group, indicating that both modes of treatment are effective for the majority of patients with anorexia (Robin et al., 1996).

Group Psychotherapy

Group treatment for anorexia is also widely used as a primary mode of treatment or as an adjunct to individual and family therapies. A typical outpatient group (Hendren, Atkins, Sumner, & Barber, 1987) may have approximately 5–8 members and meet weekly for an hour. Because of the similarity of many issues between anorexia and bulimia, patients with these disorders are often included in the same group. Group process may vary with the orientation of the therapist from more task-oriented, cognitive-behavioral groups to more process-oriented, interpersonal groups. The group setting offers numerous advantages: In open groups, more experienced members can model effective and honest working through of issues, which may assist in challenging the denial of illness characteristic of anorexia. Additionally, the group acts as a source of support for its members, removing some of the stigma of having an eating disorder. Finally, the group offers a variety of viewpoints for discussion of issues, facilitating empathy and working-through of difficulties. Some encouraging data on group therapy for anorexia have been reported (Hendren et al., 1987).

Family Interventions

In developing a treatment plan for a child with anorexia, it is important to remember that, in virtually all cases, anorexia affects the entire family. Patterns of family interaction, established when the child had an eating disorder, are unlikely to change easily. Hence, even if change is made in individual or inpatient therapy, the child is returning to an environment that potentially provokes the eating disorder behavior. To address this problem, family therapy is a frequent component of treatment for anorexia.

Family therapy for anorexia first involves an assessment of the family unit, family relationships, and family interaction patterns. This may be particularly enlightening if done during a meal. A frequently seen pattern is that of enmeshment, in which family relationships are too strong and boundaries too weak, resulting in members talking and feeling for each other and failing to allow individual development. The task of the family therapist in these cases is to identify the most common problems seen in families who have children with anorexia: enmeshed relationships, inappropriate boundaries, inconsistent enforcement of rules by parents, communication problems, and coalitions within the family. Once problems are identified, the therapist must then encourage individuation of family members (in the case of enmeshed relationships), strengthen the parental subsystem (in the case of inappropriate boundaries), foster consistency of rules, facilitate open communication, and show the family the danger of unspoken coalitions between a child and one parent against another family member (Minuchin, 1974).

Medication

Although several medications have been suggested as potential treatments for anorexia, "results from double-blind trials do not find a 'magic bullet' drug that provides a significant remission of the anorexic symptom complex" (Weltzin et al., 1993, p. 222). Antidepressant medications such as amitriptyline (Elavil), clomipramine (Anafranil), nortriptyline (Pamelor), and fluoxetine (Prozac) have been used for patients with comorbid anorexia and depression. There have been some reports that medication use enhances response to psychotherapy and that multifaceted approaches combining medication and psychotherapy are more effective than psychotherapy alone (Brambilla, Draisci, Peirone, & Brunetta, 1995).

■ Bulimia Nervosa

□ CLINICAL DESCRIPTION

Diagnostic Considerations

The essential characteristics of Bulimia Nervosa are binge eating (consuming a large amount of food with little perceived control over this eating behavior) and compensatory behavior (purging, exercising, or fasting to rid the body of calories). Adolescents with bulimia follow a binge-purge cycle in which binge eating is followed by purging of the digestive system by vomiting or use of laxatives. In some cases, fasting or exercise is also used as a method of restricting weight gain. According to DSM-IV, adolescents with bulimia feel a lack of control over eating binges, average at least two bulimic episodes a week for at least three months, try to compensate for overeating by purging or exercising, and exhibit over-concern with weight. It is not uncommon to encounter a patient with an eating disorder who does not binge frequently enough to be classified as bulimic according to DSM-IV criteria. These patients are technically classified as having Eating Disorder, NOS, although their testing patterns and treatment options are similar to those of patients with bulimia.

DSM-IV divides bulimia into two subtypes: Purging and Nonpurging. The purging subtype is characterized by the use of vomiting or laxatives as compensatory behavior following binges, whereas the nonpurging subtype is characterized by exercise or fasting as compensatory behaviors. The purging subtype appears to be the more severe of the two subtypes. Girls with purging bulimia tend to have earlier age of onset, more depressive symptoms, greater risk for social phobia, greater risk of past history of sexual abuse, and more parental discord (Garfinkel et al., 1996).

Bulimia is more common than anorexia, although diagnostic uncertainty or misuse of the term *bulimia* results in different definitions being used. Bulimic "behavior", for example, is sometimes used to mean having ever binged or purged. Obviously, a single incident of this behavior is much more common than the bulimia diagnosis. Using these more lax definitions of bulimia, prevalence rates have been estimated at between 4 and 20% (Weltzin et al., 1993); as many as 20% of high school girls regularly engage in binge eating (Levine, 1987). Binge-eating and purging behavior is also not specific to the bulimia diagnosis; the Binge-Eating/Purging subtype of Anorexia Nervosa is also characterized by binges and purges. Using a stringent DSM-IV definition, bulimia has a prevalence rate of 1–3% in females (American Psychiatric Association, 1994), although prevalence in high school girls may be as high as 8% (Johnson, Lewis, Love, Lewis, & Stuckey, 1984). Bulimia is much more common in females, who outnumber males by as much as 7 to 1 (Weltzin et al., 1993) (Table 7.1).

Appearance and Features

As with anorexia, bulimia tends to occur in females between the ages of 13 and 21. Bulimia is extremely rare below the age of 11 (Lask & Bryant-Waugh, 1997). The binge episodes of bulimia usually involve the consumption of large amounts of calorie-rich foods. Binge eating is done in secret, and special efforts (e.g., hiding large quantities of food prior to a binge) may be taken to avoid detection. Adolescents with bulimia feel out of control when on a binge and may go to great lengths to obtain food. Stealing food or money to buy food may occur on college campuses where shared rooms make access to others' food or money easier. Such antisocial behavior may be so out of character for the bulimic that he or she appears driven to eat at any cost. In a minority of cases, bulimic symptoms may occur in a seasonal pattern, with exacerbation of depressive symptoms and bulimic symptoms in the fall and winter (Levitan, Kaplan, & Rockert, 1996).

Bulimia and anorexia share several similarities. Beyond the obvious fact that both involve eating behavior, both disorders are usually characterized by overconcern about weight, distortion of body image, and an unusual focus on food. Many theorists and clinicians have also implicated the family in the development and maintenance of bulimia, much the same as for anorexia. Like anorexia, bulimia generally occurs in adolescent-age females; male cases are rare but seem to share many of the characteristics of female cases (Olivardia, Pope, Mangweth, & Hudson, 1995).

Despite their shared characteristics, bulimia and anorexia have several differences. Many adolescents with bulimia are of normal weight or are obese, whereas patients with anorexia are, by definition, thin. Therefore, the weight fluctuations of adolescents with bulimia who are not diagnosed as anorexic usually range from thin (but not anorexic) to significantly overweight. Patients with anorexia tend to stay in one (unacceptably low) weight range. Because bulimia generally does not involve the extreme weight loss of anorexia, it is rarely life threatening. However, bulimia is associated with a number of problematic medical conditions such as dental erosion, electrolyte imbalance, and dehydration. Adolescents with bulimia do not typically have the rigid bodily control characteristic of anorexia; they may, in fact, complain of feeling out of control of their body at times. Adolescents with bulimia may be more extroverted than adolescents with anorexia, more aware of subjective distress, and more prone to acting-out behaviors as well (Agras, 1987; Rybicki, Lepkowsky, & Arndt, 1989) (Table 7.5).

In addition to the eating disorder symptomatology, bulimia is associated with negative social outcomes such as instability in romantic relationships (Reiss & Johnson-Sabine, 1995). Additionally, social adjustment appears to be a significant predictor of the outcome of bulimia. Women with bulimia that persists for five or more years tend to have problems with romantic relationships, job satisfaction, and family relationships (Reiss & Johnson-Sabine, 1995).

Bulimia is a persistent disorder. Symptoms can continue sporadically even after treatment has significantly reduced their frequency. As many as 50% of individuals with bulimia may show binge-purge symptoms at least once monthly, based on 5-year follow-up (Reiss & Johnson-Sabine, 1995).

Etiology

Etiological theories of bulimia resemble those for anorexia, probably because the two syndromes were often codiagnosed prior to DSM-IV (see the earlier section of this chapter on the etiology of anorexia). Less has been written about the etiology of "pure" (normal weight) bulimia.

Psychologically, bulimia may result from several factors, with body dissatisfaction usually operating as a key component (e.g., Stice, Nemeroff, & Shaw, 1996). Dissatisfaction with body size and/or shape can result from objective evidence (being overweight), negative

TABLE 7.5   Appearance and Features of Bulimia Nervosa

COMMON FEATURES

1. Significant weight fluctuation
2. Binge eating
3. Compensatory behavior (purging, exercise, or fasting)
4. Distorted body image
5. Preoccupation with food
6. Fear of loss of control
7. Knowledge of food
8. Extreme/atypical behaviors to obtain food
9. Physical complications such as dental erosion and electrolyte imbalance
10. Family problems
11. Onset between ages 11 and 22 years
12. Female
13. Depression/low self-esteem
14. Unstable relationships

OCCASIONAL FEATURES

1. Seasonal pattern

Note: The features listed above are often seen but are not universal. Some features may be diagnostically relevant or required, while others may not be required for diagnosis. "Common" features are typical of the disorder; "occasional" features appear frequently but are not necessarily seen in a majority of cases.

feedback from others, and/or a distortion of what is ideal body weight. This dissatisfaction, in turn, causes adolescents to engage in behaviors to bring their perceived body image in line with their ideal body image. These behaviors can include restriction of eating behavior and purging behavior. Restriction of food intake, in turn, can lead to feelings of severe hunger that trigger binges. Adolescents with bulimia will sometimes claim that their initial binges occurred when they were trying to restrict their calorie intake, and they lost control over their eating behavior.

A second psychological theory focuses on negative affect and cites the sensation-seeking component of a binge as an attempt on the part of the person to reduce depressed feeling states. Some adolescents gorge for the pleasure of eating, and adolescents with bulimia may use gorging to produce pleasure when they are experiencing depression and anxiety (Stice et al., 1996). This gorging, however, must then be eliminated in order to avoid long-term weight consequences. Adolescents with bulimia may also feel guilt and shame after binges, which are allayed by purging to dispose of the evidence of the binge.

Socially, bulimia may be learned by social pressures or by imitating others who engage in binge eating and purging. Girls in high school, for example, can learn purging as a way of staying thin. The knowledge that other girls are engaging in the behavior makes it more acceptable. Girls with friends or family members who have eating disorders and bulimic symptoms, for example, are more likely to show bulimic symptoms themselves (Pike, 1995). Initiation of bulimic symptoms has also been found to be associated with family pressure to lose weight (Stice et al., 1996).

Sexual abuse has been proposed as a possible cause of bulimia because of high rates of sexual abuse reported in samples of women with eating disorders (Zlotnick et al., 1996). Recent literature reviews have shown that bulimic samples report higher rates of sexual abuse compared to anorexic samples. However, sexual abuse appears to be related to psychiatric disorders in general and not specifically to eating disorders (Casper & Lyubomirsky, 1997; Wonderlich et al., 1997). Hence, sexual abuse does not appear to be a specific cause of bulimia, although it may generate psychological distress that may cause or exacerbate bulimic symptoms (Casper & Lyubomirsky, 1997).

Biological theories of the cause of bulimia borrow largely from theories of substance abuse disorders. In particular, endorphins and enkephalins have been suggested as neurotransmitters that are responsive to binges (Weltzin et al., 1993), so adolescents with bulimia may binge for the pleasant feeling created by these neurotransmitters. Further support for this theory comes from research that suggests that adolescents with bulimia may be vulnerable to other addictions and that addiction may run in the family of adolescents with bulimia (Weltzin et al., 1993). Girls with bulimia also appear to have difficulty identifying internal body states, especially states of hunger and satiety (Pike, 1995). Because they are less aware of these states, they may not receive sufficient negative feedback that they are full until well after a binge. They may then feel so full that they are uncomfortable until they purge the excess food from their system.

ASSESSMENT PATTERNS

A sample assessment battery for Bulimia Nervosa is shown in Table 7.3.

Broad Assessment Strategies

Behavioral Assessment

Parent-Report, Teacher-Report, and Child-Report.   Most broad-band parent- or teacher-report behavioral checklists include a few items about eating problems, but few of these questionnaires yield eating disorder subscales. The ASI-4 contains a Bulimia Nervosa subscale with the major DSM-IV symptoms of the disorder, but this subscale has been the subject of relatively little research.

Child-report behavioral questionnaires also do not typically include subscales specific to eating disorders. The PIY and BASC-SRP, for example, include subscales measuring somatization and self-esteem, but they do not directly measure eating disorder symptomatology. Like the observer-report questionnaires, these self-report scales can be useful in probing for associated or comorbid mood, anxiety, and other symptoms. However, syndrome-specific tests must be used in order to provide direct questions about eating disorder symptoms in a self-report format.

Psychological Assessment

Clinician-Administered.   Bulimic samples tend to score higher on both general and specific pathology measures than control samples and higher than restricting anorexic samples as well. The typical MMPI pattern for bulimia resembles that of anorexia in reflecting elements of rebelliousness, distress, and family problems, but to a greater extent. In addition to elevations across all clinical scales (with the exception of scale 5), a 2-4-7-8 pattern has been found in patients with bulimia (Rybicki et al., 1989); scales F, 1, 3, 6, 9, and 0 can be expected to be in the 60 to 70 range. Because the adolescent with bulimia often feels more out of control than the adolescent with restricting anorexia, higher scores on scales 4 and 8 are to be expected. Furthermore, the general psychopathology and distress of bulimia contribute to significant elevations on scales 2, 4, 7, and 8, which may average as high as 70–80 in this group.

Family Assessment

The family problems suggested by high scale 4 scores on the MMPI may be assessed in more detail using the FES. On the FES, adolescents with bulimia may be expected to show lower scores on subscales identified as "Supportive" by Kronenberger and Thompson (1990): Cohesion, Expressiveness, Independence, Intellectual-Cultural Orientation, and Active-Recreational Orientation (Rybicki et al., 1989). Families of adolescents with bulimia tend to be less expressive and to engage in fewer recreational, "leisure time" activities together.

Syndrome-Specific Tests

Child-Report

Binge Scale. (BS; Hawkins & Clement, 1980). The BS consists of 19 items, of which nine are added to give a total Binge score. BS scores reflect binge eating behaviors and attitudes; they correlate with dieting and self-image concerns and are unrelated to social desirability (Hawkins & Clement, 1980). Clinicians who are using the BS may want to administer only the nine scored items.

Conroy-Healy Eating Questionnaire. (CHEQ; Healy, Conroy, & Walsh, 1985). The CHEQ consists of 13 items. Like the BS, it is relatively unidimensional and sensitive to bulimic symptomatology.

Compulsive Eating Scale. (CES; Dunn & Odercin, 1981). The CES is a 32-item scale, of which 16 items are used in scoring. It yields a total score and 3 factor scores (Golden, Buzcek, & Robbins, 1986): Negative Affect (about eating behavior), Dietary Restraint, and Positive Affect (about eating behavior). Higher CES scores are related to less emotional stability and control as well as to greater suspiciousness, guilt, social desirability, and tension (Dunn & Odercin, 1981). The CES is highly related to DSM-III bulimic symptomatology (Golden et al., 1986). A total CES score of 59 or higher may be used as a clinical cutoff (Dunn & Odercin, 1981).

Bulimic Thoughts Questionnaire. (BTQ; Phelan, 1987). The BTQ assesses self-statements in three areas: "self-schema" (actually more of a measure of body image), "self-efficacy" (perceived self-control over eating), and "salient beliefs" (maladaptive beliefs related to eating and craving for food). Phelan (1987) presents data suggesting that the

BTQ discriminates among people with bulimia, obesity, and no eating disorder. The BTQ may also be used to track treatment progress in the cognitive belief modality.

Bulimia Test.   (BULIT; Smith & Thelen, 1984). The BULIT is a 36-item scale, consisting of 32 "original" items and four items that were added later. The 32 original items are added to give a BULIT total score. A factor analysis of the 32 items yielded five factor-analytically derived subscales: Binges (binging behavior and fear of binging), Feelings (emotions related to binges), Vomiting (purge-related vomiting), Food (food preferred during a binge), and Weight (weight gain or loss within a month's time). The BULIT correlates highly with the BS and EAT. It also discriminates significantly between individuals with bulimia and healthy controls (Smith & Thelen, 1984). Smith and Thelen (1984) suggest that a total cutoff score of 102 be used for classification of bulimia. Of the bulimia-focused scales, the BULIT may yield the best discrimination of bulimic and nonreferred samples (Welch & Hall, 1989) and of bulimic and obese samples (Williamson, Prather, McKenzie, & Blouin, 1990). However, because BULIT scores correlate with general psychological distress (Pike, 1995), other symptoms and distress should be taken into account in interpreting BULIT scores.

Goldfarb Fear of Fat Scale.   (GFFS; Goldfarb, Dykens, & Gerrard, 1985). The GFFS is a 10-item self-report scale that assesses the fear of being overweight, a characteristic of anorexia and bulimia. Adolescents with anorexia as well as those with bulimia have higher GFFS scores than normals, and GFFS scores are related to general psychological symptomatology in these groups.

Forbidden Food Survey.   (FFS; Ruggiero, Williamson, Davis, Schlundt, & Carey, 1988). The FFS is a 45-item self-report questionnaire that assesses emotional reactions to food types and caloric levels. Adolescents with bulimia report more negative reactions to all of the food/calorie groups of the FFS and to foods of high and medium caloric levels from the grain, meat, and milk groups in particular. This negative reaction to food in general and to high-calorie food in particular is consistent with a fear of binge eating, which typically involves high-calorie food.

Eating Disorder Inventory-2.   (EDI-2; see earlier description). Adolescents with bulimia show elevations on all of the EDI-2 scales relative to control samples, with the largest differences occurring on the DT, B, I, ID, and IA scales (Gross, Rosen, Leitenberg, & Willmuth, 1986). If the EDI-2 is given to an individual with suspected bulimia, the B subscale, as a measure of bulimic symptoms, is an excellent substitute for the CHEQ or BS (Welch & Hall, 1989).

Eating Attitudes Test.   (EAT; see earlier description). Like the EDI-2, the EAT can be useful for providing a multifactorial view of eating beliefs and behaviors in individuals with suspected bulimia. Adolescents with bulimia have also been found to score higher than nonreferred control subjects on the Dieting, Bulimia, and total scores of the EAT (Gross et al., 1986). The Bulimia subscale of the EAT can substitute for the CHEQ or BS.

Body Image Tests.   These tests involve the measurement of body image as opposed to eating behavior. Measurement of body image can be accomplished through several means: Body satisfaction questionnaires ask patients to rate their satisfaction with shape and size of body parts. Examples of such questionnaires are the Body Image Self-Evaluation Questionnaire (BISE; Lindholm & Wilson, 1988) and the Body Attitude Test (BAT; Probst et al., 1995; described earlier in this chapter). Pictoral tests of body size, such as the Body Image Silhouette (Childress, Brewerton, Hodges, & Jarrell, 1993), present the child with a set of photographs or silhouettes, from which the child must choose pictures that describe the child's actual and ideal body size. Video image distortion tests require the child to alter human body images on a video screen to show current and ideal body size (Probst, Van Coppenolle, Vandereycken, & Goris, 1992). Adolescents with bulimia show a predictable dissatisfaction with body image, but this dissatisfaction may be no greater than that of very diet-conscious ("restricting") people without bulimia (Lindholm & Wilson, 1988). Distortion of body image is greater in people with bulimia than in individuals with obesity or compulsive overeating (Williamson et al., 1990).

□ TREATMENT OPTIONS

Treatment options for Bulimia Nervosa are summarized in Table 7.6.

Medical Evaluation/Hospitalization

Although bulimia is not as immediately life threatening as is anorexia, it can create numerous physiological problems. Therefore, a thorough medical examination is indicated. In many cases, regular medical supervision or checkups are necessary as well. Hospitalization for bulimia is less frequent than for anorexia and usually occurs only in cases involving significant medical complications, severe weight loss, or constant binge-purging. Inpatient treatment typically involves a behavior management plan, intensive cognitive-behavioral and/or psychodynamic psychotherapy (individual, group, and, sometimes, family), and occasionally medication.

Psychotherapy

Cognitive-Behavioral Interventions

Most treatment for bulimia involves outpatient individual, family, and/or group psychotherapy. Psychotherapy frequently makes use of cognitive behavioral techniques, many of which are modified versions of those described for anorexia earlier in this chapter (see Peterson & Mitchell [1996] and Weiss, Katzman, & Wolchik, [1986], for more comprehensive descriptions of bulimia treatment plans).

Early in treatment, stimulus control/antecedent management (see Appendix C) strategies are implemented with the family in order to restrict the adolescent's access to binge foods such as ice cream. Stimulus control strategies include plans to restrict the amount of food in the house, to keep only nutritious food in the house, and to restrict the adolescent's access and exposure to unsupervised situations that could be tempting (ice-cream store). Rules may have to be set up about access to the refrigerator or pantry.

Goal setting and monitoring are also modified to include attention to both binges and to compensatory behaviors. Specifically, the adolescent must track urges to binge/purge and actual binge/purge episodes. Based on monitoring, the adolescent is taught to identify

TABLE 7.6   Treatment Options for Bulimia Nervosa

1. Medical Evaluation/Hospitalization
    a. Physical exam
    b. Intervention to address physical complications
    c. Restricted access to situations allowing binging or purging
2. Psychotherapy
    a. Cognitive-behavioral interventions
        (1) Assessment and joining
        (2) Psychoeducation
        (3) Goal setting
        (4) Identification of logical consequences for goal attainment
        (5) Monitoring and enforcement of eating rules by adults
        (6) Self-monitoring
        (7) Scheduling
        (8) Stimulus control strategies
        (9) Identification and restructuring of negative automatic thoughts
        (10) Relaxation techniques
        (11) Coping strategies to manage cognitions and urges related to binges
             (cognitive restructuring, thought stopping, substitution, problem solving, use
             of social support)
        (12) Self-reinforcement for lack of binge eating behavior
        (13) Addressing of family stresses
        (14) Identification and treatment of comorbid problems
        (15) Relapse prevention
    b. Psychodynamic psychotherapy
    c. Group therapy
3. Family Interventions
    a. Family therapy (typically with systemic approach focused on boundaries
       within the family)
4. Medications
    a. Fluoxetine

Note: This outline of options summarizes major treatments covered in the text. Specific treatments are
often combined into an intervention package. Refer to the text for additional descriptions of each
treatment. This table is not necessarily an exhaustive list of all treatments available.

cues that trigger binges and purges. In addition to external cues (access to food), it is important for the adolescent to learn that physiological cues (hunger) and affective cues (sadness and anxiety) are also common preludes to binges.

Scheduling of events such as mealtimes (three per day, at appropriate intervals), amount of food to be eaten (a balanced and appropriate amount at each meal), and exercise are also used to provide structure for eating and activity. Menus and calorie goals are an important part of this schedule and may, in very resistant patients, require a consultation session with a dietician. Scheduling prevents the adolescent from severe dieting, which can lead to a relapse of bulimic symptoms. Parents initially take much of the responsibility for monitoring the adolescent and enforcing the schedule, with responsibility gradually transferring to the adolescent.

In addition to these monitoring-structuring strategies, coping skills are taught to manage cues (identified earlier in the treatment plan), thoughts, or urges that could lead to binges. These include cognitive restructuring, thought stopping, substitution, problem solving, and use of social support. The adolescent is given the assignment to try out certain coping strategies to resist binges, and to report on the effectiveness of this coping during later therapy sessions.

For older adolescents who live out of the home, contracts may be used to implement a self-reinforcement program that rewards non–binge eating behavior. The patient is encouraged to continue self-monitoring and to practice techniques learned in therapy. Regular monitoring of the patient's progress using the EDI-2 or related inventories is recommended throughout therapy, and assessment results may be used to identify intervention targets or areas of improvement that can be reinforced.

The final stage of cognitive-behavioral therapy for bulimia focuses on maintenance of the improved behavior and anticipation of future problems. Cognitive-behavioral therapy has been found to be generally effective in reducing bulimic symptomatology in as few as eight brief sessions (Peterson & Mitchell, 1996; Waller et al., 1996). It may be more effective than psychodynamic or nondirective therapy alone (Fairburn, 1985; Fairburn, Kirk, O'Connor, & Cooper, 1986), although the most effective intervention probably involves the flexible use of both cognitive-behavioral and psychodynamic techniques.

Psychodynamic Psychotherapy

The use of psychodynamic techniques in conjunction with cognitive-behavioral techniques to treat bulimia is widely accepted. Psychodynamic techniques involve the exploration of the origins of the eating disorder (with a particular focus on the family), the factors maintaining the behavior, and developmental issues such as independence, intimacy, loneliness, maturing, the importance of physical appearance, and need for control. The goal of these techniques is to improve the insight of the patient into the dynamics that drive the eating disorder, so that these dynamics can be resolved and removed as triggers for maladaptive behavior. The therapeutic relationship and insight into personal issues are emphasized. Because cognitive-behavioral and psychodynamic interventions share the same goals (improved eating behavior, insight into motivating factors such as thoughts and feelings), they should be regarded as complimentary and used in conjunction.

Group Psychotherapy

Group therapies combine cognitive-behavioral, psychodynamic, psychoeducational, and process-interactional techniques to form an integrated treatment for bulimia. The cognitive-behavioral and psychodynamic components are similar to those for individual psychotherapy, with the group acting as a forum for introduction and discussion of issues. Process-interactional techniques involve group activities such as role playing and psychodrama as well as use of group interaction to facilitate insight into members' motivations for maladaptive behavior. Group therapy has been shown to be effective in relieving symptoms in many individuals with bulimia (Sykes, Currie, & Gross, 1987; Yager, 1985), although a significant proportion does not benefit from group therapy. Yager (1985) suggests that patients first be tried in individual therapy before being placed in a group so that the appropriateness of group treatment may be evaluated.

Family Interventions

Family therapy for adolescents with bulimia typically follows the same pattern and examines the same issues as family therapy for patients with anorexia. Structural family interventions emphasize components of the family such as boundaries around family subsystems (i.e., the spousal subsystem), which are observed and corrected if boundaries are overly weak or overly strong. For example, the mother may be involved in a coalition with the daughter against the father, who rigidly controls the family system. The daughter's bulimic behavior gives her control in one area of her life (weight) and arouses the concern of the mother, who becomes more enmeshed with the daughter and avoids the role of parent-spouse (partner of the domineering husband). A structural intervention would seek to strengthen the spousal-parental relationship and create appropriate boundaries between the parents and child. Behavioral interventions may also be carried out in family therapy, such as the negotiation and implementation of eating contracts and reinforcement for appropriate eating behavior.

Medication

Antidepressants (typically tricyclics [imipramine/Tofranil] and selective serotonin reuptake inhibitors [fluoxetine/Prozac, sertraline/Zoloft, paroxetine/Paxil]) have been tried as medications for bulimia (Yager, 1985). Fluoxetine has received the most support for treatment of bulimia and is an approved medication for the disorder (Bezchlibnyk-Butler & Jeffries, 1997). Antidepressant medications may also be effective in reducing depressive symptoms and, therefore, have an indirect effect on bulimia by elevating mood and reducing need for binges (Fairburn, 1985; Yager, 1985).

■ ## Pica

☐ ## CLINICAL DESCRIPTION

Diagnostic Considerations

Pica is characterized by "the persistent eating of nonnutritive substances" (American Psychiatric Association, 1994, p. 95). According to DSM-IV, the persistent behavior of Pica is manifest in repeated ingestion of the substance for 1 month. The nonnutritive items that are eaten typically include sand, dirt, clay (geophagia), starch (amylyphagia), ice (pagophagia), hair (trichophagia), gravel (lithophagia), grass/leaves (foliophagia), feces (coprophagia), paint, plaster, string, cloth, paper, metal objects, glass, plastic, and cigarette butts (Feldman, 1986). Other items ingested may be food items (lettuce, tomato seeds, coffee grounds, insects, and butter) that the child eats in inappropriately large quantities or in inappropriate form.

The most common manifestation of Pica by far is in individuals with mental retardation and/or autistic disorder. Prevalence rates as high as 10–33% in individuals with severe mental retardation and 60% in autistic groups have been reported (Feldman, 1986; Kinnell, 1985). Pica behavior also co-occurs with severe psychopathology such as schizophrenia. The frequency of Pica in these groups is large enough that the possibility of Pica should be assessed routinely in individuals with diagnoses of retardation, autism, or schizophrenia.

Appearance and Features

Pica is diagnosed most frequently in infants, young children, individuals with retardation or psychosis, and, occasionally, in pregnant women. It is extremely rare in other groups of adolescents and adults. The highest prevalence of Pica in otherwise normal children occurs between the ages of 1 and 6 years; onset age is typically 12 to 24 months (Feldman, 1986; Kinnell, 1985). Most very young children will mouth or occasionally eat nonnutritive substances. However, based on parental and sensory feedback, they quickly learn what not to eat. Pica involves the repeated eating of a nonnutritive substance. (Appearance and features of Pica are summarized in Table 7.7.)

Etiology

Several factors have been hypothesized to account for Pica. First, nutritional factors such as deficiencies in vital substances (e.g., iron) have been suggested as the motivators behind the compulsive eating behavior. This explanation has been buoyed by case studies of subjects whose Pica abated following nutritional supplements (Feldman, 1986). However, Pica behavior often does not change with a change of diet, and the nonnutritive substance ingested in Pica often does not contain the nutrients that the patient lacks. An alternative hypothesis suggests that Pica causes nutritional deficiency by impairing gastrointestinal functioning and substituting for nutritive foods.

A second group of factors hypothesized to account for Pica is psychological. Psychoanalytic views stress the emergence of Pica in individuals who are fixed at the oral phase of development, seeking gratification through oral stimulation. Social learning theories suggest modeling as a factor accounting for the adoption of the unusual eating behavior. Preliminary evidence for this view comes from studies indicating that children with pets (that presumably eat nonnutritive substances at a greater rate than humans) and with siblings diagnosed with Pica are more prone to having Pica (Feldman, 1986). Psychodynamic views focus on Pica as a response to intrapsychic and/or environmental stress; they cite as support studies indicating a higher incidence of Pica in children who are separated from a parent or who are suffering from child abuse/neglect (Prince, 1989).

TABLE 7.7 Appearance and Features of Pica

COMMON FEATURES

1. Infant/toddler age or mentally retarded
2. Onset before age 2
3. Ingestion of nonnutritive substances

OCCASIONAL FEATURES

1. Lower SES
2. Other behavior problems

Note: The features listed in the table are often seen but are not universal. Some features may be diagnostically relevant or required, whereas others may not be required for diagnosis. "Common" features are typical of the disorder; "occasional" features appear frequently but are not necessarily seen in a majority of cases.

A third group of explanations for Pica stresses the role of cultural factors in its development. Soil-eating (geophagia) in some societies, for example, is believed to promote physical well-being. The incidence of geophagia is believed to be higher in Africa because of cultural acceptance and cultural beliefs in some tribes (Prince, 1989). In much of U.S. society, on the other hand, Pica is associated with shame and humiliation; hence, Pica is often hidden and is difficult to diagnose or detect.

☐ ASSESSMENT PATTERNS

A sample assessment battery for Pica is shown in Table 7.8.

Broad Assessment Strategies

Cognitive Assessment

Clinician-Administered. An often critical component in assessing Pica is the determination of the child's level of intellectual functioning because many children with Pica (especially older children) are intellectually or developmentally delayed. To the extent that a child shows deviant scores on these tests, a significant component of the Pica may be assumed to be low intellectual and adaptive functioning.

Infants up to 42 months may be tested with the Bayley-II, whereas older children (age 2 and older) are often assessed with the SB:FE or one of the Wechsler scales (WPPSI-R for children age 3–7 or WISC-III for children age 6–17). Because many children with Pica are mentally retarded, selection of the appropriate intelligence test is crucial (see Chapter 12 for discussion of tests to use for patients with mental retardation). If a shorter IQ test is needed, the K-BIT or WASI would be appropriate.

Tests of adaptive functioning such as the VABS and ABES can provide useful estimates of the child's ability to meet the basic demands of the environment (including self-care and independent functioning), and they are required for a diagnosis of mental retardation. Children with severe mental retardation and Pica do poorly on these scales. Adaptive behavior

TABLE 7.8   Sample Assessment Battery for Pica and Rumination Disorder

COGNITIVE

1. IQ Test (Kaufman Brief Intelligence Test, Bayley-II, or Wechsler Scale)
2. Vineland Adaptive Behavior Scales

BEHAVIORAL

1. Child Behavior Checklist

FAMILY

1. Family Environment Scale

Note: Assessment instruments are intended to supplement (not substitute for) a good clinical interview and, when possible, a structured diagnostic interview.

scales indicate the extent to which the child can be expected to participate without assistance in such basic behaviors as self-care and eating.

Behavioral Assessment

Parent-Report. Because most children with Pica are young and/or retarded, self-report tests have little if any use in the assessment of Pica. Parent-report tests, on the other hand, can be quite useful. Items pertaining to Pica can be found on some major child behavior checklists (e.g., CBCL) and can be used as indicators that such behaviors should be probed in a clinical interview.

Family Assessment

Parent-Report. Because Pica occasionally occurs as a result of lax parental supervision or a stressful family environment (Minde, 1988), attention should be given to assessing family dynamics and major stresses in the environment. In addition to direct observation, family assessment measures such as the FES may be useful in identifying difficulties in the family that may contribute to the child's condition. Although no systematic research has investigated FES scores of families of children with Pica, high Conflict, low Cohesion, low Expressiveness, and low Independence scores would be expected in abusive families in which a child has Pica. Low FES Supportive factor scores and high FES Conflicted factor scores characterize these families as well.

☐   ## TREATMENT OPTIONS

Treatment options for Pica are outlined in Table 7.9.

Medical Evaluation/Hospitalization

All children with Pica should be referred to a physician for evaluation if they have not already been evaluated. Based on nutrition screening studies, the physician may prescribe nutritional supplements, which may have some effect on the Pica behavior. However, as noted before, in the great majority of cases, such supplements do little to mitigate the behavior. In addition to assessing nutritive status, the physician should evaluate the child for other negative effects of the Pica such as parasites, lead poisoning, anemia, and bowel problems.

In cases of severe or life-threatening Pica, hospitalization may be necessary for evaluation and intervention. Interventions for hospitalized children with Pica generally mirror outpatient interventions (discussed later), although the former are delivered with greater supervision, intensity, and duration. Use of medication alone (other than nutritional supplements) to treat Pica is unusual.

Behavioral Interventions

A common behavioral intervention is differential reinforcement of other behavior (DRO; Kalfus, Fisher-Gross, Marvullo, & Nau, 1987) in which the caretaker rewards the child (e.g., with verbal praise and physical affection) for every time period (i.e., 30 seconds) in which behavior other than Pica has occurred. DRO has the advantage of teaching positive

TABLE 7.9   Treatment Options for Pica

1. Medical Evaluation/Hospitalization
    a. Physical exam
    b. Nutrition studies
    c. Blood/tissue toxicity studies
2. Behavioral Interventions
    a. Differential reinforcement of other behavior
    b. Overcorrection
    c. Response prevention
    d. Antecedent management
    e. Time-out following pica behavior
    f. Aversive techniques (use with caution)
    g. Habit reversal
3. Psychotherapy
    a. Nutritional education
    b. Play therapy

Note: This outline of options summarizes major treatments covered in the text. Specific treatments are often combined into an intervention package. Refer to the text for additional descriptions of each treatment. This table is not necessarily an exhaustive list of all treatments available.

substitute behaviors to children with Pica. In addition, many therapists and parents prefer the "positive" tenor of the DRO intervention. However, DRO requires almost constant attention to the child's behavior in addition to the energy to deliver reinforcement repeatedly. Many parents cannot sustain this effort over long time periods. In addition to DRO of short time periods, tangible rewards such as food and stars can be used to reward long periods during which Pica does not occur.

Overcorrection is another intervention used to treat Pica. In this intervention, the caretaker reprimands the child, removes the substance from the child's mouth, cleans the child's mouth (or has the child clean the mouth, for example, by brushing teeth), and has the child clean the surroundings of nonnutritive substances. Although overcorrection deals directly with the Pica behavior, it can lead to caretaker-child battles and negative affect toward the caretaker.

Unlike overcorrection, which occurs after the Pica behavior, response prevention takes place in anticipation of the Pica behavior, before the child has placed the substance in the mouth. Response prevention involves blocking or pushing the child's hand away from the mouth prior to the child's placing the object in the mouth. Although response prevention takes considerable effort from the supervising adults, it has been found to be effective and to require less effort than restraints (LeBlanc, Piazza, & Krug, 1997). A more restrictive form of response prevention involves placing a screen or guard over the face or mouth. This intervention should be used with caution because it can be aversive to the child and can interfere with normal interaction with the environment.

Antecedent management (Appendix C) works at an even earlier stage than response prevention. Antecedent management involves removing the objects that are ingested by the child from the environment. Although this intervention may be effective in some cases, many children will find other substances to ingest, and certain objects (such as hair) are quite difficult to remove completely from the child's presence.

Several aversive behavioral techniques have been suggested for children with severe, intractable Pica. Time-out and physical restraint, for example, may be used to remove behavior and/or access to reinforcers (LeBlanc et al., 1997). Two other aversive techniques that have been used are exposure to aromatic ammonia following Pica behavior and spray (in the face) with a water mist following Pica behavior. Water mist treatment may be the more effective and less ethically problematic of these two treatments (Rojahn, McGonigle, Curcio, & Dixon, 1987). These more severe aversive conditioning procedures should generally be used only in cases of dangerous Pica after other behavioral techniques have failed.

For children with average intelligence and motivation to discontinue the Pica behavior, habit reversal may be an effective treatment. Woods, Miltenberger, and Lumley, (1996) describe a habit-reversal treatment that involved awareness training, competing response training, and social praise for a boy who chewed on clothing and fingernails. During awareness training, the boy learned to identify and monitor the Pica behavior. He then learned a competing response to the Pica: removing the object from his mouth and pursing his lips for one minute, whenever he put clothing or fingers in his mouth. He practiced the awareness training and competing response training in session, and his family praised him when he used the competing response *in vivo*. The treatment was effective in nearly eliminating Pica behavior.

Psychotherapy

For higher-functioning older children, nutritional education, play therapy, and traditional forms of "talking" psychotherapy may be available as treatment options. The nutritional education may take the form of teaching the child about the hazards of eating nonnutritive substances and the benefits of eating healthy food. Play and psychotherapy may address life stresses, attitudes toward eating, and controlling compulsive behavior. For children facing significant environmental stresses, simple attention to behavioral contingencies may not be sufficient to reduce the Pica behavior (Minde, 1988). Play and psychotherapy can give the child a chance to act or talk out his or her beliefs, fears, and coping strategies. With a reduction in appraised stress is expected to come a reduction in Pica behavior, which acts as a defense mechanism to deflect attention from the stress.

■ Rumination Disorder

☐ CLINICAL DESCRIPTION

Diagnostic Considerations

Rumination Disorder is characterized in DSM-IV as "repeated regurgitation and rechewing of food" (American Psychiatric Association, 1994, p. 98), without an explanatory medical problem, for at least 1 month. There must have been a period of normal functioning prior to the rumination. No age criteria are specified in the diagnostic requirements, although the typical age of onset for Rumination Disorder is between 3 and 12 months. However, in children with severe developmental delay, the disorder can begin much later in life.

Appearance and Features

Appearance and features of Rumination Disorder are listed in Table 7.10. The rumination is often associated with facial expressions and behavior indicating either that the child derives satisfaction and relaxation from the rumination activity or that the food is brought up into the mouth without nausea or disgust. The rumination behavior typically follows the adoption of a characteristic position of arching the back with the head held back and making sucking movements with the tongue. Occasionally children will stick fingers or other objects into their mouth to initiate the rumination activity. Food brought up from the stomach may be either spit out, drooled, chewed, or reswallowed. Rumination Disorder is a serious condition, with a mortality rate as high as 25% (American Psychiatric Association, 1994).

The distinction between children with and without mental retardation who develop Rumination Disorder has led some authors to speculate that there are two or more subtypes of the disorder. Mayes, Humphrey, Handford, and Mitchell (1988) review data suggesting that two subtypes of Rumination Disorder exist: Psychogenic Rumination, a disorder characterized by onset during infancy and normal developmental functioning in the vast majority of cases; and Self-Stimulating Rumination, characterized by onset at any age (including infancy and adulthood) and occurring exclusively in individuals with mental retardation. Two other types of rumination have been suggested (LaRocca & Della-Fera, 1986): an Adult Rumination type, which occurs in otherwise normal adults and may be the remnant of untreated childhood rumination; and a Bulimic type that co-occurs with Bulimia Nervosa.

The Bulimic subtype of Rumination Disorder may occur because of the frequent presence of self-induced vomiting in some individuals with bulimia. Individuals with bulimia who develop concurrent Rumination Disorder may have learned to retain the regurgitated

---

TABLE 7.10   Appearance and Features of Rumination Disorder

COMMON FEATURES

1. Repeated regurgitation
2. Weight loss/insufficient weight gain
3. Onset between 3 and 12 months of age, unless mentally retarded
4. Expression of satisfaction or lack of distress during rumination

OCCASIONAL FEATURES

1. Mental retardation/developmental disability
2. Sticking things into the mouth (to cause regurgitation)
3. Disturbed parent-child relationships (Psychogenic Rumination)

Note: The features listed in the table are often seen but are not universal. Some features may be diagnostically relevant or required, whereas others may not be required for diagnosis. "Common" features are typical of the disorder; "occasional" features appear frequently but are not necessarily seen in a majority of cases.

food in order to hide it during times of possible detection. Eventually, some food may be re-swallowed in a further attempt to avoid detection or for self-stimulating purposes. Because of the possibility of development of Rumination Disorder, some authors have suggested that all individuals with bulimia be screened for rumination symptoms (Weakley et al., 1997).

Etiology

Psychogenic Rumination Disorder

Psychogenic Rumination Disorder has typical onset between age 3 to 12 months. Major etiological theories of this disorder emphasize the role of the environment in the development of Rumination Disorder. Psychodynamic theories suggest that the caretaker interacts with the child in an immature or mechanical way, bringing little satisfaction to the child in the course of the interaction. The infant responds to this deprivation by developing difficulties with oral and feeding needs. Eventually, significant feeding problems, such as recurrent vomiting, may occur. As these problems develop, the infant may discover that it is pleasurable to rechew the regurgitated food. The regurgitation and rechewing then become a behavior pattern that provides the neglected infant with some pleasure and satisfaction, replacing that lost in the parent-infant relationship.

Research concerning psychodynamic theories of the development of Rumination Disorder has found disturbed mother-child relationships in some infants with Rumination Disorder. Familial problems such as maternal psychiatric disorder, neglect, and family stress have been cited in case studies of children with Rumination Disorder (Mayes et al., 1988). However, studies with larger samples do not always find extremely disturbed mother-child relationships (Sauvage, Leddet, Hameury, & Barthelemy, 1985), and certainly not all children with impaired mother-child relationships develop Rumination Disorder.

Learning theories of the etiology of Rumination Disorder emphasize the role of the rumination in bringing attention to the infant. The disorder emerges from one or several incidents in which the infant regurgitates food (because of some physiological reason) and receives attention from parents. Eventually, the regurgitation of food occurs to gain the reinforcement of parental attention.

Self-Stimulating Rumination

This second subtype of Rumination Disorder is assumed to be associated with cognitive rather than social factors. Age of onset of this type of rumination is much more variable than that for Psychogenic Rumination, with a range from infancy through early adulthood. In general, Self-Stimulating Rumination occurs in individuals who are considered to be severely impaired, even relative to the mentally retarded group.

Self-Stimulating Rumination is generally not the result of impaired parenting or unmet emotional needs, although this may occasionally be the case. More often, Self-Stimulating Rumination is created and maintained by environmental contingencies or by a need for self-stimulation. The self-stimulation hypothesis is particularly relevant because these children's impaired cognitive abilities may restrict them from using many of the usual internal and external sources of gratification. Deprived of these gratification sources, they revert to the simple sensory-motor gratification of rumination.

□   ## ASSESSMENT PATTERNS

Medical Examination

Assessment of Rumination Disorder must begin with a thorough medical examination to rule out any of numerous possible physical causes, including gastrointestinal (e.g., pyloric stenosis), metabolic (e.g., electrolyte abnormalities), and central nervous system (e.g., hydrocephalus) abnormalities (Mestre, Resnick, & Berman, 1983). Because of the physiological consequences of rumination (including electrolyte imbalance and malnutrition), the child should be closely followed by a pediatrician even after physical causes have been ruled out.

Broad Assessment Strategies

Cognitive Assessment

Clinician-Administered.   As with Pica, it is important to determine the child's level of cognitive functioning in the evaluation of Rumination Disorder. The major intelligence tests (Bayley-II, SB:FE, WPPSI-R, and WISC-III) are applied to Rumination Disorder in the same way that they are applied to Pica. For screening purposes, a brief intelligence test such as the K-BIT or WASI should be used.

Children with Rumination Disorder who score in the Low Average IQ range or higher (IQ of 80+) are likely to be of the Psychogenic subtype, suggesting that psychosocial factors should be extensively evaluated in follow-up testing. On the other hand, children in the Borderline range or below (less than 80 IQ) are more likely to have a Self-Stimulating Rumination Disorder. For this latter group of children, intellectual deficit and self-stimulation must be considered in addition to any psychosocial contributors to the disorder.

Family Assessment

Parent-Report.   Assessment of the parents and caretakers of children with Rumination Disorder may be of importance, particularly in the case of Psychogenic Rumination with a suspected caretaking component. Administration of parent personality and family environment tests (such as the FES) may be valuable in planning treatment. Scales reflecting caretaking and interpersonal/relationship difficulties (scales 4, 6, and 8 on the MMPI; Cohesion, Expressiveness, and Conflict on the FES) should be examined carefully for problems.

Syndrome-Specific Tests

Clinician-Administered

In infants the feeding interaction between parent and child should be closely observed. As noted earlier, infants with Rumination Disorder may appear tense and stiff when fed and will follow meals with a characteristic arching of the back and head that leads into rumination behavior. Distress during rumination is generally not observed. Other parent-child interactions should be observed as well, as an impaired parent-child relationship may suggest a dynamic driving the rumination behavior. Attention should be paid to antecedent events that predict rumination, as well as to reinforcers, particularly attention, that follow the rumination behavior. These antecedents and consequences of the rumination behavior are likely to become the major targets of a behavioral intervention.

☐ TREATMENT OPTIONS

Treatments for Rumination Disorder (Table 7.11) reflect the major features of the disorder. Because virtually all children with Rumination Disorder are cognitively limited by age or intellectual deficit, individual psychotherapy is rarely an option. Furthermore, because medical causes for the behavior are ruled out in the process of formulating the diagnosis, medication alone is usually not effective in eliminating symptoms. Hence, treatments for Rumination Disorder must rely on the child's environment and behavior to produce change.

Family Interventions

Parent-Child Relationship Therapy

This type of therapy emphasizes the need for the infant to have a warm, stimulating environment and a supportive relationship with the parent. Parents are provided support and guidance by the staff and are encouraged to modify their behavior to meet the infant's emotional and bonding needs. In particular, regular, nonthreatening, supportive interactions are encouraged, at first under supervision and later at home. This intervention is often com-

TABLE 7.11 Treatment Options for Rumination Disorder

1. Family Interventions
    a. Parent-child relationship therapy
        (1) Supervised, didactic sessions of regular, nonthreatening, supportive interactions between parent and child
        (2) Education about child development and parenting techniques
    b. Family therapy
    c. Marital therapy
2. Behavioral Interventions
    a. Punishment techniques
    b. Overcorrection
    c. Extinction
    d. Differential reinforcement of other/inconsistent behaviors
    e. Competing response training
    f. Satiation techniques

Note: This outline of options summarizes major treatments covered in the text. Specific treatments are often combined into an intervention package. Refer to the text for additional descriptions of each treatment. This table is not necessarily an exhaustive list of all treatments available.

bined with parenting skills training, which involves education about child development and parenting techniques, in addition to attention to the parent's adjustment problems.

Family/Marital Therapy

Traditional family or marital therapy for parents of children with Rumination Disorder seeks to address familial problems that drive maladaptive and nonnurturing interactions between parents and children. The role of the child and of the rumination behavior in the family system may be assessed. Then suggestions are made to modify the system to make it incompatible with the rumination behavior. In addition, work may be performed to keep marital problems within the spousal subsystem and, thus, insulate the infant from parental conflicts that may result in stress and less nurturing behavior. Overt conflict and other family stresses should be identified and minimized.

Both parent-child and family-marital therapy for Rumination Disorder have been criticized for resulting in slow progress and placing high demands on staff (Starin & Fuqua, 1987; Tierney & Jackson, 1984). Clinical experiences and case studies have shown them to be effective in individual cases, but there have been no large-scale studies. Because Rumination Disorder almost always involves some relationship issues (if not etiologically, then as a consequence of the disorder), family-based interventions are often combined with other interventions into a treatment package.

Behavioral Interventions

Punishment Techniques

Despite numerous legal and ethical issues, punishment is a frequently used technique to decrease rumination behavior. All punishment techniques involve early identification of rumination behavior followed by the administration of a noxious stimulus. Generally, the noxious stimulus is administered during rumination precursor behaviors such as lip-smacking, back-arching, sticking a finger in the throat, gagging, or the appearance of small amounts of regurgitated food. Punishment techniques differ by the nature of the noxious stimulus.

The most widely used and ethically acceptable noxious stimuli are strong negative tasting liquids such as Tabasco sauce or highly concentrated lemon juice. Treatment with these stimuli is accomplished by squirting a small quantity of the liquid into the person's mouth upon the appearance of rumination behavior. Lemon juice is especially effective because it combines a noxious taste with a reflexive pucker response that is physically incompatible with regurgitation of food. Lemon juice is also more acceptable to parents because it is a concentrate of a familiar substance.

Noxious tastes have been effective in reducing rumination behavior, although generally not as quickly or completely as shock treatments (described later). One drawback to the use of these substances is the possibility that they may irritate the mouth and surrounding area. Furthermore, if the patient is surprised by the noxious taste, a risk exists of aspirating the lemon or Tabasco juice and ruminated material into the lungs.

Electric shock is another type of noxious stimulus that has been used in research studies of the effects of punishment on Self-Stimulating Rumination. Shock is used less often for Psychogenic Rumination. Studies of the effect of shock punishment on rumination indicate that shock is a very effective treatment, resulting in rapid decreases in rumination behaviors to near-zero levels (Starin & Fuqua, 1987). Although apparently very effective, shock treatment has a number of drawbacks, including a need for the patient to be in contact with a shocking device (often resulting in limited mobility), occasional failure to maintain treatment gains at follow-up, and ethical concerns about the use of shock treatment. For these reasons, shock treatment, as well as other pain-related noxious stimuli (such as pinching), is used only in extreme, dangerous, or multiple-failure cases.

Overcorrection

Overcorrection for rumination involves responses in which the patient restores the environment to its previous state and practices desired responses. Specifically, the child must clean up the vomit, change clothes, brush teeth several times, and gargle with an oral antiseptic. Overcorrection for Self-Stimulating Rumination has been shown to be effective and is often combined with other techniques.

Extinction

This technique involves withholding the reinforcement that is maintaining the rumination behavior. Identification of the reinforcement is critical and usually requires careful behavioral assessment. In addition, a cooperative and controlled environment is required. Because the reinforcer most frequently identified (in the case of Psychogenic Rumination) is attention, extinction techniques often involve ignoring the behavior or withdrawal of social interaction. Although extinction represents a useful adjunct to other techniques, it is likely to be only moderately effective if used alone because it does not address the self-stimulating motivation for much rumination behavior.

Differential Reinforcement of Other Behavior (DRO)

DRO and Differential Reinforcement of Incompatible Behavior (DRI) share the characteristic of providing the patient with substitute responses for rumination. Most DRO protocols involve the provision of a reinforcer when the rumination behavior has not occurred for a specified period of time. It is assumed that this will result in an increase in nonrumination responses, which are reinforced. Although this technique is often effective in reducing rumination behavior, problems can arise with patients who exhibit such high levels of rumination that it is difficult to catch them not ruminating for any significant period of time. In addition, it is not always desirable to reward the behaviors in which the subject engages between ruminations; these intermittent behaviors may be undesirable or maladaptive themselves.

DRI involves reinforcing behaviors that are incompatible with rumination and that eventually replace rumination. Behaviors selected for DRI include toy play and talking. Like DRO, DRI has been shown to be moderately effective in reducing rumination behavior.

Competing Response Training

Competing response training (CRT), a component of habit reversal, is similar to DRI and can be used with older children of normal intelligence who are motivated to stop the rumination symptoms. CRT involves providing the child with an alternative response that takes the place of the rumination and is incompatible with rumination behavior. Weakley et al. (1997), for example, describe the treatment of an adolescent of normal intelligence who developed Rumination Disorder as an outgrowth of her bulimia. The adolescent was asked to chew gum following meals, when most rumination tended to occur. Because the adolescent liked gum and was motivated to stop the pain that was associated with rumination, she was cooperative with the intervention. The gum chewing rapidly took the place of rumination, with symptoms resolving in 4 weeks.

Satiation Treatments

These treatments involve feeding the patient large quantities of food, possibly resulting in sufficient esophageal stimulation to reduce the need to ruminate (although it is really not known why this technique works). Studies using satiation report some reduction in rumination, although the ability of this technique to consistently produce favorable outcomes is questionable.

Combination Treatments

A combination of the individual treatments described earlier is by far the most common plan for both Psychogenic and Self-Stimulating Rumination Disorder. Typically, a family-based intervention is combined with lemon juice (punishment technique) and DRO/DRI. Because of their multidimensional approach, these packages are likely to have the greatest efficacy in reducing rumination behavior.

■ Feeding Disorder of Infancy or Early Childhood

☐ CLINICAL DESCRIPTION

Diagnostic Considerations

Feeding Disorder of Infancy or Early Childhood (FDI) is a syndrome characterized by a failure to eat adequately prior to age 6, causing weight stagnation or loss (Table 7.12). If the weight stagnation or loss is severe, the child may meet criteria for a related syndrome, nonorganic failure-to-thrive (NOFT). NOFT is characterized by weight below the fifth percentile for age, normal head circumference, malnourished appearance, failure to gain weight for at least one month, abnormal social development, developmental delays, and the absence of an organic syndrome to explain the weight problems (Green, 1989; Kelley & Heffer, 1990; Ramsay, 1995; Tibbits-Kleber & Howell, 1985).

In addition to NOFT, FDI can be associated with Reactive Attachment Disorder of Infancy or Early Childhood (RAD; see Chapter 16) because feeding and attachment are closely interrelated in infants and toddlers. Children with FDI have been found to have higher rates of attachment problems compared to healthy children. Furthermore, the mothers of children with FDI have a higher incidence of insecure attachments to their own mothers (Drotar,

TABLE 7.12 Epidemiology and Course of Feeding Disorder of Infancy or Early Childhood

---

Prevalence: Probably less than 4% in general population; may account for as many as 2–5% of pediatric admissions.

Sex Ratio (Male:Female):   1:1

Typical Onset Age: 3–24 months of age; onset is diagnostically required prior to age 6.

Course: Onset sometimes occurs after a discrete event (illness, surgery, switching to a different type of food), but other children show chronic feeding problems from very early ages. Malnutrition and developmental delay can result from poor intake and low weight. Placement of gastrostomy tube (G-tube) or nasogastric tube (NG tube) is sometimes required to deliver nutrition directly to the stomach. Many children respond to a multidimensional medical-behavioral plan; remission without intensive behavioral intervention is sometimes seen (probably as a result of some change in parental behavior). Long-term outcomes of behavioral problems and cognitive delays have been reported in severe cases.

Common Comorbid Conditions: 1. Reactive Attachment Disorder
2. Oppositional-Defiant Disorder (toddlers and preschoolers)

Relevant Subtypes: 1. Posttraumatic Feeding Disorder
2. Attachment-Based FDI

1995). A subtype of FDI that is characterized by poor attachment has been proposed (Chatoor & Egan, 1983) but is not recognized in DSM-IV.

Appearance and Features

The characteristics of FDI (Table 7.13) are most apparent during the parent-child feeding interaction, which can take several forms. Typically, the feeding problem behaviors of the FDI child involve pushing food (or utensils) away from the mouth, refusal to open the mouth, throwing food (or utensils or dishes), spitting food out, screaming, squirming, turning the head away from food, trying to get out of the chair, or failure to attend to the food. Initial maladaptive parental responses are things such as criticism, screaming at the child, stuffing food into the child's mouth, giving the child increased attention during food refusal, distracting the child from the meal with a toy, looking exasperated, feeding the child too quickly, or not allowing the child to choose the type of food to be eaten next.

Frequently, the child is initially difficult to feed because of temperament problems, oral-motor problems, gastrointestinal problems (such as reflux), or illness. Difficult or slow-to-warm-up temperaments may be characteristic of the majority of children who develop FDI (Reifsnider, 1996). Alternatively, the family environment may be characterized by chaos, neglect, or conflict, which upsets the child and causes reduced appetite and reduced feeding behavior. In some cases, parents do not notice or do not respond to their child's feeding rhythm and feed the child too quickly or too slowly, provoking a negative response from the child. Other parents misjudge infant cues of satiety, mistakenly thinking that their child is hungry when he or she is not. This can lead to over- or underfeeding,

TABLE 7.13   Appearance and Features of Feeding Disorder of Infancy

COMMON FEATURES

1. Failure to eat adequately
2. Loss of, or failure to gain, weight
3. Onset prior to age 6
4. Maladaptive feeding behavior: pushing food away from mouth, refusal to open mouth, throwing food, spitting food out, trying to get away from the meal, failure to attend to the food
5. Power struggles with caretaker around feeding issues

OCCASIONAL FEATURES

1. Difficult temperament
2. Oral-motor or oral-sensory problems
3. History of illness with adverse impact on feeding behavior (illness can no longer be the cause of the feeding problems)
4. Attachment abnormalities
5. Abnormal/negative care or home environment (abuse, neglect, chaotic family, conflictual family environment, separation from caretaker)
6. Inadequate stimulation from environment
7. Lethargy
8. Ambivalent or disinterested attitude of parent toward child, especially at meals
9. Failure of parent to respond to social cues of child
10. Developmental (especially language) delay
11. Parental psychopathology: insecurity, depression, dependence
12. Lack of parenting knowledge

Note: The features listed in the table are often seen but are not universal. Some features may be diagnostically relevant or required, whereas others may not be required for diagnosis. "Common" features are typical of the disorder; "occasional" features appear frequently but are not necessarily seen in a majority of cases.

which causes the infant to associate feeding with unpleasantness (Fischhoff, 1989). Another common presentation is characterized by an atypical feeding schedule. Children who are allowed to eat small amounts constantly ("graze") during the day may never develop sufficient hunger to eat a nutritious and caloric meal. On the other hand, children whose meal and snack schedule is chaotic may not develop the normal cycles of hunger that are associated with specific mealtimes.

Regardless of their initial cause, a child's feeding problems are often frustrating and a concern to parents, provoking feelings of inadequacy, anxiety, and anger. The parent's reaction then reflects these feelings and creates conflict or a lack of connection between parent and child during meals. If meals then become unpleasant or ungratifying, the child will lose interest in mealtime interaction. Ultimately, negative feeding interactions may cause the infant to associate feeding with discomfort and distress, leading to fussiness and avoidance at mealtimes.

Toddlers and preschoolers with FDI may begin to use eating as a means of exerting control over their environment. Such children use eating as a means of controlling parental attention and as a way of expressing anger. If this dynamic is present, the child often has associated oppositional and defiant behaviors outside of mealtimes.

As a result of negative interactions with the child, parents may develop negative feelings and parenting practices toward the child. Parental anxiety and depression is a significant risk. Parents may also become more avoidant of the child and engage in less interaction with the child. In extreme cases, nurturant behaviors may be almost absent, with interactions reduced largely to monitoring and commands directed at the child. The resulting parent-child relationship may become characterized largely by harsh commands and power struggles on the one hand, and avoidance and reduced interaction on the other hand. For example, interactions between children with FDI and parents are characterized by more conflict and fewer positive interchanges as compared to control families (Puckering et al., 1995).

The course of FDI can be serious. Infants and children with severe FDI can be listless, withdrawn, apathetic, and irritable. Malnutrition, growth deformity, and developmental delays are a significant risk. For infants in this category, immediate medical intervention is essential. Infants with FDI may have a higher incidence of psychiatric symptoms and achievement problems later in development (Drotar, 1995). Cognitive delay or impairment occurs in many cases of FDI (Puckering et al., 1995; Ramsay, 1995), and the effects can be irreversible in severe cases. Cognitive delay appears to result from both a combination of malnutrition and lack of stimulation from the environment.

Etiology

Drotar (1995) suggests that failure to thrive may emerge from a critical combination of risk factors in the parent (such as psychopathology or distress), the child (such as temperament), and the child's social context (family and community). No one factor has been found to be consistently responsible for FDI, suggesting that FDI is probably caused by multiple factors that interact in a unique way in each case.

In many cases, FDI seems to be caused by problems in parent-child relationships or in problematic contingencies surrounding feeding behavior. When neglect is involved, the child experiences a lack of stimulation, which could cause growth deficits by way of neuroendocrinological mechanisms (Tibbits-Kleber & Howell, 1985). Less severe variants of neglect occur when the parent ignores the child during meals. When conflict is present, the child's emotional upset may interfere with appetite and with the focused behavior needed to orient to the mealtime interaction. Grazing and other problems with scheduling interfere with the normal development of hunger at certain times of the day, leading to lower calorie intake at mealtimes.

In other cases, parental psychopathology, low intellectual functioning, or inability to change behavior leads to maladaptive parent behavior at feeding times. Some parents are unable to read their child's cues. Others express their anger or frustration at the child by "forcing" him or her to eat. Parents with borderline intellectual or social functioning may simply not know how to feed the child or how to create the structure to facilitate normal feeding schedules and interactions. Bad advice from parents, friends, or quasi-professionals may also result in poor feeding behavior on the part of the parent. Parents may believe that they should restrict their child's intake or that they should feed their child in a way that will cause malnutrition.

Chatoor and Egan (1983) presented a theory of the development of NOFT that integrates some of these parent-child relationship issues. According to this theory, infants (especially those with difficult temperaments) sometimes challenge their mothers with food refusal during the normal process of differentiation that occurs between 6 and 12 months of age. Rather than responding with accommodation to their infants' developing autonomy, vulnerable mothers respond to this food refusal with feelings of distress and uncertainty, turning to more forceful feeding methods in order to achieve feeding goals. The combination of the mother's lack of understanding of the child's autonomy needs and the child's willful temperament causes conflict and power struggles around feeding. In support of this theory, there is evidence that difficult child temperament and maternal failure to match the child's temperament with her behavior is a factor in some NOFT/FDI cases (Reifsnider, 1996).

Problems with eating and swallowing mechanics are another possible cause of FDI. Infants may have difficulty with the process of chewing and swallowing food, causing difficulty with eating solids. In other cases, some infants have an oversensitive oral area or an oversensitive gag reflex; such problems cause oral defensiveness, in which the infant resists the placement of solids in the mouth area as a result of hypersensitivity. Even in infants without these problems initially, failure to introduce solids until late in development (after 1 year of age) can cause problems with sensory or motor oral functioning (Ramsay, 1995).

Some feeding disorders occur after an illness or surgery, which disrupts the child's schedule; other illnesses, such as reflux, are directly associated with feeding problems. In some cases, illnesses with no apparent overlap with feeding can impact on infants' ability to feed. For example, infants with cardiac or lung problems may have difficulty with sustained sucking and swallowing because the short interruption in breathing robs their body of oxygen (Ramsay, 1995). In other cases, negative experiences involving the nose, mouth, or throat can cause a posttraumatic feeding disorder, in which the child gags and refuses food (Benoit, Green, & Arts-Rodas, 1997). Even after illnesses are treated successfully, parents and children must relearn proper feeding behavior. Failure to do so can result in the emergence of FDI. FDI is not diagnosed if a current illness is solely responsible for the child's eating problems.

☐   ASSESSMENT PATTERNS

Broad Assessment Strategies

Cognitive Assessment

Clinician-Administered. Because of the risk of malnutrition, lack of stimulation, and developmental delay, sensory, motor, and cognitive assessment should be considered for children with FDI. Tests such as the Bayley-II may indicate intellectual and motor deficits. The VABS can provide insights into the child's development of adaptive behavior. Overall, it is important to track these children cognitively because of the long-term intellectual risks of malnutrition.

Family Assessment

Parent-Report. Formal psychological assessment may be helpful in understanding parental contributions to the dynamics underlying maladaptive family interactions. Mothers of children with NOFT have been the target of some study, and the results of this research may be applied to mothers of children with FDI. No assessment research exists on fathers of children with NOFT/FDI.

Maternal defensiveness and denial may appear on the MMPI as an elevated L (for low SES mothers) or K (for higher SES mothers). Additional elevations for distressed mothers may be expected on scales 2 and 7, reflecting emotional upset and/or depression. An elevated scale 4 likely indicates troubles in the current family or family of origin and should be followed up by an FES. Difficulties with empathy and nurturance may be manifest in a 4–5 codetype for women. Scales 3 and 0 indicate the mother's social presentation; mothers with a high 3 and low 0 are likely to be selfish and needy/dependent in relationships. They may be unable to give their infant sufficient stimulation because they themselves are in need of attention and validation from others. Mothers with a low 3 and high 0 may be reclusive, introverted, and avoidant of any social relationships. Elevations on scales 6 and 8 suggest a more pathological process underlying the FDI, with suspiciousness, anger, attributional biases, and lack of cognitive control driving the maladaptive parent-child interaction.

Assessment of the marital relationships of parents of children with FDI often reveals troubled marriages. Mothers of children with FDI report significantly lower marital satisfaction on the Dyadic Adjustment Scale (Spanier, 1976). In one study, 36% of partners of mothers of children with NOFT were substance abusers, a value three times as high as that for controls (Benoit, Zeanah, & Barton, 1989). Similar problems may be expected on the FES, with some mothers elevating the Conflict and Control subscales in conjunction with deficits on Cohesion, Active-Recreational Orientation, and Intellectual-Cultural Orientation. Defensive mothers, on the other hand, may report high Cohesion and low Conflict.

Syndrome-Specific Tests

Clinician-Administered

Infant Feeding Behaviors-Rater.   (IFB-R). The IFB-R (Benoit et al., 1997) is a clinician rating scale of infants' problem behaviors at mealtimes. The IFB-R yields a total raw score that indicates behaviors characteristic of feeding problems. The IFB-R has been successfully used to document change in treatment for feeding disorders (Benoit et al., 1997).

Working Model of the Child Interview.   (WMCI). The WMCI (Zeanah & Benoit, 1995) is a semistructured interview that measures parents' perceptions of and relationships with their infants. It is useful in the assessment of attachment and parent perceptions of the child. Based on the interview, the clinician rates parents' perceptions of their infants in several areas, eight of which are recommended for clinical use: richness of perceptions, openness to change, intensity of involvement, coherence, acceptance, caregiving sensitivity, fear for (infant's) safety, and infant difficulty. An overall rating classifies the parent's perception of the child into one of three categories: balanced (rich and full impressions), disengaged (emotionally aloof and detached), or distorted (confused or contradictory). WMCI overall ratings are correlated with Strange Situation categories and are stable across time (Zeanah & Benoit, 1995). The length of the WMCI (1 hour for interview and additional time for coding) limits its clinical utility, but the research and theory associated with the WMCI can be helpful in organizing clinical impressions.

☐ TREATMENT OPTIONS

Treatment options for FDI are outlined in Table 7.14.

Medical Evaluation/Hospitalization

Initial treatment must focus on the medical needs of the child with FDI. Many of these children are undernourished or neglected and require immediate medical evaluation and treatment. Medical treatment typically consists of measures to monitor and increase nourishment

TABLE 7.14 Treatment Options for Feeding Disorder of Infancy

1. Medical Evaluation/Hospitalization
   a. Evaluation for physical causes
   b. Enforced, monitored feeding or tube placement

2. Behavioral Interventions
   a. Desensitize the child to food cues
   b. Do not force the child to eat
   c. Do not allow "grazing"
   d. Restrict access to nonnutritional foods
   e. Ignore resistant or oppositional behavior
   f. Praise eating behaviors
   g. Reduce distractions during mealtimes as much as possible
   h. Allow toddlers to feed themselves
   i. Do not allow access to desserts or snacks until the child has eaten the food required for the meal
   j. Model eating behavior during the child's meals, and allow the child to eat in the presence of other people who are eating
   k. Regulate the child's movement, orientation, and focus during meals
   l. Follow meals with interesting reinforcers
   m. Preface meals with a calm-down time
   n. Set a clear schedule and clear eating goals for the child and family
   o. Increase the level of intellectual stimulation in the environment

3. Family Interventions
   a. Support for the parent
   b. Education about nutrition, child development, behavioral parenting skills, and behavioral interventions for FDI
   c. Family therapy
   d. Marital therapy
   e. Parent psychotherapy

4. Home Monitoring and Protective Removal
   a. Temporary separation of parent and child
   b. Home visits by social worker or home health nurse
   c. "Parental holiday" while child is hospitalized

Note: This outline of options summarizes major treatments covered in the text. Specific treatments are often combined into an intervention package. Refer to the text for additional descriptions of each treatment. This table is not necessarily an exhaustive list of all treatments available.

and body weight, which may range from a specific diet and feeding plan to placement of a gastrostomy tube (G-tube). In severe cases, inpatient hospitalization is necessary, with feeding by or under the supervision of nursing personnel. If the infant thrives in the hospital environment after failing to gain weight at home (up to 2 weeks may be needed to notice this), intervention with parents is essential prior to hospital discharge to prevent a recurrence of weight loss and feeding problems.

Behavioral Interventions

Behavioral treatments are a universal part of treatment for FDI. These interventions are typically integrated with nutritional and medical recommendations to form a multidisciplinary plan. A typical behavioral treatment plan for FDI is as follows:

1. Desensitize the child to food cues. Children with FDI are encouraged to handle and play with food in order to desensitize them to food and feeding cues. In addition to playing with and handling food, children may be desensitized by introducing food in a hierarchy of texture.

2. Encourage, but do not force, the child to eat. *Never* force a utensil into the child's mouth.

3. Do not allow the child to "graze" during the day. "Grazing" involves nibbling at snacks or drinking from a bottle throughout the day so that the child is not hungry at mealtimes. A typical feeding day for a child with FDI involves three meals and two to three snacks, which must be eaten at certain, discrete times. Thirty minutes are allotted for meals and 15 minutes for snacks.

4. Restrict access to nonnutritional foods unless the child is meeting eating goals. Some children with FDI will satisfy hunger with cola or water. Access to these should be denied.

5. Ignore resistant or oppositional behavior during mealtimes. This ignoring should be done by looking away and remaining silent for 5 seconds or until the behavior stops.

6. Praise eating behavior, even for small bites or attempts.

7. Unless absolutely necessary, do not use toys or other attention-getting devices to reward the child during mealtime. These often distract the child from the meal interaction.

8. Allow toddlers to take more responsibility for the feeding interaction. This may be accomplished by letting them feed themselves and choosing the order in which they eat food from their plate. Finger food is often appealing to toddlers.

9. Do not place desserts or other snacks on the child's plate until the child has eaten the food required for the meal.

10. Allow the child to eat in the presence of other people who are eating, unless this is too distracting to the child.

11. Remove toys and other distractions from the feeding area.

12. Regulate the child's movement, orientation, and focus during meals. The child should be placed in an appropriate chair (belted in a high chair for older infants and young toddlers) and should not be allowed to leave the table until mealtime is over. For extremely active children who try to escape to another room, a gate may need to be placed at the room entrance, or (in the hospital) the room door may need to be closed.

13. Follow meals with interesting reinforcers. Meals should be followed by access to an interesting activity, which is delayed if the child does not meet feeding goals.

14. Preface meals with a calm-down time. Children will not be hungry if they are extremely active or distracted immediately before a meal. A buffer time of quiet, interesting activity prior to the meal promotes relaxation and orientation to the meal activity.

15. Set a clear schedule and clear eating goals for the child and family. Charts and diaries should be used to monitor feeding, to provide structure, and to remind the parent of the schedule.

16. Increase the level of intellectual stimulation to help to offset developmental delays. Although developmental delay is a risk in infants with FDI, intellectual stimulation in the environment appears to confer a buffering effect. To increase stimulation, parents are encouraged to read books to the child, to play with interesting toys, and to expose the child to enriched experiences (such as trips to the zoo and children's museum).

Family Interventions

All interventions for FDI should include support for and education of the parents (Ramsay, 1995). In providing support, the mental health professional should allow the parent to vent and should express acceptance of the difficulties of feeding a child with FDI. Educational techniques should include information about nutrition, child development (especially pertaining to feeding and temperament), behavioral parenting skills, and behavioral interventions for FDI. As a part of this education, parents should be taught to adjust their parenting behavior to fit their child's temperament (Reifsnider, 1996). Less skilled or more overwhelmed parents may require a more structured approach with regular reminders and clear charts. In some cases, it is helpful for the feeding specialist to first demonstrate the behavioral plan and then assist the parent with the components of the behavioral plan; the parent should then perform the plan repeatedly until it is overlearned.

More traditional marital and family techniques to address FDI are typically used when there is a need to address family conflict, marital conflict, or attachment problems. Family and/or marital conflict may require structural and behavioral techniques to set clear boundaries, expectations, and goals. If attachment problems are present, family interventions for RAD (see Chapter 18) or parent-child relationship therapy (described for Rumination Disorder earlier in this chapter) are indicated.

Home Monitoring and Protective Removal

Some severe cases of FDI warrant more extreme interventions, such as temporary separation of parent and child, required home visits by a social worker, or even removal of the infant from the parents' care. This decision is usually made based on a combination of four factors: the severity of abuse/neglect, medical status of the child, willingness of the parent to change through psychological intervention, and psychological stability of the parent.

In some cases of children with FDI who are refusing to eat during a hospitalization, a "parental holiday" may be suggested as a way to break the cycle of negative parent-child interactions at mealtimes. This "holiday" serves several purposes: First, it allows the parents to be away from the stressful situation of hostile interaction with their child. A reduction of stress often results in more patience and tolerance on the part of the parent. Second, the "holiday" allows greater control of feeding interactions, which are usually conducted by a feeding specialist in the absence of the parent. Third, the time spent away from the parent may result in a weakening of the child's association of the parent with certain adversarial mealtime behaviors. Ideally, when the parent is returned to the mealtime interaction (typically after 1–3 days), the cycle of adversarial interaction is broken.

Many parents are, understandably, vehemently opposed to separation from their child in the form of a parental holiday. They see that their child is "sick" enough to be in the hospital and want to be there to support and monitor the child. Also, parents may feel that a parental holiday gives the message that their child's FDI is their fault. Thus, they regard the holiday as a further sign of their failure and possibly as the precursor to permanent separation. Hence, the parental holiday must be suggested with tact, understanding, and support. Parents should be given a chance to express their concerns. Ideally, a trusted doctor or nurse should be present or should make the suggestion of a holiday. Finally, the rationale for the holiday should be explained, with reassurance that the parents are not being blamed for the problem.

■ References

Agras, W. (1987). *Eating disorders.* New York: Pergamon.

American Psychiatric Association. (1994). *Diagnostic and statistical manual of mental disorders, fourth edition.* Washington, DC: Author.

Benoit, D., Green, D., & Arts-Rodas, D. (1997). Posttraumatic feeding disorders. *Journal of the American Academy of Child and Adolescent Psychiatry, 36,* 577–578.

Benoit, D., Zeanah, C. H., & Barton, M. L. (1989). Maternal attachment disturbances in failure to thrive. *Infant Mental Health Journal, 10,* 185–202.

Bezchlibnyk-Butler, K. Z., & Jeffries, J. J. (1997). *Clinical handbook of psychotropic drugs.* Toronto: Hogrefe & Huber Publishers.

Brambilla, F., Draisci, A., Peirone, A., & Brunetta, M. (1995). Combined cognitive-behavioral, psychopharmacological, and nutritional therapy in eating disorders. *Biological Psychiatry, 32,* 59–63.

Bruch, H. (1978). *The golden cage: The enigma of anorexia nervosa.* Cambridge, MA: Harvard University Press.

Bruch, H., Czyzewski, D., & Suhr, M. (1988). *Conversations with anorexics.* New York: Basic Books.

Burns, T., & Crisp, A. H. (1984). Outcome of anorexia nervosa in males. *British Journal of Psychiatry, 145,* 319–325.

Candy, C. M., & Fee, V. E. (1998). Underlying dimensions and psychometric properties of the Eating Behaviors and Body Image Test for preadolescent girls. *Journal of Clinical Child Psychology, 27,* 117–127.

Casper, R. C., & Lyubomirsky, S. (1997). Individual psychopathology relative to reports of unwanted sexual experiences as predictor of a bulimic eating pattern. *International Journal of Eating Disorders, 21,* 229–236.

Chatoor, I., & Egan, J. (1983). Nonorganic failure to thrive and dwarfism due to food refusal: A separation disorder. *Journal of the American Academy of Child Psychiatry, 22,* 294–301.

Childress, A. C., Brewerton, T. D., Hodges, E. L., & Jarrell, M. P. (1993). The Kids' Eating Disorders Survey (KEDS): A study of middle school students. *Journal of the American Academy of Child and Adolescent Psychiatry, 32,* 843–850.

Commerford, M. C., Licinio, J., & Halmi, K. A. (1997). Guidelines for discharging eating disorder inpatients. *Eating Disorders, 5,* 69–74.

Dancyger, I. F., Sunday, S. R., & Halmi, K. A. (1997). Depression modulates non-eating-disordered psychopathology in eating-disordered patients. *Eating Disorders, 5,* 59–68.

Deep, A. L., Nagy, L. M., Weltzin, T. E., Rao, R., & Kaye, W. H. (1995). Premorbid onset of psychopathology in long-term recovered anorexia nervosa. *International Journal of Eating Disorders, 17,* 291–297.

Drotar, D. (1995). Failure to thrive (growth deficiency). In M. C. Roberts (Ed.), *Handbook of pediatric psychology* (2nd ed.). New York: Guilford.

Dunn, P., & Odercin, P. (1981). Personality variables related to compulsive eating in college women. *Journal of Clinical Psychology, 37,* 43–49.

Fairburn, C. G. (1985). The management of bulimia nervosa. *Journal of Psychiatric Research, 19,* 465–472.

Fairburn, C. G., & Beglin, S. J. (1995). The assessment of eating disorders: Interview or self-report questionnaire? *International Journal of Eating Disorders, 16,* 363–370.

Fairburn, C. G., Kirk, J., O'Connor, M., & Cooper, P. J. (1986). A comparison of two psychological treatments for bulimia nervosa. *Behavior Research and Therapy, 24,* 629–643.

Feldman, M. D. (1986). Pica: Current perspectives. *Psychosomatics, 27,* 519–523.

Fischhoff, J. (1989). Reactive attachment disorder of infancy. *Treatments of psychiatric disorders: A task force report of the American Psychiatric Association* (pp. 734–746). Washington, DC: American Psychiatric Association.

Gallucci, N. (1987). The influence of elevated F scales on the validity of adolescent MMPI profiles. *Journal of Personality Assessment, 51,* 133–139.

Garfinkel, P. E., Lin, E., Goering, P., Spegg, C., Goldbloom, D. S., Kennedy, S., Kaplan, A. S., & Woodside, D. B. (1996). Purging and nonpurging forms of bulimia nervosa in a community sample. *International Journal of Eating Disorders, 20,* 231–238.

Garner, D. M. (1991). *The Eating Disorder Inventory-2.* Odessa, FL: Psychological Assessment Resources.

Garner, D. M., & Garfinkel, P. E. (1979). The Eating Attitudes Test: An index of the symptoms of anorexia nervosa. *Psychological Medicine, 9,* 273–279

Gleaves, D. H., & Eberenz, K. P. (1995). Correlates of dissociative symptoms among women with eating disorders. *Journal of Psychiatric Research, 29,* 417–426.

Golden, B. R., Buzcek, T., & Robbins, S. B. (1986). Parameters of bulimia: Examining the Compulsive Eating Scale. *Measurement and Evaluation in Counseling and Development, 19,* 84–92.

Golden, N., & Sacker, I. M. (1984). An overview of the etiology, diagnosis, and management of anorexia nervosa. *Clinical Pediatrics, 23,* 209–214.

Goldfarb, L. A., Dykens, E. M., & Gerrard, M. (1985). The Goldfarb Fear of Fat Scale. *Journal of Personality Assessment, 49,* 329–332.

Green, W. H. (1989). Reactive attachment disorder of infancy or early childhood. In H. I. Kaplan & B. J. Sadock (Eds.), *Comprehensive textbook of psychiatry, Volume 2*

(5th ed., pp. 1894–1903). Baltimore, MD: Williams & Wilkins.

Gross, J., Rosen, J. C., Leitenberg, H., & Willmuth, M. E. (1986). Validity of the Eating Attitudes Test and the Eating Disorders Inventory in bulimia nervosa. *Journal of Consulting and Clinical Psychology, 54,* 875–876.

Hawkins, R. C., & Clement, P. E. (1980). Development and construct validation of a self-report measure of binge eating tendencies. *Addictive Behaviors, 5,* 219–226.

Healy, K., Conroy, R. M., & Walsh, N. (1985). The prevalence of binge eating and bulimia in 1063 college students. *Journal of Psychiatric Research, 19,* 161–166.

Hebebrand, J., Himmelmann, G. W., Herzog, W., Herpertz-Dahlmann, B. M., Stienhausen, H. C., Amstein, M., Seidel, R., Deter, H. C., Remschmidt, H., & Schafer, H. (1997). Prediction of low body weight at long-term follow-up in acute anorexia nervosa by low body weight at referral. *American Journal of Psychiatry, 154,* 566–569.

Hendren, R. L., Atkins, D. M., Sumner, C. R., & Barber, J. K. (1987). Model for the group treatment of eating disorders. *International Journal of Group Psychotherapy, 37,* 589–602.

Herpertz-Dahlmann, B. M., Wewetzer, C., Schulz, E., & Remschmidt, H. (1996). Course and outcome in adolescent anorexia nervosa. *International Journal of Eating Disorders, 19,* 335–345.

Herzog, D. B., Field, A. E., Keller, M. B., West, J. C., Robbins, W., Staley, J., & Colditz, G. A. (1996). Subtyping eating disorders: Is it justified? *Journal of the American Academy of Child and Adolescent Psychiatry, 35,* 928–936.

Herzog, W., Schellberg, D., & Deter, H. C. (1997). First recovery in anorexia nervosa patients in the long-term course: A discrete-time survival analysis. *Journal of Consulting and Clinical Psychology, 65,* 169–177.

Hewitt, P. L., Flett, G. L., & Ediger, E. (1995). Perfectionism traits and perfectionistic self-presentation in eating disorder attitudes, characteristics, and symptoms. *International Journal of Eating Disorders, 18,* 317–326.

Horesh, N., Apter, A., Ishai, J., Danzinger, Y., Miculincer, M., Stein, D., Lepkifker, E., & Minouni, M. (1996). Abnormal psychosocial situations and eating disorders in adolescence. *Journal of the American Academy of Child and Adolescent Psychiatry, 35,* 921–927.

Johnson, C. L., Lewis, C., Love, S., Lewis, L. D., & Stuckey, M. (1984). Incidence and correlates of bulimic behavior in a female high school population. *Journal of Youth and Adolescence, 13,* 15–26.

Kalfus, G. R., Fisher-Gross, S., Marvullo, M. A., & Nau, P. A. (1987). Outpatient treatment of pica in a developmentally delayed child. *Child and Family Behavior Therapy, 9,* 49–63.

Kaufman, A. S., & Kaufman, N. L. (1990). *Kaufman Brief Intelligence Test.* Circle Pines, MN: American Guidance Service.

Kelley, M. L., & Heffer, R. W. (1990). Eating disorders: Food refusal and failure to thrive. In A. M. Gross & R. S. Drabman (Eds.), *Handbook of clinical behavioral pediatrics* (pp. 111–127). New York: Plenum.

Keyes, A., Fidanza, F., Karvonen, M. J., Kimura, N., & Taylor, H. L. (1972). Indices of relative weight and obesity. *Journal of Chronic Disease, 25,* 329–343.

Kinnell, H. G. (1985). Pica as a feature of autism. *British Journal of Psychiatry, 147,* 80–82.

Kronenberger, W. G., & Thompson, R. J., Jr. (1990). Dimensions of family functioning in families with chronically ill children: A higher order factor analysis of the Family Environment Scale. *Journal of Clinical Child Psychology, 19,* 380–388.

LaRocca, F. E. F., & Della-Fera, M. A. (1986). Rumination: Its significance in adults with bulimia nervosa. *Psychosomatics, 27,* 209–212.

Lask, B., & Bryant-Waugh, R. (1997). Prepubertal eating disorders. In D. M. Garner & P. E. Garfinkel (Eds.), *Handbook of treatment for eating disorders* (2nd ed., pp. 476–483). New York: Guilford.

LeBlanc, L. A., Piazza, C. C., & Krug, M. A. (1997). Comparing methods for maintaining the safety of a child with pica. *Research in Developmental Disabilities, 18,* 215–220.

Levine, M. P. (1987). *How schools can help combat student eating disorders.* Washington, DC: National Education Association.

Levitan, R. D., Kaplan, A. S., & Rockert, W. (1996). Characterization of the "seasonal" bulimic patient. *International Journal of Eating Disorders, 19,* 187–192.

Lindholm, L., & Wilson, G. T. (1988). Body image assessment in patients with bulimia nervosa and normal controls. *International Journal of Eating Disorders, 7,* 527–539.

Maloney, M. J., McGuire, J., & Daniels, S. R. (1988). Reliability testing of a children's version of the Eating Attitude Test. *Journal of the American Academy of Child and Adolescent Psychiatry, 27,* 541–543.

Mayes, S. D., Humphrey, F. J., Handford, A., & Mitchell, J. F. (1988). Rumination disorder: Differential diagnosis. *Journal of the American Academy of Child and Adolescent Psychiatry, 27,* 300–302.

Mestre, J. R., Resnick, R. J., & Berman, W. F. (1983). Behavior modification in the treatment of rumination. *Clinical Pediatrics, 83,* 488–491.

Mickalide, A. D., & Anderson, A. E. (1985). Subgroups of anorexia nervosa and bulimia: Validity and utility. *Journal of Psychiatric Research, 19,* 121–128.

Minde, K. (1988). Behavioral abnormalities commonly seen in infancy. *Canadian Journal of Psychiatry, 33,* 741–747.

Minuchin, S. (1974). *Families and family therapy.* Cambridge, MA: Harvard University Press.

Neumarker, K. J. (1997). Mortality and sudden death in anorexia nervosa. *International Journal of Eating Disorders, 21,* 205–212.

Olivardia, R., Pope, H. G., Mangweth, B., & Hudson, J. I. (1995). Eating disorders in college men. *American Journal of Psychiatry, 152,* 1279–1285.

Oyebode, F., Boodhoo, J. A., & Schapira, K. (1988). Anorexia nervosa in males: Clinical features and outcome. *International Journal of Eating Disorders, 7,* 121–124.

Peterson, C. B., & Mitchell, J. E. (1996). Cognitive-behavior therapy. In G. O. Gabbard & S. D. Atkinson (Eds.), *Synopsis of treatments of psychiatric disorders* (2nd ed.). Washington, DC: American Psychiatric Press.

Phelan, P. W. (1987). Cognitive correlates of bulimia: The Bulimic Thoughts Questionnaire. *International Journal of Eating Disorders, 6,* 593–607.

Pike, K. M. (1995). Bulimic symptomatology in high school girls: Toward a model of cumulative risk. *Psychology of Women Quarterly, 19,* 373–396.

Piran, N., Lerner, P., Garfinkel, P. E., Kennedy, S. H., & Brouillette, C. (1988). Personality disorders in anorexic patients. *International Journal of Eating Disorders, 7,* 589–599.

Prince, I. (1989). Pica and geophagia in cross-cultural perspective. *Transcultural Psychiatric Research Review, 26,* 167–197.

Probst, M., Van Coppenolle, H., Vandereycken, W., & Goris, M. (1992). Body image assessment in anorexia nervosa patients and university students by means of video distortion: A reliability study. *Journal of Psychosomatic Research, 36,* 89–97.

Probst, M., Vandereycken, W., Van Coppenolle, H., & Vanderlinden, J. (1995). The Body Attitude Test for patients with an eating disorder: Psychometric characteristics of a new questionnaire. *Eating Disorders, 3,* 133–144.

Puckering, C., Pickles, A., Skuse, D., Heptinstall, E., Dowdney, L., & Zur-Szpiro, S. (1995). Mother-child interaction and the cognitive and behavioral development of four-year-old children with poor growth. *Journal of Child Psychology and Psychiatry, 36,* 573–595.

Ramsay, M. (1995). Feeding disorder and failure to thrive. *Child and Adolescent Psychiatric Clinics of North America, 4,* 605–616.

Reifsnider, E. (1996). Helping children grow: A home-based intervention protocol. *Journal of Community Health Nursing, 13,* 93–106.

Reiss, D., & Johnson-Sabine, E. (1995). Bulimia nervosa: 5-year social outcome and relationship to eating pathology. *International Journal of Eating Disorders, 18,* 127–133.

Robin, A. L., Bedway, M., Siegel, P. T., & Gilroy, M. (1996). Therapy for adolescent anorexia nervosa: Addressing cognitions, feelings, and the family's role. In E. D. Hibbs & P. S. Jensen (Eds.), *Psychosocial treatments for child and adolescent disorders: Empirically-based strategies for clinical practice.* Washington, DC: American Psychological Association.

Robinson, P. H., & Holden, N. L. (1986). Bulimia nervosa in the male: A report of nine cases. *Psychological Medicine, 16,* 795–803.

Rojahn, J., McGonigle, J. J., Curcio, C., & Dixon, M. J. (1987). Suppression of pica by water mist and aromatic ammonia. *Behavioral Modification, 11,* 65–74.

Ruggiero, L., Williamson, D., Davis, C. J., Schlundt, D. G., & Carey, M. P. (1988). Forbidden Food Survey: Measure of bulimics anticipated emotional reactions to specific foods. *Addictive Behaviors, 13,* 267–274.

Rybicki, D. J., Lepkowsky, C. M., & Arndt, S. (1989). An empirical assessment of bulimic patients using multiple measures. *Addictive Behaviors, 14,* 249–260.

Sagardoy, R. C., Ashton, A. F., Mateos, J. L. A., Perez, C. B., & Carrasco, J. S. D. (1989). *Psychotherapy and Psychosomatics, 52,* 133–139.

Sauvage, D., Leddet, I., Hameury, L., & Barthelemy, C. (1985). Infantile rumination: Diagnosis and follow-up study of twenty cases. *Journal of the American Academy of Child Psychiatry, 24,* 197–203.

Small, A., Madero, J., Gross, H., Teagno, L., Leib, J., & Ebert, M. (1981). A comparative analysis of primary anorexics and schizophrenics on the MMPI. *Journal of Clinical Psychology, 37,* 773–776

Smith, M. C., & Thelen, M. H. (1984). Development and validation of a test for bulimia. *Journal of Consulting and Clinical Psychology, 52,* 863–872.

Spanier, G. B. (1976). Measuring dyadic adjustment: New scales for assessing the quality of marriage and similar dyads. *Journal of Marriage and the Family, 38,* 15–28.

Starin, S. P., & Fuqua, R. W. (1987). Rumination and vomiting in the developmentally disabled: A critical review of the behavioral, medical, and psychiatric treatment research. *Research in Developmental Disabilities, 8,* 575–605.

Stice, E., Nemeroff, C., & Shaw, H. E. (1996). Test of the dual pathway model of bulimia nervosa: Evidence for dietary restraint and affect regulation mechanisms. *Journal of Social and Clinical Psychology, 15,* 340–363.

Sykes, D. K., Currie, K. O., & Gross, M. (1987). The use of group therapy in the treatment of bulimia. *International Journal of Psychosomatics, 34,* 7–10.

Tibbits-Kleber, A. L., & Howell, R. J. (1985). Reactive attachment disorder of infancy (RAD). *Journal of Clinical Child Psychology, 14,* 304–310.

Tierney, D., & Jackson, H. J. (1984). Psychosocial treatments of rumination disorder: A review of the literature. *Australia and New Zealand Journal of Developmental Disabilities, 10,* 81–112.

Vacc, N. A., & Rhyne, M. (1987). The Eating Attitudes Test: Development of an adapted language form for children. *Perceptual and Motor Skills, 65,* 335–336.

Wagner, E., & Wagner, C. (1978). *The interpretation of psychological test data.* Springfield, IL: Charles Thomas.

Waller, D., Fairburn, C. G., McPherson, A., Kay, R., Lee, A., & Nowell, T. (1996). Treating bulimia nervosa in primary care: A pilot study. *International Journal of Eating Disorders, 19,* 99–103.

Weakley, M. M., Petti, T. A., & Karwisch, G. (1997). Case study: Chewing gum treatment of rumination in an adolescent with an eating disorder. *Journal of the American Academy of Child and Adolescent Psychiatry, 36,* 1124–1127.

Weiss, L., Katzman, M. K., & Wolchik, S. A. (1986). *You can't have your cake and eat it too: A program for controlling bulimia.* Saratoga, CA: R & E Publishers.

Welch, G., & Hall, A. (1989). The reliability and discriminant validity of three potential measures of bulimic behaviors. *Journal of Psychiatric Research, 23,* 125–133.

Weltzin, T. E., Starzynski, J., Santelli, R., & Kaye, W. H. (1993). Anorexia and bulimia nervosa. In R. T. Ammerman, C. G. Last, & M. Hersen (Eds.), *Handbook of prescriptive treatments for children and adolescents* (pp. 214–239). Boston, MA: Allyn & Bacon.

Williamson, D. A., Prather, R. C., McKenzie, S. J., & Blouin, D.C. (1990). Behavioral assessment procedures can differentiate bulimia nervosa, compulsive overeater, obese, and normal subjects. *Behavioral Assessment, 12,* 239–252.

Wilson, G. T., & Smith, D. (1989). Assessment of bulimia nervosa: An evaluation of the Eating Disorders Examination. *International Journal of Eating Disorders, 8,* 173–179.

Wonderlich, S. A., Brewerton, T. D., Jocic, Z., Dansky, B. S., & Abbott, D. W. (1997). Relationship of childhood sexual abuse and eating disorders. *Journal of the American Academy of Child and Adolescent Psychiatry, 36,* 1107–1115.

Woods, D. W., Miltenberger, R. G., & Lumley, V. A. (1996). A simplified habit reversal treatment for Pica-related chewing. *Journal of Behavior Therapy and Experimental Psychiatry, 27,* 257–262.

Yager, J. (1985). The outpatient treatment of bulimia. *Bulletin of the Meninger Clinic, 49,* 203–226.

Zeanah, C. H., & Benoit, D. (1995). Clinical applications of a parent perception interview in infant mental health. *Child and Adolescent Clinics of North America, 4,* 539–554.

Zlotnick, C., Hohlstein, L. A., Shea, M. T., Pearlstein, T., Recupero, P., & Bidadi, K. (1996). The relationship between sexual abuse and eating pathology. *International Journal of Eating Disorders, 20,* 129–134.

□ **CHAPTER 8**

Somatoform Disorders

■ **Somatoform Disorders**

□ CLINICAL DESCRIPTION

Diagnostic Considerations and Features

Children frequently complain of aches, pains, and various other physical symptoms that cannot be definitively linked to a physical condition. These functional somatic complaints occur in as many as 20% of children who present to pediatric clinics with physical symptoms (Robinson, Greene, & Walker, 1988; Walker, McLaughlin, & Greene, 1988). Headaches and abdominal pain are the most common somatic complaints in children (Fritz, Fritsch, & Hagino, 1997). When an organic cause is not found for the symptoms, the diagnostic focus often moves to the psychological realm with a search for stressors or behavior problems that might explain the condition. The vast majority of functional somatic complaints disappear spontaneously or are "cured" with a general antibiotic or other drug whose effect may be more placebo than disease related. Some functional somatic complaints, however, persist and develop into significant problems. These psychological disorders of persistent, pervasive physical complaints are categorized as Somatoform Disorders.

Somatoform Disorders are characterized by physical symptoms that suggest an illness or other organic problem, when careful physical evaluation reveals no physical cause for the symptoms. In the absence of a physical cause, psychological factors are assumed to be producing the symptomatology. However, the presence of a known stressor (or other psychological factor) is *required* only for the diagnosis of Conversion Disorder. Pain Disorder requires that psychological factors have an important role, but these factors do not need to be specified.

Children will sometimes intentionally fake medical symptoms in order to adopt the sick role, to gain a reward (such as attention), or to avoid some unpleasant event (such as school). When symptoms are intentionally produced, a Somatoform Disorder is not diagnosed. The

Somatoform Disorder diagnosis is reserved only for symptoms which are unintentional or not consciously produced.

The intentional production of symptoms, although not a Somatoform Disorder per se, can have deleterious psychosocial and physical consequences. Thus, such behavior should be carefully assessed and followed. Intentionally produced physical symptoms may be an attempt to escape from a dangerous environment (e.g., abuse) or may signal a state of desperation or upset in the child. For these reasons, a careful psychological and social evaluation of the child and the child's environment is warranted. Often, it is found that the parents are subtly reinforcing the child's illness behavior; usually the prime reinforcers are attention and nurturance.

If a reward for illness behavior can clearly be identified, the disorder falls under the category of Malingering. Occasionally, however, children will intentionally produce symptoms for no apparent reinforcement. Such voluntary adoption of a sick role without an associated reward is categorized as Factitious Disorder. Children with Factitious Disorder seem to have a self-concept consistent with the sick role, and they will produce symptoms to place themselves in this role. Often, such children have recently had an illness or have observed someone with an illness, and this past experience may be responsible for the motivation to intentionally produce symptoms.

Regardless of whether symptoms are believed to be intentionally or unintentionally produced, significant physical complaints or symptoms should be taken very seriously. Most children with Somatoform Disorders have had numerous medical tests to rule out plausible physical causes. It is extremely important that these tests be conducted carefully and exhaustively. Historically, studies have found that as many as 27–46% of children and 13–34% of adults diagnosed with one type of Somatoform Disorder (Conversion Disorder) actually had a physical disease (Couprie, Wijdicks, Rooijmans, & Van Gijn, 1995; Lehmkuhl, Blanz, Lehmkuhl, & Braun-Scharm, 1989). Although the accuracy of Somatoform Disorder diagnosis appears to be increasing (Couprie et al., 1995, found that only 4% of their more recent Conversion Disorder sample turned out to have an actual physical disease), caution must still be exercised with regard to the rule-out of physical causes. Rule-out of physical causes should always precede psychological intervention.

Although careful medical examination is necessary prior to making a diagnosis of Somatoform Disorder, the exam may have the unfortunate effect of legitimizing the physical nature of the symptoms or of terrifying the child into thinking that he or she has a major illness. Because the symptoms are not intentionally produced and seem to have been taken very seriously by the medical establishment, most children and their parents are extremely reluctant to accept the diagnosis of Somatoform Disorder. They assume that physical monitoring and physical treatment will stop, so if any undiagnosed physical illness is actually present, it will develop unchecked. Furthermore, most children and parents have difficulty understanding the difference between a Somatoform Disorder and a Factitious/Malingering Disorder. Hence, a statement that the symptoms have no physical cause is often interpreted as an accusation that the child is intentionally producing the symptoms. Such a perceived accusation may cause defensiveness in both parent and child, further complicating psychological assessment and treatment. For these reasons, Somatoform Disorder should be diagnosed and explained by a team of experienced professionals. Appearance and features of Somatoform Disorders are listed in Table 8.1.

TABLE 8.1   Appearance and Features of Somatoform Disorders

COMMON FEATURES

1. Physical symptoms without physical basis
2. Not intentional
3. Recent stressor
4. Defensiveness about psychological explanations for symptom
5. Age 6 and older
6. Failure of lab tests to support physical complaints
7. Presence of an illness model
8. Secondary gain
9. Past history of somatic complaints
10. Focus on somatic sensations ("body scanning")
11. Family dysfunction
12. Family focus on illness issues

OCCASIONAL FEATURES

1. School rejection/teasing
2. Covert/subtle parental support for symptom
3. La belle indifférence
4. Presentation with neurological complaint

Note: The features listed in the table are often seen but are not universal. Some features may be diagnostically relevant or required, whereas others may not be required for diagnosis. "Common" features are typical of the disorder; "occasional" features appear frequently but are not necessarily seen in a majority of cases.

Etiology

Some theorists hypothesize that Somatoform Disorders develop as coping mechanisms against intrapsychic or environmental stress. Psychodynamic theories cite the role of somatization defenses in "converting" psychological conflict into physical symptoms. Instead of experiencing uncomfortable thoughts and feelings, individuals develop physical symptoms that occupy their attention. Unhappiness over parents' divorce, for example, becomes transformed into an inability to walk. The inability to walk serves as an outlet for the conflict over experiencing parental divorce.

Somatization is a primitive defense mechanism that occurs in cases of overwhelming stress and insufficient or maladaptive coping resources. In cases of moderate stress or adequate resources, children tend to engage in more adaptive coping, such as problem solving, seeking social support, or distraction. However, high stress and inadequate resources can lead to a feeling of being trapped and out of control. At these times, more adaptive coping fails to work, leaving the individual with primitive, defensive coping responses such as somatization.

Other theorists have emphasized learning paradigms to explain Somatoform Disorders. Social learning theories, for example, stress the importance of imitation in the development of a Somatoform Disorder. Children who observe their parents or siblings having gastric pains, for example, may scan their own abdominal sensations for anything resembling a pain. Upon finding a possible pain sensation, they may then model the behavior of the other family member. Some evidence exists for this theoretical view: Children with conversion symptoms are often found to have a family member with a similar symptom (Lehmkuhl et al., 1988; Volkmar, Poll, & Lewis, 1984). In addition, Somatoform Disorders sometimes mimic previous physical disorders that a child no longer has.

Classical conditioning paradigms may also explain the emergence of a Somatoform Disorder. According to a stress-based classical conditioning paradigm, severe stressful events cause normal stress-related physiological changes and discomfort (Selye, 1956), which eventually become associated with any stress. Later, when stress occurs, the person reports significant physical discomfort, even if the actual physical changes are minimal or absent. More severe or prolonged stresses create greater feelings of discomfort such that traumatic or chronic stress could produce a Somatoform Disorder.

According to an illness-based classical conditioning paradigm, the child may experience an actual physical illness, with illness symptoms occurring normally in response to certain stimuli. For example, a child with the flu might vomit after eating. In rare cases, however, the connection between the stimulus (eating) and response (vomiting) may persist even after the actual physical illness (flu) is gone because there has been such a significant association of the stimulus and response (as a result of duration of illness, severity of symptoms, or intensity of the child's response). This continuing connection between certain stimuli and illness responses, in the absence of the original illness, would form the basis for a Somatoform Disorder. Illness-based classical conditioning paradigms seem to explain many of the Somatoform Disorders that arise following apparently legitimate severe physical illnesses. Between 10% and 60% of children with Conversion Disorder, for example, have had a previous genuine illness or injury (Fritz et al., 1997) that could form the basis for a conditioning paradigm.

Finally, family theories cite the role of the Somatoform Disorder in the family system. Some families, for example, structure their interactions around somatic topics. Children raised in these environments "scan" their bodies for problems, which then become the topic of family attention. Sufficient attention to a problem can make it the focus of attention to the point that the child believes that the illness is real.

In other cases, somatic symptoms deflect family attention from difficult issues, particularly conflict. These families invest all of their energy into concern over the "sick" child, leaving no energy or time for family conflict. Furthermore, the presence of the sick child can allow the family to adopt the role of a "family of an ill youngster." This role can be a source of family activity and can distract the family from other issues that may lead to conflict. In particular, the integrity of the marital subsystem may be violated by the sick child, leaving the parents no time for spousal activities such as romance, fun, and sex.

Support for family etiological theories comes from studies showing that children whose parents have Somatization Disorder are far more likely to have emergency room visits and to miss school compared to other children. If one sibling shows somatization symptoms, other children in the family are also likely to show such symptoms, along with missed school and hospitalization. Finally, parental substance abuse and antisocial behavior are related to somatization symptoms in children (Livingston, Witt, & Smith, 1995).

Six types of Somatoform Disorders are recognized in DSM-IV: Conversion Disorder, Pain Disorder, Somatization Disorder, Hypochondriasis, Body Dysmorphic Disorder, and Undifferentiated Somatoform Disorder. Conversion Disorder is the most common Somatoform Disorder in children and adolescents, followed by Pain Disorder. These two disorders will be covered in more detail.

■ Conversion Disorder

□ CLINICAL DESCRIPTION

Diagnostic Considerations

Conversion Disorder is the most common and most commonly studied Somatoform Disorder in children, although its exact incidence in the childhood population is unknown (Regan & Regan, 1989). According to DSM-IV, the hallmark of a Conversion Disorder is "one or more symptoms or deficits affecting voluntary motor or sensory function that suggest a neurological or other general medical condition" (American Psychiatric Association, 1994, p. 457) in the absence of sufficient physiological cause. Usually, conversion symptoms are manifest by a loss of sensory or motor functioning. The conversion symptoms must affect the person's daily functioning or must cause distress. In addition, known psychological stressors must precede the development or exacerbation of the conversion symptoms. It is important to note that when symptoms are limited to pain, Conversion Disorder is *not* diagnosed. These latter conditions typically are diagnosed in the Pain Disorder or Somatoform Disorder NOS category.

Conversion Disorder is extremely rare before age 6 and may peak at age 11–13 in childhood (Grattan-Smith, Fairley, & Procopis, 1988). Estimates of adult prevalence are in the 1–3% range (American Psychiatric Association, 1994). The disorder may be more common in girls (Lehmkuhl et al., 1989), although the data for this should be considered preliminary.

Most Conversion Disorders present as apparent neurological abnormalities. Possible seizures (pseudoseizures) and walking/gait problems seem to be most common, although limb paralysis and sensory-loss symptoms (usually visual or auditory disturbances) are often seen as well. Pseudoseizures comprise 15% to 50% of all Conversion Disorders, making them one of the most common presenting complaints (Fritz et al., 1997). These events resemble genuine seizures to a greater or lesser degree, but they share several characteristics in common. First, the EEG shows no seizure activity during an apparent seizure; evaluation to determine this usually consists of a video EEG, in which the child is simultaneously videotaped and EEG-monitored until a seizure occurs. Pseudoseizures also can often be brought on by suggestion or stress, although these may cause genuine seizures as well.

Appearance and Features

Six broad features are relatively common in cases of Conversion Disorder (Grattan-Smith et al., 1988; Siegel & Barthel, 1986; Steinhausen, Aster, Pfeiffer, & Gobel, 1989; Thomson & Sills, 1988):

1. *Identifiable stress.* Most stressors associated with Conversion Disorder fall into two categories: school/peer and family (Leslie, 1988). Examples of these stressors are separation from parent, academic failure, peer relationship problems, chronic parental discord, and parental unemployment (Lehmkuhl et al., 1989; Volkmar et al., 1984).

Despite the hypothesis that Conversion Disorders arise in order to protect the individual from a catastrophic internal conflict or stress, stressors preceding the development of Conversion Disorder are not always catastrophic or traumatic. In fact, children and adolescents with Conversion Disorders show no greater prevalence or severity of stressors than do children with other DSM-IV disorders (Lehmkuhl et al., 1989). However, as many as 90% of children with a Conversion Disorder have some significant family, peer, or school stress (Siegel & Barthel, 1986). Relatively common school stressors such as teasing by peers and poor academic performance are often cited as responsible for the development of a Conversion Disorder. Because problems with peers or academic achievement may occur in as many as 50% of cases of Conversion Disorder (Leslie, 1988; Thomson & Sills, 1988), the school should be routinely considered as a potential source of the stress underlying the disorder. In addition, because of the possibility of a stressful family situation, the family should routinely be assessed. Common stresses seen in the families of children with Conversion Disorder are parental discord, parental divorce (Volkmar et al., 1984), sexual abuse (Leslie, 1988; Volkmar et al., 1984), and psychiatric impairment of a parent (Lehmkuhl et al., 1989).

2. *Presence of a model for the conversion symptoms* (44–66% of cases [Grattan-Smith et al., 1988; Siegel & Barthel, 1986; Steinhausen et al., 1989; Thomson & Sills, 1988]). Children who observe illness behavior in siblings, parents, or friends are more prone to exhibit this behavior themselves. According to social learning theory, a person is more likely to engage in a behavior if he or she observes another person receiving reinforcement for the behavior. However, if a child's imitation of illness behavior is intentional or conscious, it is not diagnosed as Conversion Disorder but falls in the Factitious Disorder or Malingering category. Alternatively, the presence of an illness model may provide a constant reminder for the child of the possibility of illness; children may eventually come to believe that they are sick from the suggestion of illness in the environment. Evidence exists that children with Conversion Disorder are more likely to have a physically ill parent than are children with other psychiatric disorders (Steinhausen et al., 1989). Children with somatizing parents are more likely to somatize themselves (Livingston et al., 1995). Children often develop illness symptoms very similar to those of the illness model (Volkmar et al., 1984).

3. *Characteristics of family environment* (56% of cases [Siegel & Barthel, 1986]). Family issues may cause or maintain Conversion Disorder in several ways: First, the family may be the source of the precipitating stressor, such as family conflict, loss of a family member, abuse, or neglect. Second, the illness behavior may serve an important role in organizing family life. Third, the illness of a family member may provide a model for the child's Conversion Disorder.

Several types of family units have been described as typical of families of children with Conversion Disorders (Grattan-Smith et al., 1988; Seltzer, 1985). Anxious families have a preoccupation with disease and disease processes. Communication between family members often turns to topics of illness, pain, and even death. In many cases, these families have had medical histories with serious illnesses in relatives and friends. In the extreme, this illness-interaction process becomes a shared experience of family members, fostering bonding and communication at the price of excessive somatic focus. The tacit communication among members of these families is that serious physical disorders are imminent and disabling. Combined with high levels of stress and hyperattention to bodily symptoms, this attitude could lead to a mistaken belief that some bodily function has been lost.

A second type of family, the chaotic family, is characterized by a lack of organization, rules, and responsibilities (Seltzer, 1985). Children in these families fear being lost in the chaos. Therefore, they are highly reinforced by any event that brings attention or focuses the family. Their somatic complaints bind the family's attention in a single area, bringing some organization to family life. In addition, because it is more difficult to garner social support in a chaotic environment, these children are less able to depend on family members at times of stress. This lack of social support, normally a vital coping resource, makes the child more likely to use primitive coping behaviors such as somatization.

Compensating families are characterized by a desire to appear normal or ideal. This desire is brought on by a fear that the family is vulnerable to conflict, lack of support, and even disintegration (Seltzer, 1985). For example, 44% of families of children with conversion disorder in one sample used illness issues to avoid addressing family stress and conflict (Siegel & Barthel, 1986). Such families appear at first to be mutually supportive, normal, and well adapted; they will go to great lengths to convince the medical team that this is the case. Further investigation, however, reveals defensiveness about family problems and rigid resistance to any type of change. The rigid controls in these families often take the form of authoritarian parenting or strict moral values. Dissent from family unity is not tolerated, which hampers the children's development of feelings of independence. Transitions characteristic of independence (beginning school, changing schools, entering peer groups, puberty, adolescent issues) are particularly problematic and may be the precipitating incident for the development of the Conversion Disorder. The family usually denies conflict or stress, avoiding difficult topics by focusing on the "sick" child. Children who are raised in compensating families have considerable difficulty managing conflict or stress in social situations. Hence, they are vulnerable to overreaction or avoidance of stressful events; either situation may lead to social rejection and further use of somatization defenses.

4. *Secondary gain for the symptom.* Although intentional production of symptoms would rule out Conversion Disorder in favor of Factitious Disorder or Malingering, secondary gain does not always imply intentionally produced symptoms. Secondary gain is common in Conversion Disorder, occurring in as many as 40–50% of cases (Siegel & Barthel, 1986). Because the child is often not aware of the existence or significance of secondary gain, the clinician must take the lead in the search for possible sources of gain. In many cases, secondary gain is related to avoidance of a stressful situation such as peer conflict, teasing at school, growing up, and family conflict. In other cases, the secondary gain comes from increased attention or more positive social interactions. Regardless of the role of the secondary gain, the child will be more reluctant to give up the conversion symptom as long as the gain persists. Hence, identification of the source of secondary gain suggests one facet of intervention to remove the conversion symptoms: Removal of secondary gain for the symptom heightens the chances for therapeutic success.

Two points are important to remember when secondary gain is identified: First, the presence of secondary gain does not guarantee the presence of a Conversion Disorder. Many children with bona fide physical diseases receive considerable secondary gain in the form of attention, gifts, and special treatment. Second, removal of the secondary gain is not necessarily sufficient to cause removal of the conversion symptom. If the child believes that he or she has an illness, the disorder may persist even in the face of uncomfortable conditions.

5. *La belle indifférence.* La belle indifférence is a condition in which a person appears emotionally unconcerned with the loss of function in a Conversion Disorder. Hypothetically, la belle indifférence results from a denial of the stress that the patient is managing by using somatization defenses. This denial of problems manifests itself in a blasé attitude toward one's physical condition and life situation. Patients with la belle indifférence may appear calm, accepting, and even happy in the face of overwhelming functional impairments.

Despite widespread case studies and theoretical speculation, la belle indifférence appears to be the exception rather than the rule in cases of Somatoform Disorder in children (Kronenberger, Laite, & LaClave, 1995; Regan & Regan, 1989), occurring in only 19–30% of cases (Grattan-Smith et al., 1989; Siegel & Barthel, 1986), although one study reports la belle indifférence in 50% of their sample (Volkmar et al., 1984). In fact, rather than being unconcerned with their disorder, evidence exists that many children with Somatoform Disorder are distressed by their condition and suffer deficits in self-esteem and general happiness (Kronenberger et al., 1995; Robinson et al., 1988). Furthermore, children with actual physical disease may display an emotional unconcern as a defense mechanism. Hence, the presence of la belle indifférence does not always imply functional impairment. La belle indifférence is probably best thought of as characteristic of rigid denial defenses exhibited by children with either Conversion Disorder or actual physical illness.

6. *Illness-based classical conditioning factors.* Some children develop a Conversion Disorder after an apparently genuine physical illness. Siegel and Barthel (1986), for example, reported that 33% of their sample of children with conversion disorder had a significant past history of somatic complaints. Classical conditioning occurs when a reflexive response during the period of genuine illness becomes associated with a stimulus that would, in a healthy child, not be associated with the response. For example, a child with a knee injury may experience excruciating pain (response) when walking (stimulus). When the injury heals, the child should be able to walk without pain. However, in some cases, the child may, during the period before the injury is healed, begin to associate bending the knee during walking with pain in the knee joint. Then, when the injury has healed, bending the knee continues to be associated with pain. The child then reports pain with walking, despite the fact that the knee has healed. Between 10% and 60% of children with Conversion Disorder have had a previous genuine illness that could form the basis for a classical conditioning response (Fritz et al., 1997).

Etiology

Etiological factors in the development of Conversion Disorder mirror those for Somatoform Disorders in general. However, the diagnostic stipulation of a causal stress underscores the assumption that the Conversion Disorder is at least in part the result of a stressful situation.

☐ ASSESSMENT PATTERNS

A sample assessment battery for Conversion Disorder is shown in Table 8.2.

Broad Assessment Strategies

Psychological Assessment

Clinician-Administered. The MMPI/MMPI-A can be a valuable tool in the assessment of Somatoform Disorders because it provides information on personality dynamics and de-

TABLE 8.2   Sample Assessment Battery for Conversion Disorder and Pain Disorder

PSYCHOLOGICAL

1. Personality Inventory for Youth (Children) or MMPI/MMPI-A (Adolescents)
2. Piers-Harris Self-Concept Scale
3. Children's Depression Inventory

BEHAVIORAL

1. Behavioral Assessment System for Children (Parent-Report, Teacher-Report, and Self-Report)

FAMILY

1. Family Environment Scale

SYNDROME-SPECIFIC (PAIN)

1. Body Outline for Shading of Pain Areas
2. Visual Pain Intensity Scale (Pain Thermometer; Oucher)
3. Verbal Pain Intensity Scale (1–10 Rating)
4. McGill Pain Questionnaire

Note: Assessment instruments are intended to supplement (not substitute for) a good clinical interview and, when possible, a structured diagnostic interview.

fenses that may not be understood or readily admitted by the child. A "conversion V" (scales 1 and 3 elevated with scale 2 relatively low) would be expected from an adolescent with a Conversion Disorder. Such an MMPI profile is typical of a somatically focused child who lacks insight and is likely to deny psychological problems. If scales 2 and 7 are very low (less than 40–45 T-score), la belle indifférence is likely to be present. Elevations on scales 6 and 8 should be carefully examined because they may be indicative of distorted thought processes underlying or contributing to the somatization problem. On the validity scales, elevations on L or K may show some defensiveness, denial, or lack of insight into psychological processes. It is important to note that many adults and adolescents with actual physical problems will show the "conversion V" profile because of the many somatic items on scales 1 and 3. There is no foolproof way to distinguish patients with actual physical illness from those with Conversion Disorders based on MMPI profiles alone. However, when scales 1 and 3 exceed T-scores of 80, the likelihood of a diagnosis of Conversion or other Somatoform Disorder becomes much greater.

Child-Report.   On the PHSCS (Piers, 1984), children with Somatoform Disorder score lower on Behavioral Self-Esteem than physically ill children with no psychiatric diagnosis but higher than physically ill children with a diagnosis of depression. One study found children with Somatoform Disorders to show average Piers-Harris subscale T-scores in the 54–58 range, compared to depressed physically ill children, who score in the 48–52 range, and to physically ill children with no psychiatric diagnosis, who score in the 58–63 range

(Kronenberger et al., 1995). However, most self-esteem scales do not reliably differentiate children with Somatoform Disorder from children with physical disorders.

Based on their findings, Kronenberger et al. (1995) drew several conclusions about the self-report of children with Somatoform Disorder: First, children with Somatoform Disorder show a wide range of self-esteem scores on the Piers-Harris; some have a "belle indifférence" level of very high esteem, whereas some are clearly in distress with low self-esteem. Overall, children with Somatoform Disorders show slightly lower self-esteem than other children with a physical illness. Second, children with Somatoform Disorder rarely appear depressed on depression inventories, although their depression scores may be slightly higher on average than those of children with no psychiatric diagnosis.

Behavioral Assessment

Parent-Report and Teacher-Report. Most parent- and teacher-report behavioral questionnaires include subscales designed to assess somatic complaints made by children. Typically, these subscales consist of a variety of neurological, gastrointestinal, and pain complaints. Factor-analytically, they tend to load with anxiety and other internalizing scales. Obtaining parent- and teacher-report of symptoms is often helpful in the assessment of a Somatoform Disorder if the child is prone to denial when undergoing psychological evaluation.

The Achenbach scales, for example, include a Somatic Complaints subscale that measures a variety of diverse illnesses and somatic complaints. In order to elevate the Somatic Complaints subscale, a child must either have a bona fide illness with wide-ranging somatic effects or a tendency to make many complaints of illnesses. In addition to the Somatic Complaints scale, children with Somatoform Disorders will often show low scores on the competence scales (Activities, Social, and School), reflecting the deleterious impact of Somatoform Disorder on daily functioning. Analysis of other CBCL/TRF subscales can provide insight into whether other symptom clusters (especially Anxious/Depressed, Withdrawn, and Social Problems) are contributing to the somatoform symptoms. Those comorbid problem areas may provide fertile ground for further evaluation and intervention.

Like the Achenbach scales, the BASC parent- and teacher-report scales include a Somatization subscale. The BASC Somatization subscale contains items about pain, trouble breathing, neurological symptoms, and gastrointestinal complaints; most items are pain or discomfort related. Children who elevate the BASC Somatization subscale either have wide-ranging illnesses with many physical symptoms, or they tend to amplify the physical symptoms that they do have, or they develop physical symptoms in response to psychogenic causes. Other BASC subscales that are particularly important in interpreting the results of the Somatization subscale are the Anxiety and Depression subscales. Children who elevate one of these two subscales along with the Somatization subscale often are showing an Anxious-Depressed syndrome that includes physical complaints; alternatively, this pattern may occur in a seriously ill child who is experiencing internalizing adjustment problems.

The Conners' scales include a Psychosomatic subscale in the long version of the parent-report scale; no other versions (including all teacher-report versions) have a Psychosomatic subscale. The Psychosomatic subscale in the CPRS is a brief (6-item) measure of aches, pains, and fatigue. Although this subscale has content validity and seems to be useful, there is less coverage of somatization and internalizing problems on the Conners' scales than on the Achenbach, BASC, and PIY.

Child-Report. Like their parent-report and teacher-report counterparts, the self-report versions of the Achenbach (YSR) and BASC (BASC-SRP; 12–18-year-old version only) include somatization subscales. The content and interpretation of these subscales closely resembles that of the parent-report versions.

The PIY includes a Somatic Concern scale that is divided into three component subscales: The Psychosomatic Syndrome subscale contains nine items that measure the child's self-report of being tired, sick, aching, and needing a doctor more than other children. Children who elevate this subscale tend to perceive themselves as being more sickly and uncomfortable than other children. The Muscular Tension and Anxiety subscale consists of ten items reflecting muscular tenseness and physiological manifestations of panic and anxiety, such as twitching, backache, trouble breathing, dizziness, feeling hot, racing heartbeat, chest pains, cramps, and a lump in the throat. This scale is elevated in children who have panic symptoms and anxiety attacks. The Preoccupation with Disease subscale consists of eight items that measure the extent to which the child talks or worries about illness and has specific illness symptoms; it tends to be elevated for children who are constantly focused on illness issues.

Family Assessment

Child-Report and Parent-Report. On the FES, compensating families would be expected to score low on the Expressiveness and Conflict subscales, reflecting their discomfort with psychological insight and expressed emotion. It is notable, however, that many families will self-report high scores on the Expressiveness subscale, despite clearly being repressed in their emotional expression. Scores on the Cohesion subscale may be high or low, depending on whether the family is enmeshed or disengaged, respectively. Likewise, scores on the Organization and Control subscales may be high or low, depending on the level of rigidity or chaos in the family system. In some families, Supportive and Conflicted factor scores are low, showing the low level of expressed negative emotion but also the low level of overall support for individual members of the family. On the other hand, the Supportive factor may be artificially high in families who deny problems and claim to be perfect. Overall, no typical family profile exists because there are numerous types of families of children with Conversion Disorders. The value of family assessment lies in the identification of the type of family for the planning of treatment.

☐ TREATMENT OPTIONS

Medical Evaluation/Hospitalization

Children with Conversion Disorders often come to the attention of mental health professionals during or following intense pediatric evaluation, which may include hospitalization. Frequently, the child has had extensive medical testing, which is inconclusive or negative. In many cases, interventions are initiated in the pediatric hospital environment, as medical evaluations are beginning to conclusively rule out a physical cause for the symptoms. Hence, the interventions described next are sometimes initiated or completely carried out in the hospital environment (Table 8.3). Alternatively, children may be sent to outpatient treatment for the conversion symptomatology once the full medical workups are

TABLE 8.3   Treatment Options for Conversion Disorder and Pain Disorder

1. Medical Evaluation/Hospitalization
2. Psychotherapy
   a. Play therapy
   b. Psychodynamic psychotherapy
   c. Hypnotic techniques
   d. Coping skills training to manage pain components
3. Behavioral Interventions
   a. Operant conditioning behavioral treatments
   b. Classical conditioning behavioral treatments
4. Family Interventions
   a. Family therapy
5. Multidimensional Techniques
   a. Extended Illness Coping Plan
      (1) Meeting of family and medical team to disuss findings and recommendations
      (2) Physical therapy/occupational therapy
      (3) Sleep hygiene intervention
      (4) Schoolday schedule
      (5) Evening schedule
      (6) Agreement on rules of illness behavior
      (7) Operant conditioning behavioral techniques
      (8) Classical conditioning behavioral techniques
      (9) Regular meetings with psychotherapist; referrals for individual or family therapy as needed
   b. Coping approach (see Schulman, 1988)

Note: This outline of options summarizes major treatments covered in the text. Specific treatments are often combined into an intervention package. Refer to the text for additional descriptions of each treatment. This table is not necessarily an exhaustive list of all treatments available.

complete. In severe cases that do not respond to other interventions, psychiatric hospitalization may be necessary (Kronenberger et al., 1995).

If treatment is initiated in the pediatric hospital, it is important to see some dedication to the treatment plan as well as some improvement prior to hospital discharge. One study of adults showed that 96% of those who improved during a medical hospital stay had good eventual outcome, compared to only 30% of those who did not improve. Patients with more recent symptom onset had faster improvement (Couprie et al., 1995).

Psychotherapy

Psychotherapeutic techniques use insight, teaching, and the therapeutic relationship to reduce stress and to challenge somatization defenses. These techniques are one of the most widely used approaches to managing Conversion Disorder, although their efficacy when used alone is suspect. Outpatient psychotherapy is recommended for 30–70% of children with Conversion Disorder (Goodyer & Mitchell, 1989; Kotsopoulos & Snow, 1986; Kronenberger, Laite, & LaClave, 1991), usually as part of a treatment package. Some tentative evidence exists that outpatient psychotherapy alone may be less effective than inpatient treatment (Kotsopoulos & Snow, 1986). Furthermore, families often fail to follow through on recommendations to enter psychotherapy because they believe that their child's symptoms are entirely the result of physical causes.

Play Therapy

Psychodynamic play therapy can allow the child to express illness-driving conflicts in a supportive and secure atmosphere. Young children respond particularly well to play therapy techniques because of their nonthreatening and nonconfrontative quality. Confrontational techniques often fail with children, who respond to them with intensified illness behavior and denial. Play therapy for children with Conversion Disorder should be generally nondirective, although the therapist should take an active role (prior to the session) in selecting play items that will elicit themes related to the Conversion Disorder. Play should be nondirective in order to allow the child to feel secure in displaying stresses and concerns in a nonjudgmental atmosphere. Toys that should be available are a play medical kit (with stethoscope, syringes, tubing, bandages, etc.), house and family figures, peer figures, and puppets. Children who have difficulty beginning play with the therapist are usually easily engaged in the care of a "sick" puppet or "family" member. Themes of attention for symptoms, family conflict, peer conflict, and rejection should be carefully monitored and eventually interpreted for the child. Theoretically, it is believed that the child relieves some of the tension from inner conflicts and stresses through the play, removing the underlying cause of the conversion symptom.

Psychodynamic Psychotherapy

For older children and adolescents, psychotherapeutic discussion of stresses involving school, peers, and family can be helpful. It is not unusual for children to resist discussion of stressful issues, especially if they see psychotherapy as an acknowledgment that their problem is psychological. Once a trusting therapeutic bond is formed, however, children with Conversion Disorders often seem relieved to have someone with whom to discuss their problems. Progress in this case is made with a combination of support, acceptance, emotional working-through of inner conflicts, and active problem solving to reduce external stress. In the case of peer stress, role playing and social skills training are two techniques that can increase perceptions of efficacy and decrease perceptions of threat.

Hypnotic Techniques

Hypnotic states, relaxed states, and suggestion are commonly used for the management of Conversion Disorders. Because Conversion Disorders are assumed to result from an unintentional psychological-somatic process, altered states of consciousness may offer a means of controlling the symptom by accessing the psychological process that is maintaining it. The use of hypnotherapy varies widely based on the training and theoretical orientation of the clinician (LaClave, Kronenberger, Baker, & Morrow, 1993). Hypnotherapy is recommended for as many as 50% of Conversion Disorder cases in some settings (Kronenberger et al., 1991).

Hypnotherapy for Conversion Disorder can take several forms. In all cases, hypnotic induction is performed, followed by deepening into the hypnotic state. Once in the hypnotic state, suggestions of relaxation and symptom removal may be made to relieve the conversion symptom (Olness & Gardner, 1988). Suggestions are often metaphorical rather than direct. For example, a child who cannot bend her arm may receive the suggestion to imagine the arm as a hinge that bends freely. Because it is important that children feel some control over the symptom removal, they are often taught self-hypnosis, which they practice between hypnotherapy sessions.

Self-hypnosis is often not effective when secondary gain, internal conflict, or external stress hinder the child's motivation to overcome the problem. In these cases, other treatment components or an additional abreaction/catharsis component must be added to the hypnotherapy (Gross, 1983). Hypnotic abreaction/catharsis occurs when the child is hypnotically regressed to the time of the stressors. The child then reexperiences the behaviors, sensations, cognitions, and emotions connected with the stressful event. By reexperiencing and mastering the stressful event, the child may achieve a sense of insight, completion, and control (Gross, 1983). This technique has some risks, however, because it involves the reexperiencing of what obviously was a psychologically harmful event. Thus, abreaction/catharsis should be performed carefully by a trained hypnotherapist.

Other techniques, such as relaxation and suggestion, share many characteristics with hypnosis. Because relaxation is assumed to be incompatible with feelings of tension and stress, stress- and anxiety-based conversion symptoms may be reduced when the child is in a relaxed state. In addition, the teaching of relaxation techniques may increase the child's feeling of control over the body. Suggestion involves administering a treatment such as hypnotherapy, relaxation, or placebo while giving the child verbal and nonverbal cues that the treatment will cure the conversion symptom.

Case studies (e.g., Gross, 1983; Olness & Gardner, 1988) indicate that some children do respond to hypnotherapy and related techniques, but many other children show no response to these interventions. The appropriateness of hypnotherapy for any individual case probably depends on factors such as hypnotizability, resistance to hypnosis, and secondary gain for symptoms.

Behavioral Interventions

Behavioral treatments for Conversion Disorders follow one of two models of conditioning. *Operant conditioning behavioral treatments* are based on the assumption that the conversion symptom is reinforced by contingencies in the child's environment. Hence, operant treatments for Conversion Disorders begin with an assessment of gains that the child is receiving for the conversion symptom. These gains are best assessed in two ways: First, the child and family should be asked what the child can no longer do because of the conversion symptom. Initial answers to this question are often limited to descriptions of the functional loss (e.g., "I can't bend my leg") and must be probed to gather information regarding what activities (e.g., "I can't go to gym class") have been lost because of the symptom. Regardless of whether children and families attach positive or negative valence to the lost activity, any change must be considered as a possible reinforcer for the symptoms. A second way of assessing secondary gain is to ask how the child's environment has changed since the emergence of the conversion symptom. Factors such as attention, change in family roles, escape from difficult situations (e.g., bullying at school), and tangible reinforcement should be considered.

Once possible sources of secondary gain are identified, these sources are modified or removed. Provisions are made for the child to engage in as many activities as possible, taking the level of functional impairment into account. A child with difficulty walking, for example, can be provided with crutches, a walker, or a wheelchair in order to attend school. Normal activities and chores are resumed, and positive reinforcement is given for behavior characteristic of a lessening of the conversion symptom. A critical component of this treatment package is a lack of attention for the conversion symptom. If the child complains about the symptom, caretakers should give a brief supportive response that expresses understanding and a belief in the child's ability to manage normal behavior in spite of the conversion symptom. The conversion symptom is not allowed to be used as an excuse for avoiding an activity whenever possible.

Classical conditioning behavioral treatments differ from operant conditioning treatments. Classical conditioning treatments are based on the assumption that the illness symptoms were initially a reflexive or natural response to some cause (such as a disease process or actual physical problem). However, the illness symptoms became associated with neutral stimuli (e.g., going to school) in the child's environment during the period of the actual disease or physical problem. Then, when the disease process was over, the illness symptoms continued to occur in response to the formerly neutral stimuli (now called conditioned stimuli). For example, a child may have a bona fide seizure disorder and experience several seizures in school in response to neurologically based seizure activity (a natural disease process). The child is eventually put on an effective regimen of antiseizure medication and the seizures are stopped. However, the child continues to show seizure-like episodes in school, which are confirmed by video EEG monitoring to be pseudoseizures (a Conversion Disorder in which the child appears to have seizures without any neurological basis). The seizure behavior (an illness symptom) has been associated with the school environment (a previously neutral stimulus; now called a conditioned stimulus) because both were present during the actual neurological activity that caused the bona fide seizures in the first place. However, actual neurological activity (the physiological process) is now no longer necessary to cause the association of school and seizure symptoms. They have been paired by the classical conditioning experience.

Classical conditioning treatments involve gradually exposing the child to the conditioned stimulus (the formerly neutral situation that became associated with the illness response), while preventing, ignoring, or discouraging the illness response. An *in vivo* desensitization plan is developed, in which the child is exposed to increasingly strong or stressful representations of the conditioned stimulus. Because the disease or physical process that naturally caused the illness response is no longer present, the child's illness complaints are no longer forced to occur by a reflexive, physiological process. The child is exposed gradually, starting with weak representations of the conditioned stimulus, so that the illness complaints are less likely to occur. Over time and treatment, the illness complaints are "trained out" of the child's repertoire as the child is desensitized to the conditioned stimulus.

In the previous example, the child could be brought to school at off hours, then for brief, closely monitored time during the school day, and eventually integrated into the entire school day. Seizure behavior would be given the minimal necessary attention, with the assumption that it would go away eventually as the child had more experience with the conditioned stimulus (school) in the absence of the physiological process (neurological seizure activity) that originally drove the illness response. The treatment closely resembles *in vivo* desensitization for phobias because both types of treatment are based on the principles of classical conditioning.

Family Interventions

Some involvement of the family is common in the treatment of Conversion Disorder. Family members may be participants in a behavioral plan, or they may be brought into formal family therapy. Family therapy typically aims to increase family insight into interaction patterns such as enmeshed interactions and avoidance of conflict. Structural aspects of the family system must be attended to as well: Boundaries should be clear between the child subsystem and the parental subsystem, and individual family members should have some measure of independence. Communication between family members should be direct and honest. Finally, the role of the child's illness in the family must be understood, and changes in the family system must occur (see Minuchin, 1974, for a discussion of specific family techniques to address somatization).

Multidimensional Interventions

In practice it is rare to see only one type of intervention used to treat a child with a Conversion Disorder. Most treatment packages for children with Conversion Disorders include a behavioral component and a psychotherapeutic component. If the family system is felt to have qualities that are contributing to the disorder, a family therapy component is indicated. Two specific multidimensional approaches will be described in detail to illustrate these techniques.

Extended Illness Coping Plan

The Extended Illness Coping Plan (EICP; Kronenberger, 1999) is one example of a systematic, multidimensional treatment plan used to integrate medical, behavioral, and other treatment components in the care of a child with a Somatoform Disorder. In this plan, the mental health clinician works closely with the medical team, often on a pediatric unit, to address the somatic symptoms. The first step of the EICP is evaluating the child for suitability for the plan. Five major requirements must be met:

1. Serious, persistent illness symptoms of duration greater than one month.
2. Evaluation and intervention by multiple pediatric subspecialties or intensive work by a single subspecialty or primary care physician.
3. More than one visit to hospital or a single hospitalization of duration greater than 2 days.
4. Severe functional limitations, including one of the following:
    a. Greater than 25% of school days missed during duration of illness
    b. Severely limited independent functioning (difficulty leaving bed, chair, or house)
    c. Significant impact on social functioning (isolated, withdrawn)
    d. Significant impact on activities or achievement
5. Age greater than or equal to 6 years.

These requirements essentially ensure that the illness symptoms are serious, persistent, and have received substantial medical attention. Interestingly, there is no requirement that the illness symptoms be definitively shown to be the result of a Somatoform Disorder, and the EICP is also used for children with bona fide chronic physical disorders (such as cancer and spina bifida) who are experiencing severe functional limitations. However, the primary use of the EICP is for Conversion and Somatoform Disorders.

Following the determination of eligibility criteria for the EICP, treatment proceeds as follows:

1. *The primary medical team and mental health clinician meet with the family to explain medical findings and recommendations for the EICP.* At this meeting, the family is told that the treatment team believes that there is a psychological component to the child's physical symptoms. It often helps to explain that the EICP is used with children who have documented physical illness (cancer is often used as an example) and that the medical team will continue its involvement in exactly the same way that it would be involved if the EICP was not used. By keeping the medical team involved with the child, it is hoped that both child and family will be less defensive and more amenable to change.

2. *Implementation of regular physical therapy and/or occupational therapy.* Physical and occupational therapy provides activity and stimulation to the child, encouraging a return to greater activity level and functioning. As the child builds greater stamina, he or she may feel better. The presence of continued physical intervention also prevents the child from feeling abandoned by the medical team and gives the child a way to "save face." Often, children believe that they actually had an illness and that the physical therapy "cured" them of it. Physical therapy also gives the child a sense of competence and ability to overcome the impairment.

3. *Implementation of a sleep hygiene intervention.* Often children with Conversion and Somatoform Disorders experience distortions in the sleep-wake schedule. Restoration of a normal sleep-wake schedule is important to reducing fatigue and improving feelings of alertness. A goal time is set for waking, usually based on the school day (6 or 7 A.M. is commonly used); if the child's sleep-wake schedule is significantly distorted, gradual approximations (e.g., wake up an hour earlier each day) may have to be used to reach this goal wake-up time. A rigid wake-up schedule is drawn up and enforced with scheduled times to be showered, dressed, groomed, and to eat breakfast.

Similarly, a bedtime schedule is developed with a target time for bedtime and a schedule of events leading up to bedtime. Evening hygiene is described with goal times for completion of each evening hygiene task. Ideally, the child should be ready for bed 30–60 minutes before the actual bedtime, with subdued, "wind-down" activities such as reading or listening to music allowed in this window of time.

Not surprisingly, the child is often resistant toward or uninterested in these wake-up and bedtime goals. Therefore, the parent must take charge of monitoring and enforcing the new rules. Contingencies must be drawn up, and the child should not be permitted to deviate from the target times and goals. In some cases, hospitalization is necessary to accomplish this component of treatment. If the child is already in the hospital, nurses often assume the responsibility for implementing this component of treatment.

4. *Implementation of a "schoolday" schedule.* In addition to the sleep-wake schedule, the child's schedule during school hours (8 A.M. to 3 P.M. is usually used) is designed to maximize activity while reducing reinforcement for illness. Ideally, the child goes to school after breakfast for a full school day. However, in many cases, the child stays at home or is in the hospital. If this is the case, the child must begin schoolwork immediately following breakfast. Interaction with parents is minimized unless the parents have a direct teaching role toward the child. The child may have access to tutors or nurses, but there is no television, radio, reading for pleasure, telephone, or other pleasant activity allowed. Essentially, the home or hospital environment should mirror the rules of school. Unrestricted television, radio, and telephone are (obviously) not allowed in school, and (except for breaks) they are not allowed during the school day during the EICP.

An extensive schedule with expectations and goals is drawn up for the child during the school day. Rest periods may occur as needed or may be scheduled for the child, but access to preferred or interesting activities does not occur until schedule goals are met. Expectations are very minimal at first with an increase each day. If the child protests the lack of access to favored activities, it is explained that if the child is so ill that a rest period is needed, then quiet rest, without distraction of any kind, must be required for the child to recuperate.

5. *Implementation of an "evening" schedule.* Following the end of the schoolday schedule, the child's evening schedule begins. Parents are allowed unlimited access to the child, but the child's other privileges and access to favored activities do not begin until the child has met all of the goals of the schoolday schedule. If some goals have not been met, they become "homework" to be completed in the evening hours prior to any privileges. The child may also be assigned normal afternoon and evening tasks to complete, and rest periods or fun periods may also be scheduled.

If the child has attended school during the day, he or she can have unlimited access to favored activities (within reason) as long as homework and afternoon/evening tasks are finished. If the child has stayed home from school, he or she must remain inside for the evening, and television/radio/telephone/reading privileges are curtailed but not completely withdrawn. This curtailing of privileges is explained not as punishment but as limiting activity so that the child may recuperate.

6. *Agreement on rules of illness behavior.* The child, family, mental health clinician, and medical team discuss appropriate illness behavior for the child in the household. Discussions of illness and pain should be limited to the following: child requests for support or treatment, information about change (positive or negative) in condition, information about new symptoms, positive statements about treatment progress, and a limited period of time (30 minutes) scheduled each evening for the child to vent about the illness. Constant discussion of the illness or constant complaining, on the other hand, conveys no new information, cannot help the child, and should not be allowed. It is explained to the parent that once illness information has been imparted, an identical repetition of the same illness complaint accomplishes nothing (note that the child is allowed to report changes and treatment needs). Therefore, these repetitions should be discouraged.

7. *Use of operant conditioning behavioral techniques to reward positive behavior and ignore illness-related behavior.* Attention for the child's physical symptoms is to be avoided by parents, and parents should reward the child for healthy statements and healthy behavior. In some cases, tangible reward systems may be set up to encourage the child to achieve goals.

8. *Use of classical conditioning behavioral techniques to desensitize the child to return to normal daily functioning.* The implementation of the schedule in steps 3–5 may involve a gradual desensitization of the child to certain behaviors or situations if needed.

9. *Regular meetings with the psychotherapist to monitor the progress of the EICP.* Referrals for psychotherapy or family therapy are also made as needed.

10. *Return to normal functioning.* Treatment goals are met when the child has returned to normal daily functioning, and the EICP is discontinued.

Schulman's Coping Approach

A similar multidimensional technique for managing Conversion Disorders, the coping approach, was suggested by Schulman (1988). The coping approach involves 10 components:

1. Review existing medical evidence with the physician and family.

2. Continue medical care and tracking of the patient's condition in case future medical tests are warranted.

3. Review with the family previous treatments that have been effective in relieving the somatic symptoms.

4. Review with the family the extent to which the child has altered or eliminated normal life activities.

5. Tell the family that because everything has been tried with no significant effects, the most reasonable course of action is for the child to return to a normal schedule (i.e., school, living at home, etc.). Essentially, the rationale here is that because nothing more can be done, the child should learn to function in as normal a fashion as possible with the conversion problem. Families are usually very resistant at this step and may be expected to offer numerous reasons for not being able to carry out this recommendation.

6. Discuss with the family that there are many children who, despite actual physical illness, participate in normal life activities. The family may be provided with examples of good coping on the part of these physically ill children. This step addresses some of the family concerns raised in step 5.

7. Point out that difficulty with coping is understandable, but a failure to *attempt* to cope is unreasonable and self-defeating. The child must leave the hospital environment eventually.

8. Working with the medical team and the family, set up rules of illness behavior. First, the child is to avoid somatic complaints such as verbal complaining, grimacing, and body contortions; the parents will ignore these complaints. Second, every few days for a brief period of time, the child is permitted to describe to the parents any somatic concerns that he or she has. The parents will relay these concerns to the medical team. This is important for the continued monitoring of the child's medical condition. Third, a gradual return to normal daily function is planned by the staff and parents, and the parents are to carry out this plan without deviation.

9. Help parents to see how their child's somatic problems have affected their own lives, and plan a return to normal life for the parents. At this point, the therapist must be careful to observe any parental/family dynamics that will jeopardize the therapeutic plan; family therapy may be warranted if the symptom is likely to be maintained by the family system.

10. Discuss with the child any problems that he or she anticipates with the plan, and suggest ways to cope with the return to normal life. Resistance on the part of the child may suggest the need for individual psychotherapy (Schulman, 1988).

Schulman's (1988) treatment package combines behavioral and cognitive-behavioral interventions with the possibility of psychotherapeutic and family therapy interventions to arrive at a comprehensive approach to managing Conversion Disorder. He provides several examples of the implementation of this approach and reports no cases of symptom substitution (Schulman, 1988).

■ Pain Disorder

□ CLINICAL DESCRIPTION

Diagnostic Considerations

A second common childhood Somatoform Disorder is Pain Disorder. Pain Disorder is characterized by complaints of pain in the absence of a somatic explanation for the pain or for its intensity. Like a Conversion Disorder, the pain must either cause distress or interfere with daily functioning. Furthermore, evidence of a role for psychological factors in the development of the pain symptoms is required, although the factors need not be specified. Pain Disorder can and often does co-occur with actual physical problems; when this is the case, Pain Disorder Associated with Both Psychological Factors and a General Medical Condition is diagnosed. This diagnosis requires that the reported intensity of pain or impairment clearly exceeds what would be expected from the physical problem. Therefore, determining the intensity of the pain and the extent of functional impairment is often critical to this diagnosis. Pain Disorders that do not co-occur with actual physical problems are coded as Pain Disorder Associated with Psychological Factors. DSM-IV reports that Pain Disorder is "relatively common" (American Psychiatric Association, 1994, p. 460), but prevalence in children is not known.

Appearance and Features

Pain Disorder can have broad effects on the functioning of the individual. Children with Pain Disorder often miss school and other activities. Many are shuttled from doctor to doctor in an attempt to find the cause of the disorder. Family concern and family conflict may be concurrent with or may result from the child's pain complaints. Pain may interfere with the child's concentration and cause irritability or sadness. These factors may contribute to social isolation and low self-esteem in some children.

The most common sites for Pain Disorder are (in order) stomach (recurrent abdominal pain), head (headache), and joints/extremeties. Recurrent abdominal pain (RAP) is the most common type of Pain Disorder. It tends to occur in children whose families focus on illness issues and frequently make complaints about somatic or emotional distress (Walker, Garber, & Greene, 1993). Children with RAP tend to have persistent symptoms of somatic complaints over years and experience more functional limitations than healthy children (Walker, Garber, Van Slyke, & Greene, 1995).

□ ASSESSMENT PATTERNS

A sample assessment battery for Pain Disorder is shown in Table 8.2.

Broad Assessment Strategies

The broad assessment strategies for Conversion Disorder apply to Pain Disorder as well. Like Conversion Disorder, Pain Disorder is frequently accompanied by some apparent decrease in functioning. Perhaps the only difference in assessment that may be anticipated would be higher scores for children with Pain Disorder on internalizing (anxiety, depression) subscales. These higher scores would reflect the anxiety, irritation, and hopelessness that many of these children feel when the medical establishment is unable to cure their pain.

Syndrome-Specific Tests

Child-Report

It is often helpful to administer the child a self-report measure of pain (see Katz, Varni, & Jay, 1984, and Savedra & Tesler, 1989, for a review of specific measures of pain). Many aspects of pain may be assessed, but three of the most commonly assessed pain components are location (where is the pain?), intensity (how badly does the pain hurt?), and quality (what does the pain feel like?). Having the child shade in the painful area on a body outline can provide the clinician with an estimate of the localization of the pain. Use of different colored crayons to represent different severity levels of pain can add a severity dimension to the body outline shading task (Savedra & Tesler, 1989).

Many unidimensional self-report measures of pain intensity exist as well. These measures can be divided into visual scales, verbal scales, and numerical scales. Visual pain intensity scales use pictures to anchor the pain scale. Often these pictures are of faces (Beyer, 1984; McGrath, DeVeber, & Hearn, 1985), although other objects such as ladders (Jeans & Johnston, 1985) and thermometers (Katz et al., 1982) are sometimes used as well. The Oucher scale (Beyer, 1984) and nine face scale (McGrath et al., 1985), for example, present the child with several pictures of faces with expressions ranging from happy to pain/cry; children point to the face that best characterizes their pain. The Pain Ladder (Jeans & Johnston, 1985), on the other hand, asks children to point to the place on a ladder that typifies the level of pain. The bottom of the ladder is classified as no pain, whereas the top is classified as pain that is as bad as it can be. The Pain Thermometer (Katz et al., 1984) asks children to point to the place on a thermometer that represents their level of pain. Higher temperatures represent greater pain. More simple visual pain scales consist simply of a line with one end signifying extreme pain and the other end signifying no pain; children make a mark along the length of the line that characterizes their pain (Savedra & Tesler, 1989). Line scales can be scored by using a ruler to measure millimeters from the "no pain" beginning of the line. Many of these visual pain intensity scales include a numerical scale in addition to the visual component, and all of the intensity scales yield numerical scores. The visual scales have the advantage of requiring less verbal ability in the child.

Verbal scales rely exclusively on verbal descriptions of the pain, which are usually anchored to a numerical value. Savedra and Tesler (1989), for example, describe a scale used by McGrath and Unruh (1987) to assess children's pain. This verbal pain scale consists of six verbal statements ranging from "no pain" to "pain—I can't ignore it but I can do my usual activities" to "pain—such that I can't do anything." Children choose one of the six statements, which are coded on a 0 (no pain) to 5 (extreme pain) scale for scoring (Savedra & Tesler, 1989). Other verbal pain intensity scales use only a numerical scale to characterize pain. Asking a child to rate pain on a scale of 1–10 is an example of such a pain scale.

In addition to location and intensity, the quality (subjective sense or "feel") of the pain may be assessed. For example, pain may be described as "shooting," "dull," "sharp," "pressured," or "hot." The McGill Pain Questionnaire (Melzack, 1975) is one questionnaire designed to assess pain quality issues.

Other-Report

Children's pain may also be assessed by behavior rating scales such as the Observational Scale of Behavioral Distress (OSBD; Jay & Elliott, 1984). Such scales require no effort on the part of the child and eliminate self-report bias. However, they do not tap the subjective component of pain and, thus, should be regarded as incomplete or supplementary measures. When a child is suspected of significant self-report bias, a pain behavior rating scale such as the OSBD may be considered.

Despite the availability of numerous pain assessment scales, little formal pain assessment research has been done with children with Pain Disorder. Regarding pain location, no typical pattern of assessment results is seen. Some children will vary the pain location (a red flag for the diagnosis of Pain Disorder), whereas others will be consistent. Clinical experience suggests that children with Pain Disorder generally report very high levels of pain intensity, which can at times seem outrageous. One child, for example, after being asked to rate his pain on a scale of 1 to 10, groaned and said, "20." Furthermore, no typical result can be stated for assessment of pain quality in Pain Disorder. Although the value of pain assessment in the differential diagnosis of Pain Disorder is unclear, routine pain assessment is recommended in order to track treatment efficacy and to assist the child with self-monitoring of improvement of symptoms.

☐　　TREATMENT OPTIONS

Because Conversion Disorder and Pain Disorder share in common components such as somatic focus and secondary gain, most treatments for Conversion Disorder are appropriate for Pain Disorder with minimal modifications (see Table 8.3). Play therapy, behavior modification, hypnotherapy, family therapy, and multidimensional techniques are all widely used.

In addition to these techniques, the teaching and modeling of coping with pain may help these children. Such a coping-skills approach begins with an assessment of the level of pain, using one of the standardized pain instruments. Next comes an evaluation of the child's coping strategies, using an interview, parent-report, observation, and possibly a coping scale such as the KIDCOPE (Spirito, Stark, & Williams, 1988). The effectiveness of individual coping strategies is likely to vary from one child to another, making individual assessment very important. Coping strategies that are ineffective in managing pain are discouraged, and more effective coping strategies are taught. For example, the child is encouraged to purposefully use strategies such as distraction, social support, problem solving, and information seeking to attempt to manage the pain. Coping strategies are practiced, and a live model or videotape may be used to teach the use of the strategies. The effectiveness of these strategies is tested by readministering a standardized pain measure and looking for decreases in reported pain. Because the effectiveness of the coping-skills approach is dependent on the child's motivation, resistance on the part of the child may necessitate the use of other interventions before the coping-skills approach can be effective.

■ Hypochondriasis, Somatization Disorder, and Undifferentiated Somatoform Disorder

☐ CLINICAL DESCRIPTION

This subgroup of Somatoform Disorders shares in common the patient's belief that he or she has a physical problem, in the absence of any physical findings. In the case of Hypochondriasis, the person believes (or fears) that he or she has some serious, specific disease. This belief persists despite medical evidence to the contrary. Although Hypochondriasis can occur in children, it is relatively rare, with age at onset usually in early adulthood. In many cases, apparent childhood Hypochondriasis may actually be the result of the child's response to the *parent's* fear that the child is ill.

Unlike Hypochondriasis, Somatization Disorder involves recurrent, multiple physical symptoms, typically without the belief that one has some specific disease. A diagnosis of Somatization Disorder requires at least eight of a large number of possible physical symptoms in four areas: pain symptoms (at least four), gastrointestinal symptoms (at least two), sexual symptoms (at least one), and neurological symptoms (at least one). The large number and variety of physical symptoms are often the most clinically striking feature of this syndrome. Symptoms may change or abate, but the child generally has some set of physical complaints virtually all of the time for several years. Somatization Disorder typically occurs in females between the ages of 10 and 20. It is often related to some environmental stressor, intrapsychic conflict, or anxiety. Little research exists on this disorder in children, and it is relatively rare (less than 1% prevalence) in adults as well (American Psychiatric Association, 1994).

Undifferentiated Somatoform Disorder is diagnosed for children with one or more physical complaints which last at least 6 months, affect daily functioning or distress, and do not have a physical explanation. Because the symptom pattern cannot fit that of another Somatoform Disorder, pain and neurological complaints rarely fit this diagnosis. Children with single, long-lasting physical complaints of other types will often receive the Undifferentiated Somatoform Disorder Diagnosis. In addition, most children who do not have enough symptoms to qualify for the Somatization Disorder diagnosis receive the Undifferentiated Somatoform Disorder Diagnosis. Hence, the Undifferentiated Somatoform Disorder category encompasses a rather heterogeneous and diverse group of clinical presentations, ranging from children with specific unexplained physical complaints to children who nearly meet the Somatization Disorder diagnostic criteria.

■   **Body Dysmorphic Disorder**

☐   CLINICAL DESCRIPTION

Diagnostic Considerations

Body Dysmorphic Disorder (BDD) is characterized by an excessive focus on an imagined physical defect. The target of focus may be an actual physical problem, but the person's concern and distress is out of proportion to the problem. The person's concern must cause significant distress or problems in daily functioning. Common targets of this concern include facial defects, hair, skin, muscle size, breast size, genitalia size, and body proportions.

As may be expected, appearance-related preoccupations are exceedingly common in adolescence, but the point at which one of these preoccupations becomes a BDD is not clearly spelled out in DSM-IV. DSM-IV suggests that the amount of lost time and loss of daily functioning resulting from the symptoms should be used in distinguishing between appearance concerns and a BDD. Age at onset of BDD is usually during or after late adolescence; BDD appears to be very rare in preadolescent children (Table 8.4).

There is substantial overlap between BDD and Obsessive-Compulsive Disorder (OCD), Social Phobia, and Depressive Disorders. As many as 60% of individuals with BDD qualify for current Major Depressive Disorder (Phillips, 1996), whereas 35% have a lifetime diagnosis of Social Phobia (Phillips, McElroy, Hudson, & Pope, 1995). Using the DSM-IV field trial sample for OCD, Simeon, Hollander, Stein, Cohen, & Aronowitz, (1995) found that 12% had a lifetime history of BDD. In samples of patients with BDD, from 30% to over 50% have significant symptoms of OCD (Hollander, Cohen, & Simeon, 1993; Phillips et al., 1995). Patients with BDD and OCD score similarly on measures of obsessive-compulsive symptoms, depression, and anxiety (McKay, Neziroglu, & Yaryura-Tobias, 1997). However, individuals with BDD and OCD appear to have poorer insight into their disorder and more severe symptoms than those with OCD alone (Simeon et al., 1995), and individuals with OCD alone tend to have more somatic symptoms of anxiety compared to those with BDD (McKay et al.,

TABLE 8.4   Epidemiology and Outcome of Body Dysmorphic Disorder

Prevalence: 1–4%

Sex Ratio (Male:Female):   1:1 to 1:4

Typical Onset Age: Adolescence (typically around 17 years)

Course: Profound impact on day-to-day functioning, with checking behaviors, hiding the "defect," and social avoidance commonly seen. As many as one-third may attempt suicide. Most seek appearance-altering treatments including surgery or dermatological treatment.

Common Comorbid Conditions: 1. Major Depressive Disorder
                                    2. Obsessive-Compulsive Disorder
                                    3. Social Phobia
                                    4. Substance Use Disorders

Relevant Subtypes: Not Delusional vs. Delusional

1997). Some have suggested that BDD is a subtype or variant of OCD, but this hypothesis is controversial (McKay et al., 1997; Phillips, O'Sullivan, & Pope, 1997).

Appearance and Features

Patients with BDD show significant discomfort with their imagined defect. They often try to hide the defect and to hide their preoccupation with it. In many cases, their distorted view of the defect reaches the level of a delusion. Most patients also have delusions of reference that other people are paying undue attention to their defect (Phillips, 1996).

Individuals with BDD often change their behavioral patterns because of the symptoms. They may spend hours examining the "defect" in front of a mirror, or they may feel compelled to look at themselves whenever they pass a reflective surface. Alternatively, they may avoid mirrors in order to reduce distress over the imagined problem. Social withdrawal, social avoidance, and impaired social interactions are present in most adolescents with BDD. In many cases, social avoidance is severe and may reach the level of social phobia. Adolescents with BDD will often seek reassurance about their appearance, either with direct requests or in less direct, attention-seeking ways.

Suicide attempts are a significant risk in adults with BDD, with rates as high as 30% (Phillips, 1996). However, little research is available on children and adolescents. Suicide may be a greater risk when BDD symptoms are comorbid with depressive symptoms. Additionally, BDD symptoms with a delusional quality may increase the risk of a suicide attempt.

Most people with BDD seek medical (or other appearance-altering interventions) rather than psychological treatment. Surgical and dermatological treatments are very common. As many as 30–40% may have plastic surgery (Table 8.5).

TABLE 8.5   Appearance and Features of Body Dysmorphic Disorder

COMMON FEATURES

1. Preoccupation or excessive focus on imagined physical defect
2. Obsessive-compulsive features
3. Attempts to hide defect
4. Excessive examination of defect in mirrors
5. Social withdrawal or social avoidance
6. Reassurance seeking
7. Seeking surgical, dermatological, or other medical treatment
8. Suicidal ideation

OCCASIONAL FEATURES

1. Preoccupation is delusional in quality
2. Delusions that others are paying undue attention to defect
3. Suicide attempts

Note: The features listed in the table are often seen but are not universal. Some features may be diagnostically relevant or required, whereas others may not be required for diagnosis. "Common" features are typical of the disorder; "occasional" features appear frequently but are not necessarily seen in a majority of cases.

Etiology

Biological Theories

Biological theories of BDD hypothesize that a neurotransmitter deficit in the serotonergic system causes BDD symptoms to arise. Evidence cited for this theory is the effectiveness of serotonin reuptake inhibitors in treating BDD and the overlap of BDD with depressive disorders and OCD.

Psychological Theories

Cognitive-behavioral theories emphasize the role of distorted beliefs, thoughts, and perceptual processes in the development of BDD. Evidence exists, for example, that individuals with BDD tend to pay considerable attention to their bodies in general and to their imagined defect in particular. They hold the mistaken assumption that other people place the same degree of attention and value on their defect as they do. Individuals with BDD also place a strong value on being perfect in appearance. As a result of these beliefs, individuals with BDD have negative self-statements about their appearance and imagined defect. These thoughts and self-statements become so routine that they are believed by the individual. Behaviors such as hiding, watching, or checking the defect may be negatively reinforcing because they are associated with a reduction in anxiety about the defect (Rosen, Reiter, & Orosan, 1995; Veale et al., 1996).

☐ ASSESSMENT PATTERNS

Syndrome-Specific Tests

Clinician-Administered

Body Dysmorphic Disorder Examination.   The Body Dysmorphic Disorder Examination (BDDE; Rosen & Reiter, 1996) is a 34-item, semistructured interview consisting of questions about body image, perceived defects, and symptoms of BDD. The interviewer makes ratings for each item, based on the interviewer's judgment of the patient's responses; 28 of the 34 items pertain to the severity of specific BDD symptoms (rated on a 1–6 scale, if the symptom is present) in various areas. A total score may be obtained by adding the 28 symptom items. Although Rosen and Reiter (1996) note that no patient in their BDDE sample received a total score under 66, they caution that using 66 as a cutoff would produce an unacceptably high number of false positives. Hence, there is no cutoff clinical score for the BDDE, and specific items should be examined to assist in diagnosis. Administration time is about 30 minutes.

The BDDE appears to be a valid and reliable measure. Individuals with BDD score higher on BDDE total score than other clinical and nonclinical groups. BDDE total scores correlate with measures of negative body image and low self-esteem. The BDDE is sensitive to treatment changes in BDD symptoms, and it seems to be a better measure of BDD than other body image scales (Rosen & Reiter, 1996).

Self-Report

Modified Yale-Brown Obsessive-Compulsive Scale. The Modified Yale-Brown Obsessive-Compulsive Scale (M-Y-BOCS) is a version of the Yale-Brown Obsessive-Compulsive Scale (see Chapter 6) modified to focus on the imagined body defect as the content of the obsessive-compulsive symptoms (Phillips, 1993). Hence, it measures distressing thoughts and compulsions related to the imagined defect. It is sensitive to treatment changes (Neziroglu & Yaryura-Tobias, 1993) and may be a good measure of the degree to which BDD symptoms have obsessive characteristics.

☐ TREATMENT OPTIONS

Medication

Typically, medications for Obsessive-Compulsive Disorder and mood disorders are considered for application to BDD because of the frequent overlap of symptoms of these disorders with BDD. In particular, serotonin reuptake inhibitors have shown promise in treatment of BDD with improvement rates of 40–70% reported in the literature (Phillips, 1996). For example, there are case reports of clomipramine (Anafranil) and fluoxetine (Prozac) used effectively to treat BDD in adolescents and young adults with BDD (Heimann, 1997; Phillips et al., 1997).

Psychotherapy

Cognitive-Behavioral Interventions

Cognitive-behavioral interventions integrate cognitive techniques with exposure to the "defect" and prevention of responses to hide or avoid the "defect." These treatments have shown some promise in the treatment of BDD (Phillips, 1996).

In a typical treatment plan, individuals first learn about distorted beliefs, perceptions, and thoughts, consistent with a cognitive-behavioral model of BDD. Individuals then learn to monitor their thoughts and behaviors related to the BDD in a cognitive-behavioral diary. Next, exposure and response prevention are accomplished by removing the behaviors that are typically used to reduce anxiety about the defect, while not avoiding the knowledge and perception of the presumed defect. These behaviors include checking, hiding the defect, avoiding social situations, and seeking reassurance. At the same time, individuals learn to more accurately appraise their appearance (by focusing on all aspects of appearance, not just the defect) and to more accurately view the behaviors and attention of others. For individuals with symptoms too severe to allow *in vivo* exposure, imaginal techniques may be used at first. Alternatively, individuals may construct a hierarchy of anxiety-producing situations related to the BDD, with gradual exposure to increasingly more feared components of the hierarchy. Throughout the exposure treatment, relaxation and coping techniques are used to help individuals manage anxiety. Cognitive distortions are reviewed and challenged. Using cognitive-behavioral treatment plans, Rosen et al. (1995), Veale et al. (1996), and McKay et al. (1997) report significant reduction in BDD symptoms with maintenance of gains at follow-up. Symptoms were reduced by 50% on average with significant improvement in up to 80% of treated cases (Rosen et al., 1995; Veale et al., 1996).

■ References

American Psychiatric Association. (1994). *Diagnostic and statistical manual of mental disorders, fourth edition.* Washington, DC: Author.

Beyer, J. E. (1984). *The Oucher: A user's manual and technical report.* Charlottesville, VA: University of Virginia Alumni Patent Foundation.

Couprie, W., Wijdicks, E. F. M., Rooijmans, H. G. M., & van Gijn, J. (1995). Outcome in conversion disorder: A follow-up study. *Journal of Neurology, Neurosurgery, and Psychiatry, 58,* 750–752.

Fritz, G. K., Fritsch, S., & Hagino, O. (1997). Somatoform disorders in children and adolescents: A review of the past 10 years. *Journal of the American Academy of Child and Adolescent Psychiatry, 36,* 1329–1338.

Goodyer, I. M., & Mitchell, C. (1989). Somatic emotional disorders in childhood and adolescence. *Journal of Psychosomatic Research, 33,* 681–688.

Grattan-Smith, P., Fairley, M., & Procopis, P. (1988). Clinical features of conversion disorder. *Archives of Disease in Childhood, 63,* 408–414.

Gross, M. (1983). Hypnoanalysis in conversion reaction. *Medical Hypnoanalysis,* 160–165.

Heimann, S. W. (1997). SSRI for body dysmorphic disorder. *Journal of the American Academy of Child and Adolescent Psychiatry, 36,* 868.

Hollander, E., Cohen, L. J., & Simeon, D. (1993). Body dysmorphic disorder. *Psychiatric Annals, 23,* 359–364.

Jay, S. M., & Elliott, C. (1984). Behavioral observation scales for measuring children's distress: The effects of increased methodological rigor. *Journal of Consulting and Clinical Psychology, 52,* 1106–1107.

Jeans, M. E., & Johnston, C. C. (1985). Pain in children: Assessment and management. In Lipton S. & Miles J. (Eds.), *Persistent pain: Modern methods of treatment* (Vol. 5, pp. 111–127). London: Grune & Stratton.

Katz, E. R., Sharp, B., Kellerman, J., Marston, A., Hirschman, J., & Siegel, S. E. (1982). Beta-Endorphin immunoreactivity and acute behavioral distress in children with leukemia. *Journal of Nervous and Mental Disease, 170,* 72–77.

Katz, E. R., Varni, J. W., & Jay, S. M. (1984). Behavioral assessment and management of pain. In M. Hersen, R. Eisler, & P. Miller (Eds.), *Progress in behavior modification* (Vol. 18, pp. 163–193). New York: Academic Press.

Kotsopoulos, S., & Snow, B. (1986). Conversion disorders in children: A study of clinical outcome. *The Psychiatric Journal of the University of Ottawa, 11,* 134–139.

Kronenberger, W. G. (1999). *Extended illness coping plan.* Unpublished treatment plan manuscript, Indiana University School of Medicine, Indianapolis, IN.

Kronenberger, W. G., Laite, G., & LaClave, L. (1991). *Somatoform disorders in pediatric populations: Self-perceptions and recommendations.* Paper Presented at the Indiana University Department of Psychiatry Grand Rounds Series.

Kronenberger, W. G., Laite, G., & LaClave, L. (1995). Somatoform disorders in pediatric populations: Self-perceptions and recommendations. *Psychosomatics, 36,* 1–6.

LaClave, L., Kronenberger, W. G., Baker, E., & Morrow, C. (1993). Use of hypnosis following training in a psychiatry residency and psychology internship program. *International Journal of Clinical and Experimental Hypnosis, 41,* 265–271.

Lehmkuhl, G., Blanz, B., Lehmkuhl, U., & Braun-Scharm, H. (1989). Conversion disorder (DSM-III 300.11): Symptomatology and course in childhood and adolescence. *European Archives of Psychiatry and Neurological Sciences, 238,* 155–160.

Leslie, S. A. (1988). Diagnosis and treatment of hysterical conversion reactions. *Archives of Disease in Childhood, 63,* 506–511.

Livingston, R., Witt, A., & Smith, G. R. (1995). Families who somatize. *Journal of Developmental and Behavioral Pediatrics, 16,* 42–46.

McGrath, P. A., DeVeber, L. L., & Hearn, M. T. (1985). Multidimensional pain assessment in children. In Fields, H. L., Dubner, R., & Cervero, F. (Eds.), *Advances in pain research and therapy* (pp. 387–393). New York: Raven Press.

McGrath, P. J., & Unruh, A. M. (1987). *Pain in children and adolescents.* New York: Elsevier.

McKay, D., Neziroglu, F., & Yaryura-Tobias, J. A. (1997). Comparison of clinical characteristics in obsessive-compulsive disorder and body dysmorphic disorder. *Journal of Anxiety Disorders, 11,* 447–454.

McKay, D., Todaro, J., Neziroglu, F., Campisi, T., Moritz, E. K., Yaryura-Tobias, J. A. (1997). Body dysmorphic disorder: A preliminary evaluation of treatment and maintenance using exposure with response prevention. *Behavior Research and Therapy, 35,* 67–70.

Melzack, R. (1975). The McGill Pain Questionnaire: Major properties and scoring methods. *Pain, 1,* 277–299.

Minuchin, S. (1974). *Families and family therapy.* Cambridge, MA: Harvard University Press.

Neziroglu, F. A., & Yaryura-Tobias, J. A. (1993). Exposure, response prevention, and cognitive therapy in the treatment of body dysmorphic disorder. *Behavior Therapy, 24,* 431–438.

Olness, K., & Gardner, G. G. (1988). *Hypnosis and hypnotherapy with children* (2nd ed.). Philadelphia: Grune & Stratton.

Phillips, K. A. (1993). *Body dysmorphic disorder modification of the YBOCS, McLean Version.* Belmont, MA: McLean Hospital.

Phillips, K. A. (1996). Body dysmorphic disorder: Diagnosis and treatment of imagined ugliness. *Journal of Clinical Psychiatry, 57,* 61–64.

Phillips, K. A., McElroy, S. L., Hudson, J. I., & Pope, H. G., Jr. (1995). Body dysmorphic disorder: An obsessive-compulsive spectrum disorder, a form of affective spectrum disorder, or both? *Journal of Clinical Psychiatry, 56,* 41–51.

Phillips, K. A., O'Sullivan, R. L., & Pope, H. G. (1997). Muscle dysmorphia. *Journal of Clinical Psychiatry, 58,* 361.

Piers, E. V. (1984). *Piers-Harris Children's Self-Concept Scale Revised manual 1984.* Los Angeles, CA: Western Psychological Services.

Regan, J. J., & Regan, W. M. (1989). Somatoform disorders. In C. G. Last & M. Hersen (Eds.), *Handbook of child psychiatric diagnosis* (pp. 343–355). New York: Wiley.

Robinson, D. P., Greene, J. W., & Walker, L. S. (1988). Functional somatic complaints in adolescents: Relationship to negative life events, self-concept, and family characteristics. *The Journal of Pediatrics, 113,* 588–593.

Rosen, J. C., & Reiter, J. (1996). Development of the Body Dysmorphic Disorder Examination. *Behavior Research and Therapy, 34,* 755–766.

Rosen, J. C., Reiter, J., & Orosan, P. (1995). Cognitive-behavioral body image therapy for Body Dysmorphic Disorder. *Journal of Consulting and Clinical Psychology, 63,* 263–269.

Savedra, M. C., & Tesler, M. D. (1989). Assessing children's and adolescents' pain. *Pediatrician, 16,* 24–29.

Schulman, J. L. (1988). Use of a coping approach in the management of children with conversion reactions. *Journal of the American Academy of Child and Adolescent Psychiatry, 27,* 785–788.

Seltzer, W. J. (1985). Conversion disorder in childhood and adolescence: A familial/cultural approach. Part I. *Family Systems Medicine, 3,* 261–280.

Selye, H. (1956). *The stress of life.* New York: McGraw-Hill.

Siegel, M., & Barthel, R. P. (1986). Conversion disorders on a child psychiatry consultation service. *Psychosomatics, 27,* 201–204.

Simeon, D., Hollander, E., Stein, D. J., Cohen, L., & Aronowitz, B. (1995). Body Dysmorphic Disorder in the DSM-IV field trial for Obsessive-Compulsive Disorder. *American Journal of Psychiatry, 152,* 1207–1209.

Spirito, A., Stark, L. J., & Williams, C. (1988). Development of a brief coping checklist for use with pediatric populations. *Journal of Pediatric Psychology, 13,* 555–574.

Steinhausen, H. C., Aster, M., Pfeiffer, E., & Gobel, D. (1989). Comparative studies of conversion disorders in childhood and adolescence. *Journal of Child Psychology and Psychiatry and Allied Disciplines, 30,* 615–621.

Thomson, A. P. J., & Sills, J. A. (1988). Diagnosis of functional illness presenting with gait disorder. *Archives of Disease in Childhood, 63,* 148–153.

Veale, D., Gournay, K., Dryden, W., Boocock, A., Shah, F., Willson, R., & Walburn, J. (1996). Body dysmorphic disorder: A cognitive-behavioral model and pilot randomised controlled trial. *Behavior Research and Therapy, 34,* 717–729.

Volkmar, F. R., Poll, J., & Lewis, M. (1984). Conversion reactions in childhood and adolescence. *Journal of the American Academy of Child Psychiatry, 23,* 424–430.

Walker, L. S., Garber, J., & Greene, J. W. (1993). Psychosocial correlates of recurrent childhood pain: A comparison of pediatric patients with recurrent abdominal pain, organic illness, and psychiatric disorders. *Journal of Abnormal Psychology, 102,* 248–258.

Walker, L. S., Garber, J., Van Slyke, D. A., and Greene, J. W. (1995). Long-term health outcomes in patients with recurrent abdominal pain. *Journal of Pediatric Psychology, 20,* 233–245.

Walker, L. S., McLaughlin, F. J., & Greene, J. W. (1988). Functional illness and family functioning: A comparison of healthy and somaticizing adolescents. *Family Process, 27,* 317–320.

CHAPTER 9

Schizophrenia

■ **Schizophrenia and Psychosis**

□ CLINICAL DESCRIPTION

Diagnostic Considerations

The diagnostic criteria for schizophrenia in children are essentially the same as for adults. These criteria include some combination of delusions, hallucinations, incoherence, disorganized behavior, and negative symptoms such as flat affect. Symptoms must be of sufficient severity to result in a significant decrease in adaptive functioning. Depending on the predominant symptoms, children are diagnosed into one of five types of schizophrenia: Catatonic (predominantly motor disturbance), Disorganized (predominantly disorganized behavior and affect disturbance), Paranoid (predominantly delusions), Undifferentiated (schizophrenic symptoms that do not meet criteria for the first three categories), and Residual (residual symptoms but no active delusions, hallucinations, disorganized speech, disorganized behavior, or negative symptoms). Most children and young adolescents with schizophrenia fall into the Paranoid and Undifferentiated subtypes (McClellan & Werry, 1992).

Before 1980, childhood schizophrenia and autism were frequently grouped together under the title "childhood schizophrenia." This grouping occurred in spite of the fact that the symptom pictures of the two disorders are different and that there is little overlap between cases (Kolvin, Berney, & Yoeli, 1990). Research prior to 1980 (and some research following 1980) often combined children with schizophrenia and autism, obscuring the symptom picture and empirical correlates of each of these disorders. Recent research suggests that, although some children with autistic disorder develop schizophrenic features, the diagnostic separation of the two disorders is warranted (Kolvin et al., 1990; McClellan & Werry, 1992). Schizophrenia should be diagnosed in a child with a Pervasive Developmental Disorder (such as autism) only if hallucinations or delusions are prominent during a period of 1 month or more (American Psychiatric Association, 1994).

Schizophrenia appears to be rare in preadolescent children, with prevalence increasing throughout adolescence and into adulthood (Table 9.1). Childhood schizophrenia almost never occurs before age 6, and it continues to be extremely rare before age 9 (McClellan & Werry, 1992; Watkins, Asarnow, & Tanguay, 1988). Prevalence estimates of childhood schizophrenia have been in the range of 0.03% of the child population (Kolvin et al., 1990). Schizophrenia is 50 times as rare before the age of 15 as after the age of 15 (Kolvin et al., 1990). Hence, in preadolescent children, schizophrenia should be diagnosed cautiously and only after ruling out more likely explanations such as organic causes, drugs, attention-seeking behavior, Obsessive-Compulsive Disorder, and oppositionality.

Although schizophrenia is quite rare in preadolescent children, schizophrenic-like behaviors or symptoms are more common. These behaviors are unusual, incoherent, or lack reality testing, but they do not have the pervasive and long-lasting quality of schizophrenia. Children under extreme stress will sometimes decompensate into incoherence, delusions, hallucinations, and disorganized or catatonic behavior. When provided with structure and support, traumatized children lose these symptoms within days or a couple of weeks. Children who display this symptom pattern (for a period of 1 day to 1 month) are diagnosed as having a Brief Psychotic Disorder With Marked Stressors. If no stressors are identified, the diagnosis Brief Psychotic Disorder Without Marked Stressors is made (American Psychiatric Association, 1994).

When the child shows psychotic behavior for 1 to 6 months, a diagnosis of Schizophreniform Disorder may be made. This diagnosis acknowledges the presence of schizophrenic symptoms that do not meet the schizophrenia criterion of lasting longer than 6 months (American Psychiatric Association, 1994). Schizophreniform Disorder may repre-

TABLE 9.1   Epidemiology and Course of Childhood-Onset Schizophrenia

Prevalence: Extremely rare before age 12, with no prevalence estimate in this age group, but probably lower than 0.05%. Prevalence increases dramatically in late adolescence (age 15 and older), peaking at 1% to 1.5% in adulthood.

Sex Ratio (Male:Female):   May be more common in males in childhood; 1:1 in adults

Typical Onset Age: 15–35 years (earlier in men than in women)

Course: Earlier (before age 10), gradual onset is related to greater severity and chronicity of symptoms. In most cases, psychotic episodes are followed by gradual recovery and then recurrence of psychotic episodes throughout life. Gradual deterioration of functioning is often seen, although a small percentage (probably fewer than 30%) are able to function adequately in the environment with minimal symptoms.

Common Comorbid Conditions: None

Relevant Subtypes:
1. Paranoid Type
2. Disorganized Type
3. Catatonic Type
4. Undifferentiated Type
5. Residual Type
6. Type I (positive symptoms) vs. Type II (negative symptoms)

sent a number of conditions, ranging from the development of schizophrenia to a behaviorally caused cluster of strange behavior that is reinforced by the child's environment.

Another presentation that resembles schizophrenia occurs when a child or adolescent is drawn into someone else's delusion, usually held by a caretaker or other person with whom the child has bonded. This condition is diagnosed as Shared Psychotic Disorder or Folie à Deux (American Psychiatric Association, 1994). Parents have considerable influence over the ways in which their children perceive and interpret the world. A child who is repeatedly exposed to a parent's delusion may, therefore, come to believe it because of allegiance to the parent as well as because of "evidence" presented by the parent. Shared Psychotic Disorder in adolescence usually happens during overidentification with an impaired peer or peer group. In most cases children and adolescents with Shared Psychotic Disorder do not show evidence of hallucinations, bizarre behavior, or grossly inappropriate affect, and they do not develop delusions other than the one that is believed by the psychotic individual with whom they have bonded. However, they tenaciously hold to their delusion as long as they remain with the individual who is the source of the delusion. Separation of the child or adolescent from the individual who is the source of the delusion generally results in the disappearance of the delusion, although the child or adolescent may initially be resistant to giving up the delusion. Bonding with healthy individuals often helps the child to reach this goal.

The early stages of a childhood-onset bipolar disorder or psychotic depression are extremely difficult to differentiate from the early stages of schizophrenia because the disorders share symptoms of emotional lability, odd behavior, social problems, and disinhibited behavior. Furthermore, mood disorders can be accompanied by psychotic symptoms. No empirically validated models exist for differentiating the early stages of mood and schizophrenic disorders, but clinical experience suggests that reports of significant and persistent hallucinations may be more characteristic of schizophrenia. Mood instability, especially cycling of depression and hypomania, are more characteristic of a bipolar disorder or cyclothymia. In addition, if psychotic symptoms occur only during periods of mania or depression, a mood disorder diagnosis is more likely. Initially, however, both schizophrenia and bipolar disorder should be considered as possible diagnoses for such cases, and the child should be closely watched for clearer, more differentiated symptoms of one disorder or the other. Bipolar disorder or psychotic depression are commonly mistaken for schizophrenia (Volkmar, 1996).

Finally, children with autistic disorder can, at times, display behaviors that resemble schizophrenic symptoms. For example, social withdrawal, bizarre movements, and unusual verbalizations are common to both schizophrenia and autism. However, there are major differences between schizophrenia and autism. Perhaps the largest difference is that the onset of childhood schizophrenia tends to occur relatively late in the childhood years (at least 8–12 years of age with increasing rates in adolescence), whereas that of autism occurs relatively early in the childhood years (Watkins et al., 1988). In fact, schizophrenia is virtually absent before age 6, whereas autism is almost always noticed or diagnosed before age 6 (American Psychiatric Association, 1994; Gelfand, Jenson, & Drew, 1988; Watkins et al., 1988). In a combined sample of children with autism and children with schizophrenia, for example, Watkins et al. (1988) found that 83% of the children had symptom onset either before age 2 years, 7 months or after age 8 years, 11 months. All children with onset before age 9 received a diagnosis of Pervasive Developmental Disorder.

In addition to differences in age of onset, schizophrenia and autism differ in other ways. First, virtually all children with autistic disorder show a pervasive lack of social responsiveness, whereas children with schizophrenia are usually socially responsive, even if their responses are sometimes unusual (Gelfand et al., 1988). Second, children with autistic disorder tend to display early language deficits at a higher rate than do children with schizophrenia, although a high percentage of children with schizophrenia also have language deficits (Watkins et al., 1988). Third, many children with autistic disorder display echolalia, which is extremely rare in children with schizophrenia (Watkins et al., 1988). Fourth, children with autistic disorder tend to have more resistance to change, over- or underresponsivity to stimuli, and self-injurious behaviors than children with schizophrenia have (Kolvin et al., 1990; Watkins et al., 1988). Fifth, the majority of children with autistic disorder score in mentally retarded ranges on intellectual ability tests, whereas only a minority of children with schizophrenia score in mentally retarded ranges on IQ tests (Gelfand et al., 1988; Kolvin et al., 1990). Sixth, children with autistic disorder have fewer delusions and hallucinations than do children with schizophrenia (Gelfand et al., 1988). Although the differential diagnosis of autism and schizophrenia is relatively straightforward, the disorders do co-occur in a minority of cases (Watkins et al., 1988). In order for a dual schizophrenia-autism diagnosis to be made, the child must have significant hallucinations or delusions for a period of 1 month or more (American Psychiatric Association, 1994).

Most instances of odd or bizarre behaviors seen by clinicians are isolated symptoms that arise in children for a variety of reasons unrelated to schizophrenia. Children in general tend to have looser control over their behavior than do adults, particularly when they have an "externalizing" problem such as ADHD, Conduct Disorder, or Oppositional-Defiant Disorder. A child with externalizing tendencies who is sufficiently upset may engage in behaviors that would be considered psychotic in adults. Such behaviors as screaming incoherently, falling to the ground, flailing around, and making bizarre statements may be symptoms of an externalizing behavior problem as opposed to schizophrenia. When this is the case, the apparently "psychotic" behaviors tend to follow environmental restrictions or frustrations, to occur only when provoked, to occur as a single symptom (not as a cluster of psychotic symptoms), to result in secondary gain, and to disappear when the provoking situation and secondary gain are removed.

Appearance and Features

Developmental Appearance

Some symptoms that would be considered psychotic at adult ages are normal at younger ages. It is not at all uncommon, for example, for a child under the age of 6 or 7 to have an imaginary friend. Thus, it is a challenge to differentiate normal childhood fantasies from schizophrenic hallucinations at these early ages. One factor that may differentiate fantasies from hallucinations is the degree to which the child retains contact with the environment. For example, a normal child who is playing with imaginary superhero friends is usually responsive to adults and treats the imaginary "friends" differently from actual child friends. In addition, older children can (if they want to) directly tell an adult that they know that their fantasy world really does not exist (although they may sometimes be reluctant to admit it). On the other hand, a vivid perception and the insistence in an older child that the fantasy is actually present are more typical of hallucinations. However, acknowledged child hallucinations are much less suggestive of psychosis than hallucinations in an adult (Kemph, 1987; McClellan & Werry, 1992).

Oddities in thought processing, including loose associations and illogical thinking, are more prevalent in developmentally normal children before age 6 or 7. Children under age 6, for example, often have difficulty identifying the source of their memories (whether something actually happened or they were told that something happened). Preschool children are also more prone to accept illogical explanations for events and to offer such explanations themselves. Such children may also hold tenaciously to beliefs that would be considered delusional in an older child or adult (Volkmar, 1996). Developmentally normal childhood fears can also take on a delusion-like appearance. A persistent belief that a "robber" is under the bed, for example, is developmentally appropriate for a 4-year-old. A similar fear in an adult may be considered a hallucination or delusion.

In developmentally normal children, significant and recurring hallucinations, illogical thinking, loose associations, and delusions are rarely seen after age 6. After age 7, these symptoms are often suggestive of a severe disorder, possibly schizophrenia or one of the similar disorders discussed earlier in this chapter.

Children with schizophrenia may follow several developmental paths. A minority have autistic features during infancy and toddlerhood, developing schizophrenia in the school-age or adolescence period (Watkins et al., 1988). Many children who later develop schizophrenia show developmental delays in social skills, visual-motor coordination, and language functioning during the toddler and preschool years (Asarnow, Brown, & Strandburg, 1995). Asarnow and Ben-Meir (1988), for example, found that children with schizophrenia had poorer premorbid adjustment than children with depression, particularly in the areas of IQ and social functioning. McClellan and Werry (1992) report that 54–90% of children with schizophrenia have poor premorbid functioning, characterized by social withdrawal, personality oddities, cognitive delays, and sensory-motor abnormalities.

Onset of schizophrenia in early school ages is usually slow and chronic (80–94% of cases; Asarnow & Ben-Meir, 1988; Eggers & Bunk, 1997; Kolvin et al., 1990). After age 6, more classic schizophrenic symptoms such as thought disorder (incoherence, loose associations, poverty of content), inappropriate affect, and hallucinations may begin to emerge, although these are uncommon before age 8 or 9. Development of classic symptoms often follows a progression from an unusual affective appearance (e.g., stoic looking, flat affect) to social isolation and social adjustment problems and, eventually, to the emergence of disorders of thought and perception (Fish, 1986; McClellan & Werry, 1992). Younger children with early symptoms of schizophrenia often present with odd verbalizations, behaviors, and beliefs.

Thought disorder, inappropriate affect, and hallucinations become more prevalent after age 9 (Watkins et al., 1988). Loose/impaired association is seen in approximately half of children with schizophrenia, whereas flat or constricted affect occurs in 60% of cases (Kolvin et al., 1990). In late adolescence, symptoms such as delusions, catatonia, and poverty of thinking may emerge; delusions and hallucinations become more prominent (McClellan & Werry, 1992). Appearance and features of schizophrenia in childhood are listed in Table 9.2.

The duration and severity of schizophrenic symptoms vary widely from child to child. Some children have a relatively constant presentation of social withdrawal, inappropriate affect, and delusions. Others cycle between periods of more florid symptoms (hallucinations,

TABLE 9.2   Appearance and Features of Schizophrenia in Childhood

COMMON FEATURES

1. Onset after age 9
2. Slow, chronic onset
3. Unusual verbalizations, behaviors, and beliefs (in younger children)
4. Delusions (in adolescents)
5. Primarily internal auditory hallucinations (in younger children)
5. Disorganized thought
6. Flat or constricted affect
7. Premorbid social withdrawal, personality oddities, cognitive delays
8. Peer rejection

OCCASIONAL FEATURES

1. Loose association
2. Deficits in preschool social and language functioning
3. Self-injurious behavior
4. Behavior dangerous to others
5. Guarded, suspicious social attitude

Note: The features listed in the table are often seen but are not universal. Some features may be diagnostically relevant or required, whereas others may not be required for diagnosis. "Common" features are typical of the disorder; "occasional" features appear frequently but are not necessarily seen in a majority of cases.

bizarre behaviors, and thought disorder) and periods of relative calm (although rarely normal behavior). The florid symptom periods can range from one week to three months, whereas the remission periods can range from 3 months to several years. Generally, "positive" symptoms such as hallucinations, delusions, and thought disorganization are more likely to change with cycles, whereas "negative" symptoms such as apathy and withdrawal persist to a certain extent even in remission periods. Other children exhibit symptoms only in certain environments (e.g., in large crowds) or only when stressed. Because of these differences in symptom duration, type, and severity, careful attention to these issues should occur in the initial interview.

Perceptual Features: Hallucinations

Auditory hallucinations are a common feature of childhood schizophrenia, occurring in 80–85% of cases. Visual hallucinations are less common but still are found in about one-third of cases (Volkmar, 1996). When voices are heard, the identity of the voice may be known or unknown. Usually, the voice is telling the child to do something (command hallucinations) or is calling the child names (persecutory hallucinations).

Hallucinations can be persistent in some children and transient in others. For example, Garralda (1984b) found that 69% of a sample of hallucinating children had hallucinations over a decade later. Likewise, Del Beccaro, Burke, & McCauley, (1988) found 52% of their sample of hallucinating children to still have hallucinations 2–6 years later. The mean duration of the hallucinations in the Del Beccaro study was 3 years, 4 months (Del Beccaro et al., 1988). The relationship between hallucinations and other behavioral problems is unclear, although Del Beccaro et al. (1988) report that children with hallucinations have significant additional problems in the areas of somatization and schizoid behavior.

In addition to schizophrenia, hallucinations may be caused by a variety of organic conditions. Because of the rarity of full-blown schizophrenia in preadolescent children, organic causes should be carefully investigated at the initial evaluation, especially if the onset of the hallucinations is rapid in an otherwise well-functioning child. Delirium and neurological disease should be evaluated, particularly if the child had a preexisting serious physical illness such as lupus, cancer, or diabetes. Toxic exposures (accidental poisonings, allergic reactions) are other causes that require investigation in such cases. Children with ADHD who present with an agitated state, visual hallucinations, and paranoia, for example, should be carefully evaluated for psychostimulant overdose.

Cognitive Features

Delusions tend to be characteristic of schizophrenia at later ages, but some young adolescents experience them. Somatic delusions, including those of illness or body image, are sometimes seen and may be difficult to differentiate from symptoms of a Body Dysmorphic Disorder. Another common delusional topic concerns beliefs about religion, death, supernatural creatures, or the afterlife. Young adolescents with schizophrenia, for example, may believe themselves to be a special agent of God or the devil. Magical thinking and loose associations are also common components of schizophrenia in late childhood and early adolescence. Delusions are seen in about half to two-thirds of cases, although the frequency of disorganized/illogical thought processes is unclear (Volkmar, 1996).

Behavioral Features

In addition to disorders of perception, children with schizophrenia display clear disorders of behavior. They may injure themselves, others, or animals for bizarre reasons or for no reason at all (Fish, 1986). At times, their verbalizations range from egocentric to odd to bizarre. Because of their undercontrolled behavior and poor judgment, older children and adolescents with schizophrenia can possibly be dangerous and erratic, injuring people or animals without regard to the effects of their behavior. The death rate of children and adolescents with schizophrenia is 5–10%, far higher than the population average (McClellan & Werry, 1992). Children with schizophrenia are also at increased risk for violent behaviors such as suicide or homicide.

Social Features

Socially, children with schizophrenia are often avoided or teased by peers because of their poor social skills, odd appearance, and odd behavior. Some children with schizophrenia respond to peer rejection with further withdrawal and adoption of a guarded, suspicious attitude toward others. Social communication may be minimal and hindered by absent or inappropriate facial expressions. Their poor judgment and low insight may lead to behaviors that peers find inappropriate and selfish. Unfortunately, isolation and rejection put the child with schizophrenia even more at risk for the development of psychotic symptoms because of a lack of social support, modeling, or peer encouragement of appropriate behaviors (Fish, 1986).

Long-Term Features

The prognosis for children with schizophrenia is generally poor. Younger age of onset (especially before 10 years of age) is associated with greater severity and chronicity, as are slow onset, poor premorbid functioning, and low intelligence (Kolvin et al., 1990; Werry & McClellan, 1992). There is controversy over the importance of family environment for long-term prognosis. Some authors stress the importance of family characteristics such as expressed emotion, whereas others find that family environmental components are not important for prognosis (Kolvin et al., 1990).

In mid- to late adolescence, persistent childhood schizophrenia evolves to closely resemble schizophrenia in the adult form. Disorders of thought, perception, communication, and social relationships become more evident as the child gains cognitive capacity and the ability to engage in concrete or formal operational thinking. At age 15 and above, conceptualizations of adult schizophrenia apply more clearly to the behavior and dynamics of the adolescent (Volkmar, 1996).

Etiology

Childhood schizophrenia has been the subject of less etiological research than adult schizophrenia. Hence, comments about the etiology of childhood schizophrenia are more tentative and often use downward extensions of findings from adults. Because childhood schizophrenia resembles adult schizophrenia and because it is sometimes responsive to medication, biological causes have been proposed for schizophrenia in childhood.

Genetic theories of schizophrenia have received considerable support in adult family and twin studies. Results of this research show both a high heritability value for schizophrenia and a tendency for schizophrenia to run in families. Studies have shown that 40–50% of monozygotic (identical) twins of schizophrenic adults are schizophrenic, compared to only 10–15% of dizygotic twins and 10–15% of children of schizophrenic parents (Kaplan, Sadock, & Grebb, 1994). Knowledge of a child's family history of schizophrenia can, therefore, be very helpful in evaluating risk for schizophrenia.

The effectiveness of medications that block the neurotransmitters dopamine and serotonin has also been taken as evidence that childhood schizophrenia has a biological cause. Most biochemical theories have focused on overactivity of the dopamine system in the development of schizophrenia because most antipsychotic medications act primarily to block postsynaptic dopamine receptors. Furthermore, amphetamine overdose, which produces massive release of dopamine in the brain, can cause psychotic symptomatology.

In addition to biological theories, family theories have been advanced to account for the development of childhood schizophrenia. Various components of family environment, such as open, extreme expression of hostility ("expressed emotion") and the presence of a parent who gives the child messages of both acceptance and rejection at the same time ("double bind") have been proposed as factors in schizophrenia development or recurrence. However, these have received only weak and sporadic support (Gelfand et al., 1988).

Perhaps the ripest area of speculation is a "diathesis-stress" model of the development of childhood schizophrenia. According to this model, the child has a biological propensity or weakness ("diathesis") to develop schizophrenia, which may be consistent with one of the biological theories described previously. This diathesis must be activated by an environment that is characterized by stress or contingencies that encourage the emergence of schizophrenic behavior. For example, a child with a family history of schizophrenia may carry a genetic, anatomical, or biochemical propensity to engage in some unusual behavior and unusual thinking. Stress in the environment may result in an increase in disorganization of the child's behavior and thinking. When these thoughts and behaviors emerge, they may be "encouraged" by the environment through reinforcing attention or the withdrawal of an aversive stimulus (e.g., less teasing by peers, who are driven away by the strange behavior). This results in more abnormal behavior, more stress, and more activation of the propensity to behave and think strangely. As this dynamic develops, it may have neurobiological effects on the brain, modifying the body's propensity to engage in schizophrenic behavior. Eventually, the behavioral, environmental, and biological factors combine to favor the emergence of schizophrenia.

Overall, the biological and diathesis-stress theories are the most widely accepted explanations for the development of childhood schizophrenia. Hence, the clinician should attend to both biological and environmental issues in evaluating the child for etiological factors related to the emergence of schizophrenia.

ASSESSMENT PATTERNS

Broad Assessment Strategies

Cognitive Assessment

Clinician-Administered—Intellectual Ability. Because schizophrenia frequently affects quality of thought, researchers have hypothesized that IQ testing results of individuals with schizophrenia may differ systematically from those without schizophrenia. Specifically, it is not unreasonable to expect a drop in IQ scores following the onset of schizophrenia (Fish, 1986; Kolvin et al., 1990). Studies typically find mean WISC-R VIQ, PIQ, and FIQ scores in the 85–95 range for samples of children with schizophrenia, with no VIQ-PIQ difference (Asarnow & Ben-Meir, 1988; Caplan, Foy, Asarnow, & Sherman, 1990a; Caplan, Perdue, Tanguay, & Fish, 1990b). Intuitively, WISC-III scales requiring association and higher-order thinking, such as Similarities and Comprehension, would be expected to be impaired in children with schizophrenia. In addition, tests that are more responsive to social problem solving, such as Comprehension and Picture Arrangement, may be hypothesized to be lower for children with schizophrenia. These hypotheses have not been extensively investigated, although Fish (1986) suggests that a drop of 2–9 scaled score points on the Comprehension subtest in several years is typical of a child with schizophrenia. Children with schizophrenia score lower on measures of concentration and memory, such as the Freedom from Distractibility/Working Memory factor (FFD/WM) on the WISC-III and WAIS-III, than on other clusters of subtests.

In addition to differences in IQ between children with schizophrenia and children with no diagnosis, studies indicate that certain IQ measures relate to schizophrenic symptomatology. WISC-III FIQ, VIQ, and FFD, for example, correlate negatively with the number of loose associations, but PIQ is not related to loose associations (Caplan et al., 1990a, 1990b). In addition, IQ scores have been found to be negatively related to negative symptoms of schizophrenia, such as social withdrawal and flat affect (Bettes & Walker, 1987). Surprisingly, IQ scores have not been found to be related to illogical thinking (Caplan et al., 1990a, 1990b).

Clinician-Administered—Adaptive Behavior. Frequently, children with schizophrenia experience deficits in adaptive behavior areas such as social interaction, academic skills, self-care skills, and communication skills. Administration of an adaptive behavior scale such as the VABS or ABES can be helpful in identifying areas of adaptive skill weakness. These areas can be specifically targeted in behavioral plans to improve the child's functioning in the environment. The ABES, for example, has a companion workbook specifically designed to provide intervention suggestions for the adaptive skill covered by each ABES item (McCarney, 1995).

Psychological Assessment

Clinician-Administered. Projective testing data (Table 9.3) can be a great help in evaluating a child with suspected schizophrenia. Projective tests allow for open-ended responses, which often elicit disorganized or unusual responses from children with schizophrenia. Furthermore, repetitive thought-behavior patterns may emerge in projective testing. Analysis of these thematic patterns allows the clinician to generate hypotheses about the nature of the thought disorder affecting the child. Thus, projective testing can provide the clinician with a view of the child's organizational, thought, and perceptual processes. Hypotheses regarding these internal processes may then be integrated with behavioral data reported by parents and other adults. It is generally not appropriate to use projective data in isolation without integration with these other sources of information.

TABLE 9.3   Sample Assessment Battery for Schizophrenia in Childhood

PERSONALITY

1. Rorschach
2. Thematic Apperception Test
3. Sentence Completion Tests
4. MMPI-A (age 14 and older)

BEHAVIORAL

1. Behavior Assessment System for Children (Parent-Report, Teacher-Report, and Self-Report)
2. Child Symptom Inventory—4 (Parent-Report and Teacher-Report)
3. Personality Inventory for Youth

Note: Assessment instruments are intended to supplement (not substitute for) a good clinical interview and, when possible, a structured diagnostic interview.

Organized, coherent, appropriate responses to projective testing are usually not consistent with an active thought disorder. However, schizophrenia should not be ruled out based on projective testing data alone. Some children with schizophrenia can maintain an organized presentation throughout projective testing, particularly if they are not stressed by the experience. Other children fluctuate between different degrees of thought disorder. On a "good" day (not during a psychotic episode), these children may do fine on projectives, whereas on a "bad" day (especially if during a psychotic episode), they may give a plethora of strange responses. In general, however, a discrepancy between behavioral data indicating schizophrenia and projective data suggesting appropriate thought should act as a red flag to slow the diagnosis of schizophrenia. Overall, projective testing can allow the clinician to evaluate thought and perceptual processes in more detail than can be gained by behavioral observation or structured self-report.

Perhaps the most common projective test for children with schizophrenia is the Rorschach. Children with schizophrenia give varying numbers of responses to the 10 cards. A high proportion of F responses ("high" in this context means more then 1 S.D. above the mean; see Exner & Weiner, 1995, for norms by age) combined with a low number of total responses ("low" in this context means more than 1 S.D. below the mean) may be suggestive of a child who is rigidly maintaining cognitive control by constricting the content and process of thought and perception. Very few responses may also be suggestive of a depressive component, particularly if the child appears flat or withdrawn. On the other hand, many responses and few F responses could indicate cognitive loosening, impulsivity, emotional undercontrol, and an inability to control cognitive content and process.

Perceptual distortion may be manifest by several Rorschach indices. Low numbers of popular (P) responses indicate an inability to perceive even the most blatant and mundane interpretation of a visual stimulus. However, many children with schizophrenia are able to identify several popular responses. In fact, a total lack of popular responses is more likely to suggest either malingering, misunderstanding of the task, or extreme stress. More diagnostic is the form quality of the child's responses, reflected in the F+%, X+%, and X–% indices of the Rorschach. An X+% (the proportion of responses with good or ordinary form quality) of 70–80% with a standard deviation of 10% is typical of nonclinical children at different ages (Exner & Weiner, 1995). Exner and Weiner (1995) state that X+% scores of less than 60% indicate markedly unconventional perceptions that probably affect adjustment. However, clinical observations suggest that a 50% value could be used as a more conservative indicator. When a low X+% is coupled with an X–% (the proportion of responses with poor form quality) of 30% or higher, the child is distorting perceptions significantly, probably impairing adjustment. Such a pattern is consistent with schizophrenic perception and thinking, although it should *not* be the major basis for a diagnosis. Alternative explanations for X+%<60% and X–%>30% include misunderstanding of the task, oppositionality, low IQ, anxiety, and depression.

There is a major difference between poor form quality (coded "–") and unusual form quality (coded "u"). Poor form quality reflects true distortions in perception. Unusual form quality, on the other hand, reflects unusual perceptions that, by and large, are not distorted. Hence, a record with many unusual form quality responses may indicate a child with unique or egocentric, but not grossly distorted, ways of perceiving ambiguous stimuli. Children with high numbers of unusual form quality responses and low numbers of poor form quality responses tend to have low X+% scores *and* low X–% scores. In some cases a child with malingering schizophrenia will give large numbers of unusual form quality responses. This response pattern indicates that the child is attempting to appear psychiatrically impaired by giving strange responses. However, such a response pattern would suggest that the child has intact reality testing, which is guiding the selection of responses and conforming to the appearance of the blot.

Exner and Weiner (1995) note several other areas in which disordered thinking affects Rorschach scores. Perhaps the most obvious of these is the special score coding for Rorschach answers. Special scores are assigned to answers that reflect unusual ways of identifying Rorschach responses or of describing responses. In most cases these unusual responses consist of strange statements that are assumed to reflect a breakdown in the thinking or perceptual process. Because these breakdowns can occur as a result of a thought disorder, special scores can indicate the presence of schizophrenic distortion of thought. Six "critical" special scores receive attention as possible indicators of schizophrenic thinking (Exner & Weiner, 1995): Deviant Verbalizations (neologisms or redundancies), Deviant Responses (inappropriate phrases, irrelevant phrases, or circumstantial responses), Incongruous Combinations (combination of inappropriate images into a single whole, such as a snake with six legs), Contaminations (two impressions fused into one, such as a bat-fly to refer to a single space on the blot), Fabulized Combinations (an implausible relationship between two details, such as a frog driving a truck), and Inappropriate Logic (strained reasoning used to justify an answer). Although young (age 6 and under) children average as many as six of these responses, older children and adults average only one to three. More than eight critical special score responses, however, is unusual at any age. More than four such responses would be considered high for a child over the age of 12.

In addition to the six critical special scores, Exner (1986) reports that human movement answers with poor or no form quality (M-answers) are typical of schizophrenic adults. The extent to which this observation corresponds to children with schizophrenia, however, is unknown. M-answers indicate the possibility of negative interpersonal skills and social relationships. More than two M-answers are extremely unusual in individuals without schizophrenia.

Other Rorschach scores that are sometimes seen in children with schizophrenia are high numbers of abstract responses, low numbers of human content responses, and high numbers of imaginary (parenthesized) human responses. Absent or distorted human content responses may suggest few, poor, or unusual social relationships. A preponderance of chromatic color responses can indicate an emotional or impulsive component to the schizophrenia. On the other hand, achromatic color or shading responses may be driven by a depressed or painful component. Finally, unusual content, fantasy content, and a large number of morbid responses can provide some insight into bizarre thought content of the child.

Over all, the responses of the child with schizophrenia to the Rorschach often have an unusual quality. Verbalizations may be bizarre, contents may be unusual or perseverative, and form quality may be poor. Analysis of the characteristics of Rorschach responses provides insight into cognitive processing and cognitive content. It must be remembered throughout the interpretation process, however, that some unusual verbalizations or distortions are normal for young children. Use of the standardized Exner (Exner & Weiner, 1995) system can allow the clinician to compare a child to normative samples of nonreferred peers. These comparisons are vital in determining if a Rorschach protocol reflects unusual responses or merely age-appropriate responses. Furthermore, despite its utility in the assessment of the child with schizophrenia, the Rorschach should be used only as a hypothesis-generating device following extensive interviewing and behavioral data gathering.

In addition to the Rorschach, the TAT can provide information concerning the child's thought and perceptual processes. TAT stories provide the clinician with a sense of the child's scripts for interpreting the events of daily life. For children over age 6 or so, scripts involve a plausible progression of events that occur in a story-like form. They indicate the child's expectations of how events occur in the world, usually based on past experience or recollections of stories told by others. At the most basic level, a script involves an initial scene followed by an event. Based on the event, an outcome occurs. This outcome may then become an event that leads to yet another outcome, and so on. "Characters" in the script are things that act or produce change in the story; they are usually people, animals, or objects.

The characters and events in the child's stories often reflect some aspect of the child's fantasy or reality life. Thus, they indicate the child's internalized structures for interpreting reality. For the child with schizophrenia, story scripts may be rambling, purposeless, confused, or disjointed. This presentation reflects a disorganization of thought and the basic building blocks for interpreting events (scripts). Other children with schizophrenia tell markedly impoverished stories or simply describe the TAT cards. This constriction of thought occurs as a defense against disorganization produced when thought is allowed to flow freely. Less common is the child with schizophrenia who tells stories that are linear and purposeful but with bizarre themes. Children who show this latter pattern are more likely to be traumatized, malingering, or to have overly active fantasy lives.

As with the Rorschach, the TAT is valuable as a hypothesis-generating device and as a source of added information in the assessment of the child with schizophrenia. However, it should not be used alone for diagnostic purposes independently of behavioral/interview assessment techniques. Bizarre or disjointed TAT stories can reflect conditions other than schizophrenia, such as brain damage, mental retardation, depression, or oppositionality. Furthermore, the clinician must adopt a developmental view when interpreting TAT stories. Children under the age of 6 will often tell brief, stereotypical, or disjointed stories. Such stories in a 13-year-old would be considered indicative of depression, oppositionality, mental retardation, or schizophrenia. Between the ages of 6 and 12, children acquire improved verbal and storytelling skills, and their repertoire of scripts increases. Hence, TAT stories improve greatly between these ages.

Many other projective techniques are used to assess children with suspected schizophrenia. The most popular of these other techniques are sentence completion tests and drawing tests. The responses given by children with schizophrenia to sentence completion tests reflect their disorder of thought and perception. For example, the child with schizophrenia may perseverate on an unusual or bizarre theme in all sentence completion responses. In other cases, responses may not logically follow the theme of the beginning of the sentence. Very impaired children may make up their own sentence and ignore the beginning of the sentence given to them to complete. Analysis of the child's responses on the sentence completion test can indicate specific problems with organization of thought as well as specific thought contents.

Projective drawing techniques range from self-portraits, to drawings of the family, to open-ended drawings of anything. The drawings of the child with schizophrenia may reflect disorganization, attention problems, or bizarre thought/perceptual processes. Some children with schizophrenia leave critical elements off of drawings (e.g., body without a head), whereas others make drawings with strange or painful themes (e.g., a graphic drawing of a killing or suicide). Drawings can sometimes serve as a starting or connection point for therapy, with the child explaining the drawing to the therapist. Child and therapist can then explore thoughts and feelings related to the drawing.

Behavioral Assessment

Parent-Report/Other-Report. Children with schizophrenia score higher (usually in the 69+ T-score range) than psychiatric controls on the Achenbach scales (Del Beccaro et al., 1988). In particular, the Thought Problems, Somatic Complaints, and Withdrawn subscales are likely to be elevated in a child showing classic schizophrenic symptoms. These subscales, however, consist of items characteristic of several nonschizophrenic syndromes and are, therefore, not specific to schizophrenia. The Thought Problems subscale has a strong obsessive-compulsive component, whereas the Somatic Complaints subscale is driven largely by somatization items. The Withdrawn subscale reflects depression as well as general social problems. Specific CBCL and TRF findings should be probed in a clinical interview.

The BASC Atypicality scale includes items with the greatest overlap with positive symptoms of schizophrenia. These include questions about hallucinations, loss of control, and loss of touch with reality. However, the Atypicality scale contains items that reflect other disorders including pervasive developmental disorders (self-stimulating behavior), pica, and habit disorders. Hence, elevation of the Atypicality scale could indicate other unusual behaviors in addition to schizophrenic symptoms. The BASC Withdrawal, Leadership, and Social Skills scales include items consistent with the negative symptoms of schizophrenia, as well as the social maladjustment characteristic of the disorder. Therefore, elevation of the Atypicality and Withdrawal scales, combined with low Leadership and Social Skills scale scores, would be expected for the child with schizophrenia. It must be remembered, however, that this scale configuration could be consistent with other disorders.

Both the CSI-4 and ASI-4 parent and teacher versions include subscales that screen directly for DSM-IV schizophrenia symptomatology. The Schizophrenia subscale consists of five items asking about delusions, auditory hallucinations, illogical/bizarre thought processes, inappropriate emotion, and odd behavior; the ASI-4 adds a sixth item about negative symptoms (loss of interest, social withdrawal). The CSI-4 also includes subscales for depressive disorders, pervasive developmental disorders, and anxiety disorders, and the ASI-4 includes subscales for depressive disorders, anxiety disorders, schizoid personality, bipolar disorder, and substance use. These subscales can be helpful in identifying alternative diagnoses to explain the child's symptomatology. Because of their broad symptom coverage and correspondence to DSM-IV symptomatology, these scales provide excellent screening information to assist in evaluating the child's schizophrenic and related problems. Although they have less supporting empirical research than many other behavior questionnaires, they can provide valuable information to be probed in interview.

Self-Report. Like its parent- and teacher-report counterparts, the YSR includes Thought Problems, Somatic Complaints, and Withdrawal subscales that would be expected to be elevated for a child with schizophrenia. However, the caution about diagnostic specificity applies to the YSR as well as to the CBCL and TRF: No YSR subscale consists of a majority of items that overlap with specific schizophrenic symptomatology. Furthermore, there is no YSR profile that is diagnostically specific for schizophrenia.

Interpretation of the self-report version of the BASC also mirrors that of its parent- and teacher-report counterparts. The Atypicality scale reflects odd symptoms, including those of schizophrenia and other less common disorders. Elevations on the Locus of Control subscale suggest that the child feels little control over self or environment. The Social Stress, Relations with Parents, and Interpersonal Relations subscales reflect social functioning and negative symptoms. Elevated Atypicality, Locus of Control, and Social Stress scale scores, combined with low Relations with Parents and Interpersonal Relations subscale scores, would, therefore, be characteristic of (although not diagnostically specific for) a child with schizophrenia.

On the PIY, children with schizophrenic symptomatology tend to elevate the Reality Distortion (RLT) scale, and T-scores greater than 70 on this scale are likely. The RLT scale is composed of two subscales, and analysis of these subscale scores can provide additional insight into the child's self-reported symptomatology. The Feelings of Alienation subscale of the RLT scale consists of items reflecting lack of connection to others or to reality, along with unusual or distressing behaviors, thoughts, and feelings. The Hallucinations and Delusions subscale contains items about hallucinations, delusional beliefs, and loss of mental control. Although children who feel alienated and unhappy may elevate the Feelings of Alienation subscale, elevation of the Hallucinations and Delusions subscale suggests the presence of serious symptomatology that could be characteristic of schizophrenia. In addition to the RLT scale and subscales, the Social Withdrawal and Social Skills Deficits scales may provide information about social functioning and negative symptoms of schizophrenia. Specifically, the Isolation subscale of the Social Withdrawal scale measures symptoms characteristic of the withdrawal and isolation seen when a child or adolescent shows negative symptoms of schizophrenia.

Syndrome-Specific Tests

Clinician-Administered

Kiddie Formal Thought Disorder Rating Scale. The Kiddie Formal Thought Disorder Rating Scale (K-FTDS; Caplan et al., 1989) is an observer-rating scale of four types of thought disorder derived from DSM-III: illogical thinking, loose association, incoherence, and poverty of content of speech. It is administered by playing the Kiddie Formal Thought Disorder Story Game (Caplan, Guthrie, Fish, Tanguay, & David-Lando, 1989) with the child and then coding the child's answers to the game. The Kiddie Formal Thought Disorder Story Game is a 20–25-minute technique that consists of three parts: In the first part, the child listens to an audiotaped story and then must repeat it and answer questions based on it. In the second part, the child is asked to make up a story based on one of four topics. The third part is identical to the first part. Responses to the game are typically videotaped for later coding (Caplan et al., 1990b).

The child's responses to the three parts of the story game are coded into the four thought disorder categories based on operational definitions and examples for each category. A total score may be derived by summing the category scores. Interrater reliability for the K-FTDS is reported to be good (Caplan et al., 1990b). Illogical thinking, loose association, and total scores discriminate between schizophrenic and normal samples (Caplan et al., 1989, 1990a, 1990b). Clinically, the K-FTDS has limited utility because its coding procedure can be time-consuming.

□   TREATMENT OPTIONS

Behavioral Interventions

Behavioral treatments (Table 9.4) for childhood schizophrenia focus on the child's external behaviors, with less emphasis on internal thought or perceptual processes. Three types of behavioral treatments are widely used to treat childhood schizophrenia: environmental structure, contingency management, and adaptive skill interventions. Contingency management interventions target schizophrenic symptoms and aim to reduce their frequency and severity. Adaptive skill interventions use behavioral principles to improve the child's basic social, self-care, and organizational skills.

Environmental Structure Interventions

Environmental structure interventions increase the predictability, organization, and scheduling of the child's daily life. This is accomplished in several ways: First, the child's work-

---

TABLE 9.4   Treatment Options for Schizophrenia in Childhood

1. Behavioral Interventions
    a. Environmental Structure
    b. Contingency Management
        (1) Definition and Operationalizing Symptoms
        (2) Identification of Antecedents and Consequences
        (3) Differential Reinforcement of Other Behavior
        (4) Differential Reinforcement of Incompatible Behavior
        (5) Ignoring Symptoms
        (6) Antecedent Management
    c. Adaptive Skills Interventions
2. Medication
    a. Neuroleptics
3. Psychotherapy
    a. Play Therapy
4. Family Interventions
    a. Family Therapy
5. Inpatient Hospitalization

Note: This outline of options summarizes major treatments covered in the text. Specific treatments are often combined into an intervention package. Refer to the text for additional descriptions of each treatment. This table is not necessarily an exhaustive list of all treatments available.

ing and living spaces are organized, and a map or other description of this organization is provided for the child. Regular periods of reviewing the organization of living spaces and restoring the spaces to the proper organization are built into each day. These provide consistent review and maintenance of structure in the child's environment. Second, the child's daily schedule is kept as predictable and active/interesting as possible. Social, mental, and physical activity is encouraged, and withdrawal is discouraged. The schedule is drawn up no later than the morning of the day that it is to occur, and it is reviewed with the child each morning. Finally, events that may interfere with structure, such as family conflict, access to negative models, stress, and breakdowns of communication between adults, are removed.

Environmental structure interventions encourage internal structure of thought processes by providing the child with positive models of external structure. In addition, the structure and predictability reduce the level of stress that may provoke psychotic behavior. Because little is required from the child in these interventions, they are relatively undemanding and can be used with more impaired children. However, environmental structure interventions make significant demands on the adults in the child's environment. Hence, the adults must be capable of functioning at a sufficient level to initiate and sustain these interventions. Environmental structure interventions are commonly used on inpatient units.

Contingency Management Interventions

Contingency management interventions assume that schizophrenic behavior, like any other behavior, can be reduced by altering the contingencies that support or allow the behavior. A variety of specific behavioral techniques are used in contingency management interventions for schizophrenia, including operationalizing and defining symptoms, analysis of antecedents and consequences, differential reinforcement of other behavior (DRO), differential reinforcement of incompatible behavior (DRI), ignoring, and antecedent management.

Contingency management behavior therapy for schizophrenia begins with a detailed analysis of the child's schizophrenic behaviors. First, the behaviors are listed, operationally defined, and broken down into molecular parts. For example, if the child is making strange statements, the word *strange* is operationally defined as including certain themes or components. Examples are gathered, until the therapist and parents are in agreement as to exactly what constitutes a strange statement.

Next, the antecedents and consequences of the behavior are investigated. The therapist, parent, and (sometimes) child discuss what typically happens before and after each of the target schizophrenic behaviors. If detailed information is needed, the parent may keep a diary of occurrences of the behavior, antecedents, and consequences for a week or two. This diary technique may identify antecedents and consequences of which the parent was unaware.

Once antecedents and consequences are identified, baseline monitoring may begin. This monitoring consists of tracking the number of occurrences of the target behavior over time, before intervention occurs. Usually, only one or two circumscribed schizophrenic behaviors are initially chosen for monitoring.

Following baseline monitoring, an intervention is designed and implemented. This intervention involves a manipulation of antecedents and consequences in order to discourage the occurrence of the target behavior. If the behavior appears to have a function (e.g., seeking attention, making friends) in the environment, other means for achieving the function may be developed. For example, consequences are modified by rewarding the nonoccurrence of the behavior (differential reinforcement of other behavior, or DRO) or by rewarding the occurrence of behaviors that are incompatible with the target behavior (differential reinforcement of incompatible behavior, or DRI). To reduce attention for the schizophrenic behavior, the behavior is ignored as much as possible during the behavioral intervention plan. Typically, reinforcement is delivered on a fixed-interval schedule, in which the child is rewarded if the behavior does not occur for a certain period of time (depending on the initial frequency of the behavior, this time period may range from 5 minutes to a full day).

Alternatively, antecedents may be changed so that the most common eliciting situations for the behavior occur less frequently (antecedent management, see Appendix C). For example, in the case of a child who displays schizophrenic behaviors following loud arguments between parents, intervention may consist of reducing family conflict.

The implementation of the intervention occurs concurrently with continued monitoring of the target behavior. If the target behavior responds to the intervention, the intervention may continue unchanged. On the other hand, if the target behavior does not respond to intervention, the intervention may be modified in order to have a greater effect. In such cases, reinforcers may have to be modified to improve their salience and power for the child.

When a criterion level is reached for the target behavior, the intervention is faded by increasing the intervals between reinforcement, reducing the amount of reinforcement, or implementing a variable interval or variable ratio schedule, with the interval/ratio gradually increasing. A new target behavior is then selected, and the process begins again.

Examples of target schizophrenic behaviors are inappropriate affect, reports of hallucinations, random babbling, and odd behavior or statements. For example, a child who laughs at random or inappropriate times may be put on a behavioral plan that begins with monitoring of the inappropriate laughter. Following the monitoring period, the child is then instructed about when laughter is and is not appropriate. A reinforcer (i.e., 5 extra minutes of TV time) is then given for each instance of appropriate laughter, with punishment (i.e., 5 fewer minutes of TV) for inappropriate laughter. Other than announcing the punishment, inappropriate laughter would be ignored.

Adaptive Skills Interventions

Adaptive skills interventions attempt to address social, organization, and self-care deficits commonly shown by children with schizophrenia by teaching and encouraging demonstration of the skills in the home and school environment. These interventions begin by defining clear goals and expectations for social interaction and self-care, which are tailored to each child's individual symptomatology and current level of adaptive skills. Examples of these goals are eye contact, interacting with others, showing appropriate affect, understanding the communication of others, maintaining a clean working and living space, and practicing appropriate hygeine. Careful evaluation of the child's adaptive behavior (using one of the instruments described in the Assessment Patterns section of this chapter) is a good first step to identifying adaptive behavior areas for intervention.

After adaptive behavior goals are identified, the child is taught to monitor opportunities to show the behavior and to evaluate instances in which he or she demonstrated the goal behavior. Modeling, rehearsal, and education are used to practice and demonstrate goal behavior in therapy sessions, and the child is expected to record and evaluate progress toward the goal. Adults in the family and school environment also learn to identify the goal behaviors and to reward the child when goal behaviors occur, using contingency management techniques such as those described earlier in this chapter.

Because social skills training is almost always needed as a part of an adaptive skills package, children participate in structured social skills learning experiences. As with other adaptive skills interventions, social skills interventions for children with schizophrenia begin with education about schizophrenia, social skills, and social interaction. Specific skills are then targeted for learning, practice, and improvement in the environment. For children with significant deficits, targeted social skills would include eye contact, smiling, physical space, voice volume and inflection, content of conversation, compliments, acknowledgments, conversational openers, assertive requests, and ignoring. More advanced children might learn skills such as reading social cues, starting and ending a conversation, giving and receiving compliments, expressing oneself nonverbally, asking questions to others, answering questions when asked, expressing emotions, entering a group or conversation, disagreeing with others, setting limits on others and resisting peer pressure, anticipating what others are thinking and feeling, developing empathy, and persuading others.

Social skills are taught using an introductory explanation followed by practice techniques such as modeling, role playing, repeated rehearsal of the skill, and feedback from the therapist or group. Reinforcement is used to encourage participation and effective learning of the skill. Finally, the child is required to demonstrate the social skills in the environment, with reinforcement from parents and/or teachers. Social skills interventions are often implemented in a group format, which offers more opportunities to practice interaction as well as to form relationships with others. Social skills group interventions for children with schizophrenia may be modified based on those developed by LeCroy (1994) and Forman (1993).

Evaluation of Behavioral Techniques

Behavioral techniques have the advantage of being straightforward and easy to evaluate for efficacy. However, they do not directly address the internal, subjective, cognitive components of schizophrenia, which are a major part of the disorder. Furthermore, some children with schizophrenia report having little control over their behavior during a psychotic episode. Therefore, they have little ability to purposefully respond to a reinforcement schedule.

Over all, behavioral techniques are most likely to be effective for children who have more of a behavioral than a thought disorder, for children who exhibit schizophrenic behaviors for attention, and for children with schizophrenia whose symptoms have an oppositional-defiant quality. Behavioral therapy can also be a useful adjunct to medication by encouraging the emergence of appropriate behaviors at a time when the medication is causing a reduction in negative behaviors. Behavioral techniques may also be more effective during periods of time between psychotic episodes.

Medication

Although the use of medication for adolescents with schizophrenia is widely accepted and supported by adult research, the use of medication for preadolescent children who show schizophrenic symptoms is a more complicated issue. Some object to medication use with children younger than 12 or 13 because of the early stage of research and the potential negative side effects of neuroleptic medication. Nevertheless, clinical experience, case study, and preliminary research support the use of neuroleptics with some children with schizophrenia (Campbell & Cueva, 1995). In addition, the social and developmental consequences of not controlling schizophrenic symptoms at an early age can be significant. Hence, although the documented efficacy of medication derives largely from preliminary studies with children and extensive studies with adolescents and adults, the potential positive effects of medication for a child with schizophrenia often warrant that medication be considered as a component of treatment.

Different neuroleptic medications appear to be helpful for different children with schizophrenia, and there has been no consistent evidence supporting the superiority of one neuroleptic over others (McClellan & Werry, 1992). Choice of the neuroleptic is usually dependent on the child's major symptoms, vulnerability to side effects, and eventual response (or lack thereof) to the specific medication. Haloperidol (Haldol) and thioridazine (Mellaril) have historically been among the most popular neuroleptics prescribed for children with schizophrenia. More recently, risperidone (Risperdal) has seen wider use and preliminary empirical efficacy with children and adolescents (Armenteros, Whitaker, Welikson, Stedge, & Gorman, 1997). Clozapine (Clozaril) has been used with treatment-resistant children (Turetz, Mozes, Toren, & Chernauzan, 1997), but fears of severe side effects (agranulocytosis) limit its utility in children. There are reports that risperidone and clozapine may be more effective for negative symptoms, at least in adults (Bezchlibnyk-Butler & Jeffries, 1997). Other new antipsychotic medications such as olanzapine (Zyprexa) are seeing increased use with children, with hopes that their side effects will be milder than those of the older neuroleptics.

The primary effect of most neuroleptics in children with schizophrenia is to decrease positive symptoms such as hallucinations, delusions, hyperactivity, and disorganized thought. Negative symptoms, such as flatness and withdrawal, do not respond as well to neuroleptic medication, even for medications that have some effect on them, such as Risperdal.

The largest drawback to the use of medication for children with schizophrenia is the presence of potentially severe side effects. Side effects vary somewhat from one neuroleptic to another, but certain effects are common: Fatigue, drowsiness, sedation, akathisia (constant movement), and tardive dyskinesia are a few of the more common effects (Bezchlibnyk-Butler & Jeffries, 1997). Ultimately, the decision to use medication involves a weighing of the benefits and risks. In general, failure of psychological interventions, severe symptoms, significant functional impairment, long duration, and/or presence of dangerous behavior are characteristics that argue in favor of using medication. Because these characteristics occur in many children with schizophrenia, use of medication for treatment is frequently warranted.

Psychotherapy

Play Therapy

A variety of psychotherapeutic interventions have been attempted with children with schizophrenia, with varying success from child to child. Play therapy, for example, allows the child with schizophrenia to play in an unstructured, accepting therapy situation (Axline, 1969; Gelfand et al., 1988). The therapist acts as a facilitator for the child's growth and as a source of acceptance. The rationale for play therapy is the belief that children with schizophrenia have not internalized an acceptance of themselves as worthwhile, valuable persons. By playing in a nondirective, accepting atmosphere, they have a chance to explore themselves and to have their sense of self validated by the therapist. Play therapy may be effective for psychotic children who have been neglected, rejected, or traumatized; in such cases, social structure and attachment problems may be responsible for their core difficulties. However, the utility of play therapy for the majority of children with schizophrenia has not been established.

Family Interventions

Family therapy focuses on the role of the child's schizophrenic symptoms within the family system and the role of family conflict in exacerbating schizophrenic symptoms. In some cases the child's symptoms may deflect attention from other family issues. Alternatively, the symptoms may serve the psychological needs of one or more family members. For example, a child with schizophrenia may serve the needs of a mother who has an intense need to care for a dependent person. The child's symptoms may bring the child attention from the mother and preserve the family system by allowing the mother to retain her caretaking role. On the other hand, family conflict may create distress within a vulnerable child, resulting in disorganization of thought and bizarre behavior. Family therapy attempts to change the family system so that the child's symptoms no longer are needed to preserve the integrity of the system. In addition, the behavior of the family is modified in order to reduce the child's distress and psychotic behavior. Family therapy probably applies to a proportion of cases of childhood schizophrenia, but it rarely addresses all of the key issues and symptoms of schizophrenia. Additionally, family therapy may address environmental factors that reduce the ability of the family to implement interventions such as medication compliance and behavioral therapy.

Inpatient Hospitalization

Children with severe schizophrenic symptoms sometimes require hospitalization to stabilize their behavior and return them to a minimally adaptive level of functioning. Usually, these children have seen a worsening of symptoms despite efforts at behavioral or psychopharmacological treatment. In other cases, children are hospitalized because their psychotic symptoms render them unmanageable or dangerous in the home environment. Because many children with schizophrenia experience periodic psychotic episodes, periodic hospital treatment for stabilization is sometimes required. For children with milder psychotic symptoms, every effort should be made to avoid hospitalization, so that they do not receive the message that they are very sick. Hospitalization may also expose the child to negative peer behavior models. Children with milder symptoms can often be managed with outpatient therapy or medication.

Inpatient treatment generally involves the use of intense milieu behavioral therapy (see environmental structure section earlier in this chapter) combined with trials of medications to determine the most beneficial medication and dose. Behavior therapy is usually administered by the unit staff, who follow a behavior plan devised by a mental health professional. This plan typically involves the allocation of privileges and access to favored activities based on compliance with target behaviors (see contingency management section earlier in this chapter). In many cases, the target behaviors consist of compliance, behavioral control, and positive interaction with peers. Although these targets are not psychotic symptoms per se, they presumably encourage more appropriate behavior that is inconsistent with psychotic behavior. For longer hospitalizations, children and adolescents may also be given responsibilities (ranging from "jobs" to schoolwork and homework) that provide them with a sense of structure and accomplishment.

In addition to behavior therapy in the context of the unit milieu, inpatient placements generally include components of individual, group, or family therapy. The effectiveness of these interventions in addressing schizophrenic symptoms is unclear, but they can be valuable for postdischarge planning. For example, the child can be prepared in individual therapy for difficulties that are likely to be encountered following discharge. Likewise, parents can be educated, and family changes can be encouraged to prevent schizophrenic behavior at home. Psychoeducation of the parent and child about the symptoms and treatments of schizophrenia is a common component of such individual and family therapies in and out of the hospital.

Over all, inpatient placements can provide the intensive, consistent environment necessary to regulate persistent, severe, and bizarre schizophrenic behavior. However, in addition to temporarily stabilizing behavior, inpatient treatment should aim to produce lasting change in the child's behavior once the child is returned to the home environment. Hence, work with parents and outpatient follow-up is critical to the long-term efficacy of inpatient therapy for children with schizophrenia.

■ References

American Psychiatric Association. (1994). *Diagnostic and statistical manual of mental disorders, fourth edition.* Washington, DC: Author.

Armenteros, J. L., Whitaker, A. H., Welikson, M., Stedge, D. J., & Gorman, J. (1997). Risperidone in adolescents with schizophrenia: An open pilot study. *Journal of the American Academy of Child and Adolescent Psychiatry, 36,* 694–700.

Asarnow, J. R., & Ben-Meir, S. (1988). Children with schizophrenia spectrum and depressive disorders: A comparative study of premorbid adjustment, onset pattern and severity of impairment. *Journal of Child Psychology and Psychiatry, 29,* 477–488.

Asarnow, R. F., Brown, W., & Strandburg, R. (1995). Children with a schizophrenic disorder: Neurobehavioral studies. *European Archives of Psychiatry and Clinical Neuroscience, 245,* 70–79.

Axline, V. M. (1969). *Play therapy.* New York: Ballantine.

Bettes, B. A., & Walker, E. (1987). Positive and negative symptoms in psychotic and other psychiatrically disturbed children. *Journal of Child Psychology and Psychiatry, 28,* 555–568.

Bezchlibnyk-Butler, K. Z., & Jeffries, J. J. (1997). *Clinical handbook of psychotropic drugs.* Toronto: Hogrefe & Huber Publishers.

Campbell, M., & Cueva, J. E. (1995). Psychopharmacology in child and adolescent psychiatry: A review of the past seven years. Part II. *Journal of the American Academy of Child and Adolescent Psychiatry, 34,* 1262–1272.

Caplan, R., Foy, J. G., Asarnow, R. F., & Sherman, T. (1990a). Information processing deficits of schizophrenic children with formal thought disorder. *Psychiatry Research, 31,* 169–177.

Caplan, R., Guthrie, D., Fish, B., Tanguay, P. E., & David-Lando, G. (1989). The Kiddie Formal Thought Disorder Scale (K-FTDS): Clinical assessment, reliability, and validity. *Journal of the American Academy of Child Psychiatry, 28,* 408–416.

Caplan, R., Perdue, S., Tanguay, P. E., & Fish, B. (1990b). Formal thought disorder in childhood onset schizophrenia and schizotypal personality disorder. *Journal of Child Psychology and Psychiatry, 31,* 1103–1114.

Del Beccaro, M. A., Burke, P., & McCauley, E. (1988). Hallucinations in children: A follow-up study. *Journal of the American Academy of Child and Adolescent Psychiatry, 27,* 462–465.

Eggers, C., & Bunk, D. (1997). The long-term course of childhood-onset schizophrenia: A 42 year follow-up. *Schizophrenia Bulletin, 23,* 105–117.

Exner, J. E. (1986). *The Rorschach: A Comprehensive System Volume 1: Basic Foundations* (2nd ed.). New York: Wiley.

Exner, J. E., & Weiner, I. B. (1995). *The Rorschach: A Comprehensive System Volume 3: Assessment of Children and Adolescents* (2nd ed.). New York: Wiley.

Fish, B. (1986). Antecedents of an acute schizophrenic break. *Journal of the American Academy of Child Psychiatry, 25,* 595–600.

Forman, S. G. (1993). *Coping skills interventions for children and adolescents.* San Francisco: Jossey-Bass

Garralda, M. E. (1984b). Hallucinations in children with conduct and emotional disorders: II. The follow-up study. *Psychological Medicine, 14,* 597–604.

Gelfand, D. M., Jenson, W. R., & Drew, C. J. (1988). *Understanding child behavior disorders* (2nd ed.). New York: Harcourt Brace Jovanovich College Publishers.

Kaplan, H. I., Sadock, B. J., & Grebb, J. A. (1994). *Kaplan and Sadock's synopsis of psychiatry: behavioral sciences, clinical psychiatry* (7th ed.). Baltimore, MD: Williams & Wilkins.

Kemph, J. P. (1987). Hallucinations in psychotic children. *Journal of the American Academy of Child and Adolescent Psychiatry, 26,* 556–559.

Kolvin, I., Berncy, T. P., & Yoeli, J. (1990). Schizophrenia in childhood. In M. Hersen & C. G. Last (Eds.), *Handbook of child and adult psychopathology: A longitudinal perspective* (pp. 99–113). New York: Pergamon.

LeCroy, C. W. (1994). Social skills training. In C. W. LeCroy (Ed.), *Handbook of child and adolescent treatment manuals.* New York: Lexington.

McCarney, S. B. (1995). *The Adaptive Behavior Evaluation Scale Home Version Technical Manual—Revised.* Columbia, MO: Hawthorne Educational Services.

McClellan, J. M., & Werry, J. S. (1992). Schizophrenia. *Pediatric Psychopharmacology, 15,* 131–148

Turetz, M., Mozes, T., Toren, P., & Chernauzan, N. (1997). An open trial of clozapine in neuroleptic-resistant childhood-onset schizophrenia. *British Journal of Psychiatry, 170,* 507–510.

Volkmar, F. R. (1996). Childhood and adolescent psychosis: A review of the past 10 years. *Journal of the American Academy of Child and Adolescent Psychiatry, 35,* 843–851.

Watkins, J. M., Asarnow, R. F., & Tanguay, P. E. (1988). Symptom development in childhood onset schizophrenia. *Journal of Child Psychology and Psychiatry, 29,* 865–878.

Werry, J. S., & McClellan, J. M. (1992). Predicting outcome in child and adolescent (early onset) schizophrenia and bipolar disorder. *Journal of the American Academy of Child and Adolescent Psychiatry, 31,* 147–150.

CHAPTER 10

Pervasive Developmental Disorders

Beginning with DSM-IV, PDDs are placed on Axis I. DSM-IV contains five categories of PDDs: Autistic Disorder, Rett's Disorder, Childhood Disintegrative Disorder (CDD), Asperger's Disorder, and PDD Not Otherwise Specified (PDDNOS). Like autism, the other PDDs are characterized by serious communication problems and social deficits.

■ Rett's Disorder

□ CLINICAL DESCRIPTION

Rett's Disorder emerges following normal prenatal and early infant (e.g., the first few months) development. After about age 6–18 months, however, the infant experiences slowed head growth, loss of purposeful hand movement, the emergence of stereotypical movement (facial grimacing, wringing of hands, grinding teeth), loss of interest in social interaction, poor coordination, slow movement, and loss of language skills. Slowed head growth may persist until as late as age 4, and a decline in hand movement skills may persist until age 2½. Little recovery of these pervasive losses occurs throughout the life span, resulting in significant impairments in language, social functioning, and motor functioning. Hence, the disorder has an appearance of progressive decline in the early years. Seizures, gait disturbance (and poor gross motor coordination in general), and spasticity often emerge during school-age years. The muscular/movement component of the disorder often progresses to the extent of rigidity, muscle wasting, and inability to ambulate without assistance (American Psychiatric Association, 1994; Kaplan, Sadock, & Grebb, 1994).

Children with Rett's Disorder resemble children with autism somewhat in their language and social delays. However, they typically show more motoric problems than children with autism, and their loss of language is more complete and permanent. In children with Rett's Disorder, the loss of formerly present movement skills and social involvement is apparent, whereas children with Autistic Disorder fail to develop social orientation from infancy. Rett's

Disorder occurs only in girls and has a "neurological" appearance. It is rare, with prevalence less than 0.01% (American Psychiatric Association, 1994; Kaplan et al., 1994).

The cause of Rett's Disorder is not definitively known, although there is speculation about an X-linked genetic etiology. Neurologically, children with Rett's Disorder experience cerebral atrophy and disease in the substantia nigra area of the brain (Kaplan et al., 1994).

☐ ASSESSMENT PATTERNS

Children with Rett's Disorder have severely delayed language skills, typically at a one-year age level. Social interaction skills are similarly impaired. Hence, administration of cognitive or personality/behavioral testing is rarely necessary to identify such a severe deficit. Tests of adaptive behavior, such as the VABS or ABES, may be helpful in documenting adaptive skill deficits and competencies, although these typically reveal very low levels of adaptive skills.

☐ TREATMENT OPTIONS

Behavior therapy for troublesome behavioral symptoms of Rett's Disorder borrows largely from techniques used for Autistic Disorder (reviewed later in this chapter). Family therapy and psychoeducation may help parents and family members to understand and deal with the loss of functioning and severe deficits that accompany the disorder. Medication is often a component of treatment to assist with managing seizures and dangerous behaviors (e.g., self-injurious behavior), and involvement of a neurologist is, therefore, routine. Physical and occupational therapy may be used to treat movement and muscular symptoms of the disorder. No known treatment halts or reverses the progression of Rett's Disorder.

■ **Childhood Disintegrative Disorder**

☐ CLINICAL DESCRIPTION

Childhood Disintegrative Disorder (CDD) emerges following normal infant and early toddler development (age 2 or older). In the late toddler–early preschool years, children with CDD lose many of their early skills in the language, social, play, adaptive functioning, and motor areas. This "disintegration" in functioning is accompanied by social and communication deficits or by odd behaviors that appear autistic. Anxiety and increased dependency often accompany these symptoms. Neurologically, seizures are associated with CDD but are not an inevitable feature of the diagnosis (American Psychiatric Association, 1994).

Unlike children with autism, children with CDD have at least two years of normal development and a deterioration from previously average levels of functioning. Furthermore, their social-communication-behavior deficits need not be as severe as those of children with autism, and deficits in only two of the three (social, communication, or behavior) areas are required for diagnosis. Many children who were previously classified as "late" or "childhood" onset autism in previous diagnostic systems are now diagnosed with CDD. Because many children diagnosed with Rett's Disorder and Autistic Disorder will also meet the milder CDD criteria, CDD can only be diagnosed when Rett's and Autistic Disorder are ruled out. Like Rett's Disorder, CDD is rare, occurring in fewer than 0.001% of the population (Kaplan et al., 1994).

The cause of CDD is unknown, but its appearance suggests a neurologic dysfunction. CDD-like symptoms can accompany other progressive neurological disorders.

☐ ASSESSMENT PATTERNS

Cognitive testing of the child with CDD typically reveals IQ levels below 70, with language significantly impaired. Strategies resembling those for the assessment of Autistic Disorder can be employed with little modification for the child with CDD. Adaptive behaviors should be assessed with the ABES or VABS to identify levels of impairment in language, social behavior, play, motor skills, and self-care.

☐ TREATMENT OPTIONS

Treatment of CDD is similar to that for Autistic Disorder. Neurological features of the disorder should be followed closely by a psychiatrist or neurologist, and the emergence of seizures should be monitored closely.

■ Asperger's Disorder

☐ CLINICAL DESCRIPTION

Diagnostic Considerations

Asperger's Disorder is characterized by significant social and behavioral deficits *without* significant language, cognitive, or adaptive functioning deficits. Typical social deficits of the child with Asperger's Disorder are lack of empathy/reciprocity, impaired or absent peer relationships, lack of social interest, and impaired social nonverbal interaction (e.g., lack of eye contact). Typical behavioral deficits involve the presence of a restricted range of stereotyped behaviors, interests, or routines. Children diagnosed with Asperger's Disorder are often socially unresponsive and withdrawn (although inappropriate gregariousness is sometimes seen), with very circumscribed interests and activities. Their problems cause significant impairment in daily functioning, particularly in the social arena. However, their language, performance in school, and testing data all suggest no major problems with verbal intellectual ability, language (including language developmental milestones), or adaptive behavior. Like CDD, Asperger's Disorder can only be diagnosed when Autistic Disorder and Rett's Disorder are ruled out.

The Asperger's Disorder diagnosis suffers from ambiguity in how symptoms can be interpreted, as well as from a history of nebulous criteria referring to Asperger's Syndrome. Prior to DSM-IV, Asperger's Disorder was not a recognized, operationally defined Axis I diagnosis in the DSM system, leading to vast differences in how clinicians used the undefined term *Asperger's Syndrome*. These unstandardized, variably defined criteria for Asperger's Syndrome persist in the informal diagnostic systems of some clinicians and laypersons, which are then confused with DSM-IV diagnostic criteria. A second problem is potential ambiguity in interpretation of certain Asperger's Disorder diagnostic criteria. Some clinicians use the Asperger's Disorder diagnosis synonymously with mild to moderate social skills deficits and restricted interest patterns, whereas others reserve the diagnosis for a more severe impairment in these areas.

Close reading of the DSM-IV diagnostic criteria suggests that the intent is that the symptoms refer to severe impairments in the social and behavioral areas, and that the syndrome should be relatively unusual in the general population. Prevalence estimates are hindered by reliability problems, but preliminary prevalence estimates of 0.01% are reported (Klin, Sparrow, Volkmar, Cicchetti, & Rourke, 1995; Wing, 1981). Clinicians should remember that many other diagnoses (e.g., disruptive behavior disorders and Attention-Deficit/Hyperactivity Disorder) have social deficits as core or associated features, so social deficiencies could be associated with another diagnosis as opposed to Asperger's Disorder.

Asperger's Disorder is not merely a deficit in social skills. Children with Asperger's Disorder retain the oddity and dysfluency of social interaction even when they have learned social skills by rote. Thus, the social disconnection and restricted interest components of the disorder seem to persist throughout the life span, although individual symptoms may improve with treatment and experience. Outcome for Asperger's Disorder is better than that for Autistic Disorder, probably because Asperger's Disorder is not associated with mental retardation and language deficits.

Appearance and Features

Often, the most noticeable characteristic of children with Asperger's Disorder is their apparent obliviousness toward the perspective of others and the basic rules of social interaction. They often appear unaware of the impact that their behavior has on others or on the thoughts and feelings of others. This lack of awareness resembles an oversight more than callousness or lack of caring. As a result of their lack of awareness of the perspective of others, their social interactions with others often are one-sided and egocentric. They may be withdrawn into their own interests at one point and inappropriately familiar and intrusive with strangers or peers at another point.

Increasing the oddity of their interactive style, children with Asperger's Disorder often focus on their own very circumscribed interests, which may include topics such as mechanical objects, historical occurrences, and/or circumscribed factual areas (baseball cards, stock prices). Typically, a child will have an exceedingly detailed knowledge of one or a few very specialized areas, without an overall comprehension or perspective (Wing, 1981). In the vast majority of cases, the areas of interest for children with Asperger's Disorder tend to involve many rote verbal facts, as opposed to nonverbal or motor skill areas.

Unlike children with autism, children with Asperger's Disorder show an awareness of the presence of others and alter their behavior as a result. Many children with Asperger's Disorder are interested in meeting and interacting with others, although their interactions are characteristically one-sided and focused on their own narrow interests. They often have difficulty reading the nonverbal social cues of others, causing further problems in the normal give-and-take of social interaction. Frequently, children with Asperger's Disorder appear to be more interested in the (egocentric) social interaction than they are in the actual social relationship with the other person. Hence, they seem to lack connection with others while simultaneously craving social interaction based on their own terms.

In addition to social interaction oddities, the speech and language of children with Asperger's Disorder are also often characteristically atypical. Speech patterns lack the rhythm and flow of typical social interaction, instead appearing pedantic or flat. Pedantic speech (in which the speaker uses a monologue consisting of vocabulary that is formal and typical of book writing, using a precise and formal speech pattern) occurs in two-thirds to three-fourths of children with Asperger's Disorder, compared to one-third or less of children with normal-intelligence Autistic Disorder (Ghaziuddin & Gerstein, 1996).

The speech content of the child with Asperger's Disorder is also typically character-ized by an odd egocentrism that can seem tangential at times. For example, a question about how a child is feeling today may lead to a response about the current value of a par-ticular baseball card. Although this progression may seem tangential to the listener, to the child with Asperger's Disorder, baseball cards may be a central issue in most or all topics and, therefore, could form the basis of a valid response to any question. Some children with Asperger's Disorder will show a hyperlexia (use of extensive language with impaired com-prehension of what is being said), although hyperlexia is not a universal characteristic of Asperger's Disorder. Beyond content, the language of the child with Asperger's Disorder is notable for its length and lack of focus. Many children with Asperger's Disorder will talk at great length on their subject of interest, providing many details without an overarching, co-herent organization or main idea. Attempts to shorten or divert their topics with nonverbal cues are often unsuccessful because they fail to recognize those cues.

Motor skills are often delayed, with parents describing the child as clumsy. Handwrit-ing and drawing are usually poor, unless the child approaches them with obsessive, detail-oriented slowness. Clinicians should be alert to the trade-off between accuracy and speed in the motor skills of children with Asperger's Disorder. Some children learn to avoid clum-siness or poor coordination by moving very slowly, especially in pencil work.

Neuropsychological research emphasizes the nonverbal and comprehension deficits ap-parent in the behavior of many children with Asperger's Disorder, causing some to speculate that a great many children with Asperger's Disorder may manifest a Nonverbal Learning Disability (NVLD) (Rourke, 1995a). NVLD is a neuropsychological syndrome character-ized by weaknesses in tactile perception, visual perception, motor skills, novel problem solving, attention to complex visual stimuli, visual memory, concept formation, comprehen-sion, and mathematics. Conversely, children with NVLD show strengths in rote learning and memory, simple verbal skills, rote facts and fund of information, and simple language skills. Essentially, nonverbal and higher-order novel problem-solving and comprehension skills are impaired whereas rote, overlearned verbal details are strong. Of particular relevance for As-perger's Disorder is that children with NVLD demonstrate difficulties with social judgment, nonverbal social cues, and fluid, reciprocal social interaction. Research suggests that many of the neuropsychological characteristics of NVLD (including deficits in motor skills, visual-perceptual skills, nonverbal reasoning, concept formation, and visual memory) are also found in children with Asperger's Disorder (Klin et al., 1995).

Etiology

Asperger's Disorder appears to run in families, leading to hypotheses of a genetic etiology. Frequently, close family members of the child with Asperger's Disorder, such as parents, will be identified as having similar traits (Klin et al., 1995). Another possibility is that Asperger's Disorder represents an extreme of temperamental characteristics of withdrawal and social disconnection. At the present time, however, no definitive etiological data have been developed.

☐ ASSESSMENT PATTERNS

Broad Assessment Strategies

Cognitive Assessment

Clinician-Administered—IQ and Neurocognitive Testing.   Children with Asperger's Disorder often show a pattern of lower scores on cognitive tests of novel, nonverbal, visual-perceptual skills and higher scores on cognitive tests of verbal, fund of information skills. As a result of research showing significant overlap between Asperger's Disorder and NVLD, some specialists recommend an extensive cognitive or neuropsychological battery for most or all children with suspected Asperger's Disorder. Such a battery would begin with an intellectual test such as a Wechsler scale. As expected from NVLD research, the WISC-III scores of children with Asperger's Disorder typically show a pattern of higher Verbal than Performance IQ (Klin et al., 1995).

Tests to identify nonverbal, visual-perceptual weaknesses include the WASI Matrix Reasoning subtest (nonverbal logical reasoning), the Developmental Test of Visual-Motor Integration (visual-perceptual skills, fine-motor coordination skills, and visual-motor skills; Beery, 1997), Test of Nonverbal Intelligence—Third Edition (visual perception and nonverbal logical reasoning; Brown, Sherbenou, & Johnson, 1997), Matrices subtest of the K-BIT (nonverbal logical reasoning), Visual Memory subtests of the Wide Range Assessment of Memory and Learning (visual memory; Sheslow & Adams, 1990), and Rey-Osterreith Complex Figure Test (visual-spatial organization and planning; Meyers & Meyers, 1995). Children with Asperger's Disorder should show lower scores on these tests. Conversely, children with Asperger's Disorder typically score higher (usually in the average range or above) on tests emphasizing rote verbal skills such as the Vocabulary subtest of the K-BIT (one-word expressive vocabulary and definitions), the California Verbal Learning Test for Children (word memory score on Trials 1–5, which is a measure of simple verbal memory and learning; Delis, Kramer, Kaplan, & Ober, 1994), and Peabody Picture Vocabulary Test (receptive one-word vocabulary, Dunn & Dunn, 1997).

On achievement testing, children with Asperger's Disorder generally score higher on tests of reading, factual knowledge, and simple written language (e.g., spelling), compared to their scores on tests of mathematics, reasoning, and comprehension. Hence, achievement testing is generally recommended for the child with Asperger's Disorder. On the WJ-R, deficits on the Calculation and Applied Problems subtests of the Mathematics cluster would be expected of the child with Asperger's Disorder, compared to higher scores on the Reading, Written Language, and Knowledge cluster. In some cases, children with Asperger's Disorder will have difficulty with the Passage Comprehension subtest of the Reading cluster, reflecting difficulty with comprehension. However, this discrepancy is not always seen because children can sometimes compensate for comprehension deficits with their strong vocabulary. On the WIAT, children with Asperger's Disorder usually show low scores on the Mathematics composite and higher scores on the Reading and Written Language composites. In some cases, the comprehension and organization problems shown by such children will lower their scores on the Reading Comprehension, Written Expression, and Language cluster (Oral Expression and Listening Comprehension) subtests, but this is not universally seen.

Cognitive or neuropsychological testing can be extremely important for understanding the cognitive strengths and weaknesses of the child with Asperger's Disorder, and a neuropsychological phenotype (similar to NVLD, with nonverbal/comprehension weaknesses and rote verbal strengths) appears to characterize a great many children with the disorder. However, the neuropsychological phenotype is neither specific to nor diagnostically required for Asperger's Disorder. Hence, although an NVLD pattern may support an Asperger's diagnosis (or the lack of an NVLD pattern may raise some questions about the presence of an Asperger's diagnosis), cognitive testing results alone should not be used to make or rule out the diagnosis. They should be seen as additional, very important data to be considered when making the diagnosis in the context of historical, interview, observational, and other testing data. Such data can also be valuable in differentiating Asperger's Disorder from Autistic Disorder because many nonretarded children with Autistic Disorder show the reverse cognitive psychological profile, with strong nonverbal functioning, compared to weaker verbal functioning. Additional information about NVLD assessment and its application to Asperger's Disorder is found in Klin et al. (1995) and Rourke (1989).

Clinician-Administered—Adaptive Functioning. Adaptive functioning tests can be useful for evaluating the extent of problems in social functioning and other areas of adaptive functioning. Diagnostically, the child with Asperger's Disorder must show impairment in social functioning but no significant impairment in other adaptive behavior areas (such as self-care skills and communication skills). Administration of an adaptive functioning test such as the VABS or ABES can provide valuable information about the severity and nature of the social deficit, while also confirming that no other significant adaptive behavior deficits exist (that would preclude the Asperger's Disorder diagnosis). Children with Asperger's Disorder show predictable deficits (greater than 1 standard deviation below the mean, and usually greater than 2 standard deviations below the mean) in social adaptive behavior while scoring in average ranges (higher than 1 standard deviation below the mean) on adaptive functioning subtests of self-care and communication.

Behavioral Assessment

Parent- and Teacher-Report. Of the major broad-band behavior checklists, only the ECI-4 and CSI-4 include an Asperger's Disorder subscale. This subscale consists of re-worded DSM-IV criteria for each of the four social impairment symptoms and four restricted interest/odd behavior symptoms of Asperger's Disorder. There has been little research to validate this subscale, but clinical experience suggests that rigid application of scale cutoffs results in many false positives (children screening positive for Asperger's Disorder when they do not have it); false negatives (children screening negative for Asperger's Disorder when they do have it) appear to be less common. Nevertheless, the subscale does seem to capture the symptoms of Asperger's Disorder and is useful as a screening instrument for further evaluation.

On the CBCL and TRF, children with Asperger's Disorder would be expected to score lower on the Activities and Social competence subscales while elevating the Withdrawn and Social Problems subscales. Elevation of the Thought Problems and Attention Problems subscales is also commonly seen, reflecting the social oddity, narrowed interests, and inappropriate social behavior of children with Asperger's Disorder. The Anxious/Depressed subscale should be carefully inspected, as some children with Asperger's Disorder experience internal upset as a result of repeated failures in social interaction experiences.

The parent and teacher versions of the BASC include two scales that reflect social skills: Social Skills (measuring specific social skills such as helping others, engaging in reciprocal interaction, and politeness) and Leadership (measuring the tendency to be outgoing, creative, confident, and respected by others). Low scores (reflecting deficits) on both of these scales would be expected of the child with Asperger's Disorder. Similarly, the BASC Adaptability scale (measuring flexibility, adjustment to changes, and coping ability) is typically a low score for children with Asperger's Disorder. None of the BASC problem scales contain items that relate to core Asperger's Disorder diagnostic symptoms, although elevations on some of these scales could indicate specific emotional or behavioral problems concurrent with Asperger's Disorder.

Self-Report.   Preadolescent children with Asperger's Disorder often have poor insight and may show little awareness of the impact of their behavior in the environment. Therefore, they are often unreliable reporters of their behavior on self-report questionnaires. If use of a self-report instrument is desired, the PIY is recommended because of its validity scales and good coverage of social problems. Clinicians should be careful to check for elevations on the DEF (defensiveness or social desirability) or INC (inconsistent responding) scales, which may warn of problems with insight and understanding of the items.

TREATMENT OPTIONS

Behavioral Interventions and Psychotherapy

Treatment of the social deficits and restricted/stereotyped behaviors characteristic of Asperger's Disorder is typically accomplished by teaching children patterns of appropriate behavior and then reinforcing appropriate behavior when it occurs in the environment. The process of teaching appropriate social behaviors borrows heavily from traditional social skills training programs, beginning with showing children examples of basic adaptive social behaviors such as eye contact, smiling, physical space, communicating with nonverbal cues, voice volume and inflection, recognizing nonverbal cues of others, empathy and perspective-taking, content of conversation, listening to others, compliments, acknowledgments, conversational openers, assertive requests, and ignoring. Children are also taught to recognize their own odd behaviors and cues from others that their behavior is inappropriate. Verbal explanations, videotape, and live demonstration are used to train the children in how and when to use these skills. A rote, straightforward approach, in which the child learns a strategy for self-monitoring and implementing the skills, is best for children with

Asperger's Disorder. After learning the skills by rote, the children practice the skills with the therapist or in a group setting, with reinforcement for successful attainment of the skills. Finally, children are helped to use the skills in the real-world environment, with reinforcement by parents and teachers. Traditional social skills programs such as those proposed by LeCroy (1994) and Forman (1993) can be modified to fit the symptoms shown by a group of children with Asperger's Disorder.

Special Educational Services

Children with Asperger's Disorder frequently experience learning and social problems in school. Education of teachers about the child's diagnosis and cognitive profile is a valuable first step in designing an intervention to promote the child's academic and social adjustment in the classroom. If the child shows the NVLD syndrome, teaching and therapeutic interventions for NVLD would be warranted. Examples of these interventions include teaching the child using rote, clear strategies that minimize the level of inference and novel problem solving required. Short, sequential verbal explanations are generally better understood than pictorial, nonverbal, inferential explanations. Children with Asperger's Disorder and NVLD generally understand details and parts better than overarching ideas and wholes. Thus, starting with the details and working toward the main ideas using clear verbal steps is most effective in their learning. Some content, such as heavily nonverbal, conceptual information, may have to be simplified or deleted from their learning program. Other treatments for children with NVLD can be tailored to each individual classroom and social situation (Rourke, 1995b).

■ Autistic Disorder

☐ CLINICAL DESCRIPTION

Diagnostic Considerations

Autistic Disorder (or autism) is considered the "prototype" PDD and has received clinical and research attention for decades. The DSM-IV definition of Autistic Disorder focuses on three major symptom areas: impairment in social interaction, impairment in communication, and restricted or stereotyped activities, interests, and behaviors. Social interaction impairment is characterized by lack of appropriate nonverbal social behavior (e.g., eye contact), lack of peer relationships, and lack of socioemotional empathy or reciprocity. Communication impairment is shown by language delay, stereotyped/inappropriate use of language, inability to initiate or sustain conversation, and markedly reduced imaginative play. Examples of restricted interests and behaviors are distress at change in routine, stereotyped motor behavior, focus on odd objects, and extreme interest in a circumscribed activity. Onset age for autism has been changed in each of the last three DSMs. In DSM-IV, age of onset is placed at 3 years or younger (Table 10.1).

Other criteria for autism are occasionally used, but the differences between autism definitions are largely in the amount of emphasis put on particular symptoms. Nevertheless,

TABLE 10.1 Epidemiology and Course of Autistic Disorder

Prevalence: 0.05–0.1%

Sex Ratio (Male:Female): 3–4:1

Typical Onset Age: Infancy or toddlerhood; always before age 4

Course: About 75% are unable to function independently as adults and have mental retardation. Approximately 10% function sufficiently well to live a relatively normal independent life but retain elements of social avoidance and awkwardness. Failure to develop functional communication and normal imaginative and toy play prior to age 5 are associated with negative outcomes.

Common Comorbid Conditions: 1. Mental Retardation
2. Seizure Disorders

Relevant Subtypes: 1. High Functioning (IQ > 80)

disagreement over an autism diagnosis can result from the use of different definition systems (Morgan, 1988). In addition to differing definitions of autism, the diagnosis of autism is further complicated by conditions that consist of autistic-appearing features but that have not been defined as autism per se (Ornitz, 1989). DSM-IV has taken a step toward diagnostic improvement by clarifying the differences between Autistic Disorder, Rett's Disorder, CDD, and Asperger's Disorder.

Mental retardation frequently co-occurs with autism, perhaps in more than 75% of cases of autism (Morgan, 1990; Ornitz, 1989). However, the bulk of children with mental retardation are not autistic, despite the fact that they may show some autistic behaviors. One characteristic that frequently differentiates children with autism and mental retardation is that children with Autistic Disorder tend to have better motor coordination than children with mental retardation. In addition, children with Autistic Disorder usually do not show the uniformly delayed development seen in children with mental retardation. Instead, children with Autistic Disorder often develop isolated abilities at or before normative ages. Finally, children with mental retardation often show social interest and development of relationships, whereas children with Autistic Disorder do not.

There is a growing realization that autistic features are more common in children than was once believed. However, the prevalence of the full-blown Autistic Disorder depends on the definition used to define the disorder (Ornitz, 1989). Using the early, more rigorous definitions of autism, only 1 in 10,000 children would be diagnosed with the disorder (Morgan, 1990). However, using more modern definitions (Ritvo & Freeman, 1978), autism affects 4–5 out of every 10,000 children, and there are 3–4 autistic males for every autistic female (Morgan, 1990; Lotter, 1966; Ornitz, 1989; Wing, Yeates, Brierley, & Gould, 1976).

Little agreement exists on subtyping of children with Autistic Disorder. Authors do agree, however, that children with Autistic Disorder form a somewhat heterogeneous group. Some authors suggest that children with Autistic Disorder may be divided into subgroups based on intelligence (Newsom & Rincover, 1989). Children with Autistic Disorder who are severely and profoundly retarded typically have negative outcomes, with little growth in intelligence, modest communication skills, and lifelong problems with social interaction (Morgan, 1990). As many as 60–75% of children with Autistic Disorder may face this outcome, especially without intensive intervention (Morgan, 1990; Newsom & Rincover, 1989). These children typically can learn, at most, self-care skills, following instructions, simple social conventions, and very basic communication. Independent living is not a reasonable goal for children with comorbid Autistic Disorder and severe mental retardation, and intervention programs should be geared toward the modest gains that they are capable of making. Failure to develop communicative language by age 5 and failure to achieve normal toy play are both associated with particularly poor prognosis (Morgan, 1990; Ornitz & Ritvo, 1976).

A second group of children with Autistic Disorder scores in mildly retarded or higher ranges on intelligence tests (Newsom & Rincover, 1989). These children have considerably more potential than the former group, and some of them will achieve a nearly normal level of functioning, especially if they develop communicative language before age 5 (Morgan, 1990). In general, these children tend to be easier to teach basic self-care and communication skills. Thus, the emphasis (and hard work) is on teaching them higher-level skills that are needed for normal functioning in society. Such goals as social skills, average vocabulary and grammar, and independent living may be encouraged in this latter group of children with Autistic Disorder. Children with Autistic Disorder who have near-normal intelligence (defined in various ways, but typically as IQ > 80) are sometimes called "high functioning," although there is no universally recognized definition of this subgroup.

Because of their higher potential, children with Autistic Disorder who score in higher IQ ranges (mild mental retardation and higher) have a wider range of outcomes. If early intervention is neglected or if the child is in an impoverished environment, outcome may resemble that of the moderately to severely retarded group. On the other hand, intensive, early intervention may result in impressive gains in functioning. However, children with Autistic Disorder rarely achieve a completely normal level of functioning. Rather, children with high-functioning autism tend to retain some elements of shyness, introversion, poor social judgment, and impaired empathy (Ornitz & Ritvo, 1976). Approximately 5–17% of children with Autistic Disorder are able to achieve this high level of functioning and live a relatively normal, independent life (Rogers, 1998).

Because children with high-functioning autism have IQ values at or near the average range and less severe symptoms than other children with Autistic Disorder, there is sometimes difficulty in differentiating them from children with Asperger's Disorder, which also is characterized by average IQ and milder PDD symptoms. However, there may be some differences between the groups that can assist with differential diagnosis. Higher-functioning children with Autistic Disorder tend to have weaker verbal than nonverbal skills (or, in some cases, approximately equivalent verbal and nonverbal skills), whereas children with Asperger's Disorder tend to have weaker nonverbal than verbal skills. Children with Asperger's Disorder also tend to engage in more pedantic speech patterns than children with high-functioning autism. Children with high-functioning autism often have their disorder noticed and diagnosed earlier in life (before age 3), whereas Asperger's Disorder is often not clearly noticed until school-age years. Children with Asperger's Disorder are more often described as clumsy with late-developing motor skills, whereas children with Autistic Disorder often develop motor skills on time or early. Children with high-functioning autism show more significant disorders of communication and language, especially during early development, whereas those with Asperger's Disorder do not (American Psychiatric Association, 1994; Ghaziuddin & Gerstein, 1996; Klin et al., 1995).

Appearance and Features

Despite disagreement over the relative importance of specific diagnostic criteria, common features of autistic appearance and behavior (see Table 10.2) are well agreed upon. Controversy arises when authors designate some symptoms as more important than others, or when authors attempt to group symptoms into meaningful categories.

The earliest conceptualization of autism by Kanner (1943) emphasized five features of the disorder: (1) inability to relate to social stimuli, (2) need for sameness and order in the environment, (3) failure to use language to communicate, (4) fascination with objects, and (5) potential for normal cognitive development. The latter characteristic has been abandoned, but the first four persist in modern definitions of autism. In DSM-IV, the three categories of autistic symptoms are impairment in (1) reciprocal social interaction, (2) communication, and (3) repertoire of activities and interests. Ornitz and Ritvo (1976) emphasized five symptom categories: disturbances of (1) perception, (2) developmental rate, (3) relating to people and objects, (4) speech and language, and (5) motility.

TABLE 10.2   Appearance and Features of Autistic Disorder

COMMON FEATURES

1. Impaired social interaction: poor eye contact, failure to orient to a speaker, discomfort with physical touching, lack of interest in social interaction, refusal/inability to follow social rules, lack of imitation, lack of empathy
2. Impaired/absent peer relationships
3. Impaired communication: language delay, echolalia, pronoun reversal
4. Unusual or inappropriate tonal quality of speech (flatness, sing-song)
5. Impaired use of objects: stereotyped use of objects, focus on one quality of an object (e.g., touch), resistance to novel use of objects
6. Disturbance of motor behavior: arm flapping, hand waving, head banging, whirling, rocking, swaying, scratching, toe walking
7. Attachment to routine
8. Hyper- and/or hyporesponsivity to sensory input
9. Repetitive, stereotypic play without imagination or fantasy
10. Inappropriate or flat affect
11. Self-stimulating behavior
12. Disturbances of developmental rate
13. Mental retardation
14. Onset before age 3

OCCASIONAL FEATURES

1. Negative/impaired relationship with caretakers
2. Unusual attachment behavior toward caretakers
3. One or two extremely well developed, narrow, encapsulated abilities
4. Seizures

Note: The features listed in the table are often seen but are not universal. Some features may be diagnostically relevant or required, whereas others may not be required for diagnosis. "Common" features are typical of the disorder; "occasional" features appear frequently but are not necessarily seen in a majority of cases.

The following description of autistic features reviews the basic features of autism without judging their relative importance. Not all children with Autistic Disorder will have all of these features, and the manifestation of the features may occur at varying degrees of severity:

Impaired Social Interaction.   One set of features of autism involves impairments in interaction with others (American Psychiatric Association, 1994; Ornitz & Ritvo, 1976). Children with Autistic Disorder often have poor or absent eye contact and do not orient normally to a person who is interacting with them. When picked up or touched, their response is unusual, ranging from ignoring to actively resisting the social contact. They may stiffen when held by a parent or pull away from physical contact as though it were an aversive stimulus. Reciprocal social interaction with these children is extremely difficult to initiate and maintain. They often show little interest in their social environment, will not abide by the rules of social interaction, and do not initiate their own social interactions. When they do show interest in a person, the interest may be unusual, such as fascination over a body part or a piece of clothing. Over- or underreaction to social interactions is the general rule for children with Autistic Disorder.

Children with Autistic Disorder also have difficulty understanding or sympathizing with another person's thoughts or feelings, which is sometimes referred to as impairment in "theory of mind." They seem to lack a basic sense of the perspective of others. For example, children with Autistic Disorder will sometimes ignore the distress of others or will react not out of sympathy but out of fear or irritation. They may act in ways that provoke anger or upset in other children, apparently oblivious that their actions will have that effect. Similarly, they show a blunted or absent response to the affection of others. Attention and praise often have a limited impact on them (especially prior to psychosocial treatment), and some children rarely seek reassurance or comfort from others.

A lack of imitation and unresponsiveness to social reinforcement make children with Autistic Disorder extremely difficult to teach. Much of a child's learning is dependent on imitation and social shaping of behavior. These venues are, at least initially, largely unavailable to children with Autistic Disorder. Because of their detached, oblivious social behavior, they rarely have friendships among peers, and they may alienate or upset their caretakers.

On the other hand, some children with Autistic Disorder do show attachments to their caretakers or other familiar people, although the attachment may be demonstrated in unusual ways. For example, the child may engage in a favorite ritual when reunited with a parent. Alternatively, the child may ignore a caretaker until the caretaker leaves and then throw a tantrum. Newsom and Rincover (1989) report that as many as half of children with Autistic Disorder cuddle when held by a caretaker and show a social smile.

Impaired Communication.   Children with Autistic Disorder almost always have problems with communication, beginning with a delay in the acquisition of communicative language skills. In the most severe cases of autism, this begins as total mutism (roughly 1 in 4 children with Autistic Disorder is mute [Morgan, 1990]). About half of children with Autistic Disorder speak very little and use only primitive gestures to communicate (Newsom & Rincover, 1989).

Often, however, the child verbalizes in an abnormal way. For example, the child may vocalize syllables that initially have no meaning but are eventually recognized by the parent to reflect internal states or needs. At later ages, phrases may be used by the child that have completely different meaning to the child than their meaning in the language. For example, the child may say, "The train is leaving" when he or she wants to go for a ride in the car. Other children engage in echolalia, in which they repeat phrases that they hear, without modifying the information to convey any measure of communication. Another unusual characteristic of the speech of children with Autistic Disorder is pronoun reversal, which occurs when the child with Autistic Disorder substitutes "you" for "me" and "me" for "you." For example, if the child is thirsty, he or she may say "you want a drink of water."

When speech occurs, it may be accompanied by odd inflections (e.g., total flatness or sing-song, meaningless tonal quality) and unusual or absent expressive mannerisms (such as a lack of facial expression). Verbal and nonverbal communication modes may not be congruent, as when a child monotonously states that he or she is very happy or intensely angry. Likewise, a child may attempt to indicate an object without pointing, an action that even mentally retarded children very easily learn. These impairments in simple communication and language make social interaction with children with Autistic Disorder difficult and at times uncomfortable.

Impaired Use of Objects. Children with Autistic Disorder tend to relate to objects in unusual ways. Stereotyped, rigid, or self-stimulating behaviors in relation to objects are common. For example, a child may carefully feel the texture of a surface for an hour, repeatedly stroking and patting it. Some children with Autistic Disorder spin or twirl objects repeatedly. Repetitive, ritualistic play with objects is common, and the child may become extremely distressed if he or she is encouraged to play with the object in a novel way. For example, children with Autistic Disorder may become preoccupied with parts of objects, showing excruciating attention to simple details. However, they may ignore major details, such as the child who plays with the tail of a stuffed animal but ignores the head. Creative, imaginative play with objects, seen in normal 3-year-olds, is often absent in children with Autistic Disorder. Children with Autistic Disorder can become very attached to unusual objects, such as a potato chip bag, while ignoring objects that typically elicit attachment behaviors, such as blankets and stuffed animals. The features described here, along with a preference for their environments to be structured, have been interpreted by some authors to indicate a need for a rigid sameness in the environment (Ornitz, 1989), as well as control over idiosyncratic details.

Disturbances of Motor Behavior. Children with Autistic Disorder frequently engage in a number of unusual, apparently purposeless motor behaviors. For example, a child with Autistic Disorder may flap his arm for no apparent reason or may repeatedly wave her hands in front of her face. Self-harming/self-stimulating behaviors may also be exhibited, as when a child bangs his or her head against the wall for hours or scratches part of the body until it bleeds. Whirling, rocking, and swaying behaviors also are common, as is walking up on the toes. These motor behaviors are intermittent and may occur without any significant change in the environment. Some authors also note that observation of a spinning top tends to elicit motility disturbances (Ornitz & Ritvo, 1976). The stereotyped, intense, unpredictable, repetitive nature of behavior of children with Autistic Disorder has caused some authors to suggest that the behavior is performed in order for the child to receive vestibular or proprioceptive input (Ornitz, 1989).

Attachment to Routines.   Children with Autistic Disorder show a strong attachment to routines, and they may become extremely agitated or upset if small deviations occur. This is related to their general resistance to any environmental change (Schopler, Reichler, De Vellis, & Daly, 1980). Even meaningless details may be extremely important to the child with Autistic Disorder, such as the cup that is used for drink at breakfast each morning or the steps in getting ready for school.

Problems with Sensory Input and Responsiveness.   Hyper- and hyporeactivity to sensory stimuli are common in children with Autistic Disorder, although the stimuli that elicit them are unpredictable. Knowledge of what stimuli normal children find preferable or aversive is often of little help in identifying what stimuli a particular child with Autistic Disorder will relate to. Loud sounds sometimes elicit no response from the child with Autistic Disorder, whereas certain quiet sounds may cause extreme distress. Hence, a child who has loudly banged on a can may wail and cover his or her ears at the sounds of two pieces of paper rubbing together.

In the tactile area, young children with Autistic Disorder seem to prefer smooth surfaces and textures, avoiding rough textured objects and foods (Ornitz, 1989). This tactile hyperresponsivity sometimes results in significant feeding problems, as the child refuses textured, solid food in favor of milk and baby food. In extreme cases, this can cause failure-to-thrive and dangerous weight loss. Also in the tactile arena, painful stimuli may elicit no response, whereas simple tactile stimuli, such as the touch of an adult, may result in extreme agitation.

Sensory input may be focused on irrelevant details of objects, as when a child repeatedly feels the texture of a book page but shows no interest in the words or pictures on the page. In other cases, sensory input may be overly focused on minute details; for example, a child may notice the briefcase of a stranger but pay no attention to the new person. Children with Autistic Disorder will also often try to create their own sensory stimuli, sometimes in atypical ways. For example, the child may repeatedly scratch a surface with his or her ear close to it.

It is often difficult to predict what auditory, tactile, or visual stimuli an individual child with Autistic Disorder will ignore and what stimuli he or she will find aversive. Such stimuli tend to differ from child to child and from time to time within the same child, although there is some within-child constancy. However, several authors note that children with Autistic Disorder in general tend to prefer proximal (touch, taste, smell) sensory stimulation over distal (hearing, seeing) sensory stimulation (Ornitz & Ritvo, 1976; Schopler et al., 1980). Hence, they will often engage in extensive, inappropriate touching, smelling, and mouthing of objects.

Unusual Play.   Unusual play is manifest in several other characteristics of autism, but it deserves individual mention because it is often reported by parents of children with Autistic Disorder. The play of children with Autistic Disorder is often repetitive, stereotypic, and lacking in creativity. Imaginative play is frequently absent, and coordinated play with other children is rarely observed, especially at younger ages.

Inappropriate Affect.   The emotional displays and responses of children with Autistic Disorder are often blunted, absent, inappropriate, or overly intense (Schopler et al., 1980).

For example, a child may show no reaction to pain or to separation from a caretaker but become vehemently angry if the floor is vacuumed. Emotional responses to the upset of others are also often blunted, exaggerated, inappropriate, or absent.

Self-Stimulating Behavior. The self-stimulating behaviors of children with Autistic Disorder include rocking, head banging, kicking, arm waving, and self-injurious behavior. The purpose of these behaviors is apparently to provide sensory input, although the reason for this input is unclear.

Disturbances of Developmental Rate. Children with Autistic Disorder achieve some milestones early, others on time, and others very late (Ornitz & Ritvo, 1976). The affected developmental milestones tend to vary from child to child, although motor development is usually normal or only slightly delayed (Newsom & Rincover, 1989). For example, a child with Autistic Disorder may say a first word early in development but then not use language for communication until age 4 or 5. The achievement of some developmental milestones at or before appropriate ages, combined with the often normal or attractive appearance of children with Autistic Disorder, caused some authors (Kanner, 1943) to speculate that children with Autistic Disorder have normal intelligence but have difficulty expressing it. A substantial body of research, however, suggests that this is not the case (Ornitz, 1989).

Intellectual Functioning. As many as 75–80% of children with Autistic Disorder are mentally retarded, scoring below 70 on tests of intellectual functioning. In many cases, children with Autistic Disorder refuse to cooperate sufficiently to be tested; this almost always reflects low functioning rather than oppositionality (Morgan, 1990). Combined with severe delays in adaptive communication, self-care, and judgment skills, these intellectual deficits are pervasive and have a major impact on the child's development. Occasionally, a child with Autistic Disorder will show normal development or even extraordinary skills in a very defined area, such as computation, memory, or music. However, this talent is typically well encapsulated and should not be used as an indicator of general intelligence.

Considerable confusion has resulted from the early definitions of autism, which included potential for normal intelligence as a common feature (Morgan, 1990). This feature is not present in any modern definitions. In fact, it is now assumed that a diagnosis of autism almost always connotes some cognitive impairments.

Relative Nonverbal Strengths. In many cases, children with high-functioning (IQ > 80) autism (who do not qualify for a diagnosis of Asperger's Syndrome) demonstrate strengths in perceptual-organizational, nonverbal reasoning, and verbal tasks that require less processing or production. More elaborate verbal tasks (those that involve more novel information or a more extensive, organized, or flexible response) are often quite difficult for these children.

Associated Neurological Problems. There is a high rate of comorbidity of autism and seizure disorders, particularly at later ages (Ornitz & Ritvo, 1976). As many as 25% of children with Autistic Disorder may develop seizures, usually in adolescence (Ornitz, 1989; Ornitz & Ritvo, 1976). Childhood seizures are associated with poorer outcome (Morgan, 1990).

Age of Onset. Most parents report noticing autistic symptoms in their child before the age of 2½ years, even if they do not bring the child to professional attention until much later (Ornitz, 1989). Onset before age 3 is diagnostically required, and many authors believe that "autism is probably present at birth" (Ornitz & Ritvo, 1976, p. 610). Before 18 months, parents may notice that their child responds strangely to being held (rigid or limp), does not respond to social or other stimulation, has a delayed social smile, vocalizes rarely, and cries little. Nevertheless, the full autistic syndrome is typically not noted by parents before age 18 months. After 18 months, developmental delays become much more obvious. Children who clearly have onset of autistic symptomatology after age 3 probably suffer from one of the other Pervasive Developmental Disorders or a different disorder.

Etiology

Family Theories

Historically, parents of children with Autistic Disorder were described as aloof, intelligent, cold, perfectionistic, achievement oriented, and wealthy (Morgan, 1990; Ornitz & Ritvo, 1976). Presumably these characteristics suggested that the parents (particularly the mother) were unresponsive to the needs of their children. The children, with their needs ignored and in an uncomfortable state, internalized an image of the environment as hostile and withdrew into their own world. Initial evidence for this explanation was anecdotal and based on selective clinical observations. Follow-up empirical studies have not supported this characterization of parents of children with Autistic Disorder. No significant differences have been found between parents of children with Autistic Disorder and control parents (Morgan, 1990; Ornitz, 1989). Other family etiology theories, which postulated parental hostility, rejection, and disturbed family dynamics, have also not received empirical support (Ornitz & Ritvo, 1976). However, there is some evidence that having a child with autism may contribute to family stress and parental problems (Ornitz & Ritvo, 1976).

Biological Theories

With the fall of family etiology theories has come the rise of biological theories of autism. These theories postulate that autism is the result of a genetic-neurological-physiological defect that causes the symptoms of the disorder. Twin studies support a genetic basis for the disorder, with monozygotic twins showing higher concordance rates than dizygotic twins. Furthermore, autism cuts across geography, culture, and racial populations, suggesting a biological cause as opposed to a cultural one (Ornitz & Ritvo, 1976).

Additional support for the biological theory comes from neurological and physiological studies. These studies find an abnormally large number of neurologic soft signs in children with autism, with 40–75% of children showing soft signs (Ornitz & Ritvo, 1976). EEG, sleep, and REM studies have been contradictory and inconclusive. However, many children with Autistic Disorder are found to have abnormal EEG, and a significant minority develop seizures (Morgan, 1990). A host of biochemical studies has suggested some possible abnormality of serotonin or dopamine levels in children with Autistic Disorder, although this finding awaits further support (Newsom & Rincover, 1989; Ornitz & Ritvo, 1976).

A subgroup of biological theories posits that some or all of the symptoms of Autistic Disorder (as well as other disorders, such as some learning disorders) stem from dysfunction in the interpretation, organization, and integration of information from the various senses. As the child with Autistic Disorder develops, input from the senses is not processed accurately or adequately, leading to developmental delays, impaired sensory sensitivity, and inappropriate behavior. Advocates of sensory integration theories cite as evidence symptoms such as hyporeactivity or hyperreactivity to stimulation, tactile defensiveness (hypersensitivity to touches and textures), self-stimulating behaviors, odd movements, and self-reports of high-functioning autistic people who complain about difficulty organizing and interpreting sensation. Hypothetically, these problems are caused by central nervous system deficiencies, which do not allow proper integration and experience of sensory information. Touch, hearing, and movement/location of the body in space (vestibular and proprioceptive systems) are the sensory systems most often implicated in theories of sensory integration dysfunction, although taste, smell, and sight sensory problems have also been reported. Sensory integration theories have received considerable attention in treatment programs designed for physical, occupational, and speech/language therapies. However, research evidence on the primary biological substrate and validation of these theories remains to be seen.

Behavioral Theories

Behaviorists argue that autism develops because children with Autistic Disorder do not find social stimuli to be reinforcing. As an infant, the typical child learns that social stimuli (e.g., interaction, praise, imitation) are rewarding by pairing them with intrinsic reinforcers such as food, comfort, and warmth. For various reasons (biological predisposition, environmental contingencies, parental behavior), this pairing does not occur in children with Autistic Disorder, resulting in a lack of social interaction or interest. This lack of social interest then leads to severe problems because the child does not learn from the environment how to behave like a socialized human being. The problems grow progressively larger as the child continues to fail to learn through observation of and interaction with the social environment. Finally, the child's behaviors appear bizarre because of their continuing divergence with "typical" human behaviors, which can only be learned in a social context through modeling and social reinforcement (Lovaas, 1979).

Support for the behavioral view has come largely from studies indicating that children with Autistic Disorder do not find their social environment to be reinforcing. When children with Autistic Disorder are taught to attend to their social environments, behavior change often occurs. Behavioral interventions have brought about dramatic changes in the behavior of children with Autistic Disorder (Lovaas, 1979).

Some behavioral studies have been criticized because they focus only on higher-functioning children with Autistic Disorder, ignoring those with lower IQs that suggest more significant neurological abnormalities. Behavioral theories also do not fully explain why many children in impoverished or neglectful environments do not develop autism, whereas other children in supportive and nurturant environments do develop the disorder. Over all, however, behavioral factors may be implicated in some role in the maintenance of some autistic symptoms.

□   ASSESSMENT PATTERNS

Assessment of a child suspected to be autistic should include medical, mental health, and educational personnel. Frequently the child's primary care physician is already involved in the medical side of a diagnostic assessment. Educationally, teachers and speech-language pathologists are routinely enlisted from the school system to assess the child and to implement recommendations.

The mental health component of the assessment of a child suspected to have autism consists of at least three parts: specific testing of autistic symptomatology, cognitive testing, and testing of adaptive functioning. The cognitive and adaptive functioning tests are required to make a diagnosis of mental retardation, and they also provide valuable information about the child's information processing and behavior. Syndrome-specific tests are helpful in making the initial autism diagnosis and in identifying the autistic features present in an individual child (see Table 10.3).

Broad Assessment Strategies

Cognitive Assessment

Clinician-Administered—IQ Testing. Because most children with Autistic Disorder are either mentally retarded (Morgan, 1990; Ornitz, 1989; Ornitz & Ritvo, 1976) or have focal strengths and weaknesses, intelligence testing should be a routine part of the assessment of the child with Autistic Disorder. IQ scores of less than 70 are generally negative prognostic indicators for future development (Morgan, 1990). Three-quarters of children with autism and mental retardation (50–60% of all children with Autistic Disorder) will have IQs less than 50 (Morgan, 1990).

Parents sometimes express surprise when told that their child has not only Autistic Disorder but also mental retardation. Rather than mental retardation, the child's poor performance may have been suspected to be the result of emotional problems, withdrawal, in-

---

TABLE 10.3   Sample Assessment Battery for Autistic Disorder

COGNITIVE

1. Broad intelligence test (Bayley-II, SB:FE, or Wechsler scale)
2. Nonverbal intelligence test (WASI Matrix Reasoning, K-BIT Matrices, or TONI-3)
3. Vineland Adaptive Behavior Scale
4. Adaptive Behavior Evaluation Scale

BEHAVIORAL

1. Symptom Inventory-4 (Parent-Report and Teacher-Report)

SYNDROME-SPECIFIC

1. Childhood Autism Rating Scale
2. Aberrant Behavior Checklist

Note: Assessment instruments are intended to supplement (not substitute for) a good clinical interview and, when possible, a structured diagnostic interview.

attentiveness, or refusal to complete items that the child is capable of doing (Morgan, 1990). However, there is no evidence that apparent mental retardation in the child with Autistic Disorder is caused by these problems (Morgan, 1990; Ornitz, 1989; Ornitz & Ritvo, 1976). In fact, the refusal of the child to participate in testing is indicative of later mental retardation (Morgan, 1990; Ornitz & Ritvo, 1976).

The selection of a scale to use in assessing the child with Autistic Disorder is often crucial in obtaining valid data. If significant mental retardation is suspected (IQ below 55), the Bayley-II should be used, or, for older children, the SB:FE. Given the heavy reliance of the SB:FE on verbal communication, the Bayley-II may be more appropriate for low-functioning, young children with Autistic Disorder. For older (age 8 or above) children with suspected higher IQs (above 55), the WISC-III may be used.

Although overall low IQ is to be expected in many children with Autistic Disorder, isolated areas of good performance are occasionally found. Areas that involve rote responses or little use of communicative language (such as WISC-III Digit Span) are most likely to be discrepant with otherwise low scores. On the other hand, subtests that rely heavily on complex verbal communication, reasoning, and expression (such as WISC-III Vocabulary and Comprehension) are likely to be uniformly low. Tests of perceptual-organizational skills and nonverbal reasoning are found to be strengths in some children with Autistic Disorder.

Because of the difficulty that many children with Autistic Disorder have with processing extensive verbal information and with formulating lengthy or complex verbal responses, it is often valuable to give a less elaborate verbal cognitive test. Simple expressive and receptive vocabulary tests, such as the Peabody Picture Vocabulary Test-III (Dunn & Dunn, 1997) and the Vocabulary subtest of the K-BIT, for example, can sometimes identify strengths in less complex verbal areas.

For the nonverbal segment of cognitive testing, professionals should remember that the WISC-III does not include a direct measure of nonverbal logical (e.g., matrix or analogy) reasoning. To fully assess the child's nonverbal abilities, addition of a nonverbal matrix reasoning test (such as the WASI Matrix Reasoning subtest, the K-BIT Matrices subtest, or the Test of Nonverbal Intelligence [Brown et al., 1997]) to the testing battery is warranted.

Clinician-Administered—Adaptive Functioning. In addition to testing of cognitive abilities, testing of adaptive behavior is both useful in understanding the functioning of the child with Autistic Disorder and essential in making a diagnosis of mental retardation. The VABS and/or ABES can be particularly useful in the assessment of the child with Autistic Disorder. Information from these scales should be used in combination with the child's IQ scores to form a profile of cognitive and adaptive strengths and weaknesses. Children with Autistic Disorder give a variety of scores on adaptive functioning scales, but, as with IQ testing, composite scores tend to be below 70. Scores on communication and social subscales are usually quite low, and scores for scales reflecting self-care, organization, and self-direction are frequently significantly below average as well. Motor skills scores are variable and may be average for some children with Autistic Disorder.

Adaptive behavior scale scores are essential in making residential, schooling, and training recommendations for children with Autistic Disorder. It should never be assumed that a child with low IQ has poor adaptive functioning without first administering an adaptive functioning test. Adaptive behavior testing often leads directly to recommendations to improve specific adaptive behavior weakness areas, which can be monitored by readministration of the adaptive behavior test. The ABES, for example, has a companion intervention manual that suggests treatment options for specific adaptive behavior deficits.

Behavioral Assessment

Parent- and Teacher-Report.   Of the major broad-band behavior checklists, only the ECI-4 and CSI-4 (but not the adolescent version, the ASI-4) include an Autistic Disorder subscale. This subscale consists of reworded DSM-IV criteria for each of the four social impairment symptoms, four communication symptoms, and four restricted interest/odd behavior symptoms of Autistic Disorder. Clinical experience suggests that rigid application of scale cutoffs in a clinic setting results in many false positives (children screening positive for Autistic Disorder when they do not have it), whereas false negatives (children screening negative for Autistic Disorder when they do have it) are less common. Nevertheless, the subscale does capture the symptoms of Autistic Disorder and is useful as a screening instrument for further evaluation.

On the CBCL and TRF, children with Autistic Disorder would be expected to score lower on the Activities and Social competence subscales while elevating the Withdrawn and Social Problems subscales. Elevation of the Thought Problems and Attention Problems subscales is also commonly seen, reflecting the social oddity, narrowed interests, and inappropriate social behavior of such children. Other subscale elevations could indicate associated anxiety or aggressive behavior.

The parent and teacher versions of the BASC include two scales that reflect social skills: Social Skills (measuring specific social skills such as helping others, engaging in reciprocal interaction, and politeness) and Leadership (measuring the tendency to be outgoing, creative, confident, and respected by others). Low scores (reflecting deficits) on both of these scales would be expected of the child with Autistic Disorder. Similarly, the BASC Adaptability scale (measuring flexibility, adjustment to changes, and coping ability) is typically a low score for children with Autistic Disorder. The BASC Atypicality scale includes several items about self-stimulating or ritualistic behavior as well as odd behavior; elevations of this scale are common with autistic populations. As with the CBCL, elevations on other BASC scales could indicate associated emotional or behavioral problems being concurrently experienced by the child with Autistic Disorder.

Syndrome-Specific Tests

Clinician-Administered

Autism Behavior Checklist.   The Autism Behavior Checklist (ABC; Krug, Arick, & Almond, 1980) is a 57-item rating scale of the behavior of children with Autistic Disorder. Initial scale development and norms were based on the ratings of 1,049 professionals, although the final format of the scale potentially can be applied to parent ratings. Each item is rated for presence/absence, with 1–4 points assigned to symptom presence based on an empirically derived weighting scheme. Items are added to give five scales (sensory, relating, body and object use, language, and social self-help) and a total score. Summary scores can be compared to normative groups by age and diagnosis. Autistic groups receive average total scores of 78, whereas other diagnostic groups average 45 (Krug et al., 1980).

The ABC is part of the Autism Screening Instrument for Educational Planning (ASIEP), which includes tests of vocal behavior, interaction skills, educational skills, and novel learning skills (Krug et al., 1980; Teal & Wiebe, 1986). The ABC appears to be the most diagnostically useful of the ASIEP tests (Teal & Wiebe, 1986), and it is certainly the most widely researched (Morgan, 1988). The ABC was extensively developed, using items and information from existing autism scales, combined with feedback from numerous clinical experts. It has good psychometric properties.

Behavior Observation Scale for Autism. The Behavior Observation Scale for Autism (BOS; Freeman, Ritvo, Guthrie, Schroth, & Ball, 1978) is a second measure developed specifically for the measurement of autistic symptoms. The BOS consists of a list of 67 behaviors that are coded based on observation of the child with Autistic Disorder in a standardized setting. The behavioral items were selected based on Ritvo and Freeman's (1978) definition of autism. Observations are made during nine intervals of 3 minutes each, and each behavior is scored on a 0–3 scale of frequency for each interval. Standardized stimuli (a top, noises, lights, and tactile stimuli) are presented at the beginning of the middle seven intervals. Freeman et al. (1978) have identified BOS behaviors that are predictive of autism, and they note that different behaviors may be indicative of autism at different ages. Freeman, Schroth, Ritvo, Guthrie, and Wake, (1980) factor analyzed BOS scores, but their results have not been used widely to create summary scales. Interrater reliability and validity appear to be good (Morgan, 1990), and the list of BOS behaviors is a helpful summary of behaviors that can be casually observed by the clinician during a clinical interview of the child.

Behavior Rating Instrument for Autistic and Atypical Children. Like the BOS, the Behavior Rating Instrument for Autistic and Atypical Children (BRIAAC; Ruttenberg, Dratman, Fraknoi, & Wenar, 1966; Wenar & Ruttenberg, 1976) relies on observer ratings of behavior. Children are rated on eight scales of development (Relationship to an Adult, Communication, Drive for Mastery, Vocalization and Expressive Speech, Sound and Speech Reception, Social Responsiveness, Body Movement, and Psychobiological Development). Each scale gives a score up to 10, and scales can be added to give a total score (Wenar & Ruttenberg, 1976). The BRIAAC is primarily based on Kanner's (1943) conservative definition of autism, which may not apply to all DSM-IV cases. Because the BRIAAC is relatively easy to rate, score, and interpret, it may be easily applied in the clinical setting. However, it requires some familiarity with the child's daily functioning.

Childhood Autism Rating Scale. The Childhood Autism Rating Scale (CARS; Schopler et al., 1980) is an observer rating scale consisting of 15 "scales," each of which is a general area of autistic symptomatology: impairment in human relationships, imitation, inappropriate affect, bizarre use of body movement and persistence of stereotypes, peculiarities in relating to nonhuman objects, resistance to environmental change, peculiarities of visual responsiveness, peculiarities of auditory responsiveness, near receptor responsiveness, anxiety reaction, verbal communication, nonverbal communication, activity level, intellectual functioning, and general impressions. Each area is rated on a 1 (normal) to 4 (severely abnormal) scale based on the child's age and developmentally appropriate behavior. Observations and ratings are made during a structured diagnostic session.

Three types of scores are obtained from the CARS: First, the scale raw scores may be interpreted to find particular problem areas. Second, the scales may be added to give a total score between 15 and 60. Third, the number of scales with scores of 3 or greater may be counted. Schopler et al. (1980) suggest using a criterion for severe autism of total score greater than 36 and five or more scales rated 3 or higher. Children with total scores of less than 30 are considered nonautistic, whereas those with scores greater than 29 who do not meet autistic criteria are considered "mildly to moderately autistic" (Schopler et al., 1980, p. 97).

The CARS was not developed according to any one set of diagnostic criteria but instead incorporates items from numerous diagnostic systems of autism (Morgan, 1988; Schopler et al., 1980). Reliability and validity are good to excellent, and developmental considerations increase the utility of the scale. Teal and Wiebe (1986) found that the CARS had higher discriminant validity than the E-2 and the ASIEP. Morgan (1988) reports that "when all measures of reliability and validity are considered for the (ABC, E-2, BRIAAC, CARS, and BOS), the CARS clearly emerges as the strongest scale in terms of demonstrated psychometric properties" (p. 149). Norms are available for the CARS based on large samples, and the scale is relatively straightforward to learn and give. However, it must be administered by a trained evaluator and its administration can be time consuming.

Parent-Report

Diagnostic Checklist for Behavior-Disturbed Children, Form E-2. The Diagnostic Checklist for Behavior-Disturbed Children, Form E-2 (E-2; Rimland, 1971) consists of 80 parent-completed questions assessing behaviors in several areas: social interaction, speech/language, motor skills, intelligence, reaction to stimuli, medical history, family environment, and physiological data.

Each symptom of autism on the E-2 that is endorsed by the parent is assigned a positive point, whereas each question answered in the nonautistic direction is given a negative point. Some questions can yield either positive or negative points depending on the answer, whereas other questions give only positive points. Positive and negative points are added to give a total score. Hence, a score of +15 would indicate a child whose parent endorsed 15 more autistic items than nonautistic items. E-2 scores of +20 or higher are considered indicative of autism. The +20 criterion seems to reflect agreement with the more strict Kanner (1943) criteria of autism as opposed to DSM-IV. Hence, some children with legitimate DSM-IV autism diagnoses may not elevate the E-2 sufficiently to meet the +20 criterion. In addition to the total score, E-2 responses may be divided into behavior and speech scores (Rimland, 1971), although little has been done with these specific scores.

Rimland (1971) has accumulated a large database to support the validity of the E-2. He has found that, using the E-2 +20 criterion score, only 10% of children with suspected autism, psychosis, or a related severe behavior problem are actually diagnosed as autistic. Teal and Wiebe (1986) found that E-2 scores correctly classified 85% of children with Autistic Disorder and 95% of retarded children. The E-2 has clinical utility because it is relatively "cheap" to obtain (parents can complete it in the waiting room) and provides easily interpreted data.

Questionnaires for Behavior in Mentally Retarded Children. Because of the high occurrence of mental retardation in children with autism, behavior checklists specific to mental retardation are frequently useful for children with comorbid Autistic Disorder and mental retardation. The Aberrant Behavior Checklist (ABC) and similar checklists are reviewed in Chapter 12 (Mental Retardation).

☐ TREATMENT OPTIONS

Family Interventions

Parent Intervention. Autism has effects on the family and parents, and parents are vital for the success of behavioral therapies for autism. Hence, attention in treatment must be given to family issues and to the adjustment of parents. This is often accomplished by a combination of psychoeducation, support, and recommendations presented to the parents. The parents of a child with Autistic Disorder face enormous stresses: loss (of the idealized healthy child), guilt, fear, sadness, concern over the future, strain of the child on the family environment, and effort in caring for the child (Newsom & Rincover, 1989). Many coping strategies are used by parents to deal with these stresses, but two of the most dangerous and most common are wishful thinking and denial. Parents who engage in denial and wishful thinking have difficulty coming to terms with the reality that their child has an autistic disorder. They may point out behaviors that lead them to believe that the child is not mentally retarded or that the child has advanced intelligence. They may believe that their child will "grow out" of the disorder or that a miracle cure exists. The sensitive clinician listens to the beliefs of the parents and investigates their claims without confronting them in a way that raises their defensiveness.

Most parents have misconceptions of autism based on outdated books and errors in the media. One common misconception, for example, is that the child with Autistic Disorder constructs an elaborate inner reality in which he or she "lives" in withdrawal from the real world. Related to this is the belief that the child with Autistic Disorder has high intelligence but simply cannot express it. Other misconceptions are that autism is caused by a cold family and that autism is always accompanied by phenomenal abilities in certain specific mental areas.

With these background issues in mind, treatment begins with psychoeducation. The parents should be informed about the child's condition as directly, completely, realistically, and sensitively as possible. They should be informed about the child's current level of functioning, strengths/weaknesses, and prognosis, with appropriate caution that nobody has all of the answers. Results of formal testing can be helpful in organizing the presentation to the parents, who should be provided with a sketch of their child's cognitive, adaptive, social, motor, and behavioral functioning.

The clinician must also be prepared in this initial session to gently dispel myths held by the parents about their child's condition. Explaining the probable biological etiology of autism is usually helpful in reducing self-blame, emphasizing that the parents are part of the solution, not part of the problem. In addition, parents are generally most concerned with two issues: treatment and prognosis. They should be told that these are related issues (prognosis depends in part on treatment), and they should be informed of the most likely outcomes. At the very least, parents should understand that autism is pervasive, chronic, and debilitating. However, they should also understand that, regardless of anticipated prognosis and severity, intensive intervention should be implemented to help the child as much as possible.

Common treatments to be discussed with parents include medication, special education, behavior modification, and joining support groups. Parents should also be warned about the stress of the child with Autistic Disorder on the family. For example, the needs of the other children in the family may intensify as the child with Autistic Disorder receives increasing attention. Stress management, family therapy, or individual therapy may be warranted if the situation becomes unbearable. Finally, parents should be given an opportunity to ask questions and express feelings. These questions and feelings can be diagnostic of future problems for the parents and for the implementation of behavioral plans (Morgan, 1990; Newsom & Rincover, 1989).

Behavioral Interventions

Special Considerations for Children with Autistic Disorder

Behavioral modification has been shown to be effective in improving many symptoms, as well as the overall functioning, of children with Autistic Disorder (Lovaas et al., 1974; Lovaas, 1987; Rogers, 1998). Behavioral treatment is likely to be most effective when it is started at a young age (before age 4) with a child whose IQ is at least 50. However, behavioral techniques produce some change in almost all children with Autistic Disorder.

Behavioral modification with children with Autistic Disorder is complicated by the fact that many children with Autistic Disorder initially tend to respond poorly (or not at all) to secondary or social reinforcers (Lovaas, Schreibman, & Koegel, 1974). Secondary reinforcers have no rewarding qualities in and of themselves but come to be paired with more basic rewards and, thus, acquire rewarding qualities through association. Money, praise, and social interaction, for example, are secondary reinforcers. Primary reinforcers, on the other hand, have basic biological rewarding properties and, thus, do not have to be learned. Food and electric shock are examples of a primary reinforcer and a primary punisher, respectively. A second complicating factor in behavioral modification with children with Autistic Disorder is that they usually have deficits in the social learning modalities of observation, communication, and imitation. These deficits hinder modeling, demonstration, and verbal explanation of behavioral goals.

The goals that can be achieved with behavioral interventions are dependent, in part, on the level of intellectual functioning of the child. Children functioning intellectually in the severely/profoundly mentally retarded range (roughly corresponding to IQ < 40) may have more modest behavioral goals of basic self-care skills, compliance with basic commands, basic social interaction behaviors, and reduction of harmful behaviors. Children in higher IQ ranges (especially for IQ > 60 or 70) begin with similar modest goals but may also be expected in many cases to achieve goals such as higher language and social skills. Although it is important not to set goals too low, goals set too high will only frustrate and disappoint the parent, staff, and child (Newsom & Rincover, 1989).

Techniques for Reduction of Interfering and Dangerous Behavior

Regardless of which IQ group the child falls into, the first behaviors chosen for intervention are usually behaviors that are dangerous or that interfere with the learning of appropriate behaviors (Lovaas, 1987; Lovaas et al., 1974; Morgan, 1990). These are typically self-stimulating or self-injurious behaviors such as spinning, twirling, head banging, rocking, self-scratching, and self-hitting. The cause of such behavior is unknown, but it is usually reinforced by attention and sensory feedback (Lovaas et al., 1974).

Seven interventions are widely used to address these behaviors (Lovaas, 1987; Lovaas et al., 1974; Morgan, 1990). First, *time-out* is sometimes tried as an initial intervention. However, time-out is unsuccessful for many low-functioning children with Autistic Disorder because they do not mind separation from social contact. In higher-functioning children with Autistic Disorder, the time-out intervention may be sufficiently aversive to produce behavior change. The evaluation of whether time-out is effective is based on change in the children's behavior over a 1–2-week period of pairing time-out with self-stimulating or self-injurious behaviors. Time-out periods for children with Autistic Disorder may last from 5–10 minutes, with additional minutes given for noncompliance during time-out.

A second intervention, *differential reinforcement of other behaviors,* can be used to modify behaviors, as long as the reinforcer is powerful and salient. As noted previously, secondary reinforcers may not have an initial effect on the behavior of a child with Autistic Disorder. Primary reinforcers such as food (e.g., M&Ms), on the other hand, can sometimes encourage a desirable behavior. The behavior to be rewarded must be one that can substitute for or is incompatible with the undesirable behavior.

A third behavioral technique for children with Autistic Disorder, *positive practice,* involves repeatedly performing ("practicing") behaviors that are incompatible with the response. For example, the child who is head banging could repeatedly be required to hold his head absolutely still. Positive practice, however, is a huge strain on caretakers, who must usually force the child to engage in the practice behavior. Furthermore, because of the child's communication deficit, it is sometimes unclear whether he or she understands the goal of the intervention. Because positive practice can lead to physical battles, emotional upset, and possibly injury, it should be used judiciously.

Ignoring is a fourth technique for managing autistic behavior. Lovaas et al. (1974) present convincing data showing that ignoring self-stimulating behavior results in a reduction of such behavior. Unfortunately, it is difficult to identify the children that will respond to ignoring and those who will not. A basic rule is that if attention seeking is involved, ignoring *may* work. However, ignoring is often contraindicated if the child is hurting himself or herself, hurting another person, or destroying property.

Response prevention, a fifth technique for reducing dangerous or destructive behavior, involves actively intervening to prevent the child from performing the behavior. In most cases, this intervention involves the use of direct physical restraints or indirect clothing (or other material) restraints. An advantage of response prevention is that it prevents the dangerous behavior without presenting an aversive stimulus (other than the restraint itself). However, it can be exhausting or dangerous to parents or staff. Furthermore, the child could injure himself or herself in an attempt to escape, particularly when nonhuman physical restraints are used (e.g., material tied around the wrists). When response prevention is used, the child is given frequent opportunities to be out of the physical restraint. If the child does not engage in the dangerous behavior, the restraint is not replaced. However, if the child returns to the dangerous behavior following removal of the restraint, he or she is then placed back in the restraint.

Antecedent management (Appendix C), a sixth intervention for addressing dangerous behavior, involves removing the stimuli or situations that provoke the behavior. For example, if the behavior occurs only in a certain room (e.g., head banging on the brick of the fireplace), the child is not permitted to be in that room without supervision. Antecedent management is a useful technique for dangerous behaviors that occur only in well-defined situations that are infrequent and can be easily avoided or removed.

Finally, direct *punishment* is the most effective way to reduce self-stimulating or self-injurious behaviors (Lovaas et al., 1974). As with reinforcement, however, primary punishers must often be used because most secondary punishers have no meaning to the child with Autistic Disorder. Electric shock is one example of a primary punisher. Use of contingent electric shock typically results in rapid elimination of the problem behavior, but it is unacceptable to most parents and poses ethical problems. The only accepted use of electric shock for children with Autistic Disorder is in severe situations when the behavior is dangerous and when other interventions have been ineffective. Even in these cases, such procedures are best used only under supervision of the guardian and a human rights committee (Morgan, 1990). Some clinicians recommend an alternative punishment technique of saying "no" loudly, paired with a mild slap on the thigh (Lovaas, 1987). Although not as effective as shock, this technique does result in behavior change. The risk, however, of such a technique is that an angry or upset parent could use it inappropriately, indiscriminately, or with too much force. Such behavior may also induce aggression in a child with Autistic Disorder. Hence, this less objectionable punishment must be carefully used as well.

Teaching Learning Readiness Skills

After dangerous and interfering behaviors are brought under control, the child can be taught basic skills that form the building blocks for later learning. Among such skills are communication, attention, observation, imitation, compliance, and self-care. By mastering these learning readiness skills, the child will be better prepared to notice, acquire, and process incoming information from the environment. Rather than improving one specific behavior, this improved information acquisition and processing can help the child to learn many adaptive ways of behaving in the environment.

Lovaas et al. (1974) and Newsom and Rincover (1989) summarize several procedures for improving learning readiness. One such skill is *learning that adults are sources of contingent reward and punishment.* This may be accomplished by having the adult simply give the child a piece of candy whenever the child seeks proximity or basic interaction with the adult.

Another learning readiness skill is *attending to the adult.* Children with Autistic Disorder often do not observe or make eye contact with adults, which prevents them from further learning. Eye contact is encouraged by giving the child a piece of candy when the child happens to look at the adult. For children with extremely low initial frequencies of eye contact, an attractive object may be held in front of the adult while the adult makes an orienting request (e.g., saying "look!"), causing the child to look at the adult. The candy is then administered. Later, the object is still held and the orienting request is made, but the child must look at the adult's eyes to receive the reward. Finally, the object is gradually faded (e.g., moved a greater distance from the adult or exposed for a shorter duration) but the orienting request continues, and the child must make eye contact in response to the request alone. The attention response is then generalized to other people by allowing them to dispense the reinforcement.

Like attention, *compliance* is a very basic concept that must be taught to children with Autistic Disorder. Children with Autistic Disorder should first be taught to comply with very simple, single-step commands (sit, wait, come here) before they are asked to comply with more extensive requests. Newsom and Rincover (1989) and Lovaas (1987) suggest several ways to teach compliance: First, during 10-minute practice sessions, the child is asked to comply with a simple command about twice a minute. Compliance is rewarded with praise and a piece of candy. Noncompliance is ignored. In the case of a child who cannot perform the behavior even once, he or she may be physically guided through the behavior, or successive approximations may be rewarded. A second strategy is based on the assumption that noncompliance and escalation is an attempt to escape the situation. Hence, the child is not allowed to escape (which would reward the noncompliance if it were allowed to occur) until he or she complies. Instead of escape, the prompts and commands continue to occur during the noncompliance and escalation. A third strategy, for particularly resistant children, is the administration of a punishment such as a loud reprimand during noncompliance. However, the reprimand could soon lose its punishing status as the child habituates to it. Overall, reinforcement is most effective, but it requires considerable practice and patience.

A fourth learning readiness skill is *imitation*. Like attention and compliance, imitation is taught at a very basic level by pairing it with primary reinforcers. Initial behaviors to be imitated are simple gestures, which are immediately rewarded with a piece of candy and praise. Most children with Autistic Disorder, however, will either not spontaneously imitate or will only imitate randomly and sporadically. Two strategies to address this problem are to physically help the child imitate and to reward successive approximations to the behavior that the child is imitating. The adult must vary the gesture to be imitated, or the child will simply learn to perform a single gesture and not to imitate what is seen. Once simple imitation is learned, more complex imitation can be undertaken.

Finally, *language* is an extremely important learning skill, particularly when the goal is achievement of a near-normal level of functioning. Lovaas et al. (1974) describe a procedure in which language may be shaped in mute or near-mute children with Autistic Disorder. First, the child is reinforced with candy for any vocal utterance. Second, the child is reinforced only when the vocalizations follow the speech of the therapist. Third, the child is reinforced only when the vocalizations approximate the sound of the therapist. Fourth, the child is taught an increasing number of phonemes and to combine these phonemes into words. Once words are learned, the child is taught to use the words to label objects. Next, comprehension (as opposed to simply pairing words and objects) is encouraged by teaching the child to generalize the use of words. Finally, the use of sentences is taught by gradually encouraging the child to combine words in simple and meaningful ways (Lovaas et al., 1974).

Teaching Social Behaviors

Learning readiness skills may also be seen as very basic social behaviors. Building on these simple learned behaviors, behavior therapies for autism expand these rudimentary behaviors into approximations of appropriate social behaviors. Several social behaviors and concepts are key learning goals for the child with Autistic Disorder: proximity seeking, social reinforcement, modeling, affect, and play. In all cases, the desired behavior is operationally defined and paired with a reinforcer until the child is regularly performing it. If a child has trouble with initial trials, modeling or physically guiding the child through the behavior may be used. Eventually, as the child learns the more basic principles of social interaction, these are used to teach more complex principles, such as conversation. These more complex principles must be initially broken down into simple parts before growing into approximations of the ultimate goal (e.g., conversation of one sentence, then two, then three, and so on).

For example, social reinforcement is taught to the child with Autistic Disorder by pairing the social reinforcement with a more basic reinforcer. Initially, social reinforcers such as praise, social affection, and proximity have little or no value to the child with Autistic Disorder. However, primary reinforcers, such as food, fulfillment of needs/wants, and access to favored activities, have considerable meaning to the child. The first step in teaching social reinforcement, then, is to identify a social stimulus that is to be rewarding (e.g., a single praise word, such as *good;* or proximity to peers). Next, a primary reinforcer is identified, such that it can be easily paired with the social stimulus. Finally, a response of the child must be chosen (e.g., standing within 5 feet of a peer; or coming over to an adult when the word *good* is said). Then the social stimulus and primary reinforcer are paired in discrimination trials. That is, multiple events are allowed to happen in the child's environment, but the child is reinforced only after responding to the social stimulus (Lovaas, 1987; Newsom & Rincover, 1989).

To improve peer relationships, the child may be required to interact with a peer before an adult will give him or her access to a favored object or activity (Newsom & Rincover, 1989). Such trials must be repeatedly practiced for extended periods of time, and even then a lack of generalization and extinction are realistic risks. The risk of these problems may be lowered, however, by introducing multiple social stimuli (e.g., multiple adults saying "good") or by gradually reducing the reinforcement ratio (e.g., from every response to every fifth, every tenth, and so on) once the child has learned the basic principle.

Teaching Functional Language and Language Development

Koegel and Koegel (1996) propose a functional communication program that goes beyond the teaching of language as a learning readiness skill. Their language program is predicated on the assumptions that children with Autistic Disorder do not naturally solicit language learning experiences from their environment and that their disruptive behavior often serves a communicative function. To address these problems, children are taught to ask questions that allow them to learn about language through the naturally occurring events in their environment (self-initiated queries). For example, children are taught to ask questions such as "what," "where," and "whose." This learning takes place in a gamelike fashion, using exposure to preferred objects as reinforcers after children ask appropriate questions about the objects. Eventually, the children are rewarded for asking questions without prompting. By asking these questions, they become active participants in soliciting language learning experiences.

The second major component of Koegel and Koegel's program involves teaching children with Autistic Disorder to use communication to replace disruptive behavior. Parents and therapist first try to identify the function of disruptive behavior by recording antecedents and consequences of the behavior. Once the function is identified, parents then verbally label the function of the child's behavior immediately prior to or during disruptive behavior. Eventually, the child is taught to use language to describe the function or need that was previously being met by disruptive behavior. When parents respond by meeting the child's verbally labeled need, the function of the disruptive behavior is eliminated.

Koegel and Koegel (1996) describe an extensive plan for improving independent functional language skills. Their results indicate that children's language learning improves markedly with the training, and disruptive behaviors appear to decline. Other behavioral methods are used to enhance motivation and articulation, further improving the child's independent language functioning.

Teaching Pivotal Skills

Pivotal Response Training (PRT; Schreibman & Koegel, 1996; Schreibman & Pierce, 1993) aims to teach children with Autistic Disorder key skills that can be used to improve behavior and interaction across a wide variety of situations and behavior variations. Such an approach is hypothesized to improve the generalization of positive behaviors and to promote behavioral improvement when reinforcers (and parents) are not present. Three pivotal skills are targeted in PRT: motivation, responsivity to multiple cues, and self-management. Once these skills are learned, the child will be in a position to learn a variety of other adaptive behaviors.

The first pivotal skill taught in PRT is motivation. The PRT intervention program avoids the use of food reinforcers as motivators. Rather, the pivotal skill of motivation is taught with techniques such as giving the child choices in the environment, giving the child access to favored toys, reinforcing approximations/attempts resembling the target behavior, and repeatedly testing and rewarding the child for performance of overlearned tasks (to give success experiences). Parents also improve motivation by giving clear, brief, task-relevant instructions only when the child is paying attention.

A second pivotal skill, responsivity to multiple cues, involves attending to more than one characteristic of a stimulus (such as size, color, and texture) at a time. Schreibman and Pierce (1993) teach children to use multiple cues by giving trial problems in which two or more aspects of an object must be considered in order to solve the problem. For example, a child may be asked to pick the red cup from an array of a red pencil, a green cup, and a red cup. Both "red" and "cup" must be considered to solve the problem correctly. Correct responses are reinforced. The child learns to attend to multiple aspects of situations, improving attention to details and functioning in the complex social environment.

The final pivotal skill, self-management, consists of selecting a behavior, monitoring it, and giving reinforcement when goals are met. These components are initially completed by the parent, with a gradual transfer of responsibility to the child. Initially, the child is an active participant in the identification of target behaviors and reinforcers, with the parent guiding the process. In order to clearly describe the target behavior, parents are encouraged to identify for the child appropriate and inappropriate examples of the target behavior. For example, if loudness of voice is the target behavior, the parent may ask the child at various times if the child has used his or her "inside" (e.g., appropriate for inside settings) voice. The child is rewarded for accurate responses to the question. After the child has clearly mastered the identification of the target behavior, he or she is encouraged to keep track of positive and negative instances of the behavior, either casually or with a more formal (e.g., wrist counter) method. Again, accurate monitoring is reinforced. Finally, parental supervision, monitoring, and reinforcement are faded gradually as the child meets criteria for successful monitoring and implementation of the skill (Schreibman & Koegel, 1996).

PRT is appealing because it devotes constant attention to the generalization of learning to actual functioning across various settings in the environment. Because the program relies more on internal and/or social motivation, however, it may not be appropriate for low-functioning children or for children who have few reinforcers besides food (although Schreibman & Koegel, 1996, report success with some children who have IQ < 70). Nevertheless, the program has potential for higher-functioning children with Autistic Disorder and for children who have progressed through the early stages of behavioral management. Schreibman and Koegel (1996) describe a structured, 25-hour, parent-training treatment plan for teaching PRT.

Evaluation of Behavioral Interventions for Autism

Studies of both PRT and Lovaas's behavioral program have reported significant improvement in the behavior of children with Autistic Disorder, although Lovaas's program has received somewhat more empirical support to date (Rogers, 1998). Several differences exist between these behavioral programs. One major difference is that PRT emphasizes parents as the deliverers of the intervention, whereas Lovaas has typically used trained therapists. PRT also focuses more on general skills for teaching specific behaviors, as opposed to focusing on the specific behaviors themselves.

Schreibman and Koegel (1996) report that families learning the pivotal skills of motivation and responsivity engaged in more family leisure activities and showed more positive affect than families who were teaching individual target behaviors to their child with Autistic Disorder. Children exposed to PRT also showed improvements in behavior and language both with and without their parent present. Additionally, the pivotal skill of self-management was found to reduce stereotypic behaviors, with some evidence of generalization across settings and behaviors.

Working with all but the most profoundly impaired children with Autistic Disorder, Lovaas has presented results from an intensive program that showed that 47% of his autistic sample achieved "normal" (IQ > 90, placement in normal first grade class) intellectual and educational functioning. IQ scores for Lovaas's treatment group were, on average, 30 points higher than controls (Lovaas, 1987). These gains were maintained at follow-up several years later (McEachin, Smith, & Lovaas, 1993). Children with higher pretreatment mental age had better outcome, suggesting that this treatment may be more effective for children with higher IQ; nevertheless, the mean IQ for children in the study was only 53 (Lovaas, 1987). Rogers (1998) reviews several other studies showing similar positive outcomes using variations of Lovaas's program or similar programs based on applied behavior analysis (ABA). In addition to higher IQ, intervention prior to age 5 appears to be related to more positive outcomes from behaviorally based programs (Rogers, 1998).

If there is a downside to intensive, therapist-delivered behavioral programs, it is their time-consuming, expensive, and intensive nature. Lovaas (1987) estimates that his program costs $40,000 per child, but he notes that the cost of lifelong institutionalization is in the millions of dollars per child. Children are identified before age 3½ or 4, and they are given 40 hours per week of intensive therapy by trained therapists for at least 2 years. Parents are also trained and expected to work intensively with their children. Children must be enrolled in preschools with teachers willing to implement the behavioral program (Lovaas, 1987).

Although they are time-consuming and expensive, behavioral techniques are currently a primary treatment for autism. In many cases, the intervention is too intensive and time-consuming for the parents to manage alone, and the child must be placed in a program to obtain comprehensive behavioral treatment. Day-treatment programs or school-based programs may be effective for higher-functioning children with Autistic Disorder, but a full-time residential placement may be necessary for more severely retarded, dangerous, or disruptive children with Autistic Disorder. Regardless of what type of program is chosen, an intensive, behavioral focus is extremely important, particularly for the younger child. "Warehouses," which simply monitor the children and keep them out of trouble, result in more negative outcomes. In general, psychiatric hospitalization is warranted only in the case of acute, severe behavioral problems or medication management problems. Most psychiatric hospitals cannot provide the years of treatment needed for the child with Autistic Disorder.

Medication

Medication is usually prescribed for associated features of autism, such as dangerous behavior, psychotic behavior, aggressiveness, hyperactivity, sleep disturbance, and lack of behavioral control. By addressing these problems, the child is often in a better position to learn from the environment or from a behavior modification plan. Social behavior and communications may then result, not directly from the medication but indirectly from the child's ability to better engage the environment while taking the medication.

The medications most commonly used with children with Autistic Disorder are neuroleptics. These medications are generally used for purposes of calming or slowing overly active, aggressive, self-injurious, or "out of control" children. Haloperidol (Haldol) and thioridazine (Mellaril) are frequently prescribed for aggressive-active children with Autistic Disorder, although development of tardive dyskinesia should be watched carefully (Ornitz, 1989). Fenfluramine has also produced some positive results in controlling hyperactivity and stereotypic behavior (Morgan, 1990). More recently, risperidone has produced remarkable improvement in some children with Autistic Disorder, and large-scale studies with risperidone are forthcoming. Conventional sedatives and stimulants rarely have a positive effect on symptoms (Ornitz, 1989).

Overall, it appears that medication is effective for controlling aggression and hyperactivity in many children with Autistic Disorder. Risperidone, haloperidol, or fenfluramine should be strongly considered for children with extremely disruptive or dangerous behaviors.

Referral to Other Professionals

Speech/Language Therapy

Because language deficits are a hallmark of Autistic Disorder, children with the disorder often benefit from extra attention with learning and using language. Understanding words and communication, using communication to accomplish goals, and understanding the communication of others are examples of intervention targets commonly addressed in speech/language therapy. Improved articulation, sign language, and use of nonverbal communication

TABLE 10.4   Treatment Options for Autistic Disorder

1. Family Interventions
   a. Parent Psychotherapy
      (1) Education about autism causes and treatments
      (2) Parenting stress management
2. Behavioral Interventions
   a. Reduce interfering and dangerous behavior
      (1) Time-out
      (2) Differential reinforcement of other behaviors
      (3) Positive practice
      (4) Ignoring
      (5) Response prevention
      (6) Antecedent management
      (7) Punishment techniques
   b. Teach learning readiness skills
      (1) Learn that adults are sources of reinforcement
      (2) Attend to the adult
      (3) Learn to comply with requests
      (4) Imitation
      (5) Adaptive use of language
   c. Teach social behaviors
   d. Teach functional language
      (1) Self-initiated queries
      (2) Replacement of disruptive behavior with functional expressive language
   e. Teach pivotal skills
      (1) Motivation
      (2) Attention and response to multiple cues
      (3) Self-management
3. Medication
   a. Risperidone
   b. Haloperidol
4. Referral to Other Professionals
   a. Speech-language therapy
   b. Sensory integration training
      (1) Auditory integration training

Note: This outline of options summarizes major treatments covered in the text. Specific treatments are often combined into an intervention package. Refer to the text for additional descriptions of each treatment. This table is not necessarily an exhaustive list of all treatments available.

may be additional goals for children with severe language impairment. With improvement in language expression and usage comes improvement in behavior and social function.

In addition to language learning and usage experiences, speech/language therapy also may involve the use of devices to promote understanding and communication. For example, schedule displays, which show a series of planned events with pictures, are used to show a daily schedule or sequence of events to the child with Autistic Disorder. A communication board (which may be computer-based) uses pictures to allow the child to communicate or to make choices. Involvement of a speech-language pathologist can help with the design and implementation of these language-based interventions.

Sensory Integration Training

Sensory integration training (SIT; Ayres, 1979) is sometimes suggested for children who show unusual reactivity to stimuli and/or poor processing of incoming sensory information. SIT involves efforts to expose the child to sensory experiences in a way that helps the child to modulate the incoming sensory information while processing it more accurately and usefully. SIT therapists typically assume that a central nervous system (CNS) dysfunction causes sensory integration problems in the first place, and SIT acts to reorganize and rehabilitate the CNS to process sensory information in a more organized and accurate way. Therapeutic exposure to multisensory information (while encouraging an organized and appropriate response) allows this rehabilitation to occur. Typically, SIT is conducted by an occupational therapist or physical therapist with specialized experience in SIT techniques.

One type of SIT that has been suggested for use with children with Autistic Disorder is auditory integration training (AIT; Berard, 1993). Proponents of AIT recommend its use for children with Autistic Disorder who have difficulty modulating and interpreting auditory stimulation. Hypersensitivity to different sound frequencies, differences in processing bilateral hearing sensation, and disorganized processing of auditory stimuli are examples of problems that AIT is hypothesized to correct. AIT involves audiometric testing followed by a program of listening to music. The frequency of the music is varied and filtered (using an AIT device) based on the results of the audiometric test to improve the child's processing of sounds across the frequency spectrum. In addition to Autistic Disorder, AIT has been used for learning disorders and other psychiatric disorders.

AIT is typically conducted by an audiologist, speech-language pathologist, or occupational therapist with specialized AIT training. Some preliminary research has shown AIT to improve behavioral and intellectual-language functioning in children with Autistic Disorder, although AIT may not accomplish more than any exposure to patterned sound or music (Bettison, 1996). Concern has been raised about the safety of the AIT devices for hearing, but there is not sufficient research to draw any definitive conclusions about safety. Like SIT, AIT has not received substantial empirical verification and, therefore, remains a topic for additional efficacy research.

■ References

American Psychiatric Association. (1994). *Diagnostic and statistical manual of mental disorders, fourth edition.* Washington, DC: Author.

Ayres, J. (1979). *Sensory integration and the child.* Los Angeles: Western Psychological Services.

Bayley, N. (1993). *Bayley Scales of Infant Development: Second Edition.* San Antonio: Psychological Corporation.

Beery, K. E. (1997). *Developmental Test of Visual-Motor Integration (VMI) Administration, Scoring, and Teaching Manual* (4th ed., revised). Parsippany, NJ: Modern Curriculum Press.

Berard, G. (1993). *Hearing equals behavior.* New Canaan, CT: Keats Publishing.

Bettison, S. (1996). The long-term effects of auditory training on children with autism. *Journal of Autism and Developmental Disorders, 26,* 361–374.

Brown, L., Sherbenou, R. J., & Johnsen, S. K. (1997). *Test of Nonverbal Intelligence* (3rd ed.). Austin, TX: Pro-Ed.

Delis, D.C., Kramer, J. H., Kaplan, E., & Ober, B. A. (1994). *California Verbal Learning Test Children's Version.* San Antonio, TX: Psychological Corporation.

Dunn, L. M., & Dunn, L. M. (1997). *Peabody Picture Vocabulary Test* (3rd ed.). Circle Pines, MN: American Guidance Service.

Forman, S. G. (1993). *Coping skills interventions for children and adolescents.* San Francisco: Jossey-Bass

Freeman, B. J., Ritvo, E. R., Guthrie, D., Schroth, P., & Ball, J. (1978). The Behavior Observation Scale for Autism: Initial methodology, data analysis, and preliminary findings on 89 children. *Journal of the American Academy of Child Psychiatry, 17,* 576–588.

Freeman, B. J., Schroth, P., Ritvo, E., Guthrie, D., & Wake, L. (1980). The Behavior Observation Scale for Autism (BOS): Initial results of factor analysis. *Journal of Autism and Developmental Disorders, 10,* 343–346.

Ghaziuddin, M., & Gerstein, L. (1996). Pedantic speaking style differentiates Asperger Syndrome from High-Functioning Autism. *Journal of Autism and Developmental Disorders, 26,* 585–595.

Kanner, L. (1943). Autistic disturbances of affective contact. *Nervous Child, 2,* 217–250.

Kaplan, H. I., Sadock, B. J., & Grebb, J. A. (1994). *Kaplan and Sadock's synopsis of psychiatry: Behavioral sciences, clinical psychiatry* (7th ed.). Baltimore, MD: Williams & Wilkins.

Kaufman, A. S., & Kaufman, N. L. (1990). *Kaufman Brief Intelligence Test.* Circle Pines, MN: American Guidance Service.

Klin, A., Sparrow, S. S., Volkmar, F. R., Cicchetti, D. V., & Rourke, B. P. (1995). Asperger syndrome. In B. P. Rourke (Ed.), *Syndrome of nonverbal learning disabilities: Neurodevelopmental manifestations.* New York: Guilford.

Koegel, L. K., & Koegel, R. L. (1996). The child with autism as an active communicative partner: Child-initiated strategies for improving communication and reducing behavior problems. In E. D. Hibbs & P. S. Jensen (Eds.), *Psychosocial treatments for child and adolescent disorders: Empirically based strategies for clinical practice.* Washington, DC: American Psychological Association.

Krug, D. A., Arick, J., & Almond, P. (1980). Behavior checklist for identifying severely handicapped individuals with high levels of autistic behavior. *Journal of Child Psychology and Psychiatry, 21,* 221–229.

LeCroy, C. W. (1994). Social skills training. In C. W. LeCroy (Ed.), *Handbook of child and adolescent treatment manuals.* New York: Lexington.

Lotter, V. (1966). Epidemiology of autistic conditions in young children: I. Prevalence. *Social Psychiatry, 1,* 124–137.

Lovaas, O. I. (1979). Contrasting illness and behavioral models for the treatment of autistic children: A historical perspective. *Journal of Autism and Developmental Disorders, 9,* 315–323.

Lovaas, O. I. (1987). Behavioral treatment and normal educational and intellectual functioning in young autistic children. *Journal of Consulting and Clinical Psychology, 55,* 3–9.

Lovaas, O. I., Schreibman, L., & Koegel, R. L. (1974). A behavior modification approach to the treatment of autistic children. *Journal of Autism and Childhood Schizophrenia, 4,* 111–129.

McEachin, J. J., Smith, T., & Lovaas, O. I. (1993). Long-term outcome for children with autism who received early intensive behavioral treatment. *American Journal on Mental Retardation, 97,* 359–372.

Meyers, J. E., & Meyers, K. R. (1995). *Rey Complex Figure Test and Recognition Trial.* Odessa, FL: Psychological Assessment Resources.

Morgan, S. B. (1988). Diagnostic assessment of autism: A review of objective scales. *Journal of Psychoeducational Assessment, 6,* 139–151.

Morgan, S. B. (1990). Early childhood autism: Current perspectives on definition, assessment, and treatment. In S. B. Morgan & T. M. Okwumabua (Eds.), *Child and adolescent disorders: Developmental and health psychology perspectives* (pp. 3–45). Hillsdale, NJ: Erlbaum.

Newsom, C., & Rincover, A. (1989). Autism. In E. J. Mash & R. A. Barkley (Eds.), *Treatment of childhood disorders* (pp. 286–346). New York: Guilford.

Ornitz, E. M. (1989). Autism. In C. G. Last & M. Hersen (Eds.), *Handbook of child psychiatric diagnosis* (pp. 233–278). New York: Wiley.

Ornitz, E. M., & Ritvo, E. R. (1976). The syndrome of autism: A critical review. *The American Journal of Psychiatry, 133,* 609–621.

Rimland, B. (1971). The differentiation of childhood psychoses: An analysis of checklists for 2218 psychotic children. *Journal of Autism and Childhood Schizophrenia, 1,* 161–174.

Ritvo, E., & Freeman, B. J. (1978). Current research on the syndrome of autism. *Journal of Autism and Childhood Schizophrenia, 8,* 162–167.

Rogers, S. J. (1998). Empirically supported comprehensive treatments for young children with autism. *Journal of Clinical Child Psychology, 27,* 168–179.

Rourke, B. P. (1989). *Nonverbal learning disabilities: The syndrome and the model.* New York: Guilford.

Rourke, B. P. (1995a). Introduction: The NLD syndrome and the white matter model. In B. P. Rourke (Ed.), *Syndrome of nonverbal learning disabilities: Neurodevelopmental manifestations.* New York: Guilford.

Rourke, B. P. (1995b). Treatment program for the child with NLD. In B. P. Rourke (Ed.), *Syndrome of nonverbal learning disabilities: Neurodevelopmental manifestations.* New York: Guilford.

Ruttenberg, B. A., Dratman, M. L., Fraknoi, J., & Wenar, C. (1966). An instrument for evaluating autistic children. *Journal of the American Academy of Child Psychiatry, 5,* 453–478.

Schopler, E., Reichler, R. J., DeVellis, R. F., & Daly, K. (1980). Toward objective classification of childhood autism: Childhood Autism Rating Scale (CARS). *Journal of Autism and Developmental Disorders, 10,* 91–103.

Schreibman, L., & Koegel, R. (1996). Fostering self-management: Parent-delivered Pivotal Response Training for children with Autistic Disorder. In E. D. Hibbs & P. S. Jensen (Eds.), *Psychosocial treatments for child and adolescent disorders: Empirically based strategies for clinical practice.* Washington, DC: American Psychological Association.

Schreibman, L., & Pierce, K. (1993). Achieving greater generalization of treatment effects in children with autism: Pivotal response training and self-management. *The Clinical Psychologist, 46,* 184–191.

Sheslow, D., & Adams, W. (1990). *Wide Range Assessment of Memory and Learning.* Wilmington, DE: Wide Range, Inc.

Teal, M. B., & Wiebe, M. J. (1986). A validity analysis of selected instruments used to assess autism. *Journal of Autism and Developmental Disorders, 16,* 485–494.

Wenar, C., & Ruttenberg, B. A. (1976). The use of BRI-AAC for evaluating therapeutic effectiveness. *Journal of Autism and Childhood Schizophrenia, 6,* 175–191.

Wing, L. (1981). Asperger's syndrome: A clinical account. *Psychological Medicine, 11,* 115–130.

Wing, L., Yeates, S. R., Brierley, L. M., & Gould, J. (1976). The prevalence of early childhood autism: Comparison of administrative and epidemiological studies. *Psychological Medicine, 6,* 89–100.

CHAPTER 11

Learning, Motor Skills, and Communication Disorders

Specific (as opposed to pervasive) developmental disorders are coded in three broad areas in DSM-IV, all of which fall on Axis I: Motor Skills Disorder (Developmental Coordination Disorder), Communication Disorders (Expressive Language Disorder, Mixed Receptive-Expressive Language Disorder, Phonological Disorder, and Stuttering), and Learning Disorders (Reading Disorder, Mathematics Disorder, and Disorder of Written Expression).

■ Motor Skills Disorder

□ CLINICAL DESCRIPTION

Only one motor skills disorder is identified in DSM-IV, and there is no provision for a "not otherwise specified" category. Developmental Coordination Disorder is assigned to children who perform substantially below their expected level on daily tasks that involve coordinated movement. The expected level of coordination depends on the child's chronological age and intelligence. DSM-IV does not provide extensive criteria on how to judge a person's coordination level, although factors such as developmental milestones, handwriting, and sports are suggested as a basis for judgment. Developmental Coordination Disorder can only be diagnosed when the coordination problem significantly affects the child's daily activities.

□ ASSESSMENT PATTERNS

Assessment of the child with a motor skills disorder requires, at a minimum, measures of IQ and motor skills. Assessment of IQ is relatively straightforward and may be accomplished with one of the major intelligence tests (see Chapter 1). IQ scores provide a benchmark for intellectual development and possible global delays that would be better explained by a more pervasive disorder such as mental retardation. IQ subtests that involve a strong motor component should not be used to estimate the child's intellectual functioning, as these will be confounded with the child's motor skills deficit. Hence, many of the nonverbal subtests of the Wechsler scales and other IQ tests should be interpreted with caution. Verbal scale scores, on the other hand, are usually unaffected by motor skills and may be a better index of intellectual functioning. Nonverbal tests with less of a motor component include the Matrix Reasoning subtest of the WASI, the K-BIT Matrices subtest, and the Test of Nonverbal Intelligence—3 (Brown, Sherbenou, & Johnsen, 1997).

Assessment of motor skills, on the other hand, is less well defined. Because DSM-IV does not require the administration of a standardized motor skills test, the documentation of a motor skills deficit may be accomplished by interviewing the parent and observing the child's movement on fine and gross motor tasks. Asking the child to walk, stand on one leg, skip, hop, jump, walk with eyes closed, handle objects of various sizes, and write something are all examples of tasks that can indicate coordination problems.

If a more standardized measure of motor ability is desired, several tests may provide relevant information. The McCarthy Scales of Children's Abilities (McCarthy, 1972), a standardized, normed measure of cognitive abilities in children aged 2½ to 8½ years, provides both an overall estimate of cognitive ability and measures of motor coordination. Hence, it can be used to obtain the baseline level of intelligence and the degree of motor coordination in a single assessment. Because the McCarthy is standardized and provides normative data, the child's normative motoric ability relative to other abilities can readily be obtained. Children who score substantially lower on the Motor scale of the McCarthy relative to the Verbal scale, Perceptual-Performance scale, Quantitative scale, and Memory scale are likely to have a Developmental Coordination Disorder. The number of standard score points that represents "substantially lower" performance is left to the clinician. A 15–20-point difference is likely to be meaningful. One caution in the use of the McCarthy is the age of the test, with norms that are several decades old.

The Developmental Test of Visual-Motor Coordination (VMI; Beery, 1997) is another motor skills test. The VMI measures the child's ability to copy various designs. To help with interpretation, the VMI also includes subtests that are focused on visual perception alone (no motor coordination skills required) and motor coordination alone (minimal visual-perception skills required). VMI scores may indicate fine motor coordination problems, especially with using a writing tool.

The Bruininks-Oseretsky Test of Motor Proficiency (Bruininks, 1978) is a comprehensive test of motor functioning for children age 4 to 14 years. Subtests of the Bruininks-Oseretsky measure Gross Motor Skills (yielding a Gross Motor Composite, consisting of the Running Speed and Agility [shuttle run], Balance [stand on one leg, perform other walking balance activities], Bilateral Coordination [move hands, arms, legs, and feet in various synchronized movements], and Strength [jumping, sit-ups, push-ups] subtests) and Fine Motor Skills (yielding a Fine Motor Composite, consisting of the Response Speed [catching a falling stick], Visual-Motor Control [paper cutting, copying, drawing within lines], and Upper Limb Speed and Dexterity [hand and finger speed and dexterity] subtests). An overall battery composite is derived from the Gross Motor Skills, Fine Motor Skills, and Upper Limb Coordination (visual-motor coordination and speed of movements of arms, hands, and fingers) subtests. A short form of the Bruininks-Oseretsky yields a single score of motor proficiency in less than half of the time of the total battery. The Bruininks-Oseretsky is helpful for obtaining an extensive and rigorous standardized battery of gross and fine motor skills scores.

If the clinician is unable to test the child or wants parental interview data, the VABS includes a Motor Skills scale that may indicate the presence of coordination problems. Regardless of what method is used to indicate the coordination deficit, the deficit must be manifest in daily living for the Developmental Coordination Disorder to be diagnosed.

☐ TREATMENT OPTIONS

Treatment of a child with Developmental Coordination Disorder requires extensive consultation and referral to other professionals. First, the child should be evaluated by a pediatrician for possible organic contributors to the coordination problem. Referrals to physical therapists, occupational therapists, or to physicians specializing in motor deficits are also indicated. In many cases, occupational therapy services are available through the school system, so the child should be brought to the attention of special education authorities. In addition to making appropriate referrals, the mental health clinician's role in the process is to recommend daily activities that can enhance coordination learning and to monitor any ill effects of the coordination problem on psychological-emotional functioning.

■ Communication Disorders

☐ CLINICAL DESCRIPTION

Diagnostic Considerations

The communication disorders involve deficits in oral production and/or language comprehension ability, which must be of sufficient severity to interfere with daily functioning. For the expressive or receptive language disorders, standardized test data are required. A communication disorder cannot be diagnosed when the symptoms are exclusively a result of a pervasive developmental disorder, mental retardation, impoverished environment, or a physical condition. Disorders that involve the comprehension or production of language are sometimes also caused aphasias, dysphasias, or language impairment.

Expressive Language Disorder (ELD) involves deficits in the expression of language. These deficits must be documented by expressive language test scores that are substantially lower than scores on tests of nonverbal intelligence and receptive language. The magnitude of discrepancy required for diagnosis is not specified. Children with ELD have a variety of presentations. Some have a restricted vocabulary when talking, using overly simple words for their age. Other children with ELD manifest deficits in grammar, misusing sentence structure, word placement, or tense when they express themselves orally. A final common presentation of ELD is word-finding difficulty. Children with this latter difficulty speak haltingly because they cannot seem to find the words to express their thoughts. When the missing words are provided for the child, the child recognizes them. Often, the child is able to use simple language without word finding difficulty, but more complex words present greater problems. Estimates of the prevalence of ELD are in the 3–5% range (American Psychiatric Association, 1994).

Mixed Receptive-Expressive Language Disorder (MLD) is diagnosed when the child's receptive and expressive language abilities are delayed. As with ELD, MLD requires administration of expressive language, receptive language, and nonverbal intelligence tests. Scores in the expressive and receptive language areas must be lower than the nonverbal intelligence score. Again, the magnitude of the difference is not specified in DSM-IV. Children with MLD resemble those with ELD in their oral-verbal presentation. However, superimposed on the expressive language deficits are problems in the understanding of vocabulary and/or sentence structure or syntax. Hence, the child's comprehension lags as well as language production. MLD is less common than ELD, with estimated prevalence of less than 3% (American Psychiatric Association, 1994).

Phonological Disorder (PD) is diagnosed in children who do not articulate appropriate sounds for their age. Unlike ELD and MLD, a standardized test is not required for diagnosis, although either structured observation or testing can be helpful. Children with PD may be unable to produce certain speech sounds, although a more common presentation is the slurring or substitution of sounds. For example, the child may use the /f/ sound instead of the correct /th/ sound, saying "free" instead of "three." It is important to note the distinction between PD, which is a disorder of sound *production,* and some types of reading disorders, which are disorders of sound (phonological) *recognition or awareness.* Children with PD may or may not have problems with phonological awareness; conversely, children with deficits in phonological awareness may have no difficulty with sound production. Hence, clinicians should carefully evaluate if a phonological problem is one of awareness and/or production. If a PD is associated with a deficit in phonological awareness, dyslexia (reading disorder) is a risk. Severe PD is associated with a higher risk of reading disorder and spelling problems (Pennington, 1991). PD is rare in older children, although it may affect as many as 3% of children under age 7 (American Psychiatric Association, 1994).

Finally, stuttering is characterized by halting speech in which words and sounds are repeated, prolonged, or separated many times throughout the oral speech pattern. Children who stutter sometimes try to avoid their problem by interrupting the speech of difficult words or by substituting other words in the place of words that they have trouble pronouncing. They may have difficulty finding the word they want to say, although more often they know what they want to say but have trouble saying it.

Stuttering is often embarrassing to children and misunderstood by adults, who may take it as a sign of developmental delay or retardation. In fact, there is no evidence that stuttering is associated with dyslexia (Pennington, 1991). Stuttering may disappear in certain situations, such as when singing or talking to a doll. Teasing and embarrassment are common, and social withdrawal is a significant risk. Estimated prevalence in children under age 12 is 1%, decreasing with age.

Etiology

Although knowledge about the etiology of the communication disorders is not definitive at this point, most theories focus on neurological explanations. Dysfunction of the temporal lobes and planum temporale has been suggested as responsible for language disorders because these brain areas are responsible for language comprehension (especially Wernicke's area), phonological processing, expressive language, and speech (especially Broca's area). Language processing also involves activity and communication among multiple brain areas, so problems that interfere with this communication may cause language deficits (Teeter & Semrud-Clikeman, 1997).

☐ ASSESSMENT PATTERNS

Cognitive Assessment

Although intellectual assessment is required only for ELD and MLD, it is generally wise to obtain IQ and specific cognitive information on any child with a suspected communication disorder. These data can assist the clinician in ruling out or confirming the effects of other cognitive factors on the language problem. One of the Wechsler intelligence scales or the SB:FE is usually most appropriate for the intellectual assessment. Most children with communication disorders will score in the low average to normal ranges on overall measures of IQ, although the distribution spans from mentally deficient to very superior.

The Wechsler Performance IQ or SB:FE Abstract/Visual Reasoning Area Scores may be used as the measure of "nonverbal intelligence" for diagnosis of ELD and MLD. Other intelligence tests that focus exclusively on nonverbal functioning may also be used to obtain an estimate of nonverbal intelligence. These include the Matrices subtest of the K-BIT, the Test of Nonverbal Intelligence—Third Edition (TONI-3; Brown et al., 1997), the Leiter International Performance Scale—II (Roid & Miller, 1997), the Comprehensive Test of Nonverbal Intelligence (Hammill, Pearson, & Wiederholt, 1996), and the Universal Nonverbal Intelligence Test (UNIT; Bracken & McCallum, 1998), all of which provide reliable, valid estimates of a child's nonverbal reasoning and other nonverbal cognitive skills.

On the Wechsler scales or SB:FE, specific verbal subtest scores may be examined to document deficits in expressive and receptive language ability. On the Wechsler scales, children with ELD and MLD often have lower scores on subtests that call for extensive use of expressive language, such as Vocabulary and Comprehension. Information and Similarities, which call for less expression, may be slightly higher. Furthermore, the child with ELD/MLD typically has a higher Performance than Verbal IQ. The SB:FE Vocabulary, Comprehension, and Absurdities subtests use receptive language (e.g., pointing to pictures) items for lower age ranges and expressive language (e.g., oral expression) for higher age ranges. Hence, their interpretation varies based on the age of the child. For children older than 6, these three tests primarily reflect expressive language and are likely to be affected in the child with ELD or MLD.

An achievement test is another common component of a testing battery for a possible communication disorder. In addition to assisting in the understanding of the communication disorder per se, an achievement test can help to identify other problems, particularly in the learning area. Many items of the Knowledge subtests of the WJ-R call for the use of expressive language in response to pictures. The child's responses to these items can be used as additional data concerning the presence of an MLD or ELD. Likewise, the WIAT Oral Expression and Listening Comprehension subtests measure more complex and elaborate components of expressive language and receptive language, respectively. The WJ-R Word Attack supplemental subtest is very helpful for identifying children with PD who also have problems with phonological awareness (and, therefore, risk for reading disorder).

Over all, the child with ELD may be expected to show low scores on the Wechsler Vocabulary and Comprehension subtests, expressive picture vocabulary tests, and the WIAT

Oral Expression test, with higher scores on receptive vocabulary tests, the WIAT Listening Comprehension test, and measures of nonverbal ability (e.g., Performance IQ or matrix reasoning tests). The child with MLD will show low scores on all of the foregoing tests except for nonverbal ability measures. Some discrepancy in this testing pattern is expected, but the overall impression is one of expressive and/or receptive language deficit.

Behavioral Assessment

Most of the major broad-band behavior checklists do not include scales specifically designed to measure learning, motor, or communication disorders. However, because communication disorders can be stressful and frustrating to children and families, administration of the Achenbach, Conners', SI-4, and/or BASC scales may be warranted to rule out associated child or family problems. Additionally, children with MLD and ELD frequently have difficulty with self-report questionnaires. Lack of understanding of items, socially desirable responding, and inconsistent responding are seen with some regularity when such children are asked to complete a written questionnaire. Hence, results of such tests should be interpreted cautiously, and validity scales should be inspected carefully.

Syndrome-Specific Tests

Receptive Vocabulary Measures

Although the broad cognitive and achievement tests contain some verbal items, more focused testing of language and communication skills may help with the specific documentation of expressive and receptive language deficits. The Test of Auditory Comprehension of Language—Revised (TACL-R; Carrow-Woolfolk, 1985) and Peabody Picture Vocabulary Test—Third Edition (PPVT-III; Dunn & Dunn, 1997) are individually administered, standardized, normed measures of receptive vocabulary. For both tests, the child is shown a group of pictures and asked to point to the picture that best fits a word or sentence. No verbal response is required. The PPVT-III and TACL-R test the child's ability to comprehend verbally presented information and to match this information with visual stimuli. Because they require no verbal production, they are relatively "pure" measures of receptive vocabulary. Both tests provide an overall receptive vocabulary score using a mean of 100 and a standard deviation of 15. The TACL-R provides additional scores for Word Classes and Relations (mostly simple nouns, verbs, adjectives, and some word relations represented in pictoral form), Grammatical Morphemes (short sentences in which a grammatical concept is represented on the picture), and Elaborated Sentences (more complex sentence themes shown on the picture). Children with ELD typically score in average ranges on the PPVT-III and TACL-R, or their scores on these scales are substantially higher than their scores on expressive vocabulary measures. Children with MLD show deficits on the PPVT-III and TACL-R that are consistent with their expressive language deficits but discrepant with their nonverbal ability.

Unlike the TACL-R and the PPVT-III, the Token Test for Children (DiSimoni, 1978) is a measure of receptive language that focuses on the child's comprehension, memory, and ability to respond to auditory commands. Children are told verbally to complete various tasks in sequence, requiring attention to stimuli, understanding the verbal command, behavior consistent with the verbal command, and memory of the verbal command. Poor performance on the Token Test may suggest receptive language weaknesses and possibly an MLD.

Expressive Vocabulary Measures

In many cases, expressive vocabulary deficits are adequately documented with the Vocabulary and Comprehension subtests of the Wechsler scales. However, clinicians desiring a more detailed view of expressive vocabulary may give an expressive picture vocabulary test such as the Expressive One-Word Picture Vocabulary Test (EOWPVT; Gardner, 1990), Expressive Vocabulary Test (EVT, Williams, 1997), or Vocabulary subtest of the K-BIT. Each of these tests presents the child with a picture, and the child must name the subject depicted. Virtually all pictures may be identified with a single word. For the EVT, the examiner gives the child a synonym for the picture, and the child must provide another name for the picture. On the other hand, the K-BIT Vocabulary test includes a "definitions" component that can be affected by spelling skills. Expressive picture vocabulary tests are advantageous for assessing children who have problems understanding verbal questions (such as those used on the Wechsler Vocabulary subtest) and children with word-finding difficulties. Unlike verbal subscales on more extensive intelligence tests (e.g., the Wechsler scales), expressive picture vocabulary tests require only single-word or very brief answers. Thus, they measure more unelaborate, discrete expressive (single-word) verbal skills as opposed to tests that measure more elaborate, extended (explanatory sentences) expressive verbal skills.

In addition to tests that focus on expressive or receptive vocabulary skills, several tests measure various characteristics of expressive and receptive language in a single battery. Examples of these tests include the Clinical Evaluation of Language Fundamentals—Third Edition (Semel, Wiig, & Secord, 1995) and the Test of Word Knowledge (Wiig & Secord, 1992). Both of these batteries yield measures of receptive and expressive language.

Articulation and Auditory Discrimination Tests

Rather than focusing on language comprehension or expression, the Goldman-Fristoe Test of Articulation (GFTA; Goldman & Fristoe, 1986) and the Goldman-Fristoe-Woodcock Diagnostic Auditory Discrimination Test (GFWADT; Goldman, Fristoe, & Woodcock, 1974) measure more discrete and primary characteristics of speech and auditory function, respectively. The GFTA is a measure of speech articulation that can be helpful in identifying a PD. The GFWADT measures speech-sound discrimination and can, therefore, be helpful in ruling out this process in a language disorder.

☐ TREATMENT OPTIONS

Children with communication disorders should be evaluated by medical, speech, hearing, and educational personnel in addition to the mental health clinician. Therefore, the first intervention is often to seek consultation and assistance from professionals in these areas. Speech and language therapy is necessary for children with a communication disorder. Special educational interventions, enrichment programs, and tutoring are indicated for children with ELD and MLD. The case management of the actual communication disorder treatment frequently occurs in the speech/language or educational setting.

Long-term involvement of the mental health clinician with a child with a communication disorder usually occurs only when the child has a concurrent behavioral-emotional disorder or when ongoing testing is needed. In some cases, behavioral-emotional problems are related to the child's difficulty with communication. In other cases, the child's behavior problems co-occur with the communication disorder but do not appear to be causally related to it. Treatment for co-occurring or associated behavior problems sometimes must be modified to accommodate the child's communication problem.

■ Learning Disorders

□ CLINICAL DESCRIPTION

Diagnostic Considerations

DSM-IV recognizes three specific learning disorders and allows for a "Not Otherwise Specified" designation for other disorders of learning. Reading (Reading Disorder), mathematics (Mathematics Disorder), and writing (Disorder of Written Expression) areas are given their own diagnostic categories. In each case, the skill in question must be tested by an individually administered, standardized test of achievement in that area. The score obtained on that test must be substantially lower than the score that would be expected given the person's age, education, and intelligence. Typically, this "expected" score is obtained from an individually administered, standardized IQ test such as a Wechsler scale. The IQ-achievement discrepancy is diagnostic of a learning disorder because it implies that the child is not assimilating academic information at a rate consistent with his or her intellectual ability. Furthermore, the deficit must be manifest in the child's daily activities. If an achievement area other than reading, math, or writing is affected, the disorder is diagnosed as Learning Disorder Not Otherwise Specified.

The DSM-IV diagnosis "Learning Disorders" is somewhat synonymous with the more widely used category of "Learning Disabilities." In addition to being diagnostic entities, Learning Disabilities are educational designations that are defined legally by national and state governments. The use of the term *learning disability* is much more widely recognized than the term *learning disorder,* perhaps because learning disability terminology has been used more often in clinical, research, educational, and political circles than has DSM terminology. Hence, most of what is known about learning disorders is based on learning disability research. Because of this fact, the remainder of this chapter will use learning disability terminology and learning disability research, although statements about learning disabilities may be assumed to apply directly to the DSM-IV learning disorders. The abbreviation LD will be used to refer to the learning disabilities designation.

The prevalence of LDs varies considerably based on the criteria used, but estimates are in the range of 5–15% (see Table 11.1; Gelfand, Jenson, & Drew, 1988; Pennington, 1991; United States Department of Education, 1995). Estimates by the U.S. Department of Education set LD prevalence at about 5–6% based on legal definitions (United States Department of Education, 1995). Children with learning disabilities also appear to be at risk for behavioral problems in both the internalizing (depression, withdrawal, anxiety) and externalizing (aggression, hyperactivity) areas, although their risk is less than that of children with mental retardation (MR) (Thompson & Kronenberger, 1990).

TABLE 11.1   Epidemiology and Course of Learning Disorders

Prevalence: 5–10% (Reading Disorder 2–5%, about half of all learning disabled children)

Sex Ratio (Male:Female):   2–4:1

Typical Onset Age: Usually identified in preschool through second grade, although precursors or predisposition may be present earlier

Course: For children with reading and writing disorders, some problems with language, often specifically in phonemic awareness, are often noticed at ages 3–5. Diagnosis is rarely made prior to first or second grade. There is a higher than usual risk of behavioral-emotional problems through the school years. Most experience some learning difficulty into adulthood, at least in the form of having to expend more effort when working on the subject of learning weakness. Many complete college, although they are less likely to do well in subjects and professions that focus on their area of weakness.

Common Comorbid Conditions: 1. Attention-Deficit/Hyperactivity Disorder
      2. Other learning disorders (e.g., Disorder of Written Expression may be comorbid with Reading Disorder)

Relevant Subtypes:
      1. Reading Disorder
        a. Phonological (almost all cases)
        b. Memory, visual, or comprehension (minority of cases)
      2. Disorder of Written Expression
      3. Mathematics Disorder
        a. Acalculia/dyscalculia
        b. Gerstmann's syndrome
        c. Overlap with nonverbal learning disability

     A key issue to be considered in any discussion of LD is its definition. Definitional problems appear to have arisen for at least four reasons: First, LD has been used at times as a label to explain any learning problem or, in some cases, behavioral problem in children. Second, people without proper training, including some in the popular media, have advanced definitions of learning disability that are not supported by research. For example, dyslexia has become a very popular "self-diagnosis" for people with reading or writing difficulty. Third, legal definitions of LD have varied with court decisions, changes in laws, and use of the definition to control state funding for programs. Fourth, DSM-IV definitions of learning disorders are sufficiently vague as to allow multiple interpretations.

     This definitional and diagnostic confusion has resulted in multiple definitions of LD in the legal, mental health, and educational arenas. Legally, the most widely accepted definition occurs in the Individuals with Disabilities Education Act (IDEA; Public Law 101-476) of 1990, which reauthorized and superseded the former legal definitions of LD (Public Laws 94-142 [Education for All Handicapped Children], 98-199, and 99-457). This law defines a learning disability as a disorder in written or spoken language that results in an imperfect ability to listen, think, read, write, spell, or do math. Children who have learning problems as a result of visual problems, hearing problems, MR, motor problems, or environmental deprivation cannot be classified as LD under this law. Additional clarification is made on a regular basis by the U.S. Department of Education as well as by specific state educational agencies. IDEA also mandates special services and a free education for children with LD.

Clinically, learning disabilities are assumed to reflect deficits in the child's processing of information that are critical for learning in a regular (unmodified) classroom environment. Because academic information is not processed adequately, the child does not learn at a pace consistent with expectations based on his or her age or intellectual ability. To address these processing inadequacies, the child must receive extra instruction, more time, different methods of instruction, reduced learning load, or modified expectations for performance.

Psychometrically, the major issue in LD definition is the exact nature of what is meant by a "discrepancy" between IQ and achievement testing. DSM-IV defines "substantially below" as a difference of more than 2 standard deviations between the intelligence and achievement test scores. However, DSM-IV also states that a 1–2 standard deviation difference may be used for LD diagnosis in certain situations. Sattler (1990) describes several methods that have been used to define learning disability on the basis of psychological testing:

1. LD may be defined as low achievement regardless of level of intelligence. This definition, however, is inappropriate because it classifies most children with mental retardation as having LD. Furthermore, children could be classified LD if their achievement was consistent with their ability. Contrary to this definition, there is almost universal agreement that children with learning disabilities should be achieving below expectations and that children with mental retardation should not be classified as LD.

2. LD may be defined as a discrepancy between Verbal and Performance IQ scores. This definition is also inappropriate because it says nothing about the child's school achievement. LD is an academic achievement-based disorder.

3. LD may be defined as school performance significantly below age or grade level. Thus, a child in the fifth grade who is only achieving at a second grade level would be classified as LD. A major issue within this definition is the number of years discrepancy that can result in the LD diagnosis. Some clinicians use a fixed 2-year criterion, but this criterion is extremely difficult to meet at the lower grades and easier at the higher grades. Thus, Sattler (1990) recommends using a discrepancy of 1 year for grades 1 and 2, 1½ years for grades 3 and 4, 2 years for grades 5–8, and 3 years for grades 9–12.

4. LD may be defined as a difference in standard scores between an IQ and an achievement test, with the assumption that the IQ test measures "ability" as opposed to achievement. Usually, a value of 1 to 1½ standard deviations (15–22 points for the commonly used IQ and achievement tests) is used as the criterion for a significant difference. Another criterion is often added to this classification method: The achievement score must be below a certain value. Without this criterion, a child with very high achievement (e.g., score of 130) but even higher IQ (e.g., score of 150) could be classified LD even though the child may be doing very well in school (gifted children, however, can have learning problems and underachievement; whether this is the same type of a problem as an LD, however, is a subject of some debate). Thompson and Kronenberger (1990), for example, used the 20th percentile on an achievement test as a cutoff for LD. Another suggested criterion is an achievement test score of at least ⅔ to 1 standard deviation below the mean (standard score of 85–89 or lower).

Another problem with this criterion is the selection of what IQ score is to be used as the comparison IQ score. The Full Scale IQ score is probably most often used, and it is probably the most reasonable score to use when the discrepancy between Verbal and Performance IQ is not significant. However, when there is a significant difference between Performance and Verbal IQ scores, the Full Scale IQ score has little meaning and should, therefore, be used (if at all) with caution. Some clinicians select the higher of the two (VIQ or PIQ) scores as most representative of the child's "highest potential." However, especially in the case of PIQ, the degree to which this potential should be expected to be reflected in schoolwork is unclear. Other clinicians select the VIQ if there is a discrepancy, reasoning that verbal skills relate more closely to potential to learn in school. There is no firm rule in these cases, except that clinical flexibility in the selection of comparison IQ score is very important. In a majority of cases, this flexibility will lead to the selection of the FIQ score if there is no VIQ-PIQ discrepancy and to the flexible use of various cognitive testing scores if a VIQ-PIQ discrepancy exists.

5. LD may be defined based on statistical models used to calculate the child's most likely ability and achievement test scores, the statistical significance of the difference between the scores, and the frequency with which such a difference occurs in the population. Because use of this criterion requires considerable calculation or use of reference tables, computer scoring programs are typically used to provide this statistical information.

In the first step of statistically testing for LD, the child's ability and achievement test scores are statistically corrected, taking into account the principle of regression to the mean. Regression to the mean is a phenomenon in which people who achieve scores significantly above or below the average (mean) score in the population will tend to receive scores closer to the average population score if they are retested on similar material. In other words, extreme scores are less likely to occur to the same degree on retesting. For example, a child who scores 140 on an IQ test is far more likely to score 135 (5 points closer to the mean of 100) than 145 (5 points more distant from the mean of 100) on a readministration of the test (assuming no retest effects). From this phenomenon, it is inferred that the child's "true" score on the test (meaning the child's average score if he or she took the test hundreds of times) will fall closer to the mean than the child's actual score on the test. Corrections based on regression to the mean have a greater impact on more extreme scores than on scores that fall closer to the population mean.

The second step of statistically testing for LD involves calculating the statistical significance of the difference between the IQ and achievement test scores. This significance value expresses the probability that the discrepancy (difference between IQ and achievement scores) would occur by chance alone. If the probability is below a certain value (usually 1/20 to 1/100), the discrepancy between IQ and achievement test scores is assumed to be "real," in the sense of not being due to chance alone.

The third step of statistically testing for LD is the identification of how frequently such a discrepancy occurs in the population. Differences that are statistically significant (e.g., "real," as in the previous paragraph) are not necessarily rare in the population. Knowledge of the rarity of a discrepancy gives an index of the degree to which the child's ability-achievement profile deviates from that of his or her peer group.

Defining IQ-achievement discrepancies based on statistical models is usually prohibitively time-consuming without the use of computer scoring. With computer scoring, such as that available for the WISC-III and WIAT, however, use of statistical models is becoming more widespread. For the most part, methods 4 and 5 yield very similar results. It must also be remembered that the use of standardized IQ and achievement tests restricts the behaviors that are sampled to the items within these tests. If the child's LD area is not sufficiently sampled on an achievement test, the results will be misleading.

Appearance and Features

Because numerous categories of LDs exist, the appearance and features of a child with an LD (see Table 11.2) vary depending on specific diagnosis. In addition to the DSM-IV diagnoses, several subtyping systems of learning disabilities have been proposed, each of which has a unique appearance and features. Forness (1990), for example, empirically classified LD subtypes into five categories: Non-LD Pattern (children who underachieve in school or relative to grade but not relative to IQ), Production Deficits (children with difficulty retrieving information or translating cognition into verbal or nonverbal production), Verbal Organization Disorders (deficits in understanding or use of language), Nonverbal Organization Disorders (poor visuospatial achievement), and Global Disorders (deficits across a range of achievement areas). Although these categories have the strength of being empirically derived, they are not widely used in clinical or educational settings.

Learning disabilities may also be broadly classified into behavior problems, perceptual problems, and information processing problems (Gelfand et al., 1988). Behavior problem LDs occur when the child's behavior interferes with the learning process, creating a learning deficit. The most common of these is Attention-Deficit/Hyperactivity Disorder with an associated LD. Perceptual problem LDs involve problems in visual perception and auditory perception. These perception problems are not sensory difficulties but rather difficulties in discrimination, identification, association, sequential ordering, and perception. Finally, information processing LDs reflect problems in one or more cognitive processing areas: short-term memory, long-term memory, attention problems, organization and categorization of verbal or nonverbal material, and self-motivation deficits (Gelfand et al., 1988). The three broad areas and multiple subtypes of LDs are not mutually exclusive and, in fact, often overlap.

The most widely used LD subtyping systems, however, mirror DSM-IV by dividing types of LDs based on the academic subject that is impaired. Disorders of reading, written language, and/or mathematics are most common. Another disorder of learning, Nonverbal Learning Disability (NVLD), will also be briefly covered here, although NVLD tends not to be a primary academic learning problem and is not recognized in DSM-IV (see also Asperger's Disorder in Chapter 10).

TABLE 11.2 Appearance and Features of Learning Disorders

COMMON FEATURES

1. Discrepancy between intelligence and achievement/performance in a specific academic area (usually reading, mathematics, or writing)
2. Variability depending on area of deficiency (reading, mathematics, or writing)

OCCASIONAL FEATURES

1. Risk of behavior problems, especially in situations requiring use of the impaired skill

Note: The features listed in the table are often seen but are not universal. Some features may be diagnostically relevant or required, whereas others may not be required for diagnosis. "Common" features are typical of the disorder; "occasional" features appear frequently but are not necessarily seen in a majority of cases.

Reading Disorder

Reading Disorder (also known as dyslexia) is characterized by reading deficits in the context of average intellectual potential. In most cases, Reading Disorder is also accompanied by problems with spelling. Reading Disorder is the most common of the learning disorders, with prevalence estimated at between 2.5% and 7.5%; approximately half of the 5.25% of children identified as LD by U.S. schools have a Reading Disorder. There are approximately two to five males with Reading Disorder for every female with the disorder (Pennington, 1991; Spafford & Grosser, 1996).

In most cases, Reading Disorder is a result of impairment in processing sound-symbol relationships, including blended sounds and sequences of sounds (phonological processing). Phonics, the translation of a visual stimulus (letters) into a meaningful sound (pronunciation) is where the primary problem occurs for almost all children with Reading Disorder. Children with Reading Disorder almost always have difficulty with phonemic awareness, the awareness and use of the sound segments of spoken and written language. Even when they are able to use phonics accurately, their processing is slower and less efficient.

Because phonics is so difficult for children with Reading Disorder, they must devote most of their concentration and mental processing to sounding out words. As a result, they give less attention to word recognition and comprehension of the reading passage. Reading tasks, such as word recognition and phonics, that become fluid and automatic for other children are more effortful and deliberate for children with Reading Disorder. Ultimately, this causes their reading to be slower, more mechanical, more effortful, and less fluid. As a result, the basic tasks of reading place more demands on their attention and memory, interfering with their ability to comprehend individual words and passages, and leading to mental fatigue.

Children with Reading Disorder may try to infer words from their context in a passage, making educated guesses about reading content rather than attending to the actual letters in the word. Problems with sequencing of letters in words and with sequencing of words and sentences are also often seen. Related problems occur with spelling, which requires awareness of the individual sounds in spoken words and the division of the sounds into associated letters (Pennington, 1991; Sattler, 1990; Spafford & Grosser, 1996).

Less commonly, children with adequate phonics skills will demonstrate problems with memory, visual processing, or comprehension that interfere with their reading skills, causing Reading Disorder. In the case of memory skills, children with deficits in short-term working memory have difficulty retaining information while engaging in another simultaneous mental task. Such children do not efficiently transfer information that they have just read into memory, causing them difficulty with comprehension and retention of the reading material. Such children often complain that they are "just reading the words" without understanding what they have read. In other cases, the visual-memory problem interferes with sight reading of very familiar words and with rapid perception of the sequence of letters. Although relatively rare as a primary cause of Reading Disorder, this deficit does sometimes occur alone and, more commonly, can stem from and add to the problems caused by phonological processing deficits. Children with a primary comprehension problem have difficulty translating individual words into coherent, joined ideas. They tend to focus on details, missing the "big picture." In some cases, such children will learn well by rote, but they may miss the general principle contained in a series of words that they have memorized. It is also possible that this latter presentation could be part of a nonverbal learning disability.

Children with Reading Disorder often have a history of delayed phonemic awareness (the knowledge that words consist of separate sounds) as preschoolers. They may have some trouble naming specific objects, relative to stronger nonverbal reasoning and verbal reasoning skills. Attention and memory problems are also commonly seen in the preschool period (Spafford & Grosser, 1996; Teeter & Semrud-Clikeman, 1997).

Mathematics Disorder

Although not uncommon, Mathematics Disorder has been the subject of less research and clinical attention compared to Reading Disorder. Two broad types of learning disability are associated with Mathematics Disorder: specific mathematics weaknesses and nonverbal learning disabilities. Specific mathematics weaknesses are shown by a child's difficulty mastering basic operations such as addition, subtraction, multiplication, and division, as well as more advanced mathematics concepts and arithmetic operations/rules such as fractions, percentages, and probability. Short-term memory, comprehension of mathematics concepts, and difficulty learning the rules of mathematics operations are examples of problems that can cause this type of mathematics disorder.

Subtypes of specific mathematics weaknesses have been suggested by several authors. Acalculia is the inability to perform mathematics calculations and operations (e.g., multiplication), as a result of language, visual, or primary calculation deficits. Gerstmann's syndrome is characterized by poor calculation skills, left-right confusion, finger agnosia, and poor handwriting. Dyscalculia consists of a deficiency (but not total deficit) in the ability to do calculations, caused by impairments in language (verbal), writing (graphical), reading (lexical), understanding of concepts (ideognostical), or fundamental calculation ability (operational) (Spafford & Grosser, 1996).

Nonverbal learning disability (NVLD), on the other hand, is not a subtype of Mathematics Disorder but is another type of learning disability that has mathematics weakness as one characteristic. NVLD is a neuropsychological syndrome characterized by weaknesses in tactile perception, visual perception, motor skills, novel problem solving, attention to complex visual stimuli, visual memory, concept formation, comprehension, and mathematics. Conversely, children with NVLD show strengths in rote learning and memory, simple verbal skills, rote facts and fund of information, and simple language skills. Essentially, nonverbal and higher-order novel problem solving and comprehension skills are impaired whereas rote, overlearned verbal details are strong. Hence, the nonverbal, conceptual side of mathematics is difficult for children with NVLD, who attempt to master mathematics by memorizing answers to problems. Although this rote learning strategy may work in the early school grades, by third to fourth grade, the child is struggling with mathematics work (Rourke, 1995).

Disorder of Written Expression

Children with a Disorder of Written Expression have fundamental problems spelling words, following the rules of written grammar, and using written language to express ideas. Spelling problems often reflect phonological deficits and may be associated with Reading Disorder, as noted previously. Difficulty with written expression, on the other hand, may result from comprehension deficits, difficulty with creating novel written information, or difficulty translating from an oral-auditory to a visual-written modality.

Etiology

Biological Theories

Developmental lag theories state that some children with LD have learning problems because their neurological development is progressing more slowly than that of their peers. This appears at first to be a reasonable assumption because most human traits show variability, with a fraction of humans falling at the very low and the very high ends of a frequency distribution. Neurological development is one of those normally distributed human traits, and children with LD could be those children in the lower tail of the distribution. Research support for this position comes from studies suggesting that children with LD have neurological immaturities and immaturities in other psychological testing (Gelfand et al., 1988; Sattler, 1990). According to developmental lag theories, children with LD will eventually catch up to their peers in many abilities.

Despite the appeal of developmental lag theories, most evidence suggests that children with LD never reach their peers' level in their area of learning weakness (Gelfand et al., 1988; Sattler, 1990). Because the label *developmentally delayed* implies a developmental lag theory, clinicians should use it with caution because it may imply to parents that their child will catch up with other children and become relatively normal. Although this is a possibility for a few children, it can rarely be forecasted with much certainty and appears to be uncommon for Reading Disorder (Pennington, 1991).

Neurological theories state that LD is a reflection of structural damage or improper development of the nervous system. Such problems could occur during the prenatal or neonatal period, as the nervous system is developing. Alternatively, head injury, lack of oxygen, seizures, alterations in blood flow, exposure to toxins, and nutrition all may contribute to these structural-neurological problems. Empirical support for a neurological hypothesis comes from studies indicating EEG abnormalities in some children with LD. Furthermore, studies have found a link between Reading Disorder and some structural abnormalities in the left superior posterior temporal lobe (planum temporale), which may be responsible for phonemic awareness, rapid naming, and comprehension. In people without Reading Disorder, the planum temporale is larger in the left hemisphere, but symmetry in planum temporale size between hemispheres is more often found for those with Reading Disorder (Pennington, 1991; Teeter & Semrud-Clikeman, 1997). Nevertheless, although group research is suggestive, known neurological causes are not found in many individual children with learning disorders.

Genetic theories suggest that LDs are genetically determined, with genetic traits manifesting themselves in the neuroanatomy and neurophysiology of the child. These structural-physiological characteristics, in turn, are manifest as an LD. Support for the genetic theory is found in studies that show that learning disabilities run in families and that LD concordance rates are higher for identical (71% for Reading Disorder) than for fraternal (49% for Reading Disorder) twins (Teeter & Semrud-Clikeman, 1997). Results of twin, family, and adoption studies suggest that the heritability of Reading Disorder (reflected largely by phonological processing problems) is approximately 50% but that there is no single genetic cause. There have been findings suggesting that genes on chromosome 15 or chromosome 6 may cause Reading Disorder for a minority of individuals (Pennington, 1991).

The results of some familial studies have been criticized by those who note that the high rates of LDs within families could reflect family environment as much as genetics. In addition, identical twins share a prenatal environment that could account for their LD as much as genetics. Nevertheless, parents often adopt a genetic explanation for their child's learning disability, suggesting that the child is "just like me." Hence, genetic theories have received tentative support but need further research.

Psychological Theories

Psychological theories of LDs propose that environmental factors affect the neurological development, behavior, motivation, and thought processes of the child in a way that interferes with learning. For example, the family may devalue education, or educational success may not be rewarded (or may be punished out of control issues or jealousy) in the family. Alternatively, the child may live in an impoverished environment, resulting in a delay in cognitive development. Extreme stress may interfere with attention, memory, and motivation. Sattler (1990) summarizes research support showing that environmental factors such as socioeconomic status (SES), family size, school, parental education, family conflict, and motivation are related to academic performance. Furthermore, children with learning disabilities have more behavioral problems (Thompson & Kronenberger, 1990), perhaps contributing to or causing the learning disability. Wallach, Wallach, Dozier, and Kaplan (1977) demonstrated that children from low SES households had weaker phonemic awareness, which is a predictor of reading skill in grade school. Lower SES families may engage in less oral reading with children, interfering with phonemic awareness (Wallach et al., 1977).

☐   ASSESSMENT PATTERNS

Broad Assessment Strategies

Cognitive Assessment

Clinician-Administered—IQ Testing.   Diagnosing LD requires, at the very least, an intelligence and an achievement test (Table 11.3). More specific tests, including some focused cognitive or neuropsychological tests, are often critical in understanding the underlying problems contributing to the learning disorder. First, however, administration of an individual, standardized intelligence test is essential in the diagnosis of LD. Because most children being evaluated for LD are over the age of 4, the Wechsler instruments (WPPSI-R, WISC-III) are usually the tests of choice.

Although WISC-III/WPPSI-R scores should never be used alone to diagnose LD, some patterns of subscale scores tend to be characteristic of LD groups. Sattler (1990) reviewed studies and rank-ordered WISC-R subscales from easiest to most difficult for children with LD: Picture Completion, Picture Arrangement, Block Design, Object Assembly, Similarities, Comprehension, Vocabulary, Coding, Digit Span, Arithmetic, Information. Of note is that the easiest four subtests form the Perceptual-Organization (PO) factor of the WISC-III and that two of the hardest three subtests form the Freedom from Distractibility/Working Memory (FFD/WM) factor of the WISC-III. In addition, the most difficult four subtests form the so-called "ACID" (Arithmetic-Coding-Information-Digit Span) profile of

TABLE 11.3   Sample Assessment Battery for Learning Disorders

COGNITIVE

1. Intelligence test (Stanford-Binet:Fourth Edition or Wechsler scale)
2. Achievement test (Wechsler Individual Achievement Test or Woodcock-Johnson—Revised)
3. California Verbal Learning Test for Children
4. Kaufman Brief Intelligence Test

BEHAVIORAL

1. Behavior Assessment System for Children (Parent-Report, Teacher-Report, and Self-Report)
2. Conners' Rating Scales
3. Personality Inventory for Youth

Note: Assessment instruments are intended to supplement (not substitute for) a good clinical interview and, when possible, a structured diagnostic interview.

subscales. Low scores on the ACID profile are considered to be typical of LD. Finally, the Verbal Comprehension (VC) subtests (Similarities, Comprehension, Vocabulary, and Information) are generally in the middle of the range.

By definition, children with LD usually score in the average (90–109) range on Full Scale IQ, although IQ scores tend to fall in the lower end of the average range (90–95). Children with LD also tend to have higher PO (or Performance) IQ scores than VC (or Verbal) IQ scores, and the FFD/WM Index score is usually lowest. The Processing Speed (PS) score often falls between the FFD/WM and VC scores for children with LD. There is some evidence that Full Scale and Verbal IQ scores drop slightly over time for children with LD, which may reflect a general tendency for language and academic functions to fail to keep up with the trajectory of same-aged peers (Schmidt, Kuryliw, Saklorske, & Yakulic, 1989).

WPPSI-R patterns may vary somewhat from WISC-III patterns because of differences in content. Freedom from distractibility (which does *not* emerge as a WPPSI-R factor, unlike the WISC-III; Sattler, 1990) may be cautiously inferred from the Sentences, Arithmetic, and Animal House subtests of the WPPSI-R.

The Wechsler scales can be valuable adjuncts in delineating the specific nature of an LD. Children with a significant language component to their Reading Disorder, for example, score higher on Performance IQ than on Verbal IQ. Children with Mathematics Disorder and visual-spatial weaknesses, on the other hand, score higher on Verbal IQ than on Performance IQ. Children with an NVLD often show very low PO scores (especially on Block Design and Object Assembly), with much higher scores on verbal subtests and Digit Span. More specific LD problems may also be inferred from subtest scores. For example, low scores on Digit Span, Coding, and Picture Arrangement could indicate a sequential processing deficit.

It is sometimes necessary to use a test other than one of the Wechsler scales for a child with LD. The SB:FE is often the substitute test of choice. Interpretation strategies for this and other substitute tests are found in Sattler (1990).

In addition to the major intelligence tests, more specific cognitive ability tests can provide valuable information about factors contributing to the child's learning disability. The K-BIT, for example, provides estimates of verbal and nonverbal IQ but is shorter, uses more pictorial stimuli, and requires much less elaborate production of answers (verbal and nonverbal) and processing of auditory stimuli (instructions) than the Wechsler scales. Children who have strong basic verbal and nonverbal skills for discrete, straightforward problems, therefore, may perform better on the K-BIT than on the WISC-III. Similarly, children who have more difficulty with elaborate language production and comprehension may perform poorly on the WISC-III but do better on the more structured, visual K-BIT. Such a discrepancy would show intact abilities within the verbal and/or nonverbal areas.

Like the K-BIT Matrices subtest, matrix reasoning tests such as the WASI Matrix Reasoning subtest, the Test of Nonverbal Intelligence—Third Edition (TONI-3; Brown, Sherbenou, & Johnsen, 1997) and the Universal Nonverbal Intelligence Test (UNIT; Bracken & McCallum, 1998) can provide excellent indices of a child's nonverbal logical reasoning skills. The WISC-III and WPPSI-R do not have a matrix reasoning subtest, relying instead on perceptual-organizational subtests to tap a child's nonverbal logical reasoning ability. However, children with learning disabilities may perform differently on tests of perceptual organization and nonverbal logical reasoning. Both types of tests are required to indicate whether a child's problem is with visual organization or logical reasoning.

In the case of a Disorder of Written Expression, it is often helpful to evaluate the child's visual motor integration and speed. The Coding subtest of the Wechsler scales can provide one measure of visual motor speed. Visual motor integration may be assessed using a test such as the Developmental Test of Visual Motor Integration (see description under the Motor Skills Disorder section of this chapter). If visual-motor integration, speed, or coordination deficits are present in a child with a Disorder of Written Expression, it is likely that some of the writing difficulties are coordination and integration based. In such cases, involvement of an occupational therapist to address the motor skills problem is warranted.

Memory tests are another recommended component of many cognitive batteries for children with learning disabilities because the learning process involves transfer of information into short-term memory and from short-term to long-term memory. The California Verbal Learning Test for Children (CVLT-C; Delis, Kramer, Kaplan, & Ober, 1994) is a brief (approximately 20–30 minutes, not including a 20-minute delay period) measure of short-term verbal memory, verbal learning with repetition, proactive/retroactive interference effects, memory organization, and delay memory. CVLT-C scores can indicate how well a child learns with single and multiple repetitions, how a child organizes incoming memory, and the effect of factors (such as decay and interference) that may interfere with memory. Only verbal memory is measured by the CVLT-C. The Wide Range Assessment of Memory and Learning (WRAML; Sheslow & Adams, 1990) is a broad memory test assessing visual, verbal, and learning components of memory. WRAML scores can supplement CVLT-C scores by providing visual memory indices, as well as scores showing the child's ability to remember sentences and stories. One WRAML subtest measures the child's ability to remember associations between sounds and pictorial symbols, which bears some resemblance to phonetic learning (sound-letter association). Research has shown that children with Reading Disorder have difficulty with memory tests (Teeter & Semrud-Clikeman, 1997).

Specific language-focused cognitive tests are also commonly used in test batteries for learning disorders, especially when reading or writing difficulties are suspected. Tests of expressive and receptive vocabulary were described earlier in this chapter under the Communication Disorders section.

Clinician-Administered—Achievement Testing.   In addition to the intelligence test, an individually administered achievement test is typically required in order to make the LD diagnosis. Ideally, the achievement test chosen will have several subtests assessing the child's problem area, such that analysis of subtest scores will not only indicate the presence of a problem but also tell something about the nature of the problem. Failure to find an achievement-intelligence discrepancy could indicate that the achievement test did not tap the child's reported problem area (or that an LD is not present).

Two excellent global achievement tests for an LD evaluation are the WJ-R and the WIAT. The WJ-R has several advantages in the assessment of a child with LD. First, it covers an extremely wide age range, from age 2 years through adulthood. Hence, children just beginning school and even children in preschool can be tested using the WJ-R with little likelihood of floor effects. However, preschool testing of achievement differs from achievement testing of a child who is of school age. In particular, the preschool child does not have formal school experiences that can be tested for retention and learning. Hence, achievement must be inferred based on acquisition of preschool skills. For example, the preschool items of the Dictation subtest of the WJ-R involve copying marks (resembling letters) and staying within lines when using a pencil. The extent to which these skills will be predictive of later spelling and punctuation Dictation items may vary from child to child. One would not want to draw strong conclusions about future spelling ability based on copying and staying within lines, even though these skills are somewhat correlated. In other words, an assumption is made that the "preschool" WJ-R items reflect basic processes that are predictive of later achievement. However, because the child has not yet undergone formal schooling, his or her performance on these items does not directly reflect ability to learn in the school environment.

A second advantage of the WJ-R is the extensive body of scores that it yields. In addition to standard scores, the WJ-R gives age equivalent, grade equivalent, percentile, confidence interval, and Relative Mastery Index (RMI) scores. The RMI is a measure of the percentage of mastery of a topic obtained by the tested child when the average child would score a 90%. For example, an RMI of 95 on Calculation indicates that, when the average child has achieved a 90% mastery level of Calculation, the tested child is likely to show 95% mastery of Calculation. The RMI can be useful in predicting how much of an achievement area the child with LD is likely to have learned when his or her classmates are considered to have mastered it at a 90% mastery rate.

A third advantage of the WJ-R is the use of subtests within the cluster areas to identify specific problems within learning areas. For example, within the Reading cluster, the Letter-Word Identification subtest (LWI) evaluates identification and pronunciation of words, whereas the Passage Comprehension (PC) subtest measures comprehension of word meanings in the context of sentences and paragraphs. A child who does well on LWI but poorly on PC may have more of a comprehension than a word identification problem. Supplementary subtests can be extremely helpful in a more specific analysis of problems. The Word Attack (WA) subtest, for instance, is a supplementary reading subtest that asks the child to read unfamiliar "nonsense" words. Because the WA "words" are unfamiliar to the child, the child must read them phonetically; "sight" or recognition reading is of no help on WA. Hence, a low score on WA coupled with a high score on LWI (which consists of familiar words that can be read based either on recognition or pronunciation) could indicate that the child is reading adequately by sight but has poor phonetic reading skills. Such a profile would be characteristic of a Reading Disorder.

Like the WJ-R, the WIAT is an excellent test for the assessment of ability-achievement discrepancy, although its age range is substantially smaller than that of the WJ-R (age 5 years to 19 years, 11 months). Children with LD tend to receive low scores on one or more of the WIAT clusters relative to their Full Scale IQ score. Unlike the WJ-R, the WIAT includes no supplementary subtests. A useful feature of the WIAT is its ability to be used as a brief screening test by eliminating some of the more lengthy and complex subtests.

Choosing between the WJ-R and the WIAT in the assessment of the child with LD can be done on the basis of several considerations. Both tests allow the fine-grained analysis of subtests to probe deficits within broad achievement areas, such as reading. Similarly, both tests give extensive standard scores, confidence intervals, grade equivalents, and percentiles based on excellent standardization samples. However, the WJ-R has a wider age range and, thus, a wider range of items than the WIAT. Thus, for very young children, very impaired children, and very bright children, the WJ-R may be the test of choice.

On the other hand, the WIAT is designed to allow analysis of very specific abilities within each subtest. Furthermore, the WIAT was conormed with the WISC-III, so WIAT scores can be directly linked to WISC-III scores. In other words, a "predicted" score for each WIAT area can be calculated from the WISC-III IQ score, and the statistical significance of the IQ-achievement difference can be calculated. Hence, in addition to using a 15-point discrepancy for LD diagnosis, the clinician could calculate based on conormed data whether the IQ-achievement difference is statistically significant.

Within cluster areas, there are advantages to each of these achievement tests as well. For example, the supplementary WA subtest on the WJ-R allows the testing of phonetic reading ability; there is no similar subtest on the WIAT. The WJ-R, therefore, provides a better measure of phonetic reading. Furthermore, the Knowledge subtests on the WJ-R (Science, Social Studies, and Humanities) tap school achievement knowledge areas that are not covered by the WIAT and, thus, provide better coverage of fund of academic information. On the other hand, the Oral Expression and Listening Comprehension subtests on the WIAT do not have counterparts on the WJ-R Achievement Tests (there are, however, counterparts to these subtests in the WJ-R Cognitive Battery). The WIAT Reading Comprehension subtest requires the child to identify critical ideas and details in paragraphs, whereas the WJ-R Passage Comprehension subtest essentially measures the child's knowledge of what single word should fit in a particular place in a paragraph. Finally, the WIAT Spelling subtest measures only spelling skills, whereas the WJ-R Dictation subtest measures not only spelling but also plurals and punctuation. If a specific measurement of spelling skills is desired, then the WIAT is preferable. Hence, selection of the appropriate achievement test for the child with LD requires the integration of the referral question with what is known about these major achievement tests.

In addition to the WJ-R and WIAT, there are several other achievement tests with good psychometric properties and clinical usefulness. The Kaufman Test of Educational Achievement (K-TEA; Kaufman & Kaufman, 1985; a 1997 normative update is also available from the publisher) and the Peabody Individual Achievement Test-Revised (PIAT-R; Markwardt, 1989; a 1997 normative update is also available from the publisher) are widely used tests in LD assessments. Like the WJ-R and the WIAT, the K-TEA and PIAT-R include measures of reading, mathematics, and written language. Their subtests vary slightly but not substantially from ones included in the WJ-R and WIAT. Like the WIAT, the K-TEA has the advantage of identifying very specific academic areas for intervention, and a brief form is available (Kaufman & Ishikuma, 1993).

Most other broad achievement tests should be used with caution or for screening purposes only. For example, the extensively used Wide Range Achievement Test—Third Edition (WRAT-III; Wilkinson, 1993) is quite brief but provides less extensive and reliable data than the WJ-R or WIAT. The main value of the WRAT-III is its brevity and utility as a screening instrument. However, evaluation of LD should not rely exclusively on a screening instrument. Hence, the clinician evaluating a child for LD should use one of the four established tests described previously whenever possible. Most local and state departments of education will provide a list of acceptable achievement tests on request; clinicians who are doing extensive work for the schools should verify that their achievement test is consistent with the goals of the special education department of the local school system.

In some cases, assessment of a very narrow achievement area is all that is called for in an evaluation. When this is the case, a more specific achievement test may be used. The Sequential Assessment of Mathematics Inventories (SAMI; Reisman, 1985), KeyMath Diagnostic Arithmetic Test (Connolly, 1988), and Woodcock Reading Mastery Test-Revised (WRMT-R; Woodcock, 1987) are examples of good tests focused in the mathematics and reading areas. Specific tests such as these can provide a briefer but more in-depth view of a focused achievement area. However, many poorly designed, poorly standardized, and poorly normed tests exist in this specific achievement test area. Because such tests often yield information that is less useful than information obtained with the WJ-R or WIAT, these tests should be used warily.

Integration of Intelligence and Achievement Tests. Once the intelligence and achievement testing data are obtained, the clinician must integrate them into a formulation about the existence and nature of a learning disability. Several steps can facilitate this process:

1. *Selection of a comparison ability test score.* First, the child's score on an ability (typically IQ) test, to be used for the basis of comparison, must be selected. If there is no VIQ-PIQ difference, it is usually wisest to use the FIQ score. This score tends to be the most reliable measure on the test (Wechsler, 1991). However, if there is a significant VIQ-PIQ discrepancy, the FIQ loses meaning. In this case, either the VIQ or PIQ should be chosen as the comparison score. Because the VIQ tends to be the most similar to and the most correlated with achievement, this score will often be the one chosen. However, in some cases, the examiner may wish to choose the PIQ for comparison purposes. Such a situation may occur when a child has verbal production difficulties. WISC-III index (factor) scores may also be used for purposes of comparison. For example, use of the Verbal Comprehension index score may be warranted if Freedom from Distractibility problems (reflected in the Arithmetic subtest on VIQ) confound the VIQ.

If the comparison IQ is less than 70, LD cannot be diagnosed. Analysis of scores may proceed in this case, but the child should not be diagnosed LD.

2. *Identification of normative achievement deficits.* Following selection of the IQ score, normative achievement deficits are identified. These deficits occur in achievement cluster areas (e.g., reading, math, written language, language, knowledge) relative to norms. Typically, a cutoff score of 85 is used for a "deficit," although scores of 90 and 80 are also used. A compromise may be to designate scores between 80 and 89 as "mild deficits" whereas scores below 80 are designated as "severe deficits."

3. *Identification of intelligence-achievement discrepancies.* Next, the selected IQ score is matched to the achievement cluster area scores. Numerous ways exist to calculate "significant" discrepancies (see section earlier in this chapter). Areas that are both normative achievement deficits (see step 2) and intelligence-achievement discrepancies are possible LDs.

In some cases, a clinician may want to use specific achievement subtest (as opposed to composite achievement cluster) scores to identify an intelligence-achievement discrepancy. This analysis may be done, but because of the lower reliability of individual subtests relative to cluster scores, conclusions will be more tentative.

4. *Analysis of subtest scores within the LD area.* Once the possible LD area is identified, subtest scores and items within the LD area may be examined to analyze in detail the nature of the LD. Subtest scores differing by 15 or more points are generally considered to be discrepant, although the reliabilities of the subtests must be considered in choosing a cutoff for discrepancy. Statistical significance may be calculated if necessary, although the 15-point criterion is usually sufficient for the major achievement tests.

5. *Explanation of residual deficits and discrepancies.* Some achievement areas will meet the criterion for a normative achievement deficit or an intelligence-achievement discrepancy but not both. These achievement areas are not typically considered areas of learning disability. Normative achievement deficits that are not intelligence-achievement discrepancies occur when a child is achieving below peers but in line with expectations based on IQ. Such children have low IQ and similar achievement. On the other hand, intelligence-achievement discrepancies that are not normative achievement deficits typically occur when a high-IQ child is achieving at age-appropriate (but not IQ-appropriate) levels. Hence, the child is underachieving relative to IQ but not relative to age. Explanation to parents of the differences between LD and these residual problems is essential.

Behavioral Assessment

Parent-Report/Other-Report. Substantial evidence exists that children with learning problems are at risk for behavioral problems (Thompson & Kronenberger, 1990). There are three possible explanations for this finding: First, behavioral problems, such as symptoms of ADHD, may interfere with the child's ability to learn. Second, the child's learning problems may lead to frustration, boredom, and low self-esteem that result in behavioral problems. Third, some other factor, such as neurological damage, may cause both learning and behavioral problems. Often, there is interplay between all three of these explanations, which have reciprocal, interactive, and dynamic effects on the child.

Because of the risk and importance of behavior problems, children with suspected LD should be routinely assessed for behavior problems. Elevated scales on behavior checklists may suggest areas in which behavior is maladaptive and needs clinical attention. Furthermore, most behavior checklists include items and subscales about the child's behavior during learning activities. Results from these subscales may help to show the interplay between the child's LD, learning behavior, and problem behavior related to learning. There is no typical pattern of behavior problems for children with LD, although many of them show symptoms of ADHD (especially the inattentive type). Any significant elevation found with behavioral problem testing may be further probed with syndrome-specific test batteries described in other chapters. If a behavior problem is found, knowing the time of its emergence (especially if it predated or postdated learning problems) can be extremely helpful in evaluating the etiology of the LD and behavior problem.

The Conners' scales (both parent and teacher versions) include a Cognitive Problems subscale, which measures poor achievement in school, difficulty sustaining mental effort, and attention problems. This scale would be expected to be elevated for a child with an LD. Concurrent elevations of the ADHD Index and DSM-IV ADHD symptom subscales could indicate either that ADHD is comorbid with the learning disorder or that ADHD is responsible for the learning problems.

On the teacher version of the BASC, children with LDs tend to elevate the Learning Problems and Study Skills subscales, which measure poor academic performance and organization/effort, respectively. The parent version of the BASC does not include either of these scales. Both teacher and parent versions of the BASC include an Attention Problems scale, which closely resembles the DSM-IV ADHD Inattentive criteria. Although children with LD tend to elevate this scale, it is less characteristic of the core LD problems than are the teacher-report Learning Problems and Study Skills subscales. Extreme elevation of the Attention Problems subscale should trigger follow-up evaluation of whether the child has ADHD.

Self-Report.   Self-report scales should be used with caution because the child's LD may indicate some difficulty reading or understanding items. Hence, the caveats expressed for children with communication disorders also apply to children with LDs.

The BASC-SRP includes several subscales that reflect areas of risk for children with LDs, although no subscale asks specifically about core LD problems. Negative attitudes toward teachers and school are measured by the Attitude to Teachers and Attitude to School subscales, respectively. Children whose learning problems cause them to dislike or distrust teachers and school would be expected to elevate these subscales. The Sense of Inadequacy, Self-Esteem, and Self-Reliance subscales, on the other hand, can provide information about the child's global self-concept. Children who feel inferior, incompetent, and dependent as a result of their LD would elevate the Sense of Inadequacy subscale while giving low scores on the Self-Esteem and Self-Reliance subscales. Other BASC-SRP subscales measure anxiety, depression, and related psychological problems, providing information about possible comorbid disorders. Over all, the BASC-SRP is a valuable measure for assessing the impact of the LD on the child's self-concept, beliefs, and psychological well-being.

The PIY has less coverage of self-esteem than the BASC, but it includes a Cognitive Impairment scale that asks about core difficulties associated with LDs (poor achievement, memory problems, feeling low in intelligence, learning problems). The Social Withdrawal and Social Skills Deficits scales can provide additional information about the child's social adjustment, whereas other scales screen for various problems with psychological well-being. Children with LD elevate the Cognitive Impairment scale; concurrent elevations of the Social Withdrawal and Social Skills Deficits scales could indicate negative effects of the LD on social functioning or possibly the presence of a mild Pervasive Developmental Disorder.

☐ TREATMENT OPTIONS

Treatment options for LD are outlined in Table 11.4.

Referral to and Consultation with Other Professionals

Placement Decisions

The most common treatment for children with LD is special educational planning. This planning may range from regular class placement with some special attention to placement in LD classes for the problem academic areas. Individualized attention and tutoring are also frequently used. The goal of most clinicians and schools is to place the child in the "least restrictive environment," which typically means the environment that resembles as closely as possible that of children without LDs. Many children with LD, for example, attend regular classes but are given additional time in "resource rooms" where they have access to more structured learning with smaller student-to-teacher ratios (often individual instruction).

Some children who do not meet exact criteria for LD diagnosis may nevertheless show skills or achievement deficiencies that can be remediated at school. These should also be identified by the clinician and presented to the school. Many schools are willing to accommodate (within reason) the learning needs of individual students, even if a formal LD cannot be diagnosed.

The mental health clinician is rarely involved with the details of these special educational services, although the clinician holds a powerful position as advocate for these services in

---

TABLE 11.4 Treatment Options for Learning Disorders

1. Referral to and Consultation with School Experts
   a. Placement decisions
      (1) Resource room
      (2) Access to tutor
      (3) Teaching at a different pace
      (4) Clinician-school collaboration
   b. Special educational interventions
      (1) Reading Disorder: improve sight reading, build vocabulary, learn prefixes/roots/ suffixes, special phonics programs (e.g., multisensory, sounds-in-words)
      (2) Disorder of Written Expression: teach spelling rules, teach word prefixes/roots/ suffixes, practice/repetition, naturalistic writing exercises, outlining, dictation-fading techniques
      (3) Mathematics Disorder: practice with affected area, use pictures and analogies to communicate concepts concretely, teach math rules for checking answers
2. Co-Occurring Behavior Problems
   a. Address using techniques specific for each behavior problem

Note: This outline of options summarizes major treatments covered in the text. Specific treatments are often combined into an intervention package. Refer to the text for additional descriptions of each treatment. This table is not necessarily an exhaustive list of all treatments available.

appropriate cases. It is important to remember that the final decision belongs to the school and not to the clinician. Hence, a collaborative relationship with the school is essential. Often, the communication of findings and recommendations is easily accomplished by mail and phone, but if disagreement exists between the clinician, school, and parents, a face-to-face meeting may be necessary. Such a meeting may enlighten the clinician about other issues (such as parental embarrassment or school resources) that enter the decision-making process. In such complex cases, a school counselor or school psychologist can be an excellent liaison between the parents, clinician, and school.

Special Educational Interventions

Numerous special educational strategies exist to promote learning for children with LDs. Although these strategies differ depending on whether the child has a Reading Disorder, Mathematics Disorder, or Disorder of Written Expression, they typically involve two intervention processes: modifying the learning process to accommodate the child (e.g., more time on tests, less emphasis on certain material, limitations on homework) and requiring the child to put more effort into remediating the areas of weakness (under the supervision and teaching of special educators). Although general principles of intervention are reviewed later, a complete discussion of intervention strategies is beyond the scope of this book. Spafford and Grosser (1996) provide an excellent discussion of special educational interventions for learning disorders.

Reading Disorder.   Educational interventions for Reading Disorder aim to improve the child's sight reading and phonics. Sight reading may be addressed by vocabulary-building exercises, sight-reading exercises (Spafford & Grosser, 1996, note, for example, that 200–300 words make up 80% or more of the reading typically encountered by grade school children), and learning word roots, prefixes, and suffixes. Programs to improve phonics (e.g., Lindamood-Bell Reading Program, Fernald-Keller Approach, Gillingham-Stillman Approach) typically provide the child with extra experience that integrates several senses into phonemic awareness. For example, the child might trace a letter as he or she says the letter sound and looks at a picture of a letter (tactile, auditory, and visual senses). Other phonics programs (Clay, 1993; Iversen & Tumner, 1993) use words with slightly different phonemes (e.g., *c*at-*b*at) to demonstrate phonemic differences in reading. This sounds-in-words learning process typically proceeds from beginning word sounds to ending word sounds to middle word sounds to sequencing of sounds. Both vowels and consonants are learned.

Unfortunately, because there has been no systematic program of outcome studies comparing the various techniques used to address Reading Disorder, it is not possible to identify which strategies will work best for most children. At an individual level, multiple strategies are usually used. If comprehension is the child's main problem, the interventions are somewhat different, focusing on giving the child a system for organizing and retaining the material that has been read.

Disorder of Written Expression.   Because spelling problems frequently involve deficits in phonemic awareness and word recognition, interventions for Reading Disorder are often used for children whose Disorder of Written Expression involves mostly spelling errors. Spelling skills can also be promoted by teaching the child spelling rules (e.g., "*i* before *e* except after *c*"), spelling of word roots (as well as prefixes and suffixes), and mnemonic strategies for remembering the spelling of specific irregular words. Strategies to make spelling gamelike and to promote repetition learning also are used for children with spelling deficits.

When the Disorder of Written Expression consists of a deficit in written expression (communicating ideas in writing), strategies such as keeping a journal, writing out gift lists, and other naturalistic writing exercises are often used. Learning to write an outline before writing a paper as well as similar organizational strategies are used to promote a logical, sequential, comprehensive flow in writing. For children with good verbal expression and poor written expression, a verbal-to-writing intervention can be used. This intervention consists of several steps. First, the child dictates to an adult, who writes what the child says. Next the child dictates to a tape recorder, and later transposes his or her own words into writing. Then the child dictates only a few sentences into the tape recorder and writes the sentences before dictating a few more, and so on. After this step is mastered, the tape recorder is removed, and the child says the words out loud, pausing to write them periodically. Finally, the child gradually says the words more and more silently, until the child is writing while thinking (but not saying) the words.

Mathematics Disorder.   Mathematics Disorder can be caused by and is characterized by many potential problems and errors. Hence, an essential first step is to identify precisely where the child's errors are occurring. For example, a child may have difficulty with multiplication tables or with the concept of borrowing in subtraction. Once the errors are identified, several techniques are used to help the child. Concrete objects, pictorial representations (e.g., graphs), analogies, and logical explanations are used to make abstract concepts more meaningful. Strategies for translating word problems into arithmetic problems can also be directly taught (e.g., the words *and* and *together* usually mean that things will be added, as in "How many pencils did Jim and Tom have together?"). Learning math rules through practice is another technique that is often used. To make the practice more palatable, math games and reward systems are frequently used. In some cases, the math rules help the child to check his or her work (e.g., the digits in multiples of 9 always add up to 9 or a multiple of 9). In the case of very severe disorders, certain mathematics content may have to be altered or dropped from the student's curriculum.

Atypical Learning Disorders.   Some children have cognitive problems that do not fit well into one of the three learning disorders (e.g., short-term memory problem). For these children, treatment is guided by extensive evaluation to understand the nature of the problem. Treatment techniques then attempt to provide the child with external accommodations and experience to function adequately in the classroom while also improving their area of weakness.

For Nonverbal Learning Disabilities (NVLD), several suggestions for treatment are provided by Rourke (1995). These NVLD treatment suggestions include the following: Teach the child in a sequential, predictable, rote fashion; encourage the child to apply familiar problem-solving strategies to new situations; teach algorithms for dealing with new or unfamiliar situations; directly teach appropriate social and nonverbal material in a rote fashion with practice to make the child's learning more fluid and automatic; teach the child to attend to visual as well as auditory-verbal information; teach visual-organizational skills; teach appropriate use of verbal material in a social context; encourage contact with novel situations and problems; encourage structured, clear, goal-oriented peer interactions (situations in which group roles and behavior are clearly defined and supervised, the group must work together, and the group has a clear goal); and teach comprehension skills.

Psychotherapy/Behavioral Interventions

In many cases, the behavior problems of the child with LD are as much of a concern as the LD itself. When a behavior problem is identified, the contribution of the LD to the problem must be considered. Nevertheless, intervention for the behavior problem often follows the same procedures as for children without LD with a similar behavior problem.

■ References

American Psychiatric Association. (1994). *Diagnostic and statistical manual of mental disorders, fourth edition.* Washington, DC: Author.

Beery, K. E. (1997). *The Beery Buktenica Developmental Test of Visual-Motor Integration (VMI) manual.* Parsippany, NJ: Modern Curriculum Press.

Bracken, B. A, & McCallum, R. S. (1998). *Universal Nonverbal Intelligence Test (UNIT).* Itasca, IL: Riverside Publishing.

Brown, L., Sherbenou, R. J., & Johnsen, S. K. (1997). *Test of Nonverbal Intelligence—Third Edition.* Austin, TX: Pro-Ed.

Bruininks, R. H. (1978). *Bruininks-Oseretsky Test of Motor Proficiency manual.* Circle Pines, MN: American Guidance Service.

Carrow-Woolfolk, E. (1985). *Test for Auditory Comprehension of Language* (Revised Edition). Allen, TX: DLM Teaching Resources.

Clay, M. M. (1993). *Reading recovery: A guidebook for teachers in training.* Portsmouth, NH: Longman.

Connolly, A. J. (1988). *Key Math: A diagnostic inventory of essential mathematics.* Circle Pines, MN: American Guidance Service.

Delis, D.C., Kramer, J., Kaplan, E., & Ober, B. A. (1994). *California Verbal Learning Test, Children's Version (CVLT-C) manual.* San Antonio: Psychological Corporation.

DiSimoni, F. (1978). *Token Test for Children.* Chicago: Riverside Publishing.

Dunn, L. M., & Dunn, L. M. (1997). *Peabody Picture Vocabulary Test—Third Edition.* Circle Pines, MN: American Guidance Service.

Forness, S. R. (1990). Subtyping in learning disabilities: Introduction to the issues. In H. L. Swanson & B. Keogh (Eds.), *Learning disabilities: Theoretical and research issues* (pp. 195–200). Hillsdale, NJ: Erlbaum.

Gardner, M. F. (1990). *Expressive One-Word Picture Vocabulary Test—Revised.* Los Angeles, CA: Western Psychological Services.

Gelfand, D. M., Jenson, W. R., & Drew, C. J. (1988). *Understanding child behavior disorders* (2nd ed.). New York: Harcourt Brace Jovanovich College Publishers.

Goldman, R., & Fristoe, M. (1986). *Goldman-Fristoe Test of Articulation.* Circle Pines, MN: American Guidance Service.

Goldman, R., Fristoe, M., & Woodcock, R. W. (1974). *Goldman-Fristoe-Woodcock Diagnostic Auditory Discrimination Test.* Circle Pines, MN: American Guidance Service.

Hammill, D. D., Pearson, N. A., & Wiederholt, J. L. (1996). *Comprehensive Test of Nonverbal Intelligence.* Austin, TX: Pro-Ed.

Iversen, S., & Tumner, W. E. (1993). Phonological processing skills and the reading recovery program. *Journal of Educational Psychology, 85,* 112–126.

Kaufman, A. S., & Ishikuma, T. (1993). Intellectual and achievement testing. In T. H. Ollendick & M. Hersen (Eds.), *Handbook of child and adolescent assessment* (pp. 192–207). Needham Heights, MA: Allyn & Bacon.

Kaufman, A. S., & Kaufman, N. L. (1985). *Manual for the Kaufman Test of Educational Achievement (K-TEA) Comprehensive Form.* Circle Pines, MN: American Guidance Service.

Kaufman, A. S., & Kaufman, N. L. (1990). *Kaufman Brief Intelligence Test manual.* Circle Pines, MN: American Guidance Service.

Markwardt, F. C. (1989). *Manual for the Peabody Individual Achievement Test—Revised (PIAT-R).* Circle Pines, MN: American Guidance Service.

McCarthy, D. A. (1972). *Manual for the McCarthy Scales of Children's Abilities.* San Antonio: Psychological Corporation.

Pennington, B. F. (1991). *Diagnosing learning disorders: A neuropsychological framework.* New York: Guilford.

Reisman, F. T. (1985). *Sequential Assessment of Mathematics Inventories.* San Antonio, TX: Psychological Corporation.

Roid, G. H., & Miller, L. J. (1997). *Leiter International Performance Scale-Revised.* Wood Dale, IL: Stoelting Co.

Rourke, B. P. (1995). Treatment program for the child with NLD. In B. P. Rourke (Ed.), *Syndrome of nonverbal learning disabilities: Neurodevelopmental manifestations.* New York: Guilford.

Sattler, J. M. (1990). *Assessment of children* (3rd ed.). San Diego, CA: Author.

Schmidt, H. P., Kuryliw, A. J., Saklofske, D. H., & Yackulic, R. A. (1989). Stability of WISC-R Scores for a sample of learning disabled children. *Psychological Reports, 64,* 195–201.

Semel, E., Wigg, E. H., & Secord, W. (1995). *Clinical Evaluation of Language Fundamentals—Third Edition.* San Antonio, TX: Psychological Corporation.

Sheslow, D., & Adams, W. (1990). *Wide Range Assessment of Memory and Learning.* Wilmington, DE: Jastak.

Spafford, C. S., & Grosser, G. S. (1996). *Dyslexia: Research and resource guide.* Needham Heights, MA: Allyn & Bacon.

Teeter, P. A., & Semrud-Clikeman, M. (1997). *Child neuropsychology: Assessment and interventions for neurodevelopmental disorders.* Needham Heights, MA: Allyn & Bacon.

Thompson, R. J., Jr., & Kronenberger, W. G. (1990). Behavior problems in children with learning problems. In H. L. Swanson & B. Keogh (Eds.), *Learning disabilities: Theoretical and research issues* (pp. 155–174). Hillsdale, NJ: Erlbaum.

United States Department of Education. (1995). *Sixteenth annual report to Congress on the implementation of the Individuals with Disabilities Education Act.* Washington, DC: U.S. Government Printing Office.

Wallach, L., Wallach, M. A., Dozier, M. G., & Kaplan, N. E. (1977). Poor children learning to read do not have trouble with auditory discrimination but do have trouble with phoneme recognition. *Journal of Educational Psychology, 69,* 36–39.

Wechsler, D. (1991). *Manual for the Wechsler Intelligence Scale for Children—Third Edition.* San Antonio, TX: Psychological Corporation.

Wiig, E. H., & Secord, W. (1992). *Test of Word Knowledge.* San Antonio, TX: Psychological Corporation.

Wilkinson, G. S. (1993). *Wide Range Achievement Test* (3rd ed). Wilmington, DE: Wide Range, Inc.

Williams, K. T. (1997). *Expressive Vocabulary Test manual.* Circle Pines, MN: American Guidance Service.

Woodcock, R. W. (1987). *Manual for Woodcock Reading Mastery Tests—Revised (WRMT-R).* Circle Pines, MN: American Guidance Service.

CHAPTER 12

Mental Retardation

■ **Mental Retardation**

☐ CLINICAL DESCRIPTION

Diagnostic Considerations

Excluding the personality disorders, mental retardation (MR) is the only other diagnosis that can be made on DSM-IV Axis II. The rationale for placing MR on Axis II is to ensure "that consideration will be given to the possible presence of…Mental Retardation that might otherwise be overlooked when attention is directed to the usually more florid Axis I disorders" (American Psychiatric Association, 1994, p. 26). In practice, there is also risk that genuine Axis I disorders will be overlooked in a child with MR.

Outside of professional circles, it is widely believed that MR is diagnosed based only on intelligence testing information. In fact, a diagnosis of MR requires significant deficits not only in intellectual functioning, but also in adaptive functioning. DSM-IV identifies 11 areas of adaptive functioning (communication, self-care, home living, social skills, use of community resources, self-direction, academic skills, work, leisure, health, and safety) and requires deficits in two of them in order to make the MR diagnosis. Hence, it is not possible for a person who functions well in society to be diagnosed as mentally retarded.

For the MR diagnosis to be met, a child must have an IQ (presumably Full Scale IQ, although DSM-IV encourages flexibility in cases of significant ability scatter) of 70 or lower on an individually administered IQ test. Less rigorous (and less valid) group IQ tests cannot and should not be used for diagnosing MR. When it is not possible to obtain an IQ measure (e.g., because the child is uncooperative or cannot do the test at all), a diagnosis of Mental Retardation, Severity Unspecified, is made.

Unlike the IQ criterion, no specific score or type of adaptive functioning test is required for the MR diagnosis. Hence, the clinician could presumably make the diagnosis based on clinical impression of level of adaptive functioning. However, because several tests of adaptive functioning exist, it is wise to use a standardized, normed measure of adaptive functioning. A cutting score of 2 standard deviations below the mean on two adaptive functioning subscales (each representing one of the DSM-IV adaptive functioning areas) would meet the adaptive functioning criterion, although a case could be made for meeting this criterion if several critical subscale (e.g., communication, daily living) scores were close to 70 and the overall adaptive functioning score was less than 70. In addition to the standardized normed measures of adaptive behavior, tables of representative adaptive behavior for different ages and degrees of MR have been published in several places (Gelfand, Jenson, & Drew, 1988; Sattler, 1990).

Within the MR category, DSM-IV subtypes exist based on severity of the IQ deficit. Mild MR is diagnosed when IQ scores range from approximately 50–70; Moderate MR is diagnosed for IQ scores from approximately 35–55; Severe MR is diagnosed when IQ falls between 20 and 40; and Profound MR is diagnosed for children with IQ below 25. The overlap in the IQ scores is deliberate and allows the clinician some discretion in classifying borderline cases. The decision about which category to diagnose in these borderline cases depends on validity concerns about testing, level of adaptive functioning, behavioral observations during testing, and global clinical impression. For example, a child with an IQ of 53 who had an outlying low score on a subtest that he or she did not seem to understand (thus artificially lowering the overall IQ score) may be diagnosed as Mild MR, especially if adaptive functioning is in the 55–70 range.

The adaptive functioning areas identified in the DSM-IV definition of MR are identical to those used for the other widely accepted definition of MR, which has been proposed by the American Association on Mental Retardation (AAMR, 1992). The AAMR definition also requires intellectual deficits for a diagnosis of MR but deviates from DSM-IV in the characterization of subtypes of MR. Rather than using IQ ranges, classification in the AAMR system is based on the degree of supports needed to function well intellectually, adaptively, psychologically, emotionally, and physically, taking into account etiological and environmental influences on the individual's disorder. The four classification levels for MR are intermittent (need for support during stressful or transition periods but not constantly), limited (less intense, consistent supports needed but time limited for changing situations), extensive (long-term consistent support at work and/or home), and pervasive (very intense, long-term, constant support needed across most or all situations) (AAMR, 1992).

In the educational system, MR subtypes had been defined in the past based on the expected academic achievement of the child with MR (Gelfand et al., 1988). The educable category roughly corresponded to the Mild MR category; the trainable category corresponded to the Moderate and Severe categories; and the custodial category was reserved for children with Profound MR. These categories are rarely used anymore because of concerns that they did not accurately describe the potential of all individuals in each category.

Mental Retardation is a relatively common disorder. Estimates of prevalence are usually in the 1–3% range, although a 1% prevalence rate seems to be more widely accepted (see Table 12.1). MR prevalence estimates of 3% may not take adaptive functioning into account and may be based on faulty assumptions about life expectancy for MR populations (Aman, Hammer, & Rojahn, 1993; Harris, 1995). The majority of children with MR fall into the upper (IQ of 40–70) ranges of MR intellectual functioning; approximately 50–85% of children with MR have IQ of 55–70, whereas another 10–30% are in the 40–55 range (American Psychiatric Association, 1994; Baroff, 1986).

TABLE 12.1   Epidemiology and Course of Mental Retardation

Prevalence: 1–3%

Sex Ratio (Male:Female):   Probably more frequent in males

Typical Onset Age: Infancy or toddlerhood; usually diagnosed before kindergarten to first grade; diagnosis is earlier for more severe retardation

Course: Highly variable and closely related to severity of retardation. Individuals in the mild range may complete basic schooling, work in structured jobs, and live somewhat independently with moderate supervision by family or a case manager (in rare cases, minimal or no supervision is required). Individuals in the moderate range may complete a modified, adaptive skill-focused school curriculum, work in a highly structured job or sheltered employment setting, and live in a supervised setting. Individuals in the severe and profound ranges typically learn only basic adaptive skills, rarely work in a systematic job setting, and live in a closely supervised home, residential, or institutional setting. Decline in function varies by etiological cause; certain genetic disorders (e.g., Down's syndrome, Fragile X) are associated with intellectual decline in early adulthood.

Common Comorbid Conditions:
1. Anxiety or Mood Disorder
2. Self-Injurious or Aggressive Behavior (especially at lower IQ ranges)
3. Pervasive Developmental Disorders
4. Seizure disorders (lower IQ ranges)

Relevant Subtypes:
1. Mild (IQ/adaptive functioning range approximately 50–70)
2. Moderate (IQ/adaptive functioning range approximately 35–55)
3. Severe (IQ/adaptive functioning range approximately 20–40)
4. Profound (IQ/adaptive functioning range approximately 25 and lower)

Appearance and Features

Mental Retardation is heterogeneous in etiology, appearance, behavioral-psychological features, and outcome. The appearance and associated behavioral features of children with MR (see Table 12.2) vary so widely that it is difficult to characterize a typical presentation. Some children with MR are quiet, polite, confident, and compliant; others are aggressive, oppositional, anxious, and hostile. Some children are extremely sociable, whereas others may be withdrawn. Over all, however, there appears to be a somewhat elevated risk of behavior problems in the population of children with MR. Significant problems with aggressive behavior, self-injurious behavior, stereotypic behavior, overactivity, and language disorders are reported in MR populations (Aman et al., 1993; Jacobson, 1982). These behaviors may occur at greater frequencies in more intellectually impaired and older groups.

Intellectually, children with MR tend to be concrete, to have poor problem-solving skills, to have deficient verbal and social skills, and to do poorly in novel situations. Developmentally, children with MR show significant delays in the achievement of intellectual,

TABLE 12.2   Appearance and Features of Mental Retardation

COMMON FEATURES

1. Significantly below average cognitive functioning (less than 2nd percentile across areas)
2. Significantly below average adaptive functioning (less than 2nd percentile in two major areas)
3. Developmental delay
4. Socially responsive
5. Risk of behavior problems (Axis I)
6. Need for special education

OCCASIONAL FEATURES

1. Known neurological involvement or disorder
2. Unusual appearance/soft signs
3. Need for structured support or caretaking environment throughout life

Note: The features listed in the table are often seen but are not universal. Some features may be diagnostically relevant or required, whereas others may not be required for diagnosis. "Common" features are typical of the disorder; "occasional" features appear frequently but are not necessarily seen in a majority of cases.

social, and motor milestones. They typically talk later than do average children, and their vocabulary grows more slowly. Socially, most are responsive, attached, and oriented to interaction, but social understanding and social skills are often poor. Children with MR frequently violate basic social conventions and exhibit unusual behavior in social situations as a result of disinhibition, poor self-monitoring, and skills deficits. Children with mild to moderate MR may be taught some adaptive behaviors, but they typically require more practice and guidance than average children.

As with behavior, the appearance of a child with MR can vary from unusual to completely normal. A large subgroup of children with MR, however, have clearly unusual physical appearances characterized by neurological soft signs, unusual facial features, and poor motor coordination. Neurological soft signs and unusual appearance are often associated with a biological cause. Examples of unusual appearance include webbed digits, small head, eyefolds, flat nose, large and protruding ears, short stature, and protruding tongue.

Etiology

Biological Theories

Mental Retardation is believed to be caused by an interaction of biological and environmental variables, with the nature and relative influence of the variables changing from person to person. In some cases, biology appears to be largely responsible for the MR condition, with environment exerting only mild influences on the individual's level of functioning within the MR category. In other cases, environment appears to strongly influence or contribute to a biological vulnerability. In most cases of mild MR, etiology is not known, whereas biological factors (especially genetics) account for the condition in the majority of children with moderate, severe, or profound MR (Matson, Applegate, Smiroldo, & Stallings, 1998).

With improved research and diagnostic procedures, identifiable biological causes are being found for a greater proportion of cases of MR in all categories. These biological causes can be grouped into five broad categories that account for at least 15–25% of total cases (Gelfand et al., 1988; Grossman, 1983):

1. *Postnatal infection/toxic exposure.* Certain infections (e.g., meningitis) can attack or have effects on the child's developing nervous system, causing permanent damage that is reflected in MR. Toxic substances can have similar effects. These effects are particularly pronounced at earlier ages, when the nervous system is showing the greatest development.

2. *Metabolic disorders.* These disorders [such as phenylketonuria (PKU)] are characterized by the body's inability to correctly metabolize or eliminate chemicals, resulting in a toxic internal biochemical environment for the child. This toxic environment causes neurological damage and MR. In some cases, the child is born with normal functioning, but the metabolic disorder poses a future risk. Hence, control of the disorder can reduce or prevent MR.

3. *Genetic factors.* These factors are often the cause of metabolic, neuroanatomical, or neurophysiologic abnormalities that can be traced to the genes or chromosomes of the child. The most common known genetic cause of MR, Down's syndrome, usually involves a third chromosome 21 and occurs in approximately one out of every 700 live births. Down's syndrome is associated with variable levels of functioning, ranging from mild to severe MR. The second most common known genetic condition causing MR is Fragile X syndrome, which is caused by a damaged X chromosome. Fragile X syndrome occurs in one out of every 1,000 males and is less frequent and less severe in females. Approximately 80% of males with Fragile X (as compared to 30% of females) will have below average intelligence, with MR being common (Stone, MacLean, & Hogan, 1995; Teeter & Semrud-Clikeman, 1997).

4. *Prenatal factors.* Because much of the child's neurological development occurs before birth, a host of prenatal factors (including infection, nutrition, and impaired biological development) can affect the child's neurological integrity and functional status. Microcephaly and severe forms of spina bifida are two such conditions.

5. *Injury or trauma.* These factors include birth difficulties (lack of oxygen during birth, premature birth, traumatic injury during birth) and later physical injury (closed head injury, lack of oxygen) that have neurological effects functionally manifest as MR.

Psychological Theories

In addition to biological causes, MR can result from or be strongly influenced by psychological-environmental factors. The most widely accepted psychological cause of MR is environmental deprivation. Infants placed in environmentally deprived situations (typically characterized by unchanging sensory stimulation, lack of social contact, and restricted movement) for long periods are at significant risk for MR. Early, severe, extended deprivation is usually required to cause significant MR, whereas milder versions of MR may be caused by a combination of environmental causes and an initial propensity toward a lower IQ range.

☐   ASSESSMENT PATTERNS

Before psychological testing begins, medical and sensory tests should be completed. First, the child should be evaluated by a physician to investigate biomedical conditions such as lead poisoning, infection, and genetic disorder. Second, the clinician should attend to the hearing and vision capacity of the child. In some cases, sensory deficits can be misdiagnosed as MR because the child does not perceive the environment accurately, leading to learning deficits and inappropriate behaviors. Any other factors felt to account for the MR should be thoroughly investigated by the clinician or another professional. A sample psychological testing battery is shown in Table 12.3.

Broad Assessment Strategies

Cognitive Assessment

Clinician-Administered—IQ Testing.   The most critical component of cognitive diagnostic testing for MR is the intelligence test, which is required for the MR diagnosis. The choice of intelligence test is crucial and should be made based on preliminary information obtained by the clinician. For children with estimated IQ levels of 50 and above, the instruments of choice are usually the Wechsler intelligence scales. Children age 3–7 can be tested with the WPPSI-R; children between the ages of 6 and 17 can be tested with the WISC-III.

When testing with the Wechsler scales, several issues must be considered. First, the Wechsler scales experience floor effects in the 40–50 IQ range; at or below these scores, they simply give the floor IQ. Hence, they are not useful with children in the severe to profound

TABLE 12.3   Sample Assessment Battery for Mental Retardation

COGNITIVE

1. Intelligence test (Bayley-II, Stanford-Binet:Fourth Edition, or Wechsler scale)
2. Vineland Adaptive Behavior Scales
3. Adaptive Behavior Evaluation Scale
4. Kaufman Brief Intelligence Test
5. Leiter International Performance Scale, Universal Nonverbal Intelligence Test, or Comprehensive Test of Nonverbal Ability

BEHAVIORAL

1. Conners Parent and Teacher Rating Scales
2. Behavior Assessment System for Children (Parent and Teacher)

SYNDROME-SPECIFIC

1. Aberrant Behavior Checklist

Note: Assessment instruments are intended to supplement (not substitute for) a good clinical interview and, when possible, a structured diagnostic interview.

range of MR. If the child fails to score more than 0 or 1 raw score point on the first three or four subtests of a Wechsler scale, the clinician should probably select a different intelligence test. Second, the floor for the Wechsler scales extends farther and is more valid as the child with MR becomes older than the lower age range on the test. In other words, there are fewer "easy" items on the WISC-III for a 6-year-old than there are for a 12-year-old. Hence, a more valid result is obtained for the 12-year-old with MR. This problem can be easily handled in the 6-year-old age range, when the child can be given either the WPPSI-R or WISC-III. At test overlap ages, children with MR should be given the "easier" (in the sense of having more items for younger mental ages) WPPSI-R rather than the "harder" WISC-III. Third, in addition to the overall Full Scale IQ, the Wechsler scales give Verbal and Performance IQ scores, Index scores, and subscale scores. Hence, it is possible to identify strengths and weaknesses in the profile, which may lead to hypotheses about the nature and treatment of the disorder.

In some cases, use of the Wechsler scales to assess intelligence is contraindicated for the child with MR. For example, if a child's suspected IQ is less than 50, the Wechsler scales may not provide an accurate IQ. Furthermore, at the lower end of the age range for the WPPSI-R (age 3 years), the child may be able to complete few items, giving an unreliable indication of intelligence. In addition, a child may have trouble understanding the tasks of the Wechsler scales, or the examiner may want a second measure of IQ because of validity concerns with a previously administered Wechsler scale. For children with these issues, one of two intelligence tests are usually substituted for the Wechsler scale: the SB:FE or Bayley-II.

The SB:FE can be administered to individuals of age 2 years to 24 years. Because of this extensive age range, it includes items that may be in the developmental range for children with severe and profound MR who are over the age of 6. Hence, for children above age 6 who are suspected of being severely or profoundly retarded, the SB-IV is often a more appropriate test than a Wechsler scale. In this age range, it can give IQ scores as low as 36. However, for children under age 6, the SB:FE has floor effects comparable to those of the WPPSI-R. These floor effects become extreme at age 3 years, 6 months, rendering the test meaningless for children with MR below this age. For children under 3½ years, the lowest SB:FE IQ that can be obtained is a 66, and at age 2, the lowest IQ is 95 (Sattler, 1990).

For children with MR who are under age 3½, the test of choice is often the Bayley-II. The Bayley-II yields a Mental Developmental Index (MDI) and a Psychomotor Developmental Index (PDI), as well as a Behavior Rating Index, which is less relevant to MR. The MDI may be used as an approximation of IQ, although IQ at very young ages is minimally predictive of IQ at later ages. Nevertheless, the MDI and PDI of the Bayley-II average 3 standard deviations below the mean for children with Down's syndrome, showing the utility of the Bayley-II for children with MR (Bayley, 1993). Like the Wechsler scales, the Bayley-II scores have a mean of 100 and standard deviation of 15.

For children at or below age 42 months, Bayley-II scores reach a floor level at a standard score of 50. Hence, children with index scores that may be below 50 will receive a score of 50. In addition to being the test of choice for children with MR who are under age 3½, the Bayley is the test of choice for older children who are so impaired (severe or profound MR) that they cannot complete either the Wechsler or SB:FE scales. For children over 3½, an MDI cannot be obtained (because the norm tables end at age 42 months), but a developmental age equivalent can be obtained from Table B.2 (p. 325) in the Bayley-II manual (Bayley, 1993). This developmental age can give some idea of level of functioning.

In addition to the three intelligence tests covered earlier, another good intelligence test for children with developmental delays or MR is the McCarthy Scales of Children's Abilities (McCarthy, 1972; age 2½ to 8½). When using the McCarthy, however, clinicians should attend to the possibility of outdated content or norms (both of which were obtained in the late 1960s to early 1970s). On the other hand, the Kaufman Assessment Battery for Children (K-ABC; Kaufman & Kaufman, 1983; age 2½ to 12½), which is an otherwise good test, should typically not be used to assess MR because of floor effects. For children with severe sensory handicaps, consult Sattler (1990) for testing procedures.

Children with severe language impairments but stronger nonverbal skills should be tested using a predominantly nonverbal intelligence test in addition to or instead of the other IQ tests. Such tests include the Universal Nonverbal Intelligence Test (Bracken & McCallum, 1998), the Leiter International Performance Scale—II (Roid & Miller, 1997), and the Comprehensive Test of Nonverbal Intelligence (Hammill, Pearson, & Wiederholt, 1996). For children with very brief attention spans and problems understanding complex directions, the K-BIT and the Test of Nonverbal Intelligence-3 (Brown, Sherbenou, & Johnsen, 1997) can provide reliable brief/screening IQ values with relatively few demands on the child. In addition to providing information about the IQ of a child who could not complete a Wechsler or SB:FE scale, these brief and nonverbal tests serve a second very important function: checking on the validity of the MR diagnosis. In some cases, children who struggle with longer, more extensive, verbally based IQ tests (such as the Wechsler or SB:FE scales) show much stronger scores on briefer, less demanding tests or on nonverbal tests. In such cases, the MR diagnosis may not accurately characterize the child's adequate function on less elaborate, less verbal, more nonverbal tasks.

By diagnostic definition, the child with MR must score a 70 or below on an intelligence test. Special provision may be made for the SB:FE because it has a different standard deviation, and a cutting score of 68 can be used. With the Bayley, interpretation typically stops with the MDI, but the SB:FE and Wechsler subscales should be interpreted for strengths and weaknesses. Children with MR generally show a uniform depression across subscales, but some children have areas of greater competence.

Cognitive testing can also include achievement and neuropsychological testing. Achievement testing is warranted if the child is placed in an academic setting and a baseline or follow-up measure of learning is desired. This is usually the case for most children in the mild and moderate MR ranges. Typically, achievement testing scores mirror IQ scores for children with a diagnosis of MR.

Clinician-Administered—Adaptive Functioning. Intellectual functioning is only the first half of the MR diagnostic picture. Concurrent with intellectual testing, it is essential to assess the child's adaptive functioning. Adaptive functioning may be defined as the degree to which the child functions and cares for himself or herself independently, adequately, and effectively in the social, academic, work, home, and community environments. As with IQ, adaptive behavior scores must be considered relative to a child's age; what is expected of a child at age 5 will be very different from what is expected at age 15. A developmental, normative sense of adaptive behavior is, therefore, important.

Numerous informal measures of adaptive behavior exist, such as clinical impressions and lists of expected behaviors at various ages. Clinical impressions, although providing useful information, should not be the only basis for assessing adaptive behavior in an MR evaluation. At the very least, these impressions should be compared to tables that list examples of adaptive behaviors for children of various ages and various levels of functioning (see Gelfand et al., 1988; Sattler, 1990). For a diagnosis as important as MR, however, it is important to get a valid, standardized, normed assessment of the child's adaptive behavior. For this purpose, several adaptive behavior scales have been created. The Vineland Adaptive Behavior Scales (VABS) and the Adaptive Behavior Evaluation Scale (ABES) provide items and scores based on both normal and impaired development of adaptive functioning; thus, they are useful for both MR and nonreferred populations. The AAMR Adaptive Behavior Scales-School:2 (ABS-S:2), on the other hand, is geared more specifically to an MR population.

The VABS is an interview measure that yields four subscales: Communication (receptive and expressive language, written language), Daily Living Skills (hygiene, personal care, independence in personal living), Socialization (social behavior), and Motor Skills (gross and fine motor coordination). Subscales can be combined to give an Adaptive Behavior Composite. All VABS scales can be scored relative to norms (basic norms are from a group of individuals without MR, although other comparison samples are available) to give standard scores (mean = 100; standard deviation = 15). Children with MR tend to score 70 or below on all subscales of the VABS. The VABS has been one of the most widely used scales for assessing adaptive functioning in children with MR and other developmental delays, although its subscales do not correspond exactly to the adaptive areas currently identified by AAMR and DSM-IV criteria.

The ABES differs from most other adaptive functioning scales in adopting a questionnaire (as opposed to interview) format. This makes it much easier to administer to parents and teachers, although the advantages of interview administration are lost. ABES subscales are based on the adaptive behavior areas identified by the AAMR and DSM-IV for diagnosis of mental retardation: Communication Skills, Self-Care, Home Living, Social, Community Use, Self-Direction, Health and Safety, Functional Academics, Leisure, and Work. Scaled scores (mean of 10, standard deviation of 3) are provided for each of the 10 subscales, and an overall composite score (mean of 100, standard deviation of 15) is also given, based on a large, nonclinical, nonrepresentative sample. Although less often used, the ABES is valuable for its correspondence to diagnostically required adaptive behavior areas and for its questionnaire format.

The ABS-S:2 (Lambert, Nihira, & Leland, 1993) is an adaptive behavior scale for individuals age 3–18. It is designed to be completed by teachers or other staff in schools. The ABS-S:2 is briefer than the VABS (15–30 minutes) and can be given as an interview or on computer. The ABS-S:2 has two parts, the first of which measures adaptive behavior and the second of which measures social and behavior problems. Part I (adaptive behavior) of the ABS-S:2 asks questions from nine domains (independent functioning, physical development, economic activity, language development, numbers and time, prevocational/vocational activity, self-direction, responsibility, and socialization) that are combined to give a total score. The subscale and total scores are converted to standard scores based on large normative samples of students with and without developmental disabilities.

In addition to the very widely used VABS, ABES, and ABS, other adaptive behavior scales exist, such as the Adaptive Behavior Inventory for Children (ABIC; Mercer & Lewis, 1982) and the Scales of Independent Behavior (SIB; Bruininks, Woodcock, Weatherman, & Hill, 1984). Children with MR score below 70 (2nd to 3rd percentile) on most adaptive behavior subscales and composite scores, relative to children with no diagnosis. If children with

MR are used as the normative group, the adaptive behavior score is typically within 1 standard deviation of the MR norm group. Unlike children with Autistic Disorder, who occasionally elevate physical-motor adaptive behavior subscales, children with MR tend to uniformly depress all adaptive behavior subscales. When IQ and adaptive functioning scores are below 70 and the onset of the problem is before age 18, a diagnosis of MR is warranted.

Behavioral Assessment

Parent-Report/Other-Report. There is no typical MR pattern on the broad-band behavior rating scales, although children with MR and developmental disabilities tend to have elevated profiles (Thompson & Kronenberger, 1990). Based on estimated dual diagnosis (e.g., diagnosed with MR and another DSM diagnosis) rates of 15–30% (Aman et al., 1993), as many as one-third of children with MR may be expected to score in clinical ranges on these tests. Scales that may show the highest elevations in MR populations include measures of Learning Difficulty, Hyperactivity, Inhibition/Withdrawal, and Social Problems.

The Conners' scales contain a subscale that is sensitive to achievement problems and difficulty in school. The CPRS and CTRS Cognitive Problems subscale measures difficulty sustaining effort and completing work (more heavily emphasized on the CPRS), attention/concentration problems, and poor achievement (more heavily emphasized on the CTRS). Other Conners' subscales can be helpful in identifying comorbid hyperactivity-impulsivity (Hyperactivity subscale), aggression/oppositionality/irritability (Oppositional subscale), shyness/anxiety (Anxious-Shy subscale) and social isolation problems (Social Problems subscale) in the child with MR. Children with MR almost always elevate the Cognitive Problems subscale, and elevations of some pattern of the other subscales are common. Hence, the Conners' scales can be of assistance in measuring both core cognitive and associated behavioral-diagnostic components of MR.

On the BASC, children with MR elevate the Learning Problems and Study Skills subscales on the Teacher Report Form (there are no congruent subscales on the other BASC forms), reflecting their core cognitive deficits. Other BASC subscales are extremely useful for identifying the child's associated weaknesses and areas of psychological symptoms. Subscales measuring social behavior and skills (Withdrawal, Social Skills and Leadership) are valuable for characterizing the child's behavior with others. More symptom-focused scales in the internalizing (Depression, Anxiety, Attention Problems, Somatization) and externalizing (Aggression, Hyperactivity, Conduct Problems) areas allow the assessment of potential comorbid disorders. The Atypicality subscale provides information about self-stimulating/habit behaviors, loss of touch with reality, thought disorganization, self-destructive behavior, and odd behavior. In sum, the BASC provides broad information about a variety of problems for which the child with MR may be at risk.

Syndrome-Specific Tests

Aberrant Behavior Checklist

The Aberrant Behavior Checklist (ABC; Aman & Singh, 1994) is a 58-item behavior rating scale completed by parents, teachers, or other caretakers for children age 6 and older. Items are rated on a 0–3 scale of problem severity and fall into five subscales: Irritability,

Lethargy, Stereotypy, Hyperactivity, and Inappropriate Speech. Norms based on teacher ratings of a nonrepresentative sample of children may be used to convert raw scores to T-scores. Unlike broad-band behavior rating scales developed for children without MR, the ABC includes items and scales of behaviors that are more commonly seen in MR populations (e.g., Stereotypy subscale).

Other MR-Specific Tests

Numerous other broad-band behavior rating scales exist for use with MR or other developmentally disabled adolescents and adults, such as the Reiss Screen for Maladaptive Behavior (Reiss, 1988), the Diagnostic Assessment for the Severely Handicapped-II (DASH-II; Matson, 1995), the Emotional Disorders Rating Scale (which applies to children as well as adolescents and adults; Feinstein, Kaminer, Barrett, & Tylenda, 1988), and the Prout-Strohmer Assessment System (Prout & Strohmer, 1989). Most behavior scales developed specifically for MR populations include questions about common MR behaviors such as stereotypic and self-injurious behaviors (Aman & White, 1986), in addition to standard internalizing (depression, anxiety, withdrawal, somatization) and externalizing (hyperactivity, hostility, aggression) problems. In general, however, MR-specific scales are not as well normed and have weaker psychometric properties than behavior-rating scales developed for use with other populations of children.

☐   TREATMENT OPTIONS

Treatment for the child with MR focuses on two broad target areas (Table 12.4): associated behavioral-emotional problems and intellectual-adaptive deficits. Admittedly, this division is somewhat artificial because the intellectual-adaptive deficits of children with MR often contribute to their behavioral-emotional problems. Likewise, the behavioral-emotional problems hinder children's adaptive behaviors, resulting in further intellectual-adaptive deficit. However, the identification of behavioral-emotional components and co-occurring diagnoses allows the application of more specific treatment techniques to the child with MR.

Treatment of Comorbid Behavioral-Emotional Disorders

Behavioral Interventions

When a co-occurring DSM-IV disorder or behavior problem is identified in a child with MR, an effort should be made to apply specific treatment techniques for that disorder. In many cases, the treatment requires some modification to accommodate to the child's lower level of cognitive functioning and understanding of the situation. In addition, children with MR sometimes respond more slowly to treatment and may require more intensive, more straightforward, less cognitive procedures (e.g., more learning trials, simpler contingencies). The extent to which treatment procedures will have to be modified depends on the child's age and severity of retardation. Adolescents with mild MR may be able to manage some limited cognitive techniques. Those with moderate MR probably will not respond to cognitive techniques, but they may respond easily to behavioral treatments. Children with severe or profound retardation require very basic behavioral techniques and very modest goals.

TABLE 12.4   Treatment Options for Mental Retardation

1. Treatment of Associated or Comorbid Behavioral-Emotional Problems

    a. Using techniques specific for each behavior problem with modifications to account for intellectual deficits:
       (1) Reduce, simplify, or eliminate cognitive interventions
       (2) Set appropriate goals and timing expectations
       (3) Use concrete, immediate reinforcement

    b. Behavioral techniques
       (1) Differential reinforcement
       (2) Ignoring
       (3) Antecedent management
       (4) Shaping
       (5) Time-out
       (6) Modeling
       (7) Positive practice
       (8) Punishment

    c. Play therapy for modeling purposes

    d. Medication (for aggressive or self-injurious behavior)

2. Treatment of Intellectual-Adaptive Deficits

    a. Special education
       (1) Enriched experience, structure, and skills training

    b. Behavioral interventions
       (1) Communication training
       (2) Other behavioral techniques
           (a) Reinforcement
           (b) Modeling
           (c) Shaping
           (d) Task analysis

    c. Realistic goals for adaptive functioning

Note: This outline of options summarizes major treatments covered in the text. Specific treatments are often combined into an intervention package. Refer to the text for additional descriptions of each treatment. This table is not necessarily an exhaustive list of all treatments available.

Most of the time, accommodation of disorder-specific treatment procedures to MR requires extensive use of behavioral techniques (Aman et al., 1993). Because these techniques require only a basic level of functioning and little if any processing of internal cognition, they are well suited to even the most impaired child. However, the effectiveness of behavioral techniques depends on the child's environment and on the ability of the people in that environment to adhere to contingencies. In some cases, if the child's behavior is severe and the home environment's ability to manage the behavior is limited, inpatient hospitalization is required to create the behavioral-therapeutic milieu. If behavior problems persist even after extensive attempts at behavior modification, residential placement or institutionalization may have to be considered.

The most common behavioral techniques used for children with MR are differential reinforcement, ignoring, antecedent management, shaping, time-out, modeling, positive practice, and punishment. Differential reinforcement is used to encourage goal behaviors (by rewarding them) while discouraging negative behaviors by ignoring them. Ignoring is effective for behaviors performed to gain the attention or behavior of another person; however, if the attention-seeking behavior is sufficiently dangerous or maladaptive, ignoring may need to be modified or eliminated from the behavior plan. Antecedent management requires the identification of the trigger situation for a behavior and modification (or removal) of that situation to stop the behavior. Shaping and modeling are used to demonstrate for the child successive approximations to a goal, rewarding the child at each step. Time-out is used both to remove the child from a situation in which the maladaptive behavior occurs and to discourage the child from performing the behavior; alternatively, time-out may consist of removing an object from the child's presence when the object is the trigger for inappropriate behavior. Positive practice involves repeatedly practicing appropriate behaviors many times (e.g., walking into the bathroom and sitting on the toilet) until they become automatic or learned by rote.

Finally, punishment is typically administered with methods such as a water mist, loud noise, face washing, physical restraint, mild slap on the hand, or electric shock. The use of such punishment techniques is controversial. Use of any severe punishment technique should be implemented only for dangerous or similarly severe behaviors that do not respond to any other technique and have been thoroughly reviewed and approved by other professionals, with special attention to matters of ethics. Examples of behavioral targets for punishment procedures are self-injurious behavior, severe aggressive behavior, rumination, and pica. Punishment should also never be used alone because reinforcement is necessary to develop substitute behaviors in the child (Matson et al., 1998).

Psychotherapy

Traditional cognitive and psychodynamic psychotherapy techniques are rarely used with children with MR because their limited insight makes progress in the cognitive arena difficult (Kendall & Braswell, 1993). Adolescents with mild MR may be appropriate for cognitive-behavioral psychotherapy. Play therapy may also be effective in some specific cases as a means of modeling social interaction and other desired behaviors, as well as a teaching tool for basic living principles. For example, the therapist-child relationship in play therapy may serve as a prototypic authority relationship for the child. In another case, puppet play may be used to teach sharing behavior or rules of social interaction. In general, however, play, cognitive, and psychodynamic therapies should not be used without concurrent behavioral interventions to address the child's behavior problems in the environment.

Medication

Medication is sometimes used to treat severe behavior problems in children with MR. Although there have been few well-controlled studies with MR populations, most psychotropic medications appear to work in the same way with MR as with non-MR populations (Aman et al., 1993). One common application of medication in the MR population is for aggressive or destructive behavior. Neuroleptics, such as haloperidol (Haldol), chlorpromazine (Thorazine), and thioridazine (Mellaril), are often used to reduce these acting-out behaviors. Methylphenidate (Ritalin) appears to be effective only in some individuals with mild and moderate MR, whose symptoms are solely the result of ADHD (Aman et al., 1993).

Treatment of Intellectual-Adaptive Deficits

Special Education

Children with MR have difficulty with intake, processing, and storage of information. Because this process is vital for schooling, interventions to improve learning usually occur in the context of special education. Special educational programs use detailed teaching, motivational, and behavioral principles to teach children with MR at a pace consistent with their ability.

Early intervention is critical for improving intellectual and adaptive functioning. Parents should be trained to provide their child with structure, experience, and skills training to promote development in the infant, toddler, and preschool years. Out-of-home interventions include programs modeled after Head Start, which identify children at risk for developmental delays and then expose them to enriched learning experiences in a preschool-like setting. It appears that early, intense intervention with ongoing follow-up results in the most positive outcome for children's intellectual and adaptive functioning.

Behavioral Interventions

Behavioral techniques can be quite effective in improving the adaptive behavior of children with MR. Depending on the severity of MR, adaptive skills may need to be taught at a very basic level. Specific interventions to address adaptive behavior can be found in a companion intervention manual to the ABES (McCarney, McCain, & Bauer, 1995). Other interventions to develop adaptive behavior skills in children with MR rely heavily on communication and behavioral principles. In some cases, these interventions closely resemble those for Autistic Disorder.

Communication training programs have the therapist (or teacher) demonstrate appropriate requests and social interaction during actual situations in which the child should be using communication to gain a favored toy or activity. The child is then rewarded for imitating the therapist by gaining access to the desired item or task. For example, the first few times when the child is reaching for a ball, the therapist could say, "I want the ball," as the ball is handed to the child. Later, the child would have to say the sentence in order to receive the ball. A similar program requires the therapist (or teacher) to describe verbally the child's behavior by commenting or by making a request that mirrors the child's attempt to gain a favored object or activity (Matson et al., 1998). Other communication skills interventions, such as pivotal response training, are described in Chapter 11.

Behavioral techniques to teach adaptive behavior to the child with MR use a variety of techniques, including reinforcement, modeling, shaping, and task analysis of behavior. Reinforcement techniques follow a typical plan of identifying a reward and then pairing it with the child's production of the desired adaptive behavior. Maladaptive behavior or absence of the adaptive behavior is ignored. Modeling involves demonstrating the desired behavior for the child, at times moving the child physically through the behavior sequence.

The goal behaviors chosen and the pace of attainment of expected goals must match the child's ability level. To assist with more complex behaviors, a procedure of shaping and task analysis is used.

Shaping and task analysis begin with an assessment of what the child can do. Simple goals are then identified and broken down into discrete learning steps (Sattler, 1990). For example, brushing the teeth involves knowing where to find a toothbrush, identification of the correct toothbrush, holding the toothbrush, using toothpaste, putting the toothbrush into the mouth, moving the toothbrush, brushing all teeth, brushing for a specified period of time, and performing all of these activities without direct supervision. Each learning step is demonstrated (at times by physically moving the child to perform the correct behavior) and reinforced repeatedly with praise or another reinforcer (candy is often used as a reinforcer, although presumably not for toothbrushing). Behaviors that interfere with learning of the target behavior may be ignored, punished, or redirected (Aman et al., 1993). Once several parts of the skill are learned, the child is required to perform larger chunks of the skill in order to be reinforced. After the whole skill is learned, reinforcement is gradually faded by administering it less often and with less intensity. Simple skills such as dressing and washing hands, as well as complex skills such as answering social questions and interacting with people, may be taught in this fashion (Gelfand et al., 1988).

Four principles that must be remembered throughout behavioral intervention with the child with MR are (1) goals must be kept modest, (2) behavior must be broken down into discrete steps, (3) learning must be paced with the ability level of the child, and (4) the behavioral plan must be consistently followed. Unfortunately, following all four of these principles is often challenging for parents and institutional staff. Parents may complain that the child's achievements are insignificant, that the plan is not working, or that the plan is too difficult to follow. The clinician must be sensitive to these complaints because they may indicate that the plan will be spontaneously modified or dropped by the parents. Continued severe family stress may suggest that family therapy is warranted. If the plan is implemented in school or an institution, the greatest risk is inconsistent implementation by staff. All staff should be informed of the plan and given an opportunity for input. One staff member should be responsible for monitoring the plan and dealing with problems.

■ References

Aman, M. G., Hammer, D., & Rojahn, J. (1993). Mental Retardation. In T. H. Ollendick & M. Hersen (Eds.), *Handbook of child and adolescent assessment* (pp. 321–345). Needham Heights, MA: Allyn & Bacon.

Aman, M. G., & Singh, N. N. (1994). *Aberrant Behavior Checklist: Community* (Supplementary Manual). East Aurora, NY: Slosson Educational Publications.

Aman, M. G., & White, A. J. (1986). Measures of drug change in mental retardation. In K. Gadow (Ed.), *Advances in learning and behavioral disabilities* (pp. 157–202). Greenwich, CT: JAI Press.

American Association on Mental Retardation. (1992). *Mental retardation: Definition, classification, and systems of supports* (9th ed.). Washington, DC: Author.

American Psychiatric Association. (1994). *Diagnostic and statistical manual of mental disorders, fourth edition.* Washington, DC: Author.

Baroff, G. S. (1986). *Mental retardation: Nature, cause, and management* (2nd ed.). New York: Wiley.

Bayley, N. (1993). *Bayley Scales of Infant Development: Second Edition.* San Antonio: Psychological Corporation.

Bracken, B. A., & McCallum, R. S. (1998). *Universal Nonverbal Intelligence Test (UNIT).* Itasca, IL: Riverside Publishing.

Brown, L., Sherbenou, R. J., & Johnsen, S. K. (1997). *Test of Nonverbal Intelligence—Third Edition.* Austin, TX: Pro-Ed.

Bruininks, R. H., Woodcock, R. W., Weatherman, R. F., & Hill, B. K. (1984). *Scales of Independent Behavior (SIB).* Allen, TX: DLM Teaching Resources.

Feinstein, C., Kaminer, Y., Barrett, R. B., & Tylenda, B. (1988). The assessment of mood and affect in developmentally disabled children and adolescents: The Emotional Disorders Rating Scale. *Research in Developmental Disabilities, 9,* 109–121.

Gelfand, D. M., Jenson, W. R., & Drew, C. J. (1988). *Understanding child behavior disorders* (2nd ed.). New York: Harcourt Brace Jovanovich College Publishers.

Grossman, H. J. (1983). *Classification in mental retardation.* Washington, DC: American Association on Mental Deficiency.

Hammill, D. D., Pearson, N. A., & Wiederholt, J. L. (1996). *Comprehensive Test of Nonverbal Intelligence.* Austin, TX: Pro-Ed.

Harris, J. C. (1995). *Developmental neuropsychiatry.* New York: Oxford.

Jacobson, J. W. (1982). Problem behavior and psychiatric impairment in a developmentally disabled population I: Behavior frequency. *Applied Research in Mental Retardation, 3,* 121–139.

Kaufman, A. S., & Kaufman, N. L. (1990). *Kaufman Brief Intelligence Test manual.* Circle Pines, MN: American Guidance Service.

Kaufman, A. S., & Kaufman, N. L. (1983). *K-ABC: Kaufman Assessment Battery for Children.* Circle Pines, MN: American Guidance Service.

Kendall, P. C., & Braswell, L. (1993). *Cognitive-behavioral therapy for impulsive children* (2nd ed.). New York: Guilford.

Lambert, N. M., Nihira, K., & Leland, H. (1993). *AAMR Adaptive Behavior Scales - School: Second Edition.* Austin, TX: Pro-Ed.

Matson, J. L. (1995). *Diagnostic assessment for the severely handicapped.* Baton Rouge, LA: Scientific Publishers.

Matson, J. L., Applegate, H., Smiroldo, B., & Stallings, S. (1998). Mentally retarded children. In R. J. Morris and T. R. Kratochwill (Eds.), *The practice of child therapy* (3rd ed.). Boston: Allyn & Bacon.

McCarney, S. B., McCain, B. R., & Bauer, A. M. (1995). *The Adaptive Behavior Intervention Manual—Revised.* Columbia, MO: Hawthorne Educational Services.

McCarthy, D. A. (1972). *Manual for the McCarthy Scales of Children's Abilities.* San Antonio: Psychological Corporation.

Mercer, J. R., & Lewis, J. F. (1982). *System of Multicultural Pluralistic Assessment.* San Antonio: Psychological Corporation.

Prout, H. T., & Strohmer, D.C. (1989). *Prout-Strohmer Personality Inventory manual.* Schenectady, NY: Genium Publishing Corp.

Reiss, S. (1988). *Test manual for the Reiss Screen for Maladaptive Behavior.* Orland Park, IL: International Diagnostic Systems.

Roid, G. H., & Miller, L. J. (1997). *Leiter International Performance Scale—Revised.* Wood Dale, IL: Stoelting Co.

Sattler, J. M. (1990). *Assessment of children* (3rd ed.). San Diego, CA: Jerome M. Sattler, Publisher.

Stone, W. L., MacLean, W. E., Jr., & Hogan, K. L. (1995). Autism and mental retardation. In M. C. Roberts (Ed.), *Handbook of pediatric psychology* (2nd ed.). New York: Guilford.

Teeter, P. A., & Semrud-Clikeman, M. (1997). *Child neuropsychology: Assessment and interventions for neurodevelopmental disorders.* Boston: Allyn & Bacon.

Thompson, R. J., Jr., & Kronenberger, W. G. (1990). Behavior problems in children with learning problems. In H. L. Swanson & B. Keogh (Eds.), *Learning disabilities: Theoretical and research issues* (pp. 155–174). Hillsdale, NJ: Erlbaum.

CHAPTER 13

Tic Disorders

□ CLINICAL DESCRIPTION

Diagnostic Considerations

A tic is a "sudden, rapid, recurrent, nonrhythmic, stereotyped motor movement or vocalization" (American Psychiatric Association, 1994, p. 103). Although they may be suppressed for varying periods of time, tics are experienced as involuntary impulses. Examples of tics are eye blinking, grimacing, coughing, hitting self, vocalizations, and verbalizations. Because they feel involuntary and can appear unusual, they are often associated with distress or social difficulty for the child.

Three major types of tic disorders are identified in DSM-IV, each of which must begin before age 18 in order to be diagnosed. Tic disorders that begin in adulthood are classified as Tic Disorder, Not Otherwise Specified. Tourette's Disorder (also called Tourette's Syndrome, or TS) is a tic disorder involving several motor and at least one vocal tics. The tics must be frequent (defined in DSM-IV as occurring many times a day, nearly every day), and the disorder must be of long duration (defined in DSM-IV as lasting more than one year). Furthermore, characteristics of the tics, such as number, frequency, location, complexity, and severity, change over time. Chronic Motor or Vocal Tic Disorder (CTD) is less severe than TS in that it involves either motor or vocal tics, but not both. As with TS, these tics must be frequent, and the disorder must be of long duration. CTD may be a less severe form of TS caused by the same underlying disorder. The final DSM-IV tic disorder is Transient Tic Disorder (TTD), which is characterized by one or more motor or vocal tics. Unlike TS and CTD, however, TTD has a duration of less than one year.

The prevalence of TS and CTD is 3–5 in every 10,000 people, with prevalence increasing to as high as 0.5% when mild TTDs are considered (Table 13.1; American Psychiatric Association, 1994; Leckman & Cohen, 1996). However, simple tics that do not qualify for diagno-

TABLE 13.1   Epidemiology and Course of Tic Disorders and Tourette's Disorder

Prevalence: 0.03–0.05% for Tourette's Disorder; as high as 1% for any tic disorder

Sex Ratio (Male:Female):   2:1 to 4:1

Typical Onset Age: 2–13 years, peaking between 7 and 11 years

Course: TS and severe cases of CTD can last through childhood and be associated with attention problems, learning problems, social difficulties, and mood disorder. TTD and minor tics frequently remit spontaneously, although a fraction of cases do develop into CTD or TS. The frequency and intensity of motor and vocal tics usually peak between ages 7 and 15, declining for most children after age 12. Complete remission in adulthood is sometimes seen, although mild symptoms often persist with some periodic flare-ups. Some severe cases of TS can persist through adulthood.

Common Comorbid Conditions: 1. Obsessive-Compulsive Disorder
2. Attention-Deficit/Hyperactivity Disorder
3. Mood Disorders

Relevant Subtypes: 1. Tic Subtypes: Motor vs. Vocal, Simple vs. Complex
2. Tourette's Disorder
3. Chronic Motor or Vocal Tic Disorder
4. Transient Tic Disorder

sis are much more common. It is estimated that 10–20% of children will display a transient tic at one time or another (Cohen, Leckman & Riddle, 1997; Leckman & Cohen, 1996).

Two diagnoses that share similarities with Tic Disorders are Stereotypy/Habit Disorder and Obsessive-Compulsive Disorder. In these disorders, the person feels compelled to perform a behavior, but the behavior is ultimately voluntary. Tics, on the other hand, are involuntary and usually unwanted. Furthermore, compulsions and habits may be more regular, rhythmic, and anxiety reducing than are tics.

Appearance and Features

Tics may be grouped into several categories based on their appearance (see Table 13.2). *Motor* tics involve movements, whereas *vocal or phonic* tics involve words or sounds. *Simple* tics are usually brief and unelaborated, whereas *complex* tics are coordinated and longer-lasting. Examples of simple motor tics are shoulder-shrugging, eye blinking, twitching, or head nodding. Complex motor tics involve elaborate movements such as facial gestures, hitting, and stomping feet. Simple vocal tics are typically manifest as coughing or grunting, whereas complex vocal tics consist of words. Examples of complex vocal tics are coprolalia (use of socially unacceptable words), echolalia (repeating what is heard), palilalia (repeating what one just said), saying words out of context, or screaming words (Kurlan, 1989; Ollendick & Ollendick, 1990). In addition to the motor/vocal and simple/complex tic categories, Kurlan (1989) describes the phenomenon of sensory tics. Sensory tics are feelings of abnormal sensation (pressure, tickle, temperature) in the body. The person attempts to remove these "tics" by movements that themselves may appear as motor tics.

Tics can range from being barely noticeable to overt and embarrassing. Complex vocal tics, particularly coprolalia, can be both humiliating and disruptive, requiring special

TABLE 13.2   Appearance and Features of Tic Disorders

COMMON FEATURES

1. Involuntary, rapid movements or vocalizations
2. May be suppressed for a time
3. May be diverted into different (but similar) behaviors
4. Onset between ages 2 and 13
5. Tics occur many times a day
6. Tics can range from barely noticeable to obvious
7. Aggravated by stress, excitement, or fatigue
8. Child can anticipate the tic
9. Avoidance of social situations

OCCASIONAL FEATURES

1. Attempt to disguise tic into apparently normal activity
2. Social rejection

Note: The features listed in the table are often seen but are not universal. Some features may be diagnostically relevant or required, whereas others may not be required for diagnosis. "Common" features are typical of the disorder; "occasional" features appear frequently but are not necessarily seen in a majority of cases.

arrangements for children with this type of tic. Uninformed children and adults often mistake complex vocal tics for intentionally rude and disruptive behavior. Their responses, therefore, often consist of punishment and avoidance; children may ridicule and reject the child with the disorder. Although coprolalia is commonly dramatized in media portrayals of TS, it only occurs in 10–30% of children with TS (American Psychiatric Association, 1994; Harris, 1995; Sallee & Spratt, 1999).

The frequency and intensity of tics vary with time. TTD usually begins with tics in the arms, head, or neck. These tics may change in form and may come and go without clear reason or pattern. At the onset or early in the course of TTD, there is no clear way to predict whether the disorder will spontaneously remit, continue without progressing, or develop into CTD or TS. Many children with TTD experience remission of their symptoms and do not progress to CTD or TS (Leckman & Cohen, 1996). TTD does not tend to be associated with other behavioral problems and comorbid diagnoses to the extent seen for TS and CTD (Cohen et al., 1997).

Onset of TS is typically between the ages of 2 and 13 years, with an average onset age of 7 years (American Psychiatric Association, 1994; Cohen et al., 1997). TS almost always begins with a simple motor tic that is often, but not always, located in the upper half of the body (often in the neck or head), with an eye blink tic being the most common (Harris, 1995). Vocal and other motor tics may then emerge, change, and disappear. There is a wide variety of presentation of tics in different cases of TS, ranging from relatively mild tics that the child can frequently camouflage to severe, complex motor and vocal tics. However, most cases of TS are so mild that they do not receive clinical attention (Cohen et al., 1997; Harris, 1995). Tics generally increase during times of stress, major life change, emotional excitement, or fatigue (Sallee & Spratt, 1999). In many individuals, decreases in tic behavior occur during activities requiring attention and concentration, or during sleep (American Psychiatric Association, 1994; Brunn, 1984; Ollendick & Ollendick, 1990).

The course and outcome of Tic Disorders is variable, although most patients see improvement of symptoms after age 12. Vocal tics are most likely to completely remit, and motor tics tend to improve as well. In cases in which tics were mild and transient, remission is most likely. For children with TS, about one-third have complete remission of symptoms by adulthood, and another one-third see significant improvement (Harris, 1995). Despite improvement for most children with TS, some children with severe TS continue to have significant symptoms as adults. In some cases, children with TS experience increased obsessions and compulsions around the time that their tic symptoms are improving (Cohen et al., 1997; Leckman & Cohen, 1996).

Children with tic disorders often report that they can anticipate tics and, usually, suppress them for a time. However, they have a subjective sense of the tics "building up" when they are suppressed, and they have a period of increased tic behavior following suppression. Children will also attempt to disguise tics by blending them into apparently normal motor or vocal activity. Because they can sometimes suppress or disguise tics, children with tic disorder expend considerable amounts of energy holding back tics in order to avoid attention or humiliation in public. When they then enter a safer situation, such as the home environment or nurse's office, they may let out the tics in a burst of activity. Unfortunately, the amount of energy required to withhold tics distracts these children from learning or social situations, causing further difficulties for them (Sallee & Spratt, 1999). In some cases, the child will suppress tics during a clinical interview. Hence, the failure to observe tics during interview does not mean that tics are never present. Parents and other observers must be enlisted to provide an accurate view of the child's tic suppression/expression pattern.

Children with tic disorders may manifest a variety of other behavior problems, and the risk of associated problems increases with the severity of the disorder. Children with TS are most at risk for associated problems, with half or more having comorbid psychiatric diagnoses. Two psychiatric disorders most often noted as co-occurring with TS and CTD are Attention Deficit/Hyperactivity Disorder (ADHD) and Obsessive-Compulsive Disorder (OCD) (Cohen et al., 1997). Up to 50% of children with TS show symptoms of OCD (Kurlan, 1989), and 30–50% have ADHD (Cohen et al., 1997; Harris, 1995). Neurological, physiologic, and genetic factors appear to be responsible for this comorbidity (Cohen et al., 1997). In clinically referred samples, depression (73%) has been frequently found, and children with tic disorders have been described as anxious and tense as well (Wodrich, Benjamin, & Lachar, 1997). Sleep disorders also appear to be common (Harris, 1995). Motor coordination and learning problems are present in up to 30% of children with TS seen in clinical settings (Cohen et al., 1997; Sallee & Spratt, 1999).

Tic disorders may also lead to social difficulties, such as peer rejection, low self-esteem, feelings of alienation, and isolation (Bronheim, 1991). Children with TS have been found to have poorer peer relationships than children with diabetes, indicating that it is the nature of the tic symptoms, and not the stress of a chronic disease in general, that affects the child's peer relationships (Bawden, Stokes, Camfield, Camfield, & Salisbury, 1998). The presence of OCD, ADHD, or social dysfunction in a child with a tic disorder requires modification of assessment expectations and treatment plans.

Etiology

Biological Theories

Five major findings support the hypothesis that TS has a physiological or genetic etiology:

1. Neurological and neuropsychological findings suggest that problems in the frontal lobes, striatum, and basal ganglia are related to the presence of TS (Peterson & Klein, 1997). Interestingly, these areas are also implicated in ADHD and OCD, two disorders that are often comorbid with TS. Children with TS tend to do more poorly on neuropsychological tests that are sensitive to frontal lobe, executive functioning. They also have a higher incidence of neurological symptoms, including soft signs and abnormal EEG patterns. Although CT (computerized tomography) and MRI (magnetic resonance imaging) studies have not produced consistent results, PET (positron emission tomography) and SPECT (single photon emission tomography) studies have suggested abnormal metabolism in the frontal and striatal brain areas, as well as in the basal ganglia, for children with TS (Harris, 1995; Sallee & Spratt, 1999).

2. TS tends to occur in children who have a family member with a tic disorder, an obsessive-compulsive disorder, or ADHD. Studies have shown an over 50% concordance rate for TS in identical twins, as compared to about 10% for fraternal twins (Price, Kidd, Cohen, Pauls, & Leckman, 1985). In many cases, an autosomal dominant gene appears to be responsible for TS, although this gene does not have complete penetrance. Other environmental and physiological factors, such as the presence of certain sex hormones, appears to affect the phenotypic presentation of the gene (American Psychiatric Association, 1994; Cohen et al., 1997; Harris, 1995), and other patterns of genetic inheritance of TS are likely (Sallee & Spratt, 1999).

3. In some cases, prenatal experiences appear to be related to TS, possibly by affecting neural development. For example, mothers of children with TS report more life stress, nausea, and vomiting during pregnancy (Leckman et al., 1990).

4. Specific psychotropic medications can be quite effective in reducing tics. Psychopharmacological evidence suggests that problems in dopaminergic neurotransmission may underlie TS because the most effective TS medications block dopamine transmission, whereas tics are exacerbated by medications that facilitate dopaminergic transmission (Harris, 1995).

5. There appears to be a small subgroup of children who develop comorbid OCD and TS symptoms as a result of an infection-triggered autoimmune disorder. This disorder begins with a bacteriological infection that causes an immune response that results in brain impairment and emergence of the OCD/TS symptoms. Symptoms often improve after immunosuppressant treatment in these cases (Allen, Leonard, & Swedo, 1995).

Behavioral Theories

Although physiological theories of the etiology of TS and CTD have received the most research support, behavioral factors may contribute to the expression of tic disorders. In the case of very mild and/or transient tics, behavioral factors may be solely responsible for the development of tics (Matthews, Eustace, Grad, Pelcovitz, & Olson, 1985). Behavioral theories characterize tics as behaviors that are reinforced by the environment. Tics that are followed by reinforcing attention, for instance, are likely to recur. In a classical conditioning paradigm, the tic may be part of a reflexive fear response that becomes classically conditioned to a particular type of situation such as a social gathering. Eventually, the social gathering becomes directly paired with the tic behaviors even in the absence of the feeling of fear. Despite the intuitive appeal of these behavioral theories, behavioral treatments for tic disorders have received more attention than behavioral causes of tic disorders.

☐ ASSESSMENT PATTERNS

A sample assessment battery for tic disorders is shown in Table 13.3.

Broad Assessment Strategies

Cognitive Assessment

Clinician-Administered. Psychological assessment of the child with a tic disorder usually includes at least basic IQ and achievement testing. Based on initial findings from these tests, additional neuropsychological testing may be ordered. In many cases, therefore, testing will begin with a brief IQ test such as the K-BIT or WASI, progressing to the WISC-III if necessary.

On the WISC-III, children with TS generally score in normal ranges for Full Scale (FIQ), Performance (PIQ), and Verbal (VIQ) IQ (Bornstein, 1990; Bornstein, Baker, Bazylewich, & Douglas, 1991; Bornstein & Yang, 1991; Dykens et al., 1990). Children with comorbid TS and ADHD score 10–15 IQ points lower than children with TS who do not have ADHD, placing their group IQ mean in the low average range (Dykens et al., 1990). Medication for TS does not appear to have a significant effect on IQ (Bornstein & Yang, 1991).

Children with TS often show strengths in abstract thinking and verbal knowledge (Similarities, Comprehension, and Vocabulary subtests, and the Verbal Comprehension

TABLE 13.3   Sample Assessment Battery for Tic Disorders

COGNITIVE

1. Wechsler Abbreviated Scale of Intelligence

BEHAVIORAL

1. Personality Inventory for Youth
2. Behavior Assessment System for Children (Parent-Report and Teacher-Report)

SYNDROME-SPECIFIC

1. Tourette Syndrome Global Scale
2. Yale Global Tic Severity Scale

Note: Assessment instruments are intended to supplement (not substitute for) a good clinical interview and, when possible, a structured diagnostic interview.

factor), accompanied by a weakness in processing speed (Coding subtest and Processing Speed factor; Bornstein et al., 1991; Dykens et al., 1990). Weaknesses in attention, concentration, and processing speed are most common when TS is accompanied by ADHD. Children with CTD will often show assessment patterns similar to those of children with TS. Children with TTD, as a group, usually score in normal ranges.

Children with TS typically have average achievement testing patterns on reading and written language tests, with deficits in mathematics (Bornstein, 1990; Bornstein et al., 1991; Bornstein & Yang, 1991; Dykens et al., 1990). As with IQ, children with TS and accompanying ADHD score lower than those without ADHD (Dykens et al., 1990), and there is no difference based on medication status (Bornstein & Yang, 1991).

On neuropsychological testing, there appears to be a subgroup (20–50%) of children with TS who show mild to moderate deficits on tests involving performance skills such as motor speed, perceptual organization, and visuographic skills (Bornstein, 1990; Bornstein & Baker, 1991; Bornstein et al., 1991). This impaired subgroup of children with TS has more frequent and severe tic symptoms (Bornstein et al., 1991) as well as physiological abnormalities (Bornstein & Baker, 1991).

Psychological Assessment

Child-Report. Because children with TS and CTD tend to have co-occurring behavioral and psychological problems, personality and behavior problem testing is often warranted. Such testing should target social problems, depression, low self-esteem, and anxiety, which may contribute to or result from the tics. Adolescents, for example, may be expected to show MMPI and MMPI-A patterns characteristic of depression (elevated scale 2), anxiety/rumination (elevated scales 7 and 8), or social maladjustment (elevated scales 4 and 0). The configuration of these scales suggests the relative importance of each of these problems.

Younger children may show deficits on scales of self-esteem, reflecting their unhappiness over the disorder. Children with TS tend to score lower on the PHSCS Behavior subscale than controls, indicating that they are unhappy with their behavior and have more behavior problems (Edell-Fisher & Motta, 1990). Children with TS also scored lower on the Tennessee Self-Concept Scale (TSCS; Fitts, 1965) than did controls (Edell-Fisher & Motta, 1990). Most evidence supports the hypothesis that children with TS have specific behavioral self-esteem problems as opposed to a global self-esteem deficit (Edell-Fisher & Motta, 1990). Edell and Motta (1989) did not find tic severity to be correlated with global PHSCS self-esteem scores.

Behavioral Assessment

Parent-Report. On parent-completed behavioral checklists, children with tic disorders may be expected to show a range of results. Behavior subscales reflecting overactivity, obsessive-compulsive problems, depression, and social functioning are the most likely to show elevations. The ECI-4, CSI-4, and ASI-4 each have items asking about motor tics and vocal tics, but the duration of the tics is not specified. Furthermore, parents will sometimes endorse the SI-4 tic items to reflect compulsions and ritualistic behaviors as opposed to tics. Children with tic disorders also frequently show elevations of the SI-4 ADHD subscale and the obsessive-compulsive items.

Although the parent-report and teacher-report BASC scales do not have items or sub-scales designed specifically to measure symptoms of tic disorders, several BASC subscales are sensitive to associated features of tic disorders. Children with comorbid hyperactivity and attention problems elevate the BASC Attention Problems and Hyperactivity subscales. Problems in social functioning, especially rejection by or avoidance of peers, may be shown by low Leadership and high Withdrawal subscale scores. Obsessive-compulsive symptoms (which are common in children with tic disorders) are contained on the BASC Atypicality scale, which also contains other infrequent psychiatric symptoms. Depression symptoms may be indicated by elevated Depression or Withdrawal subscale scores.

On the CBCL, elevations of the Thought Problems subscale usually reflect the un-usual, compulsive nature of the tics, as well as obsessive-compulsive tendencies that often accompany TS. Elevations on the CBCL Withdrawn, Anxious/Depressed, and Attention Problems subscales could indicate problems with social relationships, unhappiness, and at-tention, respectively. Such difficulties commonly result from the stress of having TS and from the response of peers to the tics.

Child-Report. Tic disorders take an emotional toll on children, causing both distress and frustration, in addition to common comorbid syndromes such as ADHD and OCD. For these reasons, child self-report measures can be of help in identifying the impact of the tic disorder on the child's psychological well-being. The PIY has two items about twitching that are not clearly defined as tics per se and that fall on the Somatic Concern scale. Children who are upset about their tic disorders would be expected to elevate the PIY Psychological Discomfort scale. Associated ADHD symptoms and learning problems would be indicated by elevated Impul-sivity and Distractibility scale and Cognitive Impairment scale scores, respectively. Shyness, withdrawal, and isolation would result in an elevated Social Withdrawal scale score, whereas outright peer rejection and neglect would be shown by an elevated Social Skills Deficits scale score. Family problems may be indicated if the Family Dysfunction scale is elevated.

On the BASC, children with tic disorders may elevate the Atypicality subscale, reflect-ing their feeling of being out of control of compelling impulses. Elevation of the Social Stress subscale combined with a low score on the Interpersonal Relations subscale could indicate that their relationships with peers are being harmed by their symptoms. The self-report version of the BASC is also very helpful in understanding the self-esteem of the child with a tic disorder. Feelings of positive self-worth are indicated by a high Self-Esteem subscale score, whereas the belief that the child is confident, independent, and decisive would be shown by a high Self-Reliance score. Both of these subscales tap areas of possi-ble self-esteem problems for the child with a tic disorder.

Syndrome-Specific Tests

Clinician-Administered

Simple Frequency Counts. Simple frequency count measures involve counting the number of tics that the child produces in a defined period of time. To provide standard con-ditions for the counts, the child is given a task that requires mental focus, such as the Cod-ing or Symbol Search subtests from the WISC-III. Observation periods range from 5 minutes to 1 hour, with 10–15 minutes being most typical.

Tourette Syndrome Global Scale. The Tourette Syndrome Global Scale (TSGS; Harcherik, Leckman, Detlor, & Cohen, 1984) assesses behavior in two areas: the Motor and Phonic Tic Domain and the Social Functioning Domain. In the Motor and Phonic Tic Domain, tics are scored according to type (simple, complex, motor, phonic), frequency, and degree of disruption. Frequency and degree of disruption are scored on a six point scale (0–5), with higher scores indicating greater impairment. A total tic domain score is obtained by adding the products of all of the Frequency and Disruption scores. The Social Functioning Domain of the TSGS consists of three areas (behavioral problems, motor restlessness, and level of school functioning), which are rated on a 0 to 25 scale, again with higher scores indicating greater impairment. Scores on the TSGS are related to behavioral and cognitive impairment (Bornstein et al., 1991; Ollendick & Ollendick, 1990).

Yale Global Tic Severity Scale. The Yale Global Tic Severity Scale (YGTSS; Leckman et al., 1989) allows the clinician to rate the severity of tics along the dimensions of number, frequency, intensity, complexity, and interference. Each of these five dimensions is rated on a six-point scale (0–5), with higher scores indicating greater problems. Scores are obtained for Total Motor, Total Phonic, and Total Tics. The YGTSS also includes items pertaining to the type of tics and global impairment as a result of tics. It appears to have good reliability and validity and is easy to administer (Leckman et al., 1989).

Parent-Report and Self-Report

Tic Symptom Self-Report. The Tic Symptom Self-Report (TSSR; Cohen, Leckman, & Shaywitz, 1984; Leckman & Cohen, 1999) is a parent-report measure of the frequency and severity of a child's tics over a one-week period prior to the completion of the scale. A self-report version of the TSSR has been used with adults and appears to be applicable to adolescents. The TSSR has shown moderate correlations with clinician-report measures of tic severity, such as the YGTSS (Leckman & Cohen, 1999).

☐ TREATMENT OPTIONS

Overview

The first step in the treatment of a tic disorder is deciding whether to treat at all. Very minor tics that do not meet DSM-IV criteria and some very mild forms of TTD may not need immediate treatment. For brief, minor tics, parents might be advised to continue discretely monitoring the tic but to reduce overt attention to it. If the tic persists or meets criteria for CTD or TS, the child may be brought back for treatment. The most widely used treatments for TS and CTD are behavioral and pharmacological, although family therapy and individual psychotherapy are helpful in some cases (Table 13.4).

Behavioral Interventions

Behavioral techniques that have been used to treat tics include psychoeducation, massed practice, self-monitoring, contingent reinforcement, relaxation, environmental change, and

TABLE 13.4   Treatment Options for Tic Disorders

1. Behavioral Interventions
   a. Psychoeducation
   b. Massed practice
   c. Self-monitoring
   d. Reinforcement contingencies
   e. Relaxation techniques
   f. Environmental change
   g. Habit reversal
2. Medication
3. Psychotherapy
   a. Hypnotic techniques
4. Family Interventions
   a. Family therapy

Note: This outline of options summarizes major treatments covered in the text. Specific treatments are often combined into an intervention package. Refer to the text for additional descriptions of each treatment. This table is not necessarily an exhaustive list of all treatments available.

habit reversal. Although each of these techniques has produced successes in specific cases, habit reversal appears to be the most promising of the behavioral treatments (Ollendick & Ollendick, 1990).

Psychoeducation

Psychoeducation for tic disorders (Dedmon, 1986; Fisher, Conlon, Burd, & Conlon, 1986) involves informing the child and family about the nature of tics as well as the negative impact that the tics can have on personal, familial, and social functioning. The aim of psychoeducation is to facilitate understanding of the tic behavior as unintentional and not as something to be punished. In more mild cases, families are informed of the common nature of transient tics and asked to return only if the tics intensify. By improving understanding of the tics in these mild cases, it is hoped that the negative collateral impacts of the tic can be minimized and that potentially reinforcing attention to the tic will decrease.

Massed Practice

Massed practice (Turpin, 1983) is a technique that requires the child to produce tics voluntarily for an extended period of time. Following brief rest periods, more voluntary production of tics is performed. This practice is hypothesized to reduce tics by fatiguing muscles or by making the production of the tic aversive to the child. Despite early widespread use of this technique, outcome studies question its effectiveness (Sallee & Spratt, 1999).

Awareness Training and Self-Monitoring

Awareness training is a technique in which a child is taught to detect tics and the events that precede them. For example, the therapist and child might discuss how the tic looks to an observer and how the tic feels to the child. Once the tics are clearly defined, the child demonstrates awareness of tics, by saying "tic" or by making a note in a notebook after each tic occurs (Carr & Bailey, 1996).

Self-monitoring (Ollendick, 1981) follows awareness training and consists of having the child record the frequency or intensity of tics. A wrist-counter or notebook may be used for record keeping. Typically, self-monitoring is augmented by feedback from the therapist or significant others as to when the tic is occurring. Finally, the child learns to identify situations in which the tics are more likely to occur or are more likely to be severe. Documentation of the tics is hypothesized to increase the child's awareness of them, leading to internal motivation to stop them.

Contingent Reinforcement

Reinforcement interventions provide praise or other rewards for the absence of tics or for the production of a behavior that is incompatible with tics. When tics do occur, they are either ignored or punished. Parents are encouraged to provide favorable comments and attention to the child's decrease in tics and compliance with behavioral program. Azrin and Peterson (1990) also suggest the use of a "habit inconvenience review," in which the therapist and child discuss the embarrassment, inconveniences, and effort that were caused by the tics. This review reminds the child of the intrinsic rewards of reducing the tic behavior. Tangible rewards are also frequently arranged with parents for documented decreases in the tic behavior (Azrin & Peterson, 1990).

Carrying out a reinforcement program requires extensive parent training to deliver the intervention accurately and effectively. Parents are encouraged to reduce stresses in the family, increase support for the child, and reinforce the absence of tic behaviors. Reinforcement contingencies, particularly contingent attention, may be the most appropriate treatment for TTD and mild CTD. However, reinforcement alone tends to produce only short-term and situation-specific gains for TS (Ollendick & Ollendick, 1990).

Relaxation Techniques

Relaxation techniques involve the teaching of progressive muscle relaxation, breathing, imagery, and relaxing self-statements (Azrin & Peterson, 1990). Children are instructed to practice the relaxation at home, eventually applying the relaxation techniques whenever a tic is imminent (Azrin & Peterson, 1990). Relaxation techniques attempt to address the anxiety and stress that underlie and exacerbate tics. Relaxation may also reduce tics by giving the child greater control over the muscle groups that produce tics. Furthermore, muscles in a state of relaxation may be less likely to contract and produce tics. Typically, relaxation techniques are used as components in multifactorial behavior therapy packages (Ollendick & Ollendick, 1990).

Environmental Change

Environmental change interventions seek to make the environment as nonthreatening and accommodating as possible for the child with a tic disorder (Bronheim, 1991; Dedmon, 1986). Many of these interventions are applied in the school setting in order to reduce the stress of a setting that is social (risk of embarrassment), structured (difficult to escape), and anxiety provoking (involves evaluation). Environmental change in the school is accomplished by modifying classroom rules, educating teachers, educating peers, and communicating understanding to the child. For example, the child may be allowed to leave the room periodically to "let out" tics. Alternatively, the child may be permitted to leave the room during traditionally "quiet" times, such as tests (Bronheim, 1991; Dedmon, 1986). Other environmental interventions target deficits associated with the tic disorder, such as a learning disability or attention deficit. Ideally, as environmental stress is reduced, tic frequency and associated problems decrease.

Habit Reversal and Competing Response Training

Habit reversal consists of five components that address tics (Azrin & Nunn, 1973; Azrin & Peterson, 1990): awareness training, self-monitoring, relaxation training, contingency management, and competing response training (Azrin & Peterson, 1990). The core component of habit reversal, however, is competing response training.

Competing response training consists of the practice of a competing response that prevents the tic from occurring (Azrin & Nunn, 1973; Azrin & Peterson, 1989, 1990). The competing response must be opposite to the tic movement, inconspicuous, and not distracting for the child (Azrin & Peterson, 1990). Azrin and Peterson (1990) suggest that most competing responses consist of the tensing of muscles that control movement opposite to the tic, although other responses are possible. For example, a child with a head shaking tic would tense the neck muscles that hold the head still; an eye blink tic would be controlled by a systematic, voluntary eye blink (Azrin and Peterson, 1989). One tic is initially identified as the competing response target. Then the child practices the competing response, applying it *in vivo* for 1 minute when the child anticipates the tic or has just exhibited the tic (Azrin & Peterson, 1990). The competing response prevents the tic and may act as a punisher for the urge or tendency to have a tic (Ollendick & Ollendick, 1990).

Habit reversal and related methods have received empirical support for children with transient tics, CTD, and TS (Azrin & Nunn, 1973; Azrin & Peterson, 1989, 1990; Carr & Bailey, 1996). Turpin (1983) summarizes Azrin's results reporting an 80% success rate at 18-month follow-up, and other authors report similar results (Carr & Bailey, 1996). In the largest study of the effectiveness of habit reversal, Azrin and Peterson (1990) report an average reduction of 93% in tic frequency in 10 children with TS. Half of the children showed no tic symptoms either at the clinic or at home, and 20% had a complete remission in both environments. The average therapy time was 20 sessions, and the program was equally effective for motor and vocal tics (Azrin & Peterson, 1990).

Medication

Pharmacological treatments are a frequent intervention for moderate to severe tic disorders. A decision to treat with medication should be based on the severity of the tics, the extent to which tics interfere with normal functioning, and the existence of other conditions (Kerbeshian & Burd, 1988). Most knowledge of pharmacological treatments for tic disorders is based on experience with TS.

Numerous medications, predominantly neuroleptics, are used to treat TS. The most frequently used and most well-studied medication is haloperidol, although other medications, such as clonidine, pimozide, fluphenazine, sulpiride, flunarizine, and clonazepam, are also used to treat TS (Kerbeshian & Burd, 1988; Leckman & Cohen, 1996; Micheli et al., 1990; Robertson, Schnieden & Lees, 1990; Shapiro et al., 1989). Although less well studied, the newer medications risperidone and guanfacine also appear to produce significant improvement in tic symptoms (Chappell et al., 1995; Lombroso et al., 1995). Response rates to these medications are all more effective than response to placebo. Within medications, haloperidol is usually more effective than pimozide or clonidine for tics (Harris, 1995), although at least one study has shown pimozide to be superior to haloperidol (Sallee, Nesbitt, Jackson, Sine, & Sethuraman, 1997). Considerations such as co-occurring conditions or side effects may argue against haloperidol use (Kerbeshian & Burd, 1988; Shapiro et al., 1989).

Approximately 70–80% of children receiving haloperidol or pimozide show an improvement in symptoms, with average symptom reduction rates of about 70% (Leckman & Cohen, 1996). Shapiro et al. (1989) reported a 65% decrease in tics with haloperidol and a 60% decrease in tics with pimozide. A median tic decrease rate of 50% was reported by Lombroso et al. (1995) for children taking risperidone. Other researchers report improvements using medications such as clonidine (Leckman et al., 1991), sulpiride (Robertson et al., 1990), and flunarizine (Micheli et al., 1990), generally with less improvement than seen with haloperidol, pimozide, and risperidone. Importantly, some children with TS improve on placebo, although to a lesser extent than with medication (Leckman et al., 1991). One study reported a decrease of 43.4% in tics for the placebo group (Shapiro et al., 1989).

Over all, the literature appears to support haloperidol as a first line of pharmacological treatment for TS (Ollendick & Ollendick, 1990). Depending on side effects and other symptoms, however, other medications may be used (Kerbeshian & Burd, 1988). Haloperidol, for example, is faster acting than clonidine but may cause more extrapyramidal side effects. Likewise, pimozide is associated with fewer sedating and extrapyramidal effects than haloperidol, but it has potential negative cardiac side effects.

Choice of medication is also affected by the presence of comorbid disorders, particularly ADHD. Clonidine may be more effective than haloperidol for cases of tic disorder and ADHD (Kerbeshian & Burd, 1988), and the combination of clonidine and clonazapam may treat tic symptoms better than clonidine alone (Steingard et al., 1994). Guanfacine produces similar effects to clonidine in reducing impulsivity and tics, with fewer hypotensive and sedative effects (Chappell et al., 1995).

The use of methylphenidate (Ritalin) for combined ADHD and tic disorder is a topic of some controversy. Studies show that methylphenidate reduces hyperactive and aggressive behavior, and some authors report minimal increases in tics (Gadow, Sverd, Sprafkin, Nolan, & Ezor, 1995). However, there is evidence of some increase in motor tic symptoms when taking methylphenidate (Gadow et al., 1995; Riddle et al., 1995).

For combined tic and seizure disorders, clonazepam may be the medication of choice (Kerbeshian & Burd, 1988). In cases when tic disorders and other disorders co-occur, haloperidol and another psychotropic medication may be combined, provided that there are no negative interactions (Kerbeshian & Burd, 1988). Informed flexibility in medication is the general rule for TS, trying medications sequentially until an appropriate treatment is found.

Psychotherapy

Hypnotic Techniques

Hypnotherapy may be particularly promising for tic disorders because it emphasizes relaxation and control over bodily functioning (Young & Montano, 1988). Hypnotherapy with relaxation and mastery images is antithetical to the tic behavior as well as distracting and pleasant for the child. Children who are taught self-hypnotic techniques can learn to apply this intervention to tics *in vivo*. Some studies (Kohen & Botts, 1987; Young & Montano, 1988) report positive outcomes for hypnotherapy to address tic disorders. However, as with relaxation techniques, well-controlled outcome studies of hypnosis techniques are sparse. Hypnotherapy may also be used as a component of a behavioral treatment package in order to address relaxation and mastery goals (Young & Montano, 1988).

Psychodynamic and Play Therapy

Individual psychotherapy and play therapy are typically not used as the major treatments for a tic disorder, unless psychological factors are clearly contributing to the disorder. For example, individual psychotherapy may be necessary for the child who is reluctant to give up the tic symptom or for the child for whom the tic has created other problems such as depression or social maladjustment. However, medication and behavioral interventions are typically tried first.

Family Interventions

Family therapy is rarely used as a first or only treatment for tic disorders, largely because of the success rates of behavioral and pharmacological therapy. However, the clinician must be prepared to use family therapy if significant family issues emerge in the assessment. Family therapy may also be necessary if the tic serves a role in the family system such that the family sabotages other interventions (Prata & Masson, 1985). The tic may also be a major stressor in the family, demanding therapeutic attention.

■ References

Allen, A. J., Leonard, H. L., & Swedo, S. E. (1995). Case study: A new, infection-triggered, autoimmune subtype of pediatric OCD and Tourette's syndrome. *Journal of the American Academy of Child and Adolescent Psychiatry, 34,* 307–311.

American Psychiatric Association. (1994). *Diagnostic and statistical manual of mental disorders, fourth edition.* Washington, DC: Author.

Azrin, N. H., & Nunn, R. G. (1973). Habit-reversal: A method of eliminating nervous habits and tics. *Behavior Research and Therapy, 11,* 619–628.

Azrin, N. H., & Peterson, A. L. (1989). Reduction of an eye tic by controlled blinking. *Behavior Therapy, 20,* 467–473.

Azrin, N. H., & Peterson, A. L. (1990). Treatment of Tourette Syndrome by habit reversal: A waiting-list control group comparison. *Behavior Therapy, 21,* 305–318.

Bawden, H. N., Stokes, A., Camfield, C. S., Camfield, P. R., & Salisbury, S. (1998). Peer relationship problems in children with Tourette's disorder or diabetes mellitus. *Journal of Child Psychology and Psychiatry and Allied Disciplines, 39,* 663–668.

Bornstein, R. A. (1990). Neuropsychological performance in children with Tourette's Syndrome. *Psychiatry Research, 33,* 73–81.

Bornstein, R. A., & Baker, G. B. (1991). Neuropsychological performance and urinary phenylethylamine in Tourette's Syndrome. *The Journal of Neuropsychiatry and Clinical Neurosciences, 3,* 417–421.

Bornstein, R. A., Baker, G. B., Bazylewich, T., & Douglass, A. B. (1991). Tourette syndrome and neuropsychological performance. *Acta Psychiatrica Scandinavia, 84,* 212–216.

Bornstein, R. A., & Yang, V. (1991). Neuropsychological performance in medicated and unmedicated patients with Tourette's Disorder. *American Journal of Psychiatry, 148,* 468–471.

Bronheim, S. (1991). An educator's guide to Tourette Syndrome. *Journal of Learning Disabilities, 24,* 17–22.

Brunn, R. D. (1984). Gilles de la Tourette syndrome: An overview of clinical experience. *Journal of the American Academy of Child Psychiatry, 23,* 126–133.

Carr, J. E., & Bailey, J. S. (1996). A brief behavior therapy protocol for Tourette Syndrome. *Journal of Behavior Therapy and Experimental Psychiatry, 27,* 33–40.

Chappell, P. B., Riddle, M. A., Scahill, L., Lynch, K. A., Schultz, R., Arnsten, A., Leckman, J. F., & Cohen, D. J. (1995). Guanfacine treatment of comorbid Attention-Deficit/Hyperactivity Disorder and Tourette's Syndrome: Preliminary clinical experience. *Journal of the American Academy of Child and Adolescent Psychiatry, 34,* 1140–1146.

Cohen, D. J., Leckman, J. F., & Riddle, M. (1997). Tourette's disorder and tic disorders. In N. E. Alessi (Ed.), *Handbook of child and adolescent psychiatry Volume Four: Varieties of development.* New York: Wiley.

Cohen, D. J., Leckman, J. F., & Shaywitz, B. A. (1984). The Tourette's syndrome and other tics. In D. Shaffer, A. A. Ehrhardt, & L. Greenhill (Eds.), *Diagnosis and treatment in pediatric psychiatry.* New York: Macmillan Free Press.

Dedmon, S. R. (1986). Helping children with Tourette Syndrome to cope in the classroom. *Social Work in Education, 8,* 243–257.

Dykens, E., Leckman, J., Riddle, M., Hardin, M., Schwartz, S., & Cohen, D. (1990). Intellectual, academic, and adaptive functioning of Tourette Syndrome children with and without Attention Deficit Disorder. *Journal of Abnormal Child Psychology, 18,* 607–615.

Edell, B. H., & Motta, R. W. (1989). The emotional adjustment of children with Tourette's Syndrome. *The Journal of Psychology, 123,* 51–57.

Edell-Fisher, B. H., & Motta, R. W. (1990). Tourette Syndrome: Relation to children's and parents' self-concepts. *Psychological Reports, 66,* 539–545.

Fisher, W., Conlon, C., Burd, L., & Conlon, R. (1986). Educating children and adults on coping with Tourette Syndrome. *Perceptual and Motor Skills, 62,* 530.

Fitts, W. H. (1965). *The Tennessee Self-Concept Scale Manual.* Nashville, TN: Counselor Recordings and Tests.

Gadow, K. D., Sverd, J., Sprafkin, J., Nolan, E. E., & Ezor, S. N. (1995). Efficacy of methylphenidate for Attention-Deficit/Hyperactivity Disorder in children with Tic Disorder. *Archives of General Psychiatry, 52,* 444–455.

Harcherik, D. F., Leckman, J. F., Detlor, J., & Cohen, D. J. (1984). A new instrument for clinical studies of Tourette's syndrome. *Journal of the American Academy of Child Psychiatry, 23,* 153–160.

Harris, J. C. (1995). *Developmental neuropsychiatry Volume Two: Assessment, diagnosis, and treatment of developmental disorders.* New York: Oxford.

Kerbeshian, J., & Burd, L. (1988). A clinical pharmacological approach to treating Tourette Syndrome in children and adolescents. *Neuroscience & Behavioral Reviews, 12,* 241–245.

Kohen, D. P., & Botts, P. (1987). Relaxation-imagery (self-hypnosis) in Tourette Syndrome: Experience with four children. *American Journal of Clinical Hypnosis, 29,* 227–237.

Kurlan, R. (1989). Tourette's Syndrome: Current concepts. *Neurology, 39,* 1625–1630.

Leckman, J. F., & Cohen, D. J. (1996). Tic disorders. In M. Lewis (Ed.), *Child and adolescent psychiatry: A comprehensive textbook* (2nd ed.). Baltimore: Williams & Wilkins.

Leckman, J. F., & Cohen, D. J. (1999). *Tourette's syndrome—Tics, obsessions, compulsions: Developmental psychopathology and clinical care.* New York: Wiley

Leckman, J. F., Dolnansky, E. S., Hardin, M. T., Clubb, M., Walkup, J. T., Stevenson, J., & Pauls, D. L. (1990). Perinatal factors in the expression of Tourette's Syndrome: An exploratory study. *Journal of the American Academy of Child and Adolescent Psychiatry, 29,* 220–226.

Leckman, J. F., Hardin, M. T., Riddle, M. A., Stevenson, J., Ort, S. I., & Cohen, D. J. (1991). Clonidine treatment of Gilles de la Tourette's Syndrome. *Archives of General Psychiatry, 48,* 324–328.

Leckman, J. F., Riddle, M. A., Hardin, M. T., Ort, S. I., Swartz, K. L., Stevenson, J., & Cohen, D. J. (1989). The Yale Global Tic Severity Scale: Initial testing of a clinician-rated scale of tic severity. *Journal of the American Academy of Child and Adolescent Psychiatry, 28,* 566–573.

Lombroso, P. J., Scahill, L., King, R. A., Lynch, K. A., Chappell, P. B., Peterson, B. S., McDougle, C. J., & Leckman, J. F. (1995). Risperidone treatment of children and adolescents with chronic tic disorders: A preliminary report. *Journal of the American Academy of Child and Adolescent Psychiatry, 34,* 1147–1152.

Matthews, M., Eustace, C., Grad, G., Pelcovitz, D., & Olson, M. (1985). A family systems perspective on

Tourette's Syndrome. *International Journal of Family Psychiatry, 6,* 53–66.

Micheli, F., Gatto, M., Lekhuniec, E., Mangone, C., Pardal, M. F., Pikielny, R., & Parera, I. C. (1990). Treatment of Tourette's Syndrome with calcium antagonists. *Clinical Neuropharmacology, 13,* 77–83.

Ollendick, T. H. (1981). Self-monitoring and self-administered overcorrection: The modification of tics in children. *Behavior Modification, 5,* 75–84.

Ollendick, T. H., & Ollendick, D. G. (1990). Tics and Tourette Syndrome. In A. M. Gross & R. S. Drabman (Eds.), *Handbook of clinical behavioral pediatrics* (pp. 243–252). New York: Plenum.

Peterson, B. S., & Klein, J. E. (1997). Neuroimaging of Tourette's syndrome neurobiologic substrate. *Child and Adolescent Psychiatric Clinics of North America, 6,* 343–364.

Prata, G., & Masson, O. (1985). Short therapy of a child with Gilles de la Tourette's Syndrome. *Journal of Family Therapy, 7,* 315–332.

Price, R. A., Kidd, K. K., Cohen, D. J., Pauls, D. L., & Leckman, J. F. (1985). A twin study of Tourette syndrome. *Archives of General Psychiatry, 42,* 815–820.

Riddle, M. A., Lynch, K. A., Scahill, L., deVries, A., Cohen, D. J., & Leckman, J. F. (1995). Methylphenidate discontinuation and reinitiation during long-term treatment of children with Tourette's disorder and attention-deficit hyperactivity disorder: A pilot study. *Journal of Child and Adolescent Psychopharmacology, 5,* 205–214.

Robertson, M. M., Schnieden, V., & Lees, A. J. (1990). Management of Gilles de la Tourette Syndrome using sulpiride. *Clinical Neuropharmacology, 13,* 229–235.

Sallee, F. R., Nesbitt, L., Jackson, C., Sine, L., & Sethuraman, G. (1997). Relative efficacy of haloperidol and pimozide in children and adolescents with Tourette's disorder. *American Journal of Psychiatry, 154,* 1057–1062.

Sallee, F. R., & Spratt, E. G. (1999). Tic disorders. In R. T. Ammerman, M. Hersen, & C. G. Last (Eds.), *Handbook of prescriptive treatments for children and adolescents* (2nd ed.). Boston: Allyn & Bacon.

Shapiro, A. K., Shapiro, E., Brunn, R. D., & Sweet, R. D. (1978). *Gilles de la Tourette Syndrome.* New York: Raven Press.

Shapiro, E., Shapiro, A. K., Fulop, G., Hubbard, M., Mandeli, J., Nordlie, J., & Phillips, R. A. (1989). Controlled study of haloperidol, pimozide, and placebo for the treatment of Gilles de la Tourette's Syndrome. *Archives of General Psychiatry, 46,* 722–730.

Turpin, G. (1983). The behavioral management of tic disorders: A critical review. *Advances in Behavior Research and Therapy, 5,* 203–245.

Wodrich, D. L., Benjamin, E., & Lachar, D. (1997). Tourette's syndrome and psychopathology in a child psychiatry setting. *Journal of the American Academy of Child and Adolescent Psychiatry, 36,* 1618–1624.

Young, M. H., & Montano, R. J. (1988). A new hypnobehavioral method for the treatment of children with Tourette's Disorder. *American Journal of Clinical Hypnosis, 31,* 97–106.

CHAPTER 14

Selective Mutism

■ **Selective Mutism**

□ CLINICAL DESCRIPTION

Diagnostic Considerations

Selective Mutism is a disorder in which a child does not speak in one or more common situations such as school or to strangers. This refusal to speak is not the result of a language or vocal deficit, but rather seems to be at least partially under the control of the child. True Selective Mutism occurs in 0.3 to 0.8 of every 1,000 children (Table 14.1) (Brown & Lloyd, 1975; Dow, Sonies, Scheib, Moss, & Leonard, 1995; Labbe & Williamson, 1984), although less severe shyness or reluctance to speak are much more common (Labbe & Williamson, 1984). Selective Mutism appears to be more frequent in immigrant children who are less familiar with the language spoken in school (Bradley & Sloman, 1975).

The diagnostic criteria for Selective Mutism focus on a refusal to speak in some situations, while speaking adequately in other situations: First, the child must show a refusal to speak in one or more social situations. School is suggested as one such situation, probably because Selective Mutism, when it is seen, often occurs at school. Importantly, the child must speak in other situations. Hence, a child who never speaks in any situation would technically not qualify for the Selective Mutism diagnosis. Second, the child must not have a communication disorder that would remove the ability to comprehend or produce speech. This criterion eliminates physical causes for the mutism and inability to speak because of severe cognitive impairment. However, it does not exclude children who have language delays but can still understand language and speak. Third, the mutism must last at least one month (which cannot be the first month of school) and must interfere with social or educational functioning. Finally, the mutism cannot be a result of a lack of knowledge of the spoken language (American Psychiatric Association, 1994).

Several authors have attempted to identify subtypes of Selective Mutism that can be useful in clinical description or treatment of the disorder. For example, children with Selec-

TABLE 14.1   Epidemiology and Course of Selective Mutism

Prevalence: 0.03–0.08%

Sex Ratio (Male:Female):   1:2 to 1:3

Typical Onset Age: 2–5 years

Course: Although few outcome studies have been completed, children with Selective Mutism (especially the anxious subtypes) are thought to be at risk for later anxiety disorders and social difficulties. Children with the resistant subtype, on the other hand, may be at risk for later oppositional and manipulative behaviors. Many children appear to adapt and to outgrow their symptoms of Selective Mutism, although some shyness, anxiety, or resistance often persists.

Common Comorbid Conditions: 1. Social Phobia
2. Separation Anxiety Disorder
3. Simple Phobia
4. Generalized Anxiety Disorder

Relevant Subtypes: 1. Anxious vs. Resistant
2. Traumatic Mutism

tive Mutism may be divided into compliant and noncompliant types (Lesser-Katz, 1988). Children with compliant-subtype mutism are passive, fearful, insecure, and exhibit dependent behavior with one or more adults. They react to new situations with immobility and stranger anxiety, preventing them from speaking. However, at home they may be oppositional and aggressive. Children with noncompliant-type mutism are passive-aggressive, actively avoidant, and hostile-withdrawn. With adults, they are often manipulative, aggressive, stubborn, defiant, and oppositional, perhaps as a result of anger toward parents. They use their mutism and withdrawal to communicate rejection of peers and/or adults, defiantly resisting any attempts to be engaged.

Similar to the compliant-noncompliant subtyping is the grouping of children with Selective Mutism based on level of anxiety. Children with speech-related anxiety are afraid to speak in social situations; their behavior resembles the compliant subtype. Children who lack speech-related anxiety are usually defiant and manipulative in withholding speech. They appear relaxed and comfortable in social situations, resembling the noncompliant subtype (Laybourne, 1989; Reed, 1963).

A second subtyping system places Selective Mutism in the context of other speech-withholding behaviors. Labbe and Williamson (1984) suggest that Selective Mutism is an extreme version of speech-reduced behavior. A more moderate problem is that of Reluctant Speech. Unlike the child with Selective Mutism, who shows complete absence of speech in certain situations, the child with Reluctant Speech shows dramatically reduced, but not absent, speech (Brown & Doll, 1988). Selective Mutism may be associated with more language delays and family pathology than is Reluctant Speech, although both fall along the speech-reduced continuum (Carr & Afnan, 1989; Wilkins, 1985).

A third subtyping of mutism is the traumatic/elective distinction (Silver, 1989). Traumatic mutism follows a significant psychological or physical stressor, such as diagnosis of a chronic illness or death of a parent. The mutism in this case is often complete, with no speech in any situation. Technically, this problem would not meet DSM-IV Selective Mutism criteria, which state that the child speaks in some situations. Furthermore, traumatic mutism rarely lasts a full month. Rather, traumatic mutism is more likely to be temporary and to spontaneously disappear (Silver, 1989).

A fourth subtyping of Selective Mutism groups children into symbiotic, passive-aggressive, reactive, and speech-phobic groups (Hayden, 1980). Symbiotic mutism is the most common and is characterized by an enmeshed relationship with the primary caretaker. The caretaker is often domineering and jealous of the child's other relationships, isolating the child by appearing to meet all of the child's needs. The other parent is generally disengaged and isolated from the caretaker-child relationship. Children with the symbiotic subtype initially appear shy and clinging, but further observation reveals that they are manipulative and controlling (Hayden, 1980; Silver, 1989). Children with passive-aggressive mutism, the next most common type, use silence to show defiance and hostility. They tend to engage in aggressive and antisocial behaviors and are the targets of blame and rejection in their families (Hayden, 1980; Silver, 1989). Reactive mutism is somewhat similar to traumatic mutism. It occurs in response to a single traumatic stressor or a chronically stressful environment. Children with reactive mutism often have associated difficulties such as depression, social withdrawal, or Posttraumatic Stress Disorder (Hayden, 1980; Silver, 1989). The least frequent subtype is speech phobic mutism, characterized by a fear of hearing one's own voice. These children sometimes exhibit compulsive or ritualistic behaviors.

Although each of these subtyping systems has advantages in describing the behavior of children with Selective Mutism, the most clinically helpful distinction is that of anxious (including symbiotic and compliant subtypes) versus resistant (including noncompliant, defiant, and passive-aggressive subtypes) mutism. These categories are not always mutually exclusive, and many children will show components of both subtypes. Nevertheless, the majority of children with Selective Mutism will tend to show behaviors mostly of one subtype or the other.

The anxious subtype of Selective Mutism appears to be the more common (based on frequent reports of comorbid anxiety) presentation of Selective Mutism, and it may be the more amenable to treatment. Children with the anxious subtype are generally inhibited, sensitive, and fearful. More than 90% of children with Selective Mutism are of the anxious subtype, with Social Phobia being the most common comorbid diagnosis. Social Phobia co-occurs with Selective Mutism in as many as 90% or more of cases (Black & Uhde, 1995; Dummit et al., 1997). This high rate of co-occurrence of Selective Mutism and anxiety disorders has led some to categorize Selective Mutism as a symptom or variant of an anxiety disorder (Black & Uhde, 1995; Dummit et al., 1997).

The resistant subtype of Selective Mutism is rare and less likely to show positive change in treatment. This subtype occurs in under 20% of cases (Steinhausen & Juzi, 1996). Fewer than 10% of children with Selective Mutism have comorbid disruptive behavior disorders such as Oppositional-Defiant Disorder and Attention-Deficit/Hyperactivity Disorder (Black & Uhde, 1995; Dummit et al., 1997).

Appearance and Features

Selective Mutism is usually first noticed in children between the ages of 2 and 5 (Black & Uhde, 1995; Shvartzman et al., 1990; Weininger, 1987). Parents may initially regard it as simple shyness, but the magnitude of the behavior becomes apparent when the child begins attending school. The vast majority of children with Selective Mutism are referred based on muteness at school and/or toward strangers. It is not unusual for children to be initially quiet and reserved when they begin kindergarten or first grade. Some children are even completely silent for the first few days of school. However, children with Selective Mutism continue this silent behavior for weeks, despite attempts by teachers and other children to encourage them to speak (Laybourne, 1989).

Children with Selective Mutism frequently speak normally at home and with a small circle of close relatives and friends (Laybourne, 1989; Silver, 1989). However, they are silent in certain situations, such as when they are with teachers, strange children, or unfamiliar adults. Although speech in these "mute" situations is not present, the child may still attempt to communicate using other means. Gestures, brief vocalizations, or whispering to a familiar person are common ways in which children with Selective Mutism attempt to communicate (Laybourne, 1989; Silver, 1989). In extremely rare cases, the child may be mute in all situations. Children with complete mutism do not meet DSM-IV Selective Mutism criteria and may be experiencing a transient reaction to trauma.

The presentation of Selective Mutism often gives the impression that these children are being controlling or dependent, causing several authors (Afnan & Carr, 1989; Brown & Doll, 1988; Lesser-Katz, 1988; Weininger, 1987) to speculate that they have additional social or behavioral problems (Table 14.2). Children with Selective Mutism may also appear socially anxious and insecure, fearing separation from familiar others and clinging to parents (Lesser-Katz, 1988; Wilkins, 1985). With peers, they are often anxious, submissive, and timid. Rejection or neglect by the peer group is often seen if the mutism persists to older ages. Depression, manipulative behavior, and developmental language disorders have also been reported as occurring with above average frequency in children with Selective Mutism (Afnan & Carr, 1989; Weininger, 1987; Wilkins, 1985). Significant language and

TABLE 14.2   Appearance and Features of Selective Mutism

COMMON FEATURES

1. Refusal/inability to speak in one or more common situations
2. Adequate motor and language development to allow speech
3. Onset between 3 and 5 years of age
4. Usually speaks to a small circle of family members
5. Use of gestures or whispering to communicate
6. Socially anxious, shy, timid
7. Clingy, protests separation from parent

OCCASIONAL FEATURES

1. Use of mutism to manipulate the environment
2. Use of mutism to get attention or to express anger
3. Developmental language disorders

Note: The features listed in the table are often seen but are not universal. Some features may be diagnostically relevant or required, whereas others may not be required for diagnosis. "Common" features are typical of the disorder; "occasional" features appear frequently but are not necessarily seen in a majority of cases.

learning disorders have been found in about 10–20% of children with Selective Mutism (Dow et al., 1995; Dummit et al., 1997).

Etiology

Theories of the etiology of Selective Mutism usually implicate biological, family, psychodynamic, or behavioral factors in the development and maintenance of the mute behavior. In some cases, the same etiological factors can lead to either anxious or resistant mutism, depending on the temperament of the child and other characteristics of the environment.

Biological Theories

Biological theories of Selective Mutism hypothesize that the mutism is a symptom of a sensitive, inhibited, or anxious temperament. These theories are supported by findings that the vast majority of children with Selective Mutism also have at least one anxiety disorder diagnosis (Dummit et al., 1997). Furthermore, studies have found that as many as 70% of family members of children with Selective Mutism qualify for an anxiety disorder diagnosis (Black & Uhde, 1995).

Family Theories

Conflict and marital disharmony are reported in many cases of Selective Mutism, causing some authors to speculate that some cases of Selective Mutism result from structural components and stresses of the family environment (Tatem & DelCampo, 1995). Structurally, family disharmony can result in the formation of a coalition by one parent and the child against the other parent. For example, some mothers of children with Selective Mutism are described as lonely, anxious, deprived, or depressed, with a resentment toward the father and a desire to be enmeshed with the child (Lesser-Katz, 1988, Silver, 1989). Enmeshment may be reflected in overprotecting the child and encouraging regression in the child. Sensing the needs and anxieties of the mother, the child rejects interaction with other people in order to maintain the symbiotic and enmeshed relationship. Speaking to others is, in effect, a rejection of the mother, and attempts to challenge this enmeshment are met with angry silence (Silver, 1989). Alternatively, the child may interpret the mother's anxiety and dependent behavior as a sign that the child is fundamentally flawed. Hence, the child fears separation from the mother because the child needs the mother for security (Atoynatan, 1986; Lesser-Katz, 1988). In other cases, the child resents the maternal enmeshment and overprotectiveness and responds with silence as a means of defiance or control. Clearly, these explanations are somewhat stereotypical and do not apply to all Selective Mutism cases. Nevertheless, they may provide initial hypotheses for investigation in cases with a clear structural family component.

Psychological Theories

Psychodynamic explanations of the etiology of Selective Mutism overlap with family theories, beginning with a focus on the mother-child relationship. Analytic theorists add to this model by hypothesizing that the child is silent because of fears of saying something forbidden or nasty. Fearing the expression of these aggressive impulses, the child chooses to be silent. This withholding of speech reflects a fixation at the anal stage of development. The source of aggressive impulses and related fears is hypothesized to be the mother-child relationship and parental discipline of the expression of id impulses (Weininger, 1987).

In the case of traumatic mutism, which often does not qualify for the formal Selective Mutism diagnosis, mutism symptoms often represent the child's defensive response to a stressor. Abused children, for example, may use silence to remain inconspicuous or to express anger in a way that is less likely to lead to further abuse. The silence may also represent a shock response to a stressor for which there is no readily available coping mechanism. In some cases, the trauma may be symbolically related to silence, as when a child who is repeatedly slapped in the face becomes mute (Silver, 1989).

Behavioral Theories

A third group of theories of the etiology of Selective Mutism focuses on behavioral contingencies driving the mutism (Afnan & Carr, 1989; Brown & Doll, 1988; Carr & Afnan, 1989). Operant conditioning explanations conceptualize mutism as a behavior that is reinforced by attention, access to favored activities, and avoidance of aversive activities (such as school) (Brown & Doll, 1988; Carr & Afnan, 1989). Classical conditioning suggests that the child has associated speech with some negative event, such as pain, humiliation, anxiety, or parental discipline for speaking. Failed social interactions could also lead to the development of mutism through this classical conditioning model. Hence, the child avoids speech in order to avoid the conditioned fear response that follows speech (Afnan & Carr, 1989; Carr & Afnan, 1989). Not speaking causes a reduction in the uncomfortable anxiety state, reinforcing the mutism. Finally, social learning theories may explain the development of Selective Mutism in a child who is modeling the behavior of a quiet parent or sibling (Brown & Doll, 1988; Weininger, 1987).

☐ ASSESSMENT PATTERNS

A sample assessment battery for Selective Mutism is shown in Table 14.3.

Broad Assessment Strategies

Children with Selective Mutism are often extremely difficult to assess because they refuse to communicate normally with the examiner. Techniques such as allowing the child to pantomime responses, whisper answers to another person, or say answers to a puppet may help at times. However, these techniques are time-consuming and violate the standardization of some tests. In many cases, a parent or familiar other person must remain in the clinician's office during interview and testing if any productive interaction is to occur.

Cognitive Assessment

Clinician-Administered. Many children with Selective Mutism have cognitive and language skills in the normal ranges. However, a subgroup of cognitively delayed children with Selective Mutism does exist. As a whole group, then, children with Selective Mutism may show a somewhat increased prevalence of cognitive or language deficit (Dow et al.,

TABLE 14.3   Sample Assessment Battery for Selective Mutism

COGNITIVE

1. Peabody Picture Vocabulary Test—Revised
2. Kaufman Brief Intelligence Test

BEHAVIORAL

1. Behavior Assessment System for Children (Parent-Report and Teacher-Report)
2. Personality Inventory for Youth (age 9 and older)

FAMILY

1. Family Environment Scale

Note: Assessment instruments are intended to supplement (not substitute for) a good clinical interview and, when possible, a structured diagnostic interview.

1995). Because of potential language and cognitive deficits, many of these children should be administered a battery consisting of a screening cognitive test such as the K-BIT or WASI, followed by a major intelligence test such as the WISC-III, WPPSI-R, or SB:FE, if more detailed information is needed. In addition, a major achievement test such as the WJ-R or WIAT is warranted for cases with academic problems.

Speech-language testing is also important to rule out language problems. A receptive vocabulary test such as the Peabody Picture Vocabulary Test-Third Edition (PPVT-III; Dunn & Dunn, 1997) may be helpful because it does not require speech. Over all, screening examination for a comorbid Communication Disorder is recommended (see Chapter 11 for a discussion of testing for Communication Disorders).

For children who will speak rarely or not at all during testing, the examiner must rely more heavily on intelligence tests with a less significant verbal component. Most Performance subtests of the WISC-III require little in the way of verbal response. Alternatively, the K-BIT is both briefer and less verbal than the more extensive IQ tests, with a nonverbal matrix reasoning component. Exclusively nonverbal tests such as the Test of Nonverbal Intelligence—Third Edition (TONI-3; Brown, Sherbenou, & Johnsen, 1997), the Leiter International Performance Scale—II (Roid & Miller, 1997), the Comprehensive Test of Nonverbal Intelligence (Hammill, Pearson, & Wiederholt, 1996), and the Universal Nonverbal Intelligence Test (UNIT; Bracken & McCallum, 1998) can provide nonverbal cognitive functioning information for children with language disorders or near-total mutism.

Although no systematic research exists on the IQ/achievement testing patterns of children with Selective Mutism, average to somewhat below average scores on Full Scale and Verbal IQ would be expected. Children who score average or above on Full Scale and Verbal IQ are withholding speech without associated cognitive deficits. Language-based achievement tests such as reading and written language should also be analyzed to see if a language deficit pervades modalities other than speech. Expressive vocabulary subtests on the WISC-III and SB:FE (WPPSI-R vocabulary mixes expressive and receptive components) may be compared to the PPVT-R to see if the child has an expressive-receptive vocabulary discrepancy.

Behavioral Assessment

Parent- and Teacher-Report. Of the major broad-band behavior checklists, only the ECI-4 has a Selective Mutism subscale (consisting of DSM-IV symptoms for Selective Mutism). However, the other major behavior checklists may be valuable for measuring withdrawal, anxiety, and other problems that are very commonly associated with Selective Mutism. The child (CSI-4) and adolescent (ASI-4) companions to the ECI-4, for example, do not contain Selective Mutism subscales, but they do have subscales for Social Phobia and Generalized Anxiety Disorder, which are frequently elevated for children with Selective Mutism. Elevation of the Oppositional-Defiant Disorder subscale could indicate the presence of the resistant subtype of Selective Mutism.

On the Achenbach scales (CBCL and TRF), depressed, shy, and withdrawn children with Selective Mutism (anxious mutism subtype) tend to elevate internalizing subscales (Carr & Afnan, 1989). For all children with Selective Mutism, the Social Problems subscale tends to be elevated, whereas the Activities and Social Competence subscales are lower than average. A similar pattern is seen on the Conners' scales, with elevations of the Anxious-Shy subscale reflecting social avoidance and fear, whereas elevation of the Social Problems scale suggests that social rejection is taking place as well.

The BASC includes several subscales that provide information about anxiety and social functioning in the child with Selective Mutism. The BASC Withdrawal subscale contains items about social avoidance, social anxiety, and shyness, including some that reflect Selective Mutism symptoms. The BASC Leadership subscale, on the other hand, consists of items that are largely the inverse of Selective Mutism symptoms and associated features: gregariousness, speaking up, joining social activities, and leading groups of peers. The Adaptability subscale can indicate problems adjusting to changes in the environment, whereas the Social Skills subscale measures knowledge and use of basic skills in social interaction. Other BASC subscales allow screening of other associated mood, anxiety, and acting-out problems.

For the BASC, Achenbach, and Conners questionnaires, elevation of externalizing subscales is rarely seen when the questions are answered by the person who is with the child in the situation in which the mutism occurs, because many externalizing behavior items involve verbalization or vocalization (e.g., argues with others). On the other hand, the respondent who is with the child (especially for the resistant subtype) in the situation in which speaking occurs (often the parent) may report significant externalizing behavior.

Child-Report. Because most children with Selective Mutism are under age 8 when they come to the attention of professionals, child self-report tests are of limited utility. However, when the child is old enough to complete a self-report inventory, an attempt to obtain structured, self-report data is often recommended. Children who are reluctant to talk may be willing to describe their symptoms on a written true-false test. On the other hand, many children with Selective Mutism (especially the resistant subtype) are avoidant and unwilling to express their feelings, raising the probability of denial of problems on self-report tests.

On the PIY, the Social Introversion subscale of the Social Withdrawal scale has content that closely matches Selective Mutism symptoms and associated problems. In addition to this subscale, children with Selective Mutism who also have difficulties with peer interaction would be expected to elevate the Social Skills Deficits scale (reflecting rejection and ignoring by peers) and the Isolation subscale of the Social Withdrawal scale (reflecting withdrawal and isolation from others). Children with language and achievement problems produce elevations of the Cognitive Impairment scale, whereas those with the resistant mutism subtype would be expected to elevate the Noncompliance subscale of the Delinquency scale. Inspection of the Family Dysfunction scale might also suggest that family issues play into the child's behavioral difficulties. Because of the risk of denial of problems, the PIY validity scales should be closely inspected. Defensiveness subscale T-scores greater than 60–65 suggest some denial or low insight on the part of the child.

Like the PIY, the self-report version of the BASC cannot be used with children under age 8, although it can be helpful for children age 8 and older. On the BASC, children with Selective Mutism would be expected to elevate the Social Stress and Sense of Inadequacy subscales, indicating social avoidance and alienation, particularly related to school and peers. Problems with social acceptance would be indicated by low scores on the Interpersonal Relations subscale, whereas difficulties with self-esteem and independence would be shown by low scores on the Self-Esteem and Self-Reliance subscales. For children with resistant, noncompliant mutism, elevation of the Attitude to School and Attitude to Teachers subscales would indicate pessimism and alienation from school and teachers, respectively.

Family Assessment

Parent-Report.   Based on theories suggesting that parental factors can sometimes play a role in the development or maintenance of Selective Mutism, assessment of the parents, marriage, and family may be warranted. Parents in an enmeshed parent-child relationship may elevate scales 2, 3, 4, 8, and 0 on the MMPI, reflecting depression, low self-esteem, alienation, anger, and need for a symbiotic relationship. On the FES, families of children with Selective Mutism may be expected to show patterns characteristic of family conflict, enmeshment, and control. Elevations on FES Cohesion, Expressiveness, Conflict, Control, Conflicted, and Controlling scales/factors are likely to be coupled with a low score on Independence. Family inventories should be given to both parents separately because differences in parental response may provide insight into family structure and differences in how the family is viewed. A mother who reports very high cohesion and a father who reports very low cohesion, for example, may indicate that the father is disengaged and the mother is enmeshed with the child. Likewise, scores on the Dyadic Adjustment Scale (DAS; Spanier, 1976) may suggest difficulties in the marriage or differences in how the marriage is perceived. DAS scores of less than 100 reflect poor marital adjustment in parents of children with Selective Mutism.

Syndrome-Specific Tests

Few tests have been developed specifically for the measurement of mutism symptoms. Dummit et al. (1997) developed a Situational Speech Scale to quantify amount of speech in different situations. Parents rate their child's frequency of speaking with various people in 14 situations including home, family, school, telephone, and in public. Ratings are made on a 0–4 scale. The Situational Speech Scale appears to provide useful information for clinical use.

□ TREATMENT OPTIONS

Treatment options for Selective Mutism are listed in Table 14.4.

Behavioral Interventions

Behavior therapy is generally regarded as the most effective treatment for Selective Mutism. In cases that do not respond to behavioral techniques, psychodynamic play therapy or family therapy may be warranted (Dow et al., 1995). Over all, a flexible, multimodal approach emphasizing work with the parents and child appears to be the best option (Silver, 1989), beginning with behavioral techniques and using play and family techniques as needed to bolster behavioral interventions. Five types of behavior therapy are used for children with Selective Mutism: stimulus fading, reinforcement contingencies, ignoring, relaxation techniques, shaping, and self-modeling.

Stimulus Fading

Stimulus fading is frequently an effective component of a behavior therapy package for Selective Mutism (Afnan & Carr, 1989; Carr & Afnan, 1989; Silver, 1989). In stimulus fading, the child is taken by someone to whom the child will talk (e.g., the mother) to the situation in which the child is mute. Initially, this situation is made as conducive as possible to talking, by removing any potential social stressors. For example, child and parent may visit the child's classroom after school, when only the child and parent will be present. The child is then encouraged to talk to the parent. Gradually, other components of the

TABLE 14.4 Treatment Options for Selective Mutism

1. Behavioral Interventions
   a. Stimulus fading
   b. Reinforcement contingencies
   c. Ignoring
   d. Relaxation techniques
   e. Shaping
   f. Self-modeling
2. Psychotherapy
   a. Play therapy
3. Family Interventions
   a. Family therapy
   b. Parent psychotherapy
4. Medication
5. Referrals
   a. Speech/language therapy

Note: This outline of options summarizes major treatments covered in the text. Specific treatments are often combined into an intervention package. Refer to the text for additional descriptions of each treatment. This table is not necessarily an exhaustive list of all treatments available.

environment are introduced, at a rate that does not stop the verbalizations of the child. The parent (as well as other reinforcers) is used to support the introduction of these additional components. In the school example, the teacher may gradually be introduced into the classroom, first hovering outside the doorway, then entering the room, then approaching parent and child, then sitting with the parent and child. The parent would introduce the teacher to the child and relay information between teacher and child (Afnan & Carr, 1989; Carr & Afnan, 1989; Laybourne, 1989; Silver, 1989).

Once the other components are introduced, the role of the parent is gradually faded, and the role of the other components are increased, again at a rate that does not significantly affect the child's verbalizations. To return to the school example, the parent would gradually stop relaying the teacher's questions to the child and the teacher would begin addressing the child directly. One or two children would then be added to the situation, and the child would be engaged by the group. The parent would then announce that he or she is moving to another area of the room. Following a period of being in the room but apart from the child, the parent would tell the child that the parent is leaving but will be back at a certain time. Finally, the situation is allowed to return to its normal state. This program must be implemented gradually, with returns to earlier stages if the child stops speaking. As few as 12 and as many as 180 sessions may be necessary to achieve the goal of speech in the target situation (Afnan & Carr, 1989; Carr & Afnan, 1989; Laybourne, 1989; Silver, 1989).

Reinforcement Contingency

Stimulus fading is often combined with a second behavioral treatment, reinforcement contingency. A reinforcement contingency approach implements the simple principle of rewarding the child for speech behavior and ensuring that reinforcement does not occur for muteness. Probably the most important part of this intervention is the selection of behaviors to reinforce. Initially, target behaviors must be relatively simple for the child to attain while requiring verbal response or an approximation of a verbal response, such as moving the lips (Laybourne, 1989; Mace & West, 1986). For example, an initial target might be a one-word response as opposed to reading a long passage. The most common reinforcer is praise, although other reinforcers such as prizes have been used (Brown & Doll, 1988; Mace & West, 1986). Logical consequences are another type of potent reinforcer. The most common logical consequence is to require the child to verbally ask for some desired item or activity in order to receive the desired item or activity. Gestures, silence, or talking to just one person would not be sufficient to receive the desired item or activity. Reinforcement contingencies have been reported to be effective in some cases (Brown & Doll, 1988; Mace & West, 1986), although they are probably best used as one component of a multidimensional behavioral program.

In some cases, peers are reinforced when the child speaks, creating an incentive for them to assist the child in speech. In one intervention, kindergarten classmates of a girl with Selective Mutism were allowed to choose a prize each time the girl spoke to a member of the class (Brown & Doll, 1988). The children were reminded of the prizes before recess each day, and prizes were distributed after recess. In a 5–6-week period, the girl's peer interactions increased, as did attempts by peers to engage her: "At various times, groups of children would gather about Amy and begin speaking to her, cheering when she would respond" (Brown & Doll, 1988, p. 114). Clearly, this intervention should be only applied to children who would benefit from the increased interaction; extremely shy or phobic children might find the attention aversive or overwhelming.

Ignoring

Ignoring the child's mute behavior and associated behavior patterns that replace speech (gestures, grunts, etc.) is another common component of a behavioral plan for Selective Mutism, particularly for children with the resistant mutism subtype. In situations when verbal communication is expected or appropriate, parents are instructed not to look at or otherwise respond to the child unless the child makes verbal statements (or an approximation of verbal interaction, if shaping techniques are used). In some cases, parents and others unintentionally reward the child's mutism by giving extra attention and help. When this is the case, the adults should be coached to ignore mute behavior, as opposed to "helping" the child with extra attention and guesses about the topic of communication.

Relaxation Training

Some children are selectively mute because of anxiety over social interaction or speaking. For these children, relaxation techniques targeting the underlying anxiety may be an effective approach to encouraging speech. Laybourne (1989) suggests that a systematic desensitization approach may be helpful for some children. In this approach, the child creates a hierarchy of anxiety-producing social situations. The child is then taught a relaxation technique, such as progressive muscle relaxation. The anxiety-producing images are then gradually paired with the relaxed state, from least anxiety producing to most anxiety producing. The child practices this technique in therapy and at home. The ultimate aim of this intervention is to encourage the child to feel relaxed in social situations, facilitating speech.

Although relaxation techniques may be helpful for some children, they are unlikely to produce much benefit unless they are combined with *in vivo* practice. Furthermore, the child with Selective Mutism may not be willing to engage in sufficient interaction with the therapist to allow the teaching of relaxation. Hence, this technique is best considered for older, motivated children with Selective Mutism who are so anxious that they cannot be helped by other techniques until their anxiety is managed.

Shaping

Shaping techniques underlie other components of behavior therapy and, thus, do not constitute a separate type of therapy per se. Shaping involves rewarding approximations of the target speaking behavior (Blake & Moss, 1967). For example, the child may be initially reinforced for moving the lips. Later the behavior target is changed to movement of lips accompanied by a whispering speech. This target is then gradually increased in loudness until the child is speaking in an audible voice (e.g., Brown & Doll, 1988). The reinforcement may vary from praise to a more tangible reinforcer, such as candy.

Shaping is often necessary in order to achieve a positive outcome for children with selective mutism. Expecting these children to speak loudly and normally with the implementation of a reinforcement contingency is often unrealistic and may produce a failure experience that makes the child more resistant to intervention. Rewarding small increases in speech performance makes the intervention less aversive for the child and allows the therapist to teach proper speech behavior.

Self-Modeling

Self-modeling refers to a group of behavioral techniques in which the child observes himself or herself demonstrating target speech and social interaction behaviors, using videotape or audiotape media (Blum et al., 1998; Dow et al., 1995). The tapes are made by having the child talk and interact in a situation in which the child has no difficulty (typically at home or with a parent alone). The child then views the tapes repeatedly and practices the behaviors in more difficult situations.

One variant of self-modeling, called feedforward, involves editing the child's tapes with segments of situations in which the child is currently experiencing difficulty with mutism and anxiety symptoms. These edited tapes show the child engaging in adaptive behavior, with sounds and/or views of the problem situation spliced in between the segments of adaptive behavior. In a well-edited tape, the child appears to be speaking and interacting apparently in the problem situation. The child then views or listens to the tape repeatedly and practices the behaviors in the target situation.

Case studies of self-modeling and feedforward interventions have produced positive results, although large-scale, controlled studies have not been undertaken (Dow et al., 1995). Both audio and video modalities have been found to be effective, and the feedforward technique has also received case study support (Blum et al., 1998). Potential difficulties with self-modeling techniques include refusal of the child to participate and difficulty in producing a well-made and/or well-edited tape. Nevertheless, self-modeling may be a helpful intervention especially for children who have difficulty responding to other behavioral interventions.

Behavior Treatment Packages

It is relatively rare to see any of the behavior techniques implemented alone. Rather, the techniques are combined into a treatment package that is tailored to fit individual needs. Children who respond well to praise, for example, should be given the reinforcement contingency of praise. In addition, a shaping component should be built into stimulus fading or reinforcement contingency conditions so that the child has achievable behavioral goals. Components should be added, deleted, or modified based on assessment of performance of the target behavior. As with all behavior interventions, the target behaviors should be observable and clearly defined; assessment of target behaviors is crucial for tracking change.

Psychotherapy

Play Therapy

The use of play therapy as an intervention for Selective Mutism is based on two assumptions: first, that the mutism represents the child's response to internal conflicts or nonacceptance of self; and second, that the mutism reflects concerns about expression and acceptance of feelings and thoughts. In the case of psychodynamically oriented psychotherapy, a third assumption is made: that feelings stemming from historical events and relationships with caretakers underlie the mutism. Play therapy aims to create an environment in which the child feels free to express feelings, manage conflicts, gain insight, and accept his or her thoughts and feelings. Using the medium of play, feelings and conflicts are initially acted out symbolically. In early sessions, the parent may need to be present in order for the child to engage in any activity at all.

Depending on the method of play therapy used, the therapist participates in an engaged but nondirective way (Axline, 1969) or in a more directive, interpreting way. In the case of nondirective play therapy, the therapist communicates warmth and acceptance of the child's thoughts, feelings, and behavior in the play, without directing or judging the play. For children who are inhibited and lack self-confidence, this acceptance provides external validation that the child internalizes into a better acceptance of self. Improvement in self-acceptance is then reflected in less anger and anxiety, as well as greater confidence to communicate with others.

In psychodynamic play therapy, the therapist interprets the child's play and talks with the child about the conflicts and emotions that are reflected in the play. By labeling the drives that are underlying the play activity, the therapist promotes insight in the child, resulting in better awareness of the conflicts that are causing the mutism. Understanding and resolution of these conflicts is assumed to be necessary for improving the mutism symptoms.

Play therapy may also be an important technique in cases of traumatic mutism. Children with this subtype of Selective Mutism have encountered some stressful event in close proximity to the development of the mutism. They use the mutism as a form of protective control over their thought and emotional states. By not allowing verbal interaction, they ward off conversations, thoughts, and feelings related to the event, and they maintain control over one aspect of their lives (speaking). These children often fear being overwhelmed with affects and stress if they talk about the traumatic event, and they see attempts to make them talk as dangerous to their well-being. Mutism may also be a safe way for them to express anger and frustration over their stresses or losses.

Play therapy allows the creation of a safe environment in which the topics and themes are under the control of the child. As the child realizes that he or she controls the therapy environment, the child can begin to process themes related to the trauma. These themes may be only superficially processed at first, with increasing depth as the child adjusts to working through the painful event. Presumably, when the trauma is worked through and mastered, the need for mutism disappears, along with the symptoms.

Family Interventions

Because of the role of the family in many cases of Selective Mutism, family therapy is often indicated to resolve family characteristics that are contributing to the mutism. In some cases, the family dynamic is that of an enmeshed parent and disengaged parent. At other times, family therapy is necessary to confront a family dynamic that rewards the child for mutism and resists change. Structural family therapy aims to restructure family relationships by drawing an appropriate boundary between the enmeshed parent and the child while engaging the disengaged parent as a contributing family member. In order to achieve these structural goals, marital therapy may be necessary to strengthen the parents' relationship (Tatem & DelCampo, 1995).

When the pathology of one parent appears to be maintaining the child's mutism and the parent subtly resists change, individual psychotherapy with the parent may be necessary. This therapy should target issues that prevent the parent from fostering independence and sociability in the child. In extreme cases, parents will stubbornly resist change and insist that there is not a problem until a parent-child separation is threatened (Atoynatan, 1986).

Medication

Medication interventions for Selective Mutism target the social anxiety symptoms along with the mutism and, therefore, typically involve serotonin reuptake inhibitors. Fluoxetine (Prozac) and fluvoxamine (Luvox) have been reported to be effective for Selective Mutism, particularly when anxiety symptoms are significant (Dow et al., 1995; Dummit, Klein, Tancer, Asche, & Martin, 1996). Medication intervention is typically combined with psychotherapy to shape positive behavior at the same time that anxiety is managed medically.

Referrals

Speech/Language Therapy

Some children exhibit mutism symptoms partly as a result of speech and language deficits (Dow et al., 1995). The child may be ashamed of speaking for fear of looking different or fear of saying something embarrassing. When testing indicates these deficits, a speech/language pathologist should be consulted to handle this component of therapy. The presence of language deficits, however, should not be thought of as precluding other psychological and behavioral treatments. The speech therapist and psychologist should consider themselves as collaborators working on two dimensions that are contributing to the mute behavior.

■ References

Afnan, S., & Carr, A. (1989). Interdisciplinary treatment of a case of elective mutism. *British Journal of Occupational Therapy, 52,* 61–66.

American Psychiatric Association. (1994). *Diagnostic and statistical manual of mental disorders, fourth edition.* Washington, DC: Author.

Atoynatan, T. H. (1986). Elective mutism: Involvement of the mother in the treatment of the child. *Child Psychiatry and Human Development, 17,* 15–27.

Axline, V. M. (1969). *Play therapy.* New York: Ballantine.

Black, B., & Uhde, T. W. (1995). Psychiatric characteristics of children with selective mutism: A pilot study. *Journal of the American Academy of Child and Adolescent Psychiatry, 34,* 847–856.

Blake, P., & Moss, T. (1967). The development of socialization skills in an electively mute child. *Behavior Research and Therapy, 5,* 349–356.

Blum, N. J., Kell, R. S., Starr, H. L., Lender, W. L., Bradley-Klug, K. L., Osborne, M. L., & Dowrick, P. W. (1998). Case study: Audio feedforward treatment of Selective Mutism. *Journal of the American Academy of Child and Adolescent Psychiatry, 37,* 40–43.

Bracken, B. A., & McCallum, R. S. (1998). *Universal Nonverbal Intelligence Test (UNIT).* Itasca, IL: Riverside Publishing.

Bradley, S., & Sloman, L. (1975). Elective mutism in immigrant families. *Journal of the American Academy of Child and Adolescent Psychiatry, 14,* 510–514.

Brown, B., & Doll, B. (1988). Case illustration of classroom intervention with an elective mute child. *Special Services in the Schools, 5,* 107–125.

Brown, J., & Lloyd, H. (1975). A controlled study of children not speaking at school. *Journal of the Association of Workers with Maladjusted Children, 10,* 49–63.

Brown, L., Sherbenou, R. J., & Johnsen, S. K. (1997). *Test of Nonverbal Intelligence—Third Edition.* Austin, TX: Pro-Ed.

Carr, A., & Afnan, S. (1989). Concurrent individual and family therapy in a case of elective mutism. *Journal of Family Therapy, 11,* 29–44.

Dow, S. P., Sonies, B. C., Scheib, D., Moss, S. E., & Leonard, H. L. (1995). Practical guidelines for the assessment and treatment of Selective Mutism. *Journal of the American Academy of Child and Adolescent Psychiatry, 34,* 836–846.

Dummit, E. S., Klein, R. G., Tancer, N. K., Asche, B., & Martin, J. (1996). Fluoxetine treatment of children with selective mutism: An open trial. *Journal of the American Academy of Child and Adolescent Psychiatry, 35,* 615–621.

Dummit, E. S., Klein, R. G., Tancer, N. K., Asche, B., Martin, J., & Fairbanks, J. A. (1997). Systematic assessment of 50 children with Selective Mutism. *Journal of the American Academy of Child and Adolescent Psychiatry, 36,* 653–660.

Dunn, L. M., & Dunn, L. M. (1997). *Peabody Picture Vocabulary Test—Third Edition.* Circle Pines, MN: American Guidance Service.

Hammill, D. D., Pearson, N. A., & Wiederholt, J. L. (1996). *Comprehensive Test of Nonverbal Intelligence.* Austin, TX: Pro-Ed.

Hayden, T. L. (1980). Classification of elective mutism. *Journal of the American Academy of Child Psychiatry, 19,* 18–33.

Labbe, E. E., & Williamson, D. A. (1984). Behavioral treatment of elective mutism: A review of the literature. *Clinical Psychology Review, 4* , 273–292.

Laybourne, P. C. (1989). Treatment of elective mutism. In *Treatments of psychiatric disorders: A task force report of the American Psychiatric Association* (Volume 1, pp. 762–771). Washington, DC: American Psychiatric Association.

Lesser-Katz, M. (1988). The treatment of elective mutism as stranger reaction. *Psychotherapy, 25,* 305–313.

Mace, F. C., & West, B. J. (1986). Analysis of demand conditions associated with reluctant speech. *Journal of Behavior Therapy and Experimental Psychiatry, 17,* 285–294.

Reed, C. F. (1963). Elective mutism in children. A reappraisal. *Journal of Child Psychology and Psychiatry, 4,* 99–107.

Roid, G. H., & Miller, L. J. (1997). *Leiter International Performance Scale-Revised.* Wood Dale, IL: Stoelting Co.

Shvartzman, P., Hornshtein, I., Klein, E., Yechezkel, A., Ziv, M., & Herman, J. (1990). Elective mutism in family practice. *The Journal of Family Practice, 31,* 319–320.

Silver, L. B. (1989). Elective mutism. In H. I. Kaplan & B. T. Sadock (Eds.), *Comprehensive Textbook of Psychiatry, Volume 2* (5th ed., pp. 1887–1889). Baltimore: Williams & Wilkins.

Spanier, G. B. (1976). Measuring dyadic adjustment: New scales for assessing the quality of marriage and similar dyads. *Journal of Marriage and the Family, 38,* 15–28.

Steinhausen, H., & Juzi, C. (1996). Elective mutism: An analysis of 100 cases. *Journal of the American Academy of Child and Adolescent Psychiatry, 35,* 606–614,

Tatem, D. W., & DelCampo, R. L. (1995). Selective mutism in children: A structural family therapy approach to treatment. *Contemporary Family Therapy: An International Journal, 17,* 177–194.

Weininger, O. (1987). Electively mute children: A therapeutic approach. *The Journal of the Melanie Klein Society, 5,* 25–42.

Wilkins, R. (1985). A comparison of elective mutism and emotional disorders in children. *British Journal of Psychiatry, 146,* 198–203.

CHAPTER 15

Gender Identity Disorder

■ **Gender Identity Disorder**

☐ CLINICAL DESCRIPTION

Diagnostic Considerations

Children develop a sense of gender identity (the awareness that one is a boy or girl) early in life, probably between the ages of 1 and 3 years (Coates, 1990; Zucker, 1989, 1990a). Gender identity is fundamental to the sense of self, stable, emotionally meaningful, and value laden, and it drives many types of behaviors, which are referred to as gender role behaviors (Coates, 1990; Money, 1994; Zucker & Green, 1996). In most cases, the gender identity of the child matches his or her biological sex. The DSM-IV diagnosis Gender Identity Disorder (GID) refers to cases in which the child's gender identity (or desired gender identity) does not match the biological sex. The diagnostic qualifier "in Children" is added to "Gender Identity Disorder" to specify that the GID is occurring in a child.

Diagnostically, the hallmark of GID is persistent discomfort or distress over biological sex and identification with the opposite sex. Identification with the opposite sex is usually manifest as desire to be (or insistence that one is) a member of the opposite sex, preoccupation with stereotypical activities or roles of the opposite sex, preference for peer interaction with the opposite sex, and strong preference for opposite-sex clothing. Distress over biological sex is shown by such behaviors as repudiation or disgust of the biological sex organ, sense of inappropriateness over one's sex, and aversion toward stereotypical activities and roles of the biological sex. The GID must cause distress or impairment in functioning in order to be diagnosed. GID behavior generally emerges in the preschool years (Bradley & Zucker, 1997). Its exact prevalence is not known, although the disorder is very uncommon and probably occurs in 0.001 to 0.01% of children (American Psychiatric Association, 1994) (see Table 15.1).

TABLE 15.1 Epidemiology and Course of Gender Identity Disorder

Prevalence: 0.001–0.01%

Sex Ratio (Male:Female): 3–5:1

Typical Onset Age: Symptoms are usually noticed by toddlerhood or early childhood; gender identity and interests become stable at about age 2–4

Course: Social isolation and rejection by same-sex peers is common, leading to adjustment problems. 70–80% have a homosexual or bisexual orientation as adolescents and adults.

Common Comorbid Conditions: 1. Separation Anxiety Disorder
2. Social Phobia
3. Generalized Anxiety Disorder
4. Depressive Disorders
5. Social Rejection or Neglect by Peers

Relevant Subtypes: 1. Gender Identity Disorder in Children
2. Gender Identity Disorder in Adolescents or Adults

The GID diagnosis occasionally comes under fire by those who regard it as psychiatric sanction for traditional gender roles. Critics contend that traditional gender roles are imposed on children whose interests would otherwise be androgenous and that GID represents the punishment for those who would transcend traditional roles. In addition, GID is criticized as a "homophobic" diagnosis assigned to boys who may be showing early signs of homosexuality. Although it is true that most boys with GID become homosexual in adolescence and adulthood, only a fraction of adult homosexuals have GID in childhood. Finally, some clinicians see cross-gender behavior as an exploratory phase of childhood. These clinicians argue that most children grow out of cross-gender behavior without intervention and that parents should allow their children to engage in this exploration as a part of normal development. For these reasons, GID is sometimes attacked as an unfair diagnosis (Zucker, 1990b).

Despite potential misuses by those who cite GID as support for traditional gender roles, the GID diagnosis has value both as a behavioral descriptor and as a target for intervention (Zucker, 1990b). First, the diagnosis is not given to children who simply favor androgenous or opposite gender activities. DSM-IV requires persistent cross-sex identification *and* persistent discomfort about one's biological sex. Boys who engage in traditional girl-role activities but do not have distress (or sense of inappropriateness) about their sex should not be diagnosed with GID. Likewise, girls who are "tomboys" typically do not express persistent and intense unhappiness with their sex. Furthermore, although tomboys may prefer boys' clothing, they can be persuaded under certain circumstances to dress in girls' clothing. Hence, the GID diagnosis need not be made for children with diverse or unusual interests.

Second, extensive cross-gender behavior and cross-gender identity in very young children are not normal (Zucker, 1989). It is true that children will, on some occasions, ask to dress like the parent of the opposite sex or will say that they are the sex of the opposite parent. However, in normal children such instances are not of the frequency, duration, and intensity seen in children with GID. Intense and persistent cross-gender identity and behavior are atypical because children tend to form gender identity at a very early age.

Finally, some evidence exists that children with GID are at risk for comorbid psycho-pathology (Bates, Bentler, & Thompson, 1979; Coates, 1990; Coates & Person, 1985; Zucker, 1989, 1990b). They often have difficulty with peer relationships, characterized by frequent rejection (Coates, 1990; Zucker, 1989, 1990b). Separation Anxiety Disorder and internalizing symptoms in general occur at high rates in boys with GID (Bradley & Zucker, 1997). Over all, there appear to be valid reasons for diagnosing and considering treatment for GID, and it is likely to remain a DSM diagnosis for some time (Bradley et al., 1991).

Appearance and Features

Boys with GID show a pattern of preferences for female clothing, activities, and behavior (see Table 15.2). They often dress in girls' or women's clothing; prefer to play with dolls; seek out girls as playmates; adopt female motor behaviors/movements (swaying hips, droopy wrist, speaking in a high or soft voice); and favor female characters in movies, books, and on TV. They may pretend that they are girls or famous females and try to make themselves appear female by using cosmetics and jewelry. A fixation on female clothing may be seen as well (American Psychiatric Association, 1994; Bradley & Zucker, 1990; Coates, 1990; Doering, Zucker, Bradley, & MacIntyre, 1989; Zucker, 1989). Research indicates that boys with GID also have a more feminine and attractive physical appearance, whereas girls with GID appear more rugged, tomboyish, and masculine (McDermid, Zucker, Bradley, & Maing, 1998).

In addition to adopting stereotypically feminine behavior and interests, boys with GID will state that they are or would like to be a girl. They avoid traditional male activities, such as rough-and-tumble play, all-boy play groups, and traditional male toys. Less common is the stated desire to lose or cut off the penis. In some cases, desire to lose the penis is manifest by hiding the penis or sitting to urinate (Zucker & Green, 1996). On very rare occasions, boys with GID engage in self-mutilation (Coates, 1990).

TABLE 15.2   Appearance and Features of Gender Identity Disorder

COMMON FEATURES

1. Distress over biological sex
2. Desire to be a member of opposite sex
3. Impaired peer relationships, social rejection
4. Preference for clothing, activity, motor behavior, and fantasy play stereotypically associated with other sex
5. Avoidance of play with same-sex peers
6. More friendships with cross-sex peers

OCCASIONAL FEATURES

1. Internalizing symptoms (separation anxiety, depression, loneliness)
2. Homosexuality in adulthood

Note: The features listed in the table are often seen but are not universal. Some features may be diagnostically relevant or required, whereas others may not be required for diagnosis. "Common" features are typical of the disorder; "occasional" features appear frequently but are not necessarily seen in a majority of cases.

Girls with GID are much less common than boys with GID, with 3–7 male GID referrals for female referral; however, this ratio is strongly affected by societal intolerance of cross-sex behavior in boys (American Psychiatric Association, 1994; Bradley & Zucker, 1997; Zucker, Bradley, & Sanikhani, 1997). Girls with GID express the desire to be a boy as well as dislike of being a girl. They may adopt behaviors (standing to urinate, insisting that they have a penis) that make this male identification apparent. In addition, their behavior and activities are stereotypically male. For example, they seek out rough-and-tumble play with boys, prefer traditionally male toys, take a male role in fantasy or play, adopt male speech patterns, and avoid feminine clothing and activities. Some girls with GID throw extremely intense temper tantrums if forced to wear feminine clothing, and they socialize almost exclusively with boys throughout their childhood (Bradley & Zucker, 1990; Zucker & Green, 1996).

Two problematic features associated with GID are increased risk of psychopathology and negative peer relations. Internalizing, overcontrolled problems such as separation anxiety disorder, clinginess, and depression have been commonly reported in boys with GID (Coates, 1990), although rates may not be as high as those reported in initial studies (Zucker & Green, 1996). The extent of associated psychopathology in girls with GID is unknown, although girls with GID may be at lower risk for social problems and psychopathology than are boys with GID (American Psychiatric Association, 1994).

In addition to having elevated risk of internalizing symptoms, children with GID, particularly boys, are at risk for poor peer relationships. Children, who can be exceedingly intolerant of differences in appearance and behavior, frequently single out boys with GID for teasing, rejection, and ostracism (Zucker, 1990b). The rejection of the other children is generally based on their observation of the feminine speech and behavior of boys with GID; taunts of "sissy" and "gay" are common (Coates, 1990). Same-sex friendships are difficult to establish because other children fear rejection by association and do not know how to interpret the unusual behavior (Coates, 1990). Some boys with GID will form relationships with girls based on mutual interests. However, these relationships may be tenuous because the boy realizes that he is "different" despite having similar interests. Unless they find an accepting group of girls or similarly rejected boys, many of these boys are socially isolated by their teen years (Bradley & Zucker, 1990). Predictably, they often admit feelings of loneliness and rejection (Coates, 1990). Social rejection is often so severe that it may underlie some of the risk for psychopathology (Zucker, 1990b).

The social relationships of girls with GID have been less well studied, although girls probably have fewer social problems than boys. Bradley and Zucker (1990) suggest that girls with GID often find a relatively socially acceptable outlet for their interests in sports participation and adoption of a tomboy appearance. They may seek out same-sex peer groups that do not engage exclusively in traditional female interests.

Prospective research (Green, 1987) indicates that most, but not all, boys with GID become homosexual as adults (Coates, 1990; Zucker, 1989). Because sexual orientation is not a GID diagnostic criterion, it is incorrect to say that all boys with GID are or will become homosexual. In addition, because there are many more homosexual men than boys with GID, the GID-turned-homosexual group is only a very small subgroup of homosexual men. However, follow-up studies suggest that a significant proportion (greater than 50% and possibly in the 70–80% range [Green, 1987; Zucker, 1989]) of boys with GID report having a bisexual or homosexual orientation as adults (Zucker, 1989). The pattern of development of sexual orientation for girls with GID may be different than that for boys, with fewer girls with GID becoming homosexual as adults. Girls who merely have traditionally male interests without GID generally develop more feminine interests at puberty. A disproportionate number of boys with GID become transsexual as adults, although the risk of transsexuality is small even within the GID population (probably less than 5% [Green, 1987; Zucker, 1989]).

Etiology

Biological Theories

Biological theories of GID are based on genetic and hormonal studies. Genetically, a higher concordance rate for GID has been found in monozygotic than dizygotic twins, with a monozygotic concordance rate of 50%. However, these twin studies do not completely account for environmental influences, and even a 50% concordance rate leaves considerable variation out of the genetic realm (Zucker & Green, 1996).

Animal studies show that prenatal hormones have an effect on later sex-typed behavior such as aggressiveness, rough-and-tumble play, and mounting (Bradley & Zucker, 1990; Money, 1994). However, most of these studies have induced stereotypic male behavior in genetic females, whereas GID occurs predominantly in boys. Furthermore, the value of generalizing from animal hormone studies to human functioning can be questioned. Certainly humans have shown much more plasticity in response to hormonal influences.

A version of these animal findings occurs naturally in humans in the case of congenital adrenal hyperplasia (CAH). CAH occurs when the adrenal glands of a female fetus secrete masculinizing hormones (androgens). In severe cases, CAH can result in significant hypertrophy of the clitoris and labia majora, at times to the point of causing the external appearance of a penis. Far more commonly, however, the effect on external genitalia is noticeable but not this extreme. Behaviorally, girls with CAH have been noted to engage in more rough-and-tumble play and to have more stereotypically masculine interests. Women with CAH also have a much higher rate of homosexual orientation and fantasy as compared to women without CAH (Bradley & Zucker, 1997; Money, 1994). Less certain, however, is the effect of CAH on gender identity (Zucker & Green, 1996).

Despite these suggestive findings, hormonal disorders are rarely found in children with GID (Zucker & Green, 1996), although this does not preclude the possibility of unknown hormonal influences before birth. Hence, evidence for a biological explanation is suggestive but speculative. Any biological influences that are found are likely to be predispositions that must be activated by environmental influences (see Money, 1994, for extensive discussion of the interplay between biological and psychosocial influences in the development of GID).

Psychological Theories

Psychodynamic/psychoanalytic theories of GID suggest that characteristics of the mother-child relationship (usually mother-son; these theories typically neglect daughters) encourage the development of GID. Stoller's (1968, 1975) "blissful symbiosis" theory, for example, attributes overly feminine behavior in many boys to an enmeshed relationship with the mother. The mother-son relationship is so intense that the boy is unable to separate himself from his mother's physical characteristics and behavior. Thus, the boy remains fixed at an early, "symbiotic" phase of development and identification with the mother. This identification includes the mother's gender identity. Despite its initial acceptance in the psychoanalytic literature, the blissful symbiosis theory has not been supported by research and case study (Bradley & Zucker, 1997).

Other authors agree with Stoller's central role of the mother but focus on separation as opposed to symbiosis. Coates (1990) contends that emotional or physical separation from the mother creates such anxiety in some boys that they adopt the mother's beliefs, behaviors, and appearance in order to feel that she is present. This fantasy of maternal presence alters the self-view of the boy, who wants to be a girl and values females over males (Coates, 1990). Object relations theorists take a similar view of GID, suggesting that GID develops following parental loss (Bleiberg, Jackson, & Ross, 1986). Children who lose their mothers (physically or emotionally) at the time that they are attempting to gain a sense of self separate from their mother are vulnerable to considerable anxiety and a threat to their sense of self. To defend against these painful experiences, the child identifies extremely strongly with the mother, in some cases adopting her gender identity and behaviors. Adoption of the female role then becomes a part of the child's identity, particularly under stresses involving loss or deprivation (Bleiberg et al., 1986).

Behavioral Theories

Behavioral influences almost certainly have some role in explaining the etiology of GID, although they are generally not thought to act alone in producing the disorder. Parents of children with GID have been found to be more tolerant of cross-gender behaviors, while being less positive about same-gender behaviors (Bradley & Zucker, 1997; Green, 1987). In more extreme (and unusual) cases, parents may strongly encourage cross-gender behaviors, while strongly discouraging same-gender behaviors. These parents may regard their son's dressing in mother's clothing as "cute." They may also relish in their child's exploration of cross-gender toys while ignoring more gender-congruent behavior. Other parents, wishing to expose their child to androgenous experiences, may unwittingly give the impression that they favor playing with cross-sex toys by encouraging exposure to them. Gender-incongruent behavior in both children and adults is often regarded as "funny," and parents may laugh as their child behaves or acts in a silly, cross-gender way. This laughter may be highly reinforcing and lead to a repetition of the behavior. Less benign behavioral influences occur when parents force their child to dress or act like a member of the opposite sex, punishing same-sex behavior. In extreme cases, parents may give the child an opposite-sex nickname or buy only clothing typical of the opposite sex. Social learning influences may arise if a child observes an opposite-sex sibling receiving special attention for his or her behavior.

Family Theories

Two major theories of family influences on GID have received attention. One theory is based on research findings that boys with GID (as well as homosexual men) tend to have a higher brother-to-sister ratio and a later birth order than control samples. Biological theorists have speculated that the antibody-hormonal environment of the mother may have been altered by multiple male births, increasing the risk of hormonal influences driving a later-born male fetus toward a propensity for GID (Zucker & Green, 1996). Alternatively, it is possible that mothers with more boys would wish for a later born child of the opposite sex; hence, the later born son would be affected by the mother's disappointment over not having a girl. This disappointment may subtly influence the behavior of a psychologically vulnerable mother who was desperately hoping for a daughter. Both the biological and the familial explanation for this birth order and sibling ratio effect have not yet been empirically supported (Bradley & Zucker, 1997).

A second theory of family influences attributes GID to maternal psychopathology and behavior. This theory holds that psychopathology in mothers of boys with GID affects parenting behaviors, which in turn affects their son's identity development. For example, mothers of boys with GID report higher levels of depression and more often meet the criteria for Borderline Personality Disorder than do mothers of controls (Coates, 1990; Marantz & Coates, 1991). Depression may be present in as many as half of mothers of boys with GID and significant borderline pathology in as many as one-quarter (Coates, 1990). In addition, mothers of boys with GID have been reported as having a strong "fear, anger, and devaluation of men. Mothers of boys with GID frequently describe their sons as... 'special, gentle, angelic, nonviolent,...and sensitive' "(Coates, 1990, p. 423). In other words, the mothers' dislike of men is apparent, and they sometimes take pains to separate their sons from this image of men in general. In some cases, fathers are the target of disparaging maternal remarks. In some cases, fathers are detached or absent from the family and have an emotionally distant relationship with their son with GID. Coates (1990) traces maternal devaluation of men to traumatic experiences with men.

The maternal psychopathology theory has been criticized because there is no evidence of such influences in many cases of GID. Certainly, other relatives and friends, as well as general societal messages, can have a profound influence on the gender identity of the child. Furthermore, theories emphasizing mothers are generally used only to explain the emergence of GID in boys. Finally, the frequency and severity of psychopathology in mothers of children with GID do not appear to be significantly greater than that in mothers of children with other psychiatric disorders (Zucker & Green, 1996). Hence, maternal psychopathology may be a nonspecific predictor of psychiatric disorder in general as opposed to Gender Identity Disorder in particular.

☐ ASSESSMENT PATTERNS

A sample assessment battery for GID is shown in Table 15.3.

Broad Assessment Strategies

Cognitive Assessment

Clinician-Administered. Rekers, Kilgus, & Rosen, (1991) report that their sample of 29 boys with gender dysphoria had a mean IQ of 108, with considerable variability within the sample (range of 72–141). No IQ subscale or achievement scores have been reported based on group or systematic research, and no data have been published regarding the cognitive status of girls with GID. Based on the scant literature available, the IQ-achievement status of children with GID as a group is expected to be average.

TABLE 15.3   Sample Assessment Battery for Gender Identity Disorder

PERSONALITY

1. Rorschach
2. Thematic Apperception Test
3. Draw-a-Person

BEHAVIORAL

1. Child Behavior Checklist
2. Behavior Assessment System for Children (Parent-Report and Teacher-Report)

FAMILY

1. Family Environment Scale

SYNDROME-SPECIFIC

1. Gender Behavior Inventory for Boys

Note: Assessment instruments are intended to supplement (not substitute for) a good clinical interview and, when possible, a structured diagnostic interview.

Psychological Assessment

Clinician-Administered.   In order to assess underlying beliefs and minimize defensiveness, projective tests may supplement the observation and interview of children with GID. On the Rorschach, boys with GID often report seeing a higher proportion of female figures (such as ballerinas, cheerleaders, and female superheros) than male figures, whereas controls do the opposite (Benziman & Marodes, 1997; Zucker, Lozinski, Bradley, & Doering, 1992). In addition, female clothing and other items related to female appearance are commonly identified by boys with GID. In more severe cases, gender confusion enters into the responses, as when a child transforms a response from one gender to another or combines gender in a percept (Coates, 1990).

Other reported characteristics of the Rorschach tests of boys with GID (as compared to controls) include higher levels of two Rorschach special scores (confabulation and fabulized combination) (Tuber & Coates, 1989) that are sometimes categorized as thought-disordered responses. Boys with GID have also been found to report more malevolent interactions between objects on the Rorschach (Tuber & Coates, 1989) and to give an initial response of butterfly to card V (whereas control boys tend to see bats; Benziman & Marodes, 1997).

Over all, the Rorschachs of boys with GID are likely to be characterized by female and female-related percepts as well as occasional hostile and unusual responses. These responses should be carefully interpreted to provide a sense of the underlying thought and emotional processes. Rorschachs of girls with GID have not been systematically studied but would be expected to be characterized by more stereotypically male responses.

Other projective tests such as the TAT and projective drawings are also occasionally used to investigate the personality dynamics of children with GID. On the TAT, boys with

GID often identify with the female figures, telling stories from their point of view. Themes of social rejection and isolation of men, combined with nurturance and competence of women, are also frequently seen on the TAT. Men may be portrayed as unimportant or malevolent. On Draw-a-Person tests boys with GID often draw the female figure first, larger, more positively, and/or more elaborately than the male figure. Stories about their drawings tend to emphasize the female figure. Boys without GID show the opposite pattern on Draw-a-Person tests (Benziman & Marodes, 1997).

Behavioral Assessment

Parent-Report.   Because children with GID may be at risk for comorbid symptoms, it is generally wise to administer a behavior problem checklist to the parents to screen for other difficulties. On the CBCL, boys with GID often score in clinical ranges, especially for internalizing problems. Coates (1990), for example, reported that 84% of her sample of 25 boys with GID scored in the clinical range on the CBCL. Most had symptoms of anxiety and depression, with half scoring in the clinical range on a measure of depressive symptoms. Two CBCL items have as their content behaving like the opposite sex or wishing to be of the opposite sex; these items can be used as an additional GID screen. CBCL results can also be used to assess the social functioning and social problems of the child. Behavior problem scales related to social functioning (Withdrawn, Social Problems) and general internalizing problems (Anxiety/Depression) would be expected to be elevated for a child with GID.

Although the BASC does not have specific items addressing GID, its extensive coverage of social adjustment and depressive symptoms make it a potentially valuable adjunct to a GID assessment. Children with GID would be expected to elevate the BASC parent-report and teacher-report Depression and Anxiety subscales, reflecting the dysphoria typically associated with GID. A high Withdrawal subscale score with a low Leadership subscale score would be characteristic of the social difficulties seen by many children with GID. Similarly, on the Conners' scales, children with GID would be expected to elevate the Anxious-Shy and Social Problems subscales, indicating dysphoria and social problems, respectively.

Family Assessment

Parent-Report.   Assessment of parents of children with GID has focused on the mothers of boys with GID. In many cases, FES results will indicate high Cohesion and Expressiveness scores, coupled with low Conflict and Independence scores. Coates (1990) suggests that many mothers of boys with GID have significant psychopathology, including depression, borderline traits, fear/anger toward men, dependency, and low self-esteem. On the Beck Depression Inventory (Beck, Ward, Mendelson, Mock, & Erbaugh, 1961), mothers of boys with GID have been found to obtain scores averaging 15.8, with 46% falling in clinical ranges (Marantz & Coates, 1991); both of these values are greater than those obtained by controls. On the Diagnostic Interview for Borderlines (Gunderson, Kolb, & Austin, 1981), 25% of mothers of boys with GID obtained scores in the borderline range; their total, affect, psychosis, and interpersonal relations scores exceeded those of controls.

Although no systematic MMPI studies of mothers of children with GID have been undertaken, some inferences can be made based on the observations of Coates (1990) and Marantz and Coates (1991). Distressed mothers would be expected to show elevations on scales 2, 4, 6, 7, 8, and 0, reflecting depression, low self-esteem, rejection of norms, anger, alienation from men or people in general, and poor or atypical social relationships. Their scale 5 score could indicate their own gender identification problems (high score) as well as passive-aggressive tendencies (low score) in acting out this identification. Higher scale 5 may typify a more aggressive, openly defiant mother who clearly rejects the female gender role. A low scale 5 could reflect a more passive, nurturant mother who is in a symbiotic relationship with her son.

Syndrome-Specific Tests

Parent-Report

In addition to the general assessment instruments, several instruments have been developed to measure symptomatology specific to GID. The Gender Behavior Inventory for Boys (GBI; Bates, Bentler, & Thompson, 1973), for example, is a parent-report questionnaire that yields four factors: Extraversion, Feminine Behavior, Behavior Disturbance, and Mother's Boy. The fourth ("Mother's Boy") factor had relatively weak internal consistency and did not discriminate between control and clinical samples. Thus, this six-item factor has been largely ignored. The remaining three factors, however, differentiate boys with and without gender dysphoria (Bates et al., 1973).

The Extraversion scale assesses friendliness and social/physical activity; the Feminine Behavior scale measures feminine and cross-gender behavior; the Behavior Disturbance scale contains diverse items relating to irritability, oppositionality, and emotional upset. Bates et al. (1973) found that boys with gender disturbance scored significantly higher on Feminine Behavior and Behavior Disturbance and lower on Extraversion than control boys. Similarly, Rekers and Morey (1989) reported that their sample of boys with gender disturbance scored significantly higher on Feminine Behavior and lower on Extraversion relative to nonreferred boys. However, they found no difference for Behavior Disturbance. GBI Feminine Behavior and Extraversion scores have also been found to be related to the severity of gender disturbance (Rekers & Morey, 1989).

☐ TREATMENT OPTIONS

In addition to treatment focused on the child's GID symptomatology, clinicians should also be alert for the presence and need for treatment of comorbid psychological problems and disorders. Social problems (ranging from rejection to withdrawal) and internalizing symptoms (including separation anxiety, social phobia, and mood disorders) are at greatest risk for co-occurrence with GID. If comorbid disorders are present, they should be addressed with appropriate techniques for each disorder. Regarding treatment for GID symptoms in particular, early intervention is much more likely to produce a positive outcome than later intervention. By adolescence, GID is very resistant to intervention, and dysphoria can be very persistent.

Behavioral Interventions

Behavior therapy for GID typically involves the use of contingency management (using attention or tangible items for reinforcement), antecedent management, and modeling/social learning to increase the frequency of same-gender behaviors and to decrease the frequency of cross-gender behaviors (Table 15.4). Intervention targets are such behaviors as play with cross-sex toys, dressing in clothing of the opposite sex, fantasy/role playing of a member of the opposite sex, peer relationships, and motoric actions (Zucker, 1989, 1990b). Goal behaviors, consequently, are play with same-sex toys, dress in gender-appropriate clothing, establishment of same-sex relationships, and gender-appropriate mannerisms.

Contingency Management

The crucial first step in contingency management for GID is the identification of the exact behaviors to be targeted. Some parents are distressed by their child's cross-sex behaviors and want all cross-sex behaviors to cease immediately. The tendency to target all cross-sex behaviors at once, however, can be overwhelming and confusing for the child. The targeting of a few clearly defined behaviors allows all parties involved to deal with a manageable group of contingencies. Clear definition of target behaviors prevents haggling over whether a specific behavior fits the "cross-sex" category or not.

Following the identification of target behaviors, a baseline level of behavior is identified. This baseline may either be a frequency count of the target behaviors or a record of amount of time spent doing the target behaviors. The baseline record allows the parents to become familiar with behavior recording systems and, in some cases, increases the insight of the parents and the child into the magnitude of the problem. It also provides an initial data point from which to evaluate the effectiveness of future interventions.

Once specific behaviors are identified, they are matched with reinforcements, and, in some instances, punishments. A common intervention, for example, involves the use of attention as a reinforcer for appropriate behavior. Parents (and, in some cases, teachers, other caretakers, or even peers) are instructed to attend to same-sex behaviors and to ignore opposite sex behaviors (Zucker, 1990b). Another intervention involves the provision of tokens or other tangible primary or secondary reinforcers for appropriate behavior. This is often combined with a response-cost intervention in which tokens are removed for inappropriate behavior. Finally, self-regulation has been suggested as an intervention that will promote generalization of same-sex behaviors to multiple contexts (Rekers & Varni, 1977). In this

---

TABLE 15.4   Treatment Options for Gender Identity Disorder

1. Behavioral Interventions
   a. Contingency management
   b. Antecedent management
   c. Modeling/social learning
2. Psychotherapy
   a. Play therapy
3. Family Interventions
   a. Marital therapy
   b. Parent intervention/training
   c. Family therapy

Note: This outline of options summarizes major treatments covered in the text. Specific treatments are often combined into an intervention package. Refer to the text for additional descriptions of each treatment. This table is not necessarily an exhaustive list of all treatments available.

intervention, the child is given a device, such as a wrist counter, and is taught to press it when engaging in a specific same-sex behavior. Initially, the child is taught this self-monitoring behavior in a controlled setting such as a lab or office. The child is then instructed to continue this recording in the natural environment. The goal is to increase the counts of appropriate behavior during each week. This intervention has been reported to be very effective (Rekers & Varni, 1977; Zucker, 1990b), although it is highly dependent on the child's motivation.

Antecedent Management

In addition to managing the reinforcements and punishments associated with same-sex and cross-sex behaviors and identification, parents can intervene by removing the items or situations that lead to cross-sex behaviors and identification, while inserting items or situations that encourage same-sex behaviors and identification. Such an antecedent management intervention might include the removal of (or limiting access to) cross-sex toys such as dolls for boys. Other antecedents commonly identified are cross-sex clothing (discouraged), membership in a same-sex club or team (encouraged), and participation in a sport associated with a particular gender role (e.g., football for boys). These interventions must be implemented carefully, in order to avoid communicating disgust or disdain of cross-gender items or activities. An attitude of asking the child to try some new things (associated with his or her traditional gender role) in addition to (or in place of) other items or activities is typically the best approach to antecedent management.

Modeling/Social Learning

To promote social learning of the gender role, parents are encouraged to model gender role-congruent behavior while communicating to the child that they value the child as a member of his or her own sex. Frequently, the same-sex parent is called on to participate with the child in activities that promote identification and acceptance of the child's biological sex and the gender role that accompanies it. More direct modeling may occur when a therapist practices gender-congruent behaviors with the child. Boys, for example, might be taught a more traditionally "masculine" way of sitting, standing, and walking.

Social learning in the context of peers can be encouraged by placing the child in same-sex peer groups, clubs, or teams. Exposure to these peer experiences should usually follow a period of learning and training about how to interact with the same-sex peer group in order to reduce the chances of failure and ostracization. More structured and monitored group interactions (e.g., scouts, teams) are also more likely to produce success because they give the child a clearly defined role. Exposure to same-sex peers provides many opportunities for modeling and social learning experiences.

Other aspects of gender role behaviors may also be discussed with the child, including stereotypic gender interests and social interaction styles. Exposure to reading material (e.g., sports page for boys) may be used to improve the child's knowledge of information that will promote positive interactions with members of the same sex. As with antecedent management, the goal is to increase the child's exposure to gender-congruent items and activities without communicating negatively about cross-gender items and activities.

Behavior therapy for GID has been reported to be effective both in the short and long term for reducing cross-gender behavior and increasing same-gender behavior (Bradley &

Zucker, 1997; Rekers et al., 1991). However, its effectiveness for changing the beliefs and affects associated with GID is less clear. Furthermore, the extent to which behavioral improvements generalize to other contexts (especially those in which the reinforcer is absent) has not been studied. Despite these problems, however, behavior therapy has been one of the most extensively studied and supported interventions for GID.

Psychotherapy

Psychoanalytic and psychodynamic psychotherapies for GID have received at least as much attention as behavior therapy, but they suffer from a lack of published empirical research. Psychotherapy interventions usually target the early parent- (usually mother) child relationship and its effects on the child's current functioning. Specific themes addressed in psychoanalytic psychotherapy mirror those thought to be linked to the development of GID: symbiosis with the mother and overidentification with the mother following real or symbolic loss (Bleiberg et al., 1986; Coates, 1990). Loss causes separation anxiety in the child, which is alleviated by the adoption of the parent's behaviors. By behaving like the parent, the child can continue to feel attached to the parent. In order to abandon their GID behaviors, then, children must work through the loss of their attachment figure (Zucker, 1990b).

In preadolescent children, psychodynamic therapy usually takes the form of play therapy, in which the child is permitted to play out fantasies and concerns. The therapist, initially a nondirective partner in the play, gradually interprets the concerns and affects that the child manifests (Bleiberg et al., 1986). Interpretations usually focus on the fear of loss of the parent and anger toward caretakers. Another common theme to be interpreted is the fear of being different from the mother, leading to a withdrawal of her love and acceptance. This interpretation is particularly likely to arise when mothers reject and devalue men. Therapeutic interpretations, coupled with the nurturance and support of the therapeutic relationship, facilitate insight and working-through of anxiety-provoking issues that underlie GID behavior.

Family Interventions

Marital Therapy

Some parents are openly or passively resistant to interventions for GID, necessitating a focus on the issues of the couple, the family, or the individual parent. Marital conflict, for example, may be played out in relationships with the children. The most common manifestation of this is for one parent to be enmeshed with the children while the other parent is disengaged from the family. In such cases, an enmeshed relationship between the child and opposite-sex parent may foster and maintain the GID. The family system resists any change in this parent-child relationship because this change would require a focus on and a change in the marital relationship. In this case, marital therapy may be necessary to address the parents' problems before work on the child's GID can begin (Bradley & Zucker, 1990).

Parent Psychotherapy

When only one parent is involved in the resistance to treatment, individual psychotherapy with the parent may be warranted. Such parental difficulties as depression, borderline personality disorder, and devaluation of men have been suggested as underlying GID (Coates, 1990). Some parents may be deriving secondary psychological gain from their child's GID, as when a socially isolated mother enmeshes with her son and derives narcissistic pleasure from his imitation of her. These longstanding problems are likely to interfere with suggestions that a parent change his or her behavior. Clinicians must be wary of parental psychopathology that could interfere with child-focused treatment plans; the initial focus of GID therapy may need to be on the problems of such parents.

Family Therapy

In some families, the child's GID is a family affair. The initial signs that family therapy may be necessary are the presence of GID in more than one child, boundary difficulties between parents and children, or evidence that family life is organized around the GID of the child. When this is the case, structural interventions (e.g., Minuchin, 1974) to address family boundary issues and strategic interventions (Haley, 1976) to alter family behaviors are necessary components of treatment. Despite their insistence that they are committed to treatment, some families are unintentionally resistant to interventions because they fear the repercussions of a change in the family system. Discussion of the family structure and the role of the GID symptoms in family life can reveal the dynamics underlying the family's resistance. Restructuring the family is usually necessary in these cases.

▪ References

American Psychiatric Association. (1994). *Diagnostic and statistical manual of mental disorders, fourth edition.* Washington, DC: Author.

Bates, J. E., Bentler, P. M., & Thompson, S. K. (1973). Measurement of deviant gender development in boys. *Child Development, 44,* 591–598.

Bates, J. E., Bentler, P. M., & Thompson, S. K. (1979). Gender deviant boys compared with normal and clinical control boys. *Journal of Abnormal Child Psychology, 7,* 243–259.

Beck, A. T., Ward, C. H., Mendelson, M., Mock, J., & Erbaugh, J. (1961). An inventory for measuring depression. *Archives of General Psychiatry, 4,* 561–571.

Benziman, H., & Marodes, S. (1997). Indicators of feminine gender identity in latency-aged boys in the Draw a Person and the Rorschach tests. *Journal of Clinical Psychology, 53,* 143–157.

Bleiberg, E., Jackson, L., & Ross, J. L. (1986). Gender Identity Disorder and object loss. *Journal of the American Academy of Child Psychiatry, 25,* 58–67.

Bradley, S. J., Blanchard, R., Coates, S., Green, R., Levine, S. B., Meyer-Bahlburg, H. F. L., Pauly, I. B., & Zucker, K. J. (1991). Interim report of the DSM-IV sub-committee on gender identity disorders. *Archives of Sexual Behavior, 20,* 333–343.

Bradley, S. J., & Zucker, K. J. (1990). Gender Identity Disorder and psychosexual problems in children and adolescents. *Canadian Journal of Psychiatry, 35,* 477–486.

Bradley, S. J., & Zucker, K. J. (1997). Gender Identity Disorder: A review of the past 10 years. *Journal of the American Academy of Child and Adolescent Psychiatry, 36,* 872–880.

Coates, S. (1990). Ontogenesis of boyhood gender identity disorder. *Journal of the American Academy of Psychoanalysis, 18,* 414–438.

Coates, S., & Person, E. (1985). Extreme boyhood femininity: Isolated behavior or pervasive disorder? *Journal of the American Academy of Child and Adolescent Psychiatry, 24,* 702–709.

Doering, R. W., Zucker, K. J., Bradley, S. J., & MacIntyre, R. B. (1989). Effects of neutral toys on sex-typed play in children with Gender Identity Disorder. *Journal of Abnormal Child Psychology, 17,* 563–574.

Green, R. (1987). *The "sissy boy" syndrome and the development of homosexuality.* New Haven: Yale University Press.

Gunderson, J. G., Kolb, J. E., & Austin, V. (1981). The diagnostic interview for borderline patients. *American Journal of Psychiatry, 138,* 896–905.

Haley, J. (1976). *Problem-solving therapy.* New York: Harper & Row.

Marantz, S., & Coates, S. (1991). Mothers of boys with gender identity disorder: A comparison of matched controls. *Journal of the American Academy of Child and Adolescent Psychiatry, 30,* 310–315.

McDermid, S. A., Zucker, K. J., Bradley, S. J., & Maing, D. M. (1998). Effects of physical appearance on masculine trait ratings of boys and girls with gender identity disorder. *Archives of Sexual Behavior, 27,* 253–267.

Minuchin, S. (1974). *Families and family therapy.* Cambridge, MA: Harvard University Press.

Money, J. (1994). The concept of Gender Identity Disorder in childhood and adolescence after 39 years. *Journal of Sex and Marital Therapy, 20,* 163–177.

Rekers, G. A., Kilgus, M., & Rosen, A. C. (1991). Long-term effects of treatment for Gender Identity Disorder of Childhood. *Journal of Psychology and Human Sexuality, 3,* 121–153.

Rekers, G. A., & Morey, S. M. (1989). Relationship of maternal report of feminine behaviors and extraversion to clinician's rating of gender disturbance. *Perceptual and Motor Skills, 69,* 387–394.

Rekers, G. A., & Varni, J. W. (1977). Self-regulation of gender-role behaviors: A case study. *Journal of Behavior Therapy and Experimental Psychiatry, 8,* 427–432.

Stoller, R. J. (1968). *Sex and gender.* New York: Science House.

Stoller, R. J. (1975). *Sex and gender, volume 2. The transsexual experiment.* London: Hogarth Press.

Tuber, S., & Coates, S. (1989). Indices of psychopathology in the Rorschachs of boys with severe gender identity disorder: A comparison with normal control subjects. *Journal of Personality Assessment, 53,* 100–112.

Zucker, K. J. (1989). Gender identity disorders. In C. G. Last & M. Hersen (Eds.), *Handbook of child psychiatric diagnosis* (pp. 388–406). New York: Wiley.

Zucker, K. J. (1990a). Gender Identity Disorders in children: Clinical descriptions and natural history. In R. Blanchard & B. W. Steiner (Eds.), *Clinical management of gender identity disorders in children and adults* (pp. 27–45). Washington, DC: American Psychiatric Association.

Zucker, K. J. (1990b). Treatment of Gender Identity Disorders in children. In R. Blanchard & B. W. Steiner (Eds.), *Clinical management of gender identity disorders in children and adults* (pp. 3–23). Washington, DC: American Psychiatric Association.

Zucker, K. J., Bradley, S. J., & Sanikhani, M. (1997). Sex differences in referral rates of children with gender identity disorder: Some hypotheses. *Journal of Abnormal Child Psychology, 25,* 217–227.

Zucker, K. J., & Green, R. (1996). Gender Identity Disorders. In M. Lewis (Ed.), *Child and adolescent psychiatry: A comprehensive textbook* (2nd ed.). Baltimore: Williams & Wilkins.

Zucker, K. J., Lozinski, J. A., Bradley, S. J., & Doering, R. W. (1992). Sex typed responses in the Rorschach protocols of children with gender identity disorder. *Journal of Personality Assessment, 58,* 295–310.

CHAPTER 16

Reactive Attachment Disorder

■ Reactive Attachment Disorder

□ CLINICAL DESCRIPTION

Diagnostic Considerations

Reactive Attachment Disorder of Infancy or Early Childhood (RAD) refers to a disturbed pattern of attachment behavior seen in some infants and toddlers. This disturbed attachment behavior takes one of two forms: (1) failure to attach or positively respond to people or (2) indiscriminate attachment to multiple people, regardless of familiarity or caretaking function. Children with the former RAD presentation are classified as "inhibited type," whereas those with the latter RAD presentation are classified as "disinhibited type."

According to DSM-IV, RAD begins before age 5 and cannot be the result of Mental Retardation or a Pervasive Developmental Disorder. In addition to abnormal social-attachment behavior, there must be some evidence of abnormal or negative care, such as abuse, neglect, or multiple change of primary caregiver. It is presumed that this abnormal or negative care is responsible for the attachment disturbance. RAD is reportedly uncommon in the general population of infants and toddlers (American Psychiatric Association, 1994), although it is more common in certain situations (e.g., extended hospitalizations, parental neglect) (see Table 16.1).

RAD frequently is seen in infants and young children with nonorganic failure-to-thrive (NOFT), a disorder in which infants and toddlers fail to grow physically and to develop socially. The symptoms of NOFT overlap substantially with the DSM-IV Feeding Disorder of Infancy (FDI) diagnosis, making NOFT and FDI roughly analogous diagnoses. FDI is characterized by a failure to eat adequately, stagnant weight or weight loss, and onset prior to age 6. Because of the substantial overlap among NOFT, FDI, and RAD, children with RAD should be routinely evaluated for FDI/NOFT, and vice versa. Evaluation and treatment of FDI are covered in detail in Chapter 7 of this book.

TABLE 16.1   Epidemiology and Course of Reactive Attachment Disorder

Prevalence: Unknown; thought to be rare

Sex Ratio (Male:Female):   Unknown; probably 1:1

Typical Onset Age: Infancy or toddlerhood; must be present before age 5.

Course: Highly variable and dependent on age at diagnosis, severity of problem, and intensity of intervention. Most children respond well to intervention and show improvements in physical health, social interaction, and cognitive development, although some retain attachment disruption even with intervention. If feeding disorder and nonorganic failure-to-thrive are present, growth deformity or mortality is a risk if left untreated. Developmental and cognitive delays are often seen but improve in many children with treatment. Less is known of long-term course, but difficulty forming attachments, intimate relationships, and appropriate social relationships is a risk. Behavior problems may emerge in early childhood and adolescence.

Common Comorbid Conditions: 1. Feeding Disorder of Infancy or Early Childhood
    (Nonorganic Failure-to-Thrive)
2. Depressive Disorders
3. Learning Disorders, Developmental Delays, Borderline Intellectual Functioning, or Mental Retardation
4. Communication Disorders

Relevant Subtypes: 1. Inhibited vs. Disinhibited
2. Etiology subtypes
    a. Hospitalism
    b. Institutionalism
    c. Neglect/Abuse
    d. Maladaptive Parent-Child Interactions

Like RAD, NOFT/FDI is thought to be caused in many cases by maladaptive parent-child relationships. These relationships may result in a lack of stimulation for the child, which could cause growth deficits by way of neuroendocrinological mechanisms (Tibbits-Kleber & Howell, 1985). In addition, maladaptive parent-child relationships often become manifest at mealtimes, resulting in abnormal feeding behavior by the child with RAD. Parents and children with NOFT/FDI frequently engage in power struggles over food, and the meal is often a time of anxiety and conflict. The resultant failure of the child to ingest adequate nutrition causes the growth deficit characteristic of NOFT (Green, 1989; Hathaway, 1989; Kelley & Heffer, 1990).

Although little doubt exists that RAD and NOFT/FDI co-occur, some confusion has existed over the exact relationship between the two conditions. Originally, RAD was defined largely as the psychiatric component of NOFT (Tibbits-Kleber & Howell, 1985) or as a "subset of nonorganic FTT" (Dulcan & Popper, 1991, p. 92). More recently, however, efforts have been made to separate the social/attachment features of RAD from the growth/feeding features of FDI, while admitting some comorbidity of the conditions. Hence, RAD and NOFT/FDI may or may not occur together.

Psychosocial dwarfism (or psychosocially determined short stature) is another medical diagnosis that co-occurs occasionally with RAD (Green, 1989). This disorder emerges at age

2–3 and is characterized by a marked decrease in growth rate following an earlier period of approximately normal growth. Height is typically below the third percentile and bone growth is clearly stunted. Although the condition cannot be the result of malnutrition or other physical disorders, growth hormone levels are often found to be abnormally low or inconsistent.

Like NOFT, psychosocial dwarfism is hypothesized to result from a maladaptive caretaker-child relationship such as that typically seen in RAD. Green (1989), for example, cites a "severely disturbed relationship between primary caretaker and child" (p. 1897) or child abuse as diagnostically important for the psychosocial dwarfism diagnosis. The effects of the parent-child relationship on stimulation and arousal adversely impact the endocrinological functioning of the child, including the regulation of growth hormone. Therefore, when the parent-child relationship problems are treated, hormone levels and growth return to normal (Green, 1989).

Appearance and Features

Appearance and features of RAD are listed in Table 16.2. Children with RAD often appear socially and developmentally delayed. For example, they may fail to smile in response to a playful person (at around 2 months), fail to engage in simple social games/play (at around 5 months), or fail to bond with a primary caretaker (at around 8 months) (Dulcan & Popper, 1991). Social delays also include lack of eye contact, extreme engagement or disengagement in social interaction, and lack of attention to the environment. Other characteristics of RAD are lethargy, slow weight gain, weight loss, thin and frail appearance, feeding

TABLE 16.2   Appearance and Features of Reactive Attachment Disorder

COMMON FEATURES

1. Failure to attach or indiscriminate attachment
2. Abnormal or negative care (abuse, neglect, separation from caretaker)
3. Nonorganic failure-to-thrive (weight loss, feeding problem)
4. Lack of stimulation from environment
5. Impaired social relationships
6. Lethargy
7. Resistance to being held
8. Lack of interest in social environment or excessive interest in strangers
9. Ambivalent or disinterested attitude of parent toward child
10. Failure of parent to respond to social cues of child

OCCASIONAL FEATURES

1. Developmental (especially language) delay
2. Parental psychopathology: insecurity, depression, dependence
3. Parental stress: marital distress, social isolation
4. Lack of parenting knowledge
5. Family conflict/family stress

Note: The features listed in the table are often seen but are not universal. Some features may be diagnostically relevant or required, whereas others may not be required for diagnosis. "Common" features are typical of the disorder; "occasional" features appear frequently but are not necessarily seen in a majority of cases.

problems, resistance to being held, poor visual tracking, lack of interest in the social environment, and fussiness (American Psychiatric Association, 1994; Richters & Volkmar, 1996).

Children with disinhibited RAD display excessive interest and positive affect with strangers. They are often overly friendly and even clingy with unfamiliar adults, becoming immediately emotionally involved with new people. These infants and toddlers are often favorites in hospitals and institutions because they are extremely friendly and accepting of adults. However, their apparent "attachment" is fleeting because of their tendency to substitute one adult for another.

In terms of cognitive development, children with RAD are at risk for communication and intellectual delays, particularly when significant neglect and/or failure-to-thrive is present. Communication problems include delays in articulation and vocabulary. Intellectually, such children frequently score in below average ranges, especially when they have been neglected by caretakers. Some studies report that as many as two-thirds of children with RAD develop a reading disorder (Hufton & Oates, 1977). In many cases, however, communication and cognitive delays improve dramatically with intervention (Richters & Volkmar, 1996).

Very little is known about infant characteristics that predate RAD, although it seems possible that these infants may tend to be temperamentally difficult. Combined with a vulnerable parent, this temperamental difficulty could lead to parental frustration, child distress, and maladaptive interactions characteristic of RAD (Tibbits-Kleber & Howell, 1985).

Because of the centrality of the parent-child relationship in the hypothesized etiology of RAD, clinical attention is usually focused on the characteristics of families whose children develop RAD. Unfortunately, the research in this area is sparse, and many characteristics are inferred from studies of related disorders such as NOFT and FDI. Although no personality type, psychiatric diagnosis, or specific behavior can be attributed to all parents of children with RAD, the following characteristics have been noted in many cases (Dulcan & Popper, 1991; Fischhoff, 1989; Lee, Kwon, Sihn, & Kim, 1996; Richters & Volkmar, 1996; Tibbits-Kleber & Howell, 1985). For the most part, these characteristics have been observed in mothers; far less is known about fathers of children with RAD:

CHARACTERISTICS OF THE PARENT(S)

1. Deficits in parenting confidence and self-esteem
2. Inadequate observation of the child
3. Ambivalence over parental role, manifest by varying interest in the child (in hospitals and institutions, shown by infrequent or brief parental visits)
4. Appearance of being under great stress, which appears to impact on caretaking ability
5. Depression, personality disorder, or similar symptoms
6. Emotional lability
7. Social awkwardness
8. Attention to child's physical but not emotional needs
9. Frustration/anger over feeding
10. Overtly hostile/adversarial marital interaction
11. One parent (often father) detached from family

12. Lack of empathy for child

13. Blaming child for problems

14. Inappropriate expectations of child, relative to developmental level

15. Social isolation

16. Financial stresses

CHARACTERISTICS OF THE PARENT-CHILD INTERACTION

1. Lack of physical or emotional nurturance

2. Inappropriate amount/timing of stimulation

3. Inappropriate reactions to child's emotional behavior

4. Failure to place infant in an interacting position

5. Lack of communication between parent and infant (e.g., parent cannot or does not read infant's cues; infant may not attempt to engage parent)

6. Adversarial or unpleasant feeding interaction

7. Inconsistency in interaction, varying from pleasant/engaged to hostile to mutual disinterest

8. Forced separation of parent and child because of illness or other problem

9. Failure of child to respond differentially to parental bids for interaction or to show preference for the parent

Parental stress and problems in parent-child interaction are often most apparent during feeding, perhaps because feeding represents a potential time of nurturance and satisfaction of the child's needs. Some parents are not sensitive to their child's feeding rhythm and feed them too quickly or too slowly, provoking a negative response from the child. This response leads to parental frustration and a continuation or worsening of the abnormal feeding interaction. Other parents misjudge infant cues of satiety, mistakenly thinking that their child is hungry or full when he or she is not. This can lead to over- or underfeeding, which causes the infant to associate feeding with unpleasantness (Fischhoff, 1989). In some cases, the child has a bona fide medical problem (e.g., reflux) that creates an initial problem with the feeding interaction. However, even after this medical problem is corrected, the history of maladaptive feeding interaction remains and can affect feeding and attachment behavior.

In other cases, characteristics of family interaction interfere with the feeding. Family conflict, for example, may emerge when the family gathers to eat, creating a tense or loud atmosphere that is not conducive to relaxed infant feeding. Other children may demand much of the parents' attention, distracting them from the infant's cues and preventing parent-infant interaction during feeding. Any of these situations can lead to an association of feeding with discomfort and distress, causing the infant to be fussy and avoidant at mealtime.

The course of RAD is variable but can be serious. In cases of NOFT/FDI or other feeding difficulties, malnutrition, growth deformity, and developmental delays are a significant risk. For infants in this category, immediate medical intervention is essential.

Social deprivation can lead to long-term difficulty forming positive attachments and friendships. In severe cases, future behavior problems and personality disturbances characterized by relationship difficulties are a risk (Tibbits-Kleber & Howell, 1985). High rates of manipulative behavior, difficulty with perspective taking, lack of respect for social rules, and difficulty with intimate relationships have been observed in older children and adolescents with histories of RAD.

Etiology

Psychological Theories

Underlying the RAD diagnosis is the assumption that children need to emotionally attach to one or a few primary caretakers. Attachment is shown by recognition, preference, and positive emotional response to a caretaker, coupled with wariness of unfamiliar people. Bowlby (1952) hypothesized that this attachment was naturally selected through millennia of evolution, and numerous theorists have emphasized the importance of early attachment for later adjustment. Observations of cognitive, emotional, and social impairment in children who have been deprived of caretakers (Spitz, 1945) convincingly showed the importance of interaction with a primary caretaker for normal development. Because attachment is thought to be a normal and adaptive behavior for the human species, deviations from this behavior are likely to be maladaptive.

RAD is associated with several environmental factors and medical presentations. Based on these factors and presentations, children with RAD may be classified into several overlapping etiological groups (Fischhoff, 1989):

1. Children who have been hospitalized repeatedly and/or extensively, either for medical or psychological problems ("hospitalism").
2. Children who have been placed in institutions and have received little attention from caretaking figures ("institutionalism").
3. Children from abusive or neglectful homes.
4. Children who fail to develop normally because of maladaptive parent-child interactions and relationships such as conflict and double-binding.

Hospitalism, institutionalism, abuse/neglect, and maladaptive interactions are thought to cause RAD because they reflect deviations in normal attachment between parent and child. In hospitals and institutions, infants have multiple caretakers, often spend less time with parents, and are not in a stable home environment. Hence, opportunities for a normal attachment relationship with a primary caretaker are lessened. These children sometimes indiscriminately attach to any caretaker, reflecting their experience of multiple adult caretakers, none of whom has a continuous primary role. Children from abusive/neglectful homes, on the other hand, may form tenuous or ambivalent attachments (if any) to their unpredictable parents.

Biological Theories

Although much of the focus in the search for the etiology of RAD has been placed on the environment, some evidence suggests that biological factors may also play a part in the onset of RAD (Richters & Volkmar, 1996). Children raised by the same parent in the same home, for example, do not all develop RAD, and only a fraction of neglected children develop RAD. This information suggests that parental factors or environmental neglect alone may not be responsible for RAD. Possible biological influences on RAD include difficult temperament, physical anomalies, and abnormalities in early social interaction reflexes (e.g., gaze, cuddliness). These influences could provoke avoidance from a vulnerable parent, as well as indicate a child with a predisposition to temperamental avoidance or irritability toward social stimulation.

ASSESSMENT PATTERNS

A sample assessment battery for RAD is shown in Table 16.3.

Broad Assessment Strategies

Cognitive Assessment

Clinician-Administered.   Observations that children with RAD may have cognitive delays suggest the need for sensory, motor, and cognitive assessment. Tests such as the Bayley-II and SB:FE may indicate intellectual and motor deficits. The VABS and ABES can provide insight into infants' development of adaptive behavior. Over all, it is important to track these infants cognitively because of the long-term intellectual risks of a lack of social-environmental stimulation.

Behavioral Assessment

Parent-Report.   Little research has been done on the typical behavior checklist profile of the child with RAD. In many cases, symptoms of RAD will be apparent at ages that are below

---

TABLE 16.3   Sample Assessment Battery for Reactive Attachment Disorder

COGNITIVE

1. Vineland Adaptive Behavior Scales

BEHAVIORAL

1. Behavior Assessment System for Children (if age 2½ or older)

FAMILY

1. Family Environment Scale
2. Parent MMPI (when possible)

SYNDROME-SPECIFIC TESTS

1. Parenting Stress Index

Note: Assessment instruments are intended to supplement (not substitute for) a good clinical interview and, when possible, a structured diagnostic interview.

the lower age bound of the major broad-band behavior checklists, so their use will not be possible. Of the major broad-band behavior checklists, the CBCL (age 2) and BASC (age 2½) have the lowest age ranges, whereas the Conners scales (age 3) apply at slightly older ages. It appears likely that children with inhibited-type RAD would show abnormal scores on most of the social subscales of the behavior checklists. Children with disinhibited-type RAD, on the other hand, would be expected to show a different pattern of scores, with either no significant pattern of elevation or an elevated pattern of scales reflecting hyperactivity, manipulative behavior, or aggression.

On the CBCL, elevations of the Social Problems (4–16-year-old version only) and Withdrawn (for children with inhibited-type RAD) subscales would be expected. On the BASC, low scores on the Leadership and Social Skills subscales (6–18-year-old versions only) with higher scores on the Withdrawal subscale would be characteristic of children with inhibited-type RAD. Children with disinhibited-type RAD, on the other hand, who are experiencing overactive, oppositional, or manipulative behavior, would elevate the Hyperactivity and Aggression subscales of the BASC.

Of the major broad-band subscales, only the ECI-4 has a subscale corresponding directly to RAD symptoms. The ECI-4 RAD subscale consists of two items, one measuring inhibited RAD symptoms and the other measuring disinhibited RAD symptoms. There has, however, been little research on this subscale of the ECI-4. Children with RAD would also be expected to elevate the feeding problems items of the ECI-4, with other ECI-4 subscale elevations showing comorbid Axis I symptoms.

Family Assessment

Parent-Report. Formal psychological assessment may be helpful in understanding parental contributions to the dynamics underlying maladaptive interactions in a family with a child who has RAD. Knowledge of parent personality and psychopathology (if present) can, therefore, be of immense assistance in understanding the child's condition and planning for treatment. Maternal defensiveness or denial may appear on the MMPI as an elevated L for low SES mothers or K for higher SES mothers. Additional elevations for distressed mothers may be expected on scales 2 and 7, reflecting emotional upset or depression. An elevated scale 4 likely indicates troubles in the current family or family of origin and should be followed up by a Dyadic Adjustment Scale and Family Environment Scale. Difficulties with empathy and nurturance may be manifest in a 4–5 codetype for women. Scales 3 and 0 indicate the mother's social presentation; mothers with a high 3 and low 0 are likely to be outgoing but more self-oriented and dependent in relationships. They may be unable to give their infant sufficient stimulation because they themselves are in need of attention and validation from others. Mothers with a low 3 and high 0 may be reclusive, introverted, and avoidant of any social relationships. Elevations on scales 6 and 8 suggest more serious suspiciousness, anger, attributional biases, and lack of cognitive control driving the maladaptive parent-child interaction.

Assessment of marital relationships in families with RAD sometimes reveals troubled marriages. Lower marital satisfaction scores on the Dyadic Adjustment Scale (Spanier, 1976) would be expected in those cases. In one study, 36% of partners of mothers of children with NOFT were substance abusers, a value three times that for controls (Benoit, Zeanah, & Barton, 1989). Similar problems may be expected on the FES, with some mothers elevating the Conflict and Control subscales in conjunction with deficits on Cohesion, Active-Recreational Orientation, and Intellectual-Cultural Orientation. Defensive mothers, on the other hand, may report high Cohesion and low Conflict. Assessment of the marital and family environment may suggest potential sources of difficulty and sources of intervention for these families.

Because of marital and family difficulties, mothers of children with RAD may either withdraw from social interaction or look for support outside of their families. Measures of social support such as the Social Support Questionnaire (Sarason, Levine, Basham, & Sarason, 1983) may provide some insight into the mother's constellation of social support. Mothers of children with NOFT, for example, report less social support from within the family but more social support from nonfamily sources (Benoit et al., 1989).

Assessment of fathers of children with RAD is also important, but much less is known about their personality characteristics. The role of the father in the family life and the status of the father-child relationship are important starting points in paternal assessment. Administration of the MMPI and FES to the father may provide some insight into his role in the family.

Syndrome-Specific Tests

Clinician-Administered

The evaluation of the family of a child with RAD should include careful observation by the clinician of parent-child and parent-parent interactions. The importance of firsthand observation cannot be overstated because parents of children with RAD may be (intentionally or unintentionally) unreliable reporters of their behavior and interactions (Fischhoff, 1989). Common characteristics of families and children with RAD (described earlier in the Appearance and Features section of this chapter) should form the backbone of this clinical evaluation.

Parent-Report

Measurement of parenting stress and parent perceptions of the difficulty of caretaking can be extremely valuable in understanding the family environment of the child with RAD. Although not specifically developed for RAD, the Parenting Stress Index (Abidin, 1995) can provide information that bears directly on these stress/perception factors. The PSI has 120 multiple choice (on a 1–4, 1–5, or Yes-No scale of agreement) items that are answered by parents of children 0–12 years of age. Subscales reflect difficult child behaviors (Distractibility/Hyperactivity, Adaptability, Reinforces Parent, Demandingness, Mood, and Acceptability subscales), parent adjustment and functioning (Competence, Isolation, Attachment, Health, Role Restriction, Depression, and Spouse subscales), and overall life stresses (Life Stress subscale). Total scores are obtained for the Child Domain, Parent Domain, and Total Stress (Child and Parent Domains) areas. Scores are converted to percentiles based on a large, nonrepresentative norm sample of mothers, aggregated across child ages 0–12 years (separate norms for total scores of different age groups can be obtained in the manual but are not routinely used in scoring). A Defensive Responding scale measures the parent's tendency to minimize stress and problems.

Parents of children with RAD would be expected to obtain higher Total Stress, Child Domain, and Parent Domain scores, as compared to the PSI norm group. Of particular interest is the Attachment subscale, which measures the parent's sense of emotional closeness to the child and ability to understand the child. The Competence subscale reflects parent confidence, comfort, and skill in child caring, whereas the Depression subscale is sensitive to the presence of depressive symptoms in the parent. Hence, elevation of the Attachment, Competence, and Depression subscales would be common in the RAD population. A high Defensive Responding subscale score could indicate that the parent is minimizing problems because of low insight, social desirability, or an intentional attempt to look good.

☐ TREATMENT OPTIONS

Treatment options are outlined in Table 16.4.

Medical Evaluation/Hospitalization

Initial treatment attention must be paid to the medical needs of the child. Many children with RAD are undernourished or neglected and require immediate medical attention. In fact, children with RAD often present with medical problems in pediatric hospitals and are

TABLE 16.4   Treatment Options for Reactive Attachment Disorder

1. Medical Evaluation/Hospitalization
   a. Evaluation for physical problems
   b. Enforced, monitored feeding or G-tube placement if nutritional/growth status is a risk
2. Environmental Interventions
   a. Provision of regular stimulation and social interaction
   b. Identification of one or two primary caretakers for the child; avoidance of multiple caretakers
3. Behavioral Interventions
   a. Treatment for feeding problems as needed, in accordance with FDI interventions
   b. Praise
   c. Pairing the attachment figure with rewarding stimulation
   d. Parent behavior training and parent-child therapy
4. Family Interventions
   a. Instrumental and social support
   b. Family therapy
   c. Marital therapy
   d. Parent psychotherapy or medication treatment
5. Home Monitoring and Protective Removal
   a. Temporary separation of parent and child
   b. Home visits by social worker, nurse, or other mental health professionals
   c. Therapeutic foster care

Note: This outline of options summarizes major treatments covered in the text. Specific treatments are often combined into an intervention package. Refer to the text for additional descriptions of each treatment. This table is not necessarily an exhaustive list of all treatments available.

only later evaluated for RAD. Medical treatment typically consists of measures to increase nourishment and body weight (if NOFT is seen), which may range from regular feeding to placement of a G-tube. If the infant thrives in the hospital environment after failing to gain weight or interact appropriately at home (and this is often the case within the first two weeks), intervention with parents is essential prior to hospital discharge to prevent a recurrence of the feeding, attachment, and social problems.

Environmental Interventions

The provision of regular stimulation is a routine psychological intervention for children with RAD. This increase in stimulation must be provided gradually to avoid overwhelming the child (Green, 1989). Placement of a mobile above the crib, coupled with frequent, regular social contact is usually beneficial. The social contact should include tactile, visual, and auditory stimulation, with extensive verbal stimulation. Ideally, this contact should occur with a small, consistent set of adults and one primary caretaker in order to increase the possibility for attachment. Assignment of a small group of primary nurses and one or two parent figures (who make regular, extended visits) is often necessary to achieve this goal (Tibbits-Kleber & Howell, 1985).

Behavioral Interventions

Behavioral treatments are typically used to address both feeding and attachment problems in children with RAD. Treatments for feeding problems are described in Chapter 7, under the FDI diagnosis. Behavioral techniques to promote attachment include the use of praise, pairing the attachment figure with rewarding stimulation, and teaching behavioral parenting skills.

Praise and pairing the attachment figure with rewarding stimulation are used to promote preference for the caretaker and proximity seeking by the child. Caretakers should reward attachment behaviors such as eye contact, proximity seeking, physical contact, and positive affect with warm praise and affection. If the child is interested in certain toys or other objects, increased access to these should also be connected to the caretaker's presence. When the caretaker has to leave, the child should be provided with a special transitional object that is connected with the caretaker's presence. Common transitional objects are blankets and stuffed animals.

Parent behavior skills training and parent-child therapy aim to teach the parent to behave in ways that promote stable attachment and social connection in the child. These interventions begin with psychoeducation of the parent about interaction with children in general and about the needs and behaviors of children with RAD in particular. Parenting skills classes about attachment, discipline, and parental stress management are helpful in this regard. Webster-Stratton's (1996) videotape-based parent-training program (see Chapter 3 for full description) is one excellent example of these techniques.

The psychoeducational component is accompanied by *in vivo* interactions between the therapist, parent, and child. The therapist observes the parent's interaction with the child and discusses this interaction with the parent. Parents should be taught to attend to the child's cues, especially cues to initiate and terminate parent-child interaction. In many cases, parents must be taught to be less directive and controlling in interactions with the child. Other parents must be taught how to observe the child with sustained, nondirective watching behavior.

Interaction components that the child finds appealing may be identified and taught to the parent. Finally, parents often benefit from observing the therapist's interaction with the child.

Family Interventions

In addition to parent training and parent-child therapy, family therapy interventions may also be helpful. These interventions may take several forms, including provision of instrumental and emotional support, restructuring of family relationships, and improvement of the marital relationship (Fischhoff, 1989; Green, 1989; Tibbits-Kleber & Howell, 1985). Provision of support may be particularly important for parents who are experiencing significant stresses. These parents may be overwhelmed with their life situation and may regard the child as yet another stressor. Assistance with coping skills such as problem solving (how to care for the child adequately in the context of current stress), cognitive restructuring (seeing the child as a source of happiness as opposed to as a source of stress), and approach-coping (attending to the behavior and needs of the child without feeling overwhelmed) may be a crucial area of needed support. Instrumental support such as financial assistance for food and materials for stimulation may also be necessary. Because providing this support requires a good therapeutic relationship, relationship building is an important component of working with parents.

Marital and family therapy should also attend to issues such as adversarial interactions between family members and disengagement of one or both parents. In some cases, adversarial interactions between spouses occur in front of the child, who withdraws from the environment in order to avoid the negative stimulation. In other cases, it is the parent(s) who withdraw from the child, engaging in avoidant or neglectful behavior. The impact of these behaviors on the child should be discussed, and alternative behaviors should be found. Parents should also be encouraged to discuss their feelings about being parents and their feelings toward the child (without the child present). The effect of the child's behavior on the parents is often an important topic; many parents have never had a chance to process their response to the child. Unrealistic expectations or attributions of the child may be challenged and reframed in order to alter the parents' emotional response to the child.

It is often also necessary to do individual work with one or both parents. In individual psychotherapy, parental psychopathology should be addressed, particularly as this psychopathology affects the parent's relationship with the child. As in family therapy, the parent should be encouraged to discuss expectations, feelings, disappointments, and frustrations related to the child. Many parents will initially deny problems, fearing that their child will be removed from their care. Hence, formation of a trusting therapeutic relationship is generally the first step in this therapy. Medication interventions may be appropriate for some types of parental psychopathology (such as severe depression).

Home Monitoring and Protective Removal

Some severe cases of RAD warrant more extreme interventions, such as temporary separation of parent and child, required home visits by a health care provider, or even removal of the child from the parents' care. This decision is usually made based on a combination of four factors: the severity of abuse/neglect, medical status of the child, willingness of the parent to change through psychological intervention, and psychological stability of the parent.

In cases of significant neglect, in-home visits by nurses and mental health professionals may be necessary to monitor the child's physical, emotional, and cognitive growth, as well as to document positive changes in the parent's behavior. Such visits should integrate the environmental and behavioral interventions described earlier.

In especially dire or intractable situations, removal of the child from the parent's care and placement in therapeutic foster care may be necessary. If the parent wants to remain involved (or to eventually regain custody), parent-child therapy and regular supervised visits should be used to improve parental behavior and to demonstrate the parent's readiness to regain custody of the child. The foster home should be small (relatively few other children), stable (little coming and going of caretakers), stimulating (but not chaotic or overly exciting), and structured.

■ References

Abidin, R. R. (1995). *Parenting Stress Index* (3rd ed.). Odessa, FL: Psychological Assessment Resources.

American Psychiatric Association. (1994). *Diagnostic and statistical manual of mental disorders, fourth edition.* Washington, DC: Author.

Benoit, D., Zeanah, C. H., & Barton, M. L. (1989). Maternal attachment disturbances in failure to thrive. *Infant Mental Health Journal, 10,* 185–202.

Bowlby, J. (1952). *Maternal care and mental health* (2nd ed.). New York: Shocken.

Dulcan, M. K., & Popper, C. W. (1991). *Concise guide to child and adolescent psychiatry.* Washington, DC: American Psychiatric Press.

Fischhoff, J. (1989). Reactive attachment disorder of infancy. *Treatments of psychiatric disorders: A task force report of the American Psychiatric Association* (pp. 734–746). Washington, DC: American Psychiatric Association.

Green, W. H. (1989). Reactive attachment disorder of infancy or early childhood. In H. I. Kaplan & B. J. Sadock (Eds.), *Comprehensive textbook of psychiatry, Volume 2* (5th ed., pp. 1894–1903). Baltimore: Williams & Wilkins.

Hathaway, P. (1989). Failure to thrive: Knowledge for social workers. *Health and Social Work,* 122–126.

Hufton, I. W., & Oates, K. (1977). Nonorganic failure to thrive: A long-term follow-up. *Pediatrics, 59,* 73–77.

Kelley, M. L., & Heffer, R. W. (1990). Eating disorders: Food refusal and failure to thrive. In A. M. Gross & R. S. Drabman (Eds.), *Handbook of clinical behavioral pediatrics* (pp. 111–127). New York: Plenum.

Lee, K. S., Kwon, U., Sihn, Y. J., & Kim, T. L. (1996). Personality, marital relationship, and social support in mothers with RAD children and normal children. *Korean Journal of Developmental Psychology, 9,* 121–134.

Richters, M. M., & Volkmar, F. R. (1996). Reactive attachment disorders of infancy or early childhood. In M. Lewis (Ed.), *Child and adolescent psychiatry: A comprehensive textbook* (2nd ed.). Baltimore: Williams & Wilkins.

Sarason, I. G., Levine, H. M., Basham, R. B., & Sarason, B. R. (1983). Assessing social support: The Social Support Questionnaire. *Journal of Personality and Social Psychology, 44,* 127–139.

Spanier, G. B. (1976). Measuring dyadic adjustment: New scales for assessing the quality of marriage and similar dyads. *Journal of Marriage and the Family, 38,* 15–28.

Spitz, R. A. (1945). Hospitalism: An inquiry into the genesis of psychiatric conditions in early childhood. *Psychoanalytic Study of the Child, 1,* 53–74.

Tibbits-Kleber, A. L., & Howell, R. J. (1985). Reactive attachment disorder of infancy (RAD). *Journal of Clinical Child Psychology, 14,* 304–310.

Webster-Stratton, C. (1996). Early intervention with videotape modeling: Programs for families of children with Oppositional-Defiant Disorder or Conduct Disorder. In E. D. Hibbs & P. S. Jensen (Eds.), *Psychosocial treatments for child and adolescent disorders: Empirically based strategies for clinical practice.* Washington, DC: American Psychological Association.

Child Clinician's Intake Summary Form

Using This Form: The Child Clinician's Intake Summary Form (CISF) is a structured, form-based tool for gathering background information about children and families. It is designed for completion by a parent, when the child is the major focus of the clinical encounter. Ways in which the CISF can be useful include the following:

1. *As a paper-and-pencil questionnaire for parents to complete prior to the first session.* Parents who can read, understand, and respond to CISF items may be given the CISF to complete in the waiting room prior to the first session. The clinician then has some basic information to structure the interview and to suggest directions for questions.

2. *As separate questionnaires for each type of information gathered by the CISF.* The CISF is organized around eight topics: Demographic Information, Presenting Problem/Referral Question, Developmental History, Medical History, Family History, Social History, Academic History, and Major Stresses and Coping Challenges. With the exception of Family History (2 pages), each topic is contained on a single page and can serve as a stand-alone questionnaire. Thus, families may be given one or more pages out of the CISF depending on specific information in which the clinician is interested.

3. *As the framework for a semistructured intake interview.* CISF questions can form the basis for an interview administered by a professional or by a trained technician. Answers can be placed in the appropriate blanks.

4. *As a training tool for new clinicians.* The CISF was developed based on a review of the literature and draws heavily from recommendations of the Quality Assurance Committee of the Riley Child and Adolescent Psychiatry Clinic. Thus, it includes information cited by professionals from the disciplines of medicine, psychology, social work, education, and nursing as essential to background information needed for a good mental health intake report. Because it is highly structured, it provides organization for students and trainees in the mental health field.

5. *As a research tool.* Because the CISF is highly structured, it is easily adapted to chart-review or prospective research. Based on the CISF, information about socioeconomic status, demographic variables, medical variables, family psychiatric history, adaptive behavior, temperament, and other variables may be derived.

Child Clinician's Intake Summary Form

Directions: This form is very important to help with our interview and evaluation process. Not all questions apply to all families; just answer questions as best as they apply to your family. Your answers will help us to better address your child's needs and to better understand your child. It takes about 15–20 minutes to complete. Use the back of pages as necessary. Thank you.

Demographic Information

Child's Name: _____   Child's Sex: M   F   Child's Date of Birth: _____

Child's School: _____   Child's Grade: _____   Today's Date: _____

Child's Race: _____   Height: _____   Weight: _____

Biological Father Information:

Name: _____   Age: _____   Marital Status: _____

Occupation: _____   Education: _____   Date of Marriage: _____

Live with Child?   Y   N   (If no, how often does the child see this person?_____)

Biological Mother Information:

Name: _____   Age: _____   Marital Status: _____

Occupation: _____   Education: _____   Date of Current Marriage: _____

Live with Child?   Y   N   (If no, how often does the child see this person?_____)

Other Male Caretaker: (circle one: Adoptive father Stepfather Grandfather Mother's boyfriend Other)

Name: _____   Age: _____   Marital Status: _____

Occupation: _____   Education: _____   Date of Current Marriage: _____

Live with Child?   Y   N   (If no, how often does the child see this person?_____)

Other Female Caretaker: (circle one: Adoptive mother Stepmother Grandmother Father's girlfriend Other.)

Name: _____   Age: _____   Marital Status: _____

Occupation: _____   Education: _____   Date of Current Marriage: _____

Live with Child?   Y   N   (If no, how often does the child see this person?_____)

Siblings and Others Living in the Household (List ALL of child's biological siblings, whether in the house or not. Also list any other people that live in the household):

Name	Age	Relationship to Child (circle one)					
_____	____	Full-sib	Half-sib	Step-sib	Uncle	Aunt	Other: _____
_____	____	Full-sib	Half-sib	Step-sib	Uncle	Aunt	Other: _____
_____	____	Full-sib	Half-sib	Step-sib	Uncle	Aunt	Other: _____
_____	____	Full-sib	Half-sib	Step-sib	Uncle	Aunt	Other: _____
_____	____	Full-sib	Half-sib	Step-sib	Uncle	Aunt	Other: _____
_____	____	Full-sib	Half-sib	Step-sib	Uncle	Aunt	Other: _____
_____	____	Full-sib	Half-sib	Step-sib	Uncle	Aunt	Other: _____

Who referred you for psychological services? _____

Do you agree with this referral?   YES   NO   Mixed Feelings

Presenting Problem/Referral Question

Please list the three biggest reasons (or problems) for which you are coming for an appointment:

1. _____

2. _____

3. _____

HISTORY OF PRESENT PROBLEM

1. Approximately how old was your child when you first noticed your child's problem? What did the problem look like then?

2. How has your child's problem changed throughout his or her growth?

3. What is your child's attitude toward his or her problems?

4. Has your child had any other behavioral or emotional problems in the past (even if they are not affecting him or her now)? Describe them.

5. Previous Therapy Experiences of Your Child (include family, school, psychotherapy, psychiatric medication)

Therapist Name	Dates	Clinic Name/Phone	Reason for Therapy	Effectiveness

6. Previous Psychological Testing of Your Child

Evaluator Name	Date	Clinic/School Name/Phone	Reason for Testing	Findings

7. Has your child ever talked about hurting or killing himself or herself or another person? Describe.

8. Has your child ever used or abused medication, illegal drugs, or alcohol? Describe.

Developmental History

1. How did the parents feel when they found out that the mother was pregnant? Was the child planned?

2. Please circle all that occurred during the mother's pregnancy with this child:

   a. Smoking
   (# of packs per day: _____)

   b. Drinking Alcohol
   (# of drinks per day: _____)

   c. Marijuana Use

   d. Cocaine/Crack Use

   e. LSD Use

   f. Other Street Drug Use
   (What Drug(s): _____)

   g. Physical abuse of mother

   h. Extreme stress on mother

   i. Major Illness of mother
   (Illness: _____)

   j. Major injury of mother

   k. Regular prenatal care

3. Other significant things or complications about pregnancy:

4. Were there any complications during your child's delivery? If so, describe.

5. Birth history:

   a. Child's weight at birth: _____   Type of birth: Vaginal   C-section

   b. Premature birth?   YES   NO   If premature, how many weeks into pregnancy at birth? _____

   c. Problems/illnesses immediately after birth: _____ Admission to hospital/neonatal ICU: YES   NO

6. At what age did your child:

   Sit:_____   Say first word: _____   Say two-word sentences:_____

   Crawl:_____   Toilet Trained: _____

   Walk: _____   Learn to read: _____

   Would you say that your child developed faster, slower, or at about the same rate as other children?

   _____

7. Circle all that apply to your child as a baby:

   a. Cuddly

   b. Irritable

   c. Cried a lot

   d. Slow to warm up

   e. Curious

   f. Active

   g. Good sleeper

   h. Tense/"on edge"

   i. Difficult to soothe

   j. Withdrawn

   k. Friendly

   l. Afraid of strangers

   m. Easy to put on a schedule

   n. Easily startled/overreactive

Medical History

1. Current medications that the child is taking:

   Name   Total Daily Dose   Times per Day   Reason

   a. _____

   b. _____

   c. _____

   d. _____

2. Past medications that your child has taken for behavior or psychological problems (list name only):

   a. _____   b. _____   c. _____   d. _____

3. Drug or Other Allergies:

   Allergy   Typical Reaction

   a. _____

   b. _____

   c. _____

   d. _____

4. Child's immunizations up to date?   YES   NO   (If no, what ones are not? _____)

5. Has your child ever had any surgeries or hospitalizations?

   Hospitalization Dates   Reason for Hospitalization/Surgery

   a. _____

   b. _____

   c. _____

6. Child's Exposure to Poisons or Toxic Substances

           Poison or   How Exposed

   Date   Toxic Substance   (Drank, Touched)   Effect on Child

   a. _____

   b. _____

7. Has your child ever had any serious and/or life-threatening illnesses or injuries?

   Dates   Illness/Injury   Hospitalization Dates

   a. _____

   b. _____

   c. _____

   d. _____

Family History

1. Does anyone in the child's immediate or extended family have the following illnesses or problems? Include brothers, sisters, father, mother, grandparents, aunts, uncles, cousins.

Illness	Circle Y or N	Relationship (father, aunt, etc.)
Depression	Y N	_____
Manic Depression	Y N	_____
Nervous Breakdown	Y N	_____
Psychiatric Hospital	Y N	_____
Delayed Reading	Y N	_____
Delayed Speech	Y N	_____
Mental Retardation	Y N	_____
Attention Problems	Y N	_____
Hyperactivity	Y N	_____
Heavy Drinking	Y N	_____
Drug Abuse	Y N	_____
Suicide	Y N	_____
Stealing	Y N	_____
School Phobia	Y N	_____
Epilepsy	Y N	_____
Felony Conviction	Y N	_____
Anxiety Disorder	Y N	_____
Bedwetting	Y N	_____
Aggressive Outbursts	Y N	_____
Schizophrenia/Psychosis	Y N	_____
Autism	Y N	_____
Eating Disorder	Y N	_____
Insomnia	Y N	_____
Any Genetic Disorder	Y N	_____
Other	Y N	_____

2. Please indicate if the following have occurred in the family:

	Date(s)	Description/Comments
Parental Divorce	_____	_____
Separation	_____	_____
Marital Problems	_____	_____
Domestic Violence	_____	_____
Excessive Conflict	_____	_____
Death of Parent	_____	_____

	Date(s)	Description/Comments
Death of Sibling	_____	_____
Death of Grandparent	_____	_____
Alcohol Abuse	_____	_____
Drug Abuse	_____	_____
Move to New Home	_____	_____
Physical or Sexual Abuse	_____	_____
Significant Illness	_____	_____
Other Changes	_____	_____

3. How is discipline handled in the family?

4. Who is most responsible for discipline?   Mother   Father   Both

5. Describe your relationships with the following extended family members.

    a. Father's Parents: Excellent   Good   Fair   Poor

    b. Mother's Parents: Excellent   Good   Fair   Poor

    c. Father's Siblings: Excellent   Good   Fair   Poor

    d. Mother's Siblings: Excellent   Good   Fair   Poor

    e. Child's Cousins: Excellent   Good   Fair   Poor

    f. Other: _____: Excellent   Good   Fair   Poor

6. Family Religion: _____

7. Other Marriages or Live-In Relationships of Biological MOTHER (past and present; include marriage to biological father, if divorced):

Partner's Name	Dates of Relationship	Children's Names	Reason for Divorce
_____	_____	_____	_____
_____	_____	_____	_____
_____	_____	_____	_____

8. Other Marriages or Live-In Relationships of Biological FATHER (past and present; include marriage to biological mother, if divorced):

Partner's Name	Dates of Relationship	Children's Names	Reason for Divorce
_____	_____	_____	_____
_____	_____	_____	_____
_____	_____	_____	_____

Social History

1. Check ALL that describe your child socially:

   _____ Other children seek him or her out for play

   _____ He or she seeks out other children for play

   _____ He or she prefers to play alone

   _____ Lots of children like him or her, AND few children dislike him or her

   _____ Lots of children like him or her, BUT lots of children don't like him or her

   _____ Other children pretty much ignore my child

   _____ My child fights a lot with other children

   _____ My child often plays cooperatively with other children

2. How many friends does your child have at home? _____

   How much time does your child play with those friends per day? _____

3. How many friends does your child have at school? _____

   How much time does your child play with those friends per day? _____

4. Does your child have a best friend?   YES   NO   (If yes) what is the best friend's name? _____

5. How does your child get along with nonparent adults? (Check all that apply.)

   _____ Friendly   _____ Better behaved than with parents

   _____ Cooperative   _____ Adults like my child

   _____ Disobedient   _____ Obedient

   _____ Disrespectful   _____ Other (describe) _____

6. How does your child get along with teachers/coaches?

   _____ Friendly   _____ Better behaved than with parents

   _____ Cooperative   _____ Adults like my child

   _____ Disobedient   _____ Obedient

   _____ Disrespectful   _____ Other (describe) _____

7. How does your child get along with brothers and sisters?

   _____ Protective of them   _____ They like him or her

   _____ Aggressive/fights   _____ Jealous

   _____ Won't share things   _____ Ignores them

   _____ Wants to be babied   _____ Other (describe) _____

   _____ Likes them

8. Has your child ever had a sexual relationship?

9. Has your child ever been arrested, accused, or convicted of a crime? What crimes?

Academic History

1. Has your child ever been in nursery or day care?   YES   NO   If so, what ages?_____

2. At what age did your child start kindergarten? _____   Start first grade? _____

3. Has your child ever been held back a grade?   YES   NO   If so, what grade(s)? _____

4. Is your child in any of the following class placements?
   _____ Resource Room
   _____ Gifted Class (What subjects? _____)
   _____ Learning Disabled or Special Education Class (What subjects? _____)
   _____ Emotionally Handicapped (EH or BEH) Class

5. What are your child's grades in the following subjects? (Approximate if unsure.)

	This Year	Last Year	Best Year Ever (Yr: _____)
Math	_____	_____	_____ (Yr: _____)
Reading	_____	_____	_____ (Yr: _____)
Spelling	_____	_____	_____ (Yr: _____)
Science	_____	_____	_____ (Yr: _____)
Social Studies	_____	_____	_____ (Yr: _____)
English	_____	_____	_____ (Yr: _____)
Other (describe)	_____	_____	_____ (Yr: _____)

6. What school subjects does your child like most? (Circle.)
   Math   Reading   Spelling   Social Studies   Science   Other:

7. What school subjects does your child like least? (Circle.)
   Math   Reading   Spelling   Social Studies   Science   Other:

8. How is your child's behavior in school? (Check all that apply.)
   _____ Disobedient   _____ Overactive
   _____ Worried/tense   _____ Withdrawn/shy
   _____ Not liked by children   _____ Popular
   _____ Not liked by teachers   _____ Class clown

9. List changes in your child's school setting during his or her life. Why were these changes made? How did your child react?

10. Have any of the following happened to your child at school? (Write number of times.)
    _____ Suspended
    _____ Expelled
    _____ Special conference for behavior problems
    _____ Switched classes because of problems

Major Stresses and Coping Strategies

1. List the three biggest stressors in your child's life right now.

   a. _____

   b. _____

   c. _____

2. Are there any other major stressors that have occurred in your child's lifetime and had a lasting effect on him or her?

3. Has your child been sexually abused?   YES   NO   If so, describe.

4. Has your child been physically abused?   YES   NO   If so, describe.

5. Has your child been emotionally abused?   YES   NO   If so, describe.

6. How does your child *usually* cope when under stress? (Circle all that apply.)

Tries to solve the problem	Ignores or pretends that there is no problem
Seeks information about the problem	Becomes anxious and/or tearful
Comes to parents for help	Becomes angry and/or throws tantrums
Goes to friends for help	Takes a positive attitude toward the problem
Gives up and accepts the problem	Gets physically ill
Jokes, makes light of the problem	Becomes manipulative or deceitful
Prays or asks God for help	Withdraws from others; tries to be alone
Refuses to talk; "holds it in"	None of the above

   Other: _____

Semistructured Mental Status Examination

Using This Form: The Semistructured Mental Status Examination (SMSE) is a form-based tool for conducting and/or recording information obtained from a mental status examination. Instructions for use:

1. The SMSE is designed for use with all ages, from preschool to adult. Hence, some questions will not be developmentally appropriate for certain ages.

2. Answers to SMSE questions or observations may be either circled on the form, or blanks are provided for open-ended answers.

3. It is not necessary to ask all questions or to proceed in any fixed order on the SMSE. Questions and observations typically considered important for a complete mental status examination are underlined on the SMSE form; if a brief interview is desired, it is recommended that the clinician focus on a subset of the underlined items.

4. Each of the major topics of the SMSE is divided into three parts. The Observations section contains information that can be obtained by watching the child's behavior and social interaction. The Queries section contains recommended questions for evaluating aspects of mental status. The Other Notes section provides space to record information that is not captured by the other two sections.

5. As with most mental status examination interviews, there is no scoring for the SMSE.

Semistructured Mental Status Examination (SMSE)

I. Demographics: Sex: M F   Race: W B A O

II. Appearance:

Observations—

Size:

   Height: Tall   Medium   Short
   Build: Thin   Medium   Heavy   Athletic   Very Obese   Malnourished

Dress and Grooming:

   Hygenic State: Clean   Dirty   Unbrushed-Hair   Sloppy
   Clothing: Appropriate   Sloppy   Formal   Peculiar   Gender inappropriate

Facial Expressions: Friendly   Tense   Anxious   Angry   Wary   Sad

   Flat   Smiling   Crying   Tearful

Initial Behavior:

   Accompanied by: _____

   Greeting: Appropriate   Inappropriate   (Notes: _____)

   Eye Contact: Appropriate   Sporadic   Avoidant

Queries—

Other Notes—

III. Attitude:

Observations—

Cooperation: Cooperative   Resistant   Argumentative   Avoidant   Reticent   Evasive

Warmth: Warm   Detached   Reserved   Appropriate

Engaging Environment: Withdrawn   Dependent   Passive   Clingy

   Guarded   Seeks Approval   Aggressive

   Dramatic   Complaining   Destructive

   Friendly   Boastful

Emotional Valence: Positive   Negative   Neutral   Enthusiastic   Distressed   Hostile

Sincerity: Honest/Sincere   Manipulative   Lying   Callous   Withholding

Queries—

Other Notes—

IV. Motor Behavior:

Observations—

Activity Level:	Low Average High Average Very High
Gross Motor:	No Apparent Problems Uncoordinated Clumsy Tremor Spasms
Fine Motor:	No Apparent Problems Uncoordinated Tremor
Repetitive Behaviors:	None (Specify: _____)
Tics:	None (Specify: _____)
Anxious Behaviors:	None Fidgety Shaking Fingernail Biting
Strength:	Unremarkable Weak Strong

Queries—

1. Take five steps forward for me. Take five steps backward for me.

   Gait: Unremarkable   Problematic (Specify: _____)

2. Stand on one foot. Now hop on one foot.

   Gross Balance/Coordination: Adequate   Problematic (Specify: _____)

3. *Close your eyes and touch your nose with your finger.*

   Gross Balance/Coordination: Adequate   Problematic (Specify: _____)

4. Show me how you (throw a ball, swing a bat, eat with a fork).

   Dominant Hand: Right   Left

5. *Grab my fingers in your hand and squeeze as hard as you can.*

   Strength: Unremarkable   Weak   Strong

6. Write your name on this piece of paper.

   Dominant Hand: Right   Left

   Fine Motor Skill: Adequate   Tremor   Clumsy

7. Draw this (a horizontal line) (a circle) (a square) (a diamond).

   Dominant Hand: Right   Left

   Fine Motor Coordination: Adequate   Tremor   Clumsy

8. Tell me about a time that you thought you might do something and then decided not to.

   Tell me about a time that you acted impulsively and then regretted it later.

   (Notes: _____

   _____)

Other Notes—

V. Thought Process:

Observations—

Speed of Thought Process:	Slow Average High
Thought Production:	No Apparent Problems Blocking Halting
Flow/Association:	Logical/Sequential Illogical Tangential Loose Circumstantial
Clarity of Thought Process:	Clear Vague

Queries—

1. <u>Tell me about a typical day for you.</u>   Logical   Sequential   Clear   Vague   Loose
2. *Tell me the steps involved in making a sandwich.*   Logical   Sequential   Clear   Vague   Loose

Other Notes—

VI. Sensorium and Intellect:

Observations—

<u>Alertness:</u>	Alert Drowsy Unconscious Stupor Variable
<u>Orientation:</u>	Person Place Time
<u>Attention:</u>	Good Average Low Average Poor Variable
<u>Vocabulary:</u>	Above Average Average Below Average (Notes: _____)
<u>Insight:</u>	Good Adequate Fair Poor
<u>Judgment:</u>	Good Adequate Fair Poor

Queries—

1. <u>Orientation</u>

<u>How old are you?</u> _____   <u>When were you born?</u> _____   <u>What is your address?</u> _____

Your middle name? _____   Your mother's name? _____   <u>What is your phone #?</u> _____

What time is it? _____   <u>What is the day of the week?</u> _____   <u>Where are you right now?</u> _____

How long have you been here? _____   What is the month/year? _____

2. Concentration

<u>Start at 100 and count backward by 7's.</u> Accurate to 65 or lower: Yes   No

  (Children)   Start at 50 and count backward by 3's.   Accurate to 35 or lower: Yes   No

<u>Spell "world." Now spell world backward.</u> Spelling: _____   (young children—substitute "cat": _____)

3. Memory

<u>Remember these three objects:</u> car   dog   house.   What were they? Car   Dog   House

  (at 1 minute) I told you to remember three objects. <u>What were they?</u> Car   Dog   House

  (at 5 minutes) I told you remember three objects. <u>What were they?</u> Car   Dog   House

Remember these numbers: 9-3-4-7 Now tell them back to me in the same order. _____

  (can also use 7-1-4-8-5, 1-4-9-2-6-3, 8-3-5-7-1-6-2).

<u>What did you have for breakfast this morning?</u> _____

<u>What did you have for dinner last night?</u> _____

Tell me two things you did yesterday afternoon. _____

What is your teacher's (boss's) name? _____

Tell me, in order, all of the places where you have lived. _____

4. Intelligence/Fund of Knowledge

<u>What are your grades in school?</u> _____

How far is it from New York to Los Angeles? _____

Tell me the three largest cities in the United States: Chicago   New York   Los Angeles

Who is the president right now? _____

Name the last four presidents. _____

Tell me two countries in Asia. _____

What does this saying mean: "The grass is always greener on the other side of the fence"?
Correct   Concrete   Overly Abstract

What does this saying mean: "Slow but steady wins the race"? Correct   Concrete   Overly Abstract

5. Insight

What problems do you think that you have? _____

What do you think is the cause of your problem? _____

What do others think is the cause of your problem? _____

Have you had similar or different problems in the past? _____

What do you think it will take to improve your problem? _____

6. Judgment

What would you do if you were given $10,000? _____

What is your ultimate goal in life (for kids, what would you like to be when you grow up)? _____

What would you do if you were the first person to notice a fire in a theater? _____

7. Substance Use

Do you think that marijuana should be legalized? Yes   No   Why or why not? _____

Are you taking any prescription or nonprescription medications at the present time (also dosages)?

_____

What effects do they have on your mood, energy level, or thoughts? _____

What kinds and how much alcohol do you drink? _____

Do you use any drugs? (Can say "illegal", but may increase denial rate.)   How often? _____

Have you ever been treated in a drug or alcohol abuse program? Yes   No

What drugs (legal and illegal) have you taken within the past few hours? Are they affecting you now?

_____

Other Notes—

VII. Thought Content:

Observations—

Delusions: None   Notable: _____

Abstraction/Reasoning: Concrete   Overly Abstract   Unremarkable

Interpretation Bias: None   Hostile   Suspicious   Naive   Hopeless   Egocentric   External

Suicidal Ideation: Denied   Vague   Elaborate   Intent

Homicidal Ideation: Denied   Vague   Elaborate   Intent

Queries—

1. Do you have any thoughts that bother you? Yes   No

How often do you have these thoughts?   Many a day   One a day   Several/Wk   Several/Mo

How controllable are they?   Easy   With Effort   Uncontrollable

2. Did you ever have a thought that you couldn't get out of your mind, no matter how hard you tried? Yes   No

Describe: _____

3. If you could have three wishes, what would they be? (1) _____

(2) _____   (3) _____

4. Tell me three lies. (1) _____   (2) _____   (3) _____

5. If you could be any animal you wanted, what animal would you be? _____

Why? _____

6. Has there ever been a time when you didn't feel like you were really a part of things that were happening to you? Yes   No

Describe: _____

7. Has there ever been a time when people said that you did things that you later did not remember?

Describe: _____

8. Tell me your earliest three memories. About how old were you? (1) _____

(2) _____   (3) _____

9. Tell me three things that you're afraid of (that scare you). (1) _____

(2) _____   (3) _____

10. Fantasy:

What is your favorite thing to daydream about?   _____

Tell me about one of your recent dreams.   _____

Tell me about one of your recent nightmares.   _____

11. What kinds of things do you do for fun? Hobbies, sports? _____

12. How much time each day do you spend working at your job? _____

Doing fun things?   _____   Working at home?   _____

13. Have you ever thought about hurting or killing yourself or someone else?   _____

If yes: _____

When was the last time that you had these thoughts?   _____

How often/how much did you have these thoughts?   _____

Do you have thoughts like that now? Yes   No

Did you ever plan to follow through on those thoughts? Yes   No

What plan did you have?   _____

Did you ever do what those thoughts told you to do? Yes   No

How many times?   _____

Did you ever tell anyone or hurt yourself so badly that you had to go to the hospital? Yes   No

Other Notes:

VIII. Sensation and Perception:

Observations—

Sensory Modalities:

Vision: Glasses   Squint   Unfocused   Blind   No Problems

Hearing: Hearing Aid   Difficulty Hearing   No Problems

Queries—

1. Has there ever been a time when your eyes or ears played tricks on you and you saw or heard things that were not really there? Visual   Auditory   None

   If Yes:

   What did you do when that happened? _____

   Did you know that they weren't real or did they seem real to you? Not Real   Seemed Real

   How did you feel when you saw/heard these things? Ego Syntonic   Ego Dystonic   No Reaction

   If Auditory:

   Were the sounds (voices) coming from inside your head or outside your head?   Inside   Outside

   Did you recognize the voices? Yes   No

   Whose voices were they? _____

   What did the voices tell you to do? _____

2. Has there ever been a time when you couldn't feel certain parts of your body? Yes   No

   If Yes:

   What parts? _____

   For how long? _____

   When did that happen? _____

   Did you see a doctor? Yes   No

   What did the doctor find out? _____

Other Notes—

IX. Somatic Functioning:

Observations—

Somatic Appearance: Sleepy Yawning Nauseous Frail Weak Hypervigilant
                      No Apparent Problems

Queries—

1. How well do you sleep at night? _____

   How many hours do you sleep on an average night? _____

   Do you nap during the day? _____

   Do you have trouble falling asleep? _____

   Do you have trouble staying asleep? _____

   Do you have trouble waking up in the morning? _____

   Do you feel that you get enough sleep? _____

   Have your sleep patterns changed recently? _____

2. How is your appetite? _____

   How many big meals do you eat each day? _____

   How many snacks do you eat each day? _____

   Have you gained or lost more than 10 pounds recently? _____

3. Have you ever had any chronic or life-threatening diseases? Yes   No

   Describe: _____

4. *Have you ever been hospitalized because of illness or injury?* Yes   No

   Describe: _____

5. Have you ever had a head or brain injury or illness? Yes   No

   Describe: _____

6. How do you feel right now; do you have any current illnesses? _____

Other Notes—

X. Mood/Affect:

Observations—

Affect Appearance:

    <u>Avoidant/Constricted Affects:</u> Blunted   Subdued   Flat   Constricted   Indifferent

    <u>Sad Affects:</u>   Depressed   Sad   Tearful   Guilty

    <u>Hostile/Resistant Affects:</u> Angry   Hostile   Guarded   Suspicious   Guilty

    <u>Worried Affects:</u>   Anxious

    <u>Inappropriate Affects:</u> Inappropriate to Topic   Incongruent Across Modality

    <u>Positive/Appropriate Affects:</u> Happy   Relaxed   Appropriate to Topic

    <u>Manic Affects:</u>   Euphoric   Labile

Queries—

1. Most mornings, how do you feel when you wake up? _____

2. We all feel sad sometimes. What kind of things make you sad? _____

   <u>How often do you get sad?</u>   Every Day   Several Times a Week   Several Times a Month
   Once Every Few Months   Never

   When you get sad, what do you do? _____

3. We all feel mad sometimes. What kind of things make you mad? _____

   <u>How often do you get mad?</u>   Every Day   Several Times a Week   Several Times a Month
   Once Every Few Months   Never

   When you get mad, what do you do? _____

4. We all feel worried sometimes. What kind of things make you worried? _____

   <u>How often do you get worried?</u>   Every Day   Several Times A Week   Several Times a Month
   Once Every Few Months   Never

   When you get worried, what do you do? _____

5. We all feel happy sometimes. What kind of things make you happy? _____

   <u>How often do you get happy?</u>   Every Day Several Times a Week   Several Times a Month
   Once Every Few Months   Never

   When you get happy, what do you do? _____

6. Would your friends say that you are: happy   sad   quiet   angry   worried

7. Would your family say that you are: happy   sad   quiet   angry   worried

8. Has there ever been a time when you felt like you were on top of the world, like you had boundless energy and that nothing could stop you?   Yes   No

    Describe: _____

9. Do you usually show your feelings or hide your feelings?   Show   Hide

Other Notes—

XI. Speech and Language:

Observations—

Speech Articulation:	None "s" like "th" "r" like "w" "r" like "l" Other: _____
	Slurred Stuttering Lisp Pronunciation Problems Incoherent
Speed:	Slow Average Fast Pressured
Loudness:	Soft Normal Loud Screaming Mumbling
Quantity:	Mute Low Average Wordy
Conversation:	Initiates Sustains Answers Only
Vocabulary:	Technical Vulgar Limited Extensive Unremarkable
Oddities:	Perseveration Incoherent Content

Queries—

1. What is this? (Point to the following; circle if correct; X if incorrect.)   Clock   Pencil   Book

2. Repeat the following after me: Methodist Episcopal (adults)   She sees the barn (children)

XII. Social Interaction and Relationships:

Observations—

Quality of Interaction during Interview: Engaging   Aloof   Distant   Pleasant   Annoying

Queries—

1. With whom do you live? _____

    Married: Yes   No   Quality of Marriage: Good   Average   Poor

    Attachments to immediate family: Appropriate   Enmeshed   Disengaged

    Children's Names and Ages: _____

    Siblings' Names and Ages (Child): _____

2. How many friends do you have? _____   Do you have a best friend?   Yes   No

    What are the names of your three closest friends? _____

    How often do you see your friends: Daily   Several Times/Wk   Several Times/Month   Rarely

    When you see your friends, how much time do you spend with them? _____

    What do you do together? _____

3. In order, who would you most like to spend time with? ____ Spouse   ____ Family   ____ Group of Friends   ____ Best Friend   ____ Children   ____ Alone

4. Tell me the three people you can most count on to give you support when you need it:

(1) _____ (2) _____ (3) _____

How satisfied are you with the support that you get from these people? (1 = Not Satisfied; 10 = Very Satisfied) _____

5. In an average day, how much time do you spend with: _____ Spouse _____ Alone _____ Family

6. What does your boss (teacher) think of you? _____

What do you think of your boss (teacher)? _____

7. Describe your mother: _____

8. Describe your father: _____

Other Notes—

XIII. Self-Concept:

Observations—

Relationship of Self-Esteem to Reality: Appropriate   Defensive   Avoidant   Inflated   Egocentric

Queries—

1. Tell me three things that you're good at:

(1) _____ (2) _____ (3) _____

2. *Tell me three things that you're not very good at:*

(1) _____ (2) _____ (3) _____

3. If you could be anybody, real or imaginary, living or dead, whom would you choose to be? _____

Why? _____

4. How would you feel if you hurt a small child? _____

5. How would you feel if you got into a fight and really hurt the other person? _____

6. What would you do if your friend wrecked your car by accident? _____

7. If you could pick any profession, what would you most want to do? _____

Other Notes—

XIV. Stress and Coping:

Observations—

Coping Style: Problem Focused   Emotion Focused   Approaching   Avoidant   Defensive

Queries—

1. What are the three biggest stresses in your life right now?

(1) _____ (2) _____ (3) _____

On a scale of 1–10, rate the stressfulness of each of these stresses.

2. What things have you done to cope with each of these three stresses?

(1) _____ (2) _____ (3) _____

On a scale of 1–10, rate the effectiveness of each of these coping strategies.

Other Notes—

Formulations and Impression:

Sample Parent Behavior Modification Training Handouts

This appendix consists of descriptions of selected common behavioral interventions, using the format of parent handouts. Please refer to appropriate chapters for a full discussion of the use and rationale for these interventions. The following notes provide additional information about three of the behavioral intervention handouts. It is assumed that therapists using these interventions have a background in mental health evaluation and intervention, with appropriate training and clinical experience.

1. Special Time

    a. The points to emphasize in introducing special time to the parent are that it is non-contingent (happens no matter what), highly predictable (scheduled no later than the morning of the day of special time), regular (ideally daily; at least five days per week), and nondirective (the child chooses the activity, within reason, and the parent lets the child take the lead in interaction). Special time is not to be used as a reward or punishment; it is not to be taken away or postponed based on the child's behavior or on the parent's schedule (within reason).

2. Positive Attention

    a. Like special time, positive attention is a relationship-building technique that is non-contingent and regular.

3. Flexible Ignoring

    a. Flexible ignoring makes it possible to ignore the child while still preventing misbehavior. An example would be the child who tugs the parent's shirt repeatedly to gain the parent's attention. The parent could ignore the child by looking away and not saying anything, while still preventing the behavior by holding the child's arms down. As noted in the flexible ignoring handout, this would allow the parent to ignore in two modalities (eye contact and verbal interaction), while not ignoring in one modality (body orientation).

GOAL SETTING

1. In goal setting, you make a clear statement of the specific behavior changes that you expect of your child. The child is an important participant in this process, whether he or she helps to identify goals or whether he or she merely is told what the expectations and goals are.

2. Goals are clear, specific statements of the major behavioral changes that you expect of your child. You use goals to keep track of the effectiveness of the things that you do to change your child's behavior. Your child uses goals to help keep track of behavior and to understand your expectations. Your therapist uses goals to monitor progress in therapy and to decide when therapy should end.

3. The following steps are used for goal setting:

   a. Pick the 3–5 major changes that you would like to see in your child's behavior.

   b. Carefully describe each goal, so that there is no mistake what you mean by it.

   c. Find a way to quantify each goal. Quantifying means finding a way to rate each goal on a numeric scale (such as a scale of 1–10). The most common ways of quantifying goals are counting behaviors, rating behaviors on a 1–5 or 1–10 scale, and keeping track of the amount of time related to a behavior. Ideally, any numeric scale has "anchors," which are descriptions of specific behaviors that go along with numbers. For example, a "5" may be defined as "satisfactory completion of one-half of homework."

   d. Baseline monitoring. Rate each goal on the scale that you have chosen. This may mean that you keep track of the goal for a week or two, or it may mean that you give your impression of the initial rating for the child.

   e. Target level. Choose a target value for the goal. This value is the level at which you will be satisfied that the goal has been achieved. Remember, perfection is rarely possible in life, so goals should not involve perfect behavior.

   f. Decide what will happen when the goals are achieved. You may want to plan rewards for achievement of goals. Your therapist may use goals to determine whether to end therapy or to change the focus of therapy.

   g. Monitor goals regularly. You will want to keep track of goals on a regular basis, until the target level for each goal is achieved. Weekly or daily ratings (see (c) above) are typically needed to accomplish this. Monitoring should be discussed with the child to promote the child's self-monitoring and insight.

4. Goal setting should be used as part of a plan to change your child's behavior. Typically, behavioral techniques will be used to help you and your child to achieve these goals.

SPECIAL TIME

1. Duration: 15 minutes

2. Frequency: Every night

3. Participants: Child and ONE Parent. *No other family members are to take part in the activity.*

4. Rules:

   a. The special time activity is to be chosen by the child. It can be anything that the child wants, as long as it fits the following rules:

   (1) Cannot be dangerous (or potentially dangerous), painful, or physically aversive to the child or any other person.

(2) Cannot be abusive or neglectful.

(3) Cannot involve the destruction of property.

(4) Cannot involve lawbreaking or behavior that would be considered unethical or immoral by a reasonable person.

(5) Cannot be beyond the constraints of reality (things that the family simply cannot do because of finances, limited access, etc.).

(6) Must be completed within the special time allotment.

(7) Cannot clearly violate any important rules of the household.

b. Special time is to be scheduled in advance (at the latest, on the morning of the day of the special time).

c. Special time must have an announced beginning and end (tell your child, "special time is beginning (or ending) now").

(1) Even if you continue playing with your child after the end of special time, announce that special time is over.

d. Special time is noncontingent. It cannot be taken away for any misbehavior on the part of the child, and it is not to be used as a reward or punishment.

5. Tests—unfortunately, many children attempt to "test" the limits of special time. Some things you may see:

a. Asking for more special time when special time is over.

b. Misbehaving immediately before special time.

c. Taunting siblings over special time.

d. Asking for outrageous things for special time.

e. Refusing to do special time.

6. Responses—your responses to the tests of your child are crucial. Some things to remember:

a. Special time must *always* occur at the appointed time. If your child acts up immediately before special time, you can postpone the punishment until after special time.

b. If your child refuses to do special time, you should still inform your child when special time starts and ends. You may then do whatever you want, provided that you are available for your child if he or she decides to go ahead with special time anyway. However, once the special time period ends, the child cannot "make up" the special time at another time.

c. It is fine to continue playing with your child after special time has ended, but you must inform your child that special time is *technically ended*. If you do not let your child know this, he or she may see special time as modifiable.

7. Effects: Special time can have the following positive effects:

a. Improved self-esteem

b. Improved relationships with parents

c. Positive mood

ANTECEDENT MANAGEMENT

1. Antecedent management is a technique that is based on a very simple principle: Take away whatever is leading to the child's misbehavior.

2. Antecedent management involves a five-step process.

   a. First, identify the situations in which your child misbehaves. What cues cause misbehavior? What objects lead to problems? For example, if a child always misbehaves when he attends church with his best friend, the antecedents are church and the presence of the best friend.

   b. Second, restrict the child's access to the objects or situations that lead to the misbehavior. In the preceding example, do not allow the child to attend church with his best friend.

   c. Third, do *not* make a big deal out of the changes. Just matter-of-factly mention them to the child; if the child is upset, a short explanation and some support should be all that is needed.

   d. Fourth, *be patient.* Behaviors can take up to a month to reduce following the removal of antecedents.

   e. Fifth, evaluate the effectiveness of removing the antecedents. Professional consultation may be helpful here.

3. Antecedent management is *not* bargaining.

   a. You (or your child) may be tempted to bargain over the replacement of whatever object has been removed. An example is the child who says that he or she will "be good" if the object is replaced.

   b. Strict antecedent management does *not* allow such bargaining. Remember, you are removing the thing that caused the problem.

   c. In some cases, bargaining may help to change your child's behavior. This may be an effective intervention as well, but it is *not* antecedent management.

4. When to use antecedent management:

   a. When the child has little control over his or her behavior.

   b. When the object/situation is causing harm or major disruption. The most common use of antecedent management, for example, is to remove the child's access to harmful objects or situations, such as knives or antisocial peers.

   c. When permanent removal of the object/situation will not be harmful (or may be helpful) to the child.

FLEXIBLE IGNORING

1. Flexible ignoring differs from the way that parents typically use ignoring to modify children's behavior. First, it is purposeful; the parent uses flexible ignoring for a specific purpose (as opposed to merely being angry or distraught). Second, it is intentional; the parent chooses situations in which to use flexible ignoring (as opposed to using it in all situations). Third, it is meaningful; the parent knows why flexible ignoring will modify the child's behavior.

2. Flexible ignoring has three components:

   a. Eyes—eye contact with the child is a powerful reinforcer; avoiding eye contact is the height of ignoring

   b. Mouth—saying things to the child can also be extremely reinforcing, even if the parent is screaming or being critical. Not saying anything at all is truly ignoring the child.

   c. Body Language—this includes facial expressions, hand, arm, and leg movements, and general tenseness. A blank facial expression and only essential movements are components of ignoring.

3. Summary: Over all, then, flexible ignoring consists of a lack of eye contact, no speaking, and minimal facial expressions/movements. In some situations, the parent may have to have eye contact, but speaking and facial expressions can convey ignoring. In other situations, the parent may have to move, but a lack of speech and eye contact can convey ignoring. For example, a child may try to break a window to get the parent's attention; the parent could hold the child back (not ignoring with body language) while still not saying anything or looking at the child (ignoring with eyes and mouth).

4. What can be ignored? Behaviors that can be ignored are those that are done primarily to seek attention from the parent. In most cases, such behaviors include:

   a. Temper tantrums
   b. Arguing
   c. Power struggles

5. What cannot be ignored? Behaviors that cannot be ignored are those that are not done for attention, those that are dangerous to the child, those that are dangerous to others (including aggression), and those that destroy property. In most cases, such behaviors include:

   a. Suicidal/self-harming threats or gestures
   b. Physical aggression
   c. Destruction of property
   d. Behaviors performed for another reinforcer (e.g., stealing, not doing homework)
   e. Risk-taking behavior

6. Why does ignoring work?

   a. Ignoring works because, in many cases, your child's defiant behavior is intended to provoke a response from you. If you respond to the behavior, it shows your child that he or she can "get to you" when he or she is mad at you. This is very rewarding to an angry child.
   b. Contrary to popular belief, ignoring is *not* giving in to the child. You may ignore the child and still set limits on his or her behavior. If the child violates a rule, he or she may receive consequences, but not in the form of your attention.

7. What to expect

   a. Most children respond to ignoring with an initial increase in angry, defiant behavior (this is called an extinction burst). This is the child's way of expressing his or her disagreement with this change in your behavior. It also shows that you are getting through to the child.
   b. Eventually, the child will learn that, to avoid ignoring, he or she must not fight and throw tantrums. When this is learned, the child's behavior will begin to improve.

8. Cautions

   a. Flexible ignoring is a powerful technique. Initially, it is best used in consultation with a professional. If used improperly, it can create additional problems.
   b. Flexible ignoring should only be used when positively reinforcing techniques are also being used.
   c. Flexible ignoring should be used sparingly, with large amounts of positive interaction interspersed.

CONTINGENCY MANAGEMENT I

1. *Contingency management* is a technical term for something that parents do with children every day: Reward children for good behavior, and punish children for bad behavior. A contingency is simply a promise to your child that if he or she engages in a certain behavior, you will do something. The "something" may be a reward or punishment, but it is dependent on the child's behavior. However, contingency management also differs from typical parenting in several ways:

   a. It is planned in advance. Most parents come up with rewards and punishments on the "spur of the moment." In most cases, this is fine. But when a child is having a significant behavior problem, the normal contingencies of parenting are not working. At these times, it is important to look carefully at what is happening and to design a plan with a trained behavior therapist.
   b. It is extremely detailed. Contingency management depends on the identification of very specific behaviors in very specific situations. For example, typically you may tell your child to "be good." However, for contingency management, you will identify a specific "good" behavior (e.g., smiling at adults) in a specific situation (e.g., school). That specific behavior will then be your goal.
   c. It is discussed with your child in advance.
   d. It focuses more on teaching good behaviors than on punishing bad behaviors. Very often, children's bad behavior is what gets our attention and bothers us. So we naturally want to change the bad behaviors first. Contingency management recognizes and challenges bad behaviors, but it does this by encouraging the child to substitute good behaviors for bad ones.
   e. It involves careful monitoring. Your therapist will probably ask you to keep track of the targeted behaviors to make sure that the contingencies are having an effect. This may be done with paper and pencil, which you will bring to each therapy session.

2. *Basics of Contingency Management*—When you do contingency management, you pick two groups of behaviors: behaviors that you would like to see more often and behaviors that you would like to see less often. You will then be selecting rewards and punishments. Finally, you will connect certain rewards to the desirable behaviors of your child and certain punishments to the undesirable behaviors of your child. As your child sees that certain behaviors result in reward, those behaviors will become more frequent (because your child will want to get the rewards). Likewise, as your child sees that certain behaviors result in punishment, those behaviors will become less frequent (because your child will want to avoid punishment). All of this makes sense. Chances are that you have tried this basic scheme before. And, chances are, you have seen this scheme work, either with one of your children, with another person's children, or perhaps with yourself, when you were a child. But, for whatever reason, contingencies may not be working with your child right now. Parents often complain that they have tried to reward and punish their child, but it just isn't working. This is typical for children with behavior problems. Don't despair. The contingencies just need some fine tuning.

3. *Pre–Contingency Management—Rules and Principles to Enhance the Power of Contingencies.* Before we can even begin to perform contingency management, we must increase your power as a contingency manager. The following rules will do this:

a. *Attitude*—Contingency management begins with the right attitude: You are *not* the enforcer, *not* a person to be feared, and *not* the "bad guy." Rather, you set some basic rules that provide your child with choices and a clear sense of what will happen following each choice. Basically, you are telling your child that if he or she chooses to do a certain behavior, then a certain thing will happen. Once your child *chooses* to do the behavior, he or she has *chosen* the response. If the child chooses a behavior that is paired with a punishment, then he or she has chosen the punishment. You, the parent, are *not* the bad guy. Your child chooses what he or she gets; you just follow through on the promised contingency. Do *not* give in to the temptation to feel guilty. As long as the contingency is clear, the child has chosen what happens. You had no part in the choice. And, like your child, *you* must follow the rules. If the contingency is set up, you *must* follow through on it, whether you are rewarding or punishing. If you do not follow through on the contingency, you are saying to your child that it is OK to break the rules. Everybody (child, parent, and therapist) must follow the contingencies once they are set up. Nobody is above them.

Of course, as a parent, you would like to see your child succeed, and it is OK to root for them to earn their rewards (and avoid punishments). It is OK to be disappointed when they do not earn their rewards. But the contingencies still occur, no matter how you or your child feel about them at the time. Do not become emotional about the behavior or the contingency—take emotion out of the interaction, and let the contingencies work their magic.

b. *Consistency*—If there is a "most important part" of contingency management, it would have to be consistency. Consistency involves following through *exactly* on the contingency that is specified. In other words, *only* reward or punish the *precise* behaviors that you have identified, and *only* use the rewards or punishments that you have set up ahead of time. *never* change the contingency after the behavior has occurred. And *always* make sure the contingency occurs if the behavior occurs. In simple terms, *don't bend the rules!*

c. *Give Your Child a Reason to Care About Rewards*—Your power as a contingency manager is directly related to how much your child wants to earn rewards. Therefore, it should be relatively easy for your child to earn rewards at first. If your child has to do too much to earn a reward, it will not be worth it to your child to change the behavior. The reward has to be worth more to your child than the difficulty of changing the behavior. In other words, your child has to feel that changing behavior is "worth it." If you ask too much, it will not be "worth it." Your child has to experience the reward in order to care about it. If the contingency is too difficult, the child will give up without ever earning a reward.

d. *Give Your Child a Reason to Care About Punishments*—A similar thing is true for punishments. In order for a punishment to mean something, your child must have something to lose. Avoid giving *big* punishments, or else you will make your child feel that there is nothing more to lose by engaging in additional bad behavior. Giving big punishments also takes away your leverage because you have nothing else to use as a punishment. Instead, give small, meaningful punishments, so that if your child protests or continues to behave poorly, you can give additional punishments. For example, rather than grounding your child for a month, make your child stay inside for a half hour. If you ground your child for a month and he or she then acts poorly, what can you do? Ground him or her for another month? Your child is unlikely to care at that point because another month seems far away. But if your child knows that he or she can escape punishment in a half hour, he or she is unlikely to act up and get another half hour of punishment.

e. *Don't Let Your Child Manipulate the Behavior Plan*—Many children will pretend that they don't care about the rewards or punishments of a contingency. Nothing could be farther from the truth. Your child is *acting* as though he or she doesn't care because he or she *hopes* that you will be fooled and will drop the contingency. The contingency stays in place whether the child likes it or not. Give rewards and punishments as agreed on and *ignore* the child's manipulations. If the child refuses rewards, make them available and don't worry about whether the child takes advantage of them.

f. *Continue to Use Other Techniques*—Don't forget about using other behavioral techniques. If the child tries to have a power struggle with you over the contingency, use flexible ignoring. If antecedents are the problem, antecedent management is appropriate.

4. *Application*—Once you understand these contingency management basics, you are ready to apply what you have learned. This is covered in Contingency Management II. However, before progressing to Contingency Management II, you must agree to the principles of Contingency Management I. Your therapist may ask you to agree to a "contract" of behavior based on these principles.

CONTINGENCY MANAGEMENT II

1. Steps of Contingency Management

a. *Step 1: Define a target behavior.* With the help of your therapist, select a behavior that is specific and observable. Be sure to describe exactly what the child does that you want to stop or to encourage.

b. *Step 2: Select an alternative behavior.* If the behavior that you selected in Step 1 is a negative behavior, you must select a positive behavior to replace it. Use the same rules that you did for Step 1 in the selection of behaviors for Step 2. If the behavior that you selected in Step 1 is a positive behavior, you might choose to skip this step.

c. *Step 3: Precontingency monitoring.* For a 1–2-week period, you will be asked to keep track of the target and alternative behaviors. You will probably be asked to monitor how often and when the behaviors occur. You may also be asked to keep track of what comes before (antecedents) and after (consequences) the behavior. *Be sure to take your monitoring seriously.* The plan cannot continue without this step.

d. *Step 4: Select reinforcers and punishments.*

(1) Reinforcers are things that result in an increase in behavior. Usually, they are things that your child perceives as rewarding and that he or she will work to earn. Examples of reinforcers are parental attention, TV, food, money, access to favored activities, and privileges.

(2) Punishments are things that cause a decrease in behavior. Usually, they are things that your child dislikes or avoids. The best punishments are things that involve the withdrawal of privileges and are relatively mild. In some cases, you may give your child privileges so that you can have something to remove as a punishment. *Never* use physical punishment as part of a contingency management plan. *Never*

use something as a punishment that you want your child eventually to like (e.g., reading a book). *Never* keep your child from enriching experiences as part of a punishment (e.g., going to the zoo). Examples of punishments are removal of TV time, removal of video game time, earlier bedtime, and time-out.

e. *Step 5: Set contingencies.* In this step, you put rewards together with favored behaviors and punishments with negative behaviors. Only one reward or punishment should be tied to each behavior. Make sure that the contingency is clear and can be carried out.

f. *Step 6: Explain the new contingency to the child.* If you think that your child cannot re-member it, use a chart or picture at home as reminders. Be sure to let your child know that certain behavior choices will be followed with contingencies. Emphasize that the rule is made and that you will not change it. Ask your child if he or she understands and answer any questions. Do *not* ask for permission to start the contingency.

g. *Step 7: Implement the contingency at home.* Once you have explained the contin-gency to your child, it is immediately in effect in the home. Remember the basic rules and guidelines of contingency management and be consistent!

h. *Step 8: Postcontingency monitoring.* You will be asked to keep track of the target and alternative behaviors. This is extremely important for modifying or ending the con-tingency.

i. *Step 9: Modify contingencies as appropriate.* Based on your monitoring, your thera-pist may or may not suggest changes in the contingencies. Remember, do *not* change contingencies without a good reason, or else your child will be forever trying to get you to change contingencies in the future.

TIME-OUT TECHNIQUES

1. Time-out has been a mainstay of parenting for thousands of years under a variety of names. It involves removing the child from a situation and placing him or her in a place that is boring. Examples of time-out are making a child go to an uninteresting room or sit on a chair in the corner.

2. When to use it: Time-out can be used for a variety of problem behaviors. Typically, you should use it immediately following a behavior that you have *specifically told* your child not to do. You need to be willing to get your child to take time-out and to make your child stay in time-out, no matter how much he or she protests.

3. Characteristics of time-out:

   a. *The rules of time-out should be explained in advance to your child.* Specifically, state what behaviors are a problem, where the time-out place is, how long the child will re-main in time-out, and the penalties for noncompliance.

   b. *Time-out setting.* The place where your child goes for time-out should be away from any excitement, noise, toys, people, or other stimulation. In other words, it should be boring. Typically, parents use a chair in the corner or a room without toys or TV. If your child is sent to a room that is filled with interesting, stimulating things, your child will not feel that he or she is being punished for misbehavior.

   c. *Lack of social interaction.* Your child's time-out should *not* allow social interaction to take place. Thus, your child should be alone, and nobody should be talking with him or her. If you find that your child constantly attempts to interact during time-out, you may have to put your child in a room with a closed door. There are precautions for this, which should be discussed with your therapist

d. *Time-out duration.* Do not make time-out too long. A good rule is one minute for each year of the child's age. Thus, a 5-year-old would receive time-out for a 5-minute period.

e. *Refusal to do time-out.* You *must* be prepared for times when your child refuses to go to time-out. A good general rule is that your child may have 5 seconds of complaining (don't tell them that they are allowed to complain, but do not punish them as long as the complaining is within reason) and 15 seconds to go to the time-out area. If the child is not in time-out within 15 seconds, announce that he or she must remain in time-out for one more minute. For each additional 15 seconds of not going to time-out, the child receives an additional minute. You may slowly count to 5 to illustrate this 15-second rule for your child. The time-out "clock" is not started until the child is in time-out *and* quiet. In some cases, the child absolutely refuses to go to time-out, regardless of the cost. If this is the case, additional privileges may have to be withheld, and you may have to physically bring your child to time-out. Consult your therapist for such interventions.

f. *Use of a timer.* It is often helpful for older children to see how long time-out will last and how close it is to ending. This is most easily done with a timer. The timer should be audible or visible (ideally both) to the child, and the end time should be easily identified by a bell. Most kitchen timers will do.

g. *Be matter-of-fact.* When announcing time-out to your child, be as calm and matter-of-fact as possible. You also want to be brief, firm, and clear. State briefly what your child has done. Then tell your child to go to time-out and how long time-out will last. If your child protests, warn about the possibility of adding time to time-out. *Do not get into a power struggle, and do not feel like you have to explain yourself.* Now is *not* the time for an explanation. Chances are that your child is not interested in an explanation anyway; he or she just wants to get out of time-out.

4. Steps of time-out:

a. Your child performs a behavior that you have warned will lead to time out.
b. Get your child's attention.
c. State that the child is receiving time-out.
d. State why the child is receiving time-out.
e. Tell the child where to go for time-out.
f. State the length of time-out.
g. Watch your child go to time-out.
h. When the child is in time-out *and* quiet, start the timer.
i. When the timer rings, the child may leave time-out.

ACTIVITY SCHEDULING

1. Activity scheduling refers to the monitoring and creation of a "calendar" of events for your child. Many behavior problems in children can be linked to problems in the child's schedule. For example, the child may be bored, have too much (or too little) freedom, may not be interested in his or her daily activities, or may feel that his or her life is too chaotic. Activity scheduling gives you more control and knowledge over what your child does. By using this knowledge and control, you can make your child's life more satisfying. This satisfaction with the daily schedule can pay big rewards in terms of better child mood and behavior.

2. Activity scheduling is a widely used, research-proven technique. It is especially effective for depression, anxiety, or oppositional behavior. In fact, activity scheduling is a part of many treatment plans for depressed children *and* adults.

3. Activity Scheduling I: Monitoring of the Daily Schedule

   a. The first task of activity scheduling is to find out what you and your child do during a regular week. For each hour from 6 A.M. to 11 P.M., write down what you and your child typically do. Do this for each day of the week. The easiest way to figure out this schedule is to write down your child's activities during the next week. If some of these activities are not the usual ones, be sure to note this. Remember, you need to write something down for *each hour* (6 A.M.—11 P.M.) of *each day.* If your child does more than one thing during the hour, summarize his or her activity as well as you can; if you are not sure what your child has done at certain times, ask the adults who have been supervising your child during that time. Just make sure that you have something for *every hour.* You don't have to give much detail. For example, if your child is at school, write "school"; if he or she is asleep, write "sleep." You will go over the schedule in greater detail with your therapist.

   b. In addition to writing down what your child does during each hour, write down who joins your child in the activity (e.g., playing video games with brother, John, and friend, Jim).

4. Activity Scheduling II: Identification of Target Activities

   a. The second task of activity scheduling is to identify activities that could be dropped from the schedule and activities that can be added to the schedule.

   b. Activities to Drop

      (1) *Nonessential, Nonpositive Activities*—*Nonessential* means that these activities are *not* important for your child's development, schooling, social functioning, or contribution to the household. *Nonpositive* means that your child does not derive clear enjoyment or benefit from the activity. For example, school and chores are *essential* activities. Having fun talking to a friend on the phone is a *positive* activity. Sitting on the couch doing nothing is a *nonessential, nonpositive* activity. Getting frustrated because brother beats your child at a video game is a *nonessential, nonpositive* activity.

      (2) *Nonessential, Nonsocial Activities*—*Nonsocial* means activities that are done alone or out of the public view, such as playing on the computer or sitting in a bedroom alone.

      (3) *Nonessential, Inactive Activities*—*Inactive* means activities that do not require much in the way of movement or effort, such as sitting on the couch watching TV.

      (4) *Nonessential, Excessive Activities*—*Excessive* refers to any activity in which your child spends three hours on a typical weekday or six hours on a typical weekend day.

   c. Activities to Add—These should, in general, be something that your child could do at least 3–4 times per week or more often. "Bigger" activities (e.g., more expensive or time consuming) are OK, but there should be relatively few of these.

(1) *Positive Activities*—These are activities that interest your child or are clearly fun to him or her.

(2) *Social Activities*—These are activities that involve interaction with other people or being in a public place.

(3) *Active Activities*—Despite the apparent repetition, not all activities are "active." Active activities require significant physical movement or effort (walking, exercising, visiting someone). Some increase in physical activity is almost always necessary for an activity schedule to succeed.

5. Activity Scheduling III: Design a New Schedule

   a. Look back at your child's schedule and determine what activities can be dropped and what activities can be added (using the activities identified in Activity Scheduling II). You do not need to drop *all* of the "Activities to Drop," and you do not need to add *all* of the "Activities to Add"; in fact, too much change can be difficult for your child. Just change a few things.

   b. Design a new "target" schedule that includes more of the activities to add and fewer of the activities to drop. *Be realistic and make a commitment to make the change in your child's schedule.*

6. Activity Scheduling IV: Implement the New Schedule

   a. Tell your child about the new schedule. Be *firm* and *positive.* Although the new schedule may include some fun things, many children resist changes in their schedule. You must be prepared to go through with the schedule whether your child likes it or not.

   b. Use contingencies, ignoring, and anything else to stick to the schedule.

7. Activity Scheduling V: Modify the Schedule with Your Therapist

COMMAND CONTROL

1. Command control increases the power of your parenting by making your requests more significant to your child. There are two ways to improve the power of your commands. The first way involves shortening your commands, so that your child can understand and respond to them. The second way involves eliminating all but the most important requests that you make. By controlling the commands that you make, you communicate to your child that the few, straightforward requests that you do make are *very* important. Parents who make fewer, clearer commands have better behaved children.

2. Shortening and clarifying commands is the first method of command control. To be as powerful as possible, your commands should have the following characteristics:

   a. Use as little emotion as possible. Commands should not be made in an angry, sad, irritable, or challenging tone. Emotion from you causes an emotional response in your child, not compliance with your request. If you feel emotional, take a deep breath and remember to be matter-of-fact when you make your request.

   b. Only ask for one thing at a time. Parents need for children to do many things, but some children (especially those who are disorganized) have difficulty if they are asked to do several things at the same time. Pick the most important thing and ask for that first. Then, when the child has done it, praise him or her, and ask for the next thing.

   c. Avoid long explanations if you are making a request. A short explanation is fine, but anything beyond a few sentences will either bore, irritate, or distract the child. Don't feel that you have to justify everything that you ask for. If your child wants an explanation beyond a basic explanation, he or she can discuss it with you after complying with your request.

    d. Don't threaten unless you plan on following through on your threats immediately. Threats should not be too extreme, or your child will feel that he or she has nothing more to lose once punishment has been given.

3. Reducing the number of commands can be a difficult task, but the following steps should help.

    a. Make a list of commands. Write down a list of all of the commands that you typically make of your child. Don't just include chores or major requirements of the household. The "little" commands are also important. These include asking your child to sit in a certain place in the clinic waiting room, asking your child to walk or talk a certain way, and any other time when you comment on your child's behavior with the intent of changing it.

    b. Rate the importance of each command on a scale of 1–10, where 1 means "not at all important" and 10 means "very, very important." You *must* rate half of your commands 5 or less and half of your commands 6 or more.

    c. Select commands for elimination. Take the lower one-third to one-fifth of your commands and look at them. These commands can probably be eliminated from your interactions with your child.

    d. Eliminate the commands. Try to no longer use these commands in interactions with your child.

    e. Monitor yourself. For the next week, keep track of how many times you accidentally use the eliminated commands. Try to reduce this number during the following week.

4. Why does command control work? Most parents report that their child's behavior is much better when they are having fun. It is when something is demanded of the child that things go bad. By taking control of commands, parents can reduce these negative interactions at the same time that they improve the behavior of the child. Shortening and clarifying commands helps the child to feel as though the command is well defined and reasonable. There is also less room for the child to resist the command with an excuse. Reducing the number of commands works because children tend to respond to unusual, important aspects of their environment and to ignore repetitive, unpleasant aspects of their environment. Some children have a low tolerance for repetitive or unpleasant interactions; these children screen out parental requests when these requests are made too often. Thus, they don't listen to your commands because they have become "immune" to them; the commands are no longer unusual or important because, in the child's eyes, they happen very often (remember, this is in the child's eyes, not from your point of view. You may not actually be giving very many commands, but your child may be sensitive to commands). An additional reason why command control works is that the child has less reason to feel that he or she is overburdened with demands. This makes the child less angry and more cooperative. There may also be fewer arguments between you and your child.

5. Points to Consider:

    a. Most parents believe that all of their commands are important. This is often true, and it is difficult to decide to shorten or reduce commands, even on small matters. Command control does not discount the importance of your commands to the child. In fact, it does just the opposite—it acknowledges that some of your commands are so important that they absolutely, positively *must* be followed. However, the price of giving extra power to these "extra important" commands is that use of some smaller commands must be suspended. Your child cannot tell what commands are important until he or she sees fewer commands and more emphasis on the major commands.

b. You may decide to renew some of your dropped commands at a later date. This is fine, but the initial stages of command control require a dramatic drop in commands in order to have a big impact on the child. Do *not* renew any dropped commands without talking to the therapist.

6. Benefits of Command Control
   a. Fewer child-parent power struggles
   b. Improved child-parent relationship
   c. Less oppositional behavior

INDEX